About This Study Guide

The purpose of this study guide is to provide you with an effective tool for finding problem material related to the topic you are studying in the textbook. The Learning Chart found in each chapter aligns the topics covered in that chapter with example problems (which are found in the textbook), review questions, multiple choice questions, exercises, and assignment problems so that you can easily find either the commentary or problem material related to a particular tax issue.

This study guide also contains the questions and solutions to the following problem material:

- Review Questions
- Multiple Choice Questions
- Exercises

Also provided in this Study Guide are the Assignment Problem questions, but the solutions to the Assignment Problems are not provided, as many instructors use them for hand-in assignments for grading. However, the DVD included with the textbook contains over 150 problems that are similar to the Assignment Problems. Solutions are provided for these problems.

Study Notes: Space has been provided in the Study Guide for you to write your own notes.

References

References are provided in the outer margin of the text beside the paragraphs to which they pertain. These references are to the following sources:

1. ITA refers to the sections of the *Income Tax Act* to be discussed in the chapter;

2. ITR refers to the Income Tax Regulations which are also found in the volume containing the Act;

3. ETA refers to sections of the *Excise Tax Act* in which provisions of the Goods and Services Tax (GST)/Harmonized Sales Tax (HST) can be found;

4. IT, IC, and ATR refer, respectively, to Interpretation Bulletins, Information Circulars, and Advance Tax Rulings, and are available on the CRA's website;

5. ITTN refers to Income Tax Technical News releases that are published by the CRA intermittently to provide current technical interpretations.

6. *Folios* refers to *Income Tax Folios* which are being published by the CRA in chapters by topic to update and replace ITs and ITTNs.

7. Cda–U.S. TT refers to the *Canada–United States Income Tax Convention (1980)*; and

An explanation of these references is provided in Chapter 1 of the textbook. References to sections of the Act are provided for exercises and assignment problems. It should also be understood that in the course of their use within the paragraph of the text, all references preceded by such specific terms as "section", "subsection", "paragraph", "subparagraph", etc., without any indication of the pertinent statute, refer to the provisions of the *Income Tax Act*. Similarly, the provisions of the Income Tax Regulations are preceded by the term "Regulation" without specifying the relevant legislation. In the margin, these references are preceded by "ITA" and "ITR", respectively.

References to the *Excise Tax Act* are usually confined to the GST/HST part of a chapter and are specifically indicated as being to that legislation. References in the margin are preceded by "ETA". An attempt has been made to integrate GST/HST with relevant transactions discussed under the *Income Tax Act* in the chapters where these transactions are discussed.

Acronyms

An alphabetical list of acronyms used in the book appears in the first section of this Study Guide, immediately following the Table of Contents. The list provides the meaning of the acronym and paragraph references where the term is used in the textbook.

Review Questions

A set of review questions is provided in this Study Guide for Chapters 2 to 19. These short-answer questions attempt to review key points made in the text or points that are not integrated into the example problems, multiple choice questions, exercises, or assignment problems in this Study Guide. Discussion notes on the review questions are provided in the Study Guide.

Multiple Choice Questions

Since multiple choice questions are common in professional examinations and can be very helpful in learning specific provisions of the Act, this Study Guide provides six or seven such questions covering the material in each chapter, starting with Chapter 2, for a total of over 100 questions. Annotated solutions are provided in the Study Guide to enhance learning through self-study.

Exercises

Exercises have been provided for each chapter in this Study Guide. These usually consist of short problems to highlight particular areas of the chapter. They are designed to be fairly narrow in scope, to provide the student with an opportunity to apply the material in the chapter to a specific problem situation. Solutions to these exercises have been provided in the Study Guide.

Assignment Problems

Assignment problems are provided for each chapter of the textbook in this Study Guide. These problems are designed to have the student apply the material discussed in each chapter of the textbook to an actual fact or problem situation. While these problems focus on the key elements of the chapter in much the same way that the solved example problems in the commentary do, the problems are not identical in their coverage or presentation. As a result, it will be necessary for the student to read the assignment problems very carefully in preparing a solution. Solutions to these problems are not available. However, similar additional problems with solutions are provided on the DVD that accompanies the textbook, as discussed below.

Assignment Problems are identified as either Type 1, 2 or 3. Type 1 problems will only deal with issues from that specific chapter. Type 2 problems will be "cumulative" and will deal with issues from that specific chapter along with issues that would have been addressed in a previous chapter. Type 3 problems will be extended "case"-type problems, intended for the more advanced student. These will be used primarily to help students identify tax issues.

Additional Problems with Solutions

Students often request additional problems with solutions that they can use on a self-study basis for preparation for tests and examinations. For this purpose, a comprehensive compilation of problems similar to the Assignment Problems and multiple choice questions in the Study Guide is provided on the DVD accompanying the textbook. There are over 150 problems and solutions on the DVD, classified by coverage of chapters in the textbook. The problems, most of which have previously been used as examination questions, will provide students with an opportunity to deal with problems of a comprehensive nature. Since these supplemental problems may cover material from several chapters, as examination questions often do, they provide an excellent source for review in preparation for examinations.

Suggested Approach

The authors suggest the following approach to the use of these materials. First, the students should identify the issue in an assignment problem that they need to research, then scan the headings of the particular chapter and use them to look for the topics that relate to that issue. Once the relevant parts of the chapter are identified, students should read the commentary, including any referenced material such as sections of the Act or Regulations and CRA publications. Reviewing any example problems to see how the provisions work will also help develop understanding.

Wolters Kluwer

Introduction to Federal Income Taxation in Canada, *2016-2017*

Study Guide

Wolters Kluwer Canada Limited
300-90 Sheppard Avenue East
Toronto Ontario
M2N 6X1
1 800 268 4522
www.wolterskluwer.ca

By
Robert E. Beam, FCPA, FCA
Professor Emeritus, University of Waterloo
Stanley N. Laiken, Ph.D.
Professor Emeritus, University of Waterloo
James J. Barnett, FCPA, FCA
University of Waterloo
Nathalie Johnstone, FCPA, FCA, MPAcc.
University of Saskatchewan
Devan Mescall, Ph.D., CPA, CA
University of Saskatchewan
Julie Robson, MAcc, CPA, CA, CPA (Illinois)
University of Waterloo

Contributors
Ling Chu, M.Tax, CPA, CMA
Wilfrid Laurier University
Christy MacDonald, Ph.D., CPA, CA
Deloitte, Kitchener
Barbara Rockx, MAcc, CPA, CA
University of Toronto
Michael Zender, B.Comm., LLB
Ernst & Young, Toronto

Published by Wolters Kluwer Limited

ISBN: 978-1-55496-872-5

Typeset by Wolters Kluwer Limited.
Printed in Canada.

The solutions provided for these problems will demonstrate the approach that can be taken for the type of example problem under consideration. The solutions can also be used as a check on the student's understanding as well as a means of providing further interpretation and explanation of the material covered. The exercises at the end of the chapter can be used in a similar manner. Once the parts of a chapter have been completed in this manner, the student should be sufficiently prepared to attempt the assignment problems relevant to a particular part or to the whole chapter. When reviewing material for examination or other purposes, the multiple choice questions at the end of each chapter can be attempted. The solutions in the Study Guide can then be checked. As well, the additional problems included on the DVD that accompanies the textbook can be attempted. Review might also focus on the approaches used to address the various types of problems presented.

Learning Goals

To be a successful tax adviser it is not enough to just know the technical material found in the Act and supporting materials. You need to understand the purpose behind the rules so you can explain to others why your tax plan does not violate either the provision as it is written or purpose behind the provision. You also need to be able to blend a number of complex provisions into a comprehensive plan to accomplish the goals of your client or employer.

Materials at the introductory level on Canadian income tax legislation are not easy to study. A conscientious effort to do the work and, particularly, to do problems and apply what has been read is essential to a good understanding of this material. The authors have attempted to meet the challenge of presenting the material by setting out the work that must be done and by explaining, as best they can, the major provisions of the legislation. The challenge of learning the material is, of course, left to the student.

Robert E. Beam
Stanley N. Laiken
James J. Barnett
Nathalie Johnstone
Devan Mescall
Julie Robson

July 2016

Table of Contents

Acronyms

Acronym	Meaning	¶
A		
AB	Active business	12,140
ABI	Active business income	12,100
ABIL	Allowable business investment loss	7,720
ACB	Adjusted cost base	7,020; 8,130
ACL	Allowable capital loss	7,020
AII	Aggregate investment income	12,335
AOC	Acquisition of control	11,090
ART	Additional refundable tax	12,335
ATR	Advance Tax Ruling	1,143
B		
BFTC	Business foreign tax credit	10,490; 11,335
Boot (expression)	Non-share/non-partnership interest consideration	16,050
C		
CCA	Capital cost allowance	5,005
CCPC	Canadian-controlled private corporation	11,212
CCTB	Canada child tax benefit	10,460
CDA	Capital dividend account	15,055
CDSB	Canada disability savings bond	9,095.50
CDSG	Canada disability savings grant	9,095.40
CEC	Cumulative eligible capital	5,210
CECA	Cumulative eligible capital amount	5,210
CESG	Canada education savings grant	9,090.20
CG	Capital gain	7,020
CGD	Capital gains deduction	13,370
CGE	Capital gains exemption	13,370
CL	Capital loss	7,020
CLB	Canada learning bond	9,090.30
CNIL	Cumulative net investment loss	13,380
CRA	Canada Revenue Agency	1,350
D		
DBP	Defined benefit pension plan	9,330.10
DPSP	Deferred profit sharing plan	9,330.30
DTC	Dividend tax credit	6,060
E		
ECE	Eligible capital expenditure	5,210
ECP	Eligible capital property	5,210
ETA	*Excise Tax Act*	
F		
FAPI	foreign accrual property income	19,545
FCA	Federal Court of Appeal	1,335
FMV	Fair market value	4,045; 16,155
FTC	Foreign tax credit	10,490; 11,335

Acronym	Meaning	¶
G		
GIS	Guaranteed income supplement	
GRIP	General-rate income pool	12,040
GST	Goods and Services Tax	1,400
H		
HBP	Home buyers' plan	9,395
HST	Harmonized Sales Tax	1,400
I		
IC	Information Circulars	1,143
IT	Interpretation Bulletins	1,143
ITA	*Income Tax Act*	1,020
ITAR	Income Tax Application Rules	1,134
ITC	Investment Tax Credit	11,350; 11,355
ITC	Input Tax Credit	1,440
ITR	Income Tax Regulations	1,136
L		
LLP	Lifelong learning plan	9,400
LLP	Limited liability partnership	18,040
LOCP	Lower of cost or proceeds	5,015.20
LPP	Listed personal property	7,015
LSC	Legal stated capital	15,055; 16,145
M		
M&P	Manufacturing and processing	11,910
MPP	Money-purchase pension plan	9,330.20
N		
NBFTC	Non-business foreign tax credit	10,490; 11,330
NCL	Net capital loss	10,040; 11,075
N-CL	Non-capital loss	10,035; 11,065
O		
OAS	Old Age Security	9,460
P		
PA	Pension adjustment	9,355
PE	Permanent establishment	11,260
PI	Partnership interest	18,060
POD	Proceeds of disposition	7,020
PRE	Principal residence exemption	7,230
PSB	Personal services business	12,155
PSBI	Personal services business income	12,155
PUC	Paid-up capital	15,025
PUP	Personal-use property	7,014
Q		
QSBCS	Qualifying small business corporation shares	13,340
R		
RDSP	Registered disability saving plan	9,095
RDTOH	Refundable dividend tax on hand	12,345
REOP	Reasonable expectation of profit	4,237
RESP	Registered education savings plan	9,090
RRIF	Registered retirement income fund	9,410
RRSP	Registered retirement savings plan	9,300

Acronym	Meaning	¶
S		
SBC	Small business corporation	13,345
SBD	Small business deduction	12,140
SCC	Supreme Court of Canada	1,340
SIB	Specified investment business	11,150
SIBI	Specified investment business income	11,150
T		
T1	Personal income tax return	
T2	Corporate income tax return	
T3	Income tax return for a trust	
TCG	Taxable capital gain	7,020
TFSA	Tax-free savings account	9,220
TOP	Tax otherwise payable	11,330; 11,335
TV	Tax value	16,060
U		
UCC	Undepreciated capital cost	5,015
UCCB	Universal child care benefit	9,135

Reading the *Income Tax Act*[1]

Reading the *Income Tax Act* is often avoided by students, because they are intimidated by the volume of words and the apparent complexity of the expression of the provisions. Keeping in mind a few simple principles and procedures of statutory interpretation and applying them in your reading of a provision will address the intimidation successfully. For an overview of the development of some of the principles of statutory interpretation in the common law as they pertain to the *Income Tax Act* (the Act), refer to ¶1,500 of the textbook. This section will take a "how to" approach that should prove helpful in reading the Act. It is broken down into four sections, each framed as a question:

How do I find something?

How do I read the legislation?

What am I missing?

Am I reading the provision correctly?

HOW DO I FIND SOMETHING?

Before you can interpret a provision of the Act, you have to be able to find it in the Act. In practice, a client will present you with a set of facts, whether complete or incomplete, and you will have to search for the provision or provisions that might apply. Here are some procedures that you should follow to find a provision:

1. Know how the Act is structured in order to recognize where something is most likely to be found.

a. Parts (particularly Part I), Divisions, Subdivisions

— For example, if the facts suggest that you are dealing with an employee and you need to determine whether an amount must be included in income, you should know that the most likely place to find a provision that would deal with that issue is in Part I, Division B, Subdivision a, subsection 6(1), which contains a number of paragraphs listing possible inclusions. After subsection 6(1), subsection 6(2) to 6(23) are what might be termed "amplification" rules, which provide clarification for a rule in subsection 6(1) or a formula for a calculation of an inclusion, rather than a new inclusion rule.

— On the other hand, if the facts of a situation require a determination of whether an amount is deductible from business income, you should know that you should look in Part I, Division B, Subdivision b, subsection 20(1) to see if the expenditure is specifically listed there. Then, if the expenditure is not listed in subsection 20(1), look in subsection 18(1) to see if it is prohibited as a current-year deduction. If it is neither prohibited nor specifically allowed, then it might be allowed on the general principle that it was incurred to earn income. This possibility may have to be researched in court decisions or other interpretations.

---

[1] The materials in this section of the note have benefited from reference to materials prepared as their course notes by Chasmar and by Laiken, as listed in the References section.

b. Know where to find the definition sections for each Division or Subdivision and for the Act and note the wording used to indicate the scope of a definition or where in the Act the definitions are applicable. For example, see

— S.248(1): Note that the opening words, often referred to as the preamble, are "in this Act", indicating that the definition is applicable to the use of the word or term anywhere in the Act. Some terms listed in subsection 248(1) will refer you to another definitions section. For example, the term "adjusted cost base" is listed in subsection 248(1), but you are referred to section 54 for the definition to be used throughout the Act.

— S.54: Here the preamble used is "in this subdivision", indicating that these definitions are applicable to the use of the word or term only in Part I, Division B, Subdivision c, pertains to taxable capital gains and allowable capital losses.

— S.74.4(1): The preamble for this definitions provision is "in this section", thereby limiting the scope of the use of these definitions to section 74.4 pertaining to transfers and loans to corporations.

2. **Look in the alphabetical Topical Index** compiled by the editors of the edition of the Act that you are using. If the word or term is used anywhere in the Act or the Regulations, it may be listed there with a provision reference.

3. **Look in the Sectional List** provided immediately before the provisions of the Act. Scanning the headings in that list in the area of the Act that you are searching may help you determine a provision that is applicable. For example, if you are searching in subsection 6(1) for a possible inclusion, looking down the list of headings of the paragraphs of subsection 6(1) may identify quickly an appropriate provision.

4. **Look at the "Related Sections" and other notes** at the end of subsections and paragraphs to see if there are any other provisions or issues to consider.

HOW DO I READ THE LEGISLATION?

Having found a provision or provisions that might apply to the facts that you are trying to analyze, the next step is to read the provision to determine if it actually does apply and what it does.

1. Does this provision apply?

a. Identify the start and end of the sentence.

— Note that, typically, each subsection of the Act is one sentence. Subsection 6(1), pertaining to amounts to be included in income from an office or employment, extends through several pages of paragraphs, each of which ends with a semicolon, until paragraph 6(1)(*l*), which ends with a period, indicating the end of subsection 6(1). On the other hand, subsection 6(1.1), pertaining to parking cost, is a much shorter subsection and, hence, a sentence of only a few lines.

b. Identify the components of the provision. There will usually be four components, as follows:

i. To whom, i.e., an individual, a corporation, a partnership or a trust, does the provision apply?

— For example, the preamble to subsection 6(1) indicates that the provision applies to "a taxpayer" who has income from an office or employment. It can be determined from the definition of "office" and "employment" in subsection 248(1) that only an individual can hold these positions.

— To keep the specific facts of your situation straight, insert the names of persons in your fact situation into the provision that describes those persons.

ii. What is the transaction, activity or event to which the provision applies, and what are the conditions for that provision to apply?

— Continuing with the use of subsection 6(1) as an example, the taxpayer must receive or enjoy one or more amounts or benefits listed in the paragraphs of subsection 6(1). Each of those paragraphs contains conditions on or a description of what must be included and some contain exceptions to the inclusion rule. For example, paragraph 6(1)(*b*) requires the inclusion of "all amounts received . . . as an allowance". This condition is followed by 11 subparagraphs describing exceptions, each with its own descriptions or conditions.

— To understand the basics of a provision, on the first read, you might ignore any exceptions. However, on subsequent reading, it is important to see if any of the exceptions apply to your fact situation.

iii. What are the consequences of the provision, if it applies, to the person who is involved in the transaction, activity or event?

— Under subsection 6(1), the taxpayer/employee must include in his or her income from an office or employment any amount determined to meet the inclusion conditions in one or more of the paragraphs of subsection 6(1).

— Other consequences may involve:

— charging a person with the responsibility to pay tax (e.g., subsection 2(1) — "an income tax shall be paid"),

— charging someone with the responsibility to withhold tax (e.g., section 153 — "every person paying . . ."),

— permitting a deduction (e.g., subsection 8(1) — "there may be deducted . . ."),

— denying a deduction (e.g., subsection 18(1) — "no deduction shall be made . . ."),

— changing the nature of income or a deduction (e.g., subsection 55(2) — where a taxable dividend is deemed not to be a taxable dividend, but to be proceeds of disposition of shares),

— changing the timing of income or a deduction (e.g., subsection 73(1), which defers an unrealized capital gain on the transfer of a capital property to a spouse or common-law partner), or

— changing the person who pays the tax on income (e.g., subsection 74.1(1), which attributes income on property owned by a spouse or common-law partner to the spouse who originally owned and transferred the property to the owner-spouse).

iv. What is the timeframe over which the provision applies?

— Under subsection 6(1), the inclusion in "the income of a taxpayer" is "for a taxation year" in which the amount is received or the benefit is enjoyed, as specified in one or more of the paragraphs of subsection 6(1).

— Under subsection 156(1), individuals must pay quarterly instalments, under specified conditions, on the 15th day of March, June, September and December, i.e., the last month in each calendar quarter.

— Under subsection 165(1), a deadline is established for filing a notice of objection in respect of an assessment.

c. Determine the meaning of the key words used in the provision by following some established principles of interpreting a statute.

    i. Grammar, including punctuation, sentence structure, and the ordinary sense of words are important in determining the meaning of words, phrases, clauses and sentences in a provision.

        — For example, the following question might be asked about the application of paragraph 20(1)(*n*): does the paragraph apply on a sale of land held as inventory?

            — The question revolves around whether the exception (within the commas in the provision) applies to the whole provision, meaning that the reserve does not apply on the sale of land held as inventory or whether that exception applies to the two-year payment requirement, such that the two-year requirement does not apply to a reserve on the sale of the land held as inventory.

            — A reasonable interpretation would suggest that the exception, following the "and" between the two conditions, should apply only to the second condition involving the two-year requirement.

    ii. What is the intention of Parliament for or the policy purpose of this provision?

        — Look at the explanatory notes that accompany the introduction of a provision or published practitioner or government commentary to determine why Parliament legislated a provision and used the words that it did.

        — Paragraph 56(1)(*n*) requires the inclusion in a student/taxpayer's income of amounts received in respect of scholarships and similar awards. Within that paragraph is an exception, often referred to as a "carve-out" that would except from the treatment of amounts as scholarships "amounts received in the course of or by virtue of *an office or employment*" [italics added]. Did Parliament intend the reference to "an office or employment" to be to that of the student/taxpayer or to that of anyone else's office or employment? The carve-out was legislated to counteract the situation in the Supreme Court of Canada decision in *Savage* (83 DTC 5409) involving an employee who received a prize for achievement, personally. Apparently, Parliament's intent in legislating the exception was to make the prize employment income of the recipient as an employee and, therefore, not subject to paragraph 56(1)(*n*). For example, where an employer offers a scholarship to the child of an employee, is it the employment of the parent that should result in the exception being applied? Would it be reasonable to interpret "an office or employment" in this general way?

        — It is important to test the reasonableness of the result of your interpretation by comparing that result to your understanding of the purpose of the provision that you are interpreting.

    iii. Are any of the words or terms used in the provision defined in the *Income Tax Act*?

        — A definition contained in the Act overrides the ordinary meaning of a word or term.

            — Check the "Related Sections" note at the end of a subsection or paragraph.

            — Be careful to note the scope of the definition by the use of words like: "in this Act", "in this subdivision", or "in this subsection".

            — Some terms used for different purposes in the Act are defined differently for a particular purpose.

— For example, the term "earned income" is defined in subsection 63(3) for the purposes of the child care expense deduction in subsection 63(1). That definition is limited to section 63. The definition reflects the type of income that the government is attempting to encourage by providing a deduction for child care expenses, i.e., employment, business and student income.

— The same term, "earned income", is defined differently in subsection 146(1) only for the purposes of section 146, pertaining to the deduction for contributions to Registered Retirement Savings Plans (RRSPs). This definition reflects the type of income that the government is attempting to encourage as the base for tax-assisted retirement savings, i.e., income that requires a certain amount of activity to generate, rather than passive investment income.

iv. Are there words used in the Act that are not defined in the Act but that derive meaning from the way in which they are used?

— Distinguish between the words "means" and "includes".

— Note how the definition of the term "capital property" in section 54 uses the word "means", indicating that this definition is comprehensive and nothing more can be considered. Note also that this definition applies to the use of the term in Subdivision c of Division B in Part I of the Act.

— On the other hand, the definition of the term "personal-use property" in section 54 uses the word "includes", suggesting that use of the term is not limited to the property specifically listed in the definition.

— Both words, "means" and "includes", can be used in the same definition, as found in the definition of the word "office" in subsection 248(1).

— Note the use of the expression "for greater certainty".

— For example, this expression is used in paragraph 256(1.2)(*b*) to expand the meaning of the concept of "control", as used in subsection 256(1), among other provisions in section 256, pertaining to associated corporations.

— A deeming rule is often used to change the ordinary meaning of a term under specified facts or conditions.

— For example, subsection 250(1) "deems" a person, who may not ordinarily be considered to be a full-year resident of Canada based on the facts, to be deemed to be a resident of Canada for a full year. One condition for that deeming rule to apply is set out in paragraph 250(1)(*b*), where the person "was, at any time in the year, a member of the Canadian Forces". That person may not have been physically present in Canada at any time in the year but is deemed to be a full-year resident.

— Distinguish between the use of the words "may" and "shall".

— Where a provision uses the word "shall", the rule is mandatory. For example, subsection 6(1) begins by stating that "there shall be included . . .".

— Where a provision uses the word "may", the rule is permissive. For example, subsection 20(1), pertaining to deductions from business or property income, indicates that "there may be deducted" specified amounts listed in the subsection. Hence, a deduction for capital cost allowance or a reserve is permissive and need not be taken to the maximum allowed or at all.

— Note the use of the words "notwithstanding" and "except".

— For example, "notwithstanding" is used in subsection 20(1) to allow certain deductions specified in the subsection despite the fact that certain paragraphs in subsection 18(1) may prohibit their deduction, by stating that "no deduction shall be made" for in respect of specified expenditures. As a specific example, paragraph 18(1)(*b*) prohibits the deduction of "an outlay or loss or replacement of capital property" or "an allowance in respect of depreciation". However, paragraph 20(1)(*a*) provides for the deduction of capital cost allowance, which represents all or part of the capital cost of a property.

— Note that paragraph 18(1)(*b*) also provides an exception to its prohibition, by the use of the words "except as expressly permitted in this Part". Paragraph 20(1)(*a*) provides for such express permission for capital cost allowance.

— Note the use of the words "and" and "or", which are often used to separate conditions in a provision. Usually, these words are used between the second-last and last conditions in a list of more than two. However, they may be inserted between each condition in a list of more than two, as is the case in paragraph 256(1)(*c*), pertaining to a rule determining associated corporations, where "and" is inserted twice to join three conditions.

— Where the word "and" is used, each one of the conditions in the list must be satisfied for the provision to apply. Hence, if one condition in the list is not satisfied, then the provision does not apply.

— Where the word "or" is used, only one of the conditions in the list must be satisfied for the provision to apply. See for example, paragraph 256(1)(*b*) pertaining to a rule determining associated corporations.

— If a requirement or condition is stated in the negative, the use of the word "or" may have the same effect as the use of the word "and" in a positive statement of the requirement. For example, look at paragraph 8(1)(*f*) pertaining to the deduction of sales expenses by an employee. There are three conditions in subparagraphs (v), (vi) and (vii), joined by the word "or". However, these conditions are preceded, in the midamble (i.e., in the middle of the paragraph), by the words "to the extent that those amounts were not . . .." This means that none of the three conditions can be satisfied by the facts if the deduction provision is to apply with the effect that the word "or" after the negative statement has the same effect as the word "and" following a positive statement.

— Consider the use of limiting terms and their effect on the meaning of words.

— Note the use of the phrase "for the purposes of" in subsection 6(2). This subsection provides a formula for calculating a reasonable standby charge for the purposes of the inclusion specified in paragraph 6(1)(*e*).

— Also, note the use of the phrase "subject to" in subsection 9(2), pertaining to a loss from business or property. The rule in subsection 9(2) is subject to the rule in section 31 which limits the loss otherwise determined by subsection 9(2) in the case of certain farming losses.

— The word "prescribed" is used throughout the Act to signal the existence of a Regulation that must be considered or a form that must be filed in complying with the provision of the Act. The word is defined in subsection 248(1).

— Look at the use of the phrase "prescribed by regulation" in paragraph 110.1(8)(*e*), pertaining to the deduction of certain donations by a corporation. The notes to that provision contain a section for "Related Regulations", which specifies the particular regulation that is prescribed.

— For an example of the use of "prescribed form", look at subsection 8(6.1), pertaining to the deduction for an eligible tool of an employee tradesperson. Paragraph (*c*) of that provision requires certification in prescribed form. The notes to that provision contain a "Forms" section which indicates that the prescribed form is T2200.

— The word "Idem" is often seen as the heading (in bold type) of a provision. It is the Latin word meaning "the same", as in the same heading.

— Look at the heading for subsection 13(2), pertaining to recapture of capital cost allowance claimed on certain passenger vehicles. This provision follows subsection 13(1) pertaining to recapture, generally, so subsection 13(2) is headed "Idem" to denote that it deals with more on recapture.

v. Can the meaning of general words used in the Act be determined by inference following an established rule of interpretation?

— Class words: where a general word, such as the word "similar", follows a list of particular or specific words (i.e., words of a class of words), the general word is to take its meaning from the context of the specific words.

— For example, see the definition of "eligible capital expenditure" in subsection 14(5). Subparagraph (*f*)(iii) lists "a share, bond, debenture, mortgage, hypothecary claim, note, bill or *other similar property*" [italics added]. A "similar" property would have to fit in the same class as the properties specifically listed.

— As another example, consider the definition of "listed personal property" in section 54. Paragraph (*a*) lists "print, etching, drawing, painting, sculpture, or *other similar work of art*" [italics added]. A "similar work of art" would have to fit the same class as the listed types of art. Would a poster be similar to a print?

vi. Are there words used in the Act that may derive their meaning from other legislation?

— Some legal terms used in the Act may derive their meaning from other Canadian statutes.

— For example, the word "corporation", by itself, is not defined in the Act. Reference to a corporate law, like the *Canada Business Corporations Act*, may be necessary.

— Similarly, the term "legal stated capital" may be defined in corporate law.

— A dictionary of legal terms can be consulted for a consolidation of these definitions.

vii. What is the role of the *Interpretation Act* in interpreting undefined words or terms used in the *Income Tax Act*?

— This legislation was enacted to provide a source of defined words or terms used in all federal statutes and regulations, including the *Income Tax Act*.

— Section 16 of the *Interpretation Act* indicates that words used in a Regulation are to be given the same meaning as the same words used in the Act to which the Regulation relates.

— Section 26 indicates that when a deadline falls on a "holiday", the deadline is considered to fall on the next day that is not a holiday.

— For example, if the 60-day RRSP deadline, which is usually March 1 in years other than a leap year, falls on a holiday, the deadline is moved to the next business day. The word "holiday" is defined in section 35, the general definitions section of the *Interpretation Act*, to include Sunday.

viii. What is the role of the courts in determining the meaning of words used in the *Income Tax Act*?

— The courts have considered and continue to consider the meaning of words and terms used in the Act.

— The meaning of the word "profit" has been considered by the courts over a period of years. In the process, the reliance on accounting principles in the determination of profit has been established.

— The basis of the meaning of the word "control", used in the context of legal control, as in provisions pertaining to acquisition of control in subsection 111(4), was established many years ago by the Exchequer Court of Canada, the intermediate-level court at the time. The same meaning of the word "control" is used in section 256, pertaining to associated corporations, but the concept has been broadened to include "control in fact", as described in subsection 256(5.1), applicable to the use of that phrase anywhere in the Act.

— In determining the meaning of a word not defined in the Act, the courts have often attempted to ascertain the ordinary meaning of a word in the context in which it is used in the Act.

— In this process of determining the ordinary meaning of a word, the courts have often consulted a standard dictionary. If you are trying to determine the meaning of a word used in the Act, but not defined in the Act or other relevant legislation and not considered in the same context by a court, you could do the same. It is best to consult a Canadian edition of a standard dictionary which is more likely to provide an appropriate meaning in the Canadian context.

— The courts attempt to determine the conventional, normal or everyday meaning or usage of a word or term. In the process the courts follow the presumption that Parliament used words of ordinary or common usage and the more common meaning of the word is used.

WHAT AM I MISSING?

1. Consider the consequences of one provision on another.

— For example, consider the impact of your determination of proceeds of disposition of property for a vendor on the ACB of the purchaser and the impact of the relationship between the parties on both proceeds and cost.

— Look for related provisions and regulations in the notes to the provision you are attempting to interpret.

2. Look for the existence of and consider the applicability of an anti-avoidance rule that is specific to the provision and/or consider the applicability of the general anti-avoidance rule (GAAR).

AM I READING THE PROVISION CORRECTLY?

Look for other sources to confirm your interpretation, such as:

— court decisions for the judicial position in common law

— CRA publications, including Interpretation Bulletins (ITs), Information Circulars (ICs), technical interpretations, etc. and their replacements in *Tax Folios* (these do not have the force of law unless they can be shown to have a basis in law, but they can be instructive in helping to know the CRA's views)

— articles in technical publications of the Canadian Tax Foundation, such as the *Canadian Tax Journal* and *Conference Reports*, while not the law, provide views of professionals in the field

EXHIBIT 1: SUMMARY OF IDENTIFYING TAX ISSUES

Gather and Sort Information

1. Who is involved and what do we know about them?

a. Draw a diagram

i. Indicate all of the parties involved and their relationships to each other.

ii. Indicate the ownership of assets both before and after any transactions.

b. Who is my "client" and what are their objectives?

i. Individual, corporation, partnership, trust

ii. What is their "business"/how do they earn income?

iii. What are my client's short-, mid- and long-term objectives and what is important to them?

c. Develop a tax profile for each of the parties

Individual

i. Age

ii. Significant relationships

iii. Estate plans

Trust

i. Type of trust — *inter vivos* or testamentary

ii. Details on the terms of the trust, settlor, trustee, beneficiaries, property held, distribution terms

Corporation

i. Canadian-Controlled Private Corporation (CCPC)

— Small Business Corporation (SBC)

ii. Private, public

Assets and liabilities of each client

i. For each significant asset identify the adjusted cost base (ACB), fair market value (FMV), undepreciated capital cost (UCC) or other tax attributes.

ii. Identify the amount and terms of any debt.

Amount and type of income being earned by each client

i. Employment/personal services business

ii. Active business income — Canadian or foreign

iii. Property/aggregate investment income — Canadian or foreign

iv. Dividends — for individuals — Canadian eligible or not eligible or foreign

— for corporations — Canadian connected or portfolio, or foreign

v. Taxable capital gains, allowable capital losses

vi. Income (loss) vs. capital gain (loss)

vii. Other income or deductions

viii. Net or non-capital losses from other years

ix. Capital gains deduction

x. Personal tax — graduated tax rates, marginal tax rate, credits applicable

xi. Corporate tax — basic tax rate, provincial abatement, small business deduction, general rate reduction, M&PP deduction, foreign tax credit, additional refundable tax, Part IV tax, refundable Part I tax, dividend refund, ITCs

Shareholders

i. Individuals, corporations, trusts or partnerships

ii. Relationships among shareholders

iii. Details of shareholdings — number of shares

iv. Legal control — voting rights

v. *De facto* control — financial or other influence

vi. Adjusted cost base (ACB), paid-up capital (PUC)

vii. Details of a shareholder agreement

viii. ABIL, capital gain deduction information

Relationships

i. With shareholders (related, affiliated, control, employees, etc.)

ii. With other corporations (related, affiliated, control, associated, connected, etc.)

iii. Employer/employee, corporation/shareholder, partnership/partner, trust/beneficiary

Liability for tax

i. Canadian residents — worldwide income

ii. Foreign residents — Canadian source

Tax risk tolerance

i. Taxpayer's risk tolerance

ii. Professional adviser's risk tolerance

iii. Risk to reputation, client/professional relationship, penalties

2. What are the transactions or events?

  a. **Identify all of the completed or planned transactions or events** — sale, purchase, loan given or received, gift given or received, benefit given or received

   i. Between shareholder and corporation

   ii. Between employees and employer

   iii. Between corporations

   iv. Between individuals

   v. Actual transactions — compliance, appeal

   vi. Proposed transactions — planning

  b. **Draw one or more diagrams** showing the transactions or events and all of the parties involved.

  c. **Draw a timeline** identifying dates of the completed or planned transactions or events

  d. **What is the taxpayer's purpose** for the transaction or events?

   i. Business planning, e.g., expansion, creditor proofing

   ii. Tax planning/avoidance, e.g., income splitting, loss utilization

  e. **What is the impact on debt or share financing?**

  f. **How is the transaction or event accounted for?**

   i. ASPE, IFRS

3. What is missing?

  a. **Identify any information** that you think is missing from what you have been given.

  b. **Look for gaps** in the tax profile or missing information about a transaction or event.

  c. **Identify/list any assumptions** you are making.

Analyze the Information

4. What is the impact on income for each party to the transaction?

   — Identify the parties — vendor/purchaser, donor/recipient, estate/beneficiary

   — Identify the types of income impacted

5. What is the impact on tax attributes for each party to the transaction?

  a. Cost, ACB, UCC, PUC

6. Does any anti-avoidance or other special provision apply?

  a. A tax benefit is realized

  b. Transactions not at arm's length or not at fair market value

  c. Transactions that allow losses to be utilized

  d. Transactions that create losses, especially transactions between related parties

  e. Income or expenses are moved to another taxpayer

  f. A benefit is conferred on another taxpayer

Identify the Tax-Related Issues

7. Based on the above, what are the issues?

a. Identify all of the issues that are supported by the facts (tax, accounting, finance, ethical, governance, business, personal, etc.)

b. Identify compliance (completed transactions) vs. planning (proposed transactions) issues

c. Are the benefits of the plan worth the cost of designing, implementing and maintaining the plan?

d. Be able to explain why these issues are relevant

8. Which issues are more important?

a. Use judgement to prioritize and group the issues in terms of importance to your role and importance to the client's objectives. Considerations include urgency, materiality and risk.

b. Ask yourself:

i. What am I being asked to do?

c. What extra value can I provide?

d. Are there important issues your client is not aware of?

e. Are there non-tax issues that must be decided first?

EXHIBIT 2: SUMMARY OF READING THE *INCOME TAX ACT*

How do I find something?

1. Know how the Act is structured in order to recognize where something is most likely to be found.

a. Parts (particularly Part I), Divisions, Subdivisions

b. Know where to find the definition sections for each Division or Subdivision and for the Act, and note the wording used to indicate the scope of a definition or where in the Act the definitions are applicable

2. Look in the alphabetical Topical Index compiled by the editors of the edition of the Act that you are using. If the word or term is used anywhere in the Act or the Regulations, it may be listed there with a provision reference.

3. Look in the Sectional List provided immediately before the provisions of the Act. Scanning the headings in that list in the area of the Act that you are searching may help you determine a provision that is applicable.

4. Look at the "Related Sections" and other notes at the end of subsections and paragraphs to see if there are any other provisions or issues to consider.

How do I read the legislation?

1. Does this provision apply?

a. Identify the start and end of the sentence.

b. Identify the components of the provision. There will usually be four components, as follows:

i. To whom, i.e., an individual, a corporation, a partnership or a trust, does the provision apply?

ii. What is the transaction, activity or event to which the provision applies, and what are the conditions for that provision to apply?

iii. What are the consequences of the provision, if it applies, to the person who is involved in the transaction, activity or event?

iv. What is the timeframe over which the provision applies?

c. Determine the meaning of the key words used in the provision by following some established principles of interpreting a statute.

i. Grammar, including punctuation, sentence structure and the ordinary sense of words are important in determining the meaning of words, phrases, clauses and sentences in a provision.

ii. What is the intention of Parliament for or the policy purpose of this provision?

iii. Are any of the words or terms used in the provision defined in the *Income Tax Act?*

iv. Are there words used in the Act that are not defined in the Act but that derive meaning from the way in which they are used?

v. Can the meaning of general words used in the Act be determined by inference following an established rule of interpretation?

vi. Are there words used in the Act that may derive their meaning from other legislation?

vii. What is the role of the *Interpretation Act* in interpreting undefined words or terms used in the *Income Tax Act?*

viii. What is the role of the courts in determining the meaning of words used in the *Income Tax Act?*

What am I missing?

1. Consider the consequences of one provision on another.

2. Look for the existence of and consider the applicability of an anti-avoidance rule that is specific to the provision and/or consider the applicability of the general anti-avoidance rule (GAAR).

Am I reading the provision correctly?

Look for other sources to confirm your interpretation.

REFERENCES

Chasmar, Hugh. *TAX 616, Statutory Interpretation, Course Notes*, MTax Program, School of Accounting and Finance, University of Waterloo.

Laiken, Stanley N. *ACC 604, Statutory Interpretation, Course Notes*, Master of Accounting Program, School of Accounting and Finance, University of Waterloo.

Identifying Tax-Related Issues

INTRODUCTION

After many years of teaching tax, we have determined that key concepts in tax can be challenging for many students to grasp. As a result, students take a surface approach to learning — memorizing the basics to meet the requirements of our tax courses — rather than developing the deeper understanding needed to become competent tax professionals who can respond to the complex and evolving needs of clients.

Decoding Project

Learning stumbling blocks are referred to as "bottlenecks" within an area of the higher education teaching and learning literature called "Decoding the Disciplines" (DtD). Underlying each bottleneck are often disciplinary ways of thinking about a subject that are natural and tacit for experts but difficult for students. "Decoding" bottlenecks, therefore, involves experts "reconstruct[ing] the steps that they themselves do when solving similar problems,"[1] so that they may be modeled for students and integrated into teaching. Thus, DtD is also a methodology,[2] as it provides a clearly-delineated, seven-step process for identifying and deconstructing bottlenecks and provides guidelines for designing instructional, motivational, and assessment strategies that support deep learning of the troublesome concepts.

During the Fall 2012 and Winter 2013 terms Jim Barnett and Julie Timmermans (Centre for Teaching Excellence at the University of Waterloo) spent time identifying topics in our undergraduate tax program that students found challenging (bottlenecks). Information gathered from students and faculty was used to develop and prioritize a list of topics that presented the greatest barriers.

Results

Students rated a list of potential bottlenecks in terms of their perceived level of importance and their perceived level of understanding. Two topics that were rated as the most important and least understood were:

1. being able to identify tax-related issues in a non-directed fact situation and

2. being able to read and understand the *Income Tax Act*.

We worked with tax faculty and tax practitioners to "decode" these bottlenecks — that is, to construct a series of steps that experts in the field would use to address these issues. By following these steps, students will be able to develop their skills faster and more completely than if they are left to figure out these steps on their own.

In the following sections we will address these two bottlenecks in detail.

---

[1] Middendorf & Pace, 2004b, p. 5

[2] Diaz & Pace, 2012

IDENTIFYING TAX-RELATED ISSUES[3]

What do we mean when we use the term "tax-related issue?" A tax-related issue is something that might have positive or negative implications and needs further analysis. Issues may relate to opportunities that can be taken advantage of or penalties to be avoided. They may be tax specific or related to financial accounting, finance, ethics, governance, business or personal matters that relate to the tax matters under consideration.

Don't wait until you reach step 7 to identify the issues. Identify them "as you gather, sort and analyze." Issues may be identified early or near the end, but never stop looking for them. Issues that are identified can be addressed, but those that are not identified represent a potential threat either as an opportunity missed or a penalty incurred; neither option is desirable.

We have decoded this bottleneck by setting out eight steps organized under three main headings:

> Gather and sort information
>
> Analyze the information
>
> Identify the tax-related issues

In this section, we will describe our approach in some detail and provide an example of how to apply it.

Gather and Sort Information

In this first section, the goal is to uncover all the information you can. You want to know about the parties involved, their relationships to each other, and the details of their actual or planned transactions.

1. Who is involved and what do we know about them?

a. Draw a diagram

Start by drawing a diagram indicating all of the parties involved, their relationships to each other, and, if there is a transaction involved, the ownership of the assets both before and after. Relationships include parent-child, brother-sister, employer-employee and shareholder-corporation.

b. Who is my "client" and what are their objectives?

It is important to know who your client is, the "business" they are in, and their short- and longer-term goals. With this understanding it may be possible to find a more tax-efficient way for them to achieve their objectives. It is also helpful to understand what they don't want to do or their tax risk tolerance (see below), as this may put some limits on what you might recommend.

c. Develop a tax profile for each of the parties

A tax profile is just an organized way of gathering all the information you need on your client. Not all of it will be directly related to the particular situation you are analyzing, but sometimes it is difficult to determine this in advance. It is best to gather too much information than not enough.

Individual

For individuals, you should know their age, significant relationships, and, if possible, their estate plans.

---

[3] Barnett, J., & Timmermans, J. (2013).

Trust

If the client is a trust, then determine whether the person who set up the trust was alive at the time (*inter vivos* trust) or whether the trust was established under someone's will on death (testamentary trust).

Who settled the trust? Who is the trustee? Who are the income and capital beneficiaries? How was the trust established? When will the property held in the trust be distributed? What discretion does the trustee have in making decisions?

Corporation

Identifying the type of corporation is crucial for determining how the income earned in the corporation is taxed. The main classifications are Canadian-controlled private corporation (CCPC) or public corporation.

Within the CCPC category, consider whether the company meets the conditions to be a small business corporation (SBC), which is important for purposes of the capital gains exemption and the allowable business investment loss provisions.

Assets and liabilities of each client

The tax value of each asset is important information. For each significant asset, identify the adjusted cost base (ACB), fair market value (FMV), undepreciated capital cost (UCC), or other tax attribute.

Debt plays a key role in financial planning. For any debt, identify the amount outstanding and the terms, such as repayment terms and restrictive covenants.

Amount and type of income being earned by each client

It is very common for different types of income to be taxed in different ways for both individuals and corporations. As a result, it is important to identify the types of income being earned by the different types of taxpayers identified above. The following is a list to consider:

Individuals

— Employment

— Business — Canadian or foreign

— Property — Canadian or foreign

— Dividends from Canadian corporations — eligible dividends and non-eligible dividends

— Dividends from foreign corporations and tax withheld at source

— Taxable capital gains and allowable capital losses, including whether QSBC shares or other types of capital property were disposed of

— Income (loss) vs. capital gain (capital loss)

— Other income or deductions

— Net or non-capital losses from other years

— Capital gains deduction

— Personal tax — graduated tax rates, marginal tax rate, credits applicable

Corporation

— Active business income — Canadian and foreign

— Personal service business

— Aggregate investment income — Canadian and foreign property income, net taxable capital gains

— Dividends from Canadian-connected and non-connected corporations

— Dividends from foreign corporations and tax withheld at source

— Income (loss) vs. capital gain (capital loss)

— Net or non-capital losses from other years

— Corporate tax — basic tax rate, provincial abatement, small business deduction, general rate reduction, M&PP deduction, foreign tax credit, additional refundable tax, Part IV tax, refundable Part I tax, dividend refund, ITCs

Shareholders

It is important to have detailed information on shareholders, particularly shareholders of closely held private corporations. This section applies to all shareholders, regardless of whether they are individuals, corporations, trusts or partnerships.

Details of shareholdings include such information as number of shares owned, what was paid for the shares (ACB), shares' voting rights, and the paid-up capital (PUC).

It should also be determined whether the shareholder has any financial or other influence that, if exercised, could result in control (*de facto*) of the corporation.

The details of a shareholder agreement are also very important.

Has the shareholder ever reported an allowable business investment loss (ABIL) or claimed a capital gain deduction?

Relationships

Relationships need to be identified. Are the parties involved related or affiliated? If the shareholder is a corporation, is it connected or associated? Is the relationship one or more of employer/employee, corporation/shareholder, partnership/partner or trust/beneficiary?

Liability for tax

Are the parties Canadian residents and, therefore, subject to tax on their worldwide income, or are they foreign residents and taxed in Canada, in some fashion, on their Canadian-source income?

Tax risk tolerance

Before making any recommendation to a client, it is important to understand their risk tolerance, particularly as it relates to tax. Some taxpayers want to pay the least amount of tax and are willing to accept some risk of reassessment in order to do this. Others want to minimize any risk of reassessment.

You also need to assess your own risk tolerance as a professional adviser. There may be some transactions that you are not comfortable supporting because of the risk involved.

Risk is not simply the risk of reassessment and potential interest and penalties; it also involves risk to reputation and relationships. A significant reassessment could damage your reputation in the community, as well as the relationship between the taxpayer and the professional adviser.

2. What are the transactions or events?

Virtually all transactions or events have tax consequences, so identify all those that are completed or proposed. Also, large transactions may be made up of a series of smaller transactions, so identify each component. Don't just consider financial transactions. Events such as marriage and death have significant tax implications as well. Here are some things to consider:

Identify all of the completed or planned transactions or events, such as a sale, purchase, loan given or received, gift given or received, and benefit given or received.

Draw one or more diagrams showing the transactions or events and all of the parties involved. You may need to draw multiple diagrams if there is a series of transactions. This will help you identify each of the components involved in each of the transactions.

Draw a timeline identifying dates of the completed or planned transactions or events. The order of transactions or when they occurred or will occur is often an important detail.

Identify the taxpayer's purpose for the transaction. Examples include business expansion, creditor proofing, income splitting, loss utilization, and estate planning. Understanding the purpose may help you identify problems or alternatives.

What impact will this transaction have on the taxpayer's debt or share financing? Will any debt covenants be broken? Will the voting control change?

How is the transaction or event accounted for under accounting standards for private enterprise (ASPE) or international financial reporting standards (IFRS)? The accounting for a transaction can have a significant impact on how the outcome is viewed, so it is important to address the accounting issues in advance.

3. What is missing?

It is important to identify any information that you think is missing by looking for gaps in the tax profile or missing information about a transaction or event. Clearly identify this information and list any assumptions you are making.

Analyze the Information

Now that you have gathered all the information, you need to analyze the transactions or events to determine the tax consequences.

4. What is the impact on income for each party to the transaction?

All transactions have more than one party involved. They may be individuals, corporations, partnerships or trusts. The transaction may, for example, be that of vendor/purchaser, donor/recipient, or estate/beneficiary, and all transactions will have an impact on income either now or in the future. It is important to identify the income effect on each of the parties involved, in the present or in the future.

The types of income are identified above.

5. What is the impact on tax attributes for each party to the transaction?

All transactions have an impact on the tax attributes of the property transferred and/or received.

These attributes include the cost, adjusted cost base (ACB), undepreciated capital cost (UCC), and paid-up capital (PUC).

6. Does any anti-avoidance or other special provision apply?

This is a crucial part of the analysis. The Act is full of special rules and exceptions that impact income and tax attributes. In particular, look for these special provisions where:

— A tax benefit is realized

— Transactions are not at arm's length or not at fair market value

— Transactions allow losses to be utilized

— Transactions create losses, especially transactions between related parties

— Income or expenses are moved to another taxpayer

— A benefit is conferred on another taxpayer

Identify the Tax-Related Issues

Now that you have gathered and analyzed the information, you need to condense it into specific issues and determine which issues are more important in light of the taxpayer's objectives, the transactions involved, and the level of risk. At this point you don't have to have all the issues resolved, just identified.

Remember what we mean when we use the term "tax-related issue" — an issue that might have positive or negative implications that needs further analysis. Issues may relate to opportunities that can be taken advantage of or penalties to be avoided. They may be tax specific or related to financial accounting, finance, ethics, governance, business or personal matters that relate to the tax matters under consideration.

7. Based on the above, what are the issues?

Identify all of the issues that are supported by the facts (tax, accounting, finance, ethical, governance, business, personal, etc.). Identify compliance (completed transactions) vs. planning (proposed transactions) issues. Assess whether the benefits of the plan are worth the cost of designing, implementing and maintaining the plan.

Be able to explain why these issues are relevant to your client.

8. Which issues are more important?

Use judgement to prioritize and group the issues in terms of importance to your role and importance to the client's objectives. Considerations include urgency, materiality and risk.

Ask yourself what you are being asked to do and what extra value you can provide; there may be important tax issues your client is not aware of.

Are there non-tax issues that must be decided first?

Case Example for Identifying Tax-Related Issues

Sherry Huang works for Pub Co Inc., a Canadian listed public company. Two years ago she was granted an option by her employer to buy 1,000 shares of Pub Co for $25 each. This year she exercised the stock option when the fair market value of the shares was $35; she sold the shares later this year for $40. The fair market value at the grant date was equal to the exercise price of $25 per share.

Sherry is in the top tax bracket while her husband, Tom, and 16-year old daughter, Rachel, are not. Her goal is to split income with her husband and daughter to reduce their overall tax burden. To accomplish this she plans to give her daughter $10,000 to buy shares on the stock exchange and to give her husband $30,000 to buy government bonds. She would like your advice on her completed and proposed transactions.

Gather and Sort Information

1. Who is involved and what do we know about them?

a. Draw a diagram

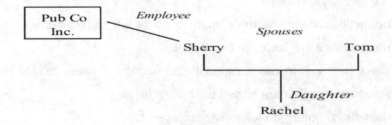

Before: Sherry has proceeds of $40,000 and owes tax on the option.

Tom and Rachel have no assets that we know of.

After: Sherry gives $40,000 away and is left with no cash and owes tax on the option.

Tom has cash of $30,000 and will potentially earn interest and a capital gain or loss.

Rachel has cash of $10,000 and will potentially earn dividends and a capital gain or loss.

b. Who is my "client" and what are their objectives?

Sherry, an individual, is your client. She is an employee of a public company, so she earns employment income. She has no other income that we know of.

Sherry wants to split income with her husband and daughter because they are in a lower tax bracket than she is.

c. Develop a tax profile for each of the parties

Individual

We don't know much about Sherry except that she is married to Tom and they have a 16-year-old daughter. We don't know anything about her estate plans.

Assets and liabilities of each client

Sherry has cash from the sale of her Pub Co shares of $40,000.

Tom will have bonds with and ACB and FMV of $30,000

Rachel will have stock with an ACB and FMV of $10,000.

Amount and type of income being earned by each client

Sherry will have employment income from the exercise of her stock option. She may also be able to claim a Division C deduction related to this stock option. These are issues to be determined.

Tom may earn interest on the bonds he buys and realize a capital gain or capital loss when he sells the bonds.

Rachel may earn dividends on the shares she buys and realize a capital gain or capital loss when she sells the shares. The dividends will be subject to the gross-up and credit as eligible dividends.

Shareholders

Neither Sherry nor Tom will be shareholders at the end of the year.

Rachel will own shares in a public company.

Relationships

Sherry is an employee of Pub Co Inc., but she is no longer a shareholder.

Sherry and Tom are spouses, so they are related and affiliated.

As their daughter, Rachel is related to both Sherry and Tom.

Liability for tax

We should confirm that Sherry, Tom and Rachel are residents of Canada and have been all year.

As residents, they will be taxed on their world income.

Tax risk tolerance

Sherry has not expressed her tolerance for tax risk. We need to ask her about this.

We need to be sure that our recommendations don't carry a financial or reputational risk that is not acceptable to either Sherry or us, as her advisers.

2. What are the transactions or events?

a. Identify all of the completed or planned transactions or events

Completed: Sherry exercised her stock option and sold the shares

Planned: Sherry will give $30,000 to Tom and $10,000 to Rachel

b. Draw one or more diagrams showing the transactions or events and all of the parties involved.

Before	After

Sherry		**Sherry**		**Tom**	
Proceeds	$ 40,000	Cash	$ -	Cash/bonds	$ 30,000
Tax owing	?	Tax owing	?		

	Rachel	
	Cash/shares	$ 10,000

c. Draw a timeline identifying dates of the completed or planned transactions or events.

All events took place this year.

d. What is the taxpayer's purpose for the transaction or events?

i. Tax planning — income splitting

e. What is the impact on debt or share financing?

None

f. How is the transaction or event accounted for?

N/A

3. What is missing?

Are Sherry, Tom and Rachel Canadian residents?

Will Sherry want the money back in the future or is this a true gift?

Analyze the Information

4. What is the impact on income for each party to the transaction?

Completed Transaction — stock option exercised

Pub Co is a listed company, therefore, employment income is recognized when option is exercised

Employment income = 1,000 shares × ($35-$25) = $10,000

Sherry's ACB in these shares becomes $25 + ($35-$25) = $35/share

Since the option price was not less than the FMV at grant date, Sherry is eligible for the Division C deduction of 50% x $10,000 employment income = $5,000

Sherry is in the top tax bracket of 46%, so her tax owing on the stock option will be 46% x ($10,000-$5,000) = $2,300.

Completed Transaction — sale of stock option shares

Proceeds (1,000 x $40)	$ 40,000
ACB (above 1,000 x $35)	(35,000)
Capital gain	$ 5,000
Taxable capital gain	$ 2,500
Tax owing @ 46%	$ 1,150

Planned Transactions — gift to Tom

Tom receives $30,000 and buys bonds to earn interest income and possibly a capital gain or loss on the sale.

Planned Transaction — gift to Rachel

Rachel receives $10,000 and buys shares to earn dividend income and possibly a capital gain or loss on the sale.

Since she will purchase public company shares, the dividends will be eligible dividends with a dividend tax credit.

5. What is the impact on tax attributes for each party to the transaction?

Tom's ACB of the bonds he purchases will be $30,000.

Rachel's ACB of the shares she purchases will be $20,000.

6. Does any anti-avoidance or other special provision apply?

The exercise of the stock option and subsequent sale of the shares does not create a tax benefit nor does it shift income to anyone else.

The gifts to Tom and Rachel do result in a tax benefit. The interest and dividends earned by Tom and Rachel will be taxed at a lower rate than if Sherry earned them. Sherry has shifted income to and conferred a benefit on her husband and daughter.

Identify the Tax-Related Issues

7. Based on the above, what are the issues?

— How is Sherry going to pay for her tax liability of $3,450 on the stock option shares?

— Since Sherry is shifting interest income (i.e., income from property) and potentially capital gain to Tom through a gift, the attribution rules will apply.

— Since Sherry is shifting dividend income (i.e., income from property) and potentially capital gain to Rachel, who is under 18, through a gift, the attribution rules will apply.

— Does Sherry really want to give this money away permanently or would she prefer to keep it for her own retirement?

— Is there a better way for Sherry to accomplish her goals?

8. Which issues are more important?

— The completed transactions (exercise of stock option and sale of shares) are important for determining how much cash Sherry has to deal with. However, estimating the tax owing is not complicated.

— The planned transactions require more research to determine what Sherry's goals are and to develop options for her to consider.

REFERENCES

Barnett, J., & J. Timmermans. (2013). *Decoding bottlenecks in tax*. University of Waterloo, Waterloo, Canada.

Dìaz, A., J. Middendorf, D. Pace, & J. Shopkow (2011). *Definition of Decoding the Disciplines*. Retrieved from: http://decodingthedisciplines.org

Dìaz, A., & D. Pace, (2012, June). *Introduction to Decoding the Disciplines*. Handouts from the preconference workshop facilitated at the Fourth Biennial Threshold Concepts Conference, Dublin, Ireland.

Middendorf, J., & D. Pace, D. (Eds.). (2004a). Decoding the Disciplines: Helping students learn disciplinary ways of thinking. *New Directions for Teaching and Learning, 98*. San Francisco: Jossey Bass.

Middendorf, J., & D. Pace (2004b). Decoding the Disciplines: A model for helping students learn disciplinary ways of thinking. In J. Middendorf, & D. Pace (Eds.), Decoding the Disciplines: Helping students learn disciplinary ways of thinking. *New Directions for Teaching and Learning, 98* (pp. 1-12). San Francisco: Jossey Bass.

Shopkow, L. (2010). What 'Decoding the Disciplines' has to offer 'Threshold Concepts.' In J. H. F. Meyer, R. Land, & C. Baillie (Eds.), *Threshold concepts and transformational learning* (pp. 317-332). Rotterdam: Sense.

Shopkow, L., A. Dìaz., J. Middendorf, & D. Pace (2012). The History Learning Project "decodes" a discipline: The union of research and teaching. In K. McKinney (Ed.), *Scholarship of teaching and learning in and across the disciplines*. Bloomington, IN: Indiana University Press.

Chapter 1

Introduction

Learning Goals

Know, Understand and Explain

By the end of this chapter you will know, understand and be able to explain:

- The different roles that professional accountants and lawyers may play in providing tax services.
- The principles that make good tax policy.
- How the perspective on income differs among economic analysis, financial reporting, and the *Income Tax Act*.
- How tax policy is created in Canada.
- The appeals process in the Canadian tax system.
- Strategies for interpreting the *Income Tax Act*.
- How to reference the *Income Tax Act*.
- The common sources of tax rules and sources for interpretation in the Canadian tax system.
- The general structure of the GST/HST.

Apply

By the end of this chapter you will be able to apply your knowledge and understanding to:

- Assess the attributes of prospective tax policies.

Exercise Questions
¶1,850 in the Study Guide

Assignment Problems
¶1,875 in the Study Guide

CHAPTER 1 — LEARNING CHART

Problem Descriptions

Exercises

1	Identify sections of the Act
2	Determine income, taxable income and basic federal tax
3	Identify components of 212(1)

Assignment Problems

1	Identify section of the Act
2	Determine income using ordering rules
3	Identify and define words/terms found in section 2

Study Notes

¶1,850 EXERCISES

Exercise 1

ITA: 8, 15, 20, 38, 69, 81, 108, 150

For each of the following items, identify the appropriate provision of the Act which deals with the item listed. Be as specific as possible in citing the reference to the Act, i.e., Part, Division, Subdivision, Section, Subsection, etc. Use of the Sectional List at the beginning of the Wolters Kluwer edition of the CANADIAN INCOME TAX ACT and/or the Topical Index at the end of the book may be helpful. However, using the DVD attached to the back cover of the textbook may provide faster search results.

(A) Definition of "taxable capital gain".

(B) Deduction for certain annual professional membership dues paid by an employee.

(C) Taxability of payments received as income from property acquired as personal injury award.

(D) Deductibility of an expense based on its magnitude.

(E) Definition of a "parent" under the Act.

(F) Definition of an *"inter vivos"* trust.

(G) Deadline for filing of a tax return for a deceased person.

(H) Taxability of a benefit received from a corporation by a shareholder.

(I) Transaction price in a non-arm's length disposition of property.

(J) Deductibility of fees for investment advice.

Exercise 2

ITA: Divisions B and C

Mr. Malcolm Miller has provided you with a list of various sources of income, losses, deductions, and credits for the purpose of determining his basic federal tax.

Income (net):

Business income	$10,000
Property income	3,000
Retiring allowance from a former employer	20,000
Employment income from new employer	60,000
Taxable capital gains (net of allowable capital losses)	20,000

Deduction and Losses:

Rental property loss	4,000

Carry forward Losses and Tax Credits:

Canada Pension Plan contributions tax credit	382
Non-capital losses from a previous year	4,000
Tuition tax credits transfer from son	80
Net capital losses from a previous year	5,000
Basic personal and spousal tax credits	3,442
Employment Insurance premiums tax credit	143
Tuition tax credit for night course on computer applications	68
Charitable gifts tax credit	550
Canada employment tax credit	174

— REQUIRED

(A) Determine the income, taxable income and basic federal tax based on the above correct information using the ordering rules in sections 3, 111.1, and 118.92. Assume that federal tax before credits is $18,529 in 2016.

(B) Cross-reference each amount to the appropriate section of the Act.

Exercise 3

Identify the following components of subsection 212(1):

(A) the person who is the subject of the provision,

(B) the activity, event, or condition that must be met for the provision to apply,

(C) the consequences of the activity or event to the person who is the subject of the provision, and

(D) the time frame for the application of the provision.

¶1,875 ASSIGNMENT PROBLEMS

Type 1 Problems

Problem 1

Identify the provision of the Act which deals with each of the following items. Be as specific as possible in citing the reference to the Act (Part, Division, Subdivision, Section, Subsection, etc.). Use of the sectional list at the beginning of the Wolters Kluwer edition of the Act and/or the topical index at the end of the book may be helpful. However, using the DVD attached to the back cover of the textbook may provide faster search results.

(A) Definition of a "person".

(B) Tax credit for donation made by a Canadian resident individual to a Canadian university.

(C) Definition of "balance-due day".

(D) Taxability of group term life insurance premiums paid by an employer on behalf of an employee.

(E) Definition of "capital dividend".

(F) Computation of income tax instalments for individuals.

(G) Definition of a "qualified small business corporation share".

(H) Prescribed requirement to file an information return for a corporation paying a dividend.

(I) Definition of a "testamentary trust".

(J) The calculation of a benefit associated with an interest-free loan from an employer to an employee.

(K) Definition of a "disposition" of non-depreciable capital property.

(L) Limitation on deduction of RRSP administration fees.

(M) General limitation on the amount of deductible expenses.

(N) Deduction from taxable income for taxable dividends that were received by a Canadian corporation.

(O) Tax payable on excess contributions to an RRSP.

Problem 2   ITA: 245; Division B, C

Ms. Irene Vanburg had a tumultuous year in 2016. She broke her engagement early in the year and quit her job. She moved to a resort area to take a waitress job and to start up a fitness instruction business. She has had the following items correctly calculated and classified as either inclusions, deductions or tax credits for the purposes of determining her taxable income and federal tax.

Income (net):

Employment Insurance benefits	$ 600
Employment income	32,600
Property income	775
Rental property income	975
Taxable capital gain (net of allowable capital losses)	100
Retiring allowance from previous employer	800

Deductions and Losses:

Business loss	(275)

Deductions, Losses, and Tax Credits:

Charitable gifts tax credit	26
Child care expenses	1,800
Canada Pension Plan contributions tax credits on employment earnings	216
Medical expenses tax credit	9

Moving expenses	1,700
Non-capital losses from previous year	600
Personal tax credit	1,721
Employment Insurance premiums tax credit	92
Canada employment credit	174

Irene has asked you to determine the income, taxable income, and basic federal tax based on the above correct information using the ordering rules in sections 3, 111.1, and 118.92. Assume federal tax before credits is $4,721 in 2016.

For your files you should cross-reference each amount to the appropriate section of the Act.

Problem 3

ITA: 2

Many words and terms used in the Act have very specific interpretations. Awareness of these interpretations is fundamental to understanding the scheme and application of the Act. These interpretations come from various sources. The primary source is statutory definition; that is, the term is explicitly defined in the Act. Common law principles also determine interpretations for terms. Many court cases have centred on the interpretation of specific words or phrases which were not explicitly defined in the statute. Once such terms are interpreted by the Courts, that interpretation becomes standard for that term. If a term is neither defined in the statute, nor the subject of a common law definition, the word or term must be assigned the meaning provided by everyday language. The definition is often that which can be found in a common dictionary.

Division A of Part I of the Act outlines who is liable for tax. This Division is a fundamental building block for the Act as it defines to whom the Act will apply. Therefore, it is essential that the terms used in this Division are clearly understood.

You have been asked to identify and define those words and terms found in section 2 of the Act, in the order of their use, which you believe require definition. Indicate the references in the Act to the source of the definition for those words or terms which you have so identified. If you use the DVD included with this text the words that are defined elsewhere in the Act are highlighted in red.

You have also been asked to identify the following components of subsection 2(3):

(i) the person who is the subject of the provision,

(ii) the activity, event, or condition that must be met for the provision to apply,

(iii) the consequences of the activity or event to the person who is the subject of the provision, and

(iv) the time frame for the application of the provision.

CHAPTER 1 — SOLUTIONS TO EXERCISES

Exercise 1

The following summary is discussed in more detail below:

Case	Topic	Part	Division	Subdivision	Provision
(A)	Taxable capital gain	I	B	c	paragraph 38(*a*)
(B)	Membership dues	I	B	a	subparagraph 8(1)(*i*)(i)
(C)	Personal injury award	I	B	g	paragraph 81(1)(*g*.1)
(D)	Expense limit	I	B	f	section 67
(E)	Parent	XVII	—	—	subsection 252(2)
(F)	*Inter vivos* trust	I	B	k	subsection 108(1)
(G)	Filing deadline	I	I	—	paragraph 150(1)(*b*)
(H)	Shareholder benefit	I	B	b	subsection 15(1)
(I)	Non-arm's length	I	B	f	paragraph 69(1)(*b*)
(J)	Investment fees	I	B	b	paragraph 20(1)(*bb*)

(A) Part I, Division B, Subdivision c, paragraph 38(*a*): — Most definitions applicable to the Taxable Capital Gains and Allowable Capital Losses subdivision of Part I, Division B are found in section 54. However, this definition is set out at the beginning of Subdivision c. Definitions of terms used throughout the Act are found in subsection 248(1). If a term is not specifically defined in subsection 248(1) or in a section elsewhere in the Act, judicial precedents should be consulted for the meaning of the word.

(B) Part I, Division B, Subdivision a, subparagraph 8(1)(*i*)(i): — Employment income and deductions are set out in sections 5 to 8 of Part I, Division B, Subdivision a of the Act. All deductions from this source appear in section 8 with the major list of deductions occurring in subsection 8(1) and further explanation or restriction of these deductions appearing in subsections 8(2) to 8(11).

(C) Part I, Division B, Subdivision g, paragraph 81(1)(*g*.1): — Income from property acquired as personal injury award is one in a limited list of items found in section 81 which are not included in computing income.

(D) Part I, Division B, Subdivision f, section 67: — Inclusions and deductions in the computation of income are generally found in Part I, Division B, Subdivisions a, b, c, d or e. In this case, however, the rule is found in Subdivision f dealing with general rules relating to the computation of income from all sources.

(E) Part XVII, subsection 252(2): — The word "parent" appears throughout the Act, so the definition is most likely to be in Part XVII on "Interpretation."

(F) Part I, Division B, Subdivision k, subsection 108(1): — Trusts and their beneficiaries are dealt with in Subdivision k of Part I, Division B. The definitions section for this subdivision is section 108.

(G) Part I, Division I, paragraph 150(1)(*b*): This is a procedural matter generally handled in Division I of Part I of the Act dealing with Returns, Assessments, Payment and Appeals.

(H) Part I, Division B, Subdivision b, subsection 15(1): — A benefit received by a shareholder, if it is to be taxed, would likely be income from property which is handled in Subdivision b of Division B of Part I. Inclusions from that source are generally listed in sections 12 to 17.

(I) Part I, Division B, Subdivision f, paragraph 69(1)(*b*): — This provision can be found in the set of general rules pertaining to the computation of income in Subdivision f of Division B of Part I because it affects the computation of income from a variety of sources.

(J) Part I, Division B, Subdivision b, paragraph 20(1)(*bb*): — Investments provide income from property and deductions from such income are generally listed in subsection 20(1).

Exercise 2

DIVISION B

Par. 3(*a*)	*Subdivision a*			
	Sec. 5, 6, 7, 8	Employment income		$ 60,000
	Subdivision b			
	Sec. 9	Business income	$ 10,000	
	Sec. 9	Property income	3,000	13,000
	Subdivision d			
	Par. 56(1)(*a*)	Retiring allowance.........................		20,000
		Total par. 3(*a*) income		$ 93,000
Par. 3(*b*)	*Subdivision c*			
	Par. 38	Taxable capital gain (net of allowable capital loss)		20,000
				$113,000
Par. 3(*d*)	*Subdivision b*			
	Ssec. 9(2):	Rental property loss		(4,000)

Division B income			$109,000
Par. 111(1)(*a*)	Non-capital loss	$ 4,000	
Par. 111(1)(*b*)	Net capital loss	5,000	(9,000)
Taxable income			$100,000

Federal tax after credits

Tax before credits			$ 18,529
	Sec. 118(1)	Personal credits	(3,442)
	Sec. 118(10)	Canada employment credit......................	(174)
	Sec. 118.7	CPP contributions credit	(382)
	Sec. 118.7	EI premium credit	(143)
	Sec. 118.5	Tuition credit	(68)
	Sec. 118.6	Tuition credit transfer	(80)
	Sec. 118.1	Charitable donation credit	(550)
Basic federal tax			$ 13,690

Exercise 3

Subsection 212(1) is a "charging provision" because it charges someone with the responsibility for paying a tax.

The components of subsection 212(1) are as follows.

(A) the person who is the subject of the provision

- "every non-resident person"

(B) the activity, event or condition that must be met for the provision to apply

- "on every amount that a person resident in Canada pays or credits or is deemed by Part I to pay or credit to the non-resident person as ..." [followed by paragraphs (*a*) to (*w*) that list types of payments, such as a management fee, interest, rent, etc.]

(C) the consequences of the activity or event to the person who is the subject of the provision

- "*shall* pay an income tax at 25% on every amount ..."

- note the use of the word "shall", indicating a mandatory payment

- note that the 25% rate can be reduced by a tax treaty which overrides the Canadian *Income Tax Act*

(D) the time frame for the application of the provision

- in the year that the amount is paid or credited is implied

Chapter 2

Liability for Tax

Learning Goals

Know, Understand and Explain

By the end of this chapter you will know, understand and be able to explain:

- The definition of person under the Act.
- Factors used to determine the residency status of a person under the Act.
- The tax liability for resident and non-resident persons.
- The effects of an existing international tax treaty on the tax liability of a person.
- Who is responsible for the collection of GST/HST and the effects of the input tax credit.

Apply

By the end of this chapter you will be able to apply your knowledge and understanding to:

- Determine the residency status of an individual, including the status of a part-year resident in a year of transition.
- Determine the residency status of a corporation.
- Advise clients and employers on the tax implications of the determined residency status.
- Determine the requirement to be GST/HST registered and collect GST/HST on goods and supplies.

Review Questions
¶2,800 in the Study Guide

Multiple Choice Questions
¶2,825 in the Study Guide

Exercise Questions
¶2,850 in the Study Guide

Assignment Problems
¶2,875 in the Study Guide

CHAPTER 2 — LEARNING CHART

Problem Descriptions

Textbook Example Problems

2-1	Resident vs. non-resident — individual
2-2	Resident vs. non-resident — corporation

Multiple Choice Questions

1	Corporate residence
2	Individual residency
3	Canadian income of non-resident
4	Canadian income of part-year resident
5	Individual residency
6	HST

Exercises

1	Individual residency — multi-part
2	Individual residency — case
3	Corporate residency — multi-part
4	Canadian income of non-resident

Assignment Problems

1	Individual residency — multi-part
2	Individual residency — case
3	Individual residency — case
4	Individual residency — case
5	Corporate residency — multi-part
6	Corporate residency — case
7	Corporate residency — case
8	Corporate residency — case
9	Transfer to France
10	Move to Chile

Study Notes

¶2,800   REVIEW QUESTIONS

(1) Canadian citizens pay tax in Canada on their world income. Comment.

(2) If a non-resident vacations in Canada for 180 days during the year, then he or she will be considered a Canadian resident for the full year. Comment.

(3) If an individual sells his or her house and then leaves the country, the person will be considered to be a non-resident. Comment.

(4) Assume that an individual resided in Buffalo and carried on a proprietorship business in St. Catharines. How would he or she pay tax on the business income earned in Canada?

(5) An individual who moves to Canada on March 31 of the year will be considered resident in Canada throughout the year since he or she was resident here for more than 183 days. Comment.

(6) Since a corporation is an artificial legal entity, it does not "reside" anywhere in the sense that an individual does. Comment on how the residency of a corporation is determined.

(7) A company was incorporated in Canada on November 30, 1965, but has been carrying on business in Bermuda since that date and all of the officers and directors have always been resident there. Comment on the company's tax liability in Canada.

(8) A company was incorporated in Canada on November 30, 1964, but has been carrying on business in Bermuda since that date and all of the officers and directors have always been resident there. In the years from incorporation to 1971 the company actively solicited orders in Canada by telephone. It stopped this activity in Canada at the end of 1971. Comment on the company's tax liability to Canada.

(9) A Canadian executive is transferred to the U.S. with his company on a five-year contract. He and his family sell all their Canadian assets and move to the U.S. in December of the year. Due to the lower personal income tax rates in the U.S., he has the Canadian company defer the payment of the bonus of $100,000 that he earned in Canada in the year until the next year when he is resident in the U.S. Comment on whether the executive will be taxed in Canada on this bonus.

(10) If a U.S. corporation has an employee located in Canada who is selling goods on behalf of the employer, then would the U.S. company be taxable in Canada?

(11) If a U.S. corporation has an agent located in Canada who is selling goods on behalf of the U.S. company, then would the U.S. company be taxable in Canada?

(12) If a person is resident in Canada, can that same person also be resident in the U.S.?

(13) If a Canadian corporation is carrying on business in the U.S. through a permanent establishment in the U.S., will the Canadian company be considered resident in the U.S. and be subject to tax in the U.S. on the total corporate income?

(14) Mr. Smith is an independent consultant who provides his services wherever he can get the work. He has been asked by a U.S. company to go to the U.S. to consult with them. He thinks that he will have to spend 25 days travelling to their many locations in the U.S. over the next year and that he will earn $50,000 for his efforts. His lawyer has told him that he will be taxed in the U.S. on this business income. What do you think?

¶2,825 MULTIPLE CHOICE QUESTIONS

Question 1

X Ltd. is a corporation which has always been managed by the *same* Board of Directors. The Board of Directors has always met where the directors reside. Based on these facts, X Ltd. will NOT be resident in Canada for income tax purposes if X Ltd. was:

(A) incorporated in Canada in 1968 and its directors are all U.S. residents;

(B) incorporated in the U.S. in 1970 and its directors are all U.S. residents;

(C) incorporated in the U.S. in 1968 and its directors are all Canadian residents;

(D) incorporated in Canada in 1964 and its directors are all Canadian residents.

Question 2

Joe is legally separated from his wife and has two adult children who live with his wife and are not dependent on him for support. Joe is leaving Canada to take a job in Germany on June 30 of this year. He plans to stay in Germany indefinitely and has purchased a home there. Which one of the following things is the most important for Joe to do to help ensure that he is not a resident of Canada for Canadian income tax purposes after he leaves?

(A) Take his wife and children with him to Germany.

(B) Give up his Canadian citizenship.

(C) Sell his Canadian home or rent it under a long-term lease.

(D) Put all his household furniture and personal effects into storage in Canada.

Question 3

Mr. Ng is *not* a resident of Canada. In the year, he had worldwide income of $200,000, including $50,000 of employment income earned in Canada (from director's fees) and $10,000 of interest on Government of Canada bonds.

What amount of taxable income must Mr. Ng report on his Canadian personal income tax return for the year?

(A) $10,000

(B) $50,000

(C) $60,000

(D) $200,000

Question 4

Jay ceased to be a resident of Canada on April 30 of the year and moved to New Zealand on that date. During the first four months of the year, he earned $25,000 of employment income in Canada and $1,000 of interest income from his bank accounts in Canada. While living in New Zealand during the remainder of the year, he earned $30,000 (Cdn. $) of employment income in New Zealand and received $2,000 of interest income from his Canadian bank accounts.

What amount of taxable income must Jay report on his Canadian personal income tax return for the year?

(A) $58,000

(B) $56,000

(C) $26,000

(D) Nil

Question 5

In which of the following situations is the person considered a non-resident of Canada for Canadian income tax purposes in the year in question?

(A) James Hill, a 25-year-old engineer living in Ottawa, accepted a six-month transfer to an office in London, England for the period July 1 to December 31, of the year in question. He returned to Canada in the following year. James is not married and has always lived at his parents' house in Ottawa.

(B) Judy Gordon, a financial analyst, lives in a house she owns in London, England. She had lived in Toronto all her life, until she started a minimum three-year contract with CS Services Inc., which started in July of the year in question. Judy is single and terminated the lease on her apartment in Toronto before moving her belongings to England when her position started in July.

(C) ERT Limited was incorporated in Canada in 1987 and, until recently, its manufacturing plant was located in Ontario. In June of the year in question, it moved all of its operations, including the manufacturing plant, to Mexico.

(D) Doug Stewart, a member of the Canadian Armed Forces, has been stationed in Germany for the last 5 years, including the year in question. Doug was born in Canada and lived in Canada prior to moving to Germany.

Question 6

CART Ltd. is registered for HST purposes. The following is a summary of the transactions for CART Ltd. for the month of December:

Account	Amount (Net of HST)
Sales (Taxable at 13%)	$250,000
Exports	100,000
Purchase of supplies from a registrant.	(30,000)
Salaries	(70,000)
Interest Expense	(20,000)
	$230,000

The HST that has to be remitted in respect of the above transaction is:

(A) $19,500

(B) $26,000

(C) $28,600

(D) $39,000

¶2,850 EXERCISES

Exercise 1

ITA: 2, 114, 115, 250(1)

Determine the form of residence, if any, for each of the following individuals.

(A) Alpha had lived all of his life in Vancouver until this year when he left with his family on August 27 to live in Los Angeles.

(B) Beta is a Canadian citizen who has lived in the United States with his family for the past nine years.

(C) Gamma lives in Niagara Falls, New York, but works Monday to Friday from 9:00 a.m. to 5:00 p.m. in an office in Niagara Falls, Ontario.

(D) Delta had lived all of his life in Dallas, Texas. He moved with his family to Calgary, Alberta, early this year to take a job with Dome Petroleum. He moved back to Dallas in the summer of this year. While in Canada he invested in the shares of a private corporation operating in Calgary. These shares were later sold during the year after he left Calgary.

(E) Epsilon was born in Philadelphia. He is now 10 years old and has never been to Canada but his mother has been consul in the Canadian Consulate there for the past 12 years.

(F) Mu is a German citizen who is married to a member of the Canadian forces stationed in Germany. She has been to Canada only for brief visits when her husband was on leave.

Exercise 2

ITA: 2, 114, 250; Income Tax Folio S5-F1-C1

The following is a summary of the statement of fact of the situation.

- Mr. O. MacDonald was about 58 years old in the year under assessment.

- He was at all material times an American citizen.

- He is a sea captain and sails tankers around the world. His employer is the Cities Services Corporation of New York and the ships bear United States registry. He is paid in United States currency from New York for the last 12 years he has been Master of the "S.S. Cities Services, Norfolk".

- Prior to six years ago, Mr. MacDonald and his wife had always lived in the United States. Until then, they owned a house in Massachusetts. In June, six years ago, they moved, with their furniture, to Fredericton, NB. Mrs. MacDonald rented a house in her name to live nearer their two youngest sons, who were attending a boarding school in Saint John, N.B. Their two oldest children were married and another was attending the Springfield (Mass.) College. Upon moving, they sold their nine-room house in the United States.

- About 15 months after their move to Fredericton, Mr. and Mrs. MacDonald purchased a house in Fredericton which was registered in joint tenancy in both their names. On the advice of an American lawyer, Mr. and Mrs. MacDonald tried to purchase a house in Canada within the year in order to avoid the American capital gains tax; unfortunately, they jointly bought this house two months too late and had to pay the tax.

- Prior to the purchase of the house Mr. and Mrs. MacDonald lived in the rented premises in Fredericton.

- Mr. MacDonald filed a T1 Income Tax Return for the taxation year immediately prior to the year under assessment on which he stated, "the above taxpayer and his family are American citizens and are merely residents of Canada. He is a U.S. ship captain and is employed full-time by a U.S. company".

- Mr. MacDonald paid a small amount of Canadian income tax for that previous taxation year after using his foreign tax credit.

- The routine into which Mr. and Mrs. MacDonald have settled over the past years is as follows: The appellant receives his orders to sail from New York. He may be gone months at a time. He may dock at U.S. ports such as Galveston, Texas, or San Francisco.

CHAPTER 2

- After Mrs. MacDonald moved to Fredericton, Mr. MacDonald retained two rooms in his sister's house in Stoneham, Mass., U.S.A. He gave his sister's number as his telephone number in the United States.

- At all material times, the appellant:

  — worked for a U.S. company;

  — was paid in U.S. currency;

  — was a member of the First Baptist Church at Wakefield, Mass.;

  — had two children living in the United States;

  — had a bank account or accounts in the United States;

  — had investments, including stocks and bonds, in the United States;

  — had a pension plan with a U.S. company;

  — intended and still intends to retire in Florida;

  — banked his pay at the First National Bank in Malden, Mass. and enough to maintain his wife and children was sent to her. The rest stayed in the United States where he still retains a chequing account in Malden.

- The appellant, during 1964:

  — had a joint bank account in Fredericton with his wife;

  — had a family phone number in his wife's name;

  — neither applied for nor received family allowance for his children;

  — neither was employed nor carried on business in Canada;

  — never belonged to a church or club in Fredericton;

  — was never a member of a Canadian union;

  — had no Canadian investments;

  — owned a car jointly with his wife with a New Brunswick registry.

- The appellant's sole connections with Canada during 1964 were:

  — his wife lived in Fredericton with one son;

  — he visited Fredericton for a total of 166 days at the following times in the year:

January 3 to February 22	51 days
June 1 to August 7	68 days
November 14 to December 31	<u>47</u> days
	<u><u>166</u></u> days

- In about a year and a half after the year under assessment the house in Fredericton was sold and Mr. and Mrs. MacDonald moved back to the United States.

- As already mentioned, during the year under assessment, her husband lived 166 days in Fredericton and spent the rest of the time at sea. While away, his pay cheques were sent directly from the New York office to a bank in Malden, Mass., and his wife received monthly cheques for living expenditures in Canada. During his vacation, his pay cheques were deposited in a joint bank account in Fredericton. His trips usually lasted three to four months, and six months when bound for foreign ports. When he was unable to come home, his wife would visit him in New York or at his sister's home in Massachusetts. Mr. MacDonald contended that, in the year under assessment, he resided with his sister and could be reached there at any time, but did not enjoy the exclusive right to the use of rooms and furniture; during that period, his wife stayed there with him for three or four weeks.

— REQUIRED

Prepare an analysis of the residence issue. Evaluate in detail the alternatives in the residence issue as they relate to this fact situation for the year under assessment. Discuss each possible degree of residence and its tax consequences. Weigh the relevance of the facts you consider and come to a conclusion on the case.

Exercise 3

ITA: 2, 250(4)

Determine the form of residence, if any, for each of the following corporations.

(A) Inch Incorporated was incorporated in 1982 in North Dakota. However, its directors are all residents of Saskatchewan where all meetings of the board of directors have been held since incorporation.

(B) Foot Limited was incorporated in Manitoba in 1972. However, it is managed in Japan where all directors' and shareholders' meetings have been held since incorporation.

(C) Yard Incorporated was incorporated in Ohio in 1967, but until five years ago all of the directors' meetings were held in Ontario and the president of the company was a resident of Ontario. However, five years ago the president moved to Ohio and from then on all directors' meetings have been held there.

(D) Mile Limited was incorporated in Nova Scotia in 1964 where all directors' meetings were held until 1971 when the directors moved to Boston where they met regularly.

Exercise 4

ITA: 2(3)

Samson Industries Inc. is a small American company located in Minneapolis, Minnesota. Samson sells various items by mail-order, mostly advertising trinkets such as pens, telephone diaries, post-it notes, and similar items, to Canadian businesses. Last year was the first year they did this and profits on its Canadian sales amounted to $76,000. The principals of Samson are worried about their liability for Canadian income tax and have come to you for advice. Advise Samson on their Canadian tax liability. Include an explanation of your rationale.

CHAPTER 2

¶2,875 ASSIGNMENT PROBLEMS

Type 1 Problems

Problem 1

Identify the criteria you will use to determine residency for individuals and the steps you will use to apply them.

For each of the following individuals, apply your criteria and determine and explain their residency status for tax purposes. Where there is a change in resident status in a year, explain how the individual will be taxed in that year and the next.

(a) Anthony entered Canada on March 1 of this year, and worked as a domestic on a southern Saskatchewan ranch for the remainder of the year. On December 15 of this year, Anthony's wife moved to Canada with their three children and all of their belongings. They plan to stay permanently in Canada.

(b) Lubie is a U.S. citizen who has lived in Detroit her entire life. For the last 10 years she has been a full-time employee in Windsor, so she commutes across the border every day. She has also traded large volumes of shares and bonds in her own stock account at a broker in Windsor.

(c) Ephran, a computer programmer with Xion Corporation in Toronto, accepted a long-term transfer to Silicon Valley, California. He committed to stay for at least five years. On May 1 of this year, he flew to California and began work on the same day. Most of his belongings remained in Toronto until July 30 of this year. His common-law spouse waited until this day, when the house was sold, the bank accounts were closed, and her contract with the Toronto Public School Board was fulfilled.

(d) Julia, a citizen of the United States, moved with her parents in August two years ago to Edmonton, Alberta. From September 1 two years ago to April 30 of last year, she attended the University of Alberta after transferring credits from her U.S. university. Her parents moved to Edmonton as a result of a job transfer. On May 1 of last year, she accepted an employment position as a mountain bike guide in Colorado and resided there until August 30 of last year. Then, she returned to Edmonton to complete her commerce degree. On June 1 of this year, Julia began full-time employment with a public accounting firm in Edmonton.

(e) Helen Huang has lived in Florida for many years and is a U.S. citizen. All her children also live in Florida. While she enjoys Florida during the winter months, she prefers the relatively cooler weather in Toronto during the other months of the year. As a result, she owns a condo along Queen's Quay in downtown Toronto. Last year, she travelled back and forth between Florida and Toronto fairly often, and when she checked her calendar she found that she had stayed in Toronto on 205 nights. Her children would sometimes come up for short visits.

Problem 2

ITA: 2, 114, 250; Income Tax Folio S5-F1-C1

The client was born and raised in Canada. After obtaining his MBA in 2002, he began working as a consultant. In July 2014, the corporation of which he was a major shareholder entered into a contract with a Canadian Crown corporation to furnish consulting advice in Nigeria. Services were to commence July 15, 2014 and end January 14, 2016. A daily rate of fees was set, but total billings were not to exceed a specified maximum. The contract also provided for moving, travel and living expenses for the client and his dependants up to a specified maximum.

All fees and expenses were paid to the client's corporation in Toronto. He continued to be a shareholder, director and officer of the corporation and he remained very interested in its activities. The corporation paid the client and was instructed to deposit these payments in the client's Canadian bank account which he continued to maintain for this purpose and for the operation of the rental property that he owned. He felt that the Canadian bank account was necessary because of foreign exchange difficulties that he might otherwise encounter. He instructed the corporation not to withhold any income taxes on these payments because he intended to give up his Canadian residence status to establish an international consulting business abroad upon termination of the Nigerian contract.

Since the client had little time before leaving for Nigeria, he quickly rented the unit that he had been occupying in a duplex that he owned, on a month-to-month basis. He intended to sell the property when the market would provide him with a reasonable profit. He arranged to have his corporation manage the renting of this property for a fee which he paid to the corporation.

He stored his major furnishings and winter clothing in Canada. His smaller household and personal effects were shipped to Nigeria. He sold his car, cancelled his auto insurance and a gasoline company credit card and obtained an international driver's licence. He retained credit cards such as American Express, Visa and MasterCard, as well as his RRSP accounts. Under the contract he was also required to maintain his provincial health insurance coverage.

When he left Canada for Nigeria, he was accompanied by his friend, Martha, who had been a part of his life for over a year before their departure. She had obtained leave from her university program of studies for the fall 2014 term. The couple took up residence in a hotel suite that was converted into an apartment at the Holiday Inn in Lagos, Nigeria. No conventional living quarters were available, because of the housing market. During his stay in Nigeria, the client obtained a Nigerian driver's licence and maintained two bank accounts and two cars. He joined sports, dining and social clubs in Lagos. He was provided with an office by the Nigerian government and he carried business cards which identified him as a consultant with that government. He promoted the consulting business of his Toronto corporation actively in Nigeria in the hope of establishing the business abroad, but he did not generate sufficient business to stay in Nigeria beyond the period of the existing contract. He did not seek to extend his visa or pay any form of tax on his income in Nigeria.

Martha returned to Canada for the winter 2015 term, and then returned to Nigeria for the summer of 2015, but returned again to Canada in September 2015 to begin a new program.

By December 2015 the client had billed the limit under the contract. He vacated his apartment, sold his cars, packed up his possessions, including some artwork, textiles and other souvenirs that he had acquired, and returned to Canada.

Prepare a memo for the tax person in your firm who will advise the client on the income tax consequences of these facts. Evaluate in detail the alternatives in the residence issue as they relate to this fact situation. Discuss each possible degree of residence and its tax consequences. State your conclusions on the case after weighing the significance of the facts considered.

Problem 3

ITA: 2, 114, 250; Income Tax Folio S5-F1-C1

The client is an electronic engineer. He was born in Erith, England, on July 7, 1976. During the relevant times the client held a valid passport for the United Kingdom of Great Britain and Northern Ireland. The passport declares him a British subject with a residence in the United Kingdom with the right of abode therein. The passport was issued on September 26, 2008 for a 10-year period.

Prior to the client's second marriage in 2011, his parents maintained a bedroom for him in Kent, England.

In 2011, the client married Cathy, a Canadian citizen residing in Canada who had no income of her own and was wholly dependent on the client. She has always resided continuously in Canada.

In June of 2011, a house near Apsley, Ontario, was purchased by Cathy with money supplied by the client. In September of 2012, Cathy borrowed money by way of a mortgage. The client guaranteed the mortgage which has an affidavit attached dated September 13, 2012 where he swore that he was not then a non-resident of Canada. For a purchase of property in Ontario, he would otherwise have had to pay a 20% non-resident land transfer tax.

During the three-year period at issue in this case, 2011 to 2013, the client regularly returned to Canada when he was not working. Each time the client entered Canada, his passport was stamped by Immigration Canada with the majority of the entries setting out a date upon which he must leave Canada. The authorized period of stay varied from five days to 45 days. On some of the stamps the word "visitor" was written in by an immigration official. Throughout the three-year period, the client was employed full-time by a non-resident corporation and all work was performed outside Canada on an oil rig at sea. All income was deposited directly into a Canadian bank.

The client indicated that he was charged in Provincial Court for failure to file an income tax return for 1981 and was acquitted (likely on the basis that he was not required to file in Canada for that year).

During the three-year period, the client indicated or claimed that he:

(a) never filed a tax return or paid income tax anywhere;

(b) was not allowed to work in Canada;

(c) was given a fixed date to leave Canada on entry (i.e., not allowed to stay in Canada);

(d) could not join OHIP, pay EI, maintain an RRSP or join a pension plan;

(e) was out of the country more than 183 days per year;

(f) had no desire to work in Canada;

(g) had a residence in Britain in the home of his mother and father;

(h) held a mortgage in Britain on his first wife's house;

(i) could not live a normal life in Canada as he had to leave every 27 days; and

(j) had a bank account with the Royal Bank of Canada both in Canada and the Caribbean.

In 2014, the client purchased a car in Canada. In 2015, the client:

(a) obtained a Canadian driver's licence;

(b) obtained a Canadian visa; and

(c) became a landed immigrant in Canada.

Prepare a memo for the tax person in your firm who will advise the client on the income tax consequences of these facts. Evaluate in detail the alternatives in the residence issue as they relate to this fact situation for the period in question. Discuss each degree of residence and its tax consequences as it applies to this fact situation. Note that in this case, residence under the common law principle could only result from a "fresh start" at a point in time in the period in question. Therefore, part-year residence would depend on there being a period of non-residence prior to a "fresh start", if any.

State your conclusion on this case after appropriately weighing the significance of the facts considered. Your conclusion should indicate whether the client became a resident at any point in the period or remained a non-resident throughout the period. If you conclude that he became a resident, indicate the point in time when the "fresh start" was made.

Problem 4

ITA: 2, 114, 250; Income
Tax Folio S5-F1-C1

The client is a mechanical engineer, born and educated in England. The client was married in England in 1980 and he and his wife, Dawn, had three sons born in 1982, 1984, and 1987. In 1985, the client and his wife and family moved to Canada where he immediately commenced employment with Imperial Oil in Sarnia, Ontario. With Imperial Oil and/or its parent corporation, Exxon Corporation, the client and his family moved to various locations throughout Canada until 2006. In 2006, while residing and working in Edmonton, Alberta, the client was offered the position as deputy manager of the Exxon refinery at Port Dickson in Malaysia. He accepted the position because it presented the opportunity to likely become manager of this same refinery within a three-year period.

At the time of his acceptance of the above position, the client and his wife were experiencing marriage difficulties. As a result of these difficulties, it was mutually agreed that the client would go to Malaysia on his own. His wife and youngest son remained in the family home in Edmonton. His older sons were living on their own by this time.

The client and his employer undertook the following steps in preparation for his move from Canada:

● his employer obtained a work permit for him in Malaysia;

● he sold his car;

● he cancelled his provincial health plan;

● his employer obtained private health insurance for him;

● he closed all of his existing bank accounts at Royal Bank;

● he opened a savings account at the Bank of Nova Scotia because this bank had a branch in Kuala Lumpur, the capital of Malaysia;

● he allowed his membership in the Edmonton Petroleum Club to lapse; and

● he allowed his participation in the Model Guided Plane Association to lapse.

The client moved to Malaysia in the last few days of September 2006. He stayed in a hotel in Malaysia for the first few weeks and then moved into a company-provided home. His employer charged him with a monthly rent of $1,000 for his use of this house. He took the following items with him from Canada to Malaysia:

● all of his clothes and personal effects; and

● an airplane kit for model guided planes and a radio control transmitter for his hobby of model guided planes.

Once in Malaysia, the client undertook to establish Port Dickson as his home. To this end, he:

- purchased a car;

- obtained a Malaysian driver's licence;

- joined the Port Dickson yacht club which was, in fact, a social/recreational club;

- joined the petroleum club at Kuala Lumpur;

- opened a chequing account at the Bank of Nova Scotia in Kuala Lumpur;

- opened a chequing account at the Standard Chartered Bank at Port Dickson;

- acquired two Malaysian credit cards;

- became a patient at a Port Dickson medical clinic and, as well, made regular visits to a dentist in Port Dickson; and

- joined the Port Dickson Golf Club in 2009.

In accordance with Exxon corporate policy, the client remained on the payroll and in the pension plan of the Canadian subsidiary. His monthly pay was deposited into his Edmonton bank account. There was no income tax withheld at source on the client's salary because the Canadian subsidiary knew that he was working full-time outside of Canada. The total cost of his salary and related benefits (including pension) were charged by the Canadian subsidiary to Exxon Corporation International.

The client made only two visits to Canada during the period from 2007 through 2012. He visited for 14 days in 2008 and 14 days again in 2010. On each of these visits, he stayed in the family home in Edmonton. During the same period, the client's spouse made eight visits to him in Malaysia. She made no visits after January 2010, but prior to that time, the length of her visits ranged from 19 days to 32 days. On each of these visits, she stayed with the client in his Malaysian home. The client and his wife remained married throughout the relevant period.

The client maintained the following Canadian investments while he was residing in Malaysia:

- his 50% interest in the family home in Edmonton;

- a 50% investment in a rental property which his wife purchased after his move to Malaysia, because she thought it would be a good investment;

- his RRSP;

- his company savings plan; and

- a few personal shares in Canadian public companies.

He did maintain his memberships in the Canadian Society of Mechanical Engineers and the Association of Professional Engineers and Geologists of Alberta.

The client became manager of the Port Dickson plant in 2009 and eventually retired from Exxon in the summer of 2013 under the terms of an early retirement package. Upon retirement from Exxon, the client returned to Edmonton to the family home. In late 2013 the client started seeking employment in Malaysia and in January 2014 he and his wife went to Malaysia hoping that he would find employment and they would both live there. His wife returned to Canada in February 2014 and he moved on to Thailand where he stayed through July 2015 (working for the 12-month period from August 2014 through July 2015). When the Thailand employment ended, the client returned to Canada. He and his wife then worked out a plan of separation.

Prepare a memo for the tax person in your firm who will advise the client on the income tax consequences of these facts. Evaluate in detail the alternatives in the residence issue as they relate to this fact situation for the period October 1, 2006 through the summer of 2013. Discuss each possible degree of residence and its tax consequences. State your conclusions on this case after weighing the relevance of the facts you have considered.

Problem 5

ITA: 2, 250(1)

For each of the following corporations, determine and explain the type of residency, for tax purposes for this year.

(a) ABI, incorporated in Montreal, Quebec, in 1980, carries on a clothing manufacturing business in Hong Kong. All directors' meetings and staff meetings are held in Hawaii, United States, each year.

(b) Nickel Company, incorporated in the Bahamas in 1966, operates a mining business in Northern Ontario. All profits are paid out as dividends directly into a Swiss bank account. All books and records are maintained in the president's office in Ontario. The company directors all live in Toronto and meet monthly for their directors' meeting.

(c) Saffron Ltd. is a 40% subsidiary of a Canadian corporation located in Houston, Texas. The products manufactured by Saffron are sold directly to the Canadian market. No revenues are earned from U.S. sales.

Problem 6

ITA: 2, 250, 253

Far Eastern Airlines is a company incorporated in Korea in 1974. Its general manager and other active officers of the company are resident in Korea and have their offices there. The directors and corporate officers of the company live in Korea as well.

During the year in question, its sole business was operating an international airline which had no landing rights in Canada. However, in that year it had raised capital on the Canadian market for its international operations by selling an issue of its stock through an investment dealer in Vancouver. The vice-president–finance of the company, who believed the stock issue would sell better in Canada, travelled from the head office in Korea to Vancouver to instruct the investment dealer.

The stock issue was highly successful and the proceeds of the issue were accumulated in a bank account in Vancouver. During the several months in the year in question when these funds were being accumulated, the company became aware of an opportunity to purchase a vast quantity of aviation fuel at a very low price. A purchasing agent was dispatched from the head office in Korea to Canada to complete the purchase using some of the funds accumulated from the stock issue. The fuel was stored in Canada temporarily in rented facilities pending shipment to San Francisco, where it could be used by aircraft landing there. Subsequently, the company was unable to make suitable arrangements for shipment. The fuel was sold to a Canadian buyer at a considerable profit. All contracts involved in the purchase and sale transactions were drawn up by a Canadian lawyer under the direction of the purchasing agent who operated from a hotel room in Vancouver during the period of the transactions.

Prepare a memo for the tax person in your firm who will advise Far Eastern Airlines on the income tax consequences of these facts. Evaluate in detail the alternatives in the residence issue as they relate to this fact situation. Discuss each possible degree of residence and its tax consequences. State your conclusions on the case after considering the relevant international tax agreement and after appropriately weighing the significance of the facts considered.

Problem 7

ITA: 2, 250, 253

Wong Computer Games Inc. (WCG) was incorporated in the state of Illinois in the last decade. The founding shareholder, Mr. Andrew Wong, is an inventor of computer simulation models. His products include a wide variety of computer games as well as some programs which have industrial applications.

Mr. Wong is the controlling shareholder of WCG. His brother owns a minority interest, as does Walter Bends, a long-time associate of Mr. Wong, who often collaborates in the development of new products. All three shareholders are resident in Chicago. In addition to Mr. Wong, the WCG Board of Directors includes George Wolf, who represents the Chicago law firm, which advises WCG, and Tony Aster who represents First National Bank of Chicago, which provides most of the financing for WCG's operations. The Board meets approximately every six months to review financial results, discuss product development and decide on strategic initiatives. The meetings are usually held in the boardroom of George Wolf's law firm.

Two years ago, Mr. Wong achieved an industry breakthrough when he developed his latest game, SuperPilot. SuperPilot is a computer game in which the operator attempts to safely land a disabled airliner. SuperPilot provided special effects which were far beyond those available in any other commercially available product. Although other WCG products were only available in the U.S. market, Wong was convinced that SuperPilot would be a global success. To ensure the competitive advantage would be maintained, Wong Computer Games Inc. took the required legal steps to ensure copyright and patent protection of the program in a variety of countries, including Canada.

By last year, SuperPilot was doing very well in the U.S. market and WCG began to launch the product in other markets. Walter Bends was assigned responsibility for the Canadian market and took a short-term lease on a Toronto apartment in March of last year. WCG established a bank account with a Toronto branch of a Canadian bank. This account was to be used by Bends for promotional expenses and other incidentals. All other expenses, including Bends' salary, continued to be paid from Chicago.

Bends attended a number of Canadian trade shows, exhibiting the SuperPilot program. Prospective purchasers were provided with SuperPilot game cartridges as a promotional item. Bends was given the authority to sign supply contracts which would permit the purchaser a one-month supply of cartridges. At the end of the one month, if the distributor was still interested, a longer-term supply contract would be required. Bends was not permitted, however, to sign any of these long-term agreements without receiving prior approval from the WCG Board. All game cartridges, including promotional cartridges, were supplied from Chicago. If the product began to sell well in Canada, the WCG Board had discussed establishing a Canadian warehouse.

By January of this year, it became obvious that SuperPilot was not going to be a Canadian success. No distributors had requested a long-term supply contract and only one, Pete's Gaming Emporium, had agreed to stock the product for one month. At the end of the month, sales had been so slow that Pete's was not interested in continuing the relationship. Bends returned to Chicago, the bank account was closed, and WCG refocused its marketing efforts on the U.S. market.

Prepare a memo for the tax person in your firm who will advise WCG on the income tax consequences of these facts. Evaluate in detail the alternatives in the residence issue as they relate to this fact situation during last year and this year. Discuss each possible degree of residence and its tax consequences. State your conclusions on the case after appropriately weighing the significance of the facts considered.

Problem 8

ITA: 2, 250, 253

Capitol Life Insurance Company ("Capitol") was incorporated in the U.S.A. in the state of Colorado at the turn of the century. Its head office had always been in Denver, Colorado. Capitol was a subsidiary of Providence Capitol Corporation which in turn was a subsidiary of Gulf & Western Industries Inc. ("Gulf"). Gulf owned approximately 600 subsidiaries, 240 of which were in turn owned by Associates Corporation of North America ("Associates"). Six of these latter corporations were Canadian companies.

Capitol was in the business of writing individual and group life and health insurance policies. Capitol also wrote creditor's group life and health insurance policies for the 240 finance companies which were part of the Gulf group of companies. Under a creditor's group insurance policy, Capitol would pay to the finance company, upon the death or disability of the borrower, the outstanding amount of the loan in the case of death or the required instalment payments in the case of disability. The costs of the insurance were effectively passed on to the borrower, either as a separate charge or as a higher interest rate.

About 25 years ago, Capitol planned to expand into Canada and obtained licences in nearly every province and obtained federal registration under the *Foreign Insurance Companies Act* ("FICA"). The FICA registration required that Capitol name a chief agent in Canada and that he be given a power of attorney. Capitol was also required to make deposits with the insurance superintendent and maintain assets in Canada. Two bank accounts were opened in Canada. The planned expansion into Canada was cancelled. However, the licences and registration were maintained. This required that Canadian representatives and agents be retained as locations for the licensing authorities to serve legal notices. All reports to the licensing authorities and all inquiries of the licensing authorities were to be passed through the Canadian chief agent. The reports to the licensing authorities were prepared in Denver and all inquiries were passed on to Denver by the chief agent. The chief agent was required to maintain copies of records required by the superintendent of insurance. None of Capitol's representatives or agents ever solicited insurance or were expected or authorized to do any business.

The chief agent countersigned the cheques on Capitol's general bank account on the requirement of the insurance superintendent. He had no means to verify the legitimacy of the cheques; as all books and records were maintained in Denver where the cheques were prepared. The agent later deposited the premiums received in an effort to streamline the former procedure of having the premiums sent to Denver and then sent back to Canada through the bank for deposit into the Canadian general account to meet licensing requirements. All investments were administered and managed in Denver.

Capitol did not have anyone in Canada who solicited insurance business, collected premiums, processed or paid claims, administered investments or countersigned any claim cheques. Capitol had five group insurance contracts under which the lives of Canadian residents were insured. These policies were all issued to affiliated companies without solicitation in Canada. Two of these policies were creditor's group insurance policies with Associates. They were each drafted in accordance with Denver law and signed in Denver by the president of Associates, who was a resident of Indiana. Associates was shown as the insured company and paid all premiums. On the insistence of the Canadian insurance authorities, the wording of the agreements was amended to reflect "a premium collection fee". The original agreement provided for a retroactive adjustment of premiums based upon past claim experience. Capitol and Associates continued to administer, interpret and apply the agreement in the same manner as the original agreement. Blank insurance certificates were also required to be issued so that they could be provided to borrowers whose loans were insured as a way of informing them of the terms of the coverage. The coverage took place independently of the issuance of a certificate to an individual. These certificates listed the Canadian head office of Capitol as being in Don Mills, Ontario, as required by the federal insurance superintendent. This office was never used as a head office. The federal insurance superintendent also required the issuance of a brochure for the information of the Canadian borrowers whose lives and health were insured.

The income that Capitol received from the Canadian insurance and investments represented a very small proportion of its total revenue. Canadian operations were not kept separately from U.S. operations, no Denver personnel were charged with Canadian operations, and there were no special Canadian claim forms or procedures. The only separation of Canadian business from U.S. operations to be found in the accounts of Capitol was to comply with the Canadian insurance authorities. All corporate meetings as well as all levels of management took place in the U.S.A.

Prepare a memo for the tax person in your firm who will advise Capitol on the income tax consequences of these facts. Evaluate in detail the alternatives in the residence issue as they relate to this fact situation. Discuss each possible degree of residence and its tax consequences. State your conclusions on this case after weighing the relevance of the facts you have considered.

Problem 9

Sally has just come to you for advice on a possible job transfer to Paris, France. She is currently working for a large private corporation located in St. Catharines, Ontario. It is now April and the president of the company has asked Sally, who is the company's computer network expert, to move to Paris for at least two years. Her time there may extend beyond two years, but that will depend on the success of the project she will be working on.

Sally is married to Harry and they have two daughters, ages six and eight. The company wants Sally to be in Paris and working by May 15, so she will have to leave by May 10 to get there and settled in time. She is planning to rent a furnished apartment when she arrives. Her children are in school and won't be done until the end of June. Harry has his own career as a school teacher and is willing to take an unpaid leave of absence for two years, but he can't leave until the end of June or middle of July at the earliest.

Sally and Harry enjoy golf and have recently joined a fairly exclusive club in the St. Catharines area, after an eight-year waiting period and after paying a large initiation fee. They do not wish to give up this membership. Their home is located just outside the city on 20 acres and they are very reluctant to sell it, as they would not be able to replace it on their return.

Both Sally and Harry grew up in the St. Catharines area and their families still live there. Sally's parents and Harry's parents are retired.

Sally and Harry both want to move to Paris, and they have come to you for tax advice on whether they could be considered non-residents of Canada, or what, if anything, they could do to achieve this result.

Problem 10

The plaintiff, Jennifer Marken, is a 21-year-old Canadian citizen and has always lived and worked in Regina except for the last two years. During these two years, she obtained a position as an English teacher for a local school in Osorno, Chile. Originally, the two-year contract could have been extended into a permanent position at Jennifer's option. However, at the end of the two-year period Jennifer's brother became suddenly ill and she opted to return to Regina and complete her education degree.

She is scheduled to appear in court next week to claim that she was a non-resident of Canada during the two-year period and, therefore, should not be liable for Canadian tax. Both the CRA and Jennifer's counsel agree on the following facts:

● Jennifer is a Canadian citizen and all of her direct family resides in Saskatchewan.

● Jennifer's fiancé visited her five times during the two-year period and lived in Chile during his summer vacations. He plans to complete his accounting designation with a Canadian firm in Saskatchewan.

● All of Jennifer's income during the two-year period ending in January of this year was paid by the Chilean school.

● Upon departing for Chile, Jennifer put all of her furniture in storage and leased her car to her younger sister on a month-to-month basis. Her household belongings were shipped to Chile.

- While in Chile, she maintained her provincial health care policy, her Canadian savings account and a Canadian American Express card. She cancelled her Canadian chequing account, and her Canadian Visa card.

- Before leaving, she cancelled all of her club memberships and abdicated her position as the honourary chair of the Beta Gamma Phi sorority.

- While in Chile she made no attempt to learn the Spanish language and did not join any Chilean organizations. She rented a one-bedroom apartment from another Canadian living in Osorno.

- Over the two-year period, Jennifer visited Canada each Christmas, at Easter, and for the marriage of her best friend. Her total number of days in Canada over the two-year period amounted to 50 days.

Jennifer's litigation counsel would like your advice on the income tax options for the two-year period during which Jennifer worked in Chile. Provide your perspective on the facts that support each place of residence and the tax consequences they entail. Weigh the relevance of the facts and conclude on the likely outcome in this situation.

 [For more problems and solutions thereto, see the DVD accompanying the textbook.]

CHAPTER 2 —
DISCUSSION NOTES FOR REVIEW QUESTIONS

(1) Canadian individuals are taxed based on residency and not their citizenship. Canadian residents are taxed on their world income.

ITA: 2(1)

(2) He or she will be deemed to be a resident only if he or she sojourned in Canada for 183 or more days during the year.

ITA: 250(1)

(3) You need to look at other factors to determine where they have a "continuing state of relationship", such as family and social ties and other personal property. The Income Tax Folio categorizes the type of facts that can be used to establish residential ties.

Income Tax Folio
S5-F1-C1 — Determining
an Individual's Residence
Status

(4) He or she would be considered to be a non-resident of Canada throughout the year. However, since he or she carried on business in Canada during the year while a non-resident, he or she would be taxable in Canada on his or her Canadian business profits for the year.

ITA: 2(3)

(5) If he or she is establishing a "fresh start" in Canada on March 31 then he or she becomes resident on that date and is taxed in Canada on his or her world income from that date. The sojourning rules would not apply since they only apply to non-residents who are in Canada on a temporary basis.

(6) The residency of a corporation is either determined by the common law test of "central management and control", or a corporation is deemed to be a Canadian resident if it is incorporated in Canada after April 26, 1965, or it meets the tests outlined in the Act if it was incorporated before that date.

ITA: 250(4)

(7) A corporation is deemed to be resident in Canada if it was incorporated in Canada after April 26, 1965. Reference to the tax treaty would be the next step but Canada does not have a tax treaty with Bermuda. Therefore, it would be resident in Canada and taxable in Canada on its world income.

ITA: 250(4)(a)

(8) Any company which was incorporated in Canada before April 27, 1965 and which carried on business in Canada in any year after that date is deemed to be resident in Canada. An extended meaning of carrying on business includes soliciting orders in Canada. The facts fit the meaning because of the continuity of the order solicitation over a period of years. Therefore, the company would be resident in Canada and taxable in Canada on its world income.

ITA: 250(4)(a)
ITA: 253(b)

(9) Subsection 2(3) refers to "employed in Canada in the year or a previous year". Therefore, section 115 of Division D requires the income from an office or employment to be taxed in Canada.

ITA: 115(2)(c)

(10) The U.S. company is soliciting orders in Canada and, therefore, is carrying on business in Canada. The corporation is, thus, taxable in Canada on the profits related to these sales.

ITA: 2(3), 115, 253

(11) Under the extended meaning of carrying on business, the U.S. company would be a non-resident carrying on business in Canada and liable for tax on its earning in Canada. However, under the Canada–U.S. tax treaty, the U.S. company would probably not be taxable in Canada because its profits are not earned from a permanent establishment in Canada.

ITA: 253

(12) Yes, a person can be a resident of more than one country since residency is determined under the laws of each country. Article IV of the Canada–U.S. tax treaty provides rules for resolving who collects the tax where a person is a resident of both the United States and Canada.

(13) Under Article VII of the Canada–U.S. tax treaty, it will only be subject to tax on the income attributable to that permanent establishment.

(14) Article XIV of the Canada–U.S. tax treaty will cause him to be taxed in the United States only if he has a "fixed base regularly available to him" in the United States Therefore, he will only pay tax in Canada on this income.

CHAPTER 2 — SOLUTIONS TO MULTIPLE CHOICE QUESTIONS

Question 1

(B) is correct. Since X Ltd. is not incorporated in Canada, it is not deemed to be resident in Canada. Since the directors are not resident in Canada, X Ltd. is not resident in Canada under the common law "central management and control" rule.

ITA: 250(4)

(A) is incorrect because X Ltd. is deemed to be resident.

ITA: 250(4)(*a*)

(C) is incorrect because X Ltd. is resident under the common law "central management and control" rule.

(D) is incorrect because X Ltd. is deemed to be resident; the common law "central management and control" rule would also apply.

ITA: 250(4)(*c*)

Question 2

(C) is correct. Generally, the CRA will consider the individual not to have severed residential ties within Canada if he has a dwelling available for occupancy.

Income Tax Folio S5-F1-C1 — Determining an Individual's Residence Status

(A) is incorrect, because taking his wife and children with him to Germany is not feasible, since the couple is legally separated and the children are not dependent on him for support.

Income Tax Folio S5-F1-C1 — Determining an Individual's Residence Status

(B) is incorrect, because giving up Canadian citizenship has little relevance in determining residency.

(D) is incorrect. Although putting all his household furniture and personal effects into storage in Canada is a residential tie, the tie is a weaker one than that cited in (C).

Income Tax Folio S5-F1-C1 — Determining an Individual's Residence Status

Question 3

(B) is correct. Only the $50,000 of employment income earned in Canada would be reported on Mr. Ng's Canadian personal income tax return for the year.

ITA: 2(3), 115

(A) is incorrect. The $10,000 interest, earned by the non-resident, is not taxable under either Part I (ssec. 2(3)) or Part XIII (ssec. 212(3), "fully exempt interest").

(C) is incorrect for the same reason as (A).

(D) is incorrect, because only residents of Canada are subject to Canadian income tax on their worldwide income.

ITA: 2(1)

Question 4

(C) is correct. Because Jay ceased to be a resident of Canada on April 30 of the year, only his worldwide income during the first four months of the year ($26,000 = $25,000 + $1,000) is subject to tax in Canada under Part I and would be reported on his Canadian personal income tax return for the year.

ITA: 2(1), 114

(A) includes income earned while not a resident of Canada: $58,000 = $25,000 + $1,000 + $30,000 + $2,000. The $30,000 of employment income earned in New Zealand and the $2,000 of Canadian interest earned from May 1 to December 31 of the year are not subject to Part I tax because Jay is not resident in Canada at that time. The $2,000 of Canadian interest is exempt from withholding tax under Part XIII.

ITA: 2(1), 114

(B) includes the salary earned in New Zealand: $56,000 = $25,000 + $1,000 + $30,000. As in (A), above, the $30,000 of employment income earned in New Zealand is not subject to tax in Canada.

(D) excludes the worldwide income earned while Jay was a resident in Canada. As discussed in (A), above, this would be reported on his Canadian personal income tax return for the year.

ITA: 2(1), 114

CHAPTER 2

Question 5

(B) is correct. Judy is a non-resident. She seems to have severed her residential ties to Canada (moving her belongings) and established new ties to London, England (buying a house).

(A) is incorrect. James is still a resident of Canada. There is no indication that James has severed his residential ties to Canada or established ties to London, England.

(C) is incorrect. Since ERT Limited was incorporated in Canada after April 26, 1965, it is deemed to be a resident of Canada.   ITA: 250(4)(*a*)

(D) is incorrect. Doug is deemed to be a resident of Canada because he is a member of the Canadian armed forces.   ITA: 250(1)(*b*)

Question 6

(C) is correct.

Sales (taxable at 13%) $250,000
Purchase of supplies from a registrant . . . . (30,000)
$220,000 × 13% = $28,600.

(A) incorrectly takes a deduction for salaries which is an exempt supply: $250,000 − $30,000 − $70,000 = $150,000. $150,000 × 13% = $19,500.

(B) incorrectly takes a deduction for interest expense: $250,000 − $30,000 − $20,000 = $200,000. $200,000 × 13% = $26,000.

(D) incorrectly includes exports (which are zero-rated) and takes a deduction for interest expense (an exempt supply): $250,000 + $100,000 − $30,000 − $20,000 = $300,000. $300,000 × 13% = $39,000.

CHAPTER 2 — SOLUTIONS TO EXERCISES

Exercise 1

(A) Alpha is a part-year resident of Canada in the year. He would be a resident until August 27 of the year when he appears to have made a "clean break" with Canada. While in Canada he would not have been sojourning, so the deeming rule would not apply.

ITA: 250(1)(*a*)

(B) Beta has no residential ties with Canada. Citizenship is not a determining factor in establishing such ties.

(C) Gamma is a non-resident of Canada and is taxable only on employment income earned in Canada.

ITA: 2(3)(*a*), 115(1)(*a*)(i)

(D) Delta is either a part-year resident of Canada or a non-resident employed in Canada, depending on the facts of his stay in Canada. He is also taxable under paragraph 2(3)(*c*) because the shares are taxable Canadian property.

ITA: 115(1)(*b*)(iv)

(E) Epsilon is deemed a resident of Canada because of his relationship to his mother.

ITA: 250(1)(*c*)(i), 250(1)(*f*)

(F) Mu is not deemed to be a resident of Canada by any of the deeming rules. She has never been resident in Canada. Therefore, she is not a resident of Canada.

ITA: 250(1)

Exercise 2

[See: *MacDonald v. M.N.R.*, 68 DTC 433 (T.A.B.).]

(A) The resident option → taxed in Canada on worldwide income for full year:

ITA: 2(1)

Criterion: residence is a question of fact dependent on the degree of permanency in the relationship between a person and a place;

Evidence:

(i) factors indicating this relationship between the appellant and Canada,

1. he sold his house in the United States and paid an American capital gains tax for not buying another residence,

2. his wife, upon arriving in Canada, rented premises pending the purchase of a house,

3. she and the children, whom the appellant was supporting to the extent of $600 per month, stayed in Canada all year-round,

4. he stayed in Canada when he was off-duty to the extent of 166 out of 180 days in 1964,

   — full-time presence is not necessary,

5. other non-determining factors,

   — joint account in Canada where pay cheques were deposited during his vacations,

   — joint ownership of a car with New Brunswick registry,

   — citizenship irrelevant;

(ii) factors detracting from a relationship with Canada,

1. a few rooms, without exclusive use, made available for him at his sister's house in the United States,

   — not a permanent abode,

   — an individual can have more than one residence,

2. U.S. citizen and previously and subsequently resided in the United States with a stated intention to return,

   — but only 1964 in question on the facts,

   — stated intention must be supported by behavioural facts,

   — worked for a U.S. company and paid in U.S. currency,

— but not determining because a Canadian resident can be involved in such a situation, providing employment services abroad for a non-Canadian company,

— memberships and investments including bank accounts, securities and pension plan in United States,

— factors may indicate U.S. residence, but not determining and also possible for a person resident in Canada,

— no Canadian memberships or investments and no application for family allowances,

— not determining factors and also possible of a Canadian resident,

— children living in United States,

— married and apparently not dependent,

— phone in wife's name in Canada,

— a factor, but hardly determining,

— neither employed in Canada nor carrying on business in Canada,

— not necessary condition for full-time residence.

(This list of factors is longer but there is more substance for full-time residence.)

(B) The deemed resident option → taxed in Canada on worldwide income for full year: ITA: 2(1)

Criterion: the condition of sojourning an aggregate of 183 days or more;   ITA: 250(1)

Evidence: his total stay in Canada in the year was only for 166 days; therefore, the condition is not met.

(C) The part-year resident option → taxed in Canada on worldwide income for part of the year   ITA: 2(1), 114, 118.91
resident in Canada with deductions applicable to the period of part-year residence and non-refundable tax credits either prorated for or applicable to the period of part-year residence (as long as not resident in Canada during some other part of the year);

Criterion: clean break or fresh start during 1964;

Evidence: neither occurred.

(D) The non-resident option → taxed in Canada on income earned in Canada: ITA: 2(3)

Criteria: employed in Canada, carried on business in Canada or disposed of taxable Canadian property in the year;

Evidence: none of these conditions occurred in the year.   ITA: 2(3)

(E) Conclusion: if the taxpayer is to be found a resident it must be as a full-time resident:

— the major factors indicate a relationship with Canada which would warrant a conclusion of such resident status.

Exercise 3

(A) Inch Incorporated is resident in Canada by virtue of the common law principle of central   ITA: 250(4)
management and control. The corporation cannot be deemed resident in Canada because it was not incorporated in Canada.

(B) Foot Limited is deemed resident in Canada because it was incorporated in Canada after   ITA: 250(4)(a)
April 26, 1965.

(C) Yard Incorporated is not resident this year by virtue of the common law principle of central management and control. Furthermore, the corporation cannot be deemed resident in Canada because it was not incorporated in Canada.

(D) Mile Limited is resident in Canada. The corporation was incorporated in Canada before   ITA: 250(4)(c)
April 27, 1965 and after that time it was resident by virtue of the central management and control rule.

Exercise 4

Canada levies tax on non-residents who carry on business in Canada. Carrying on business in Canada is distinguishable from carrying on business with Canada. While Samson solicits sales from Canadians, it does not have a permanent establishment in Canada, nor does it employ a Canadian salesperson or agent. Given these facts, Samson is not liable for Canadian income taxes on the $76,000 profit originating from within Canada.

ITA: 2(3)

Chapter 3

Employment Income

Learning Goals

Know, Understand and Explain

By the end of this chapter you will know, understand and be able to explain:

• The basic provisions of the *Income Tax Act* (the Act) that relate to employment income.

• The factors that distinguish an employee from a self-employed individual.

• What amounts must be included in employment income.

• How employment deductions are calculated.

• The special rules relating to the expenses of a commission sales person.

Apply

By the end of this chapter you will be able to apply:

• Your knowledge and understanding to calculate net employment income to real-life situations.

Review Questions
¶3,800 in the Study Guide

Multiple Choice Questions
¶3,825 in the Study Guide

Exercise Questions
¶3,850 in the Study Guide

Assignment Problems
¶3,875 in the Study Guide

CHAPTER 3

CHAPTER 3 — LEARNING CHART

Problem Descriptions

Textbook Example Problems

3-1	Employed vs. self-employed — case
3-2	Employee loan
3-3	Employee stock option
3-4	Employee stock option
3-5	Employee stock option
3-6	Standby charge and operating benefit — employer owned — employment kilometres < 50%
3-7	Standby charge and operating benefit — employer owned — employment kilometres > 50%
3-8	Standby charge and operating benefit — employer leased — employment kilometres < 50%
3-9	Standby charge and operating benefit — employer leased — employment kilometres > 50%
3-10	Deductible automobile expenses — employee owned car
3-11	Deductible automobile lease expense — employee leased car
3-12	Deductible automobile expenses — employee leased car
3-13	Comprehensive example — employment income and expenses
3-14	GST/HST rebate

Multiple Choice Questions

1	Standby charge, operating benefit
2	Car allowance
3	Home office expenses
4	Employee loan
5	Employee stock option — public
6	Commission expenses & limitation

Exercises

1	Employed vs. self-employed
2	Employed vs. self-employed
3	Taxable benefits
4	Legal expenses — deductibility
5	Employee discount
6	Moving expense reimbursement
7	Employee benefits — employer payments
8	Employee stock option — CCPC
9	Standby charge, operating benefit
10	Home office expenses
11	Personal meals while travelling

Problem Descriptions

Assignment Problems

1	Auto benefits — company owned vs. company leased
2	Stock option — comparing CCPC to public company
3	Employee benefits — multi-part
4	Employee benefits — multi-part
5	Employee loans, car expenses
6	Commission expenses & limitation
7	Employee travel expenses
8	HST rebate
9	Employed vs. self-employed — Chow
10	Offer of employment — compensation options
11	Calculate employment income — benefits, stock option
12	Compensation alternatives — salary, bonus, benefits or stock option
13	Compensation alternatives — forgivable loan, stock option
14	Auto benefits — company owned vs. leased
15	Car allowance vs. reimbursement
16	Payment on termination
17	Calculate employment income — benefits
18	Calculate employment income — expenses
19	Calculate employment income — benefits, expenses, stock option
20	Calculate employment income — travel expenses
21	Calculate employment income — comprehensive benefits
22	Calculate employment income — comprehensive expenses
23	Calculate employment income — comprehensive benefits, auto expenses
24	Calculate employment income — comprehensive benefits, auto expenses
25	Employed vs. self-employed
26	Employed vs. self-employed
27	Employed vs. self-employed, resident
28	Employed vs. self-employed, resident

CHAPTER 3

Study Notes

¶3,800   REVIEW QUESTIONS

(1) The best way to calculate employment income is to follow the format used on the personal tax return. Comment on the accuracy of this statement.

(2) It does not matter whether an individual is employed or self-employed since he or she can claim the same expenses under either category as long as the expense was incurred to earn income. Comment on the accuracy of this statement.

(3) If an individual fails any one of the tests which are used to determine employed versus self-employed status then the individual is employed. Comment.

(4) When determining whether a person is employed or self-employed, one of the subtests used in the economic reality or entrepreneur test is the "control test". What does this test involve?

(5) When determining whether a person is employed or self-employed, one of the tests used is the "integration or organization test". What does this test involve?

(6) When determining whether a person is employed or self-employed, one of the tests used is the "specific result test". What does this test involve?

(7) If a bonus cheque is received by an employee, Ms. Davis, on December 15 of this year and she chooses not to cash her cheque until January 5 of next year, then she will be able to defer the tax on the bonus until the next year since individuals are taxed on the cash basis. Comment.

(8) If a bonus is payable to an employee, Mr. Lee, on December 15 of this year and he decides that he wants to be taxed on the income in the following year instead of this year, then he can ask his employer to defer the payment of this bonus until next year and accomplish his goal. Comment.

(9) Employees are taxed on income from their employer to the extent that it is a gross payment before withholding tax or a taxable benefit. The employer can deduct, as an expense, the full amount of the gross payments before withholding tax and taxable benefits that are reported on the employee's T4. Comment.

(10) To maximize the after-tax income from a disability insurance policy to a disabled employee, the employer should not pay *any* of the premium for the coverage. Comment.

(11) On June 2 of this year, Opco loaned $10,000 to an employee and did not charge interest. The employee repaid the loan on June 30 of the same year. How many days are included for purposes of determining the deemed interest benefit?

(12) Explain the differences between a reimbursement and an allowance.

(13) Opco bought a new car for its president that cost the company $40,000 plus $5,200 for HST. How much is the standby charge for this car for a full year assuming it is driven 40% for business purposes?

(14) What are the five conditions that must be met before a sales/negotiating person can deduct expenses?

(15) What are the four conditions that must be met by an employee, who is not a sales/negotiating person, in order to allow him or her to deduct travelling expenses other than car expenses?

(16) Mr. Wang is a part-time lecturer at the University of Waterloo. He lives in a location in Toronto which is 105 kilometres away from the university. The rest of the time he has a tax consulting practice which he operates out of his home. The university pays him $0.40 per kilometre to travel to and from the university. He is issued a T4 at the end of the year for his teaching income on the basis that he is a part-time employee. How is the travel allowance of $0.40 per kilometre treated for tax purposes?

(17) Guidelines for the deductibility of expenses related to work space in the home for employees are included in subsection 8(13). Under paragraph (*a*) of this provision the expenses are allowed if one of two conditions are met. In these conditions, the words "principally" and "exclusively" are used. What do these words mean for tax purposes?

(18) Ms. Smith has come to you to ask your tax advice. She has just had a large bonus paid to her on December 31 and wants to defer some of it until next year. She is arguing that since the CRA's portion was not sent to the Receiver General until January 15 she should be able to defer that portion until the next year on the basis that it was not received until January 15 when it was sent to the CRA. What do you think?

¶3,825   MULTIPLE CHOICE QUESTIONS

Question 1

In 2016, Bob's employer provided him with an employer-owned automobile costing $34,500 (including HST) for 12 months. His kilometres for personal use were 15,000 out of a total of 20,000 kilometres. Operating costs paid by his employer during this year were $3,600 (including HST). Which one of the following statements is TRUE for 2014?

(A) Bob's minimum standby charge is $8,280.

(B) Bob's minimum operating cost benefit is $2,700.

(C) Bob's minimum operating cost benefit is $4,050.

(D) Bob can elect to use ½ of his standby charge as his operating cost benefit.

Question 2

This year, Mary earned a $50,000 annual salary as a computer repair person and received a car allowance of $3,500. The car allowance was paid to her monthly and was not based on the number of kilometres that she drove. Her employment-related expenses (all reasonable) were:

Automobile expenses (gas, parking, CCA)	$3,000
Entertainment	2,000

What is Mary's minimum employment income for the year?

(A) $53,500

(B) $50,500

(C) $49,500

(D) $49,000

Question 3

Susanne Denholm is employed as a provincial payroll tax auditor and is required by contract to maintain an office in her home. Susanne works at home most of the time and has been provided with a laptop computer and a fireproof audit bag for her files. She has not been provided with any reimbursement or allowance in connection with her home office, which occupies 10% of the square footage of her home. She incurred the following costs to maintain her home this year:

Telephone (general line)	$ 600*
House insurance	2,000
Property taxes.	4,000
Heat, hydro & maintenance	5,000
Mortgage interest	24,000

_____

* Susanne estimates that she used her telephone 50% for employment purposes during the year.

What is the maximum amount that Susanne can claim for the costs she has incurred in respect of her home office?

(A) $500

(B) $1,100

(C) $1,400

(D) $3,800

Question 4

On April 1, 2013, E Ltd. made a loan of $100,000 to Mr. Walker, a new employee of the corporation, to assist him in purchasing a residence when he moved from Quebec to commence employment in British Columbia. The loan bears interest at 2%, which is to be paid monthly. The principal of the loan is to be repaid in full on April 1, 2023. The prescribed interest rate on April 1, 2013 was 4%. Assuming that the prescribed interest rate throughout 2016 was 3% and the interest owing on the loan is paid each month, which one of the following amounts represents the increase in Mr. Walker's employment income in 2016 due to the loan.

(A) $1,000

(B) $2,000

(C) $3,000

(D) $4,000

Question 5

Tanya, an employee of a Canadian public company, received an option to purchase 1,000 common shares of her employer at $30 per share in April 2015, when the shares were worth $19 per share. In December 2016, when the fair market value was $40 per share, she exercised her options. In January 2016, she sold all the shares for $48 per share. Tanya wants to know what employee benefit she will have to report on her tax return. She wants to pay the lowest amount of taxes possible.

(A) $5,000

(B) $18,000

(C) $14,000

(D) $10,000

Question 6

Tim began employment as a commissioned salesman in July of this year and received a base salary of $60,000 and $5,000 in commissions based on sales for the year. During the year, Tim worked away from the office negotiating sales contracts. Tim is required to pay his own travelling expenses and his employer has signed a T2200 form certifying that requirement and certifying that no reimbursements are paid for any expenses Tim incurs to earn commissions. Tim incurred the following work-related costs from July through December of this year and all expenses are reasonable:

Meals and entertainment for potential customers	$14,000
Automobile costs (90% of the following amounts were for employment purposes based on kilometres driven):	
Fuel	4,000
Insurance	750
Repairs	2,250
Leasing costs for a car costing $20,000 ($500 per month)	3,000

What is the maximum deduction Tim may claim for employment expenses for the year?

(A) $5,000

(B) $9,000

(C) $14,000

(D) $16,000

CHAPTER 3

¶3,850 EXERCISES

Exercise 1

Isaac v. M.N.R., 70 DTC 1285 (T.A.B.)

The taxpayer is a qualified registered nurse, is entitled to use the traditional letters "R.N." after her name and, in answering the questions contained in her income tax return, described herself as a "private duty" nurse both in the space provided for employed persons and in the space provided for persons in business or practising a profession. Thus, in trying to answer all the official questions on her return, the taxpayer indicated, on the one hand, that she was employed "as a private duty nurse" by the Canadian Forces Hospital at Halifax and, on the other hand, that she was in business of practising her profession "as a private duty nurse" in connection with the same hospital. The basic issue to be decided is, briefly, what was the taxpayer's correct status vis-à-vis the Canadian Forces Hospital, Halifax in the taxation year in question.

The taxpayer launched the present appeal by Notice of Appeal in which she alleged (in effect) as follows: that in the relevant taxation year she was employed by the Canadian Forces Hospital, Halifax, on a day-to-day basis terminable on 24 hours' notice; that the usual so-called fringe benefits made available to and enjoyed by the regular full-time army nursing sisters such as holidays, sick pay, retirement plan, and so on, were not made available to her as a private duty nurse; that the regional surgeon's office in Halifax classified her as a "self-employed R.N."; that in her previous return she claimed and was permitted to deduct from her income expenses of a similar type to those disallowed in the taxation year now under appeal; and that several of her fellow private duty nurses employed at the Canadian Forces Base, Halifax, were employed on the same basis as she was and had claimed expenses of a similar type to those disallowed in this appeal (i.e., the type of expenses one would associate with a private duty nurse). The CRA stated that, in making the assessment now in dispute, he had acted upon the following assumptions of fact — that the taxpayer is a registered nurse and was employed by the Department of National Defence at the Canadian Forces Hospital and Base, Halifax, during the taxation year, that in the course of carrying out her engagement as a general duty nurse the taxpayer was subject to supervision and discipline by the hospital authorities, and that of the expenses allegedly incurred by the taxpayer only the amount claimed as "R.N. fees" and the amount being her contribution to the Canada Pension Plan were permitted under the Act.

The taxpayer testified, in effect, as follows: that she is a registered nurse; that in the relevant taxation year she was living in Halifax and was employed at the Canadian Forces Hospital (Stadacona Hospital), "not as a staff nurse but more or less as a private duty nurse, though my times were made up ahead of time" (the correct interpretation to be placed on the word "employed" in this appeal appears to be the key to the solution); that private duty nurses are allowed to claim as deductions from income certain expenses such as laundry, uniforms, travelling expenses, and so on; that the only difference between herself and a private duty nurse is that the hospital deducted her Canada Pension Plan contributions from the per diem amounts payable to her; that she acted as a private duty nurse at Stadacona Hospital for about five years, after which she moved from Halifax to Charlottetown and became associated with the Charlottetown Hospital as a relief nurse; that she is presently working under exactly the same conditions under which she carried on at the Canadian Forces Hospital, Halifax, i.e., "If I don't work, I don't get paid, I have no benefits or holidays. I get private duty wages (these amounted to $15 per day in Halifax and now amount to $20 per day). My time is made up. If they get full-time nurses they can let me go"; that she and other private duty nurses were hired by Stadacona Hospital (on a day-to-day basis) to fill in while the hospital "didn't have enough service nurses"; and that in the year before she was replaced the said hospital "did get a large supply of military nurses in and we were all cut down" (i.e., a number of private duty nurses were simply laid off which was easy to do because they were working on a day-to-day basis). The Hospital supplied all equipment and supplies used by the taxpayer. The Hospital hired and fired all nursing assistants and other support staff who assisted the taxpayer in the performance of her duties. The taxpayer could request the Hospital to hire additional support staff but she personally did not hire them.

The taxpayer also testified, in effect, as follows: that her time sheet in the Canadian Forces Hospital, Halifax, was made out a week in advance; that the said hospital's authority to hire civilian nurses to meet its requirements was only valid while there was a shortage of military nurses; that, as they became available, the civilian nurses were replaced; that the hospital asserted its right to dismiss civilian nurses on 24 hours' notice — "we were told that when we went there to work"; that she, herself, was not replaced by a military nurse in the taxation year, now under appeal, but later her shifts were cut down and she was eventually replaced; that she was, of course, obliged to follow hospital regulations with regard to the administration of drugs, medications, and so on, as she would be in any recognized hospital; that, when she was working at the Canadian Forces Hospital, Halifax, she was told which patients to look after; and that she did not sign any form of contract with the above hospital when she started to work there.

— REQUIRED

Is the taxpayer in this case employed or self-employed? In presenting your answer, discuss the tests that are applied by the courts in this type of situation and consider how the facts relate to these tests.

Exercise 2

ITA: 248(1); *Wiebe Door Services Ltd. v. M.N.R.*, 87 DTC 5025 (F.C.A.)

Due to the poor economy, Davies Ltd., an architectural firm, has instituted a freeze in hiring. However, the company wants to engage the services of a specific architect, Anne Capwell, to manage the completion of a specific project over a two-year period. Following negotiations between the parties, a consulting contract was signed. Ms. Capwell will be paid $4,000 per month to work at least 14 days per month (i.e., between three and four days per week) for a two-year period. The agreement stipulates that Davies Ltd. will provide Ms. Capwell with an office and pay for underground parking at Davies Ltd. Ms. Capwell has other architectural work and she estimates that she derives approximately 30% of her consulting income from other sources.

— REQUIRED

Express your opinion as to whether Ms. Capwell is considered an employee or an independent contractor.

Exercise 3

ITA: 6(1)(*a*); IT-470R

William Winter works for an extremely generous employer, Benjamin's Ltd., which paid the following amounts on behalf of William:

(a) Registered pension plan contributions (defined benefit) $1,000
(b) Provincial employer health tax 600
(c) Extended health care premiums — Sun Life 250
(d) Drug plan premiums — Mutual of Omaha 150
(e) Tuition fee for a basket weaving course offered by a local high school 75
(f) Non-cash Christmas gift which the company did expense for tax purposes 65
(g) Subsidized lunches at company cafeteria:
    Fair market value 640
    Actual cost 420
    Amount paid by William 200
(h) Membership fees in Exclusive Private Club 800
(i) Financial counselling — ABC Investment Counselling Ltd. 1,000

— REQUIRED

Comment on whether these amounts are taxable.

Exercise 4

ITA: 6, 8

Subdivision a — Income or loss from an office or employment, outlines the basic rules, inclusions and deductions when computing net income from employment.

— REQUIRED

Explain when legal expenses are deductible in computing income from employment. Identify your references and outline any related sections, other resources and other relevant information.

Exercise 5

Melanie Hughes, a division supervisor for Eli's Ltd., a large department store chain, receives a 35% discount on all merchandise purchased through Eli's Ltd. This discount is available to all executives above assistant department heads. Melanie calculated that the discount saved her $6,000 this year.

— *REQUIRED*

Discuss whether there is a benefit.

Exercise 6

John Scott, an employee of Kelly Ltd., lives in Burlington and commutes by GO Train to Toronto where Kelly Ltd. is located. John, who is bored by reading, decides to move to Toronto, about 50 kilometres closer to his work, in order to cut down his travelling time. Kelly Ltd. reimburses him for the following amounts:

Moving van costs	$2,500
Reimbursement of actual loss suffered in selling the house	5,000
	$7,500

— *REQUIRED*

Discuss whether there is a benefit.

Exercise 7

Tanya Sims, who is chairperson of her union's negotiating team, has approached you concerning the management's offer in connection with fringe benefits. The company proposes to pay one-half of the premiums of the following plans:

(a) group term life insurance;

(b) extended health care — a private plan;

(c) dental care — a private plan;

(d) an accident and sickness income protection plan — a private group plan covering up to 50% of the wages.

All of these plans have premiums which are approximately the same. The company at present does not contribute to any of these plans.

— *REQUIRED*

Discuss the tax implications of the company's proposal.

Exercise 8

Katrina Knorr was granted, in year one, an option to purchase 50,000 common shares at $1 per share from her employer, Michael Ltd., a Canadian-controlled private corporation. The shares had an estimated fair market value at this date of $1.50. However, according to the agreement, Katrina could not exercise her option until her fourth employment year. Katrina did exercise her entire option in year five; the fair market value of the shares at that time was $3. Katrina sold all the shares in year six, at $6 per share.

— *REQUIRED*

Discuss the tax implications of the above transactions.

Exercise 9

ITA: 6(1)(*e*), 6(1)(*k*), 6(2)

Ms. Singh has full use of an employer-owned Mustang GTS purchased for her use in mid-December of last year. It is now January. The original cost to the employer of this classic is $20,000, including HST. Other details of the car for the coming year are as follows:

Capital cost allowance to be claimed by employer $4,792

Operating costs for the year paid by the employer, including HST and insurance
($600) $3,500

Personal-use kilometres 12,000

Number of months available 12

Reimbursement to employer for personal use at 15 cents per kilometre $1,800

— *REQUIRED*

Compute the taxable standby charge and operating cost benefits, if the business-use kilometres are:

(a) 10,000

(b) 20,000

Exercise 10

ITA: 8(1)(*i*), 8(13); IT-352R2

Calvin Cheng, who is employed and lives in Calgary, takes a considerable amount of office work home and, therefore, has built and furnished an office in his fully paid home. On this year's tax return, he claimed the following expenses in respect of his office which represents approximately 1/8 of the home.

Estimated rental value for office space $1,000

Maintenance — 1/8 250

Taxes — 1/8 200

Insurance — 1/8 80

$1,530

— *REQUIRED*

Discuss whether Calvin's course of action was correct.

Exercise 11

ITA: 8(4), 67.1(1)

The deduction for meals under paragraph 8(1)(*f*) — (sales expenses), is restricted to those incurred while entertaining a client or a customer or a prospective client or customer.

— *REQUIRED*

Determine the condition(s) under which personal meals consumed by an employee while travelling on business are allowable. Are there any restrictions if a deduction is allowed?

¶3,875 ASSIGNMENT PROBLEMS

Type 1 Problems

Problem 1

You have come out of a meeting with Lisa, one of your personal tax clients. She is about to start a job with a public company and, as part of the compensation package, she is offered the use of a company car. She is given the choice between two options and she wants your opinion on which she should choose. The make, model, and year of the car are the same in both cases. She expects to drive about 24,000 km per year. However, she is not sure how many personal versus business kilometres she will be driving. She expects it will be either 60% business or 40% business. Assume that she is in the 41% combined (federal and provincial) marginal tax bracket.

Option 1: The company will provide a company-owned automobile that costs $35,000 (before HST of 13%). The company will cover the insurance and operating costs which will cost $8,000 per year.

Option 2: The company will provide a company-leased automobile that costs $750 per month (before HST of 13%). The company will cover the insurance and operating costs which will cost $8,000 per year.

Problem 2

You have been asked for advice on employee stock options by two different clients.

(a) Omer is part of the management team of a Canadian public company and is eligible for the employee stock option plan. A few years ago he received an option on 1,000 shares. The current price of the shares is $35, and he is optimistic that it will go up. The option requires him to pay the option price of $30 (the value at the time the option was granted) for the shares at the time he exercises his option. He plans to sell these shares when they reach $45.

He has asked you to tell him the amount of income he will have to report and when he must report as a result of exercising the option and buying the shares for $30.

(b) Hilda is part of the management team of a Canadian-controlled private company and is eligible for the employee stock option plan. A few years ago she received an option on 1,000 shares. The current price of the shares is $35, and she is optimistic that it will go up. The option requires her to pay the option price of $30 (the value at the time the option was granted) for the shares at the time she exercises her option. She plans to sell these shares when they reach $45.

She has asked you to tell her the amount of income she will have to report and when she must report as a result of exercising the option and buying the shares for $30.

Problem 3

ITA: 5(1); 6(1)(a), (b); 8(1)(m); 62; 118.2(2)(q); IT: 470R

Rishma, a good friend from your university days, has just left your office. She remembered that you have specialized in tax and has come to you for advice on an offer of employment that she has received. Motion Tech Inc., a public company, has offered her the position of VP of Human Resources. Motion Tech has a year end of November 30th. Her start date is one month from now.

She has made the following list of items that are included in the package and would like your advice on the tax consequences of each:

1. A salary of $90,000 per year, payable by direct deposit on the last day of each month.

2. A bonus payable based on the year-end results of the company. The bonus would be up to $10,000.

3. Motion Tech has a defined contribution registered pension plan where Rishma and the company each contribute 6% of her salary.

4. Since she will have to move to Waterloo to take up this position, the company will pay her an allowance of $15,000 to cover her moving expenses.

5. Motion Tech will cover the annual dues for a fitness club up to a cost of $2,000 per year.

6. The company will pay for Rishma to have her personal tax return prepared at a cost of up to $1,000.

7. The company provides a group health plan administered by Manulife, including glasses. Rishma will pay about $200 per month and the company will pay about $800 per month.

Problem 4

You are working in the finance department at Auto Supply Inc. during your co-op work term. The CFO knows you have just taken a tax course and has asked you to do some research for him. The company is looking at possible employee benefit options and would like you to write a memo explaining whether each of the following would be considered taxable benefits of the employees.

1. Free parking.

2. Wedding or birthday gifts of up to $200.

3. All-expense paid holiday won as part of a sales contest.

4. The employee uses frequent flyer points for a personal trip. These points were earned as a result of business trips.

5. The company provides an employee discount of 24% on products sold by Auto Supply.

6. The company pays to provide financial counselling for all vice presidents, including the preparation of their personal tax returns.

7. The company will pay for annual professional dues for employees. For example, accountants and lawyers.

Problem 5

ITA: 6(9), 8(1)(*j*), 80.4, 80.5

Leonard Lewis, an employee of BGE Ltd., received the following loans on January 1 of this year from his employer:

6% . . . . . $15,000 loan to purchase a car to be used primarily for employment purposes,

4% . . . . . $100,000 loan to purchase a home, and

7% . . . . . $10,000 loan to consolidate his other debts.

Leonard does not receive a mileage allowance and is specifically required by his contract to pay his car expenses. According to Leonard's travel log, he used the car for employment purposes, for 27,000 kilometres out of a total of 45,000 kilometres.

Assume that the prescribed rates for this year were:

1st Quarter — 7%	3rd Quarter — 8%
2nd Quarter — 6%	4th Quarter — 7%

Leonard paid the interest on these loans on January 15 of the following year.

Compute the interest benefit and any deduction for interest. Ignore the effects of any leap year.

Problem 6

ITA: 8(1)(*f*), 8(1)(*i*), 8(4)

Reille travels extensively with Biotech Corporation to market new pharmaceuticals throughout Canada. He is paid a base salary of $2,200 per month plus a 2% commission on gross sales. Reille was required to incur the following expenses to earn $24,000 in commission income:

Hotel and airfare	$18,000
Out of town meals	4,000
Entertainment meals	2,500
Professional dues	250
Notebook computer	3,900
Total	**$28,650**

Compute employment expenses deductible under section 8 of the Act.

Problem 7

ITA: 6(1)(*b*), 13(7)(*g*), 67.2; IT-522R

Ms. Irvine, who is employed by Susan's Super Ltd., travels extensively across Canada in her role as an internal auditor. According to the terms of her contract, she receives an accommodation allowance of $10,000 per year.

The contract states that she must use her own automobile and pay for all travelling expenses. Ms. Irvine acquired a new car, on January 5, 2016, for $32,000 plus HST at 13%. Her kilometres for business purposes were 15,000 out of a total of 21,000 kilometres.

During the year, Ms. Irvine paid the following amounts, all of which are reasonable in the circumstances and which are supported by receipts:

(a) accommodation, including meals of $4,500 (including HST)		$12,000
(b) total car expenses:	gas (including HST)	1,500
	maintenance (including HST)	500
	insurance	1,200
	licences	90
	interest on bank loan	4,000

Ms. Irvine calculated her capital cost allowance to be:

$$(\tfrac{1}{2} \times 30\% \times \$32,000) = \$4,800$$

Ms. Irvine also filed the prescribed form (T2200) which her employer had signed. Assume that the employment use of the car is reasonable in the circumstances.

Discuss the tax consequences of the allowance and related expenses plus the deductibility of the car expenses. Ignore the effects of any leap year.

Problem 8

ITA: 6(8); ETA: 253(1)

Based on the facts and solution for Problem 7 determine the potential HST rebate and income tax consequences upon receipt of this amount.

Problem 9

ITA: 248(1); *Wiebe Door Services Ltd. v. M.N.R.*, 87 DTC 5025 (F.C.A.)

Harry Chow, the owner of Chow Installation and Repair Ltd. ("Chow") has come to you for advice, but first he describes his business. Chow is in the business of installing and repairing overhead doors. Chow maintains a list of qualified installers and repair-persons and contacts them as work becomes available. Chow informed these workers that they would be considered to be running their own business, so no withholding of income tax, EI or CPP is made. Workers are paid by the job and work mostly on their own. If the person contacted refuses the assignment, Chow will call the next person on the list. The person who agrees to the job goes directly to the job site; he or she does not report to Chow's work place, except to pick up a door or parts.

Chow supplies the doors and the parts used in the repair or installation. Each worker maintains his or her own truck and tools. Chow, however, owns specialized racks made for transporting the doors and a special drill which can be used on cement. These items are available to any worker who requires them.

Chow guarantees all work for one year. Under the terms of the agreement between Chow and the workers, if a guarantee has to be honoured, the worker will be responsible to fix any defects. If any parts are required to correct the defect, the worker has to pay for them.

Harry then asks you the question he wants advice on, "What is the risk that his installers will be considered employees for tax purposes?" He has heard that some other businesses are being reassessed and are facing significant liability for withholding taxes and he wants your advice on what his risk of reassessment is. You have agreed to meet with Harry again in one week and provide him with advice on this issue. As you think about how you will approach this assignment, you decide that you need to determine whether the workers should be considered employees of Chow or independent contractors. To do this you will need to consider the tests that are applied by the courts to this type of situation, and relate the facts of this case to those tests.

Problem 10

ITA: 5, 6(1)(a), 6(1)(b), 80.4; IT-470R

Miriam, the sole tax adviser of a financial planning firm, is contemplating an offer to become Director of Taxation of Neil Manufacturing Limited (NML) of Dundas, Ontario. The offered compensation package would include the following:

- a salary of $132,000 per year, payable monthly;

- a one-time flat allowance of $25,000, payable on acceptance of the position, to help move her and her family to Dundas;

- a company contribution of 6% of her salary to a defined benefit registered pension plan;

- company payment of the premiums for extended health coverage and a dental plan provided by Star Insurance;

- company payment, valued at $900, for the preparation of her tax return by the company's accountants;

- company payment, valued at $2,500, for her membership in the Dundas Valley Golf and Curling Club;

- a company loan of $200,000 to help finance the purchase of a new home in Dundas. The loan will bear interest at 2% per year payable monthly and will be made on May 1 of this year, the closing date on the purchase of the home.

Miriam does not deal with many employment-related tax issues and recognizes the need for a corroborating opinion on the tax consequences of this compensation package. She has asked you to comment on the income tax consequences for employment income of each item in the compensation package. Assume that the prescribed rate of interest for employee loans is 1% throughout the year. Ignore any effects of a leap year.

Problem 11

ITA: 5, 6(1)(a), 6(1)(b), 80.4; IT-470R

Erin is an employee of TD-ROM, Inc., a public company. In 2016, her compensation package was as follows:

Gross salary	$59,000
Less: Payroll deductions	
Employee contribution to a registered pension plan	(3,000)
Charitable donations — United Way	(55)
Canadian Pension Plan contributions	(2,544)
Employment Insurance contributions	(955)
Net pay received	$52,446
Non-cash perks	
Employer contribution to a registered pension plan	$ 3,500
Private dental plan valued at	$ 800
Mandatory employer-paid provincial health tax	$ 450
Reimbursement of moving expenses for relocating from Edmonton	$ 900
Club membership (for company promotion)	$ 1,800
Supplier's prize for outstanding employee sales — Hawaii golf trip valued at	$ 6,000
Bonus declared but not paid	$ 2,000
Hard hat and safety glasses	$ 450

The company states that club memberships should be used for business promotion.

TD-ROM also offered Erin a stock option to purchase 1,000 corporate shares at $12 a share. On June 4, 2016, she exercised the option. As of December 31, 2016, Erin had not disposed of the shares.

February 1, 2009, Fair market value — Grant date	$11
June 4, 2016, Fair market value — Exercise date	$19
December 31, 2016, Fair market value	$16

Erin has asked you to calculate her income from employment for income tax purposes.

Problem 12   ITA: 5, 6, 7

Three senior executives are renewing their employment contracts with Global Consulting Ltd., a public corporation. The corporation has provided each of them with the following alternative compensation plans for 2016 in addition to the $145,000 base salary each receives:

(a) A cash raise of $5,000 in 2016.

(b) A bonus of $5,500 payable in 2017.

(c) Use of the company condominium in Hawaii for two weeks, valued at $3,000.

(d) A stock option arrangement to purchase 1,000 shares of Global Consulting, a public company, in December 2016, when the fair market value of the shares is $5, and the option price would be $3.50 per share. Management anticipates the share price in December 2017 will be $6.50.

The senior executives have asked you to analyze the various alternatives and provide a recommendation. You agreed to assume a marginal tax rate of 45%.

Problem 13   ITA: 6, 110(1)(*d*)

Craig Hunt is the general manager of the local professional hockey team, the Vancouver Golden Seals Ltd. (a Canadian public corporation). Assume that today's date is November 15, 2014. Craig has obtained approval from the owner of the hockey club to offer a contract to a 27-year-old free agent player who is available to the highest bidder. In addition to an offer of a $300,000 signing bonus and a $750,000 annual salary, Craig is authorized to offer the following two items as additional compensation:

(a) an interest-free employee loan of $100,000 that will eventually be forgiven by the hockey club; and

(b) a stock option to buy 100,000 common shares of Vancouver Golden Seals Ltd. Assume that on the grant date, the fair market value of the common shares is $10 per share, and that the exercise price will be $10 per share.

Craig has asked for your advice on the following:

(a) Assuming the player will exercise all shares when the FMV is $15.00 per share and then sell the shares immediately on the open market, outline the income tax consequences with respect to the stock option and explain how this will affect the player's net income for tax purposes.

(b) From the player's perspective, what, if any, are the consequences of the signing bonus and the proposed employee loan that will be forgiven in the final contract year?

(c) Assuming instead that the loan will not be forgiven, calculate the deemed interest benefit of the loan for the 2016 and 2017 taxation years. Assume the prescribed rate of interest on the loan is 6%. Ignore the effects of any leap year.

¶3,875

Problem 14

ITA: 6(1)(*a*), 6(1)(*e*), 6(1)(*e*.1), 6(1)(*k*), 6(2), 6(2.2)

Your best friend, Mitch, was at a sales conference recently. During one of the breaks, he entered into a conversation with one of the other attendees, Darly, regarding the perks provided by their respective employers. In both cases, the employer provides a car. However, Darly commented on the significant tax advantage available to her since her employer leased the car instead of buying the car. Mitch was able to obtain all of the information from Darly regarding her car.

Mitch has come to you for some "free" tax advice. He has asked you to compare the tax position he is in currently with the employer-owned car to the position that Darly is in with the leased car.

Mitch

Capital cost of the car including HST	$38,772
Capital cost allowance claimed by the employer	6,375
Operating costs paid by the employer (including HST)	4,250
Kilometres (as calculated from Mitch's log):	
Employment	8,000
Personal	10,000
Amount reimbursed to the company for the personal use at 14 cents per kilometre	$ 1,400

Darly

Lease cost including $1,650 of insurance and HST	$12,450
Operating costs paid by the employer (including HST)	2,975
Kilometres (as calculated from Darly's log):	
Employment	23,000
Personal	9,000
Amount reimbursed to the company for the personal use at 9 cents per kilometre	$ 810

Mitch wants you to calculate the minimum car benefit that would be included in employment income for 2016 for both him and Darly.

Problem 15

ITA: 8(1)(*h*.1)

Crowchild Pipelines Corporation has offered Bing Lee a base salary of $65,000. Bing must choose one of the following compensation packages for the use of his personal automobile.

(a) To receive a reasonable car allowance of $6,000 per year to compensate for the operating expenses and the depreciation of his Jeep, used to drive to remote work sites. The allowance is based on the kilometres to and from the remote location, multiplied by the number of workdays.

(b) To submit receipts for all of his operating expenses for full reimbursement. Bing estimates that his total operating expenses are $4,000 annually. However, this amount does not cover the wear and tear on his car. Bing will use his car approximately 65% of the time for employment and he will be able to claim capital cost allowance (tax depreciation) equal to $3,000.

Bing has a marginal tax rate of 45%. He has asked you to determine, with explanation, whether he would be indifferent to the choice between these two compensation packages?

Problem 16

ITA: 5, 6(3)

Chrisa had been an employee of David Hardware, a hardware product distributor, for 15 years. Chrisa sold the David hardware products directly to hardware stores. She was a salesperson and she was paid 100% by commission. Chrisa was personally responsible for all of her business expenses. Expenses, for example, for office supplies, stamps, telephone, parking, entertainment, promotion and samples, were supported by receipts and she deducted them.

During the years that Chrisa was employed by David, she sold products and developed the hardware market in her geographic area. One of the ways in which she developed the market was by "renting" floor space in various stores to display the David products. However, no receipts were received from the various stores, because in many ways the money was considered a "tip" by the managers of the hardware stores. Chrisa did not deduct these expenses. Through this process, Chrisa had significantly increased David's sales in her sales region and she had developed a loyal following in the hardware business.

CHAPTER 3

At the time of Chrisa's departure from David, David paid $15,000 to Chrisa. The conditions of the agreement surrounding the $15,000 payment were as follows:

- David was "buying back" Chrisa's sales territory;

- Chrisa agreed not to enter a similar business to that of David's business, in David's distribution area, for a period of three years; and

- David and Chrisa agreed that the $15,000 would constitute a reimbursement of capital invested by Chrisa (i.e., the amounts she had paid to the stores for the rental of floor space for David products).

Chrisa has asked you to explain the income tax implications of the receipt of the $15,000.

Problem 17

ITA: 5, 6(1), 7, 8(1)

The following information relates to Leonard, a middle-management accountant, not engaged in negotiating contracts, of a public corporation, Peter Productions Ltd. which is located in Ontario.

(A) Salary — gross		$ 80,000
Payroll deductions:		
Income taxes	$23,412	
Registered pension plan (money purchase; see (B) below)	5,500	
Canada Pension Plan contributions	2,544	
Employment Insurance contributions	955	
Charitable donations	350	
Employee's portion of benefit plans (see (B), below)	800	(33,561)
		$ 46,439

(B) The company paid the following additional matching amounts on behalf of Leonard (an equal amount was withheld from salary as the employee's contribution, as shown in (A) above):

Registered pension plan	$5,500
Dental plan — Sun Life Co.	175
Group income protection — Royal Insurance Co.	225
Extended health care — Liberty Mutual	150
Group term life insurance — General Insurance Co.	250

The group term life coverage for Leonard was $300,000.

(C) Selected additional information concerning Leonard's receipts, disbursements, and other benefits:

(i) Trip to Europe from one of Peter Productions Ltd.'s clients in appreciation of Leonard's services (including HST) .... $ 6,000

(ii) Periodic payments received from Royal Insurance under the group income protection plan during a three-month illness. This plan had been in existence since 2005 and Leonard's share of the premium since that date was $2,300   12,000

(iii) Peter Productions Ltd. paid Leonard's annual membership fee in a golf club   2,100

(iv) Early in 2016, Leonard was granted an option to purchase 1,000 of the company's shares for $2 per share. At that time the shares were trading on the market at $3 per share. Later in the year, Leonard exercised the option and acquired 1,000 shares when they were trading at $4.50 per share. In December 2016, he needed cash, so he sold the 1,000 shares for $5 each.

(v) Leonard paid the following amounts during the year:

Annual membership fee of a professional accounting body (including HST)   800

Registered retirement savings plan 3,500

Leonard has asked you to calculate his employment income for 2016, as well as his HST rebate based on that year. He want you to explain the tax implications of the HST rebate as well. For your files you also should document why you omitted any of the items mentioned above.

Problem 18

ITA: 5(1), 6(4), 8(1)(*f*), 8(1)(*j*); IT-470R

On September 1, Maria Battelio, a Calgary resident, commenced work as an investment dealer with Top Investments Corporation. Prior to September, Maria was a fourth-year commerce student at the University of Edmonton. Maria's contract of employment required that she use her own car and incur the necessary expenses to earn commission income. Maria purchased her car on September 1 for $21,000. Top Investments Corporation lent her the $21,000 for the car and she agreed to repay them $7,000 annually, without interest, on December 31 of each year. Assume that Maria's deductible capital cost allowance (net of personal use) on her automobile is $2,000.

Total distance travelled from September 1 to December 31	
Total kilometres driven	12,500
Personal kilometres driven	5,000
Maria received the following net pay in the year:	
Gross salary	$ 4,000
Commissions	18,000
Bonus	300
Employment Insurance contributions	(414)
Canadian Pension Plan contributions	(916)
Charitable donations	(280)
Income tax withheld at source	(4,200)
Net pay	$16,742
To earn commission income, Maria incurred the following:	
Meals and entertainment	$ 2,300
Client promotion materials	1,500
Gasoline and operating expenses	1,600
Total	$ 5,400

Top Investment paid for the airfare and accommodation for Maria and her spouse to attend a conference in New York. The trip cost $800 for each person attending the conference. The company also pays premiums of $400 per employee for group life insurance with coverage of $100,000. Assume a 7% prescribed rate of interest on the employee loan.

Maria would like you to calculate her income from employment. Ignore the effects of any leap year.

Problem 19

ITA: 5(1), 6(1)(*a*), 7(1), 8(1)(*f*), 8(1)(*i*)

Susanna Sculley, a marketing representative with MBI Technology Inc. (a public company), provided the following information relating to her current year's personal income tax return. Susanna's cumulative pay at year end revealed the following:

Gross pay	
Base salary	$42,000
Gross commissions	23,500
Daycare subsidy program	1,200
Deductions from gross pay	
Employment Insurance contributions	(955)
Canadian Pension Plan contributions	(2,544)
Union dues	(280)
Income tax paid	(19,800)
Net pay	$43,121
Expenses to earn commission income	
Meals and entertainment	2,300
Hotel and travel incidentals	1,780
Airfare	1,800
Total	$ 5,880

CHAPTER 3

MBI also granted Susanna a stock option, which she exercised in April of the current year. The following information relates to the stock option:

```
Number of shares for options exercised . . . . . . . . . . . . .  1,000
Fair market value — grant date . . . . . . . . . . . . . . . . . .  $1.50
Option price . . . . . . . . . . . . . . . . . . . . . . . . . . . . .  $1.80
Fair market value — exercise date . . . . . . . . . . . . . . .  $2.50
```

Susanna's employer did not reimburse her, or provide her with an allowance for the expenses incurred to earn commission income. However, MBI did expect her to take clients out for lunch and travel when necessary.

Susanna would like you to calculate her income from employment for the current year.

Problem 20

ITA: 5, 6, 7, 8

Sylvanna Chapelle, a national sales manager at Merche Tools Ltd. in Peterborough, Ontario, presented the following information for the current taxation year.

1) Gross salary	$48,000
Bonus based on sales	40,000
Less payroll deductions:	
Employee contribution to a Registered Pension Plan	(4,000)
Charitable donations — Heart Foundation	(150)
Canada Pension Plan contributions	(2,480)
Employment Insurance contributions	(931)
Net salary	$80,439

According to Sylvanna's contract of employment, she must travel to Vancouver, Edmonton, Calgary, and Regina to oversee operations in western Canada. Sylvanna must pay for travelling and promotional expenses. The company does not provide her with a travelling allowance. Instead, Sylvanna receives a bonus based on a percentage of western Canada sales. Syvanna's travelling expenses were as follows:

2) Meals while travelling out of town (45 days)	$ 1,500
Accommodation	5,200
Airfare	7,800
Taxi	500

3) Client promotion costs:	
Company logo shirts and golf balls	700
Client meals and entertainment	2,200
Holiday gifts for prospective clients	3,500
Annual golf membership	1,800

4) Sylvanna's employment contract also required her to travel to the Oshawa manufacturing plant and four other warehouse outlets in Southern Ontario. The corporation provided her with a new four-door van last year. The cost of the van, including HST of 13%, was $36,000. The company also paid $2,400 for 100% of the operating cost. Sylvanna used the vehicle for the full calendar year for both employment and weekend pleasure. Personal kilometres driven totalled 9,900 and total kilometres driven is 18,000.

5) Merche Tools also paid out the following amounts:	
Tax return preparation for Sylvanna	$ 350
Life insurance premium	150

Sylvanna would like you to calculate her income from employment for income tax purposes for the current year.

¶3,875

Problem 21

ITA: 5, 6; IT-470R

Anita Lee, Vice-President of Gary Inc., has asked for your assistance concerning the tax implications of certain amounts and benefits she received from her employer during 2016.

Salary, gross		$ 90,000
Payroll deductions:		
Income taxes	$36,000	
Canada Pension Plan premiums	2,544	
Employment Insurance premiums	955	
Group accident disability insurance premiums	110	(39,609)
Net pay		$ 50,391

Additional Information

(1) In November 2016, Anita was in a skiing accident and was unable to work for four weeks. During this period she received disability payments totalling $1,600 from Paris Life Insurance Ltd. Half of the disability insurance premiums were paid by Gary Inc. and half by Anita (see payroll deduction above). Anita has paid a total of $350 in disability insurance premiums since she commenced employment at Gary Inc. in 2013.

(2) In 2016, Gary Inc. paid $424 (including HST) for the preparation of Anita's 2015 income tax return and $530 (including HST) for Anita to see a financial planning consultant regarding retirement planning.

(3) Anita is taking courses towards her M.B.A. degree on a part-time basis during the evening. She is taking the courses on her initiative and for her own benefit. During 2016, Gary Inc. paid for the tuition for these M.B.A. courses which amounted to $1,000. Gary Inc. also paid $400 in tuition for Anita to attend a two-day computer workshop on company time to learn about the new software system that the company had just installed.

(4) Director's fees of $2,000 were received by Anita from Clint's Hi-Tech Ltd., a company owned by Anita's spouse.

(5) Birthday gift of $200 cash was received and was expensed by Gary Inc.

(6) Anita received an employee loan of $8,000 on January 15, 2016, at 1% interest to purchase a notebook computer for personal use. The interest was payable on each anniversary date of the loan, and Anita paid the interest owing on the loan on the due date in 2017. Assume that the prescribed interest rates applicable to employee loans for 2016 are: first quarter, 2%; second quarter, 1%; third quarter, 3%; fourth quarter, 2%.

(7) For 12 months, Gary Inc. paid Anita a monthly gas allowance of $250 regardless of the number of kilometres she drove. In addition, she was provided with a company-owned automobile costing $38,500 (including HST) at the beginning of January. Anita's kilometres for personal use were 16,000 out of a total of 25,000 kilometres. Operating costs paid (excluding gas) by Gary Inc. during 2016 amounted to $2,920, including insurance of $600 and HST.

(8) Anita and her spouse Clint were provided with Gary Inc.'s condo in the Bahamas for a one-week holiday during the winter. Excluding HST considerations, such accommodation during this peak period would have cost them $500 as opposed to the $100 actually paid by Anita.

(9) Anita used her frequent-flyer points accumulated as a result of her business trips (which had been paid by Gary Inc.) for her holiday in the Bahamas. She saved $800, plus $104 of HST, by using the frequent-flyer points.

¶3,875

(10) Anita bought merchandise from Gary Inc. during the year and saved $180 (excluding HST of $23) using its 30% employee discount, which is available to all employees. Gary Inc.'s mark-up is 100%.

Anita would like you to calculate her employment income for 2016. For your file you also should document the basis for your decision to include an item or not, i.e., whether it is based on the Act or on the CRA's administrative position. You decide to ignore the impact of any leap year.

Anita also wants you to recalculate her employment income assuming that the company did not provide her with a car as she used her own car instead. In this case the company would continue to pay for the operating costs of Anita's car.

Problem 22

ITA: 5, 6, 7, 8, 67.1, 67.2, 67.3; IT-352R2

Robby Beamon has recently been appointed vice-president of sales and marketing for Lori's Unpublished Books Limited, a public company. Robby has come to you for advice regarding the tax implications of his new position. During your meeting you were able to determine the following information:

Remuneration for the year:

Salary — gross		$84,800
Less: Canada Pension Plan contributions	$2,544	
Employment Insurance contributions	955	
Disability insurance premiums	600	4,099
		$80,701
Bonus based on company sales		34,000
Allowances for the year (paid monthly):		
meals, accommodation and air travel		13,000
car		6,300
entertainment		2,000
Moving allowance		15,000

Robby has summarized the following expenses related to his employment:

Gas and oil — automobile	$ 3,900
Painting (office only)	100
Licences — automobile	100
Meals (consumed while travelling away for more than 12 hours)	7,000
House insurance	800
Accommodation (while travelling on company business)	10,000
Interest expense — car loan	3,600
General maintenance (house)	300
Car insurance	1,900
Hydro	700
Air travel	4,200
Car maintenance	1,000
Supplies	700
Fuel (house)	1,200
Property taxes	4,500
Mortgage interest	24,000
Salary (to wife, including payroll taxes and employer contributions)	15,000

Lori's Unpublished Books Limited requires Robby to provide an automobile in order to carry out his duties of employment. Robby is responsible for his travelling expenses. On March 17, 2016, he acquired a new car for $46,000, including HST at 15%, financing part of the acquisition through a bank loan arranged for the same date. The capital cost allowance rate in the first year is effectively 15%. He estimates that he will drive 38,000 kilometres in the course of his employment. He expects his total kilometres to the end of the year to be 45,000. The car and the employment use are reasonable for his position and his work requirements.

Robby's contract also requires that he maintain an office in his home, since no other office is provided. He is responsible for all costs related to the operation of the office. He does not receive an allowance or reimbursement related to any of these costs. Robby has estimated that the office occupies approximately 15% of his home. This estimate is based on square footage. Robby estimates that if he had to rent a comparable amount of space he would have to pay $850 per month plus utilities.

Robby would like you to calculate his employment income for 2016, assuming that all expenses are reasonable in the circumstances and will be documented. Ignore consideration of the HST rebate.

Robby would also like you to recalculate his deductible expenses assuming the following alternatives: ITA: 8(1)

(i) the car was leased instead of purchased on March 17, 2016.

(ii) Monthly lease payments are $1,100 including HST at 15%.

(iii) Manufacturer's list price is $48,500 excluding HST.

Problem 23

ITA: 5, 6, 7, 8, 67.2, 67.3; IT-470R

Anita Flare is a skilled tool and die worker. She has been working for Car Parts Inc., a large manufacturer of parts for the automobile industry for over 10 years. Car Parts Inc. is a Canadian-controlled private corporation. Anita has become their "Jane on the Spot" as far as diagnosing and quickly retooling machinery that breaks down or needs to be updated to run a short order. Anita is single and she rents a home in north Toronto. Because Anita is required to travel for 75% of the year, Car Parts Inc. actually pays the $1,200 monthly rent on Anita's home in Toronto. Anita reimburses the company for 25% of this amount ($300 per month) through payroll deduction as set out below.

The head office of Car Parts Inc. is located in north Toronto. The company, however, has plants that are located throughout Ontario and Quebec, wherever there are large automobile manufacturing operations to be supplied with parts. When a plant requires emergency retooling or repair Anita is sent out to that location to supervise and organize the work. As stated above, this involves about 75% of Anita's total employment hours for any given year. She stays at a particular location for a period of days or weeks depending on the nature of the job involved. She is never at a site for less than 36 hours. For the balance of the year, Anita works at the head office in the research department.

Anita's final 2016 pay stub showed the following totals for the year.

Gross salary		$115,000
Payroll deductions:		
Income tax withheld	$44,200	
Canada Pension Plan contributions	2,544	
Employment Insurance premiums paid	955	
Contributions to company group RRSP	1,750	
RPP contributions on account of current service	5,000	
Union dues to Canadian Union of Automobile Workers (HST exempt)	800	
Group accident income protection insurance premiums (matched by company)	240	
Monthly rent reimbursement (as described above)	3,600	

In discussion with Anita you determined that the company also provides the following fringe benefits.

Payment of board and lodging costs at special work sites as required — at cost to company	$18,000
Bonus based on company profits for the year above budgeted targets	12,500
Provision of safety boots and company uniform consisting of five shirts and five matching pairs of pants; the shirt is embroidered with her name on the front pocket and has the company name on the back	450
Registered pension plan contributions to defined benefit plan	6,750
Monthly allowance of $150 to cover personal phone calls, laundry costs and other incidentals while travelling. (She estimates that she spends $100 per month.)	1,800
Fitness club membership dues to a club with locations across Ontario (including HST); Anita feels that it is important to her productivity to remain in top physical shape as her work can be physically demanding	805

Anita was injured on the job early in the year and received total payments of $11,500 out of the company group income protection plan for 2 months while she was recuperating. She had not previously received any payments under this plan and has paid total premiums of $2,880 into the plan since she began employment 12 years ago (this includes all of the year 2016 premiums paid through December 2016).

Due to her extensive travel, Anita's employer requires her to have an automobile for employment purposes. Anita has provided you with the following details of her automobile expenses.

	Owned car[1]	Leased car
Leasing costs[2]	n/a	$3,680
Gasoline and oil (including HST)	$2,880	1,440
Insurance	1,333	667
Maintenance (including HST)	400	240
Licence	90	30
CCA	1,207	n/a

NOTES:

[1] She owned an automobile until August 31, 2016, at which time she disposed of that vehicle and began leasing a new one. Assume that there are no tax consequences to Anita of the disposition of the automobile other than the fact that she can claim CCA in 2016 on this vehicle, as set out above, since it was a luxury vehicle.

Anita received an automobile loan to purchase the owned automobile. She received the loan on April 1, 2011, for $40,000, but has been making principal repayments annually on April 1 each year. She made the last principal repayment of $8,000 on April 1, 2016. There was no interest payable on the loan. Assume that the prescribed interest rate for employee loans was 1% for all of 2016.

During 2016, Anita drove the owned car a total of 40,000 kilometres, of which 35,000 kilometres were employment related.

[2] Anita leased the car as of September 1, 2016, at a cost of $920 a month that includes HST. The lease is for a three-year period that will expire August 31, 2019. At the time that she leased the car, the manufacturer's list price on the vehicle was $55,000 excluding all taxes.

During 2016, Anita drove the leased car a total of 20,000 kilometres, of which 18,000 kilometres were employment related.

Anita would like you to calculate her income from employment for 2016. Ignore the effects of any leap year.

For your files you should reference your findings to the appropriate section of the Act or CRA publication. Also you should indicate why you did not include any of the above amounts in your answer with the appropriate cross-reference.

She also wants you to compute the HST rebate that should be claimed and the income tax consequences of the rebate to be received in 2017.

Problem 24

ITA: Subdiv. a of Div. B,
67.1, 67.3; IT-470R

Mr. Ned Newell is employed by Snoopy-Snacks Ltd. (a Canadian-controlled private corporation). As of February 15, 2016, Ned was promoted to vice-president sales due to his hard work negotiating puppy snack contracts on behalf of the company. This promotion required Ned to relocate from the Toronto office of Snoopy-Snacks Ltd. to its Victoria, British Columbia office.

Ned has provided you with the following information regarding his 2016 income and expenses. He requests your assistance in determining his 2016 employment income for tax purposes.

Payroll details:

Gross salary		$125,000
Less:		
Income taxes	$45,000	
Canada Pension Plan contributions	2,544	
Employment Insurance contributions	955	
Registered pension plan contributions: defined benefit	6,750	
Group income protection premiums paid	120	
Group term life insurance premiums paid	180	55,549
		$ 69,451

Employer-paid amounts and fringe benefits paid by Snoopy-Snacks Ltd.:

Dental plan premiums — paid to Star Insurance Company	$ 245
Group term life insurance premiums	90
B.C. provincial health care premiums	640
Group income protection premiums	400
Monthly allowance to cover travel and automobile expenses (based on a flat monthly amount of $400 for travel and $400 for auto)	9,600
Travelling expenses for Ned and his wife to Bermuda for a sales conference. Ned's time was spent attending the conference but his wife was on vacation the entire time. No HST was payable on the trip since it was outside of Canada. One-half of the expenses related to Ned and one-half to his wife.	2,800
A birthday gift (a watch) received while in Ontario (including HST). Snoopy-Snacks Ltd. deducted the cost of this gift as a business expense.	150
Outside financial counselling fees (including HST). The counselling firm indicated that 80% of its fees relate to counselling for future retirement while the remaining 20% of its fees relate to tax preparation.	2,568

Other Information:

1. Snoopy-Snacks Ltd. provided Ned with some assistance that relates to his move from Toronto to Victoria. The details of that assistance are set out below.

a) Ned purchased a new home in Victoria just prior to his move. However, he could not take possession of that home until April 30, 2016. Snoopy-Snacks Ltd. paid Ned's rent for a Victoria apartment for the months of February through April 2016. The rent paid was $1,200 per month.

b) Ned and Snoopy-Snacks Ltd. agreed that he would receive reimbursement from Snoopy-Snacks Ltd. for one-half of the loss realized by him on the sale of his Toronto home. Ned received $16,500 as a result of this agreement.

c) Ned received an allowance of $15,000 to cover his moving expenses.

In addition to the above, Ned's employer agreed to reimburse him an amount equal to one-quarter of his annual mortgage interest payment for the first five years of his mortgage on his new Victoria home. This was intended to compensate for higher real estate prices in Victoria. For 2016, Ned received $2,000 under the terms of this agreement.

2. Ned had unlimited use of the company's private swimming pool. All management level employees are permitted to utilize this pool. The local private swimming pool charges annual fees of $1,800 per year before HST.

3. Ned had the following expenditures during 2016.

Automobile operating expenditures:

Lease payments for 12 months ($850 a month including HST of 12%)	$10,200
(lease commenced July 1, 2013 for a period of three years; deducted lease costs for 2013 were $4,585)	
Gasoline and oil	1,300
Insurance	1,050
Maintenance	180
Licence	120
Travelling expenditures:	
Meals (consumed while out of metropolitan area for greater than 12 hours)	7,200
Accommodation	12,000

CHAPTER 3

During 2016, Ned travelled a total of 36,000 kilometres, of which 22,500 kilometres were employment-related. The manufacturer's list price on his automobile was $33,000 before HST.

Ned would like you to calculate his employment income for tax purposes for 2016, cross-reference your answer to the appropriate sections of the Act and/or Interpretation Bulletins, and for your files you should indicate why you did not include any of the above amounts in your answer with the appropriate cross-reference.

Ned would also like you to compute the potential HST rebate in 2017 and the income tax conse-   ITA: 6(8)
quences upon receipt of the HST rebate. While B.C. has both PST and GST, assume an HST rate of 12%
for this purpose.

Problem 25

Sandra Rae has worked in the investment business in Calgary for 12 years and is a salaried plus commissioned employee. Recently, however, Sandra has wished for more independence in her career. The alternative of starting her own mutual fund company is neither feasible nor cost effective. A recent offer from a new investment corporation has drawn her attention.

Sandra decided to enter into a contract arrangement with Global Investments Inc. According to the agreement, a license costing $10,000 would give her the right to use the Global name on her letterheads, business cards, and any promotional materials. Sandra could also participate in selling any Global Investment product. The arrangement is peculiar. According to the agreement, Sandra is required to execute a minimum of $750,000 in sales each year before her contract can be renewed for another year. Although Global Investments has an office in Calgary, the agreement stipulates that Sandra use her own office, supplies, computer, printer, fax, telephone, and automobile. The agreement also stipulates that Sandra not work for any other investment firm, nor act as her own agent. Although Sandra will execute transactions, closing a sale requires the signature of the client, herself and a vice-president of Global Investments. Upon the close of a sale, Sandra submits an invoice to Global Investments earning her a management fee equal to 4% of gross sales.

Sandra converted her guest bedroom into a full-time and sole-purpose home office. She will not be reimbursed for any expenses incurred for setup, travelling or office expenses. She is also required to carry professional liability insurance. On the other hand, Global Investments will provide the expertise, research, promotion, and ordering materials. Last week, Global Investments placed an announcement in the newspaper introducing five new sales associates, including Sandra.

How does this new venture affect her computation of net income?

Problem 26

Betina Harty, a well-known Vancouver artist, signed a contract with the University of Calgary to beautify the campus. Betina spent all of the year in completing the beautification. During that time, she enhanced the campus with her own artwork and pieces bought at local auctions.

The University restricted Betina's choice of art to Canadian artists. As well, the University controlled the colour schemes and the types of art selected (e.g., paintings, sculptures, or murals) for the various locations on campus. However, within these requirements, Betina was permitted to exercise artistic discretion over the actual pieces chosen. This gave her a great degree of latitude over the beautification of the campus.

She could produce the art herself, purchase another artist's work and focus on any theme she desired. Betina worked at her own studio and used her own tools for her own productions. If the University did not like the art she produced or bought, she was not reimbursed costs and had to sell the art on the open market. Over the year, Betina channelled all of her energy into the University's beautification and did not produce art for any outside clients.

How should Betina's income from this contract be treated?

Type 2 Problems

Problem 27

The taxpayer, Sherry Cane, is an unmarried research analyst and senior executive for TSE Consultants in Toronto. In January 2014, TSE entered into a contract with the Iraq government, for $390,000, requiring that Ms. Cane be in Iraq from March 2014 to October 2015 to examine the long-term energy issues facing OPEC countries. TSE terminated Ms. Cane's employment and engaged her as an independent subcontractor to perform this task.

Sherry gave up her office downtown, terminated her condominium lease, moved out, and stored her furniture and personal effects at her mother's house. Further, she shipped her clothing and books to Iraq. She retained her Canadian bank account so TSE could deposit the monthly contract income of $12,000 directly into her Canadian bank account. They did not withhold any income taxes. Similarly, in Iraq, no taxes were payable, and the government provided Ms. Cane with suitable living quarters, meals, and a part-time domestic for housekeeping. Since she intended to visit her boyfriend, Shawn, and family in Canada, she retained her Visa card and Ontario Health Care. Ms. Cane wanted to retain non-residency status for obvious reasons.

While in Iraq, Ms. Cane carried her business card with the TSE logo and promoted herself as a TSE representative. Shawn, an English professor from Queen's University, spent one six-month term on sabbatical at the University of Iraq. The letters mailed to the Canadian company from Iraq, however, indicated that she wanted to come home. She also noted that the cultural differences and political uncertainties were extreme. Ms. Cane returned home on October 17, 2015, married Shawn and purchased a lovely home in Waterloo, Ontario, with her savings.

It is now October 29, 2016, and Sherry Cane is sitting in your office as you read the following Notice of Reassessment from the CRA:

> We have completed our review of your personal returns of income for the taxation years 2014 and 2015. Based on our findings, you are a resident of Canada for tax purposes. Thus, we have adjusted your computation of net income to include the receipts of income from TSE, plus a portion of the personal benefits received during your temporary stay in Iraq.

Determine whether a Notice of Objection should be filed.

Problem 28

Claire Jordan, a registered dental hygienist, would like to file a Notice of Objection with the CRA for taxation years 2013 and 2014. The CRA has reassessed Claire as a resident in Canada for 2013 and as an employee for 2013 and 2014. Claire describes herself as an independent self-employed dental hygienist. For the past two years, Claire was employed by the Canadian Forces Dental Unit to work on a day-to-day basis. Generally, the Mobile Dental Unit contracts for her, in advance, depending on the regional demand for dental cleaning and examinations.

In 2013, Claire contracted with the Canadian Forces Mobile Dental Unit to temporarily work at a Canadian Forces base in Saudi Arabia. The terms of the contract specified that she would work on a day-to-day basis depending on the demand for dental services over the next two years. Economically, the contract was very worthwhile because her room and board were provided by the government and her pay each day was $340. Despite the risk of no work, the pay she received was earned tax-free because she considered herself as a non-resident during her absence. Prior to leaving Canada, Claire sold her condominium and car and stored her furniture at her parents' home. She also cancelled her membership at the YWCA in New Brunswick and put her engagement on hold for an indefinite period. Her plan was to stay away for the full two years, assuming that all went as planned. Unfortunately, after 12 months, the Mobile Dental Unit ceased operations and Claire was scheduled to return to Canada. The Department of Finance had severely reduced the budget for National Defence. Claire was happy to return home on January 1, 2014. She married three months after her return and resumed her work with the Mobile Dental Unit in Moncton, New Brunswick.

Claire's compensation package with the mobile dental unit differs from other employees of the Canadian Forces. Other employees are assistants and support staff who are paid on a monthly basis with fringe benefits. Claire does not receive any benefits or holidays. In Canada she is paid on a day-to-day basis ($280 per day with no deductions for EI, CPP, or tax). All dental clinics are headed by a dentist who is professionally responsible for overseeing the work of both contract and salaried dental hygienists and dental assistants. The Canadian Dental Association does not permit dental hygienists to administer anaesthetic or work without supervision. The clinic provides all of Claire's tools, supplies, and support staff. If a workday is not more than 60% booked, patients are rescheduled to another day and Claire does not work. It is not unusual for the contract dental hygienists to be temporarily laid off. This does create problems because the contract specifies that Claire must be available to work at least four days per week (so she cannot work elsewhere). This has not bothered Claire because she has claimed all of her laundry, uniforms, shoes, and travelling expenses as a deduction against her self-employed business earnings. Travelling expenses are justifiable because the mobile unit moves to various remote locations outside of Moncton.

Advise Claire on the filing of a Notice of Objection in respect of 2013 and 2014. How would you treat the various expenses incurred by Claire Jordan in each of the taxation years?

 [For more problems and solutions thereto, see the DVD accompanying the textbook.]

CHAPTER 3 —
DISCUSSION NOTES FOR REVIEW QUESTIONS

(1) The personal tax return (T1 General) does not include RPP contributions, union and professional dues and other paragraph 8(1)(*i*) deductions in the calculation of employment income. These are included under the heading "Net Income" in the personal tax return. It would be misleading to use the personal tax return format for this specific purpose, because certain deductions are limited to the amount of employment income in the year, such as the home office expense deduction.

(2) An employee can only deduct those expenses that are specifically allowed under section 8 whereas a self-employed individual may deduct all expenses incurred to earn business and property income as permitted by Subdivision b. Both the employee and the self-employed individual are subject to the reasonableness test.

ITA: 67

(3) No one test is conclusive in itself. All tests should be considered together before a conclusion is reached.

(4) The control subtest in the economic reality or entrepreneur test determines whether one person is in a position to order or require not only what is to be done but how it is to be done. Where such control, by the business over the individual, does exist, an employer–employee relationship is implied.

(5) The integration or organization test examines the degree of economic dependence of the individual on the organization. Where the individual is financially dependent on the organization, then an employer-employee relationship is implied.

(6) The specific result test looks at the expected results of the work performed. An employee–employer relationship usually contemplates the employee putting his or her personal services at the disposal of his or her employer during a given period of time without reference to a specified result and, generally, envisages the accomplishment of work on an ongoing basis. On the other hand, where a party agrees that certain specified work will be done for the other, it may be inferred that an independent contractor relationship exists.

(7) The Act uses the word "received" to determine the timing of the taxation of employment income. In this case, she will be considered to have received her bonus in the year she received the cheque. Just because she chose not to cash the cheque does not change the timing of when she received the payment.

ITA: 5

(8) The Act uses the word "received" to determine the timing of the taxation of employment income. The voluntary deferment of an unconditional right to receive the bonus is not an acceptable method of deferring income.

ITA: 5
Blenkarn v. M.N.R., 63 DTC 581 (T.A.B.)

(9) Employers cannot deduct all of the taxable benefits reported on the employee's T4. Items such as deemed interest benefits and standby charges for automobiles are not deductible to the employer since they are not expenses that are incurred for the purpose of earning income.

ITA: 80.4

(10) If the employer makes *any* of the premium payments then the benefit payments received will likely be taxable.

ITA: 6(1)(*f*); IT-428

(11) The CRA follows normal commercial practice such that the first day of the contract is counted and the last day is excluded for purposes of determining the number of days of interest. In this case the number of days from June 2 to June 29 inclusive will be used to determine the benefit, that is, 28 days.

(12) A reimbursement is a payment by an employer to an employee for expenses of the employer which have been paid by the employee and which are substantiated by receipts. This is normally accomplished by submitting an expense report. An allowance is a fixed amount which is paid to an employee in excess of his or her salary without the requirement that the employee be accountable for the amount expended.

IT-522R, pars. 40, 50

CHAPTER 3

(13) The standby charge is calculated as follows:

$$\frac{20,004}{20,004} \times 2\% \times 12 \times (\$40,000 + \$5,200) = \$10,848.$$

(14) The five conditions that a salesperson must meet in order to be able to deduct expenses are: ITA: 8(1)(*f*)

    (a) he or she must be employed in the year in connection with the selling of property or negotiating of contracts for his or her employer;

    (b) under the terms of his or her contract of employment he or she must be required to pay his or her own expenses;

    (c) he or she must be ordinarily required to carry on his or her duties away from his or her employer's place of business;

    (d) he or she is remunerated in whole or in part by commissions or other similar amounts fixed by reference to the volume of the sales made or the contracts negotiated; and

    (e) he or she was not in receipt of a reasonable allowance for travelling expenses in respect of the taxation year that was not included in computing his or her income.   ITA: 6(1)(*b*)(v)

(15) The four conditions that must be met to allow an employee to deduct travelling expenses, other than car expenses, are: ITA: 8(1)(*h*)

    (a) he or she is ordinarily required to carry on his or her duties away from his or her employer's place of business or in different places;

    (b) under his or her employment contract, he or she is required to pay the travelling expenses incurred by him or her in the performance of his or her duties;

    (c) he or she was not in receipt of a reasonable allowance for travelling expenses that was not included in computing his or her income; and   ITA: 6(1)(*b*)(v), 6(1)(*b*)(vi), 6(1)(*b*)(vii)

    (d) he or she did not claim any deduction for railway company employees, salespersons, or transport company employees.   ITA: 8(1)(*e*), 8(1)(*f*), 8(1)(*g*)

(16) There is nothing in paragraph 6(1)(*b*) that would exclude this allowance from income. However, another rule would apply to cause this receipt to be exempt from tax. In order to be exempt under this provision, the allowance must meet the following tests: ITA: 81(3.1)

    (a) he must deal at arm's length with his employer;

    (b) he must have other employment or business income (not necessary in this case, since he is employed as a professor or teacher at a designated educational institution);

    (c) the amount received must be reasonable and must relate only to travel to and from part-time employment; and

    (d) the part-time location must be at least 80 km away from both the employee's ordinary place of residence and his principal place of employment or business.

(17) Neither word is defined in the Act. However, an Interpretation Bulletin interprets the word "principally" as more than 50%. Therefore, as long as the employment-use of the workspace is its main or chief purpose, the test is met. "Exclusively" is not defined in the tax law, so reference is made to other sources. *Webster's English Dictionary* defines "exclusively" as "to the exclusion of all others" which is a much more onerous test.   IT-352R2, par. 2

(18) The Act deems that taxes withheld have been received at the time the bonus was paid. Therefore, even though the company still had the government's portion of the bonus, tax cannot be deferred on it. In addition, if the amount withheld in respect of the tax was not deemed to have been received by Ms. Smith, then she would not have received credit for the payment of this tax on her personal tax return.   ITA: 153(3)

CHAPTER 3 — SOLUTIONS TO MULTIPLE CHOICE QUESTIONS

Question 1

(A) is correct: 12 × 2% × $34,500 = $8,280.   ITA: 6(2)

(B) and (C) are wrong because the operating cost benefit is computed as: 26 cents × 15,000 personal-use kilometres = $3,900. Part (B) incorrectly computes the operating cost benefit as: 15,000/20,000 × $3,600 = $2,700. Part (C) incorrectly computes the operating cost benefit as: 27 cents × 15,000 personal-use kilometres = $4,050.   ITA: 6(1)(*k*); ITR: 7305.1

(D) is wrong because he does not have more than 50% employment use.   ITA: 6(1)(*k*)(iv)

Question 2

(B) is correct: $50,000 salary + $3,500 allowance – $3,000 automobile expenses = $50,500. The car allowance is taxable because it is not based solely on kilometres driven. Since the car allowance is taxable, the automobile expenses can be deducted. The entertainment expenses are not deductible because she has no commission income.   ITA: 6(1)(*b*)(x), 8(1)(*f*), 8(1)(*h*.1)(iii)

(A) incorrectly excludes a deduction for automobile expenses: $53,500 = $50,000 salary + $3,500 allowance. The automobile expenses are deductible because the allowance is included in income.   ITA: 8(1)(*h*.1)
ITA: 6(1)(*b*)

(C) incorrectly includes a deduction for entertainment expenses: $49,500 = $50,000 salary + $3,500 allowance – $3,000 automobile expenses – $1,000 entertainment expenses. The entertainment expenses (50% × $2,000) are not deductible because she has no commission income or income from negotiating contracts.   ITA: 8(1)(*f*)

(D) incorrectly excludes the car allowance and the deduction for automobile expenses and incorrectly includes a deduction for entertainment expenses: $49,000 = $50,000 salary – $1,000 entertainment expenses.

Question 3

(A) is correct. Susanne Denholm can claim home office expenses because she is required by contract to maintain an office in her home and she works principally in her home (i.e., "most of the time"). The $500 correct amount of deductible home office expenses is calculated as follows: ITA: 8(1)(*i*)(iii), 8(13)(*a*)(i)

Heat, hydro & maintenance: $5,000 × 10% = $500

Subsection 8(13) allows deductions under paragraphs 8(1)(*f*) or 8(1)(*i*). Since Susanne does not have any commission income, she can only deduct items under paragraph 8(1)(*i*). The distinction between (*f*) and (*i*) is that under (*f*) the expenses are fixed in nature and under (*i*) they are variable in nature (like supplies deductible under (*i*)). Since the only expenses that are variable with use are the heat, hydro, and maintenance, they are the only ones deductible. The mortgage interest is not deductible under either (*f*) or (*i*), since the only interest that is deductible as an employment expense is for automobiles and aircraft.   ITA: 8(1)(*j*), 8(2)

(B) incorrectly includes a deduction for property taxes and insurance: $1,100 = $500 + $200 insurance + $400 property taxes. The insurance (10% × $2,000) and property taxes (10% × $4,000) are not considered to be supplies. However, if Susanne had commission income, 10% of her insurance and property taxes would be deductible.   IT-352R2, par. 6
ITA: 8(1)(*i*)(iii)
ITA: 8(1)(*f*)

(C) incorrectly includes deductions for insurance, property taxes and the general telephone line: $1,400 = $500 + $200 insurance + $400 property taxes + $300 general telephone line. The insurance, property taxes and the cost of the general telephone line (50% × $600) are not deductible. If Susanne had commission income, the cost of the general telephone line would still not be deductible — only long-distance calls would be deductible.   IT-352R2, pars. 6, 10(a)
ITA: 8(1)(*i*)(iii)

(D) incorrectly includes insurance, property taxes, the general telephone line and mortgage interest: $3,800 = $500 + $200 insurance + $400 property taxes + $300 general telephone + $2,400 mortgage interest. The insurance, property taxes, the cost of the general telephone line and mortgage interest (10% × $24,000) are not considered to be supplies. If Susanne had commission income, the mortgage interest would still not be deductible since the Act limits interest expense of an employee to interest on automobiles and planes.   IT-352R2
ITA: 8(1)(*i*)(iii)
ITA: 8(1)(*j*)

CHAPTER 3

Question 4

(A) is correct. The loan qualifies as a home relocation loan. The benefit is computed using the lower   ITA: 6(9), 80.4(1), 80.4(4)
of the prescribed interest rate at the time of the loan (4%) and the prescribed interest rate during the
year (3%). Therefore the employment benefit is $1,000 (3% × $100,000 – 2% × $100,000 interest paid).

(B) incorrectly computes the employment benefit using 4%: $2,000 = 4% × $100,000 – 2% ×
$100,000.

(C) incorrectly ignores the 2% interest paid in the computation of the interest benefit: $3,000 = 3%
× $100,000.

(D) incorrectly computes the employment benefit using 4% rather than 3%. The 2% interest paid is
not deducted: 4% × $100,000.

Question 5

(D) is correct. The stock option benefit is ($40 – $30) × 1,000 shares = $10,000.

(A) incorrectly subtracts a deduction (½ × $10,000) in computing the benefit ($10,000 – $5,000).
This deduction is a Division C deduction.   ITA: 110(1)(*d*)

(B) incorrectly computes the benefit based on the sales price of $48,000 ($48,000 – $30,000 =
$18,000) rather than the price of the stock at the time of purchase.

(C) incorrectly includes the taxable capital gain in the employee benefit (($48,000 – $40,000) × ½
+ ($40,000 – $30,000) = $14,000).

Question 6

(B) is correct.

Meals and entertainment (50% × $14,000)	$ 7,000
Driving costs (90% × $10,000)	9,000
Expenses eligible for deduction	$16,000

ITA: 8(1)(*f*)

Tim can either claim a deduction for these amounts to the extent of his commission income   ITA: 8(1)(*f*)
($5,000) or he can claim a deduction for his automobile costs ($9,000) alone, without the commission   8(1)(*h*.1)
limitation. The maximum deduction is therefore $9,000.

(A) is incorrect because it is the commission-limited amount.   ITA: 8(1)(*f*)

(C) is incorrect because it is the full meals and entertainment amount ($14,000) and ignores the   ITA: 67.1
$5,000 commission limitation.

(D) is incorrect because it represents the expenses eligible as a salesperson ($16,000) but ignores   ITA: 8(1)(*f*)
the $5,000 commission limitation.

CHAPTER 3 — SOLUTIONS TO EXERCISES

Exercise 1

[See: *Isaac v. M.N.R.*, 70 DTC 1285 (T.A.B.)]

Although the test had not been articulated at the time of this case, the courts are now starting with a consideration of whether there is a mutual understanding or common intention between the parties regarding their relationship. That is best reflected in a contract between the parties, but in many cases, such as this one, no written contract is in evidence. In this situation, the courts have looked at how the parties treat each other. In the case, it appears that the hospital is treating the nurse as a non-military independent contractor by paying her a fixed rate with none of the usual employee benefits. The nurse has, at least, accepted that for about five years. However, the same facts might be used to suggest that the relationship between the parties was that of an employer/part-time employee.

The following tests are applied to support the determination of the objective intention of the parties as to whether R.N. should be regarded as an employee or an independent contractor.

Economic Reality or Entrepreneur Test

In applying the control subtest, the question is whether Canadian Forces Hospital, Halifax controlled not only what was done by R.N. but how it was done. In this case the Hospital exercised control over R.N. in connection with dividing up the patients to be cared for among the available nurses and imposing routine rules and regulations with regard to the administration of drugs and other medications. On the other hand, the Hospital did not exercise any control over the method in which R.N. did her work, which requires special knowledge, skill, and judgment. Accordingly, it does not appear that the Hospital exercised sufficient control to conclude that R.N. was an employee on the basis of this test alone.

However, the application of the other subtests is particularly revealing. R.N. does not run the risk of financing the equipment, supplying other assistants necessary to carry out her duties in the Hospital or seeking out clients. R.N. used the equipment and supplies furnished by the Hospital. She neither hired nor fired any of the nursing assistants who worked under her. She could only request that the Hospital hire additional staff to assist her. The clients were patients of the Hospital. R.N. was not in a position to substitute the services of another nurse if she was unable to perform her duties. All this evidence tends to establish that from an economic reality point of view R.N. was an employee, but this test may not be definitive in this case.

Integration or Organization Test

The Hospital deducted Canada Pension Plan contributions from her pay as they did with the nurses who were employed full-time by the Hospital. R.N. appeared to be economically dependent on the hospital, although she was not precluded from offering her services elsewhere. R.N. was subject to co-ordinational control of the hospital in terms of where to perform her services and when to do so. On the other hand, R.N. was not eligible for the regular benefits of a full-time nurse such as holidays, sick pay, retirement plan, etc. She was hired on a day-to-day basis at a *per diem* rate of pay. Her services could be terminated on 24 hours notice if full-time nurses became available. On the weight of the evidence it can be argued that R.N. is an employee of the Hospital based on the integration test.

Specific Result Test

On the one hand, it was R.N.'s personal services that were at the disposal of the Hospital. Her work was done on a continuous day-to-day basis without there being any limited or specified amount of work that she had, by contract, to accomplish. She could not substitute another person to perform her duties if she was unable to do so. On the other hand, R.N. was not a full-time nurse for any specified period of time. Her time was made up on a weekly basis in advance. She could be laid off on 24 hours notice. On balance, it appears that the evidence leads to the conclusion that, by applying the specific result test, R.N. was an employee. This conclusion is consistent with that for the integration or organization test.

Conclusion

The application of the control subtest of the economic reality or entrepreneur test leads to the conclusion that R.N was not an employee of the Hospital. The application of the other subtests of the economic reality test, the integration test and the specific result test leads to the inference that R.N. was an employee of the Hospital. Thus, there is evidence to support the determination of an employment relationship. (Your own conclusion after weighing all of these tests.)

CHAPTER 3

Exercise 2

The courts generally rely on three tests to support a determination of the objective intention of the parties as to their relationship as either independent contractor or employment. In this case, a contract was negotiated that could be interpreted as establishing an independent contractor relationship. However, a contract can be written to be self-serving to both parties. Hence the need to apply the three tests to help determine the status of Ms. Capwell in relation to the architectural firm of Davies Ltd.

ITA: 248(1); *Wiebe Door Services Ltd. v. M.N.R.*, 87 DTC 5025 (F.C.A.)

(1) Economic Reality or Entrepreneur Test

(a) Control Test

The first subtest examines the day-to-day time commitment that is expected of an individual and the accountability of the individual to the corporation. In this instance, Ms. Capwell must work at least 14 days a month on the project (but the specific days appear flexible); however, she appears to be able to work under her own direction and on other projects on her days off. It does not seem to be conclusive as to whether or not Ms. Capwell is an employee given this test, but the evidence supports that she would be an independent contractor given the circumstances.

(b) Ownership of Tools

It is not clear, but Ms. Capwell appears to provide her own car, equipment, and technical expertise. We might also conclude that since she is working on the premises, many of her expenses, such as supplies and her place of work, will be covered by Davies Ltd. This test appears to support contractor status.

(c) Chance of Profit, Risk of Loss

This subtest assesses whether the individual incurs her own business risk, legal liability, and expenses. In this case, she is getting paid a flat fee of $4,000 per month, which we must assume is directly related to billable hours of work. She estimates that 30% of her contracting revenues will come from other sources, which is not entirely insignificant. This test is also not conclusive, and depending on the details, could go either way.

(2) Integration or Organization Test

This test determines whether or not the individual is economically dependent on the payer organization and is an integral part of the corporation. In this case, Ms. Capwell is not completely dependent on Davies for all of her income, but she retains an office on the premises and also receives some employee benefits in the form of underground parking. However, it's possible that the nature of the work demands she attend the company's offices. This test is inconclusive, but depending on the circumstances, slightly favours her being viewed as an employee.

(3) Specific Results Test

As the name suggests, the object of this test is to determine whether the individual's services were acquired to complete a specific task. In this case, there is no doubt that Ms. Capwell was taken on to complete a specific project, after which the contract will be fulfilled. Given this, she would appear to be an independent contractor.

Conclusion

The tests would seem to support independent contractor status, principally because of the signed contract agreeing to a flat fee for one specific project suggesting a mutual understanding or common intention to enter an independent contractor relationship.

The results of the tests do not always provide us with a definitive answer as to whether or not an individual should be viewed as an employee. However, they can help guide us to make that determination. In this case, the facts lead toward the independent contractor conclusion. Given that the contract was drafted for a specific project, and that Ms. Capwell seems to be working independently, the courts would probably allow the designation of independent contractor status.

Exercise 3

(A) Specifically exempted.

ITA: 6(1)(*a*)

(B) Exempted; provincial employer health tax.

ITA: 6(1)(*a*)

(C) and (D) Exempted, since the premium was paid to a private medical plan.

ITA: 6(1)(*a*)

(E) Taxable. The Interpretation Bulletin only exempts tuition fees where the course is primarily for the benefit of the employer.

ITA: 6(1)(*a*), IT-470R, par. 18, 19

(F) Normally, taxable, but since the payment meets the conditions, namely that the Christmas gift is under $500 and is not cash or near cash, the CRA's position is that the gift is not a taxable benefit.

ITA: 6(1)(*a*)

(G) Partly taxable: The CRA takes the position that there will be no benefit if William had reimbursed the company the actual cost ($420). Since William did not completely reimburse the company for the actual costs, then the benefit would be calculated by taking the difference between the actual costs ($420) and the amount paid by William ($200) for a taxable benefit of $220.

ITA: 6(1)(*a*); IT-470R, par. 28

(H) Taxable, but the CRA takes the position that the amount would not be taxable if the membership was principally for the employer's advantage rather than the employee's.

ITA: 6(1)(*a*); IT-470R, par. 34

(I) Taxable unless the financial counselling was in respect of re-employment or retirement.

ITA: 6(1)(*a*), 6(1)(*a*)(iv)(B)

Exercise 4

Paragraph 8(1)(*b*) allows for the deduction of legal expenses against employment income in the year, on account of legal expenses incurred by the taxpayer to collect or establish a right to salary or wages owed to the taxpayer that, if received by the taxpayer, would be required by this subdivision to be included in computing the taxpayer's employment income.

ITA: 6, 8

Paragraph 6(1)(*j*) requires any reimbursement to either be included in income or reduce the expense being claimed.

Legal expenses may also be deductible for other purposes such as to earn income from business or property or as another deduction [ITA 60(*o*), (*o*.1)], but only those expenses specifically listed in section 8 can be deducted from employment income [ITA 8(2)].

Other resources — IT-99R5, Legal and Accounting Fees; CRA Guide T4044, Employment Expenses

Exercise 5

The $6,000 merchandise discount is a taxable benefit. Administrative practice reflected in the Interpretation Bulletin does exempt discounts on merchandise, but they must be offered to all employees and not to just select groups. If there was an overall discount of 10% to all employees, it would seem reasonable in the circumstances to include only 25% in income; however, the Interpretation Bulletin is silent on this point.

IT-470R

IT-470R, par. 27

Exercise 6

None of the $7,500 is a taxable benefit. The exclusion for an eligible housing loss applies because the loss was incurred in an eligible relocation. The Interpretation Bulletin statement no longer reflects the law, according to a 2011 Tax Court of Canada decision.

ITA: 6(1)(*a*), 6(19), 6(20), 248(1) "eligible relocation"; *Wunderlich v. The Queen*, 2011 TCC 539; IT-470R, par. 35

Note that on the sale of the house, the loss cannot be greater than the actual loss to the employee, calculated as the amount by which the cost of the house exceeds the net selling price received. A reimbursement of actual moving costs is not a taxable benefit.

IT-470R, par. 37

Exercise 7

Premiums paid:

(A) Group term life insurance premiums paid by an employer are a taxable benefit.

ITA: 6(1)(*a*), 6(4)

(B) and (C) The extended health care and dental care plans are private medical plans; hence, the premiums paid by the employer are not employment income.

ITA: 6(1)(*a*)

(D) Since the sickness or accident income protection plan is a group plan, premiums paid by the employer are exempt from employment income.

ITA: 6(1)(*a*)

Conclusion:

The following rearrangement would result in a lower tax cost:

(A) Company should pay for 100% of the extended health care and dental plan.

(B) Employees should pay the provincial medical plan premiums since company payments would be taxable benefits.

(C) Employees should consider paying the sickness or accident income protection premium themselves.

CHAPTER 3

When an employer pays *any* portion of the premium for this type of plan, amounts that are paid out of the plan are taxable as employment income, less the employee's contribution to date. Conversely, if the employee pays all of the premiums, none of the amounts paid out of the plan are taxable. Since this particular plan has benefits of only 50% of the wages, the employee would be in a relatively poor cash position. The imposition of tax, even though at a lower rate, would certainly result in extreme hardship if the illness is prolonged.

ITA: 6(1)(f)

Exercise 8

Year 1 — No tax effect.

Year 4 — No tax effect.

Year 5 — No tax effect, since the employer is a Canadian-controlled private corporation.

Year 6 — Must take into employment income under Division B the following:

ITA: 7(1.1)

$$50,000 \text{ shares} \times (\$3 - \$1) = \underline{\$100,000}$$

— Will have a capital gain of
$$50,000 \text{ shares} \times (\$6 - \$3) = \underline{\$150,000}$$

— May be eligible for the capital gains deduction for qualifying small business corporation shares.

ITA: 110.6(1), 248(1)

— Since Katrina sold these shares within two years after the date of acquisition, she is not entitled to a deduction of one half of the subsection 7(1.1) inclusion. She is also not entitled to a general deduction since the exercise price of $1.00 was less than fair market value ($1.50) at the date the option was granted.

ITA: 110(1)(d), 110(1)(d.1)

Exercise 9

(a) Car benefit if business-use kilometres are 10,000

Standby charge		
$\dfrac{20,004 \text{ km}^{(1)}}{20,004 \text{ km}} \times [2\% \times (\$20,000 \times 12)] = \dots\dots\dots\dots\dots\dots\dots\dots\dots$		$4,800
Operating costs$^{(2)}$ (12,000 km × $0.26)	3,120	$7,920
Less: amount reimbursed		1,800
Total car benefit if business-use kilometres are 10,000		$6,120

ITA: 6(1)(e), 6(2)

ITA: 6(1)(k)(v)

(b) Car benefit if business-use kilometres are 20,000

Standby charge		
$\dfrac{12,000 \text{ km}^{(3)}}{20,004 \text{ km}} \times [2\% \times (\$20,000 \times 12)] = \dots\dots\dots\dots\dots\dots\dots\dots$		$2,879
Operating costs$^{(4)}$ (50% × $2,879) =	1,440	$4,319
Less: amount reimbursed		1,800
Total car benefit if business-use kilometres are 20,000		$2,519

ITA: 6(1)(e), 6(2)

ITA: 6(1)(k)(v)

NOTES

$^{(1)}$ The employee does not qualify for the standby charge reduction since the car is not used more than 50% in the performance of employment duties when the business use is only 15,000 km. Therefore, in this outcome, the value of A in the formula (i.e., 12,000 km) is deemed equal to the value of B in the formula (i.e., 1,667 × 12 rounded).

$^{(2)}$ The election method is not available to the employee, since the car is not used more than 50% for business.

ITA: 6(1)(k)(iv)

$^{(3)}$ When the business-use kilometres is 20,000, the employee qualifies for the standby charge reduction and the numerator becomes the lesser of (a) 12,000 km, and (b) 1,667 km × 12 months.

$^{(4)}$ The operating benefit election at 50% of the standby charge is the same as $0.26 × 12,000 km = $3,120. The election method is available since employment kilometres comprise more than 50% of the total.

Exercise 10

The Act would appear to deny any deduction in respect of Calvin's workspace in the home. In order for Calvin to avoid the restrictions, one of two conditions must be met, neither of which appear to be adhered to. The first alternative condition is that the work place in the home must be where the individual principally performs the employment duties. The second alternative condition is even more stringent, namely, that the work place must be used exclusively for employment income purposes and that the work place must be used on a regular and continuous basis as a meeting place for employment-connected persons.

ITA: 8(13)

If Calvin had met one of the conditions, then he would be able to deduct some of the expenses indicated as long as he met the conditions of paragraph 8(1)(i). First Calvin must have a contract with his employer indicating that he must pay for office rent and supplies and the employer completes and signs a T2200. However, of the expenses indicated, only the maintenance expense, including fuel, electricity, light bulbs, cleaning materials and minor repairs, on a prorated basis will be permitted. The imputed rent of $1,000 is not deductible; this position was confirmed in the *Thompson* case by the Federal Court–Trial Division.

ITA: 8(13)

IT-352R2, par. 2, 3
89 DTC 5439 (F.C.T.D.)

Exercise 11

Since the question refers to meal expenses for employees, you need to refer to subsection 8(4). A deduction for personal meals consumed while travelling is only allowed where the employee is away from the municipality/metropolitan area for a minimum of 12 hours. All meal costs, regardless of their nature and purpose, are also restricted by subsection 67.1(1) to 50% of the actual cost. However, long-haul truck drivers can deduct 80%.

ITA: 8(4), 67.1(1)

CHAPTER 3

Chapter 4

Income from Business: General Concepts and Rules

Learning Goals

Know, Understand and Explain

By the end of this chapter you will know, understand and be able to explain:

- The basic provisions of the *Income Tax Act* (the Act) that relate to the calculation of business income.
- The criteria for determining whether a gain is one of capital or business income.
- The underlying distinction between business income and property income.
- The rules outlining amounts to be deducted from business income for tax purposes.
- The basic provisions of GST/HST for business activity.

Apply

By the end of this chapter you will be able to apply your knowledge and understanding to:

- Start with accounting income and make the necessary adjustments to arrive at business income for tax purposes.

Analyze

By the end of this chapter you will be able to analyze:

- Different sources of income and determine whether it should be treated as capital or business income.
- A situation and determine whether reasonable expectation of profit exists.

Review Questions
¶4,800 in the Study Guide

Multiple Choice Questions
¶4,825 in the Study Guide

Exercise Questions
¶4,850 in the Study Guide

Assignment Problems
¶4,875 in the Study Guide

CHAPTER 4 — LEARNING CHART

Problem Descriptions

Textbook Example Problems

4-1	Income vs. capital
4-2	Valuation of inventory
4-3	Amortization included in cost of inventory
4-4	Reserve for services not provided
4-5	Reserve for proceeds not yet due
4-6	Schedule 1 reconciliation
4-7	Sales person's expenses
4-8	GST/HST treatment of Example Problem 4-6

Multiple Choice Questions

1	Business & property deductions
2	Business & property deductions
3	Business & property deductions
4	Business & property — legal and accounting fees
5	Income vs. capital gain
6	Business & property deductions

Exercises

1	Employee benefits — employer/employee implications
2	Income vs. capital
3	Automobile options
4	Contract termination payment
5	Income vs. capital
6	Inventory valuation
7	*Income Tax Act* references
8	Recreational facilities
9	Home office expenses
10	Deductibility of expenses
11	Bond discount
12	Schedule 1 reconciliation
13	Income reserve
14	Schedule 1 reconciliation — HST

Assignment Problems

1	Independent issues — deductibility of expenses
2	Home office
3	SR&ED
4	Sale of assets including accounts receivable
5	Debt forgiveness
6	Income vs. capital
7	Four independent issues
8	Reasonable expectation of profit
9	Schedule 1 reconciliation
10	Schedule 1 reconciliation
11	Schedule 1 reconciliation
12	Schedule 1 reconciliation

Problem Descriptions

13	Income from business
14	Schedule 1 reconciliation
15	Income from business with home office
16	Schedule 1 reconciliation — comprehensive
17	Income from business with home office
18	Income from business with SR&ED
19	Schedule 1 reconciliation
20	GST/HST implications
21	Income vs. capital, soft costs
22	Company automobile — impact on employer
23	Stock option — impact on employer
24	Employee benefits — impact on employer
25	Employee benefits — impact on employer
26	Employed vs. self-employed
27	Sales expenses of employee or self-employed
28	New job offer — employee & employer
29	Reassessment, employee compensation
30	Accounts receivable and warranty claims
31	Business start-up costs

CHAPTER 4

Study Notes

¶4,800   REVIEW QUESTIONS

(1) Mr. Fritz is a commissioned real estate client of yours. He has just bought and sold a piece of land in a "quick flip" transaction. What kind of income might this be to him: employment, business, property or capital gain?

(2) Does the Act require that the "profit" from a business be calculated in accordance with generally accepted accounting principles?

(3) Opco Ltd. is in the business of manufacturing equipment under contract for other manufacturers. One of its customers failed to live up to its contract and would not take delivery of or pay for its order. Opco took the customer to court and was awarded the amount of $100,000 as damages. Can this amount be treated as a non-taxable capital receipt by Opco?

(4) Aco Ltd. and Xco Ltd. entered into an agreement to manufacture a new product for the next 20 years. This represented 80% of Aco's business. After five years it was decided that the two parties could not work together so Xco paid Aco $500,000 to terminate the agreement. Is the receipt of this amount by Aco considered to be business income?

(5) Donald Corleone owns an illegal gambling house. He has made significant "profits" on this activity, but has not reported the income since he believes it is not taxable. Is he correct?

(6) Opco Ltd. took advantage of a program offered by the government and hired two employees whose wages were partially offset by a government subsidy. The owner felt that since he was really just getting some of his tax dollars back through this subsidy, the amount received would not be taxable. What do you think?

(7) As long as an expenditure was made for the purpose of earning income from a business or property then it is deductible. Is this statement true? Comment.   ITA: 18

(8) One of your clients is having some short-term cash flow problems and cannot pay his year-end tax liability. He decides that he will defer his payment to the Receiver General instead of trying to get another short-term bank loan. He reasons that in either case the interest will be deductible. Comment.

(9) Subsection 18(1) lists those items that are prohibited from being deducted because of the nature of the expenditure. If an expense passes those tests, will it be deductible?

(10) A client had to replace the roof on its factory at a cost of $100,000. The client deducted the cost of the roof on the basis that it was simply replacing the previous roof with a new one of the same quality. Is the cost deductible?

(11) Is the portion of the airline ticket that represents the meal subject to the 50% limitation on meal expenses?

(12) Will a company that offers a warranty with its product be able to deduct a reserve?   ITA: 20(1)(*m*.1)

¶4,825   MULTIPLE CHOICE QUESTIONS

Question 1

Which one of the following items is NOT deductible in computing the income of a corporation under Division B of the Act?

(A) Amounts paid for landscaping business premises.

(B) Interest on money borrowed to finance the purchase of a factory for use in its business.

(C) The premium on a $100,000 term life insurance policy on an employee if the beneficiary of the policy is the employee's family.

(D) Interest and penalties on late income tax payments.

Question 2

Which one of the following amounts is DEDUCTIBLE in computing the income of a corporation under Division B of the Act?

(A) $11,000 of accrued legal fees for a pending law suit. The accrual is an estimate because no work has been done to date by the lawyers.

(B) $4,000 of donations to registered charities made for no business reason.

(C) $15,000 spent on three social events in the taxation year for all employees at a particular location.

(D) $1,500 for golf club membership dues for employees.

Question 3

Which one of the following amounts is DEDUCTIBLE in computing income of a corporation under Division B of the Act?

(A) $5,000 of donations to federal political parties.

(B) $44,000 in accrued bonuses unpaid 7 months after year-end. The amounts were legal liabilities at year-end.

(C) A $10,000 increase in the financial accounting reserve for warranty expenses.

(D) The $2,000 cost of tickets for meals and entertainment at a gala fund-raising event for a registered charity.

Question 4

XYZ Ltd.'s current financial statement shows a deduction for $20,000 of legal and accounting expenses. This amount consists of the following items:

- $5,000 of legal expenses related to the purchase of an investment in shares;

- $5,000 of legal expenses incurred to dispute a tax assessment;

- $5,000 of legal expenses related to the issuance of debt; and

- $5,000 of accounting fees related to the preparation of a prospectus regarding the issuance of shares.

What amount is deductible under Division B of the Act?

(A) $7,000

(B) $8,000

(C) $15,000

(D) $5,000

Question 5

Ten years ago, Sam, a real estate agent, purchased a piece of land for $50,000. His intention at that time was to build a rental building on the land and use it to earn rental income, which he did four years ago. In the current year, he sold the land and building for $100,000 and $80,000 respectively after receiving an unsolicited offer.

Based on the facts, which one of the following statements is true?

(A) The CRA may argue that the gain on the sale of the land is a capital gain, because Sam is a real estate agent.

(B) The CRA may argue that the gain on the sale of the land is business income, because of the 10-year holding period of the land.

(C) The CRA may argue that the gain on the sale of the land is business income because of the unsolicited offer for sale.

(D) The gain on the sale of the land will likely be treated as a capital gain for income tax purposes.

Question 6

Which of the following amounts is DEDUCTIBLE in computing the income of a corporation under Division B of the Act?

(A) $13,000 of legal fees to defend a lawsuit brought by a customer.

(B) Accounting loss on the sale of a capital property.

(C) The principal amount of a mortgage on a company's warehouse.

(D) The personal and living expenses of the shareholder who works very hard in the business and is not paid a salary.

¶4,850 EXERCISES

Exercise 1

ITA: 9, 11, 18, 20

Each of the following employee perks were provided to a senior executive of IPL Engineering Services:

Value of university tuition fees for the employee's child (age 21)	$ 2,800
Out-of-town meals for a three-day management seminar	150
Entertainment meals for clients (reimbursement)	1,500
Professional dues to Civil Engineering Society	250
Notebook computer provided for employment use	3,500
Membership to Centre Health Club (client promotion)	1,400
Interest-free loan for the purchase of company stock	40,000
Premiums paid for group term life insurance	150
Reimbursement for engineering systems software	2,000

Assumptions:

(a) Prescribed rate of interest throughout the year is 1%.

(b) The senior executive takes the notebook computer home to complete IPL assignments and memos. Personal use is minimal.

— *REQUIRED*

For each of the above, *discuss and quantify* the income tax implications to the employer and to the employee.

Exercise 2

ITA: 9; IT-218R

The taxpayer corporation, Singh Enterprises Ltd., purchased a property consisting of some eight separate residential apartment buildings. When purchased, the property was ready for profit-producing operation and immediate arrangements were made for such operations.

The principal shareholder of the corporation, Sam Singh, was an individual with a long history of trading in real estate in many different countries. He fully expected that the property would increase in value in the future.

About 11 months after the purchase of the property, circumstances dictated a change in the investments of the corporation and the property was sold for a substantial profit.

— *REQUIRED*

Determine whether the profit realized by the sale of the property was income from a business or a capital gain.

Exercise 3

ITA: 9, 11, 18, 20

Samuel, an employee of the Fish Company, needs a vehicle to complete his employment duties. Samuel generally drives approximately 10,000 kilometres for personal reasons. His manager estimates that Samuel will need to drive 7,000 kilometres to complete employment duties. Samuel estimates that his total operating expenses will be $2,500. The corporation offered Samuel three alternatives:

(a) Twelve months use of a leased vehicle plus a reimbursement for 100% of the total operating expense. The leased vehicle costs the corporation $400 per month (including HST).

(b) The same vehicle can be purchased for a total cost (including 13% HST) of $22,000 and Samuel would be reimbursed for the total operating expense.

(c) Samuel provides his own vehicle and is reimbursed 54 cents for each of the first 5,000 kilometres and 48 cents for the balance of employment kilometres.

— *REQUIRED*

Assess the tax impacts for each alternative for both the employee and the employer for the current tax year.

Exercise 4

ITA: 9

Cars Limited had a franchise for the distribution in Saskatchewan of Belchfire automobiles made in Argentina. The business had grown rapidly in its 10 years of existence. However, soon after the expansion of its facilities, Argentina Motor Industries terminated the distribution agreement and voluntarily agreed to pay Cars Limited $225,000.

— *REQUIRED*

What are the tax implications to Cars Limited?

Exercise 5

Alta Management Corporation (AMC) purchased three parcels of land in July of this year at an estate auction. Immediately after, the purchase plans were in place for the development of the properties into community shopping plazas. As a result of an unsolicited offer, two parcels of land were resold for an immediate and substantial gain. The third parcel of land sat vacant for three months while the corporation waited for the development and building permits from City Hall. The city would not approve the project because of several complaints from local residents. Consequently, the property was listed for sale with a realtor, Charles Roonie. Charles is also the major shareholder of Alta Management Corporation. The sale took place, with a substantial profit, six months after the purchase of the land.

Presently, the corporation holds two other pieces of undeveloped land, which it intends to develop if the economy improves. It also manages several apartment blocks and one shopping centre. The corporation often sells property when it becomes unfeasible to develop. For this reason the company always ensures that any real estate purchased has good resale value.

— *REQUIRED*

What type of income was earned from the disposition of each real estate property? Provide reasons for your answer, and consider all factors that the courts may consider in substantiating the intent of the taxpayer.

Exercise 6

ITA: 10

Holey Mufflers Limited operates a fast-service repair shop. At the end of its fiscal year its inventory records showed the following:

Item	Number	Actual cost	FIFO cost	Replacement cost	Net realization value
Mufflers	64	$17.50	$16.25	$18.40	$15.50
Tailpipes	157	4.75	4.25	5.00	4.50
Exhaust systems	39	16.25	16.30	17.00	15.50
Shock absorbers	256	19.45	18.85	20.50	19.75
Brackets	932	1.40	1.35	1.50	1.30
Clamps	1,746	.65	.70	.75	.80

— *REQUIRED*

What values could be used for the total inventory for tax purposes? (Assume that the method of valuing inventory could change with permission.)

ITA: 10(2.1)

Exercise 7

ITA: 18(1)(*a*), 18(1)(*b*), 18(1)(*c*), 18(1)(*e*), 18(1)(*h*), 67, 248(1)

The Act restricts the deduction of certain expenses incurred. In general, the following limitations determine the deductibility of expenses from a business:

(a) Income earning purpose test

(b) Capital test

(c) Exempt income test

(d) Reserve test

(e) Personal expense test

(f) Reasonableness test

— *REQUIRED*

Cite the appropriate references for the above tests in specific provisions of the Act, including up to three related sections, ITs (primary) or Income Tax Folios, or ICs from the footnotes to those provisions in the Act.

CHAPTER 4

Exercise 8

ITA: 18(1)(*l*)

Advice Limited, a consulting firm in Calgary, owns a small lodge in the Banff area. The lodge is used throughout the year for the purposes of entertaining clients.

— REQUIRED

(A) Comment on the deductibility of maintenance costs in respect of the lodge.

(B) Reconsider the deductibility of these costs if the property is rented during the week to the public and used to entertain clients only on the weekends.

Exercise 9

ITA: 18(12)

Amina and Karim are married and work together as self-employed management consultants. They both work full-time on various projects in a 500-square-foot office located in their home. The total square footage of their home (bedrooms, kitchen, living room, and dining room) is 2,000 square feet. Amina teaches one evening course at the university each week. She earned $70,000 in consulting income and Karim earned $65,000. Other expenses, as listed below, were also incurred:

Expenses:	
Supplies and materials	$ 1,800
Computer and software lease	2,300
Total	$ 4,100
Total home overhead costs incurred during the year:	
Mortgage interest	$16,000
Utilities, water, and electricity	2,400
Property taxes	2,200
House cleaning	2,400
Home insurance	600
Total	$23,600

— REQUIRED

Advise Amina and Karim on the deductibility of their home office expenses.

Exercise 10

ITA: 17, 20(1)

Mr. M. Black is the controller with responsibility for tax compliance of International Widget Manufacturing Limited based in Calgary. He has called to ask your advice, as the company's accountant, on various matters pertaining to the company's 2016 tax return. He has asked you the following questions.

(A) On March 1, 2017, the company paid $234,000 for the benefit of 30 employees to a defined benefit registered pension plan. Of the $234,000 paid, $129,000 represents an adjustment required as a result of an actuarial valuation; the remainder was based on a current service contribution equal to 6% of each employee's wages for 2015. What is the total amount that can be deducted for tax purposes in 2016?

(B) The company paid $15,000 representation costs to obtain a special licence from the State of Montana to sell its widgets in the state. This amount was written off in the financial accounts but added back and amortized over a 20-year period in calculating income for tax purposes. How should this item be treated?

(C) The amount of $1,500 spent to connect gas lines on conversion from oil to gas in the Toronto plant was added to the cost of the building for financial accounting purposes and depreciated with the building. How should the amount be treated for tax purposes?

(D) The president's wife is employed full-time as his secretary and paid $7,000 per month. Is this amount deductible and if not, how much is deductible?

— REQUIRED

Provide brief answers to the questions posed by the controller.

Exercise 11

ITA: 20(1)(*f*)

In August 2011, Steel Blind Manufacturing Co. Ltd., a venetian blind manufacturer, issued a series of bonds at $956.71 per $1,000 par value. The issue matured in August 2016 and was redeemed at that time at par value. It bears a coupon rate of 4% to yield 5% to maturity.

— REQUIRED

How much of the bond discount can be deducted and in what year can it be deducted?

Exercise 12

ITA: 9–12, 18–20

The following information concerning the financial statements of Incredible Incubators Incorporated for its fiscal year ended September 30, 2016 has been presented to you in order to prepare tax returns.

(a) Net income after tax per financial statements	$150,000
(b) Provision for income taxes — current	25,000
— future	130,000
(c) Amortization expense	40,000
(d) Reserve for doubtful debts — deducted in 2015	10,000
deducted in 2016	15,000
(e) Interest on income taxes paid after due date	2,500
(f) Bond interest expense (including annual discount amortization of $7,500 re bonds issued this year)	39,500
(g) Landscaping costs re factory premises — debited to land account	12,000

— REQUIRED

Using the foregoing information, compute income for tax purposes for Incredible Incubators for their fiscal year ended September 30, 2016. [Ignore capital cost allowance in respect of depreciable capital property.]

Exercise 13

ITA: 9, 12(1)(*e*)(ii), 20(1)(*n*), 20(8)(*b*)

Quickturn Land Limited bought for cash 25 acres of land at a cost of $107,500 during the year. About two months later the land was sold to a developer for $250,000 consisting of a $110,000 down payment in cash and a note without interest due in one year for the balance. A real estate commission of $12,500 was paid. The company often engages in this type of transaction.

— REQUIRED

Compute the minimum net income for the company in the year of sale and the next year in respect of this transaction.

Exercise 14

ETA: 123(1), 169(1), Schedule V, Part VII

Reconsider the facts of Exercise 12.

— REQUIRED

Outline the proper HST treatment by the corporation of the items presented.

CHAPTER 4

¶4,875 ASSIGNMENT PROBLEMS

Type 1 Problems

Problem 1

You are a co-op student working in the accounting department at Crystal Enterprises Inc. and have been asked to help with the year-end tax provision. You have gone through the detailed accounts that make up the company's income statement and have made a list of items for which you have questions.

When you took them to your boss, he asked you to determine whether the accounting treatment and the tax treatment are the same, and, if they are not, what they should do.

(1) The company made charitable donations of $15,000 in the year.

(2) While looking at the accounts receivable you noticed that they had set up an allowance for doubtful accounts for $120,000, calculated, based on their past history, as 60% of the accounts receivable that have been outstanding more than 60 days.

(3) You also noticed that they wrote off bad debts of $15,000 during the year.

(4) They included in revenue $10,000 received from a customer for goods to be delivered about two months after the year end. This is not a material amount so no adjustment was made at year end to account for this as deferred revenue.

(5) You noticed that the professional fees showed legal and accounting fees of $25,000 related to the re-financing of the company's long-term debt.

(6) In miscellaneous expenses you saw that some application software of $12,000 was expensed, as was $30,000 for landscaping the grounds around their office building.

(7) The company expensed a total of $55,000 on meals and entertainment, including $18,000 for a summer picnic for all employees.

(8) They also expensed the cost of club dues for senior executives amounting to $8,000. This covered the dues for the Westmount Golf Club, the Board of Trade, and the Downtown Racquet Club.

(9) The company expensed the costs of maintaining a small lodge located in the Muskoka area of Ontario north of Toronto and used throughout the year for the purposes of entertaining clients.

(10) You know from experience that the company pays $0.60 per kilometre as the mileage rate for the use of employee-owned cars. You noticed that some of the employees are travelling a lot, with two employees driving 6,000 km in the year.

Problem 2

Victoria carries on a retail business as a sole proprietor in a commercial plaza. All the floor space is used for displays or storage so she set aside one room (estimated to be 15% of the floor space) in her house to look after the administration. She has asked you to explain what expenses she will be able to deduct related to this space.

Problem 3

Old Tech Inc. has been in business for many years. Recently, it has been significantly impacted by its competitors who are using technology to improve their products and take market share. As a result, this year, for the first time ever, they are expecting to record a loss for the year. Also, they have spent $150,000 in research to create new products that can compete effectively. These expenditures qualify as scientific research and experimental development for tax purposes. For accounting purposes this has been expensed. How should it be treated for tax purposes?

Problem 4

ITA: 22

Mr. Flint has arranged to sell substantially all of the assets of his proprietorship business, including accounts receivable valued at $36,000, to Mr. Small who will continue the proprietorship business. At the end of last year, Mr. Flint had deducted a reserve for doubtful debts of $6,500. The face value of the accounts being sold is $45,000.

What are the tax implications to both Mr. Flint and Mr. Small of using section 22 on the sale of accounts receivable?

Problem 5

ITA: 80(2)

Carson Manufacturing Inc. (Carson) is under financial stress. As a result of plummeting sales and increasing costs, it has been losing money and has now run out of cash. Last year, one of its biggest suppliers, Scott Distribution Inc. (Scott), loaned it $300,000, on commercial terms, to support them and guarantee a supply of product to them. They are expecting that they will have to sell their land and building next year to pay off some debts, including the bank. At the current time they have non-capital losses of $120,000 and net capital losses of $30,000.

The land and building have the following values:

	Land	*Building*
Fair market value	$1,900,000	$1,100,000
Cost	1,500,000	900,000
UCC		700,000

At this point it appears unlikely that Carson will be able to repay the loan, since all of their assets have been pledged to the bank as security. As a result of recent discussions, Scott has agreed to forgive the loan. Now, Carson wants to know what the impact of this forgiveness will be on Carson.

Problem 6

ITA: 9; IT-218R

A piece of land was purchased by Yacov Corporation Ltd. for the purpose of constructing a high-rise residential building. Plans were made for the development of the property, surveys were made and the land was stripped and excavated in preparation for construction. Subsequent to this work on the land, it was determined that the location was not suitable for the intended purpose, due to heavy truck traffic in the area. As a result, the property was listed for sale with the realtor who acted in the original purchase. The sale at a substantial profit took place approximately six months from the purchase.

The corporation had been newly formed when the above land was purchased. At about the same time, another piece of land was purchased and was developed into a commercial/industrial plaza which the corporation continues to own as a rental property. The principal shareholder of the corporation, Jake Yacov, owns and operates an electrical contracting business.

The Articles of Incorporation of the corporation contain the following statement of objects:

... to purchase, lease, acquire, hold, manage, develop, operate, pledge and mortgage, either absolutely as owner or by way of collateral security or otherwise, alone or jointly with others and either as principal or agent, property, real or personal, and assets generally of any and every kind of description.

No mention is made of the purchase and sale of land as a business activity.

Write a memo for the Yacov Corporation Ltd.'s file evaluating the issue of whether the sale of the land should be treated as a receipt of income or capital gain for tax purposes. Arrive at a conclusion consistent with your analysis of the facts, but indicate the basis for any areas of potential opposition to your conclusion.

Problem 7

ITA: 6(1)(*a*)

Comment on the income tax consequences for each of the following independent situations:

(a) Dan, a construction contractor, entered into a verbal agreement with his friend, Mike, last year. Dan agreed to oversee a small renovation to Mike's house in exchange for Mike's painting services.

(b) Yoko's company won a $100,000 lawsuit against a competitor for patent infringement.

(c) Isaac Corporation, a local observatory, hired Cornell for the summer. For each hour that Cornell worked, Isaac received $5 an hour from the government as part of a student employment grant. Cornell's total compensation is $10 per hour.

(d) Jessy works part-time as the residential manager in an apartment block. In exchange for the management and cleaning services she offers, she receives free rent in a two bedroom apartment. Jessy uses her own supplies and equipment. One bedroom is used as an office for carrying out her duties and meeting existing and potential tenants.

Problem 8

ITA: 18(1)(*a*), 18(1)(*h*), 248(1)

Cameron Chase purchased 200 acres of property about 30 years ago in the eastern Ontario area between Peterborough and Ottawa, as a holiday property for himself and his family. About two years later, it became their principal residence. He worked in Ottawa, both at that time and in the subsequent years; initially he commuted between the property and his Ottawa job on a daily basis. About 10 years later, he began living in Ottawa during the week and commuting home to the property only on weekends. When the property was first purchased, there was an old brick house on it which was not suitable as a residence for the family. A new house (referred to by Cameron as the D.V.A. house) was built; the family moved into it. It is clear that the family's lifestyle was such as to enjoy the rural location.

About 14 years ago (i.e., 15 years after the purchase of the property), Cameron decided to turn part of the property into a campground; eight serviced campsites and approximately twelve unserviced sites were created for this purpose. There was as well room for at least 10 other unserviced campsites more or less immediately available and potential for expansion to a much larger number (e.g., 100). Outhouses were built; a trout pond constructed; and the requisite service roads installed. The tax treatment of the expenses incurred with respect to this construction is not part of the dispute in this case.

After these initiatives had been taken, about a year or so later, Cameron sought the advice of a consultant with the Ontario Ministry of Tourism, a Mr. Bingham. The advice sought was with respect to the possibility of developing the campground and obtaining a business loan for this purpose. Cameron had applied around that time for a loan and was turned down in September of that year.

Cameron's consultations with Mr. Bingham at that time led to suggestions for the development of the campsite through the construction of additional facilities: additional serviced sites; proper toilets; laundry facilities; a store on the property; a swimming pool; an activities building which might be used by the campers in bad weather. Cameron's accountant, Mr. McCoy, prepared projections as to the proposed profitability of the venture if the proposed development took place. These projections showed losses in the first year of operations (about 12 years ago) but a profit thereafter. The projections were based on information given to Mr. McCoy by Cameron and they envisaged the obtaining of a $500,000 loan. Cameron applied to the Eastern Ontario Development Corporation, in the third year of operations, for a loan ($80,000, not $500,000). Mr. Bingham was asked to evaluate the loan application from the Department of Tourism's point of view. He was asked to consider: whether Cameron had the management capability to effect and operate the proposed development; whether there would be any negative effects on competitors in the area if the development took place; whether Cameron's marketing plans looked reasonable. Mr. Bingham's evaluation did not involve any financial analysis of the application. Mr. Bingham recommended that the loan application go forward for the next step, evaluation by the Eastern Ontario Development Corporation. Cameron was unable to obtain the loan, because the Eastern Ontario Development Corporation's funds are new money for new projects.

Cameron purchased a "pre-fab" house for $70,000 which was constructed across the road from the D.V.A. house. The family moved into that house eight years ago. Cameron indicated that he had decided to proceed with the plans for the development of the campsite by turning the D.V.A. house into the general activities building envisaged in the projected development. He planned to add laundry facilities, toilets, etc., thereto. The first year after moving in, Cameron rented the D.V.A. house to his daughter for $100 per month. This was not sufficient to cover the mortgage costs of the property. In May of that year, Cameron had a massive heart attack. He was incapacitated until at least September of that year. Cameron continued to charge the mortgage expenses of the property as a business expense.

The profit and loss record of Cameron's business never showed a profit from the first 10 years of its operation. Losses ranged from about $24,000 to $73,000, but have decreased somewhat in the last two years.

The gross income for the campground itself for the six years was minimal.

In the last five years, the campground income was reported in a combined fashion with that received from the cottage and farmhouse property; therefore, it cannot be separately identified. The record is sketchy with respect to the renting of the cottage, the farmhouse, and the D.V.A. house. That which exists does not show a vigorous and concerted effort to run a business. The D.V.A. house, as well as being rented to the taxpayer's daughter for $100 per month five years ago, was rented during a few of the winter months in the next year to some loggers and for approximately six months in that year to some miners who were prospecting in the area.

Camp Chase was listed in a Government of Ontario camping brochure published for the second season and Cameron had had some calling cards made with Camp Chase, the address, a map and rates listed thereon. No expenses for advertising of the Camp were included in his tax returns for the period of operations to date.

Determine whether expenses incurred by Cameron during the two peak loss taxation years (five and four years ago) are business expenses that are deductible for tax purposes.

Problem 9

ITA: 12(1), 18(1), 20(1); IT-442R

TalkTech Inc. is a manufacturer and wholesaler of cellular communication products. TalkTech Inc's customers are retailers who promote TalkTech Inc.'s products to the general public. TalkTech Inc. has an October 31 year-end. You are conducting a review of TalkTech Inc's year-end accounting records for its 2016 fiscal year and have been provided with the following information.

TalkTech Inc. has the following recorded reserves:

Account	*Opening*	*Additions*	*Subtractions*	*Closing*
Warranty reserve	$35,000	$10,000	$17,500	$27,500
Allowance for doubtful accounts	32,000	7,500	5,000	34,500

TalkTech Inc. provides a one-year warranty on most of its products. The warranty is for defects in workmanship or component parts. This warranty is provided as part of the purchase price of TalkTech Inc.'s products. TalkTech Inc. honours its own warranties. The 2016 addition of $10,000 represents a standard percentage of sales made in the 2016 fiscal period. The 2016 subtraction of $17,500 represents an amount actually paid to honour warranties.

The addition of $7,500 to the allowance for doubtful accounts is a result of the application of TalkTech Inc.'s annual year-end aging analysis. In conversation with the controller of TalkTech Inc. you determine that this $7,500 increase in the allowance for doubtful accounts was computed by applying the company's historical collection percentages to the aged accounts receivable balances. Also, during its 2016 fiscal period, TalkTech Inc. wrote off $5,000 (the subtraction noted above) of amounts previously expensed and included in the opening allowance for doubtful accounts. TalkTech Inc. also ended up collecting $1,500 of previously written-off bad debts.

In an attempt to attract a particular retail customer, TalkTech Inc. provided this new customer with an incentive to make a large initial purchase of its products. On April 1, 2016, TalkTech Inc. sold $300,000 worth of cellular phones to CellBlock Limited. TalkTech agreed to the following payment terms in an attempt to entice CellBlock Limited to make the purchase:

- $100,000 due and payable May 1, 2016; and

- $50,000 due and payable January 1 each year starting January 1, 2017 through January 1, 2020.

The cost of the goods sold under this contract was $180,000. The delivery date for the cellular phones sold under this contract was May 1, 2016.

One of TalkTech's customers, Phones'N'Things, was experiencing financial trouble. As a result, TalkTech Inc. had agreed to make shipments only if payments were received well in advance of the anticipated shipping dates. Under the terms of this agreement, TalkTech Inc. received $40,000 from Phones'N'Things on September 30, 2016. This payment was an advance payment for a shipment of new technology cellular phones which TalkTech Inc. expected to be shipping to customers commencing February 1, 2017. In the event that TalkTech Inc. was unable to honour its contract with Phones'N'Things, a full refund of the $40,000 was payable.

CHAPTER 4

You agree to prepare a schedule showing the effect of the above information on income for tax purposes of TalkTech Inc. for the year ended October 31, 2016. You will also determine any adjustments that would be necessary to reconcile accounting income and income for tax purposes for the year.

In addition, you agree to analyze the tax consequences if the $5,000 subtraction in the allowance for doubtful accounts in 2015 included an account receivable of $800 which was written off only because it has been outstanding for more than 180 days. In fact, it has been outstanding for one year and is part of the opening allowance of $32,000. This $800 could still be collected and there has been no serious attempt to collect it. The remainder of that customer's account is current and further sales have been made to that customer.

Problem 10   ITA: 9, 18, 20

Jordana is self-employed in the T-shirt distribution business. The following is Jordana's income statement, for the calendar year ending December 31.

Statement of Income
For the year ended December 31

Gross revenue		$60,000
Cost of goods sold		(10,000)
Gross profit		50,000
Expenses:		
Accounting and legal	$2,000	
Advertising	800	
Golf dues	3,000	
Reasonable estimated bad debt expense	2,000	
Business, taxes, and licenses	1,000	
Amortization expense	8,000	
Cycle Safety Program	1,200	
Interest	7,800	
Meals and entertainment	4,000	
Rent and lease	2,200	
Office rent	1,000	
Salaries and wages — staff	6,000	(39,000)
Net income per financial statements		$11,000

Notes:

(a) Legal fees include $500 of accrued fees for a pending lawsuit against Jordana for the sale of distasteful T-shirts.

(b) Accounting fees include the purchase of a $1,200 computerized cash register.

(c) Interest expense includes $3,000 paid to the CRA for late instalment interest.

(d) The Cycle Safety Program cost was for Jordana, who is an active environmentalist and rides her bicycle to work every day.

(e) Included in the cost of goods sold is $3,200 incurred for the purchase of shelving and lighting.

(f) Due to the nature of the transaction, the sale of Disney rights were not included in the financial statements. Jordana actively trades rights for T-shirt logos. Net proceeds from the sale of the Disney rights were $15,000, and the cost of the logo rights was $6,800.

Jordana has asked you to calculate her income from a business for tax purposes, before CCA, for the calendar year ending December 31.

Problem 11

ITA: 12(1)(*b*), 18(1)(*a*), 18(1)(*f*), 18(1)(*l*), 67.1(1)

Source Renovations Ltd. specializes in home renovations and interior design in the Montreal area. Most of the construction and finish carpentry work is subcontracted to self-employed contractors. The following information relates to the corporation's net income for the year ended July 31.

Sales revenue	$4,100,000
Direct contracting expenses	3,750,000
Gross profit	350,000
General and administrative expenses:	
Salary to Ginny (president)	110,000
Salary to spouse (accounting)	50,000
Meals and entertainment (Note a)	12,200
Advertising expenses (Note b)	4,900
Travelling expense (Note c)	19,500
Interest and bank charges (Note d)	18,000
Amortization (Note e)	8,000
Office expenses	6,000
Total expenses	228,600
Net operating profit	$ 121,400
Other:	
Gain on sale of real estate (Note f)	$ 55,000
Sale of design contracts (Note g)	19,000
Net income	$ 195,400

Ginny informed you that there was one unrecorded receivable of $14,500 for a renovation project completed on July 30.

Notes:

(a) Meals and entertainment includes:

Club dues	$ 1,800
Promotional meals and season hockey tickets	10,400
Total	$12,200

(b) Advertising expenses include:

Charitable donations	$2,200
Community promotion	650
Local advertising and mail outs	2,050
Total	$4,900

(c) Travelling expense includes both air travel and travel reimbursement to employees for business travel. The company's policy is to reimburse employees 55 cents per kilometre for the business use of their automobiles. The employees drove less than 5,000 kilometres.

(d) Interest and bank charges include:

Interest expense — operations	$ 9,400
Penalty interest for late filing prior year's corporate tax	8,100
Bank charges	500
Total	$18,000

(e) The company uses the straight-line method of amortization. The maximum capital cost allowance that may be claimed is $8,900.

(f) During the year, the company purchased two homes. After Ginny redecorated, the corporation sold the homes for a profit. The corporation has sold six homes in the last two years using the same strategy.

(g) The sale of design contracts resulted from Ginny's desire to downscale her involvement in commercial design. The gain on sale is net of all costs and expenses and is considered to be a capital gain.

(h) The salary to Ginny's spouse is considered reasonable because he spends most of his working day administering her business.

The controller of Source Renovation Ltd. has asked you to calculate the company's income from a business for tax purposes.

Problem 12

ITA: 18, 19, 20, 67.1(1), 78(4)

Duncan Ltd. is a Canadian-controlled private corporation owned by Mr. William Duncan. Mr. Duncan purchased all shares of Duncan Ltd. on July 1 of the prior year for $500,000 in an arm's length transaction. Duncan Ltd. manufactures fabrics and will continue with its June 30 year end. The following is Duncan Ltd.'s income statement for the period of July 1 to June 30 of the current year.

Duncan Ltd.
Statement of Income
For the period July 1 to June 30

Gross revenue		$6,000,000
Cost of goods sold		(4,000,000)
Gross profit		2,000,000
Expenses:		
Accounting and legal	$ 60,000	
Advertising	100,000	
Personal expense of Mr. Duncan	30,000	
Bad debts	20,000	
Business taxes and licenses	10,000	
Amortization	80,000	
Interest	90,000	
Meals and entertainment	40,000	
Rent and lease	220,000	
Office	10,000	
Salaries and wages	600,000	(1,260,000)
Net income per financial statements		$ 740,000

Notes:

(a) Legal fees include $15,000 of estimated fees for a threatened lawsuit against the company.

(b) Accounting fees include a $10,000 cost to reorganize the share capital of the company. This amount is not deductible because it is a cumulative eligible expenditure. However, a deductible claim for cumulative eligible capital of $525 is permitted.

(c) Advertising expenses include a $10,000 payment to a television station in the United States for commercials promoting the company's products to the Vancouver market.

(d) Interest expense includes $5,000 of interest paid to the CRA for late instalments.

(e) Capital cost allowance deductible under paragraph 20(1)(a) is $14,210.

(f) On July 31 in the current fiscal year, Duncan Ltd. paid $30,000 to an agent for services to raise financing. The amount is included in the advertising expense.

(g) An $80,000 bonus is included in salary and wages. The amount will be paid on January 15, next year.

(h) Included in the cost of goods sold is $50,000 incurred for the purpose of earning exempt income.

(i) On January 1 of the current year, Duncan Ltd. paid $100,000 to one of its tenants to cancel a rental lease agreement because Duncan Ltd. required the space for its own business operations. The amount has been included in the rent expense figure. The lease of property commenced on January 1 and had five years remaining at that time.

Mr. Duncan has asked you to calculate the company's income from a business for tax purposes for the year ended June 30.

Problem 13

ITA: 9, 12(1), 18(1)

A senior tax partner in your office has requested that you meet with Mr. Jehangir Dauwalla, a new client, to assist in preparing his personal income tax return. During your initial client meeting, you obtained the following information about Mr. Dauwalla's new business, which he started on June 1. The proprietorship provides hot air balloon rides and weekend leisure trips. His accounting is prepared on the cash basis.

Up and Away
Cash Flow Statement from Proprietorship
June 1 to December 31

Cash receipts (Note a)		$27,220
Cash disbursements:		
Advertising (Note b)	$ 2,200	
Charitable donations	380	
Equipment rental	3,450	
Liability insurance	2,860	
Licences (Note c)	680	
Salary paid to Jehangir	14,750	
Supplies	3,870	
Telephone — Long distance	610	(28,800)
Cash outflow		($1,580)

Notes:

(a) Payments received from customers in January for all December flights and outstanding accounts receivable total $4,650 and are not included above.

(b) Advertising includes $462 of meals and entertainment expenses relating to promoting business with clients.

(c) Licences expense includes $460 for golf memberships for Jehangir and his spouse. He has met several potential new customers through the club and feels that this cost should be deductible. The remaining amount was for business licensing.

(d) In September, Jehangir won a new car through a minor hockey association ticket raffle. The prize had an estimated fair market value of $12,500.

Jehangir has asked you to calculate his income from a business for tax purposes.

Problem 14

ITA: 18(1)(*a*), 18(1)(*b*), 18(1)(*l*), 18(1)(*n*), 67.1

Marty started a self-employed bakery business in a North Bay warehouse on March 1, and he has selected a fiscal year end of December 31. His business includes the baking and delivery of muffins and bagels to various coffee shops throughout the city.

Ma Bagels
Statement of Income
For the period March 1 to December 31

Gross revenue		$340,000
Cost of goods sold		(190,000)
Gross profit		150,000
Expenses:		
Accounting amortization (Note a)	$4,000	
Repairs and maintenance	2,800	
Annual tennis club dues	2,500	

Uncollectible bad debts (Note b)	4,200	
Political donations	1,000	
Charitable donations	8,000	
Hotel and travel	7,800	
Meals and entertainment (Note c)	3,400	
Building rent	12,000	
Salary to spouse (Note d)	40,000	(85,700)
Net income		$ 64,300

Notes:

(a) On March 1, Marty purchased a large gas oven, a computerized blender, and a used van for his business. Marty only used the van for deliveries. Assume the deductible CCA on this equipment is $2,400.

(b) Uncollectible bad debts are from Jo Jo's coffee shop. The owner has declared bankruptcy and the business closed on September 15.

(c) Meals and entertainment expenses were incurred in the attempt to gain new business with several coffee shops.

(d) Diane, Marty's spouse, worked full-time for Marty overseeing hiring, orders and delivery of all goods.

Marty has asked you to calculate his income from a business for tax purposes for the calendar year ending December 31.

Problem 15

ITA: 9, 18, 20(1)(*l*)

Traci works evenings and weekends as a computer consultant. Weekdays she is employed full-time as a network administrator with Jimac Distributors Ltd., a Canadian-controlled private corporation. Traci has an office organized for her consulting business in her four-room condominium where she takes care of paperwork as well as the assembly and repair of computers. This room is the smallest in the condominium taking up only 50 m^2 of the 400 m^2 total space. The following information was provided by Traci.

Receipts for condo fees	$1,800
Mortgage interest	5,250
Receipts for utilities (light, heat, water)	800
Telephone bills	600
Deductible CCA on computer equipment used for diagnostic purposes	1,500

The telephone is used personally and for business. Long distance bills for business total $250. All consulting revenues are deposited into her personal account but she keeps a record in her consulting journal. All payments for supplies are paid out of her personal bank account. She provided you with the following information from her cheque book.

Money received for consulting services	$35,000
Cheques issued:	
CompWorld for parts	18,000
Computer Association	50
Savoir Faire cocktail party for clients	300
Future Shop for a television and DVD player	200
Straw Warehouse for living room furniture	5,500
Computer World magazine subscription	80

Notes:

(a) By looking at Traci's last year's tax return, you notice she claimed a reserve of $500 for amounts not collected. This year, $1,200 is outstanding on doubtful customers' accounts. Traci's records indicate that she was unable to collect $300 for two jobs completed last year.

(b) At the beginning of the year, Traci had $1,500 worth of parts. At the end of the year, she held an inventory of SIMMS that had dropped drastically in price; while the original cost was $2,000, the replacement cost is only $1,200.

(c) Traci often travels to a customer's place of business to provide training, installation, and Home Page design services. Traci uses her own car and charges the customer an extra $50 (included in consulting services) for the on-site service. Assume that Traci's capital cost allowance is $600. Traci kept track of her receipts and the kilometres she drove during the calendar year.

Total kilometres driven	15,000
Kilometres for business	4,500
Gas and oil	$ 1,500
Repairs (tires and muffler)	$ 350

Traci would like you to calculate her income from business for tax purposes.

Problem 16

ITA: 18, 19, 20(1),
147.2(1)

You have been assigned to the audit team for B.B. JAMS Ltd., one of your significant clients. Below is the income statement prepared by the company's accountant for the December 31, 2016 year end.

B.B. JAMS LIMITED
INCOME STATEMENT

FOR THE YEAR ENDED DECEMBER 31, 2016

Sales	$147,840,000
Cost of sales (Note (1))	(119,859,000)
Gross profit	$ 27,981,000
General and administrative expenses (Notes (2)–(7))	(12,374,000)
Selling expenses (Note (8))	(9,311,000)
Income from operations	$ 6,296,000
Other income (Notes (9)–(10))	16,000
Net income before income taxes	$ 6,312,000
Provision for income taxes	(2,528,000)
Net income	$ 3,784,000

Notes:

Through various discussions with the accountant, you have been able to determine that the following information has been recorded in the financial statements:

(1) JAMS had a number of items of inventory that did not sell well in the current year. For accounting purposes, the accountant has recorded a reserve for inventory obsolescence. The reserve was calculated based on the carrying value of any inventory item that had not had a sale in the last 180 days. The reserve at year-end was $1,285,000.

(2) JAMS provides insurance for employees and paid the following amounts to Nat Insurance Company during the year:

$2,000,000 insurance policy on the life of the president included in insurance expense ($300 per month)	$ 3,600
$1,000,000 insurance policy on the life of the vice-president — marketing included in insurance expense	2,000
Group term life insurance for employees included in salaries and benefits ($37,000 × 12 months)	444,000
Total	$449,600

JAMS is the beneficiary of the policies on the president and vice-president. On June 1, 2016, JAMS renegotiated its bank debt, and due to the ever increasing responsibilities of the president, the bank required the insurance policy on the life of the president as part of the collateral for the loan. The premiums on the policy are equal to the net cost of pure insurance for the policy.

(3) An analysis of the professional fees for 2016 revealed the following expenses:

Legal and accounting fees related to the issuance of shares	$29,300
Legal fees related to amending the articles of incorporation	2,300
Costs incurred regarding the renegotiating of the bank loans	46,100
Costs incurred to defend the company against a wrongful dismissal charge	59,600
Costs related to the structuring of an agreement for the purchase of equipment from a foreign company	38,700
Appraisal costs to determine value of the equipment for the bank	5,100

(4) During the year, there were substantial repairs completed to the outside of the building. After the repairs some of the landscaping had to be redone. The total costs were $139,000. Of this, $23,500 relates to the landscaping costs. The entire $139,000 was included in general and administrative expenses.

(5) A review of the other expense accounts included in general and administrative expenses showed the following:

Amortization	$4,560,000
Interest on late payment of municipal taxes	900
Severance payments to four managers*	245,000
Loss from theft by accounting clerk	4,500
Donations to various registered charities	57,000

* All of the amounts were paid in the year.

(6) The salaries and benefits account shows contributions for certain employees to the company's registered pension plan. The contributions were not actually made until March 31, 2017. The pension plan is a defined contribution (money purchase) plan. The company matches the employees' contributions on a dollar for dollar basis.

	Registered pension plan	Employment compensation
President	$13,250	$250,000
Vice-president	10,250	150,000
Accountant	5,400	70,000

(7) In early November 2016, JAMS announced an early retirement package that was made available to employees over the age of 60. In order to provide employees with the time required to assess the offer, the deadline for accepting the package has been set at February 15, 2017. While no formal replies were received as of December 31, 2016, the personnel manager anticipates a high acceptance rate. She expects that the costs associated with the packages will be $672,000. This cost has been accrued in the 2016 financial statements.

(8) The following information was taken from the various selling expense accounts:

Cost of sponsoring presentations at a local theatre company	$15,000
Hockey game tickets given to customers	8,000
Meals and entertainment costs of salespeople	109,500
Staff holiday party and summer barbecue	43,800
Cost of sponsoring local little league teams	5,000
Memberships for salespeople at local golf courses	12,700

(9) The other income includes a loss on the sale of various fixed assets of $35,900.

(10) During the year, the company had cash on hand for a short period of time due to the timing of certain contract payments. The funds earned interest income of $10,400 while they were held.

Other Information:

(11) The accountant has calculated that JAMS is entitled to claim capital cost allowance and CECA of $5,835,000 in 2016. You have confirmed that this calculation is correct.

(12) In reviewing the income tax assessments, you noted that JAMS had been charged interest of $4,900 on the late payment of instalments. You discussed this with the accountant and determined that the interest was recorded in the income tax expense account.

Based on the information that you have obtained, your manager has asked you to calculate the income from business for tax purposes for JAMS for December 31, 2016. He also wants you to show all calculations whether or not they seem relevant to the final answer and comment on all items omitted from the calculation.

Problem 17

ITA: 12(1)(*a*)(ii),
18(1)(*a*), 18(1)(*b*),
18(1)(*h*), 18(1)(*l*),
20(1)(*b*)

On February 1, 2016, Wynn, a recent commerce graduate, began a self-employed, unincorporated coffee business, Chino's & Beano's Unlimited. Wynn would like assistance preparing his 2016 tax return. He has prepared a brief, unaudited statement of income.

Chino's & Beano's Unlimited
Statement of Income
For the year ended December 31, 2016

Sales revenue		$95,000
Less: Provision for returns	$1,200	
Cost of goods sold	22,000	23,200
Gross profit		$71,800
Expenses:		
Travel — meals	$1,500	
Travel — accommodation	2,000	
Travel — total operating expenses — car	2,350	
Sales manager's convention	600	
Salaries paid to staff	30,000	
Health club dues	2,200	
Child care and housekeeping expenses (nanny — single parent)	12,000	
Home office expenses (Note e)	1,400	
Telephone bills	350	
Office supplies	1,700	
Entertainment — drinks and meals	1,800	
Private dental plan — for staff members	2,400	
Restaurant structural renovation costs	21,200	
Straight-line amortization	3,800	
Total expenses		83,300
Business loss before tax		($11,500)

Wynn also supplied the following additional information:

(a) Wynn used his personal automobile for all his business travel. The $2,350 represents his total expenses for the 12-month period. His travel log included business mileage of 14,400 kilometres; the total number of kilometres driven during the 12-month period totalled 18,000 kilometres.

(b) Wynn would like to deduct all of his nanny expenses against his income since the expenses were incurred to earn income.

(c) There are no unrecorded revenues. However, Wynn feels that $380 of his accounts receivable balance is uncollectible because the customers recently declared bankruptcy. Wynn did not provide for this bad debt expense in his financial statements.

(d) The structural renovation of the coffee shop included new walls, flooring, an office for Wynn, and a kitchen.

(e) To ease the burden of being a single parent, Wynn set up a home office. Wynn uses the office to complete his administrative work in the evenings. The home office expenses relate to a proportion of heat, light and power.

Wynn would like you to calculate her net income from a business for tax purposes, ignoring CCA.

CHAPTER 4

¶4,875

Problem 18

ITA: 37; ITR: 2900(2), 2900(3), 2903

Joe's Widget Manufacturers Inc. (JWMI) is an established manufacturing company with a growing research and development (R&D) department. JWMI is a Canadian-controlled private corporation with no associated companies. The research part of the business is new and the company's accountant has no experience dealing with the tax implications of the expenditures in this area. He has correctly computed the company's net income for tax purposes before specific R&D related adjustments as $615,000 and would like your input on the impact of the transactions described below.

For the year ended December 31, 2016, the following R&D related expenditures were made.

Description	Amount
Purchase of lab machinery and lab equipment	$450,000
Purchase of a new building to house laboratory	120,000
Salaries of lab staff	100,000
Operating costs directly related to the lab	40,000

For financial accounting purposes, the salaries and operating costs, net of the investment tax credit below, have been expensed. The lab machinery, equipment and building are used 100% for R&D activities. The lab machinery and equipment have been capitalized for accounting purposes and are being amortized over an eight-year period. Thus, amortization expense of $56,250 was recorded for accounting purposes on the lab machinery and equipment. Amortization expense was recorded on the building. Capital cost allowance for the lab machinery and equipment in Class 29 has been deducted in computing net income for tax purposes.

The company is eligible for investment tax credits at a rate of 35% and has correctly determined that they are eligible for investment tax credits at this rate on all of the above expenditures with the exception of capital expenditures. For accounting purposes, the company's accountant has netted the investment tax credits against the related expenditures as follows.

Expenditure	Gross amount	ITC	Amount recorded for accounting purposes
Lab machinery and equipment	$450,000		$450,000
Building	120,000	0	120,000
Salaries of lab staff	100,000	35,000	65,000
Operating costs of lab	40,000	14,000	26,000

You have been asked to explain to JWMI's accountant what adjustments are necessary to compute income for tax purposes for the years ended December 31, 2016 and 2017.

Problem 19

ITA: 9–12, 18–20, 37, 67.1, 78, 147

The *unaudited* income statement for Lomas & Sons Limited, a Canadian-controlled private corporation, for its year ended December 31, 2016 shows the following:

Sales		$ 795,000
Cost of sales	$350,000	
General and administrative expenses	225,000	
Research and development expenditures	65,000	(640,000)
Operating income		$ 155,000
Other income		20,000
Net income before taxes		$ 175,000
Provision for income taxes:		
— current	$ 27,000	
— future	25,000	(52,000)
Net income after income taxes		$ 123,000

The information in the following notes has already been reflected in the above income statement.

(1) Payment made by company on April 1, 2017, to a defined contribution (money purchase) registered pension plan for the president of the company in respect of current employment service, allocated to 2016 expenses by the company's accountant; in addition, the president had $7,500 withheld from his compensation of $74,000 for the RPP .... $ 7,000

(2) Increase in warranty reserve on company's product (net of expense incurred; based on self-insurance warranty program) 16,000

(3) Amortization expense recorded in the financial statements 30,000

(4) Landscaping costs re: factory premises......................... 2,500

(5) Interest on bank loan obtained for the purpose of purchasing common shares in Advanco Ltd., a dividend-paying Canadian corporation 6,300

(6) Legal costs of arranging an agreement among shareholders 8,500

(7) Legal and accounting fees related to issue of shares 12,700

(8) Interest on municipal real estate taxes paid late in error 1,000

(9) Golf club membership fees.................................... 2,200

(10) Donation to United Way..................................... 3,000

(11) Meals and entertainment for clients 4,000

(12) Appraisal fees to determine selling price of fixed assets 6,200

(13) Premium on term insurance on life of president with the corporation as beneficiary; policy was not required to be assigned as collateral for corporate borrowing from the bank 2,800

(14) Management bonuses ($20,000 of the bonuses expensed in 2016, and shown as "Bonus Payable" on the Balance Sheet as at December 31, 2016 has not been paid at the time of filing the corporate tax return on June 30, 2017) 40,000

(15) Amortization of bond discount on bonds issued in 2011 3,400

(16) The company incurred current research and development expenditures of $100,000. These current expenditures will qualify the company for an investment tax credit of $35,000. The $35,000 has been deducted from the expenditure on SR&ED, as shown in the income statement.

(17) Interest and penalties on income tax assessments, expensed for accounting purposes 1,250

(18) Items included in the financial accounting statements in arriving at the net profit:

Amount paid by an insurance company on its business interruption insurance to compensate for loss of profits when company was closed down for a month during the year because of a fire 26,800

Dividends received 1,700

Volume rebates and discounts on purchases 16,000

Your manager has asked you to compute the income from business or property for tax purposes, ignoring tax deductions in respect of depreciable capital or eligible capital property for Lomas and Sons Limited in respect of its 2016 fiscal year. In addition, she wants you to comment on all items not included in your derivation of income from business or property.

Problem 20

ETA: 123(1), 161, 164, 169(1), 170(1)(*a*), 232, 236, Sched. V, Part VII

Reconsider the facts of Problem 19 and:

(A) Outline the general HST requirements applicable in this corporate situation.

(B) Indicate which of the items listed in the additional information notes represent costs incurred for:

1. taxable supplies, eligible for an ITC, and

2. exempt supplies, not eligible for an ITC.

(C) Comment on the appropriate HST treatment of the other items listed in the additional information notes and on the income statement.

Problem 21

Ryan Holeman, the president of Nine Iron Ltd., has come to your office seeking a second opinion. Nine Iron Ltd. carries on a mini golf and retail business in southern Manitoba. The CRA has reassessed Nine Iron Ltd. for the following transactions that occurred during last year:

(a) Eighteen months earlier, the company purchased two acres of land just outside of Winnipeg with the intention of possibly developing a second retail outlet. Ryan did not have firm plans when he purchased the land. At the time, he thought he could either develop the property into a mini golf and retail outlet or build a gas station with an overnight park for recreation vehicles. Unfortunately, a significant lender backed down and the company was forced to sell the land. Luckily, as Ryan had speculated, the land was sold for a profit of $90,000. The new owner plans to develop an overnight park for recreation vehicles.

(b) Nine Iron Ltd. immediately purchased a smaller plot of land within walking distance. The company is planning to build a second mini golf and retail outlet location next year. During the year, the company expensed interest and property taxes of $26,000 relating to the vacant land. The company also expensed $7,000 in architect's fees, and legal and surveying costs for the development of the amusement park. The CRA reassessed Nine Iron Ltd. for $26,000 plus $3,500 in interest charges, claiming that Nine Iron Ltd. purchased the first plot of land with the intention of trading for profit. The CRA is also disallowing the expenses incurred on the second plot.

Advise Ryan on the income tax issues that Nine Iron Ltd. must address with respect to the above transactions.

Type 2 Problems

Problem 22

Lisa has come to see you again. She came to see you last week [Chapter 3 — Problem 1] about her decision to accept a company-owned or a company-leased car. Now she wants to make sure that she understands the company's position before she makes her decision. She would like you to explain the impact on the company's income for tax purposes of leasing or owning the car.

Problem 23

You have again been asked for advice on employee stock options by two different clients [Chapter 3 — Problem 2].

(a) Omer wants you to explain the impact of the stock option on his employer.

(b) Hilda wants you to explain the impact of the stock option on her employer.

Problem 24

Rishma has left your office again. She came to see you last week [Chapter 3 — Problem 3] about her offer of employment from Motion Tech. Based on your advice to her, she has again met with the company. Now she wants to make sure she understands the company's position before she makes her decision. She would like you to explain the impact of the list of items in her offer on Motion Tech's income for tax purposes.

Problem 25

The CFO for Auto Supply Inc. has asked you to explain to him the impact of the possible employee benefits you considered in Chapter 3 — Problem 4 on the company's income for tax purposes.

Problem 26

ITA: Subdivisions a and b

Coco Hardy is an apprentice with Sepp, a design house in Toronto. In her spare time, during some evenings and on weekends, she operates a sewing service for clothing manufacturers. She has set aside a spare room in her apartment where she keeps her equipment and materials and performs her services. This room occupies approximately 20% of her apartment. She sews for many of the same companies that deal with her employer, Sepp. The demands of her employment with Sepp will continue to prohibit her from expanding her sewing services. Consequently, she has not advertised for additional sewing work. Her sewing billings average approximately $600 per month.

She and the manufacturers mutually agree upon what type of sewing is to be done in order to meet the manufacturers' production deadlines. Her hourly rates are determined by the type of sewing required for a particular manufacturer. At the end of each month, she will issue a bill to the manufacturers bearing her name, home address, and home telephone number. Her clients pay her the gross amount on the invoice which does not include HST.

Ms. Hardy has incurred some direct sewing expenses and has allocated some of her other costs to her sewing services in respect of the past year as follows:

Direct expenses:

Sewing supplies	$ 2,890
Meals and entertainment for manufacturers	500
Sewing machine repairs	425
Long distance telephone calls to manufacturers	710
Delivery of finished product	1,500
Total direct expenses	$ 6,025

Allocated costs:

Rent ($1,000 per month)	$12,000	
Utilities	2,100	
Insurance	400	
	$14,500	
Allocation to sewing room	× 20%	$ 2,900
Capital cost allowance:		
Sewing room furniture	$ 450	
Sewing machine	325	
Automobile for deliveries	1,200	$ 1,975
Total allocated costs		$ 4,875
Total		$10,900

Coco has asked you to analyze the facts and determine whether she is earning employment income or business income from her sewing service.

She also wants you to calculate her income as business income and again as employment income and comment on whether the listed expenses and allocated costs are deductible for income tax purposes under each alternative.

Problem 27

ITA: 8(1)(*f*), 8(1)(*h*), 8(1)(*h*.1), 8(1)(*i*), 8(1)(*j*), 8(3), 8(4), 18–20

Mr. Peter Rajagopal, who is a salesman in Regina, Saskatchewan, has incurred the following expenses in connection with his employment in 2016. He was not reimbursed and did not receive an allowance in respect of any of these expenses. Peter has a Form T2200, signed by his employer, attesting to all of these expenses.

(1) Peter uses one room in his home exclusively as a home office. He uses his home office most days and evenings to do paperwork and make phone calls and his home office computer is connected to his employer's computer system. He visits his office at his employer's premises approximately once a week and spends the remainder of the time on the road, making sales calls throughout Western Canada.

(2) The following expenses relate to Peter's home office which occupies 10% of the square footage of his house:

Utilities	$ 3,100
Mortgage interest	12,000
House insurance	1,150
Municipal taxes	3,050
Maintenance and repairs	2,700
Total	$22,000
10% thereof	$2,200
Capital cost allowance on computer equipment	1,035
Rental of photocopier	1,200
Office supplies	750
Cellular phone charges (used for employment-related calls only)	700
Long distance calls related to business	1,000

(3) Peter also has the following promotional expenses:

Meals (with clients in Regina, Peter's meals)	$2,000
Client's meals	$2,100
Theatre tickets	1,200
Promotional gifts	1,300
Country club membership	3,200

(4) Peter paid the following automobile expenses:

Gas and oil	$2,000
Insurance	1,100
Licence	90
Repairs	800
Parking (employment related)	320

Peter purchased the car that he uses for employment purposes on August 1, 2015 for $50,000 plus $2,500 GST and $2,500 PST. Peter did not claim CCA on the car in 2015; therefore, the capital cost allowance rate for the car is 30% in 2016. The car was driven a total of 40,000 kilometres in 2016; 32,000 of the kilometres driven related to Peter's employment use.

(5) Peter also incurred the following travel expenses (while away at least 12 hours):

Airfare	$ 4,520
Meals and accommodation (including $2,400 for meals)	4,960
Registration fees for convention in Vancouver to increase product knowledge	800
Out-of-town entertainment	3,200

(6) Interest on bank loan:

— to buy the computer equipment for the home office in (1) above	$ 320
— to buy the car in (4) above	800

(7) Peter's remuneration from employment is as follows:

Salary	$40,000
Bonus based on company sales	35,000

(8) Saskatchewan has GST of 5% and PST of 5%.

Peter has asked you to calculate his income and expenses assuming he is an employee and assuming he is self-employed. You have agreed to do this and present him with the results with two columns; one for each option and one showing the differences, if any.

Problem 28

ITA: 5(1), 6(1)(*a*), (*b*), (*c*), (*e*), (*g*), (*k*), 6(2), 7(1), 7(8), 6(9), 80.4(1), 110(1)(*d*); IT-470R

Valerie Borg is a vice-president of Program Management with an equipment leasing company in Calgary. Recently, Valerie was approached by a large public company, Key Equipment Finance Limited ("Key"), which is based in Toronto, about the possibility of joining their firm. Valerie has always been looking for opportunities for career advancement and Toronto is an ideal city for relocation.

Valerie is in the process of negotiating her compensation package. She has just received a letter outlining a proposed package from Key. The package looks very attractive, but she would like to know the tax impact on various items outlined in the letter. Valerie is also interested in knowing the tax implications of the compensation package to her future employer. She believes that if she knows the cost to the employer, she will be in a better position to negotiate.

1. An annual salary of $150,000 and bonus, tied to the company's financial performance. Calculation of the bonus is based on the firm's December year-end results, with payment to occur on June 30.

2. Key offers to loan Valerie $200,000, interest-free, to help finance a new house. In addition, Key will reimburse all of her moving costs.

3. Key will pay the premium for Valerie to join its group term life insurance plan. Key will pay the premiums for a private health plan, a dental plan, and a drug plan. The company's insurance company is Green Shield.

4. Valerie is required to travel to Europe on a regular basis. Company policy permits a spouse to accompany its executives for these trips. Valerie's husband, Matt, is a freelance writer working from home. He is very excited about going to Europe with Valerie. The main purpose of the trips will be for Valerie to oversee the company's global operations. Her husband will spend his time visiting local museums. Key will pay a portion of the travelling expenses related to Matt.

5. Key will provide a BMW to Valerie. Valerie expects to drive the car 30% for business and 70% for her personal use. Valerie will receive a company credit card to be used to pay for gas and maintenance of the car. Key will pay a monthly lease of $850, including HST. Valerie will drive the car approximately 20,000 kilometres per year.

6. Key recently installed a fitness club in its building. All employees are encouraged to use the club free of charge. The club also offers free personal training. The equivalent value for similar facilities at a private club would be $1,100 per year, including applicable taxes.

7. Key pays for counselling services related to the physical health of its employees. Valerie will be covered by this service.

8. Valerie will participate in Key's defined contribution (i.e., money purchase) registered pension plan. The company will match Valerie's contributions to the plan, which are not to exceed 50% of the maximum deductible amount.

9. Key owns a yacht and it is made available to all of its executives. This offer is extended to Valerie. She can have it free for one week each year.

Valerie would like you to explain the tax implications of the compensation package to both herself and Key.

She would also like you to describe the tax-related issues to be considered when designing an employee compensation package.

Type 3 Problems

Problem 29

Samara, the president of Eden Prospects Ltd., has come to your office for a second opinion. Eden Prospects is a national marketing firm specializing in the development and implementation of marketing plans for partners in practices of law, accounting, medicine and dentistry. Samara is on the premises daily, carrying out her duties as president and a senior adviser to clients. The CRA recently reassessed Eden Prospect's 2014 taxation year and is requesting that an additional $140,000 in taxes and $28,000 in interest and penalty charges be paid immediately for the following transactions.

(a) In December 2015, the company declared a bonus of $280,000 to Samara and several senior vice-presidents. The amount was paid in September 2016.

(b) In 2015, the corporation provided three senior executives with an interest-free loan of $240,000 for the purchase of shares of Eden Prospects Ltd. The company borrowed the funds from the bank and incurred $20,000 in interest charges. The executives began repayment in 2017. No amount was shown by Eden Prospects as a taxable benefit for these employees.

(c) The corporation pays Samara a nominal salary to act as president. Samara provides her senior advisory services to Eden Prospects through a proprietorship, Sole Trust. Every month, Samara prepares an invoice on behalf of the proprietorship for services rendered to Eden Prospects. Prospects is Sole Trust's only client. The CRA imposed a large penalty on Eden Prospects for not treating Samara as an employee and remitting Canada Pension Plan, Employment Insurance and withholding taxes.

(d) In 2015, the corporation rented a fishing lodge to carry out group think sessions with three of their most senior clients. The purpose of the sessions was to provide a comfortable setting for the company's largest clients to share marketing ideas. The sessions also helped Eden Prospects to become closer to their clients — especially while fishing and golfing. The corporation was denied a deduction for the rent of the lodge, although it was allowed 50% of the meals, entertainment and green fees.

Advise Samara by preparing a memo on the various income tax issues that both Samara and Eden Prospects must address with respect to the above transactions.

Problem 30

London City Electronics Inc. has been a client of yours since it started in business five years ago. Isabelle Joy, the founder, has been very successful with her main product, which is a valve that measures and controls the flow of liquids. It is now the middle of March and you have just started your review engagement field work for the company's December year end when Isabelle asks you to come into her office to talk to her.

The first thing you do is congratulate her on the good year she had last year. Her sales, gross profit, and net income are all up substantially over the previous year. You are surprised when she starts to complain about the poor results so far this year. She indicates that her customers are just now starting to stretch their payments because they are facing increased competition from imports. In fact, one of her customers has given London City Electronics some of its products in exchange for the amount it owed.

To compound this problem, Isabelle has had some quality control problems in her manufacturing process and she has been receiving a large number of warranty claims. Sometimes she is able to repair the valve before there is significant cost to the customer, but in some cases the customer has had financial losses as a result of the faulty valve.

Isabelle would like your advice on the tax implications of her situation.

Problem 31

Jordana Fluge and Noa Gold were finally able to hold the grand opening for their medical supply import business. It had been an expensive party, but both Jordana and Noa felt that their suppliers, customers, and new employees had appreciated it.

It seemed like a long time ago that they got the idea and started to develop their plans. In fact, the idea had been introduced to them 12 months ago during a trip they took to California to look for business opportunities. Once they returned, they began to do their own research. They had one of the local universities do some market research for them to see whether their idea was viable. The research supported their idea of importing medical supplies from a large U.S. supplier to compete against other importers for the Canadian market.

Six months ago, the U.S. supplier put them in touch with their local importer, Beam Inc., whose owner wanted to retire. Since that time, they have been busy negotiating with Mr. Beam and the supplier, finding their own leased warehouse space (Beam Inc.'s space was too small), visiting customers, setting up the office and modern control systems and assessing the employees of Beam Inc. Even before the opening, they had spent $25,000 of their own money on expenses such as:

- their initial travel costs to California (July, last year);

- market research (September, last year);

- negotiating the operating line of credit (May, this year);

- leasehold improvements, equipment (May, this year);

- travel and entertainment expenses (January to June, this year); and

- legal and accounting costs for the incorporation (June, this year).

But now it is all coming together. Jordana is going to provide the initial capital, including the personal guarantee to the supplier and the bank, and Noa is going to manage the business. They have bought the inventory, customer lists, accounts receivable, and equipment from Beam Inc. Their initial lease is for five years with two, five-year renewal options.

Advise Jordana and Noa on the tax implications of the issues raised by this situation. Assume that they incorporated a company in June, but they have not used it in any way yet, and that it is now July when they are asking for your advice.

 [For more problems and solutions thereto, see the DVD accompanying the textbook.]

CHAPTER 4 —
DISCUSSION NOTES FOR REVIEW QUESTIONS

(1) This type of transaction is commonly referred to as an "adventure in the nature of trade" and would result in business income, if the facts of the situation indicate that it has the "badges of trade". One of the indicators that a transaction is an adventure in the nature of trade is that the taxpayer has specialized knowledge in respect of the transaction. Mr. Fritz is a real estate salesperson and, hence, on the surface appears to meet this test. Since "business" is defined to include "an adventure in the nature of trade", this transaction would be classified as business income.   ITA: 248(1)

(2) There is no requirement in the Act to use GAAP for tax purposes. The courts have, on occasion, rejected conformity between income for accounting and tax purposes, particularly in cases where GAAP is at variance with the court's concept of ordinary commercial trading and business principles and practices or common law principles. However, GAAP profits are usually used as the starting point for the calculation of net income for tax purposes.

(3) No. Since the performance of this contract would have been income to Opco if the customer had completed it, the damages received would also be treated as business income.

(4) The agreement was of such importance to Aco Ltd. that it would constitute a large part of the company's total business structure. As a result, the receipt may be treated as a capital transaction on the sale of eligible capital property with no cost base. Thus, 50% of the receipt is included in business income. (See Chapter 5.)

(5) No. Income from illegal activities is taxable. Subsection 9(1) does not impose conditions on how the profit is earned. See IT-256R for the CRA's position. See, also, the cases listed in the text on this issue.   IT-256R

(6) The subsidy is taxable as if it were an expense reduction to Opco. Refer to the CRA's position.   IT-273R2

(7) There are a number of limitations that restrict the deductibility of expenses even though they may have been incurred to earn income. Expenditures that are not deductible include: ITA: 18

- capital outlay or loss;   ITA: 18(1)(*b*)

- use of recreational facilities and club dues;   ITA: 18(1)(*l*)

- political contributions; and   ITA: 18(1)(*n*)

- limitations on interest and property taxes.   ITA: 18(2), 18(3.1)

(8) A provision specifically prohibits the deduction of any amount paid or payable under the Act. As a result, the interest paid to the Receiver General will not be deductible.   ITA: 18(1)(*t*)

(9) Not necessarily. The Act also places a limitation on the amount of an outlay or expense. It can only be deducted to the extent that it is "reasonable in the circumstances".   ITA: 67

(10) If the replacement of the roof served to restore it to its original condition then the cost should be fully deductible in the year incurred. If the replacement roof was superior to the old roof, the cost could be considered capital in nature. This would result in an addition to the undepreciated capital cost pool. Then, the cost would be deductible over a number of years. An Interpretation Bulletin comments on the issue of income *versus* capital expenditures.   IT-128R

(11) No. Airplane, train, or bus fares are specifically excluded from the 50% limitation.   ITA: 67.1(4)(*a*)

(12) The reserve is only allowed if the company is the manufacturer of the product and pays an arm's length party to take over the obligations of the warranty for the company.   ITA: 20(1)(*m.*1)

CHAPTER 4

CHAPTER 4 — SOLUTIONS TO MULTIPLE CHOICE QUESTIONS

Question 1

(D) is correct. A deduction for interest and penalties on late income tax payments is denied.   ITA: 18(1)(*t*)

(A) is a deductible item. A deduction for amounts paid for landscaping business premises is allowed.   ITA: 20(1)(*aa*)

(B) is a deductible item. A deduction for interest on money borrowed to finance the purchase of a factory for use in its business is allowed.   ITA: 20(1)(*c*)

(C) is a deductible item. If the beneficiary of a $100,000 term life insurance policy on an employee is the employee's family, the cost of the insurance premium is part of the cost of the employee's remuneration package. As such, it is not denied as it is incurred for the purpose of earning income.   ITA: 18(1)(*a*)

Question 2

(C) is correct. The entire $15,000 spent on three social events for all employees at a particular location is deductible as long as the number of events does not exceed six.   ITA: 67.1(2)(*f*)

(A) The deduction for $11,000 of accrued legal fees for a pending law suit is not allowed, because it is a contingent liability. There is no legal liability to pay this amount.   ITA: 18(1)(*e*)

(B) The deduction for $4,000 of donations to registered charities is denied because it is not incurred for the purpose of earning income. The donations would be deductible in the computation of taxable income.   ITA: 18(1)(*a*), 110.1(1)(*a*)

(D) The deduction of $1,500 for golf club membership dues for employees is denied.   ITA: 18(1)(*l*)

Question 3

(D) is correct, because the Act provides an exception to the 50% rule for the cost of meals and entertainment relating to a fund-raising event the primary purpose of which is to benefit a registered charity.   ITA: 67.1(2)(*b*)

(A) is incorrect since donations to political parties are not deductible. The federal political donation would be eligible for a tax credit.   ITA: 18(1)(*n*), 127(3)

(B) is incorrect, because accrued bonuses are not deductible if they are unpaid 180 days after year-end.   ITA: 78(4)

(C) is incorrect, because the deduction for a financial accounting reserve for warranty expenses is denied.   ITA: 18(1)(*e*)

Question 4

(A) is the correct answer. The $7,000 deduction is computed as follows:

Legal expenses related to the purchase of an investment in shares	$ 0	ITA: 18(1)(*b*)
Legal expenses incurred to dispute a tax assessment	5,000	ITA: 60(*o*)
Legal expenses related to the issuance of debt ($^1/_5$)	1,000	ITA: 20(1)(*e*)
Accounting fees in connection with the preparation of a prospectus ($^1/_5$)	1,000	ITA: 20(1)(*e*)
	$ 7,000	

(B) incorrectly deducts $1,000 for the legal expenses related to the purchase of an investment in shares: $8,000 = $1,000 + $1,000 + $5,000 + $1,000.

(C) incorrectly deducts all of the legal expenses related to the issuance of debt and the accounting fees in connection with the preparation of a prospectus but none of the legal fees for the tax dispute: $15,000 = $5,000 + $5,000 + $5,000.

(D) incorrectly deducts only the $5,000 legal expenses related to disputing the tax assessment.

Question 5

(D) is correct. Most of the facts support capital gains treatment: the nature of the asset (real estate), its use and intended use (rental), the 10-year holding period and the unsolicited offer for sale. As a result, the gain on the sale of the land will likely be treated as a capital gain for income tax purposes.

(A) is incorrect. Because Sam is a real estate agent, the CRA may argue that the gain on the sale of the land is business income (not a capital gain).

(B) is incorrect. The fact that the land has been held for 10 years supports capital gains treatment, not business income treatment.

(C) is incorrect. The unsolicited offer for sale supports capital gains treatment, not business income treatment.

Question 6

(A) is correct. Legal fees to defend a lawsuit brought by a customer would be deductible. ITA: 18(1)(*a*)

(B) and (C) are incorrect because these items (accounting loss on the sale of capital property and the principal amount of a mortgage) are on account of capital and therefore not deductible. ITA: 18(1)(*b*)

(D) is incorrect because personal and living expenses are not deductible. ITA: 18(1)(*h*)

CHAPTER 4

CHAPTER 4 — SOLUTIONS TO EXERCISES

Exercise 1

Employee Perk	Employee Taxable Benefit	Employer Impact	
			ITA: 9, 11, 18, 20
Tuition fees for the child of employee	$2,800 not a taxable benefit and jurisprudence supports an exempt scholarship for the child.	Deductible as compensation expense	
Out-of-town meals	Not taxable to employee	50% deductible for employment duties	
Entertainment for clients	Not taxable to employee	50% deductible for employment duties	
Professional dues	Not taxable to employee	Deductible for employment duties	
Notebook computer for employment	Not taxable to employee	Deductible CCA for employment duties	
Membership for health club	Not taxable if employment-related	Not deductible for company	
Interest-free loan	$40,000 is subject to an imputed interest taxable benefit of $400 (deductible by the executive as was used to invest in company shares)	No impact on employer	
Life insurance premiums	$150 taxable benefit	Deductible as compensation expense	
Reimbursement for supplies	Not taxable to employee	Deductible CCA for employment duties	

Exercise 2

[See *Hiwako Investments Limited v. The Queen*, 78 DTC 6281 (F.C.A.)]

The intention of the taxpayer corporation in this case can only be inferred from the facts of the case. The nature of the asset involved in the transaction is of prime importance in this case. It was an income-producing asset that would have been regarded as a fixed capital asset had it been held longer. Normally, the increase in value on the sale of a capital asset is taxed as a capital gain. The gain represents an enhancement of value by realizing a security in the same sense that a growth stock may be sold for a gain that is regarded as a capital gain. Thus, the prospect of an increase in value does not, by itself, characterize the gain as income from business.

The nature of the activity surrounding the transaction could characterize it as an adventure in the nature of trade. However, it could be argued that an income-producing property was purchased as an investment and circumstances changed such that the investment had to be sold. This would not necessarily be regarded as a gain made in an operation of business in carrying out a scheme for profit-making.

The Court indicated that the concept of "secondary intention" does no more than refer to a practical approach for determining certain questions that arise in connection with "trading cases". If property is acquired where there is no business or the purchaser has not considered how he or she will use it, then the sale may be regarded as an adventure in the nature of trade, supporting a secondary intention to sell at a profit. However, where the property in question is an active, profit-producing property, it may be more difficult to conceive of its having been held as a speculation in the sense of an adventure in the nature of trade.

The fact that the principal shareholder of the corporation had a long history of trading in real estate does not necessarily mean that his intention in the transaction at hand was to trade. That fact could be outweighed by the income-producing capital nature of the particular property in question.

The Court held that the gain was not income from a business, based on the foregoing reasons. However, some believe that the arguments for business income are stronger in this case and that the decision in this case should be limited to its specific facts.

Exercise 3

(a) If the company leased the vehicle and provided it for Samuel, the company would be able to deduct the cost of the lease as a business expense limited by the formula in section 67.3. Samuel would have a taxable benefit that would consist of:

ITA: 9, 11, 18, 20, 67.2, 67.3

Standby charge	($400 × 12 × ⅔) =	$3,200
Operating cost benefit	(10,000 × $0.27) =	2,600
Taxable benefit		$5,900

(b) If the company purchased the vehicle, it would claim capital cost allowance using the CCA rate of 30%, limited to a capital cost of $30,000. Interest on funds borrowed would be limited by section 67.2, thus receiving a tax reduction. This option requires the company to lay out cash and the company should do an analysis of which of the first two options is better for it for the period of time the automobile is needed.

Samuel would have a taxable benefit that would consist of:

Standby charge	2% × $22,000 × 12 =	$5,280
Operating cost benefit	10,000 × $0.26 =	2,600
Taxable benefit		$7,880

(c) The allowance would cost the company $3,660, calculated as follows:

$0.54 × 5,000 km =	$2,700
$0.48 × 2,000 km =	960
Total	$3,660

This amount would be deductible as an expense for the employer as it is tied to the CRA's automobile expense deduction limits.

Samuel's operating costs incurred for business purposes = $1,029 ($2,500 × 7,000/17,000) plus depreciation. Samuel would be receiving $3,660 per year, which implies $2,631 ($3,660 – $1,029) for depreciation.

Exercise 4

The $225,000 would be considered a capital receipt based on the *Parsons-Steiner Limited v. M.N.R.* case.

62 DTC 1148 (Ex. Ct.)

The following paraphrased excerpt from that case will help explain the conclusion:

> On the whole therefore having regard to the importance of the franchise to Cars' business, the length of time the relationship had subsisted, the extent to which the appellant's business was affected by its loss both in decreased sales and by reason of its inability to replace it with anything equivalent, and the fact that from that time the appellant was in fact out of business, leads to a conclusion that this was a capital transaction. The payment in question was to replace "a capital asset of an enduring nature". It was one which Cars had built up over the years and which on the termination of the franchise they were obliged to relinquish. The payment received in respect of its loss was accordingly a capital receipt.

Exercise 5

Various factors must be examined in the determination of whether the dispositions should be considered income from a business or a capital gain.

ITA: 248(1)

Primary intention

The stated primary intention was to develop the properties into shopping plazas, thus, to earn income from these properties. However, this intention must be supported by objectively observable behavioural factors.

CHAPTER 4

Behavioural factors

Relationship of the transaction to the taxpayer's business

AMC's main business appears to be the development and management of revenue properties. It also frequently engages in the sale of undeveloped properties. The fact that these transactions are closely related to AMC's main business and the fact that its major shareholder is a realtor and, therefore, heavily involved in buying and selling land, points to treatment of the sales as income from a business.

AMC often sells property when it is not feasible to develop and, as such, purchases land with good resale value. This focus on good resale value indicates an underlying intention of selling property for a gain. This indicates a treatment of the dispositions as business income.

Number and frequency of transactions

Transactions of buying and selling undeveloped land are frequently entered into as it is AMC's business to develop land. This frequency indicates treatment as income from a business.

Conclusion

It could be argued that AMC's primary intention was to hold the third parcel of land to develop it and earn income from it; therefore, its sale should be treated as a capital gain. But because of the likely secondary intention of earning a profit on its sale, the frequency of this type of transaction, and the closeness to AMC's primary business, it is likely the court would consider all the dispositions as income from a business. The court could say that AMC held onto the third parcel for six months only in order to get the best price and therefore to make a substantial profit.

Exercise 6

Since actual cost is known it must be used. Therefore, an assumption about cost is not appropriate. Market value is probably best reflected in net realization value for this inventory. The following calculation of inventory values could be used:

Item	Actual cost	Reg. 1801 Market	Ssec. 10(1) Each item at lower of cost or market
Mufflers	$1,120.00	$ 992.00	$ 992.00
Tailpipes	745.75	706.50	706.50
Exhaust system	633.75	604.50	604.50
Shock absorbers	4,979.20	5,056.00	4,979.20
Brackets	1,304.80	1,211.60	1,211.60
Clamps	1,134.90	1,396.80	1,134.90
Total		$9,967.40	$9,628.70

Either the $9,967.40 value can be used or the $9,628.70 value can be used. However, the ending valuation method used in a particular year must be the same as that used for the end of the preceding year.

ITR: 1801
ITA: 10(1), 10(2.1)

Exercise 7

(a) The *income-earning purpose test* is found in paragraph 18(1)(*a*) — the "general limitation" re: an outlay or expense made or incurred for the purpose of gaining or producing income from the business or property. Students can list any of the following related sections, ITs or ICs in their answer:

ITA: 18(1)(*a*), 18(1)(*b*), 18(1)(*c*), 18(1)(*e*), 18(1)(*h*), 67, 248(1)

Related sections: subsections 20(1), 20(16); subsection 21(1); subsection 26(2); section 30

ITs: IT-99R5; Income Tax Folio: S3-F9-C1; IT-211R; IT-261R; IT-357R2; IT-364; IT-467R2; IT-475; IT-487; IT-521R

ICs: IC 77-11; IC 88-2

(b) The *capital test* is found in paragraph 18(1)(*b*) — no deduction is allowed for an outlay, loss, or replacement of capital, a payment on account of capital or an allowance in respect of depreciation, obsolescence or depletion except as expressly permitted by this Part.

Related sections: subsection 14(5); subsections 20(1), (10), (16); subsection 24(1); subsection 26(2); section 30

ITs: IT-187; IT-467R2; IT-475

ICs: none

(c) The *exempt income test* is found in paragraph 18(1)(*c*) — limits an outlay or expense to the extent it may reasonable be regarded as having been made or incurred for the purpose of gaining or producing exempt income.

Related sections: none

ITs: IT-467R2

ICs: none

(d) The *reserve test* is found in paragraph 18(1)(*e*) — no deduction for an amount as, or on account of, a reserve, a contingent liability or amount or a sinking fund except as expressly permitted by this Part.

Related sections: none

ITs: IT-321R (archived); IT-467R2

ICs: none

(e) The *personal expenses test* is found in paragraph 18(1)(*h*) — no deduction for personal or living expenses of the taxpayer, other than travel expenses incurred by the taxpayer while away from home in the course of carrying on the taxpayer's business.

Related sections: subsections 20(1), (16); subsection 248(1) "personal or living expenses"

ITs: no primary ITs

ICs: none

(f) The *reasonableness test* is found in section 67, which states no deduction is allowed for an outlay or expense in respect of which any amount is otherwise deductible under this Act, except to the extent that it was reasonable in the circumstances.

Related sections: subsection 8(9); subsection 248(1) "amount"

ITs: no primary ITs

ICs: none

Exercise 8

(A) The deduction of these costs are prohibited, notwithstanding the argument that the lodge was used to produce income from client business. ITA: 18(1)(*l*)

(B) The deduction of costs are allowed if they were incurred in the ordinary course of the company's business of providing the property for rent. The facts of this case *may* fit this exception. ITA: 18(1)(*l*)

Exercise 9

First, it must be determined whether any expense incurred may be deducted in respect of the home office. To make this determination, the specific conditions outlined in subsection 18(12) are that: ITA: 18(12)

(i) the office is the principal place of business; or

(ii) it is used exclusively for the purpose of earning business income and is used on a regular and continuous basis for meeting clients, customers, or patients in respect to the business.

Since Karim performs only consulting work, the home office qualifies under condition (i). Although Amina teaches in addition to consulting, it is only part-time and her principal business is consulting. Therefore, she also qualifies under condition (i). Amina and Karim are carrying on separate self-employed businesses. Since they also live together, the home office expenses would be split on an agreed basis. Assuming that the split was agreed at 50%, both taxpayers would be permitted to deduct 50% of the eligible home office expenses. Eligible home office expense is equal to 500/2,000 square feet times the total home office costs. Supplies, materials, and software would be considered business expenses, not home office expenses. Therefore, Amina and Karim may **each** deduct the following as their 50% share of the expenses:

CHAPTER 4

Home office expense (subsection 18(12))	$23,600 × 25% × 50% =	$2,950
Supplies and materials	$1,800 × 50% =	900
Computer and software lease	$2,300 × 50% =	1,150
Total		**$5,000**

Exercise 10

(A) — contribution may be made within 120 days of the end of 2016,

— an employer contribution to a defined benefit RPP is deductible where it is made on the recommendation of an actuary in whose opinion the contribution is required so that the plan will have sufficient assets to provide benefits in accordance with its terms as registered,

— in this case, both the current service contribution and the lump-sum amount based on an actuarial valuation would be deductible in 2015, if they are in accordance with the plan.

(B) A full deduction of an amount paid in the year is permitted — or a taxpayer may elect to write it off in equal amounts over the 10-year period beginning in the current year.

ITA: 20(1)(*cc*)
ITA: 20(9)

(C) The deduction of the full amount of utilities connection costs is permitted. Since the taxpayer does not own the gas lines but the utilities company does, the amount is not eligible for capital cost allowance.

ITA: 20(1)(*ee*)

(D) Salary of an owner-employee's spouse is an allowable deduction to a corporation as long as it is reasonable in the circumstances. While $7,000 per month for full-time secretarial work is probably not reasonable, some lesser, reasonable amount would be deductible in this case. The amount in excess of a reasonable amount will not be deductible to the corporation, but will be included in the recipient's income from employment.

Exercise 11

Only ½ of the discount of $43.29 may be deducted because the bond was issued at less than 97% even though within the ⁴⁄₃ × 4% or 5.33% yield range.

ITA: 20(1)(*f*)

Given that the discount is paid effectively on maturity when the principal amount is repaid, then ½ of the $43.29 or $21.65 is deductible in 2016.

Exercise 12

Net income per financial statements		$150,000
Add: Items deducted in financial statements but not deductible for tax purposes:		
Provision for income taxes — current	25,000	
— future	130,000	
Amortization expense	40,000	
Non-deductible interest — re interest on late taxes	2,500	
Bond discount	7,500	
Reserve for doubtful debts	10,000	
	$365,000	
Deduct: Items not deducted in financial statements but deductible for tax purposes:		
Landscaping costs	$12,000	
Reserve for doubtful debts	15,000	(27,000)
Net Income for tax purposes before CCA		$338,000

ITA: 18(1)(*e*)

ITA: 18(1)(*b*)

ITA: 18(1)(*t*)
ITA: 18(1)(*b*), (*e*)
ITA: 12(1)(*d*)

ITA: 20(1)(*aa*)

ITA: 12(1)(*l*)

Exercise 13

This transaction would likely involve a receipt of income because the intention is likely to make a profit on the purchase and sale of land. This would be substantiated by the frequency of transactions in land or, at least, the indication of an adventure in the nature of trade. During the year of sale the following income would be computed:

Revenue from the sale of land		$250,000
Less: cost of land	$107,500	
real estate commission	12,500	120,000
Income from the sale of land		$130,000

ITA: 9

Less: reserve for amount not due until later year*

$$\frac{\$130,000}{\$250,000} \times (\$250,000 - \$110,000) \dots\dots\dots\dots\dots \quad \underline{72,800}$$

ITA: 20(1)(*n*)

Income after reserve .... $ 57,200

* The reserve is not available, unless the sale occurred within 36 months of the end of the year in which a reserve is to be taken.

ITA: 20(8)(*b*)

Note that the minimum two-year repayment period does not apply on the sale of land which qualifies for the reserve. In the next year, the reserve of $72,800 would be taken into income.

ITA: 12(1)(*e*)(ii), 20(1)(*n*)(ii)

Exercise 14

Since the corporation is carrying on business, it is engaged in a commercial activity. Therefore, the corporation is required to register and collect HST on its supplies, i.e., sales of goods, which are "taxable supplies." As a registrant, the corporation is entitled to a full input tax credit (ITC) in respect of HST paid or payable on goods and services that it purchases exclusively for use in its commercial activity. If HST collected or collectible on its sales exceeds its ITCs, the corporation must remit the difference. On the other hand, if ITCs exceed HST collected or collectible, a refund of the excess is available.

ETA: 123(1)

ETA: 169(1)

The following is the appropriate HST treatment of the items listed:

(a) Net income per financial statements would have been increased by HST charged which is included in revenue and reduced by HST paid or payable which is included in costs. HST charged net of ITCs from HST paid or payable must be remitted.

(b) There are no HST implications for the provision for income taxes.

(c) HST paid on the purchase of depreciable property provides an ITC, as discussed in Chapter 5. When the cost of the asset is subsequently written off through depreciation or capital cost allowance, there are no further HST implications.

Landscaping goods and services would involve payment of GST/HST on taxable supplies and, hence, would give rise to an ITC.

The following costs would not involve the payment of HST, since they are for exempt supplies:

(a) interest paid on income tax due results from a financial service,

(b) bond interest also results from a financial service, and

(c) reserve for doubtful debts.

CHAPTER 4

Chapter 5

Depreciable Property and Eligible Capital Property

Learning Goals

Know, Understand and Explain

By the end of this chapter you will know, understand and be able to explain:

- The basic provisions of the *Income Tax Act* (the Act) that relate to depreciable and eligible capital property.

- The similarities and differences between the accounting and tax deductions as they relate to depreciable and capital property.

- That capital cost allowance and cumulative eligible capital amounts are the tax equivalent of accounting amortization/depreciation for capital and intangible property.

- How to classify commonly purchased assets given the information and circumstances.

- The tax implications of asset disposal as it relates to depreciable and intangible property.

- The basic provisions in the *Excise Tax Act* pertaining to GST/HST related to the treatment of depreciable and capital property.

Apply

By the end of this chapter you will be able to apply your knowledge and understanding to:

- Correctly calculate capital cost allowance and cumulative eligible capital amounts that replace accounting deductions.

- Advise taxpayers on the tax implications of the purchase and sale of these assets.

Review Questions
¶5,800 in the Study Guide

Multiple Choice Questions
¶5,825 in the Study Guide

Exercise Questions
¶5,850 in the Study Guide

Assignment Problems
¶5,875 in the Study Guide

CHAPTER 5 — LEARNING CHART

Problem Descriptions

Textbook Example Problems

5-1	Tax shield
5-2	Half-year rule
5-3	Disposal of depreciable assets
5-4	Short fiscal year
5-5	Additions and disposals over five years
5-6	Replacement property
5-7	Eligible capital property, CECA

Multiple Choice Questions

1	Luxury vehicle CCA
2	Leasehold improvements
3	CECA
4	Leasehold improvements
5	CCA
6	Patent options

Exercises

1	Choice of CCA class
2	Luxury automobile CCA
3	Sale of luxury automobile
4	CCA schedule
5	Rental property CCA
6	CCA calculations
7	CCA schedule
8	Personal CCA on automobile
9	Sale of eligible capital property
10	Purchase and sale of eligible capital property

Assignment Problems

1	Purchase and sale of assets
2	Leasehold improvements
3	Luxury automobile
4	Eligible capital property, CECA
5	Short fiscal year
6	Available for use
7	Asset disposition
8	CCA schedule
9	CCA on change of use
10	Eligible capital property transactions
11	Eligible capital property transactions
12	Five independent issues
13	CCA schedule

Problem Descriptions

14	Class 12 assets and half-year rule
15	Schedule 1 reconciliation and CCA schedule
16	Insurance and damages receipts
17	Purchase and sale of assets
18	Deductible expenses and employee benefits

CHAPTER 5

Study Notes

¶5,800 REVIEW QUESTIONS

(1) In the year of acquisition only one-half of the capital cost of an asset is added to the CCA class. Comment.

(2) If an asset is sold for less than the UCC balance in the class then there will be a terminal loss. Comment.

(3) The "cost amount" of depreciable property is the original cost of the asset. Comment.

(4) The "capital cost" of depreciable property is the original cost of the asset before any CCA is claimed. Comment.

(5) The half-year rule applies to all property acquired in all CCA classes. Comment.

(6) The half-year rule is designed to take into account the period of ownership during the year and the fact that not all assets are purchased at the beginning of the year. Comment.

(7) CCA can be claimed in the year that title and the incidence of ownership are acquired by the taxpayer. Comment.

(8) Once a CCA claim has been made a taxpayer cannot go back and change the amount of the prior year's claim. Comment.

(9) When the fiscal period of a business is less than 365 days then the CCA must be prorated for the number of days in the fiscal year. Comment.

(10) Once an asset has been disposed of, then no CCA can be claimed on that asset. Comment.

(11) A client bought a new piece of equipment that cost her $50,000. Because of the nature of the asset she has received a government grant of $15,000 to help pay for it. She thinks she can only depreciate $35,000. Comment.

(12) It has cost a client $20,000 in legal fees to obtain a patent on some new equipment. Given his profitability, he is unhappy that he can only depreciate these costs as a Class 14 asset over the 20-year life of the patent but his controller says that he does not have any choice. Comment.

(13) Mrs. Smith has incorporated her company to carry on a retail business. As part of the start-up costs she has paid $800 to have the company incorporated and $10,000 to obtain the indefinite-life franchise that she wanted. Each of these expenditures are eligible capital expenditures and since they are different they each go into their own CEC pool. Comment.

(14) Mr. Fin has come to tell you that he has decided to wind up his business and retire. He is in the process of selling all of his assets but he cannot find one buyer who will continue the business and pay him something for goodwill. He is disappointed since he has a balance of $15,000 in his CEC account that cannot be used. Comment.

¶5,825   MULTIPLE CHOICE QUESTIONS

Question 1

X Ltd. purchased a $50,000 passenger vehicle in 2016. What is the maximum amount that X Ltd. may claim as capital cost allowance for the vehicle in 2016, ignoring harmonized sales tax?

(A) $7,500

(B) $9,000

(C) $4,500

(D) $4,050

Question 2

R Ltd. owns a restaurant business which it carries on in rented premises. R Ltd. redecorated and renovated in 2016 and made $80,000 of leasehold improvements. The lease expires on December 31, 2020 (five years) and has two successive renewal options of three years each. Assuming that R Ltd. has a December 31 year-end, what is the maximum CCA that R Ltd. can claim in 2016 in respect of these improvements?

(A) $5,000

(B) $8,000

(C) $10,000

(D) $16,000

Question 3

In the year, ABC Ltd. purchased goodwill relating to a business for $100,000. Assuming ABC Limited has no other depreciable or eligible capital property, what is the maximum write-off that ABC Ltd. can claim for this goodwill in the year?

(A) $2,500

(B) $3,500

(C) $7,000

(D) $5,250

Question 4

On January 1, 2014, ABC Ltd. signed a five-year lease for retail space for a store. The lease expires on December 31, 2018, and has two successive renewal options for three years each, In 2016, ABC Ltd. made $60,000 of leasehold improvements to this space. Assuming that ABC Ltd. has a December 31 year end, what is the maximum capital cost allowance claim that ABC Ltd. can make in 2016 in respect of these improvements?

(A) $3,750

(B) $5,000

(C) $6,000

(D) $7,500

Question 5

During the year, Swiss Restaurants purchased the following assets for its restaurant and catering business:

Moulds for fancy chocolate items ($300 each) . . . . $ 1,200
An accounting program (computer software) 600
Linens for tables in the restaurants 400
Cutlery, dishes, and kitchen utensils costing less than $500 each 15,000

What is the maximum CCA claim for these assets?

(A) $8,600

(B) $16,300

(C) $16,900

(D) $17,200

Question 6

The new controller of a pharmaceutical company has asked you how the legal costs to obtain a 20-year patent on a new drug are treated for tax purposes. Which one of the following options is not available?

(A) include in Class 14

(B) include in Class 44

(C) deduct in the year incurred

(D) treat as an eligible capital expenditure

¶5,850 EXERCISES

Exercise 1

ITA: 14(5), 20(1)(*a*);
ITR: 1100

Businesses in two plazas operating on either side of a very busy city street decided to pool their promotional efforts. They also decided to build an overpass so that customers could avoid crossing the street when shopping at the plazas. The overpass was constructed at a cost of $150,000 after appropriate arrangements were made with the city because the footings to the overpass had to be placed on city property. These arrangements did not include a leasehold interest in the city property.

— *REQUIRED*

In what class of assets can the overpass be placed for capital cost allowance?

Exercise 2

ITA: 13(7); ITR: 7307(1)

Harrison Chen, an insurance salesperson, acquired a luxury antique sports car in 2016 for a capital cost of $42,000. The car will be used 40% of the time in performing his duties of employment.

— *REQUIRED*

Compute Harrison's estimated CCA in his first and second year of owning the car (ignore HST).

Exercise 3

ITA: 20(16.1), 21(1);
ITR: 1100(2.5), 1100(6)

Scott is a commission salesman who has been claiming capital cost allowance on his automobile under paragraph 8(1)(*j*). The automobile was purchased for $38,000 (including 8% PST and 5% GST) in October 2014. The undepreciated capital cost of his automobile at January 1, 2016, was $20,170. In 2016, he sold the automobile for $12,000. Scott does 75% of his driving for employment purposes out of 16,000 kilometres of total driving.

— *REQUIRED*

(A) What are the tax consequences in 2016 to Scott on the sale of the old car?

(B) What are the tax consequences in 2016 if Scott buys a new car in October 2016 for $36,000 including HST (13%)? His net commission income after deducting cash expenses for 2016 is $3,000.

Exercise 4

ITA: 20(1)(*a*); ITR: 1100;
Sched. II, III

The following balances were found in the various classes of depreciable assets on the books of Wasting Assets Ltd., as at January 1, 2016:

Class 1 (see (1) below)	$120,000
Class 8	75,000
Class 10 (truck for transportation of goods)	40,000
Class 13 (see (2) below)	42,000
Class 14 (see (3) below)	54,400

Additional information and transactions during 2016:

(1) The Class 1 undepreciated capital cost represents two buildings costing $100,000 each. One building was sold for $150,000 during 2016.

(2) The Class 13 balance relates to a long-term lease on a warehouse for 30 years with an option to renew for a further 20 years. The original cost of the leasehold improvements in 2000, when the lease was entered into, was $50,000.

(3) Class 14 consists of a patent for 20 years costing $68,000 on January 1, 2012. (Ignore the effects of the leap years in the period.)

(4) Purchases during the year:

Manufacturing equipment	$50,000
Office equipment	10,000

— *REQUIRED*

Prepare a schedule showing the maximum capital cost allowance deductions for tax purposes in 2016.

Exercise 5

ITA: 13

Liam O'Neille acquired an apartment building a few years ago for $240,000. The cost of the entire property was allocated as follows:

Land	$80,000
Building	$160,000

The UCC of the building as of the beginning of this year was $144,500, and the net rental income for last year was $4,800. Liam turned 65 years old this year and decided to begin his retirement by selling his apartment building. He received $280,000, $100,000 of which was allocated to the land and $180,000 to the building.

— *REQUIRED*

Calculate the maximum capital cost allowance that may be claimed in the current year, and compute the undepreciated capital cost, recapture, or terminal loss.

Exercise 6

ITA: 20(1)

The following are independent situations:

(a) Gimcrack Inc. purchases its sole asset, costing $100,000, on February 15. The company has a February 28 year-end. The asset purchased is a Class 8 asset.

— *REQUIRED*

Calculate the capital cost allowance that may be claimed in the taxation year under the following independent scenarios.

(i) Fiscal period is 365 days.

(ii) Fiscal period is 90 days.

(b) RSI Ltd. sells computers and has a December 31 year end. RSI Ltd. leased a warehouse this year for ten years with a renewal option of two years and a second renewal option of three years. Leasehold improvements of $25,000 were made to the warehouse during the year. RSI has no other leasehold improvement assets.

— *REQUIRED*

Calculate the maximum amount of CCA that may be claimed in this, the first taxation year.

(c) Constabulary Ltd. acquired franchise rights for the amount of $25,000 to operate a doughnut and coffee shop. The franchise is valid for a period of 15 years commencing March 1. Constabulary Ltd.'s year end is July 31.

— *REQUIRED*

What CCA or other deduction is Constabulary Ltd. allowed this year?

Exercise 7

ITA: 20(1)

Mr. E. Presley has been operating an automobile repair business since 2002. The fiscal period of the corporation ends on September 30. The business owns the following assets:

(a) A frame building used as a garage was acquired in 2006. The capital cost of the building in 2006 was $250,000. The UCC of this Class 1 asset was $208,985 as of the last year end. During the current year, renovations were made to the garage in the amount of $20,000.

(b) A warehouse adjacent to the frame building was leased. The lease has a term of five years with five options for renewal of five years each. The lease period commences April 15. The cost of leasehold improvements was $70,000.

(c) Computer equipment was acquired on April 15, 2013. The UCC at October 1, 2015 is $40,000. The equipment was used to perform analysis for repairs.

(d) Two trucks were acquired in a previous fiscal period. The UCC as of the last year end for these Class 10 assets was $25,000. One of the trucks was sold this year for gross proceeds of $10,000. The capital cost of the truck was $15,000. Selling costs incurred to sell the truck were $1,000.

(e) The rights to a licence to sell special racing car parts was purchased for $30,000. The licence is valid for a period of 15 years commencing June 1 this year.

— REQUIRED

Compute CCA for Mr. Presley's automobile repair business for the taxation year ended September 30, 2016. Ignore the leap year effects.

Exercise 8

ITA: 13(7)(*d*)

Steven purchased a car in 2014 for $14,600. His business use of the car during 250 days each year based on mileage of 16,000 kilometres in total and the fair market values of the car in each of the years to the present were as follows:

	Business use	Fair market value
2014	85%	$14,600
2015	80%	12,200
2016	90%	9,800

— REQUIRED

Compute the maximum capital cost allowance that can be claimed.

CHAPTER 5

Exercise 9

ITA: 14(1), 20(1)(*b*)

Ms. Glutton sold her unincorporated grocery business in 2016 and received $45,000 for goodwill. The business had a December 31 year-end.

— REQUIRED

If the grocery store had been purchased on January 2, 2003 with a payment of $10,800 for goodwill at that time, compute the effect of the 2016 sale on Ms. Glutton's income. Assume that maximum deductions for amortization have been made in previous years, except in the years 2005 to 2014 inclusive when no amount was claimed since the business only had losses.

ITA: 20(1)(*b*)

Exercise 10

ITA: 14(1), 20(1)(*b*)

Buylo Ltd., which has been in the same business, except as noted below, since 2008, made the following purchases and sales throughout the period 2008 to 2016.

Jan. 1, 2008	Purchased goodwill at $40,000.
June 1, 2010	Purchased a government licence with an indefinite life for $50,000.
Mar. 1, 2012	Purchased a trademark for $20,000.
Nov. 1, 2013	Purchased goodwill for $50,000.
Sept. 7, 2014	Sold 2007 goodwill for $100,000.
Aug. 3, 2016	Sold all of the remaining assets of the business to a competitor for $500,000 of which $150,000 could be attributed to the licence and $200,000 to the trademark.

— REQUIRED

Calculate the income for the 2014 and 2016 taxation years, assuming the company always took the maximum tax amortization deductions each year for its fiscal years ending December 31. Calculate the amount of cumulative eligible capital as at January 1, 2017.

ITA: 14(1), 20(1)(*b*)

¶5,875 ASSIGNMENT PROBLEMS

Type 1 Problems

Problem 1

As Controller of Acme Inc. you are in the process of completing the corporate tax return. Today, you have come to the fixed asset section and have identified three things you need to do.

(1) Calculate the maximum CCA that can be claimed, as well as any other income inclusions or deductions.

(2) Calculate the ending UCC balance in each class.

(3) Identify adjustments you will need to make to reconcile accounting income and income for tax purposes.

The following is the information in your files:

Acme Inc. has been in business for a number of years. The following are the balances in its CCA classes at the end of its last fiscal year:

Class		Note	Rate	Balance
1	Single building (NRB)	1	6%	$ 225,000
8	Multiple assets	2	20%	30,000
10	Multiple assets	3	30%	20,000
10.1	Passenger vehicle	4	30%	13,000

During the year Acme had the following transactions:

(1) It sold its building and moved into rented space. It received proceeds of $250,000 for the building which had an original cost of $275,000 and a net book value of $180,000.

(2) It sold a class 8 asset for $3,000 which had an original cost of $6,500 and a net book value of $3,600.

(3) It bought a class 10 asset for $6,000. It also sold a class 10 asset for $8,000 which had an original cost of $7,000 and a net book value of $5,500.

(4) It sold the class 10.1 asset for $15,000 which had an original cost of $45,000 and a net book value of $35,000.

Problem 2

When Acme Inc. moved out of their building they rented a building. To make it work for them they had to make leasehold improvements costing $250,000. Their lease has a term of five years with a five-year renewal period. Describe what is included in leasehold improvements. How much can Acme deduct for the leasehold improvements? What lease terms would have been ideal to maximize the tax deduction?

Problem 3

You have received a phone call from the Controller at Seaforth Consulting Inc. They have had some capital transactions and he isn't sure how to treat them for tax purposes. He has asked you to provide him with detailed notes on how to treat them on the company's tax return for its year ended August 31, 2016 and how to report it on Judy's T4 for 2016.

Seaforth, a Canadian-controlled private corporation, provides a car for its president, Judy Wall. In its 2012 fiscal year it purchased a new car for her use costing $45,000 plus HST. On December 31, 2015 they replaced this car; they sold the old one for $25,000 and bought a new one for $50,000 plus 13% HST.

The NBV of the car purchased in 2012 was $27,000 at the time of sale.

What is the impact on the company and on Judy? Assume the company claimed the maximum amount of CCA each year.

Problem 4

One of your tax clients, Mr. Green, has just left you with an assignment.

In 2011 he purchased a health food store. As part of the purchase price he paid $20,000 for goodwill. Since then he has built up the customer base, and in 2016 he sold the store. As part of the selling price he will receive $30,000 for goodwill.

Mr. Green has operated the store as a proprietorship, with a December 31st year end, since he bought it. You quickly checked your files and found that he always claimed the maximum CECA deduction.

Calculate the impact of the sale of goodwill on his income in 2016.

Also, what would the result be if Mr. Green sold the goodwill for:

(a) $20,000; or

(b) $16,000?

Problem 5

Vicky decided to purchase a used building in 2016 to be used in her new business. As part of her planning, she has asked you to tell her what tax deduction she can take on the purchase of the building on September 30th. The cost of the building is $350,000.

Calculate the maximum CCA claim:

(A) Assume she purchased the building personally and that her year end is December 31.

(B) Assume she used a corporation to purchase the building, that it was incorporated on May 1 and that the year end is December 31.

Problem 6

Huang Manufacturing Inc. has been in business for many years. It has a December 31st year end. In 2016, the company bought a new manufacturing machine at a cost of $500,000 plus HST. They received the machine on November 30th, but it took some time for them to install it, so it wasn't ready to be used until January 15, 2017.

Calculate the maximum CCA that can be claimed in 2016 and 2017 related to this machine.

Problem 7

ITA: 13, 20(16)

Silvia Fields is the self-employed operator of a VIP delivery service. Three years ago, Silvia purchased her only asset, a van, for a cost of $24,000. The van has been used 100% for business deliveries since it was purchased. The UCC balance in Class 10 at the beginning of this year is $14,280. On March 1, Silvia sold the van for $10,300 and leased a new van for $400 a month.

Sylvia would like you to explain the income tax implications of the disposition of the van.

Problem 8

ITA: 13(1), 13(2), 20(1)(a), 20(16.1); ITR: 1100(1), 1100(2.5), 1100 (3), 1101(5p), 1103(2h), 7307(1)(b); Sch. II, III

On March 1, 2015, Jennifer Lobo incorporated Lobo Enterprises Inc. (LEI) with a December 31 year-end. The corporation purchased the licence to manufacture the computer software version of the latest trivia game, "Tax is a Microcosm of Life on DVD". LEI acquired the following assets:

Manufacturing equipment	$20,000
Tools (each costing under $500)	16,000
Dies and moulds	8,000
Computer equipment and systems software	12,000
Photocopier	6,000
Office furnishings	15,000
Customer lists (expected to be used indefinitely)	4,000
Delivery van	28,000
TV commercial video tape	22,000
Chairs and tables (for the employee eating area)	2,500
Automobile (for use by sales manager)	38,000
Licence to manufacture, based on patented information, "Tax is a Microcosm of Life on DVD" for three years ending February 28, 2018	30,000

Made improvements on the building that LEI leased on March 1, 2015; the
lease was for three years with two successive options to renew of
three years and four years 9,000

During 2016, LEI made the following disposals:

Sold the photocopier .... (4,000)
Sold the automobile .... (23,000)
Sold the TV commercial video tape .... (18,000)
Sold some of the tools (costing less than $500 each) .... (5,000)

You have been asked to prepare a schedule to show the maximum capital cost allowance for the fiscal years ended December 31, 2015 and December 31, 2016, ignoring HST considerations. For file documentation, where choices are available, state the reasons for your decision. Ignore the effects, if any, of a leap year.

Problem 9

ITA: 13(7)

On January 20, 2014, a personal residence which originally cost $280,000 was converted into a rental property. At this time the property had a fair market value of $320,000. On June 1, 2016, the property was sold for fair market value of $305,000.

You have been asked to research the following question. If the building is the only asset in Class 1, which has a 4% capital cost allowance rate, how much capital cost allowance may be deducted for the years 2014 through 2016, inclusive? [Note that where an individual has income from property, the taxation year for that income is the full calendar year, i.e., there cannot be a short taxation year for that income.]

Problem 10

ITA: 14, 20(1)(*b*)

Sharp is a musician who paid $500 in 2006 for an indefinite-life licence to perform in the subway walkway areas. In 2011, Sharp decided to try a different approach to developing a following. He purchased the name of a popular local band that stopped performing earlier that year. The cost of the name was $16,128 and the appropriate amount was included in the January 1, 2012 balance below. In 2012, he purchased an indefinite-life licence from the city for $5,000 which allowed him to perform on a street corner on Saturday afternoons. In 2013, Sharp found that he wanted to spend more time in the studio, so he sold the street corner licence for $6,000. In 2016, Sharp decided to break up his band and pursue a career as an accountant. He sold the band name for $20,000.

Sharp has not yet filed his tax return for 2016. The year-end of the business is December 31. The following information is available with respect to the cumulative eligible capital account:

(a) the balance in the cumulative eligible capital account, on January 1, 2012, was $11,492, and

(b) the total cumulative eligible capital amount claimed prior to 2012 was $979.

You have been asked to prepare a schedule calculating the balance of the cumulative eligible capital account on January 1, 2017, and calculating the impact on income for 2016.

Problem 11

ITA: 14, 20(1)(*b*),
20(1)(*cc*); IT-206R

Con-Glo Corporation has been involved in various food services businesses since its incorporation in 2003. Con-Glo has a December 31 year-end. You have been asked by the controller to examine the transactions involving various intangible assets due to an impending sale of the business. The controller wants to ensure that he understands the implications on the sale. You have been provided with the following information.

Shortly after the business was incorporated, Con-Glo purchased its first family restaurant. The purchase price included $43,000 for goodwill. After operating this business for a number of years and ensuring that it was profitable, another restaurant was purchased in 2009. The purchase again included goodwill in the amount of $68,000. The second restaurant had more of a roadhouse atmosphere. The business had obtained an unlimited life liquor licence. The value of the licence at the time of the purchase was $21,133, and this amount was allocated to the licence in the purchase agreement.

Con-Glo operated the two restaurants until 2010 when it purchased a fast food franchise. The franchise was for an undefined number of years and cost $103,000.

The fast food restaurant, while successful, was too much of a drain on the time of the owners of Con-Glo and was sold in 2013. The value of the franchise agreement was determined to be $110,000.

In 2014, it was determined that the original family restaurant would be more successful if it obtained a liquor licence. In order to obtain the licence a presentation had to be made to the liquor licensing board. Con-Glo paid $29,000 in legal fees related to the presentation to the board.

In 2015, the second restaurant was sold. Con-Glo received $80,000 for the goodwill and $60,000 for the liquor licence.

Due to health problems of the owner's wife, Con-Glo is also considering a sale of the balance of their restaurants in 2016. The selling price will include $250,000 for goodwill.

The controller has asked you to prepare a schedule calculating the balance of the cumulative eligible capital account as of January 1, 2017, and determine the impact of the above transactions on income for 2009 through 2016. Assume that the opening balance on January 1, 2009, was $20,865, the 2003 to 2008 CECA deductions were a total of $11,385, and that the company took the maximum tax write-offs that it was entitled to in each of the years 2009 to 2014. (Hint: consider paragraph 20(1)(*cc*).) Assume also that Con-Glo was deemed to be in the same business in respect of its restaurant and fast food business as per IT-206R.

Problem 12

ITA: 20(1), 20(16)

For each of the following independent situations identify the deduction for CCA, amortization, or other amount.

(a) Janice Martin was an employee of Bayshore Ltd. She was required to use her car in her employment duties and at the end of last year the UCC of her car (Class 10) was $3,500. She left Bayshore during this year and began working for Executive Search Service, where she was not required to use her car. Janice sold her car this year for $3,200.

(b) Ramesh acquired a rental building on September 1 this year at a cost of $75,000. His net rental income for the four months is $2,000. He wants to claim the maximum CCA.

(c) In 2006, William acquired two rental buildings at a cost of $60,000 each. He has sold one for $90,000. The UCC of each building was $45,000. Ignore any capital gain.

(d) Colin bought a piece of land that he is renting to a farmer for pasturing his cows. The land cost $35,000 and Colin received $1,500 in rent. Is Colin restricted on the CCA he is allowed?

(e) Randi sold her rental property last year for $100,000. The allocation was $75,000 for the building and $25,000 for the land. Her legal fees for selling the property were $2,000. What are her proceeds of disposition for the building?

Problem 13

ITA: 13, 14, 20(1)(a),
20(1)(b); ITR: 1100;
Sched. II, III

Jon's Auto Parts Ltd., which manufactures small equipment, was incorporated in 1992 and had the following balances in its records concerning its capital assets as at January 1, 2016.

| | Depreciation | | CCA | |
Type of asset	Straight-line	Book value	Class	UCC
Land	Nil	$102,000		Nil
Building	40 years	900,000	1	$568,000
Equipment	5 years	163,000	8	39,000
Rolling stock — trucks, etc. (for transportation of goods)	3 years	306,000	10	170,000
Leasehold improvements (see note (1), below)	life of lease	113,000	13	165,000
Licences	5 years	70,000	14	87,393

Additional Information

(1) The Class 13 assets consist of:

— Improvements to a leased warehouse costing $100,000 in 2015. The remaining length of the lease in 2015 was six years with two successive options of four years.

— Improvements to a leased office space for head office downtown, costing $81,600 in 2014. The remaining length of the lease was five years with an option to renew for an additional one year.

(2) The licences were purchased to start on April 22, 2014, at a cost of $110,500 and had a life of five years.

(3) During 2016, the company had the following capital transactions:

Additions:
— Purchased, in June, a new concrete manufacturing building costing $1,625,000, including $325,000 for land.
— Additional expenditures re the building:

Paved parking lot for employees	$ 97,000
Erected a steel fence around an outside storage area	65,000

— Further renovations to leased office space, costing 51,000
— Purchased equipment:

Office equipment	$ 47,000
Manufacturing equipment	255,000
Radio communication equipment	60,000

— Purchased a distributing licence on March 1, 2016, for five years from a foreign manufacturing company of a related product line, cost: $240,000.
— Paid $34,500 in legal fees in reorganizing the capital structure.

Disposals:

	Cost	Book value	Proceeds
Equipment — office	$ 16,250	$ 4,225	$ 1,950
Brick building in Cl. 1 (excluding land)	1,400,000	900,000	568,000

You have been asked to prepare a schedule for tax purposes to reflect the above transactions and calculate the maximum write-off for tax purposes. (Ignore the effects of the replacement property rules in subsection 13(4) and the effects of leap years.)

Problem 14

ITR: 1100(2)

Both cutlery and word processing software are included in Class 12. Determine, by specific reference to the *Income Tax Regulations*, whether the half-year rule applies to these two items.

Type 2 Problems

Problem 15

ITA: 13, 14, 18–20;
ITR: 1100; Sched. II, III

The controller of Choleva Products Limited has provided you with the following draft income statement as well as some notes that she made during the preparation of this statement.

Choleva Products Limited

STATEMENT OF INCOME
For the year ended December 31, 2016

Sales		$ 8,300,000
Cost of goods sold (Note (1))		(6,800,000)
Gross profit		$ 1,500,000
Commission income		70,000
		$ 1,570,000
Administrative and marketing expenses (Note (2))	$500,000	
Amortization (Note (3))	80,000	
Interest on long-term debt (Note (4))	70,000	
Interest on bank indebtedness	120,000	(770,000)
		$ 800,000
Gain on disposal of property, plant and equipment (Note (3))		40,000
Net income before income taxes		$ 840,000
Provision for income taxes		(400,000)
Net income after income taxes		$ 440,000

Notes Prepared by Controller:

(1) The cost of goods sold expense includes the following amounts:

(a) A $9,000 loss from a theft by a warehouse employee;

(b) A $15,000 reserve for future decline in the value of inventory because of new products expected to be introduced by the competitor. There was no such reserve in 2015.

(2) Administration and marketing expenses include:

(a) An $11,000 increase in the reserve for warranty expenses;

(b) $4,000 of donations to registered charities;

(c) $1,500 for golf club membership dues for the Vice-President of Sales and $2,000 for meals and entertainment expenses at the golf club. The Vice-President of Sales uses the club to generate sales;

(d) $85,000 in accrued bonuses, including $62,000 paid to employees on May 31, 2017, and $23,000 paid to employees on June 30, 2017;

(e) A $15,000 year-end party for all employees;

(f) $8,000 of financing fees incurred in connection with the mortgage of the corporation's new plant, including legal fees of $6,000 and an appraisal fee of $2,000;

(g) $5,000 of legal fees in connection with the purchase of shares of another company; and

(h) $300 for an upgrade of word processing software.

(3) The fixed asset section of the controller's working papers indicate the following:

(a) The undepreciated capital cost balances at December 31, 2015 were as follows:

Class 1	$200,000
Class 8	60,000
Class 10	80,000
Class 13	37,500
CEC	5,000

(b) Gain on disposal of property of plant and equipment consists of the profit on the sale of the corporation's only Class 1 asset (proceeds: $180,000; original cost in 1992: $300,000). The land on which the building was situated was also sold for its fair market value which was equal to its cost in 1992.

(c) During 2016, the corporation made the following purchases:

- A new office building was purchased in October for $700,000. The cost of the related land was $400,000. It cost $20,000 to pave part of the land for use as a parking lot;

- New office furniture was purchased for $25,000. This purchase replaced office furniture which was sold for its $4,000 net book value (original cost: $10,000);

- An unlimited life franchise was purchased for $100,000;

- A 10-year licence to use patented information (expiring June 30, 2026) was purchased on July 1 for $20,000; and

- Improvements on its leased head office premises which were rented in 2014 for four years with two successive options to renew for five years and five years. Improvements had originally been made in 2014 in the amount of $45,000. Additional improvements were made in 2016 at a cost of $28,000.

(d) During the year, the corporation sold some small tools (each costing less than $500) for their net book value of $500.

(4) Interest on long-term debt includes:

    (a) Bond discount amortization in the amount of $2,000;

    (b) $18,000 of interest on bonds issued to buy shares in another company; and

    (c) $50,000 of interest on the mortgage on the new plant.

You have been asked to calculate the corporation's minimum income from business or property for the year ended December 31, 2016. Assume that all expenses are reasonable in the circumstances. For file documentation purposes, you have been asked to support your treatment of each item listed above with a reason or a section reference. Ignore the effects of leap years.

Type 3 Problems

Problem 16

RBL Proprietorship was heavily damaged during a recent street riot. The mobs broke in, set fire to the store, and physically assaulted the owner, Larry. Fortunately the business was insured, and the owner received the following amounts without delay:

Personal injury damage award	$ 50,000
Insurance receipts — business interruption	80,000
Insurance receipts for delivery truck destroyed	30,000
Insurance receipts for leaseholds destroyed by fire	15,000
	$175,000

The undepreciated capital cost in Class 10 is $15,000 and in Class 13, $10,000. The original cost of the truck was $35,000 and the original cost of the leaseholds was $20,000.

Larry does not understand why the damages are not treated as an expense for tax purposes. RBL plans to replace the truck immediately. The damage to the leaseholds, however, presents a challenge because the cost to repair the damage far exceeds the insurance compensation. RBL is considering relocating its business to a safer location. The company will then be able to change its image to suit a new clientele. The architect estimates that the leasehold improvements could be completed in 12 months. The total cost for the move would be as follows:

Moving costs	$ 12,000
Business interruption	48,000
Leasehold improvements	60,000
Lease cancellation penalty	4,400
Total	$124,400

Larry would like your advice on the tax implications of his plans.

Problem 17

Dundas Printing Inc. has been in business for the past 20 years. It has only been in the past three years that Bill Peach has taken over the operations from his father (who founded the company and is now retired). As a result of his new-found management freedom and changes in the marketplace, Bill has decided to expand his operations.

One of the printing presses he needed to buy would have been too expensive if he had bought it new, so he found a used press at half the price. The drawback is that it will take some time to get the press into production, since it needs some repairs to put it into workable condition. However, Bill feels that this is still a good buy since it will meet his needs for the next five years, by which time new technology will probably make it obsolete and he will be forced to buy a new machine.

Before his retirement, Bill's father drove a car that the company had purchased for his use at a cost of $45,000. The car was given to Bill for his use on his father's retirement. Bill has now decided that he is going to trade in this car for a car that he always wanted — a sports car that is going to cost $65,000 less the trade-in value of $25,000 for the old car. Bill promises to take you for a ride when it is delivered.

In order to increase his market share, Bill bought all of the assets of one of his competitors. This not only gave him access to some important customers, it also allowed him to acquire some specialized equipment and skilled operators. The vendor had wanted to sell Bill the shares of his company, but Bill had convinced the vendor to sell him the assets, instead, including goodwill of $40,000.

Bill would like your advice on the tax implications of his plans.

Problem 18

Kingston Carpets Inc. ("Kingston") has been operating a retail carpet business out of the same location for the past 18 years. It has been very successful in gaining business from the local developers, who use Kingston almost exclusively to provide their flooring. In addition, Kingston is used extensively by the area insurance adjusters for carpet replaced due to fire and other damages. This business did not come to Kingston overnight. The owners, Andy and Sue Greene, have always spent much of their time promoting their business to these markets.

Both Andy and Sue are avid golfers. They each belong to a different golf club, in order to be members at the clubs where most of their customers play. They find that golf is an activity that has paid off, since they have conducted a significant amount of business through their contacts at the golf clubs. They will often use these clubs for lunch and dinner meetings with customers, as well as for the company's seasonal holiday party.

Last year, the company bought a building across the street from its original retail store. The previous owner had been leasing out the building and had not spent much money on repairs over the last five years. As a result, while Kingston paid a relatively low price for the property, it has had to spend a considerable amount on repairs over the past year. Prior to this purchase, Kingston had been leasing its space.

To maintain their image of success, Sue and Andy both drive expensive cars and often entertain customers at their cottage or on their boat. This approach seems to work, and their customers are always asking when the next outing will be.

Besides treating their customers well, Sue and Andy also treat their employees well. All employees belong to the group benefit plan that provides extended health care, dental, life insurance, and disability coverage. Because of the low coverage from the company's group life and disability insurance, Andy and Sue have had the company take out individual policies on both of them. The beneficiary on the life insurance policies is the company, and on the disability policies the beneficiaries are Andy and Sue.

One of their valued employees was recently divorced and during the divorce her family home was sold. In order to keep her concentrating on business, Andy and Sue had the company loan her enough to buy a house. The loan was secured by the house and no interest was charged. At that time, the company did not have enough cash to make this loan so it had to borrow the funds at prime plus 1/2%.

In addition to all of this, Andy and Sue have been actively involved in a number of charitable and political activities and have made donations to both. Even these activities have turned into business opportunities. Last year, they gave a donation to a local charity and shortly thereafter they received an order for the new carpet that was to go in the charity's offices.

Advise Sue and Andy on the tax implications of their situation and that of Kingston Carpets.

 [For more problems and solutions thereto, see the DVD accompanying the textbook.]

CHAPTER 5 —
DISCUSSION NOTES FOR REVIEW QUESTIONS

(1) The full amount of the capital cost is added to the CCA class. The half-year rule makes a separate adjustment for purposes of calculating CCA in the year of acquisition, but this adjustment does not affect the capital cost.

ITR: 1100(2)

(2) A terminal loss is allowed only when the asset sold is the last asset in the class. Otherwise, the proceeds are credited to the UCC of the class under the definition of "undepreciated capital cost" and CCA is claimed on the remaining balance.

ITA: 13(21), 20(16)

(3) "Cost amount" reflects the tax value of an asset at a particular moment in time. With respect to depreciable property, cost amount is that proportion of the UCC that the capital cost of the asset is of the capital cost of all the assets in the class. Capital cost is not defined, but as used here, it means the laid-down cost which includes the actual cost plus all costs of preparing the asset for use.

ITA: 248(1) "cost amount"

ITA: 13(21)

(4) The "capital cost" is the amount that is added to the CCA class when the asset is first acquired [item A in the definition of "undepreciated capital cost"]. See (3) above for a broadly worded definition.

ITA: 13(21)

(5) Certain exceptions to the half-year rule are found in the Regulations. However, regulations for leaseholds and for classes like Classes 24, 27, and 29 provide their own version of the half-year rule.

ITR: 1100(2)
ITR: 1100(1)(*b*), 1100(1)(*t*), 1100(1)(*ta*)

(6) The half-year rule is a simple, arbitrary adjustment that is made to reflect a period of ownership during the year. It is a simpler alternative to prorating CCA for the number of days the asset is owned during the year.

(7) Normally, the statement is true. However, the "available-for-use" rules do not allow CCA to be claimed until the asset is available for use by the taxpayer.

ITA: 13(26)–(32)

(8) An Information Circular provides the CRA's position on when the CCA claim for prior years can be changed. If the change results in a lower taxable income for the year, it must be requested within the normal time limits for appeals (see Chapter 14). If the change does not result in a lower taxable income, as, for example, the case of a loss year, the change will be allowed.

IC 84-1, par. 9, 10

(9) A regulation provides for this daily proration in the case of the short taxation year of a business, as might occur, for example, in the start-up year of a corporation. The taxation year of a proprietorship is the 12-month calendar year, since there is no distinction between the proprietorship business and the individual proprietor. Hence, no proration is required in that case.

ITR: 1100(3)

(10) Normally, this statement is true. However, a regulation allows a CCA claim equal to one-half the normal CCA in the year of disposition, as compensation for the inability to claim a terminal loss on the disposal of a Class 10.1 automobile. To qualify, the taxpayer must have sold an auto that was in Class 10.1 and that was owned by him or her at the end of the preceding year.

ITR: 1100(2.5)

(11) Your client is correct. The Act reduces the capital cost of depreciable property for grants, subsidies, forgivable loans, deductions from tax, investment allowances or other assistance received on the acquisition of the property. CCA should only be claimed on actual or net cost.

ITA: 13(7.1)

(12) There are four choices available for the legal costs of obtaining the patent:

(a) deduct them as expenses of representation;

ITA: 20(1)(*cc*)

(b) deduct the costs equally over 10 years;

ITA: 20(9)

(c) capitalize them in Class 14 by an election not to include them in Class 44 and depreciate them over the life of the patent; or

ITR: 1103(2h)

(d) capitalize the costs in Class 44 and depreciate them at a 25% declining-balance rate.

Any deduction under paragraph 20(1)(*cc*) or subsection 20(9) is subject to recapture.

ITA: 13(12); IT-99R5

(13) There is only *one* CEC pool for all eligible capital expenditures for each business. Since Mrs. Smith is only carrying on one business within her corporation, the additions to the company's CEC account in the year will be 75% of $10,800.

(14) He is able to deduct the full CEC balance as a business loss in the year that he ceased to carry on business.

ITA: 24

CHAPTER 5

CHAPTER 5 — SOLUTIONS TO MULTIPLE CHOICE QUESTIONS

Question 1

(C) is correct. The maximum CCA is: $\frac{1}{2} \times 30\% \times \$30,000 = \$4,500$.

ITA: 13(7)(*g*); ITR: 7307(1)

(A) incorrectly uses the $50,000 cost of the vehicle to compute CCA: $\frac{1}{2} \times 30\% \times \$50,000 = \$7,500$.

(B) incorrectly ignores the half-year rule: $30\% \times \$30,000 = \$9,000$.

(D) incorrectly uses the pre-2001 maximum Class 10.1 cost of $27,000: $\frac{1}{2} \times 30\% \times \$27,000 = \$4,050$.

Question 2

(A) is correct. $10,000 is the lesser of $\frac{1}{5} \times \$80,000 = \$16,000$ and $80,000/8 = $10,000. For 2016, the year the cost was incurred, the maximum CCA = 50% of $10,000 = $5,000.

ITR: 1100(1)(*b*), Sch. III

(B) is incorrect. It is 50% of the $16,000 amount calculated in (A).

(C) is incorrect because the $10,000 figure does not take into account the 50% rule.

ITR: 1100(1)(*b*)

(D) is incorrect for the reasons outlined for (B) and (C) combined.

Question 3

(D) is correct. The maximum CECA claim is: $75\% \times \$100,000 \times 7\% = \$5,250$.

(A) is incorrect: $100,000/40 = $2,500. Forty years is the maximum period for amortization of goodwill for accounting purposes only.

(B) is incorrect: $\frac{1}{2} \times \$100,000 \times 7\% = \$3,500$. The $\frac{1}{2}$ rate does not apply for purposes of additions to the CEC pool.

(C) is incorrect: $7\% \times \$100,000 = \$7,000$. Only 75% of the cost is used before multiplying by 7%.

Question 4

(B) is correct because the remaining lease term in 2016 is three years and the first renewal period is three years. The maximum CCA claim is $5,000, calculated as follows:

Lesser of: (i) $\frac{1}{5} \times \$60,000$ = $12,000
           (ii) $60,000/(3 + 3)   = $10,000

For 2016, the year the cost was incurred, the maximum CCA is: 50% of $10,000 = $5,000.

ITR: 1100(1)(*b*)

(A) is incorrect, because it uses the initial 5-year term of the lease in the calculation in place of the remaining lease term of three years: $60,000/(5 + 3) = $7,500 × 50% = $3,750.

(C) is incorrect, because the greater ($12,000), as opposed to the lesser ($10,000), of the two amounts calculated has been used: $6,000 = 50% × $12,000.

(D) is incorrect, because it uses the initial 5-year term of the lease in the calculation in place of the remaining lease term of three years and ignores the 50% rule in Regulation 1100(1)(*b*): $60,000/(5 + 3) = $7,500.

Question 5

(B) is correct. Under the Regulations, dies and moulds and software are not excepted from the half   net-amount rule, but the other Class 12 items are: linens are listed in paragraph (*g*), cutlery and dishes are listed in paragraph (*b*) and kitchen utensils costing less than $500 are listed in paragraph (*c*). ½ ($1,200 + $600) + $15,000 + $400 = $16,300.

(A) is incorrect because it uses the half-year rule on all Class 12 assets: ½ ($1,200 + $600 + $15,000 + $400) = $8,600.

(C) is incorrect because it ignores the half-year rule on the dies and moulds: $1,200 + ½ × $600 + $15,000 + $400 = $16,900.

(D) is incorrect because it ignores the half-year rule on the dies and moulds and software: $1,200 + $600 + $15,000 + $400 = $17,200.

Question 6

(D) is not available, since the property is not eligible capital property.

(A), (B), and (C) are all options for the treatment of patent costs.

CHAPTER 5 — SOLUTIONS TO EXERCISES

Exercise 1

The overpass is not eligible for capital cost allowance, since the owners have no title to the land on which the footings are placed and capital cost allowance cannot be claimed on assets that are not owned (see *Saskatoon Community Broadcasting Co. Ltd. v. M.N.R.*). The cost of the overpass qualifies as an eligible capital expenditure.

58 DTC 491 (T.A.B.)

Exercise 2

Harrison's automobile is defined as a passenger vehicle for CCA purposes. Passenger vehicles with a cost in excess of $30,000 (2016 amount) must be placed into a separate CCA class, Class 10.1. The depreciation rate for class 10.1 assets is 30%. However, CCA may only be taken on the deemed capital cost of the vehicle up to a maximum of $30,000 (paragraph 13(7)(a) and ITR 7307(1)). Harrison's maximum CCA claim for the first and second year of owning the car would be calculated as follows:

ITA: 13(7); ITR: 7307(1)

Year 1

Capital cost of additions	$30,000
Less CCA (30,000 × 30% × 50%*)	4,500
UCC, end of year 1	$25,500

* Half-year rule applied.

Business use CCA (CCA × usage %) = $4,500 × 40% = $1,800

Year 2

UCC, Beginning of Year 2	$25,500
Less CCA @ 30%	7,650
UCC, end of Year 2	$17,850

Business use CCA (CCA × usage %) = $7,650 × 40% = $3,060

Exercise 3

No terminal loss can be deducted for an automobile in Class 10.1. The special "half-year rule" to compute capital cost allowance in the year of disposition applies to Class 10.1.

ITA: 20(16.1); ITR: 1100(2.5)

(A)	Jan.	1/16	UCC (Class 10.1)	$ 20,170
		2016	CCA (½ × .30 × $20,170)	(3,026)[1]
			Proceeds of disposition	(12,000)
			Terminal loss of $5,144 denied	Nil
(B)		2016	Purchase ($36,000) (new Class 10.1) max.	$ 33,900[2]
	Dec. 31/16		UCC before adjustment	$ 33,900
			One-half of net amount (½ × $33,900)	(16,950)
			UCC before CCA	$ 16,950
			CCA @ 30% of $16,950	(5,085)[3]
			Add: ½ net amount	16,950
	Jan.	1/17	UCC	$ 28,815

— *NOTES TO SOLUTION*

[1] Note that 75% of $3,026 or $2,270 is the deduction based on business use.

[2] Limited to $30,000 plus HST (13%) or $33,900, since it was acquired after 2000.

[3] Note that 75% of $5,085 or $3,814 is deductible, since CCA claimed is not subject to the limitation on sales/negotiating person's expenses.

ITA: 8(1)(f), 8(1)(j)

Exercise 4

	Cl. 1: 4%	Cl. 8: 20%	Cl. 10: 30%	Cl. 13: S.L.	Cl. 14: S.L.	Cl. 29: 50%
Jan. 1/16						
UCC	$120,000	$75,000	$40,000	$42,000	$54,400	Nil
2016 Purchases:						
— mfg. equip.						$50,000
— off. equip.		10,000				
Disposals:						
— building	(100,000)[1]					
— equip.						
Dec. 31/16						
UCC before adjustment	$ 20,000	$85,000	$40,000	$42,000	$54,400	$50,000
½ net amount	Nil	(5,000)	Nil	Nil	N/A	(25,000)
UCC before CCA	$ 20,000	$80,000	$40,000	$42,000	$54,400	$25,000
CCA	(800)	(16,000)	(12,000)	(1,250)[2]	(3,400)[3]	(12,500)
½ net amount	Nil	5,000	Nil	Nil	N/A	25,000
Jan. 1/17						
UCC	$ 19,200	$69,000	$28,000	$40,750	$51,000	$37,500

— NOTES TO SOLUTION

[1] Capital gain on disposition of building of $50,000.

[2] Lesser of: (a) ⅕ of $50,000 .... $10,000

(b) $50,000/40 (max.) .... $ 1,250 } $1,250

— not reduced by ½ because not first year of ownership.

[3] $\dfrac{\$68,000}{(20 \times 365)} \times 365 = \$3,400$

Exercise 5

The proceeds from the sale of Liam's building are greater than the UCC of the building. This would indicate that, although Liam claimed CCA in previous years, the market value of the building did not decline. Accordingly, CCA claimed in previous years must be recaptured and added to income for tax purposes in the current year. Liam must report recaptured CCA of $15,500, calculated as follows:

ITA: 13

Class 1 — 4%		
UCC, beginning of year		$144,500
Less disposition at lesser of:		
Capital cost	$160,000	
Net proceeds	$180,000	160,000
Recaptured CCA		$(15,500)

Note that no CCA may be claimed in the year of the disposition since the UCC balance in the class after recapture is nil.

Exercise 6

(a)(i) $100,000 \times 20\% \times \frac{1}{2} = \$10,000$ ITA: 20(1)

   (ii) $100,000 \times 20\% \times \frac{1}{2} \times (90/365) = \$2,466$

In (ii), CCA is prorated because the taxation year is less than 365 days.

(b) Leasehold improvements — CCA is lesser of

   (1) $25,000 \times \frac{1}{5} \times \frac{1}{2} = \$2,500$

   (2) $25,000 \times \frac{1}{12} \times \frac{1}{2} = \$1,042$

(Twelve years is the denominator; this includes the initial lease term and the first renewal period.)

(c) The franchise is for a limited term, hence it is a Class 14 asset. The CCA on Class 14 assets is computed on a straight-line basis over the remaining life of the asset. The half-year rule does not apply to Class 14. CCA allowed to July 31 (153 days) is:

$25,000 \times \frac{1}{15} \times (153/365) = \$699$

Exercise 7

ITA: 20(1)

a.	**Class 1** $(\$208,895 + \frac{1}{2} (\$20,000)) \times 4\% =$	$ 8,756
b.	**Class 13 — Leasehold Improvements**	
	Lesser of:	
	(i) $\frac{1}{10} \times \frac{1}{2} \times 70,000$ — $3,500	
	(ii) $\frac{1}{5} \times \frac{1}{2} \times 70,000$ — $7,000	
	CCA for the year	$ 3,500
c.	**Class 50 (Computer equipment)**	
	UCC, beginning of year	$40,000
	Additions	0
		$40,000
	CCA 40,000 × 55%	22,000
	UCC, end of year	$18,000
d.	Class 10 (trucks)	
	UCC, beginning of year	$25,000
	Less dispositions ($10,000 – $1,000)	(9,000)
		$16,000
	CCA 30%	4,800
	UCC, end of year	$11,200
e.	**Class 14 — Licence**	
	$30,000 \times \frac{1}{15} \times (122*/365)$	$ 668

* Number of days from June 1 to September 30.

Exercise 8

The change in use rules could be applied as follows: ITA: 13(7)(*d*)

		Cl. 10:[(1)] *30%*
2014	Purchase (85% of $14,600)	$12,410
Dec. 31, 2014	UCC	$12,410
	CCA @ 30% of [($12,410 – (½ × $12,410)]	(1,862)
Jan. 1, 2015	UCC	$10,548
2015	Disposal (5% of $12,200)[(2)]	(610)
Dec. 31, 2015	UCC	$ 9,938
	CCA @ 30% of $9,938	(2,981)

Jan. 1, 2016	UCC	$ 6,957	
2016	Purchase (10% of $9,800)[3]	980	
Dec. 31, 2016	UCC	$ 7,937	
	CCA @ 30% of [$7,937 – (½ × $980)]	(2,234)	
Jan. 1, 2017	UCC	$ 5,703	

In practice, however, the following calculation of capital cost allowance might be made:

		Cl. 10: 30%	*Business deduction of CCA*
2014	Purchase..............	$14,600	
Dec. 31, 2014	UCC	$14,600	
	CCA @ 30% of ½ ×		
	$14,600	(2,190)	85% of $2,190 = $1,862
Dec. 31, 2015	UCC	$12,410	
	CCA @ 30%	(3,723)	80% of $3,723 = $2,978
Dec. 31, 2016	UCC	$ 8,687	
	CCA @ 30%	(2,606)	[80% + ½ (90% – 80%)][4]
			of $2,606 = $2,215
Jan. 1, 2017	UCC	$ 6,081	

—NOTES TO SOLUTION

[1] Since the automobile cost less than the prescribed limit, it is placed in Class 10.   ITA: 13(7)(*g*)

[2] Lesser of proceeds at fair market value and capital cost.

[3] Since fair market value is less than cost, the increase in capital cost is based on fair market value.

[4] An increase in use for business represents an addition to the class which is subject to the half-year rule. In practice, the CCA may be computed simply as 90% of $2,606 or $2,345.

Exercise 9

The cumulative eligible capital account would be affected as follows:

Year	Opening balance	Par. 20(1)(b) deduction[1]	Ssec. 14(1) business income inclusion	Closing balance
2003	$ 8,100	$ 567		$7,533
2004[2]	7,533	527		7,006
2015	7,006	490		6,516
2016	6,516	—	$18,684[3]	
Total		$1,584		

2016 Opening balance	$ 6,516	
Sale (¾ × $45,000)	(33,750)	
Negative balance	(27,234)	
Minus: previous CECA claims	1,584	
Balance	$(25,650)	
Income inclusion:		
Previous CECA claims	$ 1,584	
⅔ × $25,650	17,100	
Total	18,684	
Untaxed: ⅓ × ¾ × ($45,000 – $10,800)	8,550	
	$ 27,234	

— NOTES TO SOLUTION
    (1) 7% of the declining balance.

    (2) No amortization deductions taken in the 2004–2013 period because of business losses.   ITA: 20(1)(b)

    (3) The sale in 2015 would result in $18,684 of business income which is equal to the sum (rounded) of par. 20(1)(b) deductions ($1,584) plus ½ of the gain of $34,200 ($45,000 – $10,800).

Exercise 10

Jan. 1, 2008	Purchase of goodwill (¾ × $40,000)	$	30,000
Dec. 31, 2008	Cumulative eligible capital amount @ 7%		(2,100)
Jan. 1, 2009	Cumulative eligible capital	$	27,900
Dec. 31, 2009	Cumulative eligible capital amount @ 7%		(1,953)
Jan. 1, 2010	Cumulative eligible capital	$	25,947
June 1, 2010	Purchase of licence (¾ × $50,000)		37,500
	Cumulative eligible capital	$	63,447
Dec. 31, 2010	Cumulative eligible capital amount @ 7%		(4,441)
Jan. 1, 2011	Cumulative eligible capital	$	59,006
Dec. 31, 2011	Cumulative eligible capital amount @ 7%		(4,130)
Jan. 1, 2012	Cumulative eligible capital	$	54,876
Mar. 1, 2012	Purchase of trademark (¾ × $20,000)		15,000
	Cumulative eligible capital	$	69,876
Dec. 31, 2012	Cumulative eligible capital amount @ 7%		(4,891)
Jan. 1, 2013	Cumulative eligible capital	$	64,985
Nov. 1, 2013	Purchase of goodwill (¾ × $50,000)		37,500
	Cumulative eligible capital	$	102,485
Dec. 31, 2013	Cumulative eligible capital amount @ 7%		(7,174)
Jan. 1, 2014	Cumulative eligible capital	$	95,311
Sept. 7, 2014	Sale of goodwill (¾ × $100,000)		(75,000)
	Cumulative eligible capital	$	20,311
Dec. 31, 2014	Cumulative eligible capital amount @ 7%		(1,422)
Jan. 1, 2015	Cumulative eligible capital	$	18,889
Dec. 31, 2015	Cumulative eligible capital amount @ 7%		(1,322)
Jan. 1, 2016	Cumulative eligible capital	$	17,567
Aug. 3, 2016	Sale of license (¾ × $150,000)		(112,500)
	Sale of trademark (¾ × $200,000)		(150,000)
Dec. 31, 2016	Cumulative eligible capital		$(244,933)
	Business income		172,433
	Non-taxed ⅓ of "gain" [⅓ × ($244,933 – 27,433)]		72,500
Jan. 1, 2017	Cumulative eligible capital	$	Nil

ITA: 14(1)

The business income in 2016 is calculated as:

The total of:

(a) the lesser of:

  (i) the negative amount . . . . $ 244,933

  and

  (ii) the total of: . . . .
  all cumulative eligible capital deductions . . . . . . $ 27,433
  less: all recaptured deductions in prior years . . .   Nil
                                                          $ 27,433

  The lesser is . . . . $ 27,433

and

(b) ⅔ of (negative amount less recaptured in deductions in
  (a)(ii)), above [⅔ × ($244,933 – 27,433)] 145,000*

Business income $172,433

* This is the same as ½ of the economic gain:

Proceeds ($100,000 + $150,000 + $200,000) . . . . $ 450,000
Cost ($40,000 + $50,000 + $20,000 + $50,000) . . . .   (160,000)

Economic gain . . . . $ 290,000

½ = ... $ 145,000

Chapter 6

Income from Property

Learning Goals

Know, Understand and Explain

By the end of this chapter you will know, understand and be able to explain:

- The basic provisions of the Income Tax Act (the Act) that relate to property income and attribution rules.

- The rules relating to the inclusion of interest income for corporations, trusts and individuals.

- The difference between eligible and ineligible dividends and its effects on the taxation of an individual.

- The distinction between property and business income.

- The purpose of integration and how it affects the overall tax paid on income earned in a corporation.

Apply

By the end of this chapter you will be able to apply your knowledge and understanding to:

- Correctly determine the amount of interest and dividends that must be included in income.

- Correctly determine the eligible expenses that may be deducted against property income.

- Advise taxpayers on the tax implications of a non-arm's length transaction as it relates to income splitting.

- Advise taxpayers on tax planning techniques to maximize deductions and minimize overall tax.

Review Questions
¶6,800 in the Study Guide

Multiple Choice Questions
¶6,825 in the Study Guide

Exercise Questions
¶6,850 in the Study Guide

Assignment Problems
¶6,875 in the Study Guide

CHAPTER 6 — LEARNING CHART

Problem Descriptions

Textbook Example Problems

6-1	Reporting interest income
6-2	Reporting interest income
6-3	Interest income
6-4	Damages received
6-5	Dividends — public company
6-6	Attribution — spouse
6-7	Attribution — child
6-8	Carrying charges on land
6-9	Rental property CCA

Multiple Choice Questions

1	Dividends — CCPC
2	Rental property CCA
3	Attribution
4	Deductible expenses
5	Dividends — CCPC, public
6	Kiddie tax

Exercises

1	Interest income
2	Attribution — spouse
3	Carrying charges on land
4	Rental property CCA
5	Rental property disposal
6	Interest expense
7	Rental property

Assignment Problems

1	Attribution — spouse, children
2	Dividends — eligible, other, foreign
3	Sale with earn out
4	Interest vs. dividend and attribution
5	Expenses of vacant land
6	Income from rental properties
7	Construction costs
8	GST/HST
9	Property income and employee loan
10	Attribution
11	Property income
12	Interest expense
13	Interest expense
14	Business and property income, attribution

Study Notes

¶6,800   REVIEW QUESTIONS

(1) Billy has come to you to tell you that he has found a great way of generating income of which only one-half is taxable as a capital gain. He buys a bond that pays interest annually and he holds it until just before the payment date and then he sells it, including the accrued interest, at a gain. Comment.

(2) One of your clients does not want to buy the compounding series Canada Savings Bonds any more since the new interest accrual rules cause the interest earned to be taxable annually rather than at maturity. Comment.

(3) Mr. Simpson owns an unincorporated business. In recognition of his wife's considerable contribution of her time and skills to the business he gives her a one-half share of the business income. Comment.

(4) Mr. Smith has guaranteed a bank loan that his wife has taken out to buy shares in a corporation carrying on a business that she is starting. He is concerned about the attribution rules. Comment.

(5) Opco Inc. recently borrowed $300,000 to buy 30 acres of industrial land. The corporation has constructed a building, shipping and receiving areas and parking for employees on this property using up 20 acres. The remaining 10 acres is available for future needs. Is all of the interest on the $300,000 loan deductible?

(6) Rent Co. Ltd. is a corporation in the residential rental business. Because of some recent purchases, its financing costs are high and it is operating at a break-even before CCA this year. However, in the prior three years it made a profit. Can the corporation claim CCA to create a loss this year to carry back to the prior years, using the carryover rules in Division C, to offset income in those years?

(7) Ms. Campbell has bought some gold as a protection against inflation. However, she did not have the cash to make the purchase so she borrowed from the bank to buy the gold. This is the first time that she has done this and she plans to hold the gold for some time. She is repaying the loan over three years. Will she be able to deduct all or some of her interest expense? Explain.

(8) You have been told of a court case where a taxpayer borrowed money initially to purchase a home, because some of the funds that he was to receive from Iran had not arrived when expected. When the funds at last arrived, interest rates had risen above that rate he was paying on his house mortgage. He then chose to invest his money at these higher interest rates instead of paying off the mortgage. He deducted the interest portion of his mortgage payments on his tax return. Comment.

(9) A client is in the process of selling his house and buying a bigger one. However, the real estate market has slowed down and in order to sell his existing house he is going to have to take back a mortgage for $100,000 at 5% for a five-year term. Since he does not have any extra cash, he is going to have to borrow that $100,000 from you in order to buy his new house. Is the interest going to be deductible on his mortgage? If not, how might he restructure the transaction to make it deductible?

(10) You have just interviewed a new client and have discovered that she borrowed to buy shares in a private corporation five years ago. The loan is still outstanding but the corporation has since gone bankrupt. Is the interest she is paying on the loan still deductible?

¶6,825 MULTIPLE CHOICE QUESTIONS

Question 1

Max is planning to invest in preferred shares of a friend's Canadian-controlled private corporation, which are paying a $12,000 dividend per year from income taxable at the low corporate rate. Assuming that Max is in the top federal tax bracket (33%) and that the provincial tax on income rate in his province is 17%, how much income tax will Max pay on this income? Also assume that the combined federal and provincial dividend tax credit is equal to the dividend gross-up.

(A) $2,580

(B) $4,980

(C) $7,020

(D) $6,000

Question 2

Wendy Jang owns three rental buildings. All of the buildings are in Class 1:

	Property		
	1	*2*	*3*
Original cost	$120,000	$ 80,000	$150,000
UCC at Jan. 1	100,000	75,000	150,000
Rental revenue for the year	58,000	22,000	20,000
Expenses for the year:			
Interest	20,000	10,000	8,000
Property taxes	13,000	6,000	11,000
Other	17,000	4,000	1,000

What is the maximum CCA that Wendy Jang can claim on the rental properties for the year?

(A) $13,000

(B) $10,000

(C) $7,000

(D) $6,500

Question 3

In the year, Mr. P made the following loans and gifts to family members to split income with his family members. Which one of the loans and/or gifts will result in income being attributed to Mr. P?

(A) A gift of $100,000 to his son, Peter, age 21. Peter invested the money in a term deposit and earned $3,000 of interest income.

(B) An interest-free loan of $100,000 to his mother-in-law, Mabel, age 81. Mabel invested the money in mutual funds and earned $12,000 of dividend income.

(C) An interest-free loan of $100,000 to his daughter, Daphne, age 28. Daphne bought a cottage and used it for personal use.

(D) A gift of $100,000 to his wife, Debbie. Debbie put the money in her non-interest bearing chequing account and paid all the family's household expenses from the account. She then used $100,000 of her own money to invest in the stock market and earned $10,000 of dividend income.

CHAPTER 6

Question 4

Which of the following items is DEDUCTIBLE by Canadian taxpayers in the computation of income from business or property in Subdivision b of Division B of the Act?

(A) Commissions paid on the purchase of an investment in common shares.

(B) The premium paid on a $100,000 term life insurance policy on the taxpayer's life which is required as collateral for a $100,000 bank loan used to purchase a $100,000 investment in common shares.

(C) Interest expenses on a loan to invest in a registered retirement savings plan.

(D) Commissions paid on the sale of an investment in common shares.

Question 5

During the year, Mike received two cheques, one in the amount of C$20,000, the other in the amount of C$8,500. The $20,000 cheque was a dividend from business income taxed at the low corporate rate of a Canadian-controlled private corporation. The $8,500 cheque was a dividend from a foreign corporation, net of the $1,500 of foreign tax withheld by the foreign country from the dividend payment. Which of the following amounts must Mike include in his income for Canadian income tax purposes in respect of these two dividend cheques?

(A) $20,000

(B) $28,500

(C) $30,000

(D) $33,600

Question 6

Ron Bordessa is 18 years of age. He inherited shares of Royal Roads Ltd., a private corporation, on his grandfather's death three years ago. Which of the following statements is true?

(A) Any dividend that Ron receives on these shares will be subject to the tax on split income.

(B) The tax on split income does not apply to any dividends on these shares because they were inherited.

(C) Any capital gains that Ron realizes on the disposition of these shares to an arm's length person, will be subject to the tax on split income.

(D) The tax on split income does not apply to any dividend on these shares because Ron has reached the age of 18.

¶6,850   EXERCISES

Exercise 1

ITA: 12(1)(*c*), 12(4), 12(11)

What would be the *first* year in which the taxpayer would have to include interest in income in each of the following cases and to which years would that interest relate?

(A) A corporation with a June 30 year-end buys a bond that pays interest semi-annually on March 31 and September 30 from its previous owner on January 1, 2016.

(B) An individual buys a compounding GIC on November 1, 2016.

(C) An individual buys a zero coupon bond, issued on January 1, 2016, in 2016.

(D) An individual buys a compound Canada Savings Bond issued November 1, 2016.

(E) On June 1, 2016, an individual buys a $1,000 bond paying $40 interest by cheque each May 31 and November 30. The bond was issued on December 1, 2015.

Exercise 2

ITA: 74.1, 74.5

(A) A husband wants his wife to have a $1,000 Canada Savings Bond that he owns paying interest at 7%. What are the consequences to the couple during the year if:

(i) he gives the bond to her without receiving any financial consideration from her in return?

(ii) he sells the bond to her for $1,000 plus accrued interest to the date of sale in return for cash?

(iii) he sells the bond to her for $1,000 plus accrued interest to the date of sale in return for a demand note which she signs payable to him without interest?

(iv) he cashes the bond lending the proceeds to her in return for a promissory note which she signs payable to him without interest but with a definite repayment period and she uses the funds from the loan to buy a similar bond?

(B) Would any of the above answers change for the current year if he undertook the same transactions with a trust set up in favour of a child aged 15 instead of his wife?

(C) Would any of the above answers change if he undertook the same transactions with a child aged 20?

Exercise 3

ITA: 18(2)

A downtown hotel bought a vacant lot adjacent to the hotel building. Comment on the deductibility of property taxes and interest paid on funds borrowed to buy the property if:

(i) the property is used as a parking lot for hotel guests;

(ii) the property was bought for potential gains on future sale but in the meantime it is being used as a public parking lot generating net revenues before the taxes and interest of 75% of the expenditures for taxes and interest;

(iii) the property was bought for future expansion of the hotel and in the meantime is being used under the same condition as in (ii) above.

Exercise 4

ITR: 1100

Mr. Provident is a salaried employee who invests in small residential rental properties. He bought Property 1 last year and at the beginning of this year the undepreciated capital cost balances for that property were as follows:

Class 1 — brick building	$148,000
Class 8 — furniture and fixtures	25,000

CHAPTER 6

This year he bought Property 2 for $150,000 including land valued at $12,500. The net income before capital cost allowance for each property this year was:

Property 1 .... $ 9,270
Property 2 3,750

— REQUIRED

Compute the maximum capital cost allowance on these rental properties for the current year.

Exercise 5

ITA: 20(1)(*a*); ITR: 1100, 1101(1ac)

Ms. Alimeag owns two residential rental properties. One produced rental revenue of $13,500 and had allowable expenses (excluding capital cost allowance) of $11,250. The other had rental revenue of $22,500 and expenses of $18,750. Data on the two Class 1 buildings are as follows:

	Property A	Property B
Capital cost	$360,000	$600,000
UCC, January 1	$330,000	$480,000

During the year, Property A was sold for net proceeds of $336,000.

— REQUIRED

(A) What is the effect of the above information on the income of Ms. Alimeag for the year?

(B) Can an election be made under subsection 13(4) if Property A is replaced by the end of the next year?

Exercise 6

ITA: 20(1)(*c*)

Nadi borrowed $140,000 at an 5.5% annual interest rate from a local financial institution to finance the following investments.

	Cost
Common shares of a public corporation paying no dividends	$20,000
Gold bullion (treated as capital)	25,000
Corporate bond (yield is 6% *per annum*)	20,000
Preferred shares (4% annual dividend) purchased in RRSP	10,000
Common shares (2% annual dividend) in spouse's name	30,000
Paintings from well-known galleries	15,000
Guaranteed Investment Certificate paying interest at 6% *per annum*	20,000
Total cost	$140,000

— REQUIRED

Assuming that the investments were held for the full calendar year, determine the deductibility of interest expense for each investment.

¶6,850

Exercise 7

ITR: 1100(11), 1101(1ac)

Capital cost allowance, recapture, and terminal loss all form part of the net income calculation for rental properties. There are two special rules that apply only to rental properties that serve to limit the treatment of capital cost allowance.

One of the special rules stipulates that each rental property having a cost of $50,000 or more must be held in a separate capital cost allowance class.

— REQUIRED

Determine the second special rule.

CHAPTER 6

¶6,875   ASSIGNMENT PROBLEMS

Type 1 Problems

Problem 1

Donna is married to Don and they have two children, Danielle, age 25, and Susan, age 15. Donna earns $250,000 annually while Don earns $100,000. Danielle works full time and earns $30,000 annually while Susan is still in high school and doesn't have any income. Donna has been looking for ways to pay less tax and a friend of hers has suggested that she take advantage of the lower tax brackets of her husband and children. With $100,000 of extra cash in her bank account she is considering the following options and would like your advice as her accountant.

(1) Loan the $100,000 to her husband at 0% interest. He would invest it in a bond earning 3%.

(2) Give the $100,000 to her husband. He would invest it in a bond earning 3%.

(3) Loan the $100,000 to her 15-year-old daughter at 0% interest. She would invest it in a bond earning 3%.

(4) Give the $100,000 to her 15-year-old daughter. She would invest it in a bond earning 3%.

(5) Loan the $100,000 to her 25-year-old daughter at 0% interest. She would invest it in a bond earning 3%.

(6) Give the $100,000 to her 25-year-old daughter. She would invest it in a bond earning 3%.

Problem 2

Victor is confused, so he has come to you for advice. He has heard that not all dividends are treated the same, so he would like you to explain how the following are taxed to decide where he should invest his money. Victor is in the top tax bracket.

(1) $1,000 of dividends from Canadian public companies.

(2) $1,000 of dividends from Canadian private companies earning active business income taxed at the low rate.

(3) $900 of dividends from foreign public companies. $100 was deducted at source and remitted to the foreign government.

Problem 3   ITA: 12(1)(*g*); IT-462

The Country Pie is a highly recognized baker of quality pies in Beamsville, Ontario. The current proprietor, Rudolph Strudel, started the business about 20 years ago with an initial purchase of equipment of $150,000 and built up the name of the company by closely supervising the pie production process. Many have said that it is this attention and his recipes that have made the business a success. Rudolph has decided to sell his business and move to the coast to get away from the pressures of running a business. An offer has been made for the assets of The Country Pie by Big Food Corporation Ltd. ("BFC"). There was a meeting of the minds as to the value of the fixed assets of The Country Pie. However, there was considerable dispute as to the value of The Country Pie name in generating pie sales after a purchase by BFC. Consequently, it is proposed that the full proceeds be determined in part by future sales.

The BFC offer is for $50,000 cash; $60,000 to be paid on the basis of sales over the next three years with any balance of the $60,000 remaining at the end of the third year payable at that time; and 25% of gross sales in the next five years. As part of the agreement, Rudolph would provide consulting services to BFC as needed during the next three years.

Rudolph would like you to explain the income tax implications of the proposal from BFC.

Problem 4

ITA: 12(1)(c), 12(1)(j), 74.1, 74.5, 82(1); IT-510, IT-511R

Mr. Wiser is contemplating investing in two different mutual funds. His investment options are set out below.

Amount	Mutual Fund	Distribution
$200,000	International Income Fund	Annual interest of 4.0%
$200,000	Canadian Dividend Fund	Annual dividend of 3.0%

Mr. Wiser contemplates holding both mutual funds for the same period of time — from purchase to December 31, 2019. Mr. Wiser is in the top federal income tax bracket (33%). Mr. Wiser's provincial tax on income rate is 17%. Assume that the combined federal and provincial dividend tax credit is equal to the dividend gross-up. Assume that the Canadian Dividend Fund receives and distributes dividends from Canadian-resident public corporations.

Mr. Wiser would like you to advise him on the following:

(A) Based on the above information, which mutual fund should he prefer?

(B) Can he achieve any advantage by purchasing the above mutual fund in the name of his 8-year-old daughter who has no other source of income?

(C) His spouse has no source of income. Can he achieve any advantage by lending $200,000 to his spouse and having her purchase a rental property earning $16,000 per year? The $200,000 loan would be evidenced by a promissory note repayable in four equal annual instalments on each of December 31, 2015 to 2018 and bearing interest at the prescribed rate of 1%.

Problem 5

ITA: 18(2)–(3)

Furniture Focus Limited provides competitive prices to consumers by using a no-frills approach to displaying its product in large stores surrounded by ample parking. Furniture Focus Limited has excess land that is not currently used in its business. This vacant land is rented to the adjacent automobile dealer who stores new cars on it.

For the year ended December 31, 2016, Furniture Focus Limited had the following operating expenses:

Sales	$35,000,000
Cost of goods sold	(20,000,000)
Gross profit	$15,000,000
Selling expenses	(5,000,000)
General and administrative expenses	(2,000,000)
	$ 8,000,000
Other income	50,000
Net income	$ 8,050,000

The general and administrative expenses include $30,000 of interest and $5,000 of property taxes on the vacant land rented to the automobile dealer. There are no other expenses connected with this land. Other income includes $10,000 of rental income paid by the automobile dealer.

Determine the income tax consequences of the various payments related to the vacant land.

Problem 6

ITA: 20(1)(a); ITR: 1100(11), 1101(1ac); Sched. II

Sara Shimizu is the owner of two rental properties, 509 Brunswick Avenue and 356 Spadina Road. These properties were purchased six years ago for $525,000 and $600,000, respectively. In 2015, 509 Brunswick Avenue was sold for $550,000. A reasonable allocation of this amount is considered to be 75% to the building and 25% to the land. The following income and expenses were incurred in renting out the two properties in 2016:

Rental	$ 60,000
Interest on mortgage	(40,000)
Operating costs	(15,000)
Promotion costs for sale of property	(5,000)
Net income	0

There are no meal or entertainment expenses included in the $5,000 of sales promotion costs. At December 31, 2015, the undepreciated capital cost of 509 Brunswick Avenue was $383,500 and that of 356 Spadina Road was $400,000.

Sara has asked you to determine her income from the property, assuming she wishes to report the least amount possible for tax purposes in 2016.

Problem 7

ITA: 18, 20

It is early January 2016 and the president of BDC Distributing Limited, a client of your firm, called recently to discuss the tax implications regarding the construction of a new building. BDC has been growing rapidly and needs new warehouse space. They have been unable to locate any suitable space in the existing buildings in town and, therefore, have decided that their only option is to build their own building. They have identified the site and have estimated the costs of the project. These projected costs (and dates of completion) are as follows:

The land that has been identified will be purchased on February 15, 2016, for $405,000. There is no significant site preparation required so construction of the building can commence immediately. The cost of the building is estimated to be $1,348,000 plus the costs noted below. It is anticipated that BDC will be able to occupy the building on October 31, 2016.

BDC currently has an architect finalizing the drawings for the building. The architect fees, which will all be paid in 2016, will amount to $7,200. There will also be fees of $2,100 for an engineer to examine the drawings.

BDC has arranged for the financing required for the project. The project will be financed with a mortgage of $875,000 and $1,000,000 of preferred shares issued on January 15, 2016. Interest on the mortgage is payable semi-annually on July 15 and January 15 at a rate of 8% *per annum*. The preferred shares pay dividends of 5% *per annum*, payable semi-annually on July 15 and January 15. There will be a number of costs incurred in order to issue the debt and shares. These costs are legal and accounting fees of $18,450, commissions of $58,300 and registration fees of $1,800 for amending the articles of incorporation to allow the issuance of the preferred shares.

The balance of the costs related to the building are summarized below:

Building insurance from April 15, 2016 @ $450 per month	$ 3,825
Property taxes from February 15, 2016 @ $770 per month	8,085
Soil testing to determine location of footings for building	1,825
Relocation expenses	34,100
Utilities service connections estimated to be completed on May 20, 2016	3,800
Mortgage insurance premium from March 1, 2016 of $325 per month	3,250
Maintenance from October 31, 2016	2,500
Utilities from October 31, 2016	6,300
Landscaping	15,500

The president would like you to advise him of the impact of the proposed transactions on their December 31, 2016 income tax return. Ignore the effects of a leap year.

Problem 8

ETA: 123(1), Sch. V, Parts VI, VII

Reconsider the facts of Problem 7. Assume that HST was paid at 13%, where applicable, in addition to the amounts shown.

The president of BDC Distributing Limited has asked you to calculate the HST consequences of the transactions presented.

Problem 9

ITA: 20(1)(*c*), 80.4(1)

Tim Markus, Vice President of Phone Lines, earned $92,000 in salary last year. In addition to his salary, he also received low-interest loans from his employer. Tim's interest rate on these loans is 0% and he owed $160,000 throughout last year. Tim used the loan to purchase a rental property (see Schedule 1). Assume a prescribed interest rate of 2% for the entire year. Five years ago, Tim invested in some common shares of a foreign corporation. He receives $18,000 in dividends (net of $2,000 with-holding tax) annually from this corporation. Last year, he also received taxable eligible dividends of $30,000 from his investment in a Canadian public company which is resident in Canada. Tim also owns $100,000 worth of 5% bonds.

Schedule 1:

Rental revenue $16,400
   Maintenance expenses 5,500
   Utilities on rental units . . . 8,200
   CCA — half-year rule 3,200

Tim has asked you to calculate his income for tax purposes for last year.

Problem 10

ITA: 12(1)(*j*), 74.1

The following are independent situations:

(a) Tony Lee gave $50,000 to his wife, Shannon, for the acquisition of shares of a Canadian company on the Toronto Stock Exchange. During the year, an eligible dividend of $5,000 cash was paid on the shares owned by Mrs. Lee.

(b) At the beginning of the year in which her daughter Carey turned 18 in December, Ellen gifted $25,000 directly to Carey. Carey invested the $25,000 in an income-bearing investment that paid her interest of $2,500 during the year. In addition to the $2,500, Carey also earned another $7,500 in interest income from monies received from her mother previously.

What are the tax consequences for the above situations?

Problem 11

ITA: Subdivision b

John Ingles has provided you with the following information related to his various investment holdings as of December 31, 2016.

Interest earned on joint bank account with his spouse (spouse contributes equally)	$ 2,000
Interest earned on his investment account (not joint) with his investment broker	800
Interest earned on 2015 personal income tax assessment	450

Interest on short-term investments:

$20,000 term deposit taken out November 30, 2016 (interest at maturity in six months)

Accrued interest from December 1 to December 31, 2016	85

$200,000 GIC purchased November 1, 2015 (interest payable at maturity on October 31, 2018)

Accrued interest from November 1, 2015 to October 31, 2016	16,000
Accrued interest from January 1, 2016 to December 31, 2016	16,214

Government of Canada Treasury Bills purchased for $9,009 on January 3, 2016

Amount received on maturity on December 31, 2016	10,000
Cash dividends received from investment in common shares of Canadian resident public corporations	24,000
Cash dividends received from common shares in US corporations (net of $3,000 of foreign withholding taxes; all in Canadian dollars)	17,000

Rental details from operation of two separate rental properties:

	Property 1	Property 2
Gross rental revenue	$ 30,000	$ 46,000
Utilities	5,000	8,000
Property taxes	2,400	3,500
Repairs	1,500	4,800
Mortgage interest	20,000	32,000
Opening UCC	$368,209	$520,225

CHAPTER 6

Interest expenses paid during 2016:

Interest on bank line of credit used for investing in shares described above $50,000

Interest on loan to acquire an automobile for his daughter for her 18th birth-
day   3,200

Interest on a parcel of vacant land (purchased in 2011, the land does not
generate any income).   10,000

Based on the above, John has asked you to calculate his income for the year. He would also like you to comment on the income tax implications of items not included in your calculations.

Problem 12

ITA: 18(2), 20(1)(c), 74.1

Your client, Ashley, has come to you for some advice on computing her net income from property.

(a) In February, Ashley sold all her investments and paid off her personal residence mortgage. On March 1, she borrowed $90,000 to reacquire many of the same investments she previously held. Many of the common shares purchased do not carry dividend rights. Her spouse has insisted that 50% of the investments be placed in his name.

(b) On April 15, Ashley purchased a government bond that pays annual interest of 2.5%. When the bond was purchased, Ashley paid accrued interest of $262.50 to the previous owner of the bonds.

(c) On June 1, Ashley borrowed $450,000 to purchase the vacant land next to her apartment block. The land is used as a parking lot and she collected monthly revenues of $2,500. She plans improvements that will double her income from the lot. Ashley's only expenses were $45,500 for interest and property taxes.

Ashley has asked you to explain the income tax implications of each item above.

Problem 13

ITA: 18(1), 20(1)(c);
IT-533

Funds are borrowed by an individual from a financial institution at a 7% *per annum* interest rate to purchase the following unrelated investments:

(a) gold coins on which gains or losses will be treated as capital gains or losses;

(b) an RRSP portfolio of investments yielding 8% in interest;

(c) a five-year GIC paying interest at 4% *per annum*;

(d) common shares of a Canadian-resident public corporation paying no dividends;

(e) preferred shares of a Canadian-resident public corporation paying 5% dividends;

(f) preferred shares of a U.S. corporation paying 6% dividends;

(g) Mindy owns 1,000 shares of International Inc., a corporation listed on the TSX, for which she paid cash. Mindy also owns the condominium she lives in that is financed with borrowed money. Mindy is planning to sell the 1,000 shares of International Inc. and use the proceeds from the sale to pay off the mortgage on the condominium. She will then borrow money to buy another 1,000 shares of International Inc.;

(h) lottery tickets which yielded $75,000 in winnings which were reinvested in short-term securities yielding 2%; and

(i) common shares of a Canadian-resident public corporation paying dividends of 6%; later in the year the shares were sold at a small gain to repay a 8% second mortgage on a principal residence.

Determine the deductibility of the interest expense in each of these unrelated cases.

Type 2 Problems

Problem 14   ITA: Division B

Trent Zalinski recently retired as a football player with the Saskatchewan Roughriders. In the current year, he received his salary of $150,000 from the team and is eligible for a CFL pension in 15 years. He and his wife Mary have settled in Weyburn, Saskatchewan, where he runs a small sporting goods store as a proprietorship. He has provided you with the following additional information.

(a) His net income from the store for the fiscal year ended December 31 was $35,000. Next year he is hoping to double that. Mary works in the store about 35 hours a week and is paid $6 per hour. This is already included as an expense in determining the $35,000.

(b) Trent's other current-year receipts are: fees received from endorsement of a brand of football equipment, $30,000; eligible dividends from Canadian public corporations, $7,200; dividends from foreign public corporations, (net of $750 withholding tax) $6,750; interest from Canadian bank, $3,000.

(c) Trent also had the following expenses: cycling trip to Cypress Hills Provincial Park with family, $2,200; interest on bank loan to acquire public company shares, $4,050.

(d) In May of the previous year, Trent purchased a five-year GIC in Mary's name. The interest rate was 6%, and it was for $10,000. None of the interest is receivable until maturity in five years.

Trent has asked you to calculate his income for tax purposes. In addition, he wants you to provide any basic tax planning advice that might be appropriate.

 [For more problems and solutions thereto, see the DVD accompanying the textbook.]

CHAPTER 6

CHAPTER 6 —
DISCUSSION NOTES FOR REVIEW QUESTIONS

(1) The principal would be separated from the accrued interest and cause the interest to be included in Billy's income as interest income. The purchaser can deduct the same amount that the vendor included in income.

ITA: 20(14)(a)
ITA: 20(14)(b)

(2) Interest accrued annually to the anniversary date of the bond is taxable, requiring tax to be paid from some other source of funds, since no interest will be received on the compound interest bond. Your client may wish to invest in the type of Canada Savings Bonds that pay interest annually. Note that the annual accrual rules may not present a cash flow problem if the holder of the bond is not taxable on the accrued interest due to a low level of total income.

ITA: 12(4)

(3) Attribution would not appear to apply to cause any income allocated to Mrs. Simpson to be reallocated to her husband since there is no attribution of business income. (It should be noted that, if she is not actively involved in the business, then she will not be a specified member of the partnership and the income from the partnership will be deemed to be income from property.)

ITA: 74.1(1)

ITA: 248(1), 96(1.8)

(4) Although the corporation is carrying on a business, Mrs. Smith is not. She will be earning property income (i.e., dividends on the shares), so the exception to the attribution rules for business income does not apply. Attribution as a result of guarantees would only cause the attribution rules to apply if the loan was not at commercial rates. If the bank is charging commercial interest rates, then the attribution rules will not apply.

ITA: 74.5(7)
ITA: 74.5(1)

(5) The interest on the 10 acres would be capitalized since it is not used in business and there is no revenue from the land.

ITA: 18(2)

(6) CCA cannot be claimed to create or increase a loss on rental property. However, those loss limitation rules do not apply to a corporation whose principal business was the leasing, rental, development or sale, or any combination thereof, of real property owned by it. In this case, Rent Co. will be able to claim CCA to create or increase a loss.

ITR: 1100(11)–(14)

(7) No interest is deductible if Ms. Campbell is considered to realize a capital gain on the sale of the gold. Since capital gains are not income from business or property, she does not meet the requirements and cannot deduct the interest. Also, there is no provision that would allow her to capitalize the interest to the cost of the gold. On the other hand, if the gain on the sale of the gold is considered to be income from business or property, the interest would be deductible. Note that the CRA would allow her to choose income treatment for these transactions.

ITA: 9(3)
ITA: 20(1)(c)
ITA: 53
IT-346R, par. 8

(8) In the *Attaie* case, the Federal Court–Trial Division agreed that the interest expense was deductible. However, the Federal Court of Appeal reversed this decision and decided that the interest was not deductible, since there was not a direct link between the borrowed funds and the income from property.

87 DTC 5411 (F.C.T.D.)
90 DTC 6413 (F.C.A.)

(9) Under the proposed plan, the interest would not be deductible since the money is not being used to earn income. However, if your client were to borrow from the bank the $100,000 needed to loan to the purchaser in order to complete the sale of his existing house, then at least the interest would be deductible up to 5%. The purchaser would then be in a position to pay the full purchase price for the new residence.

(10) Since the corporation that your client invested in has gone out of business, there is no longer a possibility of earning income from business or property. However, the amount of the lost capital would be deemed to continue to be borrowed for the purpose of earning income and, hence, would allow the interest in this case to continue to be deductible. Refer to Income Tax Folio S3-F6-C1, paragraph 1.41.

ITA: 20.1(1)

CHAPTER 6 — SOLUTIONS TO MULTIPLE CHOICE QUESTIONS

Question 1

(B) is correct. The calculation is as follows:

Grossed up dividend ($12,000 × 1.17)	$14,040
Combined tax rate	× 50%
	$ 7,020
Dividend tax credit	(2,040)
Net tax	$ 4,980

(A) incorrectly ignores provincial tax: $14,040 × 33% – $2,040 = $2,580.

(C) incorrectly ignores the dividend tax credit:

$$\$14,040 \times 50\% = \$7,020$$

(D) incorrectly ignores the gross-up and the dividend tax credit: $12,000 × 50% = $6,000.

Question 2

(B) is the correct answer. The calculation is as follows:

	Property			
	1	*2*	*3*	*Total*
UCC at Jan. 1st	$100,000	$75,000	$150,000	
Rental revenue for the year	$ 58,000	$22,000	$ 20,000	
Expenses for the year	50,000	20,000	20,000	
Income before CCA	$ 8,000	$ 2,000	(Nil)	$10,000
CCA: 4% × UCC	$ 4,000	$ 3,000	$ 6,000	$13,000
Maximum CCA [Reg. 1100(11)]				$10,000

(A) is incorrect. $13,000 is the CCA calculation ignoring the rental property restriction.   ITR: 1100(11)

(C) is incorrect. $7,000 is the maximum CCA calculation on the first two buildings only. This calculation ignores the fact that the CCA on the third property can be claimed against the net rental income on the first two properties.

(D) is incorrect. It is one-half of the $13,000 calculated in (A) above.

Question 3

(B) is the correct answer. The $12,000 of dividend income will be attributed to Mr. P. Mabel and   ITA: 56(4.1)
Mr. P are related and it can reasonably be considered that one of the main reasons for making the loan
was to reduce tax.

(A) is incorrect. The $3,000 of interest income will not be attributed. Peter is not under 18 years of
age and, therefore, attribution does not apply. If it had been a loan, instead of a gift, subsection 56(4.1)   ITA: 74.1(2)
would apply and may attribute the income.

(C) is incorrect. Even though an interest-free loan was made to which attribution would apply,   ITA: 56(4.1)
there is no property income from the cottage to attribute.

(D) is incorrect. Even though a gift was made to a spouse to which attribution would apply, there is   ITA: 74.1(1)
no property income from the chequing account to attribute.

CHAPTER 6

Question 4

(B) is correct. The premium paid on a $100,000 term life insurance policy on the taxpayer's life which is required as collateral for a $100,000 bank loan used to purchase a $100,000 investment in common shares is deductible.

ITA: 20(1)(*e*.2)

(A) is incorrect because commissions paid on the purchase of an investment in common shares are capitalized as part of the cost of the shares.

ITA: 18(1)(*b*)

(C) is incorrect because the Act does not allow a deduction for interest expense on a loan to invest in a registered retirement savings plan.

ITA: 18(11)(*b*)

(D) is incorrect because commissions paid on the sale of an investment in common shares are a selling cost deducted in computing the capital gain on the sale of the shares. One-half of a capital gain is a taxable capital gain which is computed under Subdivision c of Division B of Part I of the Act, whereas income from business or property is computed under Subdivision b.

Question 5

(D) is correct: $20,000 × 1.17 + $8,500 + $1,500 tax withheld = $33,400.

ITA: 82(1)

(A) is incorrect because it ignores the gross-up on the dividend and the foreign income: $20,000.

(B) is incorrect because it ignores the gross-up on the dividend and the foreign tax withheld: $20,000 + $8,500 = $28,500.

(C) is incorrect because it ignores the gross-up on the dividend: $20,000 + $8,500 + $1,500 = $30,000.

Question 6

(D) is correct.

(A) is incorrect because the tax on split income only applies to taxpayers under age 18 throughout the year. Since Ron is 18, the tax on split income will not apply.

ITA: 120.4 "specified individual"

(B) is incorrect because the only exemption regarding inherited shares is for shares inherited from a parent. If Ron had been under 18 at any time in the year, the tax on split income would have applied to dividends received on the shares.

ITA: 120.4 "excluded amount"

(C) is incorrect because the tax on split income does not apply to capital gains on a disposition to an arm's length person.

ITA: 120.4 "split income"

CHAPTER 6 — SOLUTIONS TO EXERCISES

Exercise 1

(A) In its June 30, 2016 taxation year, the corporation would be required to include in income the interest received March 31, 2016 for the period October 1, 2015 to March 31, 2016 plus interest accrued from April 1 to June 30, 2016. Accrued interest from October 1, 2015 to January 1, 2016 (the period prior to acquisition), which was purchased with the bond, would give rise to a deduction. *ITA: 12(3), 20(14)*

(B) The Act would require accrued interest from November 1, 2016 to October 31, 2017 to be included in income in 2017. *ITA: 12(4)*

(C) The anniversary day would be December 31, 2016. Accrued interest from the date of purchase to December 31, 2016 would be included in 2016 income.

(D) The first anniversary day would occur October 31, 2017 and accrued interest would be included at that time. The CRA has, in the past, administratively allowed Canada Savings Bond interest to be accrued on a "bond year" basis. The Act gives legislative effect to this practice. *IT-396R, par. 25; ITA: 12(4)*

(E) The $80 received each year would be included in income. On November 30, 2016, there will be an anniversary day, but all of the interest accrued to that day will have been included in income as interest received in the year. *ITA: 12(1)(c)*

Exercise 2

(A) (i) The Act would attribute the income on the bond to him even though she is legally entitled to receive it, since a gift is considered to be a transfer and is not a fair market value exchange which would be exempt. *ITA: 74.1(1), 74.5(1)*

(ii) Since a sale is also considered to be a transfer, attribution would apply except that, in this case, the transfer would be exempt because it was for fair market value consideration, as long as they elect jointly not to have the rollover apply. *ITA: 74.1(1), 74.5(1)(a), 73(1)*

(iii) This situation still involves a sale directly between husband and wife and is, therefore, a transfer subject to the attribution of income. A non-interest bearing demand note would not qualify for the exception because a commercial rate of interest was not charged. *ITA: 74.1(1), 74.5(1)(b)*

(iv) The loan of funds would result in attribution, because the exception would not apply since a commercial rate of interest was not charged on the loan. *ITA: 74.1(1), 74.5(2)*

(B) If the loan was to a non-arm's length minor or a niece or nephew who is also a minor, then attribution would apply to transfers or loans by means of a trust to or for the benefit of a minor in the same way as spousal attribution applied in part (A), above. However, there are special rules pertaining to transfers or loans to a trust which will be discussed in Chapter 18. *ITA: 74.1(2)* *ITA: 74.1(1)*

(C) Attribution of income does not apply to a transfer involving an individual who is 18 or older. However, another provision might apply to transactions (iii) and (iv) involving loans. The key condition for this rule to apply is that one of the main reasons for the loan was to reduce or avoid tax on income from property or substituted property. A loan bearing a commercial rate of interest would be exempt from attribution. *ITA: 74.1(2)* *ITA: 56(4.1)*

Exercise 3

(i) The deductibility of carrying charges is not limited because the land is being used in the course of the hotel business. *ITA: 18(2)*

(ii) The Act will limit the deductibility of carrying charges to 75% of their total (i.e., to the amount of the net revenues) so as not to create a loss by their deduction, unless the land is owned by a corporation whose principal purpose is the rental of real property (i.e., land and building) owned by it. This is not the principal purpose of a hotel corporation. *ITA: 18(2)(e)* *ITA: 18(2)(f)*

(iii) The deductibility of carrying charges may be limited in the same manner as in (ii), above, until the property is used in the business. *ITA: 18(2)*

CHAPTER 6

Exercise 4

	Class 1: 4%	*Class 1: 4%*	*Class 8: 20%*	*Total*
	Building 1	*Building 2*(1)		
UCC, January 1	$148,000	—	$25,000	
Purchases	—	$137,500	—	
UCC, December 31	$148,000	$137,500	$25,000	
CCA	5,920	2,750(2)	4,350(3)	$13,020
UCC, January 1	$142,080	$134,750	$20,650	

— *NOTES TO SOLUTION*

(1) Separate class for rental building costing $50,000 or more.   ITR: 1101(1ac)

(2) 4% of [$137,500 − (½ × $137,500)].

(3) Net rental income before CCA ($9,270 + 3,750) $13,020

CCA on rental building and leasing properties (i.e., furniture and fixtures) limited to $13,020 [$13,020 − ($5,920 + $2,750) = $4,350] . . . .   (13,020)

Net income from rental properties . . . .   Nil

Note that where less than maximum capital cost allowance is taken, the less than maximum amount should be taken in classes with relatively higher CCA rates, so that the UCC carried forward to the following year is eligible for CCA at the higher rate in that subsequent year.

Exercise 5

(A)

	Property A	*Property B*	*Total*
UCC, January 1	$330,000	$480,000	
Disposal	(336,000)	—	
UCC, December 31	$ (6,000)	$480,000	
Recapture	6,000	—	
CCA @ 4% (Class 1) — see below	—	(12,000)	
UCC forward	Nil	$468,000	
Revenue	$ 13,500	$ 22,500	$36,000
Recapture	6,000	—	6,000
Expenses before CCA	(11,250)	(18,750)	(30,000)
Net	$ 8,250	$ 3,750	$12,000

CCA (4% of $480,000 = $19,200;
limited to net above) . . . .   (12,000)

Net income from property . . . .   Nil

(B)   The rule to defer recapture applies on a voluntary disposition of a "former business property". A   ITA: 13(4), 248(1)
rental property is excluded from the definition and, hence, the deferral rule does not apply.

Exercise 6

Interest expense is deductible if there is a reasonable expectation of earning income from property.   ITA: 20(1)(*c*)

Investment	Not deductible	Deductible
Common shares		$20,000[1]
Gold bullion	$25,000[2]	
Corporate bond		20,000[3]
Preferred shares (RRSP)	10,000[4]	
Common shares		30,000[5]
Paintings	15,000[6]	
GICs		20,000[5]
Total	**$50,000**	**$90,000**

Deductible interest = $90,000 \times 5.5\% = \$4,950$

— NOTES TO SOLUTION

[1] As there is an expectation of dividend income on common shares, the interest is deductible.

[2] As capital treatment has been chosen for gains/losses on the gold bullion, the interest is not deductible.

[3] The corporate bond is income-producing and the associated interest would be deductible.

[4] The preferred shares were purchased in an RRSP; deduction of interest is disallowed.

[5] The associated interest on the common shares and GICs would be deductible, as there is the expectation of earning property income.

[6] The paintings from well-known galleries would be considered an investment for earning future capital gains and, therefore, the associated interest would not be deductible.

Exercise 7

Since the rule relates to capital cost allowance, Regulations Part XI, Capital Cost Allowances, would be a starting point. More specifically, ITR 1101(1ac) deals with the separate classes rule related to rental properties having a cost of at least $50,000.   ITR: 1100(11), 1101(1ac)

The other special rule is ITR 1100(11), which states that capital cost allowance on rental properties can only be deducted to the extent that it does not create or increase a net loss from all rental properties combined. Note that Interpretation Bulletin IT-195R4, Rental Property — Capital Cost Allowance Restrictions, provides further details.

Chapter 7

Capital Gains: Personal

Learning Goals

Know, Understand and Explain

By the end of this chapter you will know, understand and be able to explain:

- The different types of capital gains a taxpayer can incur on the sale of capital property.
- The special provisions for the taxation of capital gains as they relate to the different types of capital property.
- The meaning of a capital gain, taxable capital gain, capital loss, and allowable capital loss.
- The circumstances in which an individual can claim the principal residence exemption.
- The tax implications on the death of a taxpayer.
- The tax implications on ceasing or establishing residency in Canada.

Apply

By the end of this chapter you will be able to apply your knowledge and understanding to:

- Classify capital property into three different categories: personal use, listed personal, and other capital property.
- Correctly determine the tax implications of non-arm's length transfers.
- Correctly determine the adjusted cost base and the proceeds of disposition on the disposition of a capital property under various circumstances.
- Minimize the tax implications of disposing of more than one principal residence.
- Apply your knowledge to advise a client or employer on the tax implications on the death of a taxpayer and plan to meet the client's needs.
- Apply your knowledge to advise a client or employer on the tax implications of ceasing or establishing residency in Canada.

Review Questions
¶7,800 in the Study Guide

Multiple Choice Questions
¶7,825 in the Study Guide

Exercise Questions
¶7,850 in the Study Guide

Assignment Problems
¶7,875 in the Study Guide

CHAPTER 7 — LEARNING CHART

Problem Descriptions

Textbook Example Problems

7-1	Sale of mutual funds
7-2	Personal-use and listed personal property
7-3	Principal residence
7-4	Change in use of principal residence
7-5	Principal residence — transfer between spouses
7-6	Share transactions
7-7	Share transactions — open market and stock option
7-8	Stock dividends
7-9	Superficial loss
7-10	Share transactions
7-11	Options
7-12	Capital gains deferral
7-13	Allowable business investment loss
7-14	Allowable business investment loss

Multiple Choice Questions

1	Personal-use property
2	Principal residence
3	Change in use of principal residence
4	Stock dividend
5	Personal-use and listed personal property
6	Transactions with child
7	Transactions with spouse
8	Transactions with spouse and child
9	Death of a taxpayer
10	Becoming non-resident

Exercises

1	Principal residence
2	Principal residence
3	Change in use of principal residence
4	Personal-use and listed personal property
5	Share transactions
6	Share transactions
7	Listed personal property
8	Stock dividends
9	Arm's length
10	Non-arm's length transaction
11	Transactions with spouse
12	Becoming a resident

CHAPTER 7

Problem Descriptions

Assignment Problems

1	Stock transactions
2	Stock option — capital gain
3	Sale of mutual fund
4	Death of a taxpayer
5	Becoming resident and non-resident
6	Non-arm's length transactions, attribution
7	Non-arm's length transactions, attribution
8	Allowable business investment loss
9	Transfer of property on divorce
10	Related, affiliated, arm's length
11	Personal-use and listed personal property
12	Principal residence
13	LPP loss and ABIL
14	Option
15	Allowable business investment loss
16	Principal residence with change in use
17	Stock transactions
18	Stock transactions
19	Death of a taxpayer
20	Going non-resident
21	Non-arm's length purchase of rental property
22	CCPC stock option with attribution
23	Comprehensive
24	Going non-resident
25	Case

Study Notes

¶7,800   REVIEW QUESTIONS

(1) A client invested in a rental property some years ago and paid $10,000 as a down payment and $150,000 was in the form of a mortgage. Recently, the vacancy rate has climbed and the value of the property has fallen. She thinks that she will just walk away from the property and let the mortgage company take over the property. What will her proceeds of disposition be?

(2) As a result of a reorganization in a company in which Mr. Smith is a shareholder, he has just had a return of some of the corporation's capital. As a result, the adjusted cost base of his shares has become negative. This does not bother him since he has been told that as long as he continues to own the shares he will not have to recognize this built-in capital gain. Comment.

(3) Mr. Chan has come to you with a problem. He owns the family cottage and his wife owns the house in town. Both housing units were purchased within the last 30 years. They are thinking of selling both of these properties and moving to another province. He thought they could each claim the principal residence exemption to avoid any tax but someone has told him that they can only claim one of the residences. In general terms can you explain the rules to him?

(4) Ms. Starra bought a cottage property on a lake that has since become polluted. As a result, the value of the property has declined and she has sold it, since no one wants to go there anymore. She realized a loss on the sale and wants to claim the loss on her personal return. Can she do it?

(5) What is the "$1,000 rule" as it relates to personal-use property? Does the same rule apply to listed personal property?

(6) Mr. Davids has come to you to have his personal tax return done. He sold some shares of a public corporation that he has owned for some years and wants help in minimizing his tax on the transaction. One point that is confusing him is the stock dividend that he received this year. He does not know how to treat the dividend for tax purposes. Please help him.

(7) Under Divisions B and C, what happens when the capital losses exceed the capital gains in any one year?

(8) If you were to win a Mazda MX5 in a lottery, what would the cost base be to you given that you might want to sell it to buy a car more fitting (boring) for an accountant?

(9) Ms. Dempster has had her company buy her a car and register it in her name. The CRA discovered this and has assessed her with a shareholder benefit for $35,000, the value of the car. Ms. Dempster is going to have to sell the car to pay the tax liability. What will her cost base be on the car?   ITA: 15(1)

(10) On July 1 of this year, John Smith died leaving his wife and four children in financial difficulty. In order to earn extra income Mrs. Smith painted the basement, put carpet down, and then rented it to students. Comment on the tax issues.

(11) On July 1 nine years ago, Ms. Marr was transferred with her family to Victoria from Toronto by her employer, a large public company. She was sure that the value of her Toronto house would go up significantly so she kept it and rented a house in Victoria. It was this year that the same employer moved Ms. Marr and her family back to Toronto, at which time they moved back into their house. However, they found that the neighbourhood had changed significantly so they decided to sell the house and buy in another location. Discuss how much of the principal residence exemption she can claim on the sale of the Toronto home.

(12) Last year Ms. Milne inherited $5 million from her uncle's estate and is now appalled by the amount of tax that she has to pay on her interest income. She has always liked the Cayman Islands and has decided to move there permanently in order to avoid Canadian tax. Her only assets are $5 million of term deposits but she has heard that there is a lot of tax to pay on leaving the country. What do you think?

(13) Mr. Shiloh was transferred to Canada by his employer four years ago and is now being transferred back to the U.S. At the time he entered Canada he held shares in his U.S. employer which are listed on the TSX Stock Exchange. He still owns all these shares and is unhappy about all the tax he is going to have to pay on the deemed disposition. Advise him.   ITA: 128.1(4)

(14) Ms. Green has been told that a good way to create a capital gain is to buy shares on the stock market and then sell someone an option to buy the shares at a price slightly higher than the current market price. Her understanding is that the proceeds on the sale of the option is a capital gain. What advice can you give her?

(15) Mrs. Garland has been going south for many years and usually keeps some U.S. currency handy in case she needs it. This year, because of some unusual fluctuations in the Canadian dollar, she realized an exchange loss on her U.S. dollar transactions of $2,500. How will this be treated for tax purposes?

(16) Mr. Oats is a farmer who is fortunate enough to have farm land close to the city. Because of the prime location he has been approached to sell the land, but he is reluctant to do so since he wants to farm for the next five years. However, he is willing to sell someone an option to buy the land in five years at what he thinks is a generous price. He is to receive $50,000 for granting this option. He thinks he can defer the gain on granting the option until the year of sale by reducing the ACB of his land by $50,000. What do you think?

(17) Mr. Rollins bought a convertible debenture two years ago for $10,000 and is now in the process of converting it into common shares of the company. The debenture is convertible into 1,000 common shares. At the time of the conversion the common shares are worth $20 each. What are the tax effects of the disposition of the debenture and the acquisition of the shares?

(18) Mrs. Gleba owns 20 acres of land that have an appraised value of $100,000. She is considering selling the land to a friend for $50,000 in order to have the friend living closer to her. The two individuals are not related. What tax issues would you discuss with her?

(19) Scott was 25 years old when his father Bill gave him shares in Bell Canada as a gift. Bill had paid $1,000 for them 10 years ago and they were worth $5,000 at the time of the gift. Scott has come to you to find out how much tax he will have to pay. Discuss the tax implications to Scott and Bill of the gift.

CHAPTER 7

¶7,825 MULTIPLE CHOICE QUESTIONS

Question 1

During the year, Mina sold the following personal assets, all of which she had acquired within the last 10 years:

	Cost	Proceeds
Automobile	$20,000	$18,000
Boat	600	1,500
Painting	600	1,300
Jewellery	1,400	200

Her capital gain for the year from these dispositions is:

(A) $900

(B) $800

(C) $500

(D) $400

Question 2

Amanda sold her cottage for $130,000 in May 2016. The cottage cost her $50,000 in 2009 and qualifies as a principal residence. The only other principal residence that Amanda has owned during her lifetime was her Toronto home, which she owned from 2007 to 2015. Even though she sold it for $200,000 more than it cost, she did not report the gain on her 2015 tax return because it was her principal residence. What is the minimum taxable capital gain that Amanda must report on her 2016 tax return in respect of the sale of the cottage?

(A) $80,000

(B) $25,000

(C) $30,000

(D) $50,000

Question 3

Gary Chin purchased his first and only principal residence in 1999 for $350,000. The residence was in Toronto, and when he was transferred to Windsor because of a promotion to managing partner in 2010, he rented the residence. The residence was worth $550,000 in 2010 and he elected to be deemed not to have changed the use of the residence. Gary rented an apartment in Windsor with the expectation of moving back into his Toronto residence on retirement. On January 1, 2016, Gary received an unsolicited offer of $850,000 for the Toronto residence and sold it. Which of the following is a true statement?   ITA: 45(2)

(A) There is no taxable capital gain to report in 2010 or 2016 in respect of the principal residence.

(B) There is no capital gain to report in 2010 in respect of the principal residence. The taxable capital gain is $13,889 in 2016 in respect of the principal residence.

(C) The taxable capital gain is $100,000 in 2010 and $150,000 in 2016 in respect of the principal residence.

(D) The taxable capital gain is $250,000 in 2016 in respect of the principal residence.

Question 4

A Canadian resident individual received a stock dividend from a public corporation of one share. The dividend is a taxable dividend. The stock dividend resulted in an increase in the paid-up capital of $4 for each share issued but the fair market value of each share is $10. Which of the following statements is correct about the stock dividend received?

(A) The cost of the stock is deemed to be $4 and the individual's net income increases by $4.

(B) The cost of the stock is deemed to be $4 and the individual's net income increases by $5.52.

(C) The cost of the stock is deemed to be $10 and the individual's net income increases by $10.

(D) The cost of the stock is deemed to be $10 and the individual's net income is deemed to be $13.80.

Question 5

Donna Jailal has provided you with the following information in connection with her income tax return for the year:

Capital Gains:

Shares	$1,600
Personal-use property	700
Listed personal property	500

Capital Losses:

Shares	$ 820
Personal-use property	1,000
Listed personal property	140
Listed personal property losses from the previous year	100

What is the minimum net taxable capital gain that she must report as Division B income for the year?

(A) $370

(B) $740

(C) $870

(D) $920

Question 6

On December 31 of this year, Ms. Y gave her 6-year-old child some common shares of a public corporation with an adjusted cost base of $900,000 and a fair market value of $1,000,000. Which one of the following statements is TRUE?

(A) The attribution rule will apply to attribute to Ms. Y any future dividends received by her child on the shares. This attribution will continue until the year in which the child becomes 18 years old.

(B) The attribution rule will apply to attribute to Ms. Y any future dividends received by her child on the shares as well as any capital gains or losses if her child sells the shares. This attribution will continue until the year in which the child turns 18 years of age.

(C) Ms. Y will report no gain or loss on the transfer of property this year because it is a gift.

(D) Ms. Y will report a $100,000 taxable capital gain on the gift this year.

CHAPTER 7

Question 7

Ms. Y sells a stock (adjusted cost base $900,000) to her husband for $800,000 cash (the fair market value of the stock) and elects out of the interspousal rollover. Which one of the following statements is TRUE?   ITA: 73(1)

(A) Ms. Y will report an allowable capital loss of $50,000 which she can only deduct against taxable capital gains.

(B) Ms. Y does not have a capital loss because transfers to a spouse are made for proceeds equal to adjusted cost base.

(C) Ms. Y does not have a capital loss because of the superficial loss rules.

(D) The attribution rule will apply to attribute to Ms. Y any future dividends received by her husband on the shares as well as any capital gains or losses if her husband sells the shares.

Question 8

Mike purchased 100 shares of Pubco (a taxable Canadian corporation and public company) in 2013 for $3.11 per share plus $39 in commissions. In 2014, Mike purchased another 100 shares of Pubco for $4 per share plus a brokerage commission of $50. On March 1, 2016, when the shares were worth $6 per share, Mike gifted half the Pubco shares to his 8-year-old son and half to his wife (no special elections were filed). What is the amount of the taxable capital gain that Mike must report in 2016?

(A) $100

(B) $122

(C) $200

(D) $400

Question 9

Mr. Smith died on June 30 of this year and left his entire estate to his son, Mark. His executor has provided you with a list of assets and their fair market value at the date of death.

List of Assets	Cost	Fair Market Value
Toronto home (sole principal residence during past 23 years)	$300,000	$840,000
Rental property in London, Ontario		
— Land	50,000	100,000
— Building (UCC: $2,000)	25,000	35,000
Mutual fund units	12,000	60,000
Shares of a public companies	90,000	100,000

What is the amount that must be included in Mr. Smith's Division B income for the year of death?

(A) $59,000

(B) $70,500

(C) $82,000

(D) $352,000

Question 10

Mr. T ceased to be a resident of Canada on September 1, 2016. At that date, he owned the following assets:

	Year acquired	Cost	Fair market value Sept. 1, 2016
Rental real estate in Canada	2001	$50,000	$100,000
Registered retirement savings plan	2009	60,000	80,000
Painting	2012	6,000	10,000
Shares of a public corporation (listed) resident in Canada (owns less than 1%)	2013	10,000	40,000

Which one of the following amounts represents Mr. T's minimum taxable capital gain on the above assets for 2016?

(A) $15,000

(B) $17,000

(C) $27,000

(D) $42,000

CHAPTER 7

¶7,850 EXERCISES

Exercise 1

ITA: 40(2)(*b*), 54

Ms. Amin has come to you for advice on the tax consequences of the disposition of the following two residences in 2016:

Residence	Date of purchase	Cost	Selling price
Regina home	2005	$400,000	$517,500
Cottage	2010	250,000	375,000

— *REQUIRED*

Compute the minimum amount of taxable capital gains.

Exercise 2

ITA: 40(2)(*b*)

Peter Patel has only two residences which he wishes to dispose of in 2016. The following facts relate to those residences:

	Date purchased	Cost	Real estate commission	Estimated selling price
City home	2001	$180,000	$12,000	$247,000
Cottage	2006	90,000	6,000	164,000

— *REQUIRED*

Determine how Peter must designate residences in order to achieve the minimum capital gain.

Exercise 3

ITA: 40(2)(*b*), 45, 54, 54.1

Howard Bauer, who presently lives in Vancouver, is considering moving to Montreal. Although Howard intends to purchase a home in Montreal, he does not want to sell his fully-paid Vancouver home in case he decides to return some time in the future. Howard would rent his Vancouver home which cost him $50,000 in 2002 and now has a fair market value of $350,000.

— *REQUIRED*

Discuss the tax implications concerning Howard's Vancouver home if:

(A) Howard is self-employed; or

(B) Howard is employed.

Exercise 4

ITA: 41, 54

Karl Kim disposed of the following assets in 2016, all of which were bought within the last nine years:

	Sale price	Cost	Selling cost
Painting	$2,000	$ 300	$100
Antique clock	1,200	250	20
Outboard motor	750	500	15
Gold coin	600	1,000	10

— *REQUIRED*

Determine Karl's net taxable capital gain for the year.

Exercise 5

ITA: 53(1)(*f*), 54

Ivan Bedard purchased the following shares of Solid Investments Ltd.:

March 1, 2015	100 shares @ $30 including brokerage
June 1, 2016..................	150 shares @ $35 including brokerage
January 10, 2017	200 shares @ $26 including brokerage

On December 15, 2016, Ivan sold 200 shares @ $25 less brokerage of $75.

— *REQUIRED*

(A) Determine Ivan's taxable capital gain or allowable capital loss on his December 15, 2016 disposition.

(B) Compute the adjusted cost base of the shares on hand on January 10, 2017.

Exercise 6

ITA: 47(1)

Regan San Juan participated in the following stock transactions to December 31, 2016:

Date	Description	Share price	Number of shares	Broker fees
Jan. 1/10	Hi Growth Co. — purchased	$3.00	1,000	$70
Jun. 5/11	Hi Growth Co. — purchased	2.80	3,000	90
Aug. 5/11	Hi Growth Co. — purchased	3.80	1,500	70
Dec. 3/12	Hi Growth Co. — purchased	5.10	1,000	120
May 1/13	Hi Growth Co. — sold	7.50	3,000	420
Nov. 8/14	Hi Growth Co. — purchased	5.75	1,000	130
Jan. 9/15	Hi Growth Co. — sold	8.40	1,500	240
Jan. 10/10	Hi Risk Co. — purchased	0.25	20,000	200
Jan. 14/10	Hi Risk Co. — purchased	0.80	4,000	75
May 20/16	Hi Risk Co. — sold	0.30	24,000	150

— *REQUIRED*

(a) Compute Regan's adjusted cost base for the shares of Hi Growth Co. that he still holds at the end of 2016.

(b) Compute Regan's 2016 taxable capital gain or allowable capital loss on the disposal of the Hi Risk Co. shares.

Exercise 7

ITA: 3, 5, 6, 7, 8, 9

Fong currently earns $23,000 income from employment and $10,000 from operating a part-time coffee bar business. In 2007, Fong inherited an antique painting. At that time the heirloom was worth $9,000. Today, the painting is apparently worth $29,000.

— *REQUIRED*

What would Fong's income for tax purposes be if he sold the painting and realized a capital gain?

Exercise 8   ITA: 53(2)

Miriam Franklin decided to purchase shares in Strippit Limited, a public company, listed on the Canadian Venture Exchange. Miriam purchased 1,000 shares at $35 per share plus brokerage of $500 on December 10, 2006.

Miriam received the following dividends during the intervening years:

February 1, 2009 . . . . .   A stock dividend of 5% with a paid-up capital of $10 per share.
April 10, 2011 . . . .   A stock dividend of 10% with a paid-up capital of $10 per share.
August 1, 2013 . . . .   A stock dividend of 20% with a paid-up capital of $10 per share.

— *REQUIRED*

Determine the adjusted cost base of Miriam's shares as at December 31, 2016.

Exercise 9   ITA: 251

Which of the following individuals are not at arm's length with Ms. Gamma:

(A) her brother's wife?

(B) her niece?

(C) her husband from whom she is legally separated?

(D) an unrelated person?

Exercise 10

James Meadows is not at arm's length with his son Hayden. James wants Hayden to have a painting   ITA: 69(1)
that cost him $1,200 and now has a fair market value of $1,500. What are the consequences under the non-arm's length transfer rules to James and Hayden if:

(A) he sells the painting to him for $2,000?

(B) he sells the painting to him for $1,200?

(C) he gives the painting to him without any financial consideration?

Exercise 11   ITA: 73, 74.1, 74.2, 74.5;
                                                                          IT-511R

Alice Verwey is considering the following courses of action in transferring assets to her spouse this year:

(A) gifting to her husband shares with a fair market value of $15,000 and an adjusted cost base of $12,000;

(B) selling to her husband shares with a fair market value of $15,000 and an adjusted cost base of   ITA: 73(1)
$12,000 for cash of $15,000. An election out of the interspousal rollover was made;

(C) selling to her husband shares with a fair market value of $15,000 and an adjusted cost base of $12,000 for a $15,000 non-interest bearing promissory note with a definite repayment period;

(D) gifting to her husband $15,000 such that he purchases the shares on the open market; and

(E) lending her husband $15,000 evidenced by a non-interest bearing promissory note with a definite repayment period such that he purchases the shares on the open market.

— *REQUIRED*

Discuss the tax implications arising from the above transactions and any subsequent disposition by the spouse.

¶7,850

Exercise 12

ITA: 128.1(4), 115

Mr. Emerson, a United States citizen, entered Canada on June 1, 2011, and became resident in Canada for tax purposes. Mr. Emerson had a capital asset A which he brought with him upon his entry to Canada. The cost of the asset was $2,000 and the fair market value was $5,000 at the time of entry. In 2012, Mr. Emerson purchased another capital property B for $10,000. Mr. Emerson is considering returning to the United States on a permanent basis in 2016. He estimates that the two properties will have fair market values of $12,000 for A and $20,000 for B.

— REQUIRED

Discuss the tax consequences of Mr. Emerson's pending departure from Canada.

CHAPTER 7

¶7,875 ASSIGNMENT PROBLEMS

Type 1 Problems

Problem 1

During the year Rachael had the following transactions in common shares of Carnegie Inc., a Canadian public company. She would like you, as her tax adviser, to explain the tax consequences to her of each of the following transactions:

Date	Transaction	Price/Share	Number of Shares	Broker Fees	Notes
Jan 15/16	Purchase	$35	1,000	$700	
Feb 20/16	Purchase	37	200	150	
April 5/16	Stock dividend — 10%		120		1
Sept 16/16	Stock split		1,320		2
Nov 30/16	Sold	17	100	75	
Dec 12/16	Purchase	13	200	125	

Notes:

(1) The April 5, 2016 stock dividend resulted in an increase in paid-up capital of $30 per share.

(2) The stock split gave Rachael one share for every share she held at the time.

(3) On December 15th she received a cash dividend of $10 per share.

Problem 2

This is a continuation of Assignment Problem 2 in Chapter 3. The following two situations are not related. Once again, you have been asked for advice on employee stock options by two different clients.

(1) Omer is part of the management team of a Canadian public company and is eligible for the employee stock option plan. A few years ago he received an option on 1,000 shares. The option required him to pay the option price of $30 (the value at the time the option was granted) for the shares at the time he exercises his option.

Omer exercised the option three years ago when the shares were worth $35 and is now selling the shares for $45. He has asked you to tell him the amount of income he will have to report.

(2) Hilda is part of the management team of a Canadian-controlled private company and is eligible for the employee stock option plan. A few years ago she received an option on 1,000 shares. The option required her to pay the option price of $30 (the value at the time the option was granted) for the shares at the time she exercises her option.

Hilda exercised the option three years ago when the shares were worth $35 and is now selling the shares for $45. She has asked you to tell her the amount of income she will have to report.

Problem 3

ITA: 53

Ivy Jackson invested $2,000 on April 1, 2015, in Growth Mutual Fund sold by a major financial institution. Her investment purchased 72.788 units of the fund. On December 31, 2015, the fund allocated $96.37 of capital gains to her account. As a result, the $96.37 was reinvested in the fund to purchase 3.774 units at the market value of $25.535 per unit.

On June 30, 2016, she sold 25 of her units for a total of $718.

Ivy has asked you to calculate the effects of these events on her income for tax purposes in 2015 and 2016.

Problem 4

Brandon died on March 15, 2016. His estate is not complicated, as most of his assets were bank deposits. However, he did have 1,000 shares in a public company at the time of his death. Of these, he left 500 to his surviving spouse and 500 to his daughter. The executor would like your advice on the tax consequences to the estate and the beneficiaries of these bequests.

The shares have a fair market value at the time of death of $50 per share. Brandon's adjusted cost base at the time of his death was $20 per share.

Problem 5

The following two situations are not related:

(1) Stella moved to Canada from Greece early this year to work for a financial institution in Toronto. Her family moved with her and they bought a house in Oakville. At the time of her move, she owned shares of a public company listed on the New York Stock Exchange. These shares had a fair market value of $40,000 at the time she became a resident. She originally paid $25,000 for the shares. They are now worth $50,000.

Stella is now considering selling these shares and has asked you to advise her on the Canadian tax consequences.

(2) Harry moved to England from Canada early this year to work for a financial institution in Oxford. His family moved with him and they bought a house near Oxford. At the time of his move, he owned shares of a public company listed on the New York Stock Exchange. These shares had a fair market value of $40,000 at the time he ceased to be a resident. He originally paid $25,000 for the shares. They are now worth $50,000.

Harry is now considering selling these shares and has asked you to advise him on the Canadian tax consequences.

Problem 6

Donna has 1,000 shares in a Canadian public company that are worth $100,000 and pay a dividend of $5,000 each year. Her adjusted cost base on these shares is $70,000. She is already in the top tax bracket. For estate planning purposes she is proposing the following options, but she would like your advice as her personal tax planner before she makes a decision.

Options considered:

(1) Give the shares to her husband.

(2) Give the shares to her 15-year-old daughter.

(3) Give the shares to her 25-year-old daughter.

Problem 7

Katie has Canadian public company shares that are worth $50,000 and pay a dividend of $2,500 each year. Her adjusted cost base on these shares is $35,000. She is already in the top tax bracket. She would like your advice on the following proposed transactions:

Sell the shares to her husband

(1) Sell the shares to him for cash of $50,000

(2) Sell the shares to him for a non-interest bearing note of $50,000

(3) Sell the shares to him for cash of $40,000.

Sell the shares to her 25-year-old daughter

(1) Sell the shares to her for cash of $50,000

(2) Sell the shares to her for a non-interest bearing note of $50,000

(3) Sell the shares to her for cash of $40,000.

Problem 8

Ten years ago, Mr. Chu invested in Able Inc., a Canadian private company which is a "small business corporation". He invested $100,000 in common shares and made an unsecured loan of $60,000 with an interest rate of 5%. He has been receiving interest on this loan until recently. He has just found out that due to the bankruptcy of a significant customer and the loss of the related accounts receivable, Able Inc. is also in significant financial difficulty. Mr. Chu has come to you for tax advice.

(1) At this point, can Mr. Chu claim a loss on either the loan or the shares without disposing of the shares or debt?

(2) He has someone who is interested in buying the shares for $10,000 and the debt for $6,000. What are the tax consequences if he does this?

Problem 9

Sally and Harry have ended their 15-year marriage and are now living apart. They have sold their house and divided the proceeds, but they don't necessarily want to sell some shares that Sally owns. However, they have agreed that Sally needs to transfer 50% of her shares to Harry as part of the equalization payment.

Sally's shares have a fair market value of $40,000 and an adjusted cost base of $25,000.

They would like you to explain the tax consequences of this transfer.

Problem 10

Mr. and Mrs. Grand are married with one child, Noah, who is 16 years old. Mr. Grand owns his own business, which he operates out of a company called Father Inc. He owns all the shares. Mrs. Grand owns her own business, which she operates out of a company called Mother Inc. She owns all the shares of this company.

Identify, with reference to the Act, who is:

— Related

— Affiliated

— Arm's length

Problem 11   ITA: 41, 46

Mr. Adam Lamb sold the following assets this year, all of which were purchased within the last 10 years:

	Cost	Proceeds
Oil painting	$2,500	$ 500
Canoe	700	500
Rare coin	1,300	500
Bible produced in 1635	800	5,000
Antique car	15,000	10,000
Antique chair	300	1,200
Antique table	1,500	2,000

Mr. Adam Lamb has an unclaimed capital loss on listed personal property of $1,200 arising three years ago.

Mr. Lamb would like you to calculate his net taxable capital gain for this year.

¶7,875

Problem 12

ITA: 40(2)(*b*), 54

Mr. Doug Hart, who lives in Ontario, is contemplating moving to Switzerland. He came to you to discuss the tax consequences of disposing of his residences, as indicated below, in April 2016. He is single and ordinarily inhabits each of the residences for several months each year. He has never used his principal residence exemption since purchasing these properties.

The following information relates to the proposed 2016 dispositions.

Residence	Date of purchase	Cost	Selling price
Toronto home	2009	$160,000	$240,000
Farm in Quebec	2011	100,000	148,000
Condominium in Florida	2014	150,000	186,000

— REQUIRED

Mr. Hart has asked you to calculate the minimum amount of taxable capital gains that he will have to report in 2016.

Problem 13

ITA: 3, 41

Dave Stieb reported the following information for tax purposes:

	2014	2015	2016
Business income	$ 60,000	$ 65,000	$70,000
Property income	2,000	3,000	(1,000)
Capital gains:*			
Listed personal property	5,000	(7,000)	3,000
Personal-use property	(2,000)	5,000	4,000
Other	(8,000)**	6,000	(16,000)

---

* Brackets indicate capital loss.
** Includes a $4,000 business investment loss.

Your manager has asked you to calculate the income under Division B for each year *after* making the necessary amendments to the returns of other years. (Deal with each item line-by-line across the years, rather than computing income one year at a time.) Assume that no capital gains deduction was ever claimed.

Problem 14

ITA: 49

Doctor Wright, a general practitioner, has decided to move into a larger office. On July 1, 2015, he paid $5,000 to Devalued Properties Ltd., a developer, for a one-year option to purchase a residential building which he would use for business. On February 1, 2016, Dr. Wright sold his option to another medical practitioner, Dr. Holmes, for $2,000. On May 1, 2016, Dr. Holmes exercised the option and paid $100,000 for the building.

You have been asked to explain the tax implications in the above situation for Doctors Wright and Holmes and for Devalued Properties Ltd.

Problem 15

ITA: 3, 39, 41

Simon has the following sources of income and losses for tax purposes:

	2015	2016
Employment income	$25,000	$30,000
Property income	10,000	(4,000)
Business income — other	8,000	(9,000)
Capital gains (capital losses):		
— Listed personal property (Note 1)	4,000	(1,500)
— Personal-use property	8,000	(1,000)
— Shares — Canadian-controlled private corporation (Note 2)	(6,000)	(2,000)
— Public corporation	(12,000)	9,000

Additional Information

(1) Simon has a capital loss from listed personal property of $1,000 carried forward from 2012.

(2) These losses qualify as business investment losses. No capital gains deduction has ever been claimed.

Simon has asked you to calculate his Division B income for 2015 and 2016. (Deal with each item line-by-line across the years, rather than computing income one year at a time.)

Problem 16

ITA: 40(2)(*b*), 45(2), 54

Ms. Andrews purchased a home in Waterloo in 2006 at a cost of $86,000. She lived in the home until January 29, 2009, at which time she moved to Vancouver and rented a home in Vancouver. At the time of the move, Ms. Andrew's Waterloo residence had risen in value to $230,000. Expecting that real estate prices would continue to rise, Ms. Andrews chose to retain ownership of her Waterloo home and rented it to a third party.

In June 2015, Ms. Andrews decided she missed living in Waterloo and chose to return. She returned to Waterloo where she took up residence in her Waterloo home. At the time, the Waterloo residence had a fair market value of $294,000. In March 2016, Ms. Andrews decided she was tired of living in the city. She sold her Waterloo home for $284,000 and moved to the countryside.

Prior to filing her 2015 personal tax return, Ms. Andrews has requested your advice in minimizing the capital gains she must report on the sale of her home.

Ms. Andrews has asked you to calculate the minimum capital gain that she will have to report on the sale of her home under the following circumstances:

(A) assuming that she elects to be deemed not to have changed the use, and

ITA: 45(2)

(B) assuming that the election is not made.

Problem 17

ITA: 47, 53

Sherman Schleuter likes to invest in the stock market for the long term. While some of his investments have been failures, some have been very successful. Generally, he has been very fortunate in buying certain stocks at a relatively low price and selling them at their peak. One such stock is Headed For the Sky Corporation, a public corporation. Sherman has provided the following trade information related to this investment:

Nov. 8, 2009	Purchased 1,000 shares at initial offering price of $5.
Apr. 15, 2010	Purchased 2,000 shares at price of $3.50.
June 6, 2011	Sold 500 shares at $2.75, incurred brokerage commission of $50.
July 2, 2011	Purchased 2,000 shares at $4.
Apr. 30, 2012	Received a stock dividend of 10% of shares held; stock dividend increased corporation's paid-up capital by $.50/share.
June 20, 2013	Two-for-one stock split.
Nov. 8, 2014	Purchased 2,000 shares at $6.
Jan. 12, 2015	Received a stock dividend of 10% of shares held; stock dividend increased corporation's paid-up capital by $1/share.
Nov. 5, 2016	Sold 10,000 shares for $7.50/share, incurred brokerage commission of $650.

Sherman has asked you to calculate the taxable capital gain or allowable capital loss on the above transactions.

Problem 18

ITA: 52; 53

Ms. Plant decided to purchase shares in Schvantz Ltd., a public company. She purchased 800 shares at $25 per share plus brokerage of $690 on May 24, 2002.

The following additional transactions took place:

June 30, 2003	— Purchased 500 shares of Shtupp Metals Ltd., a public company, at $35 plus brokerage of $600.
Aug. 20, 2003	— Purchased 1,100 additional shares of Schvantz Ltd. at $30 plus brokerage of $940.
Aug. 27, 2005	— Sold 900 shares of Schvantz Ltd. at $24.50 per share plus brokerage fee of $760.

Sept. 20, 2005	— Purchased 600 additional shares of Schvantz Ltd. at $19.50 plus brokerage of $400.
Oct. 31, 2005	— Sold 200 shares of Shtupp Metals Ltd. at $32 per share plus brokerage fee of $220.
June 9, 2007	— Sold 250 shares of Schvantz Ltd. at $32 per share plus brokerage fee of $275.
May 24, 2009	— Received a 10% stock dividend from Shtupp Metals Ltd. (i.e., 30 shares) of which $20 per share issued was credited to paid-up capital.
June 30, 2011	— Sold 150 shares of Shtupp Metals Ltd. at $36.50 per share plus brokerage fee of $165.
Aug. 20, 2013	— Received 10% stock dividend from Schvantz Ltd. of which $20 per share issued was credited to paid-up capital.
Dec. 28, 2016	— Sold 350 shares of Schvantz Ltd. at $29 per share plus brokerage fee of $355, settlement date January 4, 2016.

Ms. Plant has asked you to calculate the taxable capital gain or allowable capital loss for each of the above sales.

Problem 19

ITA: 13(7)(*e*), 70(5)(*a*), 70(5)(*b*), 70(5)(*c*), 70(6)(*d*), 70(6)(*e*); ITR: 1100(2)(*h*), 1102(14)(*d*)

On July 31, 2016, Mary McArthur passed away after a lengthy illness. Mary was survived by her husband and one adult child, Margaret. Both her husband and daughter are residents of Canada. Information related to Mary's assets as at July 31, 2015, is set out below.

Description	Capital Cost/ACB	UCC	Fair market value	Beneficiary
Rental property — Toronto, Ontario				
Land	$40,000	n/a	$ 100,000	Spouse
Building (Class 3)	55,000	$15,000	145,000	Spouse
Rental property — Stratford, Ontario				
Land	25,000	n/a	45,000	Daughter
Building (Class 1)	65,000	42,000	93,000	Daughter
CBV shares (see Note below)		n/a	1,000,000	Spouse
View Canada shares (see Note below)		n/a	150,000	Daughter

Note:

Mary inherited these shares from her father upon his death in 2014. Her father had an adjusted cost base of $250,000 in the CBV shares. The fair market value of the CBV shares on the date of his death was $500,000. Her father had an adjusted cost base of $150,000 in the View Canada shares. The fair market value of the View Canada shares on the date of his death was $180,000.

The executor for the estate has asked you to calculate the minimum income and/or taxable capital gains to be reported by Mary McArthur for 2016 in respect of the above-noted assets. Ignore any available elections.

The executor has also asked you to determine the cost amounts of the above assets to the respective beneficiaries.

Problem 20

ITA: 3, 41

In Billy's attempt to sever all business and personal ties with Canada before beginning long-term and permanent employment in Beijing, he sold all his personal assets and most of his investments.

Description	Sale proceeds	Cost	Disposition costs
Personal residence	$475,000	$125,000	$3,600
Household furniture	20,000	35,000	800
Skis, bicycle, and skates	750	1,200	0
Rights to season tickets	4,000	3,500	0
Paintings	2,400	1,900	120
Chevrolet	3,600	12,000	350
Fishing lodge	45,000	31,000	4,500
Business loan — private	0	8,000	0
ABC shares (public co.)	46,000	20,000	200

Additional Information:

- All years available for a principal residence designation were used to exempt the gain on the personal residence, leaving no years available to designate the fishing lodge.

- The business loan was made to a Canadian-controlled private company, which is now in receivership.

- Billy has never claimed a capital gains exemption.

Billy has told you that his employment income is $48,000 and asked you to calculate his income for tax purposes.

Type 2 Problems

Problem 21

ITA: 13(7)(e)

On October 1, Roxanne acquired her brother's West Vancouver condominium rental property for $600,000 (ignore any land portion). Her brother has owned it for five years and had a capital gain of $250,000 on selling it to Roxanne. He will include 50% of that in his income. Roxanne believes she can earn net rental income of $9,000 annually, and $1/4$ of that amount for the final quarter of this year.

Roxanne has asked you to calculate the maximum CCA that she may claim in this first taxation year.

Problem 22

ITA: 7, 69, 73, 74.1, 74.2, 74.5, 56(4.1), 110(1)(d)

During 2015, Madame Martel exercised a stock option that she held in her employer (a CCPC). It is now November 2016. She is currently contemplating a number of scenarios in terms of the shares she received under the 2015 stock option exercise. She has asked you to explain the tax consequences of her actual and contemplated transactions.

The details of the stock option exercised during 2015 are as follows.

Number of shares purchased	Exercise price	Fair market value of shares at exercise date	Fair market value of shares at grant date
6,000	$20	$35	$20

The current fair market value of a share is $42.

Madame Martel is married and has two children (ages 21 and 15). She is expecting large dividends to be paid on the above shares in December 2016 and each December on an ongoing basis. She also expects that the shares will increase in value quite considerably over the near future. As a result, she is looking for a means of splitting income with her immediate family. She is proposing the following scenarios in terms of distributing these shares amongst her immediate family:

(1) gift the shares to her spouse and children ($1/3$ to her spouse and $1/3$ to each child);

(2) sell the shares to her spouse and children ($1/3$ to her spouse and $1/3$ to each child) for cash proceeds of $20 per share; or

(3) sell the shares to her spouse and children (⅓ to her spouse and ⅓ to each child) in exchange for a note payable of $42 per share.

The note payable described in (3), above, will be payable over five years with no interest. Since the note pays no interest and is repayable over future years, the estimated present value of the note is $25 per share.

Madame Martel has asked you to prepare a memorandum explaining the income tax consequences of her completed and proposed transactions.

Problem 23

ITA: Division B,
Subdivisions a, b, c

Mr. Richmond, a new client, has invested in rental properties, principal residences and other capital property with inheritance monies and other liquid cash. He provides you with the following information with respect to his 2016 taxation year.

Mr. Richmond is employed by Wealth Inc., a Canadian-controlled private corporation, and received the following income and benefits:

(1) Salary (net)		$49,789
Payroll deduction:		
Income taxes	$15,012	
CPP	2,544	
EI	955	
Registered pension plan (defined benefit: current service)	3,700	22,211
		$72,000

(2) Mr. Richmond paid professional fees of $500 to the Professional Engineers of Ontario.

(3) Mr. Richmond sold two lots of his stock options. He provides you with the following:

1st lot — 450 shares sold on March 15, 2016, for $26.50 per share. These shares were purchased in February 2009 for $8 at which time the shares were valued at $10.50.

2nd lot — 600 shares sold on December 5, 2016, for $25 per share. These shares were purchased on April 12, 2016, for $15 at which time the shares were valued at $21. The fair market value at the date of grant was $17.

(4) Mr. Richmond received an interest-free loan of $9,000 on March 12, 2016, to enable him to purchase shares of Wealth Inc. The loan was outstanding until the shares were sold on December 5, at which time the loan was repaid. Assume that the prescribed rate throughout the year was 7%.

In addition, during 2016, Mr. Richmond received the following income from various sources including certain capital dispositions.

(A) Mr. Richmond sold the following assets:

	Cost	Proceeds
Antique foot stool	$1,100	$ 900
Painting	950	1,500
Stamp collection	250	850

(B) During 2016, Mr. Richmond sold his two residences, in order to purchase a larger home in an expensive suburb. The following facts relate to these two residences:

	Date purchased	Cost	Commission	Proceeds
City home	2007	$95,000	$21,000	$350,000
Cottage	2002	15,500	12,000	200,000

(C) In addition to his residences, Mr. Richmond owns two rental properties. The following information pertains to these two properties:

	Wealthier St.	Richmount St.
Cost of land	$70,000	$100,000
Cost of building	$55,000	$ 80,000
UCC — January 1, 2016, Class 1	$39,000	$ 65,000

	Wealthier St.	*Richmount St.*
Rental revenue in 2016	$18,000	$ 7,600
Expenses:		
Taxes (property)	$ 2,100	$ 1,800
Other expenses	4,300	6,100
Mortgage interest	3,600	Nil
	$10,000	$ 7,900

The Richmount St. rental property was sold in November for proceeds of $250,000 less $9,000 of selling costs. Of the proceeds, $140,000 was for the land.

Mr. Richmond purchased the Wealthier St. rental property by placing a mortgage on his home. His monthly payments are $450 per month, of which $300 per month represents interest.

(D) Mr. Richmond gifted his wife $10,000 in June 2016 to allow her to invest in the stock market. Mrs. Richmond decided to be a cautious investor for the first while; as a result, she invested the $10,000 in Treasury Bills which earned $600 from June to December 2016.

(E) In addition, Mr. Richmond decided to provide his younger brother, who is 22, with a non-interest bearing loan of $5,000 to allow him to complete his Masters in Marine Biology. Mr. Richmond's brother paid his tuition fees with the funds.

(F) Mr. Richmond gifted $8,500 to each of his twin children, Dolly and Camp, aged 15. Both children placed their monies in high interest-bearing savings accounts each receiving interest of $1,050 in 2016.

(G) Mr. Richmond received dividends from the following investments:

> Wealth Inc. — a Canadian-controlled private corporation (from income
> taxed at the low corporate rate)   800

(H) Mr. Richmond owns units in Dumark Mutual Fund. He received a T3 slip from Dumark Mutual Fund indicating the following income amounts allocated to his account and reinvested in 2015:

> Capital gains $1,200
> Actual amount of dividends   347
> Taxable amount of dividends   500

Mr. Richmond had invested $20,000 in the Dumark Fund in 2015. This resulted in the purchase of 1,640.824 units of the fund. In 2015, income of $46.31 was allocated to his account and reinvested. The reinvestment resulted in the purchase of 3.845 units at the market value of $12.044 per unit. The 2016 income allocation resulted, on reinvestment of the $1,544.97, in the purchase of 119.358 units at the market value of $12.944 per unit. Late in 2016, after the income allocation, Mr. Richmond sold 1,000 units for a total of $12,881.

(I) Mr. Richmond sold a $100,000 Government of Canada bond for $115,327. This bond paid interest semi-annually at an interest rate which was much higher than current interest rates. The proceeds received of $115,327 included accrued interest of $5,327. Mr. Richmond had purchased the bonds on the open market for $98,000.

(J) In 2013, Mr. Richmond loaned $120,000 to his brother-in-law's company which was a small business corporation. The loan paid interest at commercial rates, but no interest was received in 2016 because the company went into receivership. As an unsecured creditor, Mr. Richmond received 10 cents on the dollar ($12,000) in 2016 in full payment of this loan.

(K) Mr. Richmond has a listed personal property loss, carried forward from 2010, of $500.

Mr. Richmond has asked you to calculate his Division B income according to the ordering rules in section 3 for 2016. Assume that he claimed $60,000 of his capital gains exemption in prior years. Ignore the effects of any leap year.

Problem 24

Theresa Vert is considering emigration to the United States. She has approached you to estimate the income tax consequences on her holdings of taxable capital property. Her plan is to dispose of all the real estate holdings and retain her investments in stocks and bonds. Theresa and her husband currently live in a downtown townhouse which was purchased in 1994 for a cost of $130,000. The estimated value is now $320,000. Theresa also inherited a cottage in 1995 (estimated fair market value was $55,000). The value of the cottage is now approximately $270,000.

In 1991, Theresa purchased a rental property for $105,000 of which $25,000 was allocated to the land. There is no mortgage on the property. The land and the building have a fair market value of $150,000 and $100,000, respectively. Legal costs at the time of purchase totalled $3,000 and the estimated cost of disposal is $20,000. The UCC on the building is $30,000.

Theresa also has the following investments:

• Common shares of Canadian publicly traded companies. These shares were purchased on October 19, 1995, at a cost of $140,000 and have current value of $190,000.

• A $100,000 10-year Province of Alberta 12% bond, due in five years, with interest payable annually on June 30. The bond has a current value equal to $110,000.

• A Steinway grand piano purchased at an auction for $8,000. Theresa can sell this to her piano teacher for $10,000.

Advise Theresa on the various income tax consequences of emigrating and the tax treatment of her holdings.

Type 3 Problems

Problem 25

Belleville Furniture Inc. ("Belleville") is a manufacturer of high-quality dining room furniture. This is the second generation of the Parker family that has owned the company, and the founder's son, Dave Parker, is having some problems since foreign imports are being brought into Ontario and sold at a price lower than Belleville's cost. Dave is certainly concerned about the short term, but feels that within the next eight to twelve months Belleville can adjust its sourcing of raw materials and the manufacturing process in order to reduce its costs to the point where its can be competitive, not only in the local market, but also in the Northeastern United States.

Dave's immediate problem is that when he asked the bank to increase Belleville's operating line of credit enough to cover Belleville's operational problems for the next eight to twelve months, the bank became concerned since its sole security for the operating loan is the inventory and the under 90-day accounts receivables. To maintain the existing line of credit, and to even consider the increase, the bank wants personal guarantees from both of Dave and his wife, Nancy, as well as a collateral mortgage on the company's building. As a result, Dave has you working on cash flow projections to support the loan, his lawyer is preparing the collateral mortgage, and an appraiser is preparing a valuation of the property. Dave feels that his chances of being approved are good.

Dave has agreed that he will sell the 20% interest that he personally owns in a company that operates a lumber mill that supplies Belleville. Dave bought the shares from the company on incorporation five years ago for $50,000 to help the arm's length supplier start the lumber mill. The other 75% of the company is owned by the supplier who has agreed to have his holding company buy the shares from Dave for $40,000 in cash. Dave had borrowed all the money for this investment through an interest-only demand loan with the bank. The bank has agreed to leave the full amount of the loan outstanding as long as Dave contributes the full $40,000 of proceeds into Belleville.

To prepare for its entry into the U.S. market, Belleville will set up a U.S. dollar bank account at its local bank for deposits from U.S. customers.

Dave would like your advice on the tax implications of his situation.

 [For more problems and solutions thereto, see the DVD accompanying the text-book.]

CHAPTER 7 —
DISCUSSION NOTES FOR REVIEW QUESTIONS

(1) "Proceeds of disposition" is defined to include the principal amount of the mortgage that is owed to the mortgage company. This transaction may trigger recaptured CCA or a terminal loss.

ITA: 13(1), 13(21.1), 20(16), 54 "proceeds of disposition" (*h*)

(2) Whenever the adjusted cost base becomes negative there will be an immediate capital gain. The only exception to this rule is for a partnership interest in a general partnership (but not a limited partnership).

ITA: 40(3)

(3) The principal residence exemption is restricted to one residence per family unit. The rules provide the framework for deciding which residence should be claimed for which years in order to maximize the exemption. Mr. Chan and his wife must choose one residence or the other for the exemption.

ITA: 54 "principal residence" (*c*)
ITA: 40(2)(*b*)

(4) The cottage is considered to be "personal-use property" (PUP). Any loss on the disposal of PUP cannot be deducted. The losses are considered to arise as a result of normal personal use over time.

ITA: 40(2)(*g*)(iii), 54

(5) For the purpose of calculating the capital gain or loss on any disposal of PUP the taxpayer's cost is deemed to be the greater of the adjusted cost base of the property and $1,000. Similarly, the taxpayer's proceeds of disposition are deemed to be the greater of actual proceeds and $1,000. Listed personal property (LPP) is defined to be a subset of PUP; therefore, the $1,000 rule also applies to LPP.

ITA: 46(1)
ITA: 54

(6) The dividend should be grossed up and the grossed-up amount included in income. The amount of the dividend before the gross-up will increase the cost base of the shares and effectively reduces the capital gain or increase the capital loss when the shares are sold.

ITA: 53(2)

(7) The result of the taxable capital gains minus the allowable capital losses cannot be negative. Any negative amount is a "net capital loss" that can be carried back three years or forward indefinitely.

ITA: 3(*b*) of Div. B; 111(1)(*b*), 111(8) of Div. C

(8) You would be deemed to have acquired the prize at a cost equal to its fair market value at the time you received it.

ITA: 52(4)

(9) The car has a cost base equal to the $35,000 benefit included in her income as a shareholder benefit.

ITA: 15(1), 52(1)

(10) If Mrs. Smith did not make any structural changes to the house, then there will not be any change in use. The house will still remain her principal residence. She will have to declare the rental income and can deduct the expenses that relate to it.

Income Tax Folio S1-F3-C2 — Principal Residence

(11) Since she was moved by her employer nine years ago and was still employed by that employer when she moved back this year, the Act modifies paragraph (*d*) of the definition of "principal residence" to allow her to continue to claim her house as her principal residence for more than the 4 years generally allowed on a normal change in use under the definition. All years qualify since she was still resident in Canada, as required. She still has to make the election not to have a change in use in the year they moved. As a result, on the sale of the house, she will be able to claim the full principal residence exemption.

ITA: 45(2), 54, 54.1

ITA: 40(2)(*b*)

(12) The Act causes a deemed disposition on all her property other than certain property and certain items that are subject to withholding tax. In this case the term deposits will be deemed to be disposed of, but since there is no capital gain, there would not be any tax.

ITA: 128.1(4)

(13) Mr. Shiloh will be excepted from the deemed disposition rules on the shares of his U.S. employer since he was in Canada less than 60 months in the past 10 years.

ITA: 128.1(4)

(14) The Act generally treats the sale of this option as a disposition with the cost base being nil. Therefore, the capital gain will be equal to the proceeds and will be taxed in the year the option is sold.

ITA: 49(1)

(15) The loss on foreign currency is a capital loss. However, as an individual, she must deduct $200 from the loss in arriving at her capital loss. In this case her capital loss is $2,300.

ITA: 39(2)(b)

(16) On the granting of an option there is a disposition and the ACB is deemed to be nil. He does not have the alternative of reducing the cost base.

ITA: 49(1)

(17) A rollover on the exchange of the common shares for the debentures is provided as long as the debenture had the conversion feature built into its terms and no consideration other than shares (i.e., cash) was received. The shares will have a cost base of $10 each, so the accrued gain of $10 per share will be deferred until the common shares are sold.

ITA: 51

(18) If a person sells something to someone with whom he or she does not deal at arm's length then the proceeds will be deemed to be the fair market value. Related parties do not deal at arm's length, but in this case the two are not related. However, it is a question of fact whether persons not related to each other are dealing at arm's length. In this case there is no evidence of hard bargaining and the transaction is obviously not at fair market value. Therefore, it would be unlikely that they would be considered to be dealing at arm's length and the proceeds would likely be deemed to be $100,000. Her friend will have a cost base equal to what she paid for the land of $50,000. As a result there will be double taxation.

ITA: 69, 251, 251(1)(c)

(19) At the time of the gift, Bill will be deemed to have sold the shares at their fair market value. Scott will be deemed to have received the shares at a cost to him equal to the fair market value at the time of the gift. Since the shares were a gift, the attribution rules applicable to an income-splitting loan will not apply.

ITA: 69(1)(b), 69(1)(c)

ITA: 56(4.1)

CHAPTER 7

CHAPTER 7 — SOLUTIONS TO MULTIPLE CHOICE QUESTIONS

Question 1

(C) is correct. The loss on the automobile is not allowed since it is personal-use property (PUP). The $1,000 rule means that the gain on the boat (which is PUP) is $500, the gain on the painting (which is listed personal property (LPP)) is $300, and the loss on the jewellery (which is LPP) is $400. Since the deductible portion of the $400 LPP loss is limited to the LPP gain in the year ($300), the capital gain is: $500 + $300 – $300 = $500. The $100 LPP loss can be carried over against LPP gains.   ITA: 2, 41(1), 46(1), 54

(A) is incorrect, because it ignores the $1,000 rule and computes the gain on the boat (PUP) as $900, the gain on the painting (LPP) as $700, and the loss on the jewellery (LPP) as $1,200. The LPP gain is then offset by a portion of the LPP loss, leaving the $900 gain.

(B) is incorrect, because it does not subtract the deductible portion of the LPP loss from the LPP gain: $500 + $300 = $800.

(D) is incorrect, because it deducts the full LPP loss ($400) against all the gains: $500 + $300 – $400 = $400.

Question 2

(B) is the correct answer. Since Amanda had no capital gain on her house, she must have designated it as her principal residence for all but one of the years 2007 to 2015. She therefore has two years to designate in respect of the cottage: one of the years not used on the house (say, 2015) plus 2016. Since she owned the cottage eight years (2009 to 2016), the principal residence exemption for the cottage is: $3/8 \times \$80,000 = \$30,000$ (3 = 2 years designated + "one-plus rule"). Therefore, Amanda's taxable capital gain is $25,000 ($\frac{1}{2} \times$ ($80,000 – $30,000 principal residence exemption)).

(A) is incorrect, because $80,000 is the capital gain before the exemption.

(C) is incorrect, because it uses $2/8 \times \$80,000 = \$20,000$ as the principal residence exemption: $\frac{1}{2} \times$ ($80,000 – $20,000) = $30,000.

(D) is incorrect, because $50,000 is the capital gain, not the taxable capital gain.

Question 3

(B) is correct. Because Gary made the election to be deemed not to have changed the use in respect of the property, there is deemed to be no change in use in 2010. The only disposition occurs in 2016 on the date of sale. The Act allows Gary to designate the property as his principal residence for up to four years where the election was made. The gain on the property is $500,000 ($850,000 – $350,000) and the total years of ownership were 18 (1999 to 2016) and the maximum number of years that can be designated is 16 (1999 to 2010 plus 4). Therefore, the principal residence exemption is [(16 + 1)/18] $\times$ $500,000 or $472,222. The capital gain is therefore $27,778 ($500,000 – $472,222) and the taxable capital gain is $13,889 ($\frac{1}{2} \times$ $27,778).   ITA: 45(2) ITA: 54 ITA: 45(2)

(A) is incorrect because there is a taxable capital gain to report in 2016 because not all years of ownership qualify as years eligible for a principal residence. The extension of the four-year rule does not apply, because Gary did not move back into the residence before it was sold.   ITA: 54.1

(C) incorrectly calculates taxable capital gains of $50,000 in 2010 [$\frac{1}{2}$ ($550,000 – $350,000)] and 2016 [$\frac{1}{2}$ ($850,000 – $550,000)]. The timing is wrong because there is no deemed disposition in 2010 because of the election. The amount is also wrong because 12 years (1999 – 2010) can be designated in respect of the residence.   ITA: 45(2)

(D) correctly calculates the gain in 2016 as $500,000 without claiming any principal residence exemption, resulting in a taxable capital gain of $250,000 ($\frac{1}{2} \times$ $500,000).

Question 4

(B) is correct. The amount of the dividend is $4, the increase in the paid-up capital, and this is also the cost of the shares (ssec. 53(3)). However, the individual's net income would increase by $5.52, since it is a taxable dividend: $4 × 1.38 gross-up = $5.52. ITA: 82(1)

(A) is incorrect because although $4 is the amount of the dividend, the amount included in net income is the grossed-up dividend (1.38 × $4 = $5.52).

(C) is incorrect because the amount of the dividend is not based on the $10 fair market value of the share.

(D) is also incorrect because the amount of the dividend is not based on the $10 fair market value of the share and the amount included in income is the increase in paid-up capital grossed up by 1.38, not the fair market value grossed up by 1.38.

Question 5

(C) is correct.

Shares		$1,600
Personal-use property		700
Listed personal property	$500	
Listed personal property	(140)	
Listed personal property losses of prior year	(100)	260
Shares		(820)
Personal-use property		Nil
Capital gain		$1,740
Taxable capital gain (½)		$ 870

(A) is incorrect because it deducts the $1,000 personal-use property loss: ½ ($1,740 – 1,000) = $370.

(B) is incorrect because it deducts the $1,000 personal-use property loss and does not multiply by the ½ fraction: ($1,740 – $1,000) = $740.

(D) is incorrect because it does not deduct the listed personal property loss of other years: ½ × ($1,740 + $100) = $920.

Question 6

(A) is correct. ITA: 74.1(2)

(B) is incorrect, because capital gains or losses do not attribute on loans or gifts to minors.

(C) is incorrect, because there will be a capital gain on the gift. ITA: 69

(D) is incorrect. $100,000 is the capital gain. The taxable capital gain is:

½ × $100,000 = $50,000.

Question 7

(C) is correct. There is a superficial loss because Ms. Y has incurred a loss and an affiliated person (Mr. Y) acquired the shares within 30 days of the disposition. ITA: 40(2)(*g*), 54

(A) is incorrect, because it ignores the superficial loss rule and computes the loss as ½ × ($800,000 – $900,000).

(B) is not correct, because Ms. Y elected out of the interspousal rollover. ITA: 73(1)

(D) is not correct. There is no attribution because she elected out of the subsection 73(1) rollover and received fair market value consideration (i.e., $800,000 cash). ITA: 74.5

Question 8

(A) is correct since only the gift to the son will result in a taxable capital gain.

The ACB of Mike's stock is:

100 × $3.11 plus $39 commission (incl. sec. 7 benefit)	$350	
100 × $4 plus $50 commission	450	
200	$800 = $4 ACB per share.	ITA: 47, 53(1)(*i*)

His taxable capital gain on the gift to his son is: ½ ($6 − $4) × 100 = $100.

There is no taxable capital gain on the gift to his wife, because the transfer occurs at his $4 ACB since no special election was filed.   ITA: 73(1)

(B) incorrectly excluded brokerage commissions from the ACB of his shares as: ½ ($6 − $711/200) × 100 = $122.

(C) incorrectly computes a capital gain on the gift to Mike's wife: ½ ($6 − $4) × 200 shares = $200.

(D) is incorrect, because it incorrectly computes a capital gain on the gift to his wife and does not apply the ½ fraction to compute the taxable portion of the gain: ($6 − $4) × 200 = $400.

Question 9

(C) is correct. The calculation is as follows:

	Division B income
Toronto home (no capital gain; principal residence)	—
Rental property in London, Ontario	
— Land: ½ ($100K − 50K)	$25,000
— Building: recapture = $25K − $2K	23,000
Taxable capital gain = ½ ($35K − $25K)	5,000
Mutual fund units: ½ ($60K − $12K)	24,000
Shares of a public company: ½ ($100K − $90K)	5,000
	$82,000

(A) incorrectly ignores recapture: $82,000 − $23,000 = $59,000.

(B) incorrectly multiplies the recapture by the ½ taxable capital gains fraction: $25,000 + ½ × $23,000 + $5,000 + $24,000 + $5,000 = $70,500.

(D) incorrectly includes a capital gain on the principal residence: $82,000 + ½ × ($840,000 − $300,000) = $352,000.

Question 10

(B) is correct, because the taxable capital gain is computed as follows: listed shares of a public corporation resident in Canada (= ½ × ($40,000 − $10,000) = $15,000) + painting (= ½ ($10,000 − $6,000) = $2,000) = $17,000.

The rental real estate in Canada and the registered retirement savings plan are specifically exempted from the deemed disposition rules.   ITA: 128.1(4)

(A) incorrectly excludes the taxable capital gain on the painting.

(C) incorrectly includes ½ of the gain on the RRSP ($10,000).

(D) incorrectly includes a $25,000 taxable capital gain on the rental real estate in Canada.

CHAPTER 7 — SOLUTIONS TO EXERCISES

Exercise 1

Step 1: Determine gain per year of ownership

		Regina home		Cottage
Par. 40(2)(b) gain				
P of D		$ 517,500		$ 375,000
ACB		(400,000)		(250,000)
Gain		$ 117,500		$ 125,000
Gain per year	$\dfrac{\$117,500}{12 \text{ years}}$ =	$ 9,792	$\dfrac{\$125,000}{7 \text{ years}}$ =	$ 17,857

Step 2: Assignment of no-option years

In the five taxation years 2005 to 2009, Ms. Amin owned only the Regina home. Therefore, there is no option in those years but to designate the city home as her principal residence.

Step 3: Gain determined under paragraph 40(2)(b)

The gain per year of ownership for the cottage ($17,857) exceeds that for the city home ($9,792). If all seven years are assigned to the cottage, however, one year will be wasted. Hence, the city home should be designated for one of the years 2010 to 2016.

	Regina home	Cottage
Gain	$ 117,500	$ 125,000
Exemption	(68,542)[(1)]	(125,000)[(2)]
Capital gain	$ 48,958	Nil
Taxable capital gain	$ 24,479	Nil

— NOTES TO SOLUTION

(1) $\dfrac{1 + 5 + 1}{12}$ × $117,500 = $68,542; years designated — 2005–2009 and one of 2010–2016

(2) $\dfrac{1 + 6}{7}$ × $125,000 = $125,000; years designated — all but one of 2010–2016

Exercise 2

Step 1: Determine gain per year of ownership

		City home			Cottage		
P of D...................			$ 247,000			$ 164,000	ITA: 40(2)(b)
ACB....................	$ 180,000			$ 90,000			
SC.....................	12,000		(192,000)	6,000		(96,000)	
Gain...................			$ 55,000			$ 68,000	
Gain per year............	$\dfrac{\$55,000}{16 \text{ years}}$ =		$ 3,438	$\dfrac{\$68,000}{11 \text{ years}}$ =		$ 6,182	

Step 2: Assignment of no-option years

In the five taxation years 2001 to 2005, Peter owned only the city home. Therefore, there is no option in those years but to designate the city home as his principal residence.

Step 3: Gain determined   ITA: 40(2)(b)

The gain per year of ownership for the cottage ($6,182) exceeds that for the city home ($3,438). If all 11 years are assigned to the cottage, however, one year will be wasted. Hence, the city home should be designated for one of the years 2006 to 2016.

	City home	Cottage
Gain	$ 55,000	$ 68,000
Exemption	(24,063)[1]	(68,000)[2]
Capital gain	$ 30,937	Nil

—NOTES TO SOLUTION

[1] $\dfrac{1 + 5 + 1}{16} \times \$55,000 = \$24,063$; years designated — 2001–2005 and one of 2006–2016

[2] $\dfrac{1 + 10}{11} \times \$68,000 = \$68,000$; years designated — all but one of 2006–2016

Exercise 3

When Howard rents his home, he is deemed to have changed the use of the home and a capital gain may be triggered. However, Howard can designate the home with the appropriate number of years and should not be taxed on the gain. Under this course of action, Howard would now have a rental property from which he must declare the income less all his expenses. However, a rental loss could not be generated with capital cost allowance on the home and equipment therein.

ITA: 45(1)

ITR: 1100(15))

Alternatively, Howard could elect to defer the gain until he either sells the home or rescinds his election. Note that the CRA normally permits a retroactive election at the time of sale. In this situation, Howard would not be allowed to claim any capital cost allowance on the home or the election to be deemed not to have changed the use would be invalid.

ITA: 45(2)
Income Tax Folio S1-F3-C2 — Principal Residence
ITA: 45(2)

The election would permit Howard to designate his Vancouver home as his principal residence for at least four extra years depending upon whether he is self-employed or employed.

ITA: 45(2)

(A) Self-employed

Paragraph (*d*) in the definition of a "principal residence" permits Howard to designate his Vancouver home as his principal residence for four years, while it is being rented, if he elects to be deemed not to have changed the use according to paragraphs (*b*) and (*d*) of the definition.

ITA: 54
ITA: 45(2)

Howard might consider rescinding his election after the fourth year. This course of action would enable Howard to claim capital cost allowance after the fourth year subject to the loss restrictions discussed above.

(B) Employed

The Act waives the four-year restriction discussed above if Howard (or his wife) has moved at least 40 km closer to his new work location. Howard then can designate his Vancouver home as his principal residence during all the rental years if:

ITA: 54.1

   (i) Howard subsequently resumes ordinary habitation of his home while employed with the same employer; or

   (ii) Howard subsequently resumes ordinary habitation of his home within one year from the end of the year in which he terminates employment with that employer; or

   (iii) Howard dies.

Note that "ordinarily inhabited" means any time during the year according to the CRA, but Howard cannot temporarily move back in order to qualify for this exemption.

Income Tax Folio S1-F3-C2 — Principal Residence

CHAPTER 7

Exercise 4

	Painting		Antique clock		Outboard motor		Gold coin	
P of D		$2,000		$1,200		$1,000		$1,000
ACB	$1,000		$1,000		$1,000		$1,000	
SC	100	(1,100)	20	(1,020)	15	(1,015)	10	(1,010)
CG (CL)		$ 900		$ 180		$ (15)		$ (10)

Net taxable capital gain:

LPP — Painting....................	$ 900
— Gold coin....................	(10)[1]
	$ 890
— ½	$ 445
PUP — Antique clock (½ × $180)	90
	$ 535

—NOTE TO SOLUTION

[1] Listed personal property losses, whether current or carried-over, are applied at the full capital gain (capital loss) amount.

Exercise 5

(A)
P of D 200 shares @ $25	$5,000	
ACB 200 shares @ $33[1]	$6,600	
SC	75	(6,675)
CL[2] (Superficial loss of $1,675)		Nil

(B) Adjusted cost base of shares

50 shares @ $33	=	$1,650	
200 shares @ $26	=	5,200	
superficial loss		1,675	
		$8,525 ÷ 250 shares	= $34.10

—NOTES TO SOLUTION

[1]
100 shares @ $30	=	$3,000
150 shares @ $35	=	5,250
		$8,250 ÷ 250 shares = $33

[2] Since Ivan acquired additional shares of Solid Investments within the 30-day period.

Exercise 6

(a) For identical properties, the weighted "moving average" basis is to be used to calculate the ACB of each individual property (subsection 47(1)).   ITA: 47(1)

High Growth Co.

Date	Shares Purchased	Share Price	Adjusted Cost Base	ACB/Share
Jan. 1/10	1,000	$3.00	$ 3,070	$3.07
Jun. 5/11	3,000	2.80	8,490	
	4,000		11,560	2.89
Aug. 5/11	1,500	3.80	5,770	
	5,500		17,330	3.15
Dec. 3/12	1,000	5.10	5,220	
	6,500		22,550	3.47
May 1/13	(3,000)	3.47	(10,410)	
Nov. 8/14	1,000	5.75	5,880	
	4,500		18,020	4.00
Jan. 9/15	(1,500)	4.00	(6,000)	
	3,000		$12,020	4.00

Note: The disposition of shares has no effect on the moving average cost.

(b)

HIGH RISK CO. ACB:

Jan. 10/10	(20,000 × $0.25) + $200 =		$5,200
Jan. 14/10	(4,000 × $0.80) + $75 =		$3,275
Totals	24,000 shares		$8,475
May 20/16	Proceeds	$7,200	
	ACB	(8,475)	
	Broker fees	(150)	
	Capital loss	$(1,425)	
	Allowable capital loss	$(712.50)	

Exercise 7

ITA: 3, 5, 6, 7, 8, 9

		With Sale
Paragraph 3(*a*)	Sources of income	
Sections 5–8	Employment income	$23,000
Section 9	Business income	10,000
Paragraph 3(*b*)	Taxable capital gains	
	Sale of antique painting	
	(.50 × (29,000 − 9,000))	10,000
Section 3	Net income for tax purposes	$43,000

Exercise 8

Adjusted cost base:	
1,000 shares @ $35	$35,000
brokerage	500
2009 — stock dividend — 50 shares (5% × 1,000) × $10	500
2011 — stock dividend — 105 shares (10% × 1,050) × $10	1,050
2013 — stock dividend — 231 shares (20% × 1,155) × $10	2,310
	$39,360

Shares (1000 + 50 + 105 + 231) = 1,386
ACB per share: $39,360 ÷ 1,386 = $28.40

Exercise 9

(A) Since they are related by marriage, they are not at arm's length.   ITA: 251(2)(a), 251(6)(b)

(B) Since they are not considered to be related by blood, they are at arm's length.   ITA: 251(6)(a)

(C) Since they are still legally married, they are not at arm's length.

(D) The facts of a situation can determine that two unrelated persons are not at arm's length.   ITA: 251(1)(b)

Exercise 10

	James (seller or transferor)	*Hayden* (purchaser or transferee)
(A) sale at $2,000	has proceeds of $2,000 and, hence, a capital gain of $800 (i.e., $2,000 – $1,200)	deemed [par. 69(1)(a)] to have acquired at $1,500 resulting in potential double-counting of $500 gain
(B) sale at $1,200	deemed [par. 69(1)(b)] to have proceeds of $1,500 and, hence, a capital gain of $300	acquired at $1,200 resulting in potential double-counting of $300 gain
(C) gift	deemed [par. 69(1)(b)] to have proceeds of $1,500	deemed [par. 69(1)(c)] to have acquired at $1,500

Exercise 11

(A) (i) Since a gift is a transfer, the interspousal rollover would automatically deem that Alice's proceeds of disposition are equal to her adjusted cost base ($12,000), resulting in no capital gain.   ITA: 73

(ii) Alice would be subject to the income attribution rules on any dividends from the shares, because a gift would not meet the exception, since the fair market value of the property transferred exceeded the fair market value of the consideration received and an election out of the interspousal rollover was not made.   ITA: 74.1, 74.5(1)(a)   ITA: 73(1)

(iii) Alice would also be subject to capital gains attribution for the same reason as discussed in part (A)(ii), above. There would be full capital gains attribution on all substituted property.   ITA: 74.2; IT-511R, par. 27

(B) (i) Since Alice does elect out of the interspousal rollover, the non-arm's length transfer rule, with which the transaction conforms, will apply, since the cash consideration ($15,000) was equal to the fair market value of the property transferred. A capital gain of $3,000 would be triggered.   ITA: 73(1)   ITA: 69(1)(b)(ii)

(ii) There would be no income or capital gains attribution, because Alice has conformed with the attribution rule exception. The fair market value of the property transferred did not exceed the fair market value of the consideration received and an election out of the interspousal rollover was made.   ITA: 74.5(1)(a)   ITA: 73(1)

(C) (i) Unless Alice elects not to have the provisions of the interspousal rollover apply, there will be no capital gain triggered on the transfer to her husband.   ITA: 73

(ii) Although Alice has received consideration (debt) with a face value ($15,000) equal to the fair market value of the property transferred, the interest rate must be at least equal to the prescribed rate at the time or a commercial rate. In addition, the Act requires that Alice elect out of the interspousal rollover. Therefore, Alice will be subject to both income and capital gains attribution.   ITA: 74.5(1)(b)(i)   74.5(1)(c)

(D) The result would be the same as in (A), above, since the shares would be considered substituted property for a transfer of cash for no consideration.

(E) The result would be the same as in (C), above, since the shares would be considered substituted property.

Exercise 12

Capital property A

(A) If Mr. Emerson departs prior to June 1, 2016, there will be no capital gain on the capital asset which he brought from the U.S. by virtue of the 60-month short-term exemption.   ITA: 128.1(4)

(B) If he departs subsequent to June 1, 2016, there will be a taxable capital gain on ½ of the excess of the proceeds of disposition ($12,000) over the fair market value at the time of entry ($5,000), namely, $3,500.

Capital property B

(A) First, it is necessary to determine whether the capital property acquired in Canada is exempt from immediate departure tax but will be taxed on its ultimate disposition.   ITA: 2(3)

(B) If the property is not exempted then the taxpayer will be taxed at the time of exit from Canada.

CHAPTER 7

Chapter 8

Capital Gains: Business Related

Learning Goals

Know, Understand and Explain

By the end of this chapter you will know, understand and be able to explain:

- The tax implications of selling a property through instalment payments and the options available to minimize tax.

- The tax implications of a bad debt as it relates to the disposition of a capital property.

- The deferral available when a property is replaced within the eligible time frame for both involuntary and voluntary disposition.

- The rules related to the disposition of land and building where a terminal loss occurs as a result of the sale.

Apply

By the end of this chapter you will be able to apply your knowledge and understanding to:

- Conclude whether the nature of a transaction is business income or capital gain by applying accepted behavioural factors to case facts.

- Correctly calculate the capital gains reserve that may be claimed in a given period.

- Determine the adjusted cost base of a depreciable asset, including any allowable adjustments and for non-arm's length situations.

- Correctly calculate the deferral amount and the cost base of the new property under the replacement property rules for both capital gains and recapture.

- Correctly calculate the reallocation of proceeds of disposition between the land and building when a terminal loss occurs on the building as a result of the sale.

- Correctly determine the tax implication when a capital property has a deemed disposition as a result of a change in use.

- Apply your knowledge to specific circumstances to minimize the current tax paid by the client on the disposition of a capital property.

Review Questions
¶8,800 in the Study Guide

Multiple Choice Questions
¶8,825 in the Study Guide

Exercise Questions
¶8,850 in the Study Guide

Assignment Problems
¶8,875 in the Study Guide

CHAPTER 8 — LEARNING CHART

Problem Descriptions

Textbook Example Problems

8-1	Capital gains reserve
8-2	Recapture — Involuntary Disposition
8-3	Replacement property
8-4	Replacement property
8-5	Replacement property
8-6	Disposal of building with terminal loss
8-7	Disposition of depreciable property
8-8	Election on change in use
8-9	Foreign exchange gains and losses
8-10	Schedule 1 reconciliation

Multiple Choice Questions

1	Capital gain reserve
2	Replacement property
3	Income vs. capital
4	Replacement property
5	Disposal of building with terminal loss

Exercises

1	Replacement property
2	Sale of accounts receivable
3	Sale of building with terminal loss
4	Inherited property
5	Replacement property

Assignment Problems

1	Sale of land and building, reserve
2	Dividend in kind
3	Foreign exchange
4	Income vs. capital
5	Reserves if income or capital
6	Replacement property
7	Replacement property
8	Sale of building with terminal loss
9	Sale of building with terminal loss
10	Replacement property
11	Schedule 1 with capital transactions
12	Replacement property
13	Sale of land with apple trees

Study Notes

¶8,800 REVIEW QUESTIONS

(1) Tom, Dick, and Harry formed a partnership in order to invest in a tract of land just outside a large urban area. Five years later, the partnership sold the property making a large profit. According to the partnership agreement, profits from this venture were to be split equally. Discuss whether this is an income or a capital receipt.

(2) Rachel is a real estate salesperson who invests her spare cash in "good land buys" which she occasionally finds. This year Rachel sold one of these properties and realized a large profit. Is this an income or a capital receipt?

(3) Winston White, an accountant, uses his spare time and cash to trade in low-cost mining shares listed on a Canadian stock exchange. Winston made a large profit this year on his stock market transactions. Is this profit income or capital gain?

(4) Diana purchased some land to erect a shopping centre which she intended to sell. However, zoning bylaws could not be changed and Diana sold the property at a large profit. Is this profit income or a capital gain?

(5) Doug spends his Saturday afternoons at the race track. This year Doug was extremely fortunate and his net winnings were $15,000. How will these winnings be taxed?

(6) Mr. Cole bought six acres of lake-front property 15 years ago for $24,000. This year, he sold the three acres that are not on the lake to a neighbour who wanted the woodlot. His proceeds on the three acres sold are $30,000. Discuss what the cost base of the three acres sold would be.

(7) Mr. Bosma had 20 acres of his farm expropriated by the city for industrial land in 2015. Because he disputed their value, the proceeds were not finally decided until 2016. How soon does he have to replace the land in order to defer the tax on the capital gain realized on the sale of the land?

(8) Opco Ltd. had a large piece of equipment destroyed by fire with the insurance proceeds being paid and the machine replaced in the same year. Can the replacement property rules be applied?

(9) Mrs. Smith owns 100% of Holdco Inc., which in turn owns 100% of Opco Inc. Holdco owns the building which is used by Opco in its active business and rents it to Opco under a five-year lease. Mrs. Smith wants to sell the building and buy a bigger one for the same purpose, but she has been told that the building is considered to be a rental property and, therefore, does not qualify for the replacement property rules since it is not a "former business property". She has asked for your comments.

ITA: 248(1)

(10) Mr. Carr bought and operated a parking lot for the past 10 years. He has now decided that it is time to do something different. However, instead of selling the parking lot he wants to rezone the property and develop and sell condominium apartments. On July 1 of last year, he applied for rezoning and on December 1 of last year, he received the zoning change and a building permit. By October 31 of this year, he had completed construction and sold the units. What kind of income would he have to report and when?

(11) Last year Ms. Chung sold some land that was capital property and realized a capital gain of $150,000. As part of the proceeds she took back a note for $100,000 at 12% which unfortunately was unsecured. This year she realized that the note will become a bad debt, but since she has not disposed of the note she does not think that it can be used for tax purposes. What is your advice to her? What would be the result if the land that was sold was personal-use property?

CHAPTER 8

¶8,825 MULTIPLE CHOICE QUESTIONS

Question 1

On April 1, 2016, X Ltd., with a December 31 year-end, sold a parcel of land, a capital property with an adjusted cost base of $100,000, for $600,000. The $600,000 proceeds were payable in the form of a mortgage, with principal payments of $90,000 due every six months, starting on October 1, 2016. What is the minimum taxable capital gain that X Ltd. must report in 2016?

(A) $100,000

(B) $50,000

(C) $75,000

(D) $37,500

Question 2

Mega Ltd., which has a May 31 year-end, had its land and building expropriated on June 30, 2016, and received $1 million of compensation from the government for the expropriation. Which one of the following is the deadline for Mega Ltd. to replace the property with another property costing at least $1 million in order to defer the entire recapture and capital gain on the disposition of the expropriated property?

(A) On or before May 31, 2018.

(B) On or before June 30, 2018.

(C) On or before December 31, 2018.

(D) On or before May 31, 2019.

Question 3

Steve is the proprietor of a sporting goods retail business. By chance, he discovered on the Internet a used motor boat for sale for $4,000 — a bargain price. He purchased the motor boat and immediately sold it for a profit of $3,000. He did not use the boat. Which of the following best describes the tax treatment of this transaction?

(a) The motor boat purchase is an investment, and the sale results in a taxable capital gain.

(b) The motor boat purchase is an investment, and the sale results in property income.

(c) The motor boat purchase is an adventure or concern in the nature of trade, and the sale results in business income.

(d) The motor boat purchase is an adventure or concern in the nature of trade, and the sale results in a taxable capital gain.

Question 4

Frames Inc. had a warehouse where it stored its inventory of picture frames, but a fire destroyed the Class 1 building in September 2015. The original cost of the building was $800,000 and the UCC value at the time was $540,000. The insurance company decided the building was a write-off and paid Frames Inc. $850,000 for the building in October 2016. Frames Inc. paid $950,000 to construct a new building by November 2016. What is the UCC of the building before CCA to Frames Inc. for its taxation year ended December 31, 2016, assuming they wish to minimize tax?

(a) $640,000

(b) $690,000

(c) $950,000

(d) $900,000

Question 5

Gloria owned a non-residential building, purchased in 2000, the original cost of which was $400,000, plus $150,000 for the cost of land. The UCC value of the building was $360,000, and the land and building were sold for $750,000 in 2016. The split the taxpayer used between land and building was $300,000 for building and $450,000 for land. Assuming that Gloria wishes to minimize her taxes, what are the tax implications regarding the sale?

(a) A capital gain of $300,000 and a terminal loss of $60,000.

(b) A capital gain of $240,000 and a terminal loss of nil.

(c) A capital gain of $150,000 and a terminal loss of $60,000.

(d) A capital gain of $120,000 and a terminal loss of nil.

¶8,850 EXERCISES

Exercise 1

ITA: 13(4), 44

Tax Processing Ltd.'s computer was completely destroyed in a fire in 2014. The insurance company has been disputing the claim. In the meantime, the company is renting computer time until the claim is settled. The following facts relate to the destroyed computer:

Capital cost	$50,000
UCC immediately before the fire — Class 10	17,150

During 2016, the insurance company paid $60,000 in respect of the claim. The company continued to rent computer time for another 24 months, and in 2018 it purchased a new-generation computer for $70,000.

— *REQUIRED*

Indicate the tax consequences for Tax Processing Ltd. for the above years.

Exercise 2

ITA: 20(1)(*l*), 20(1)(*p*), 22, 38, 39, 50

Reconsider Assignment Problem 4 in Chapter 4 and explain the tax implications if Mr. Flint and Mr. Small do not use the section 22 election on the sale of the accounts receivable.

Exercise 3

ITA: 13(21.1)

Sienna Research Inc. has one last building to dispose of in its liquidation process. Higher Peaks Ltd. has agreed to purchase the building for $1.28 million. The president of Sienna would like to maximize the after-tax profits of the disposition by creating a terminal loss on the building. He bragged about how the terminal loss on the building would nicely reduce the capital gain on the land. He drafted a sales contract allocating the total proceeds as follows:

Land	$ 895,000
Building	385,000
Total	$1,280,000

The capital cost of the land and building was as follows:

Land	$345,000
Building	520,000
Total	$865,000

The UCC of the building (last asset in Class 1) is $438,700.

— *REQUIRED*

The president would like you to confirm the tax implications of this disposition.

Exercise 4

ITA: 40(1)(*a*)

Mary Jane inherited a parcel of land from her father in 1993 when she inherited his proprietorship business assets. The land was used as a customer parking lot for the proprietorship business. She sold the land in 2016 for $200,000. Her father paid $30,000 for the land and the value in 1993 was $60,000. The purchaser paid 50,000 cash, with the remaining $150,000 plus interest due in 2018. Mary Jane has calculated her capital gain as $140,000.

— *REQUIRED*

Determine if Mary Jane's calculation of her capital gain is correct. Indicate if she has any other alternatives for reporting the gain. Your answer should be supported with appropriate references to the Act.

Exercise 5

ITA: 13(4)

Windswept Storage Ltd. had a brick warehouse that was completely destroyed by a tornado early in its 2015 fiscal year ended December 31. The building had cost $300,000 and its Class 3 undepreciated capital cost at the time of its destruction was $221,000. Agreement was reached on the insurance claim later in 2015 when the company received only $295,000. A new brick building was fully constructed by August 2016 for $400,000.

— *REQUIRED*

Trace the effects of these events on the balance of the undepreciated capital cost from 2015 through to the beginning balance for 2017, assuming that the proper election is made.

ITA: 13(4)

CHAPTER 8

¶8,850

¶8,875   ASSIGNMENT PROBLEMS

Type 1 Problems

Problem 1

Lev has owned his commercial property for many years, but he has now decided to sell it. The potential purchaser does not have enough cash to pay the full price of $775,000, so he is asking Lev to accept cash of $475,000 and a note payable of $300,000 with interest at 5% for the balance. The note would be repayable in equal annual amounts of $150,000 on the anniversary of the original closing. Lev has come to you for your advice on the tax consequences of this proposal.

	Cost	UCC	Proceeds	Proposed Consideration	
				Cash	Note
Land...............	$100,000		$550,000		
Building	200,000	$155,000	225,000		
	$300,000		$775,000	$475,000	$300,000

Problem 2

Adele owns 100% of Active Inc. The company owns a small piece of land that she would like to now own personally. It has been proposed that she declare a "dividend in kind" where instead of paying cash as a dividend the company will transfer the land to her name. The land is currently worth $100,000 and has an adjusted cost base of $45,000. Adele would like to understand the tax implications of this proposal.

Problem 3

When he was vacationing in Florida this year, Joe Raymer sold, for US$10,000, an asset used in his proprietorship business in Ottawa, which he purchased four years ago for C$4,000. Joe was paid in U.S. dollars. At the time of the sale, US$1 bought C$0.93. When Joe returned, he converted the U.S. currency to Canadian dollars and received C$10,200.

ITA: 39(2)

Joe has asked you to calculate the taxable capital gain or allowable capital loss, if any, arising on the above transactions.

Problem 4

Schillaci v. M.N.R., 92 DTC 1648 (T.C.C.)

Jean-Luc, the taxpayer in this case, was experienced in retail real estate, having originally been employed by a fast-food chain of restaurants. His duties were to locate, acquire and open restaurants on behalf of his employer. He acquired extensive knowledge in packaging sites for retail operations.

Two years ago, Jean-Luc began to work as an employee for Jorge, a successful builder of homes and condominiums, real estate developer for investment of rental apartments and retail plazas, and trust company owner. Jean-Luc was employed on a salary and bonus basis. At the time, Jean-Luc was also a licensed real estate broker and owned a brokerage firm.

Jean-Luc's first project for Jorge involved developing a retail complex in Toronto. He was instrumental in obtaining two anchor tenants as well as two others. This was a successful venture.

His second venture involved a strip plaza in London, Ontario. By the time Jean-Luc and Jorge were prepared to purchase the property, most of the pre-development work had been completed and two nationally recognized restaurant chains had signed letters of intent and/or offers to lease. These two tenants represented 60% of the rentable area of the plaza. With those tenants in place, other tenants were prepared to rent because of the traffic which would be generated by the presence of the two popular fast-food restaurants. As a result, financing the project would not be a problem.

All of the leases which were negotiated were of the "net-net" type — the landlord being responsible only for its financing costs. The tenants were responsible for all other costs and expenses involved with the plaza, in addition to their own businesses.

A partnership of Jorge (74%), Jean-Luc (24%), and Shloimie (2%), the long-time accountant for Jorge, was established to own the plaza. Neither Jean-Luc nor Shloimie paid for his respective interest in the partnership. Jean-Luc considered this to be a long-term project that would provide income for his children's future. Jorge and Shloimie regarded the project as an opportunity to acquire and own an income-producing property with very little investment, since most of the funds were provided by debt financing.

City planning and zoning for the plaza was approved and most of the financing was in place. Last year, about a year after the purchase by the partnership, the building was completed to the point where the tenants took possession. Shortly thereafter, the tenants completed their respective areas and were in operation and paying rent. Temporary financing was in place and permanent financing was being negotiated pending a drop in interest rates at the time.

This year, Jorge began to have financial difficulties and his assets were liquidated by his creditors. Since his creditors did not have security on the plaza project, Jorge was in a position to sell that asset in an orderly manner. Although Jorge controlled the partnership, he received Jean-Luc's consent to sell the property. Jean-Luc's share of the gain on the sale was about $157,000.

Jean-Luc filed his tax return for this year showing the gain as a capital gain.

A CRA assessor has called to indicate that she is considering a reassessment of the income in question as income from a business, an adventure in the nature of trade, or from a profit-making undertaking or concern.

As Jean-Luc's tax adviser, evaluate the fact situation and recommend a course of action.

Problem 5

ITA: 20(1)(*n*), 20(8), 40; IT-152R3

Len Jamal bought a parcel of land in 1996. It was his intention that he would relocate his proprietorship business to the land some day. However, the city continued to delay issuing permits to landowners in the area and eventually Len purchased another property to relocate his proprietorship business to. He held onto the land for a number of years but has now decided that he needs the cash and will sell the property. The details related to his purchase of the land are set out below.

Purchase Price: $4,000; Purchase Date: May 21, 1996

Len has received an offer from an acquaintance to purchase the land. The payment terms are set out below and are considered to represent fair market value.

Purchase Price: $160,000; Purchase Date: October 1, 2016

Payment terms: $40,000 down payment on purchase date; $20,000 payable on January 1 each year for the period January 1, 2017 through January 1, 2022 inclusive. Interest: Interest is payable at 6% annually on the unpaid balance.

Len is uncertain as to whether the disposition is on account of capital or income.

You have been asked to compare the income tax consequences to Len of this sale if the sale is on account of capital and, alternatively, if it is on account of income. Do not calculate the interest income. Ignore the consequences and calculation of the interest income.

Problem 6

ITA: 13(4)

Elaine Barblaik owns an apartment building which she holds for rental income. In November 2015, Elaine settled with municipal authorities on expropriation proceeds for the property including the building. The agreed expropriation proceeds for the building and the separate sale proceeds for the appliances and fixtures are indicated in the following data:

	Expropriated building Cl. 1	*Sold appliances & fixtures*
Cost	$406,000	$26,000
UCC January 1, 2015	188,500	7,250
Proceeds	362,500	2,600

Since negotiations had been prolonged, Elaine was able to anticipate the approximate date of settlement and, as a result, she was able to replace in 2016 the assets expropriated.

Replacement cost for the building and the cost of new appliances and fixtures were as follows:

Building	$1,276,000
Appliances and fixtures	46,400

Elaine would like you to calculate the undepreciated capital cost for both assets through to the opening balance on January 1, 2017 assuming no further additions are made to either class of assets.

Problem 7

ITA: 13(4), 44

During its year ended December 31, 2016, Power Boat Corporation Ltd. sold its retailing facilities in Kingston. As the sale occurred in December, business activity was at a low. New facilities were purchased in February 2017 in Parry Sound on the shores of Georgian Bay. The corporation sold its Kingston land and building for $300,000 and $200,000, respectively. This land and building had a cost in 1999 of $50,000 and $100,000, respectively. At the end of 2015, the building had an undepreciated capital cost of $55,000 for income tax purposes. In Parry Sound, the corporation purchased land and building for $75,000 and $350,000, respectively.

You have been asked to do the following:

(A) Prepare two calculations of the income tax consequences of the above move, one without an election for additional deferral and one with this election. ITA: 44(6)

(B) If the property disposed of by the corporation in 2016 had been an apartment building held for rental purposes and producing income from property:

(i) what would the tax consequences of a sale of the property have been after a replacement of the property with another apartment complex in 2017?

(ii) what would the tax consequences on an expropriation have been after a replacement of the property with another apartment complex in 2017?

Problem 8

ITA: 13(21.1)

Pidgeon Dock Ltd. (PD) sold a property in its year ended January 31, 2016. The details are as follows:

	Proceeds	**Cost**	**UCC**
Building	$300,000	$400,000	$350,000
Land	$175,000	$100,000	N/A

The building was the last remaining asset in Class 3. PD prepared its corporate tax return based on the proceeds of disposition shown above. The CRA is now auditing PD.

PD has asked you to identify and calculate any adjustment the CRA will make to their 2016 income tax return.

Problem 9

ITA: 13(21.1)

Johnny Wong had purchased a dilapidated apartment block, The Empress, 20 years ago for $220,000. At the time, the purchase price had been allocated $80,000 to the land and $140,000 to the building. The Empress is the only building Johnny owns and is considered a Class 3 asset for CCA purposes. To date, Johnny has claimed CCA of $37,000.

High Towers has acquired all the lots in the same block as Johnny's building, except for The Empress. Johnny realized that as the last hold-out he was in an enviable negotiating position with High Towers. High Towers was desperate to gain ownership of The Empress and tear it down. After receiving ever-escalating offers, Johnny agreed to accept High Towers' offer of $1,000,000.

Johnny has been asked for your advice regarding the allocation of the purchase price between the land and building.

Type 2 Problems

Problem 10

ITA: 13(4), 44

On March 1, 2015, Raymond Fan, a sole proprietor, sold his garden supply store in downtown Toronto to a competitor because of declining sales caused by competition from large suburban hardware and grocery stores. The following information relates to the sale of the business:

	Proceeds	Cost	UCC/CEC Jan. 1, 2015
Accounts receivable	$ 6,000	$10,000	—
Land	120,000	65,000	—
Building — Class 1	170,000	62,000	$28,000
Equipment — Class 8	3,000	1,200	300
— Class 10	4,000	12,000	800
Inventory	5,200	7,000	—
Goodwill	52,000	—	—

Raymond's business year-end coincided with the calendar year. Raymond has been in the same business since 1997. As of December 31, 2014, there was a balance in the allowance for doubtful accounts for tax purposes of $1,300.

Subsequent to the sale of the business, Raymond worked for his brother, Kevin, who owned a shoe store. However, Raymond became bored and when a garden supply store on a busy highway north of Toronto came on the market in late November 2016, he immediately bought it. The following information relates to his purchase of assets of the new business:

Land	$105,000
Building (built and used before 2007)	220,000
Equipment — Class 8	9,000
— Class 10	11,000
Goodwill	Nil

Raymond has asked for your help and you have decided to do the following:

(A) Compute the minimum amount Raymond must include on his 2015 tax return in respect of the sale of the business, before any election is made to defer capital gains and recapture.

ITA: 13(4), 44

(B) Show the effect on Raymond's 2015 (amended) and 2016 tax returns if he elects to defer capital gains and recapture after purchasing the new business, but does not elect for additional deferral.

ITA: 13(4), 44
ITA: 44(6)

(C) Discuss whether Raymond should have elected for additional deferral.

(D) If the above situation had been an involuntary disposition instead of a voluntary disposition, how would your answer under part (B) differ?

Problem 11

ITA: Subdivisions b and c;
ETA: 123(1), 169(1),
170(1)(a), 174, 231, 236

PITA Co. Ltd. is a nutritional consulting firm that advises manufacturers and distributors on consumers' dietary needs and preferences. For its year ended December 31, 2016, it reported net income before taxes of $900,000 for financial statement purposes. This amount included a gain on the disposition of land held as capital property of $50,000 and of a building (not the only one in the class) of $95,000. The corporation also realized an accounting loss of $20,000 on securities and of $10,000 on a trademark. These assets were acquired for the following amounts:

land . . . . $120,000 in 2005
building . . . . . .   100,000 in 2005 (UCC of the class is $125,000)
securities . . . . .   50,000 in 2014
trademark. . . . .   80,000 in 2013

The proceeds of disposition of these assets were as follows:

land $150,000
building   120,000
securities   30,000
trademark.   70,000

The corporation has reported accounting amortization of $80,000 and wishes to claim the maximum available capital cost allowance of $100,000. During 2016, the corporation also made payments in respect of interest on unpaid income taxes ($1,500), charitable donations ($10,000), and an annual employee dinner-dance in December 2016 ($14,000). During 2016, the corporation established that an unsecured $5,000 note receivable in respect of the sale (as capital property) of a parcel of land in the prior year had become a bad debt. This was not reflected in the financial statements.

PITA has asked you to do the following:

(A) Prepare a reconciliation between net income for financial statement purposes and net income for income tax purposes for the year ended December 31, 2016. Support your reconciliation with references to the *Income Tax Act*.

(B) Discuss in general terms the treatment of these items by the corporation for purposes of the HST.

Type 3 Problems

Problem 12

Sudbury Processing Inc. has had some tough times. In December 2015, just before its December 31st year end, there was a fire in its processing plant which destroyed the building and most of the contents. Tom Haskett, the owner, had to move fast to get back in operation before he lost customers to the competition.

Tom owns all the shares of Sud Holdings Inc. ("Holdings"). Holdings owns all the shares of Sudbury Processing Inc. ("Processing"), which is the operating company. Holdings also owns the land, building, and equipment used by Processing (the ones destroyed by fire).

In order to get back into business, Tom had Processing lease a new building until he could make arrangements for a new permanent home. He had some delay in making any new arrangements, because he and the insurance company had a difference of opinion on the replacement value of the building and equipment that were destroyed. They eventually agreed in March 2016, and Holdings received the cheque shortly thereafter for the building, equipment, and some repairs. However, the delay meant Tom had to make alternate arrangements for acquiring new equipment, so Processing entered into an equipment lease with an option to buy it at the end of the five-year term. Luckily, Processing had business interruption insurance, which paid it $10,000 per month for four months until it was up and running again.

In July 2016, Tom made the final decision on a new factory. He decided not to build at the old location. Instead, that land is being sold and new property is being bought with the intention of constructing a new building in the next couple of years. On the sale of the existing land, the purchaser wants a warranty that there are no environmental problems as a result of the fire. Holdings and the purchaser agreed that if there were any problems, then Holdings would pay $20,000 of the purchase price back. Rather than purchase the new parcel of land at this time, Tom has had Holdings buy an option to acquire the land at any time in the next two years for an agreed-upon price.

Advise Tom on the tax implications of Sudbury's situation.

Problem 13

Mac Tosh is 66 years old and was a self-employed apple farmer in Kelowna. Since his children did not want to take over his farming business, he sold the farm (which qualifies for the lifetime capital gains deduction) to a real estate developer for $450,000. The developer sold the crop in late August, cleared the land and began the development of a 50-unit condominium complex.

Mac Tosh paid $10,000 for the land in 1981 and planted 500 apple trees with a cost base of $2,000. He was saddened by the attitude of the developer, as the farm had been his pride and joy. Since Mac never used insecticides or fertilizers, he could earn a premium on the sale of the "organic" apples. Mac had the land appraised at $400,000 by two independent appraisers. The appraisal values were supported by the price of a piece of raw land which had recently sold in a nearby community. To compensate Mac Tosh for all his hard work over the years as well as for the current crop, the developer agreed to pay an additional $50,000 over the appraised land value. Mac Tosh's annual revenues from his apple harvest were approximately $15,000. Mac was pleased with this additional offer because it was very similar to the offer he received the previous year for his entire farm and crop from a neighbouring farmer. Mac has not had any other dispositions of capital property, and has no other sources of earned income.

Just last week, Mac received a letter from the CRA requesting further details on the sale of his farm. He was requested to submit appraisals and a statement regarding the reason behind his tax treatment of the disposition. Mac reported the entire disposition as a capital gain and offset the gain by utilizing the necessary capital gains deduction. Mac did not have any cumulative net investment losses.

Mac can't understand why the CRA wants this information. He thought that he had considered all income tax implications of the disposition of the farm. He even read a professional tax planning book. How should Mac have reported the transaction?

 [For more problems and solutions thereto, see the DVD accompanying the textbook.]

CHAPTER 8 —
DISCUSSION NOTES FOR REVIEW QUESTIONS

(1) The transaction will probably be an income receipt. The partnership appears to have been set up specifically to buy and hold the land. The partnership agreement seems to confirm that their primary intention was to make a profit, since the agreement specifically states how the income is to be split. If, after five years, they still have done nothing to develop the land to earn rental or other income, then it would appear to be a speculation gain and, therefore, income.

(2) The transaction will probably be an income receipt. Rachel has used her specialized knowledge, derived from her normal occupation, to make the large profit. This factor, combined with her trading history, would weigh heavily in favour of income treatment.

(3) Normally, stock market transactions are treated as capital gains or losses. However, his intention seems to be to make a profit in trading shares, thereby indicating an income receipt. He may elect to have these transactions treated as capital gains. However, Winston should be careful that the CRA does not subsequently deem him to be a "trader" and thereby revoke his election.

ITA: 39(4), 39(5)

(4) The transaction would probably be an income receipt. Her primary intention is to develop the shopping centre for sale which would be an income transaction. Therefore, the sale of the land prior to development would also be an income transaction.

(5) Capital receipt (not taxable). Doug's $15,000 net winnings should not be treated as income because his actions are more in the nature of a hobby, not making a profit. If this was his business, the profits would be taxable and any losses would be deductible.

IT-334R2, par. 10

(6) One way to approach this question is to assume that the cost was allocated equally to each acre. Therefore, the cost of the three acres sold would be ½ of the original cost of the six acres or $12,000. However, the CRA, in applying the law, may consider that $12,000 is too high an amount to be "reasonably regarded as attributable to that part," since the lake-front portion would usually be more valuable than the non-lake-front property assuming that access is still available to both parcels. This, then, becomes a valuation issue.

ITA: 43

(7) He has to replace the land before the end of the second taxation year after the initial year. If they finally agreed to the price in 2016 then he has until December 31, 2018 to replace the property. The initial year is the year that the "amount has become receivable as proceeds of disposition", i.e., 2016 in this case.

ITA: 44(1)(c)

ITA: 44(1), 44(2)

(8) Yes. In order for these rules to apply the destroyed equipment must be either property that was stolen, destroyed or expropriated or a "former business property". The definition of former business property only refers to real property which has a common law definition of "land and building". Equipment is not included in that definition. However, if the property is stolen, destroyed or expropriated, it only has to meet the definition of "property". In this case the equipment meets this definition and the replacement property rules can apply. Of course, any potential recapture would be offset, by the normal rules, because the purchase of the new machine was made in the year of loss.

ITA: 248(1) "former business property"

(9) Under the definition of "former business property" the advice she received was incorrect. This building qualifies as a former business property, since it is rented to a related corporation and is used in the related corporation's business.

ITA: 248(1) "former business property", 251

(10) A change in use does not include a transfer of property from one income-producing use to another. In this case the property is being transferred from earning property income to earning business income. As a result there is no income to report on July 1 of last year when zoning was applied for. However, when the property is eventually sold an assessment will need to be done at July 1 of last year since the increase in value up to that point will be a capital gain and any profit after that date will be business income from the sale of the condominiums.

ITA: 13(7), 45(1); IT-218R

(11) Ms. Chung can elect to have disposed of her note when it is established to have become uncollectible. This will result in a capital loss equal to $100,000 and the note will then have a cost equal to nil. All or some of this loss can then be carried back under Division C to be applied against the previous capital gain. If the original property disposed of was personal-use property then the debt would have been "personal-use property". Then the Act allows a capital loss only to the extent of the capital gain on the original disposition.

ITA: 50(1), 54 "personal-use property"

ITA: 50(2)

CHAPTER 8

CHAPTER 8 — SOLUTIONS TO MULTIPLE CHOICE QUESTIONS

Question 1

(B) is correct. The gain is: $600,000 – $100,000 = $500,000. The maximum 2016 reserve is computed using the lesser of the percentage of proceeds payable after the end of the year ($510,000/$600,000 or 85%, in this case) and four fifths ($\frac{4}{5}$). Since the lesser amount is four fifths, the reserve is $400,000 ($\frac{4}{5}$ × $500,000) and the capital gain is therefore $100,000 ($500,000 – $400,000). The minimum taxable capital gain is therefore $50,000 ($\frac{1}{2}$).

ITA: 40(1)(*a*)

(A) is incorrect, because the capital gain must be multiplied by $\frac{1}{2}$ to compute the taxable capital gain.

(C) is incorrect, because it uses the 85% figure to compute the reserve and does not multiply the result by $\frac{1}{2}$: $500,000 – 85% × $500,000 = $75,000.

(D) is incorrect, because it uses the 85% figure to compute the reserve: $75,000 × $\frac{1}{2}$.

Question 2

(D) is the correct answer. Since the expropriation is an involuntary disposition, the property must be replaced by the later of two taxation years from the end of the taxation year in which the disposition took place or 24 months from the end of the taxation year in which the disposition took place. Since the relevant taxation year was May 31, 2017, the two-year deadline is May 31, 2019.

ITA: 44(1)(*c*)

(A) incorrectly uses the one-year deadline which is applicable for voluntary dispositions.

(B) incorrectly uses two years from the disposition date as the deadline.

(C) incorrectly uses two years from the end of the calendar year of the disposition as the deadline.

Question 3

(C) is correct

It can be concluded from the facts that Steve's primary intention was to purchase the boat and sell it for a profit. He bought the boat and immediately sold it for a profit the way a person in the boat-sales trade would act. He did not use the boat personally or rent it out for use as a capital asset. The transaction was, in some sense, related to his sporting goods retailing business which would give Steve some insight into the purchase and sale of a boat in this way. Profit from an adventure in the nature of trade is considered to be business income.

(A) incorrectly includes the profit as a taxable capital gain, rather than business income.

(B) incorrectly includes the income as income from property, rather than income from business.

(D) incorrectly includes the profit as a taxable capital gain, rather than business income from an adventure in the nature of trade.

Question 4

(A) is correct

Involuntary disposition: They replaced within the time limit.

Replacement cost	$950,000
Deferred capital gain	(50,000)
Capital cost	$900,000
Deferred recapture	(260,000)
UCC before CCA	$640,000

(B) incorrectly ignores the deferred capital gain.

(C) incorrectly ignores all deferrals.

(D) incorrectly ignores the deferred recapture.

Question 5

(B) is correct

Result	Land	Building	Total
Proceeds	$390,000	$ 360,000	$750,000
Capital cost	$150,000		
UCC		360,000	
Capital gain	$240,000		
Terminal loss		$ 0	

Subsection 13(21.1) would disallow the terminal loss by making the proceeds on the building equal to the UCC with the remaining proceeds allocated to the building.

(A) incorrectly ignores the reallocation of proceeds.

(C) incorrectly ignores the reallocation of proceeds and calculates the taxable capital gain, rather than the capital gain, as required.

(D) incorrectly calculates the taxable capital gain, rather than the required capital gain.

CHAPTER 8

CHAPTER 8 — SOLUTIONS TO EXERCISES

Exercise 1

(A) During the years prior to the settling of the claim, Tax Processing Ltd. is deemed to own the   ITA: 44(2)
destroyed asset. Hence the company can continue to take capital cost allowance.

			Class 50: 55%
UCC before the fire			$17,150
CCA — 2014	$ 9,433		
CCA — 2015	3,473	(12,906)	
UCC before proceeds received			$ 4,244

(B) In the second year after the fire (2015) when the company received the proceeds, the company would be deemed to have sold the computer for $60,000 with the following tax consequences:

Taxable capital gain:

P of D	$60,000
ACB	(50,000)
CG	$10,000
TCG (½ × $10,000)	$ 5,000

Recapture:

UCC before proceeds received		$ 4,244
Less the lesser of:		
(i) Capital cost	$50,000	
		(50,000)
(ii) P of D	$60,000	
Recapture		$45,756

(C) In the year of purchase of the new computer (2017), which is within the 24-month time limit for an involuntary disposition, Tax Processing Ltd. would file an amended return for the 2016 year in which the taxable capital gain and recapture were recognized.

Taxable capital gain:
   ½ of the lesser of:

(i) capital gain (see above)		$10,000		
(ii) P of D	$60,000			= Nil
less replacement cost	70,000	Nil		

ACB of new computer in 2015: ($70,000 − $10,000) = $60,000   *ITA: 44(1)(f)*

Recapture: *ITA: 13(4)*

Class 50: 55%

UCC before proceeds received (see above calculation) . . . . $ 4,244
Less deemed disposal: *ITA: 13(4)(c)*
   lesser of (i) cost ($50,000)
           (ii) P of D ($60,000) $50,000

Less the lesser of:
   (i) the recapture
       ($4,244 − $50,000) $45,756
   (ii) replacement cost   70,000   45,756   4,244

UCC after proceeds received, Dec. 31, 2015 . . . .   Nil

Class 50: 55%

2017 addition:
   Capital cost of replacement property $70,000
   Less reduction for deferred gain   10,000   *ITA: 44(1)(f)*

   Deemed capital cost $60,000
   Less reduction for deferred recapture   45,756   *ITA: 13(4)(d)*

UCC before CCA $14,244
   CCA (55% of ½ × $14,244) . . . .   (3,917)

UCC after CCA $10,327

Exercise 2

If section 22 is not used, Mr. Flint must still include in income last year's reserve of $6,500. However, the loss of $9,000 will be regarded as a capital loss which is only fractionally deductible and can be offset only against taxable capital gains. Since Mr. Small has not included any amount as income in respect of these accounts receivable, he will not be allowed a deduction for a reserve or for bad debts because the conditions of the reserve for doubtful debts or the bad debt expense rules will not be met. If Mr. Small collects more than the $36,000 fair market value, the excess will be a capital gain and, if he collects less than $36,000, the difference will be a capital loss.   *ITA: 20(1)(l), 20(1)(p)*

Exercise 3

Sienna Research Inc. has what, at first, appears to be a terminal loss on the building and a capital gain on the land. When this occurs, subsection 13(21.1) reallocates the proceeds so that the terminal loss is reduced by the capital gain on the land.   *ITA: 13(21.1)*

Without adjustment	Land	Building	Total
Proceeds per contract	$ 895,000	$ 385,000	$ 1,280,000
ACB, UCC	345,000	438,700	
Capital gain, terminal loss	550,000	(53,700)	

CHAPTER 8

With subsection 13(21.1) adjustment	Land	Building	Total
Adjusted proceeds	$ 841,300	$ 438,700	$ 1,280,000
ACB, UCC	345,000	438,700	
Capital gain, terminal loss or recapture	$ 496,300	Nil	

There are no tax implications on the disposition of the building. Even though the deemed proceeds are less than the capital cost of the building, a capital loss can never arise on the disposition of depreciable property.

Exercise 4

Property received as an inheritance has an ACB equal to the FMV when acquired. In this case, the ACB is $60,000.

ITA: 40(1)(a), 69(1)(c)

Mary Jane has correctly calculated her capital gain. However, she only received $50,000 of the proceeds in 2016 and the balance is not due until 2018. Therefore, she can consider claiming a reserve under subparagraph 40(1)(a)(iii), calculated as follows:

$$\frac{\text{Amount not due}}{\text{Proceeds}} \times \text{capital gain}$$

$$\frac{\$150,000}{\$200,000} \times \$140,000 = \$105,000$$

OR

$\frac{4}{5}$ of gain

$\frac{4}{5} \times \$140,000 = \$112,000$

Capital gain = $140,000 – $105,000 = $35,000

Mary Jane can claim a reserve of $105,000. This reserve will then be included in income in 2016 and a reserve calculated based on proceeds not yet due. Mary Jane must file Form T2017 with her 2015 income tax return.

Exercise 5

				Cl. 3: 5%
Jan. 1, 2015	UCC			$ 221,000
	Disposal[(1)]			
	lesser of:			
	(a) capital cost	$300,000		
	(b) proceeds	$295,000		(295,000)
Dec. 31, 2015	UCC			$ (74,000)
	Recapture			74,000
Jan. 1, 2016	UCC			Nil
Aug. 2016	File an amended return for 2013 as follows:			

ITA: 13(4)

Jan. 1, 2015	UCC			$ 221,000
	Deemed proceeds			
	lesser of:			
	(a) capital cost	$300,000		
	(b) proceeds	$295,000 →	$295,000	
	reduced by lesser of:			
	(a) recapture			
	($295K – $221K)	$ 74,000 →	$ 74,000	
	(b) replacement cost	$400,000		$(221,000)
Dec. 31, 2015	UCC			Nil
	Recapture			Nil
Jan. 1, 2016	UCC			Nil

ITA: 13(4)(c)

			Cl. 1-NRB: 6%[2]	
2016	Purchase of new building	$400,000		
	Less: reduction above	74,000	$ 326,000	ITA: 13(4)(*c*)
Dec. 31, 2016	UCC		$ 326,000	
	CCA @ 6% of [$326,000 – (½ × $326,000)]		(9,780)	
Jan. 1, 2017	UCC		$ 316,220	

—NOTES TO SOLUTION

[1] The CRA appears to require that even if a replacement property is purchased before the tax return for the year of disposition must be filed (i.e., within six months of the taxation year-end), the recapture must be reported in the year of disposition. The taxpayer can request a reassessment if and when the replacement is purchased within the specified time limits. In lieu of paying tax initially on the recapture, the CRA will take acceptable security until the final determination of tax is made.

IT-259R3, par. 3

[2] Note how the rules allow for a replacement with an asset of another class.

ITA: 13(4)

Chapter 9

Other Sources of Income and Deductions in Computing Income

Learning Goals

Know, Understand and Explain

By the end of this chapter you will know, understand and be able to explain:

- The basic provisions of the *Income Tax Act* that relate to income and other deductions.
- How pension income is taxed.
- How to calculate the taxable portion of an annuity.
- How contributions and withdrawls from RESP and RDSP programs affect the calculation of net income for tax purposes.
- The benefits of contributing to an RESP or RDSP.
- The difference in tax treatment for spousal support and child support.
- The difference between a RRSP contribution and a contribution to spousal RRSP and when it may benefit a taxpayer.
- The taxation of contributions and withdrawls into Registered Savings Plans.
- The different tax treatments for contributions and withdrawls for TFSAs, RRSPs and RESPs.
- The tax impacts of transitioning RSPs into retirement income.
- When moving expenses are deductible and when they are not.

Apply

By the end of this chapter you will be able to apply your knowledge and understanding to:

- Calculate deductible moving expenses.
- Calculate deductible child care expenses.
- Calculate disability support deductions.
- Split pension and CPP income to minimize tax payable.
- Calculate the RRSP contribution limit for a taxpayer.

Review Questions
¶9,800 in the Study Guide

Multiple Choice Questions
¶9,825 in the Study Guide

Exercise Questions
¶9,850 in the Study Guide

Assignment Problems
¶9,875 in the Study Guide

CHAPTER 9 — LEARNING CHART

Problem Descriptions

Textbook Example Problems

9-1	Moving expenses
9-2	Child care expenses
9-3	Disability support deduction
9-4	RRSP contribution
9-5	Spousal RRSP withdrawal
9-6	Home Buyers' Plan
9-7	Retiring allowance

Multiple Choice Questions

1	Retiring allowance
2	RRSP contribution
3	Child care deduction
4	Moving expenses
5	Earned income
6	Moving expenses

Exercises

1	Definition of "earned income"
2	RRSP deduction
3	Investing in or outside of an RRSP
4	Spousal RRSP withdrawals
5	Transfers between deferred plans
6	Moving expenses

Assignment Problems

1	Moving expenses
2	Child care expenses
3	Spousal support payments
4	Transfer of RRSP on divorce
5	RRSP
6	RRSP vs. TFSA
7	RRSP
8	Moving expenses
9	Child care expenses
10	Comprehensive
11	Calculate income, provide advice
12	Comprehensive
13	Comprehensive
14	Becoming a resident
15	Comprehensive
16	Reassessment
17	Retirement package

Study Notes

¶9,800   REVIEW QUESTIONS

(1) Ms. Tang had been working for the same employer for the past 10 years and was tired of her job. She decided to quit and travel to Australia for a year. On leaving, her employer paid her a lump-sum amount of $15,000, since Ms. Tang had been a good employee of theirs and they were hoping she might come back to work for them when she returned to Canada. Ms. Tang had no intention of working for them again but was grateful for the payment. Comment on how this payment should be taxed.

(2) Mr. Everett has worked for the provincial government for the past 35 years and was now eligible for early retirement. As part of his retirement package he is entitled to a lump-sum payment for unused sick days in the amount of $20,000 and unused vacation days of $25,000. On retirement, he is going to receive a cheque for $45,000 as payment for the above amounts. How will this amount be taxed?

(3) Charles and Dee Bowan have decided to end their 12-year marriage. As part of their written separation agreement, they agree that Charles will pay Dee $3,000 per month for her personal support and maintenance, including $1,200 per month for the mortgage on the house that Dee will be living in. The original principal amount of the mortgage is $120,000. What limitations, if any, will Charles encounter when deciding the deductibility of the payments related to the mortgage?

(4) Mark and Ann have agreed to a separation agreement that requires Ann to pay $2,000 per month to Mark as an allowance for his maintenance. Initially, this payment will consist of $1,500 paid to Mark directly and $500 paid to the financial institution that holds the mortgage on his condominium. Mark may change this arrangement at any time to have the full $2,000 paid to him directly. Comment on the deductibility of these payments.

(5) Sam Sider reached an agreement with his employer to pay for his education and living expenses while he returned to university. The agreement was that, if he returned to work for his employer when he graduated, there would be no repayment of the amounts he received. If he did not return to work for his employer, the payments he received would have to be repaid in full. How would this be treated for tax purposes?

(6) Mrs. Smith, a 75-year-old widow, has applied for and received the Old Age Security Supplement. This payment is based on the fact that her income is below a certain threshold amount. She has asked you to tell her how this is treated for tax purposes.

(7) Mr. Singh, a consultant, did some work for ACME Corporation with the agreed-upon fee being $15,000. When the time came for the billing to be done, Mr. Singh sent an invoice to ACME with instructions that the cheque be made payable to his wife. What would your comments be to Mr. Singh and his wife on this arrangement?

(8) How do you determine how much of the employer's contributions to a defined benefit pension plan are deductible?

(9) Joe is confused. He is trying to understand the pension rules and he cannot understand why the limit on a money purchase pension plan is based on 18% of this year's income while the limit for an RRSP is based on last year's income. Explain this difference to him.

(10) Jennifer wanted to withdraw $20,000 from her RRSP in January in order to buy a new car. She had spent a long time accumulating this amount, but felt that it was more important to buy a car now than accumulate for retirement later. How can she minimize the tax that is withheld on the $20,000 taken out of the plan?

(11) Mr. McDonald, a widower, has died and now his executor has come in to administer the will. His only assets on his death were an RRSP worth $150,000 and his house and other personal assets worth $150,000. Both of his children were grown up so he thought that his was a simple estate. He left the RRSPs to his daughter, Kim, and the residue to his son, Jim. Is there likely to be any conflict between the beneficiaries?

(12) Joan had worked for the same employer for 15 years. Two years ago she was fired. She took legal action against her former employer on the basis that it was wrongful dismissal. This year she won her case and was awarded $40,000. She then paid her legal fees of $8,000 and contributed $32,000 to her RRSP as a retiring allowance. She is glad the case has been settled since she has not worked since her dismissal. What would you show on her personal tax return for the year based on this information?

ITA: 60(*j*.1)

¶9,825 MULTIPLE CHOICE QUESTIONS

Question 1

Max retired in 2016 and received a $100,000 retiring allowance. Max worked for his employer for the past 18 years. He never belonged to a registered pension plan or a deferred profit sharing plan during any of those years. What is the maximum amount of retiring allowance that Max can shelter from tax by transferring it to his RRSP?

(A) Nil

(B) $27,000

(C) $63,000

(D) $100,000

Question 2

Ms. Assad wants to know the maximum RRSP contribution she can make in 2016 or in the first 60 days of 2017 that will be fully deductible on her 2016 tax return. The following information was taken from Ms. Assad's 2015 tax return:

Income from employment	$44,000
RPP contributions deducted in arriving at employment income	1,000
Moving expenses	300
Taxable spousal support received	3,600
Pension income	6,000
Real estate rental income	1,400

The pension adjustment reported by Ms. Assad's employer for 2015 was $4,000. Ms. Assad also has a $1,000 unused RRSP deduction limit room which has carried forward from 2015.

What is the maximum RRSP contribution that Ms. Assad can make in 2016 or in the first 60 days of 2017 and deduct fully on her 2016 tax return?

(A) $4,920

(B) $5,000

(C) $6,000

(D) $17,000

Question 3

Meg and James Rashev were both employed full-time during the year. The Rashevs have four children: Joanne (age 17), Susie (age 14), and Sarah and Kelly (4-year-old twins). The Rashevs employed a nanny to look after their children and paid her $15,000 for the year. In addition, during July, Susie went to overnight camp for two weeks at a cost of $250 per week. The Rashevs' family income is summarized below:

	Meg	James
Salary & taxable benefits	$ 46,000	
Employment expenses [sec. 8]	(2,800)	
Business income:		
Revenues		$ 50,000
Expenses deductible for tax purposes		(32,000)
Interest income	800	1,500

Which one of the following represents the maximum child care deduction that can be claimed by the Rashevs in the year?

(A) James can claim a deduction of $12,000.

(B) Meg can claim a deduction of $15,250.

(C) James can claim a deduction of $21,000.

(D) James can claim a deduction of $15,500.

Question 4

Ms. Chiu moved from Toronto to Vancouver to start a new job. She earned $40,000 from her Toronto job and $50,000 from her Vancouver job in the year of the move. Ms. Chiu incurred the following costs of moving all of which can be substantiated by receipts:

Moving van to transport household effects	$ 5,000
Travelling costs — self, spouse and two children	3,000
Legal fees — Vancouver house	900
Legal fees — Toronto house	1,100
Loss on sale of Toronto house	25,000
Costs while waiting for Vancouver house — Hotel (20 days × $100)	2,000
Meals (20 days × $45)	900
House hunting trip (prior to Vancouver move)	800

Travelling costs consist of three meals a day for four persons over five full days, gas and other car costs, and hotel for five nights at $100 per night. The distance moved between Toronto and Vancouver was 4,430 kilometres.

Which one of the following amounts represents the maximum amount that Ms. Chiu can deduct as moving expenses on her personal income tax return for the year of the move?

(A) $12,560

(B) $15,607

(C) $16,860

(D) $17,107

Question 5

Sahar's income for tax purposes for 2015 and 2016 is as follows:

	2015	2016
Salary	$100,000	$110,000
Taxable benefits under sections 6 and 7	8,000	8,000
Travel expenses under section 8	(3,000)	(2,000)
Registered pension plan contributions under s. 8	(4,200)	(4,200)
Business losses	(1,000)	(1,200)
Rental income (net of expenses and CCA)	3,200	3,600
Spousal support paid	(12,600)	(12,000)
Net income under Division B	$ 90,400	$102,200

Which of the following statements is correct?

(A) The earned income that should be used to calculate her child care expense deduction for 2016 is $110,000.

(B) The earned income that should be used to calculate her RRSP deduction for 2016 is $106,400.

(C) The earned income that should be used to calculate her child care expense deduction for 2016 is $102,200.

(D) The earned income that should be used to calculate her RRSP deduction for 2016 is $94,600.

Question 6

Natalie Doak moved 1,000 kilometres from Winnipeg, on March 1, 2016, to a new job and earned $40,000 in her new work location. Her employer reimbursed the costs of selling her old residence and purchasing her new residence. She did not receive any allowance or reimbursement in respect of the following expenses, all of which she paid in 2016:

Moving van	$ 2,600
Travelling costs to move Natalie and family (four persons in all)	900
Cost of cleaning house in new work location	100
Cost of painting and installing new carpets and windows	10,000
Cost of maintaining vacant former residence for three months until it was sold (mortgage interest and property taxes of $3,000 per month)	9,000
Cost of changing address on legal documents	100
House hunting trips for new residence	3,000
	$25,700

Travelling costs consist of three meals a day for four persons over three full days, gas and other car costs, and hotel for two nights at $100 per night.

What is the maximum amount Natalie can claim for moving expenses in 2016?

(A) $25,700

(B) $15,982

(C) $12,600

(D) $9,007

¶9,850 EXERCISES

Exercise 1

ITA: 63(3), 146(1)

Subsection 248(1) is one of the key definition sections found in the *Income Tax Act*. Definitions are also found elsewhere in the Act.

— REQUIRED

Find the section in the Act that contains the definition for "earned income" used in the calculation of the RRSP contribution limits.

Exercise 2

ITA: 60(*i*), 146(1), 146(5)

Don Bickle contributed $5,000 to a spousal RRSP on February 15, 2017. Don's income for tax purposes for 2015 is as follows:

Salary	$70,000
Taxable benefits	1,200
	$71,200
Less: Registered pension plan contributions — defined contribution	(2,800)
Employment income — Subdivision a	$68,400
Rental loss	(5,000)
Dividend income from taxable Canadian corporations grossed up	800
Interest income — Canada Savings Bonds	400
Division B income	$64,600

Don's employer reported a PA of $6,084 in respect of 2015.

— REQUIRED

Determine the maximum amount Don can deduct on his 2016 tax return in respect of his 2017 contribution to his spouse's RRSP and the amount, if any, that he can contribute and deduct in respect of his own RRSP.

Exercise 3

ITA: Division B

A taxable investment of $15,000 in bonds yields 4% per year before tax. The same investment can be acquired in a self-directed RRSP (tax sheltered). Assume that the yield is reinvested each year at the same 4% before tax. Further assume that the investment is held for 10 years, at which time the RRSP will be cashed in and taxes paid at 46%.

— REQUIRED

Which investment approach provides the best cash return?

Exercise 4

ITA: 146(1)

Douglas has been contributing $3,000 annually to a spousal RRSP for his wife, Donna, in each of the last six years, but not this year. The RRSP has grown to $30,000 and Donna has withdrawn $10,000 of the RRSP this year. The withholding tax was $2,000.

— REQUIRED

Describe the full income tax aspects and consequences of this RRSP withdrawal.

Exercise 5

ITA: 60(*i*), 60(*j*.1)

Ivan Reimer received the following amounts for 2016, the year of his retirement:

Employment income (see (1), below)	$ 7,000
Pension income:	
Lump-sum RPP payment from a defined benefit plan	100,000
Superannuation payments (eight monthly pension payments of	
$3,000)	24,000
Old Age Security pension	6,850
Canada Pension Plan	12,460
Retiring allowance	50,000
Interest income	8,000
	$208,310

Additional Information

(1) Ivan resigned his position on April 1, 2016. The employment income for tax purposes above includes a $300 contribution to his employer's RPP.

(2) On April 1, 2016, Ivan had his employer transfer directly the lump-sum payment from the RPP to his RRSP. In addition, Ivan's employer transferred $20,000 of his retiring allowance directly to his RRSP.

(3) Ivan has been employed by the same employer for 15 years.

(4) Ivan was 65 on October 31, 2015.

(5) Ivan's employer reported a PA for him of $700 in respect of 2015. Ivan's earned income for 2015 was $120,000.

— *REQUIRED*

Determine the tax consequences of the above transactions for 2016, supported by your computations.

Exercise 6

ITA: 62

Edwin Edwards was transferred from Vancouver to Montreal by his employer on October 1, 2016. The following expenses were incurred by Edwin:

Airfare for family	$ 1,300
Moving cost of furniture	1,000
Cost of disposing of Vancouver home	
— legal fees	500
— real estate commission	10,000
Cost of purchasing Montreal home	
— prepaid realty taxes	500
— legal fees	1,000
— Quebec transfer tax	300

Edwin's employment income for tax purposes earned in Montreal during 2016 was $7,000. Edwin's employer reimbursed Edwin for $5,000 of the moving expenses.

— *REQUIRED*

Calculate the amount that Edwin can deduct as moving expenses.

ITA: 62

¶9,875 ASSIGNMENT PROBLEMS

Type 1 Problems

Problem 1

ITA: 62(3)

Diane Weber is employed as Personnel Director of B. Ltd., an international corporation. Diane was living in Vancouver at the beginning of last year, but B. Ltd. moved her to Hamilton effective December 1. Diane rented a three-bedroom townhouse in Vancouver but purchased a two-bedroom house in Hamilton on December 20. Diane has supplied you with the following information concerning her moving costs:

Air transportation for Diane	$3,000
Moving costs	3,100
Temporary living expenses (hotel and meals) in Hamilton for 20 days	2,500
Storage	1,250
Lease cancellation fee paid to Vancouver landlord	1,200
Legal fees to purchase new home	3,600
Property taxes paid from December 21–31	400
Moving allowance paid by B. Ltd.	4,000
Diane's net employment income in Hamilton December 1–31	5,600

What is the deductible amount of moving expenses that Diane can claim in her personal income tax return for the year of the move?

Problem 2

ITA: 63

Charles Hughes was a university student in full-time attendance for 30 weeks and worked as a salesman for the balance of the year. His wife, Cathy, was also employed. The Hughes have four children: Sharon 17, Shawn 14, Sally 6 and Stephen 4. Child care expenses for the year amounted to $200 per week for 52 weeks. Charles' and Cathy's receipts and withholdings are summarized below:

	Charles	Cathy
Gross salary	$23,000	$47,000
Taxable fringe benefits	850	4,000
Interest income	200	—
Scholarship	3,600	—
Student loan	2,500	—

Deductions from Charles' and Cathy's employment income were:

	Charles	Cathy
Income taxes withheld	$ 3,800	$13,700
RPP contributions	2,000	3,700

Calculate the child care expenses deduction allowed to Charles and Cathy for 2016.

Problem 3

ITA: 56(1)(b), 56.1, 60(b), 60.1

Uriah and Ursalla Underhill decided to terminate their marriage of 10 years. On June 1 Uriah moved out. From the period of June 1 to October 31, Uriah paid Ursalla $900 per month, made up of $200 for the support of herself and $700 for their two children. On November 1, Uriah and Ursalla signed a written separation agreement which confirmed the $900 a month payment. In addition the agreement provided that Uriah would pay the monthly mortgage payment of $400 on the home which is in Ursalla's name and all medical expenses for the children. During November and December Uriah made the appropriate payments as per the written agreement and paid $100 of dental bills in respect of the children.

Discuss the tax implications of the above facts for both Uriah and Ursalla.

Problem 4

Liz and Richard have ended their marriage and are now living apart. They have sold their house and divided the proceeds, but they now need to deal with Richard's RRSP. They have agreed that Richard needs to transfer $100,000 from his RRSP to Liz as part of the equalization payment.

They would like you to explain the tax consequences of this transfer.

Problem 5

ITA: 146(5)

Diana Capriati, a Canadian resident for income tax purposes, has the following income for 2014 and 2015:

	2014	*2015*
Income from employment		
Gross salary	$130,000	$135,000
Less contribution to employer's RPP	(1,500)	(3,000)
	128,500	132,000
Income from property		
Taxable dividends from Canadian public corporations	32,000	20,000
Gross-up (38%)	12,160	7,600
	44,160	27,600
Bank interest received	3,000	5,000
	47,160	32,600
Rental income — gross	25,000	30,000
Deductible rental expenses	(18,000)	(12,000)
	54,160	50,600
Other income		
Alimony payments received	10,000	10,000
Loss from business		
Share of loss from partnership	(30,000)	(20,000)
	$162,660	$172,600

Diana has asked you to determine the maximum RRSP contribution that she can deduct in 2016. Assume that Diana put $10,000 into her self-administered RRSP on February 12, 2017. Further, assume that Diana was an active member of the partnership and that her pension adjustment for 2014 and 2015 was $4,000 and $7,000, respectively. She did not make an RRSP contribution for 2015.

Problem 6

ITA: 146(1), 146.2

The following table provides information relating to three individuals who each plan to invest $4,500 per year, before tax, starting in 2016. Each individual's before-tax rate of return on a 10-year investment is 8%. Note that each has a different marginal tax rate today (Year 0). However, in 10 years, all are expected to have a marginal tax rate of 40%.

| | **Taxpayer** | | |
	A	**B**	**C**
Earned income	$65,000	$45,000	$25,000
Marginal tax rate (Year 0)	45%	40%	27%
Marginal tax rate (Year 10)	40%	40%	40%
Before-tax rate of return	8%	8%	8%

You have been asked to do the following:

(A) Compute the future value of the investment for each taxpayer assuming:

(i) The individual does not contribute to an RRSP but invests the after-tax proceeds of the $4,500 earned income in a tax-free savings account (TFSA).

(ii) The individual contributes to a self-directed RRSP and withdraws the amount in Year 10.

(B) Should each individual contribute to an RRSP or to a TFSA?

Problem 7

ITA: 60(*i*), 60(*j*.1), 146(5), 146(5.1), 146(8.2), 146(8.3), 147.3(4), 147.3(9)

Mr. Rui retired from his job with Wise and Foresighted Consulting Ltd. on February 28, 2016. Mr. Rui expects his 2016 income for tax purposes to be as follows:

Employment income		$ 7,000
Pension income:		
	Monthly superannuation (10 months of $3,450)	34,500
	Old Age Security	6,850
	Canadian Pension Plan	12,100
Farming income		20,000
Income from rental of apartment		10,800
Royalty income from books written by Mr. Rui		14,200
Interest income		12,000
Total income		$117,450

Additional Information

(1) Mr. Rui's 2016 employment income is net of an RPP contribution of $300. His PA for 2016 is expected to be $600.

(2) Mr. Rui will be 71 in February 2017. His wife is now 67.

(3) In 2016, Mrs. Rui withdrew $6,000 from her RRSP. Mr. Rui had made the following contributions to Mrs. Rui's RRSP: January 2016 — $2,000; April 2015 — $1,000; February 2014 — $1,000; December 2013 — $3,000. Mr. Rui did not deduct the January 2016 contribution in 2015.

(4) Mr. Rui's employer reported a PA for him of $7,000 in 2015. His earned income in 2015 was $66,000.

(5) Mr. Rui has unused RRSP deduction room from prior years of $5,000.

Mr. Rui has asked you to do the following:

(A) Determine the tax implications of Mrs. Rui's $6,000 RRSP withdrawal.

(B) Determine his maximum tax deductible RRSP contribution for 2016. What additional RRSP contribution should he make for 2016?

(C) What should he contribute to his RRSP for 2017?

(D) What additional planning steps would you advise him to take in connection with his RRSP in 2017?

Problem 8

ITA: 62; IT-178R3; Income Tax Folio S1-F3-C4

Sue and George Shaker lived in Halifax, Nova Scotia, while George completed his combined law and MBA degree at Dalhousie University. The Shakers purchased a home in Halifax when they first moved to Nova Scotia. Due to contracting mononucleosis in his second year of the program, George completed his degree in December 2016 rather than in the spring of 2016.

George excelled in the program and had numerous job offers. He finally accepted a job with NorthAm Co. in Toronto. In order to convince George to accept the job, NorthAm Co. offered to pay the Shakers an amount equal to any loss that they incurred on the sale of their Halifax home and provide them with a $10,000 moving allowance.

Sue has been working for an insurance company in Halifax while George has been attending school. Sue intends to find work in Toronto, but will be unable to continue working for the same insurance company.

George accepted the job with NorthAm Co. in September 2016. During October 2016, George and Sue flew to Toronto to look for a home. They spent a week in Toronto and on the fifth day managed to find and purchase a home with the purchase contract closing on December 15, 2016. The remaining two days were spent arranging for painting and cleaning of the new home. Their expenditures on that trip were:

Two Air Canada tickets (return Halifax to Toronto)	$ 1,200
Motel room, 7 days @ $75 per day	525
Meals, 7 days @ $50 per day	350
Car rental	350

George and Sue managed to sell their Halifax home. That sale closed on December 15, 2016. The statement of account from the lawyer (dated January 15, 2017) revealed the following expenses:

Real estate commission	$7,000
Legal fees, old home	2,000
Legal fees, new home	2,500
Land transfer tax, new home	1,000

The house in Halifax was sold for $140,000. The Shakers had originally paid $160,000 for the house. NorthAm Co. provided a cheque for $27,000 in February 2017 to reimburse them for the loss and the real estate commission. (NorthAm Co. did not include the legal costs when calculating the loss eligible for reimbursement.)

Subsequent to finalizing the sale of their Halifax home and George's completion of his exams, Sue and George packed up their car and drove to Toronto. The trip took 7 days due to a leisurely pace and some bad weather delays, and since their home was not ready when they arrived, they stayed in a nearby motel for 11 days.

The cost of trip and stay in motel was as follows:

Meals, 18 days @ $100 (substantiated by receipts)	$1,800
Motel room, 18 days @ $80	1,440
Gasoline (2,000 kilometres driven)	250

In late December, the Shakers paid a moving bill consisting of $5,000 for the actual move and $250 for storage. George received the $10,000 allowance for moving expenses in December 2016. He commenced work for NorthAm Co. in January 2017 at a salary of $80,000 per year. Sue commenced work for Toronto Insurance Co. in September 2017 at a salary of $85,000 per year.

Sue and George have asked you to calculate their allowable moving expenses for both 2016 and 2017 and discuss the tax treatment of the loss reimbursement. Assume that all expenditures made were reasonable and can be substantiated by receipts.

Problem 9   ITA: 63

Nina Diamond and Len Dirkfeld are married and have five children: Lindsay age 18, Trevor age 15, James age 7, Ben age 5, and Rebecca age 3. During 2016, they paid a nanny $250 per week for 50 weeks to look after their children while they worked. During July, they paid $3,000 ($1,500 each) for Trevor and James to go to an overnight summer camp for four weeks. In addition, they paid their child Lindsay $300 to babysit the other children at various times when they worked late.

Len is a physician and has his own practice. Nina worked full-time as a computer consultant during the first eight months of the year. In September, she went back to university on a full-time basis for 13 weeks. On December 11, her courses were finished and she went back to work.

Nina and Len's incomes are summarized below:

	Nina	Len
Salary	$50,000	
Taxable benefits	3,000	
Employment expenses	(800)	
Employment income	$52,200	
Business income		$120,000
Interest income	2,000	3,000
Rental income		6,000
RRSP contribution	(5,000)	(10,000)
Net income under Division B	$49,200	$119,000

Nina and Len have asked you to calculate the maximum 2016 child care deductions they can claim.

They would also like to know how your answer would change if Nina went back to university for 13 weeks on a part-time basis rather than a full-time basis. Assume Nina took a minimum of 12 hours of courses each month, but do not redo all the calculations.

Problem 10

ITA: 56(1)(*a*), 60(*b*),
60(*i*), 60(*j*.1), 60(*o*), 60.1,
62, 63, 146(1), 146(5),
146(8.2), 147.3

In late 2015, Dr. Elaine Matthews separated from her husband. She maintained full custody of the couple's only child, a seven-year-old girl. Since May 1, 2001, Dr. Matthews had been working as a public health consultant for the Oshawa region. Around the middle of 2016 she had chosen to take advantage of a severance package from the Oshawa region. She accepted a staff position at Joseph Brant Memorial Hospital in Burlington, Ontario and moved directly from Oshawa to Burlington on September 1, 2016. She sold the former family home in Oshawa on September 15, 2016. Her husband had rented an apartment in Oshawa in late July 2016.

Dr. Matthews has some experience preparing her own tax returns but she has been particularly busy in recent months. She started her 2016 return but quickly decided she simply did not have time to finish it. She requested your assistance in completing her return.

You met with Dr. Matthews to go over her tax information related to 2016 and determined that she had correctly calculated her income under Subdivisions a, b, and c of Division B to total $158,488. Included in this correct computation were the following items:

Salary (from former employer)	$ 96,000
Salary (from Joseph Brant Memorial Hospital)	60,000
Taxable benefits under section 6 of the *Income Tax Act*	1,743
Registered pension plan contributions (defined benefit plan)	(6,750)
Consulting income (reported as business income)	8,000
Interest income from investments	540
Taxable dividends from investments	1,250
Share of rental loss from childhood home inherited from her parents	(1,495)
Net taxable capital gains	4,800
Interest paid on investment loans	(2,400)
Loss from limited partnership investment (rental property)	(3,200)
	$158,488

She provided you with the following *additional details* relating to 2016:

Miscellaneous income

Severance from former employer	$ 41,538

Transfer of RPP accrued from former employer

Her former employer made a direct transfer of her accumulated RPP benefits (within prescribed limits) to her RRSP; her former employer had made vested contributions for the years 2000 through 2016	$210,000

Spousal support

Under the terms of her separation agreement signed in September 2016, Dr. Matthews paid the following amounts for support of her husband:

Support ($500 a month for September–December)	$ 2,000
Rent on his new Oshawa apartment ($750 a month for September–December)	3,000

Moving expenses from Oshawa to Burlington

Gas for house-hunting trips (four trips made during late August 2016)	$ 40

Selling costs of former Oshawa home (owned 100% by her; sold September 15, 2016):

Real estate commissions	$ 12,000
Legal fees	1,050

Costs of purchasing new Burlington home:

Legal fees	$ 850
Land transfer tax	3,250

Costs of moving herself and her household effects:

Moving van to transport belongings	$ 600
Gas to drive herself and her daughter (120 km driven)	60
Hotel (2 nights while new home was being painted and cleaned; 2 × $100)	200
Meals (same two days as above 2 × $55)	110

You have determined that the distance from her new home to Joseph Brant Hospital is 3.5 kilometres. The distance from Joseph Brant Hospital to her former home was 115 kilometres.

Care of her daughter

Part-time nanny employed January 1–August 31	$ 8,976
YMCA overnight summer camp for two weeks in July while nanny was on vacation ($200 a week)	400
Fall term (September–December) tuition fees for private school (excluding before and after school daycare)	4,000
Before and after school daycare for September–December (provided on premises of private school)	720
Fall term (September–December) transportation to private school	1,200

Registered retirement savings plan contributions

Personal contributions through employment (March–December 2016)	10,000
Personal contributions through employment (January–February 2017)	4,000

Her 2015 earned income for RRSP purposes was $120,000; her employer had reported a pension adjustment on her 2015 T4 of $9,500; she had no unused RRSP contribution room at the start of 2016 and no undeducted balance of RRSP contributions

Legal fees paid

Legal representation during separation proceedings to establish requirements to make support payments	$ 1,600
Appeal of her 2014 income tax assessment (which she won)	1,200

You have been asked to complete the calculation of her income under Division B. Show all calculations whether or not they are necessary to the final answer. Explain briefly any items not used in your calculations.

Type 2 Problems

Problem 11
ITA: 5, 6, 8, 18, 56(1)

Sibbald Kay, age 30, earned $48,000 last year as a dental hygienist for Hi Care Dental Associates. During the year, Sibbald also received director's fees of $600, and incurred the following expenses:

Uniforms purchased for employment purposes	$480
Parking expenses ($80/month)	$960
Hygienist association fees	$280

Sibbald also earned interest income of $3,200 from holding a $50,000 cash balance in T-bills and paid $1,200 in interest expense relating to a loan for an RRSP contribution. Sibbald has not repaid this loan because she believes that saving is more important. Sibbald also has 600 shares of Battery Inc. in her self-directed RRSP. During the year, she sold 400 shares at $20 for a capital gain of $6,000. She withdrew the proceeds of disposition and purchased living room furniture.

Sibbald has asked you to calculate her income for tax purposes, and provide her with tax-planning opportunities for the upcoming years.

Problem 12
ITA: Subdivision b, 248(1)

Mariah Holt, a management consultant, provided you with the following statement for the year ended December 31.

Fees received (gross)	$145,000
Salaries and benefits expense	55,500
Liability insurance expense	5,000
Office expense	1,200
Office equipment	1,000
Automobile expenses	1,000

Interest expense (loan for business use)   10,500
Professional courses   1,400
Beginning undepreciated capital cost
    Automobile (Class 10.1)   20,000
    Office equipment (Class 8)   30,500

For the year, Mariah drove her automobile 30,000 kilometres, of which 15,000 kilometres were driven for business purposes. Mariah and her sister purchased a commercial rental property on December 5. The cost of the property was as follows:

(1) land $950,000,

(2) building $500,000, and

(3) furnishings $3,000.

The rental income and expenses for the 26 days were as follows:

(1) rent $24,000,

(2) operating expenses $20,000, and

(3) interest expense $6,250.

Mariah, a single parent of two children aged three and five, paid $800 per month to a babysitter to care for the two children in her home. In January, Mariah had purchased her first home for $115,000, paid $2,400 for commissions and $1,900 to move 45 kilometres closer to her consulting office. She withdrew $20,000 from her RRSP under the Home Buyers' Plan.

Mariah has asked you to:

(a) Calculate her net income for the taxation year.

(b) Identify any area of her income that may be controversial, particularly with the CRA.

Problem 13

ITA: 5, 6, 8, 12, 20, 39, 40(2), 56, 60, 75, 146

Ms. Sui is an executive of a large public retail corporation, Clothes to You Ltd., situated in Dundas, Ontario. Ms. Sui is not married. However, she has two adopted children, ages 8 and 10, who reside with her.

Ms. Sui has provided you with the following information for 2016:

Clothes To You Ltd.:

Gross salary	$150,000
Commission income	30,000
Canada Pension Plan contributions	(2,480)
Employment Insurance premiums	(931)
Registered pension plan contributions (money purchase)	(6,000)
Income taxes deducted	(55,000)

(1) Clothes To You Ltd. provides Ms. Sui with an automobile. The annual lease cost of the car, including HST, is $18,400. Ms. Sui is reimbursed for her operating expenses when using the car for business. Clothes To You Ltd. also pays for any insurance, licence fees and repairs and maintenance related to the operation of the automobile. The operating expenses for the year totalled $6,200, including HST. She used the car 10,000 kilometres for pleasure and 30,000 kilometres for business. She is charged $200/month for the use of the car and operating costs.

(2) Ms. Sui received stock options in the year. She has the option to purchase 20,000 shares at $3.50/share. The value of the shares at the date of the issue of the option was $3.50/share. Ms. Sui has not yet exercised any of her options.

(3) Ms. Sui received a piece of artwork worth $750, including HST, from the company at Christmas time.

(4) Clothes To You Ltd. paid $1,300, including HST, for her membership in a fitness club. The corporation also paid Private Health Insurance premiums of $350.

Investment Receipts:

Interest income.	$1,100
Dividends received from Canadian-resident public corporations	7,500
Dividends from U.S. corporation — net of 15% withholding tax (in Cdn. $)	680

Other Items:

(1) Annuity payments under contract from Profound Life Assurance Co.
    The capital portion of the annuity was $650 . . . . $2,000

(2) Net proceeds on the sale of her house on March 15, 2016 —
    net of real estate commission of $12,000 . . . . $188,000

    The house cost $90,000 in 2003. She had previously sold her cottage in 2005, giving the cottage the maximum designation as a principal residence in order to have a nil taxable capital gain.

(3) At Christmas 2015, Ms. Sui gave each of her children a 6%, $2,000 five-year bond.

Expenditures/Losses:

(1) Investment counsellor's fees . . . . $ 1,100

(2) Interest on bank loan to purchase shares 850

(3) Registered retirement savings plan contribution 14,000

    Ms. Sui's earned income in 2015 was $170,000. The PA on her 2015 was $7,000.

(4) Ms. Sui incurred meals and entertainment expenses 8,300

(5) Rental loss (before CCA) 3,500

(6) Ms. Sui invested in a limited partnership tax shelter in 2016. The loss per form T5013 is $3,200. She invested $5,000 in the partnership units in early 2016.

Ms. Sui has asked you to calculate her income for tax purposes for 2016.

Problem 14

ITA: 63

Ed Sigmond was transferred from England to Ottawa by Pharmadyne Supplies Inc. on April 1, to assume the permanent position as Vice President, Canadian operations. Ed was a permanent resident of England prior to the move. His earnings for the year are as follows:

Gross salary — January 1 to March 30	$ 12,000
Income tax paid in England	(3,200)
Gross salary — April 1 to December 31	$ 62,000
Income tax withheld	(21,000)
CPP/EI withheld	(3,499)
Donations to United Way withheld	(400)

Ed's spouse, Laura, arrived in Ottawa on July 15, with three children (all seven years of age or older). On August 1, she resumed her full-time studies at the University of Ottawa, where she was awarded a $2,500 scholarship. In England, she had attended the University of Cambridge from January 1 to April 30. In England, Laura paid $1,000 per month for a nanny for the children. In Canada, she took her children to the local daycare for $1,360 per month. The Sigmonds also incurred the following moving expenses:

Airfare/lodging — house hunting in Ottawa.	$3,500
Airfare — family move	7,000
Moving van fees.	3,200
Legal fees and land transfer taxes on acquiring the Ottawa home	5,500
Meals and hotel expenses (12 days prior to employment)	3,800

Ed is having some problems in calculating his and Laura's income for Canadian tax purposes, and has come to you for assistance. He has asked you to calculate his income for tax purposes.

Problem 15

Ms. King had a busy year in 2016. During the year, she formally separated from her husband and retained custody of her five-year-old daughter, Kelly. She also decided that she needed a fresh start in another city, so she quit her job in Belleville, Ontario, and got a new job in Windsor. Ms. King and her daughter moved to Windsor, Ontario, in November 2016. She has asked you to help her estimate her 2016 personal income tax liability. In order to help you, she has prepared the following list of all the transactions which she thinks might be of interest to you.

(1) Her employment income from her employer in Belleville for the first 11 months of 2016 was $55,000. Her deductions at source included CPP/EI of $3,499 and income tax of $11,000.

Before she left the Belleville employer, a public company, she exercised a stock option that she had for 800 shares. When this option had originally been granted, the share price was $15. The exercise price of the option was $17. At the time she exercised the option, the market price was $25. She immediately sold these shares on the open market for $25.

(2) Her new employer in Windsor agreed to pay some of her moving expenses, but in order to simplify things, they were going to give her an allowance of $8,000. She was responsible, then, for her own expenses.

Her moving costs were as follows:

Moving company charges	$5,500
Gas for trip to Windsor at the time of the move (600 km driven)	75
Motel in Belleville for one night on the day of the move	75
Meals during the one-day move to Windsor	100
Lease cancellation charge in Belleville	200
	$5,950

She had made a trip to Windsor to look for an apartment for her and Kelly and she had incurred the following expenses:

Gas for trip to Windsor and return	$150
Motel costs in Windsor	150
Meals	75
	$375

(3) Her income from her new employer in Windsor during the month of December was $5,000.

(4) During the year she incurred the following expenses for the care of Kelly:

Food and clothing	$6,000
Babysitter costs while she was at work	3,000

(5) Ms. King incurred legal fees of $3,200 to establish her right, under the *Divorce Act*, to support payments in connection with the finalization of the separation agreement. She feels that this was well spent, since her lawyer was successful in getting her husband to pay child support to her for Kelly in the amount of $800 per month, starting in February 2016. So far, her husband has been making these payments on time.

She also had trouble with her 2014 tax return and had to pay her previous accountant $400 to deal with the CRA. It turns out that the CRA has correctly assessed her return.

(6) She is totally confused by the RRSP rules, so she wants you to tell her what the maximum amount is that she can contribute to her RRSP for 2016. She wants you to assume that she will make these payments within the time deadlines when you calculate her tax liability.

(7) Five years ago, Ms. King inherited some shares in a Canadian-resident public company, Facai Ltd., from her mother. She believed that the shares were capable of making money for her. She sold the shares in 2016, in order to put money into a mutual fund that a friend recommended. Her mother had paid $5,000 for these shares in 1989 and at the time of her mother's death, the shares were worth $60,000. Ms. King sold them for $180,000.

Ms. King received cash dividends from these shares during the year in the amount of $9,058.

(8) One of her good friends had been a battered wife, so Ms. King had donated $2,000 to the local registered charity which protects battered women.

(9) Ms. King gave you a copy of her 2015 tax return and it showed employment income of $55,000, child care expenses of $2,000 and taxable dividends of $10,000. She made the maximum RRSP contribution for 2015.

Ms. King has asked you to calculate her income for 2016. Explain why you omitted any amounts from your calculations. Show all calculations.

Problem 16

ITA: Division B

Cam Renaz, a self-employed geologist, is a single parent with full custody of his two daughters, Sharee and Susanna (ages 13 and 15). During the past year, Cam retained the full-time services of a nanny to care for them while he worked. Unfortunately, this was a difficult year in Cam's field and his earnings were low. To assist in financing his living expenses, he withdrew $12,000 from his RRSP. He also settled with his wife and she paid him $20,000 as a lump sum in exchange for being relieved of any liability for future alimony payments. To save even more money, Cam prepared his own income tax return, instead of using his accountant's services.

Below is a summary of Cam's income tax information:

Consulting income, net of expenses	$28,000
Car purchased — used 40% for business use	(18,000)
Nanny's salary ($1000/month)	(12,000)
RRSP withdrawals (gross)	12,000
Canadian dividends — cash amount (from CCPCs whose active business income is eligible for the small business deduction)	1,500

When Cam filed his income tax return, he deducted the nanny expense from his consulting income, and wrote off 40% of the cost of the car as business expense. He did not report the RRSP withdrawals because 20% tax was withheld at source.

When Cam received his notice of assessment from the CRA, he was shocked to see that he owed substantially more income tax. The following comments were made in his notice of assessment:

- Child care expenses are not deductible as a self-employed business expense and have been disallowed.

- Cannot deduct price of car as a business expense, and the item has been disallowed.

- Your dividend income has been increased by $270.

- Our records indicate that you withdrew $12,000 from your RRSP and received $20,000 from your ex-spouse for alimony; these amounts have been added to your income.

Cam does not understand why the CRA is assessing him this way. He particularly recalls his accountant telling him that the nanny expenses would be tax deductible.

Compute Cam's net income, considering the legislation, common law and administrative practice, and the correct income tax treatment of each of the items creating problems in Cam's income tax return.

Type 3 Problems

Problem 17

ITA: Division B

Myron Van Doulis, age 42, just left your office with his spouse, Jennifer Barnes. Over the past several years Myron, a former VP at TNS Communications, has been successfully promoted and now earns $220,000 annual salary. The couple worked assiduously for their social position; Myron encouraged his wife to learn bridge, tennis, and to work as a charitable member of the local community. Jennifer continues to pay her law society dues, hoping that someday she will return to her profession. Myron's treadmill was running at full-speed until last month when TNS was suddenly acquired by MIC International. Myron's life was in crisis when the president, accompanied by a security officer, guided him from his office with a $120,000 severance package. The presidents of TNS and MIC both agreed that Myron's work ethic and performance were less than marginal when compared with the performance of MIC's senior vice president.

While the couple's children (ages 8, 10, and 13) are in school, Jennifer has been secretly writing and working on the computer. Over the past five years, Jennifer has developed a few unique software packages for specialized legal services. Her software was tested and favourably accepted by a large international law firm. Jennifer now has a lucrative proposal from a leading software publishing company. Over the past month, Myron has had time to reflect, ponder, and examine his future needs.

Myron just finished reading the best-selling book, *Take Your Money and Run*. Given the ever-increasing debt load, Myron believes that the government will continue to raise his federal income tax rates. He also believes that the cost of health care and education will increase dramatically. The current market value of Myron's net assets are as follows:

Cash	$ 13,000
Treasury bills and bonds	120,000
Speculative stocks (cost $95,000)	4,000
RRSP: Securities	149,000
House (cost $210,000)	240,000
Bank loan for trading	(140,000)
Net assets	$386,000

Myron's most immediate concern is his severance pay. He has a few options. His marginal tax rate this year will be 50% and, in 20 years, when he retires, he estimates a marginal tax rate of 40%.

(a) In the details of Myron's severance package, MIC is willing to pay an $80,000 retirement allowance. Assume for the purposes of this case that all of the $80,000 may be contributed to his RRSP due to Myron's unused RRSP room. Myron can invest the $80,000 in the Province of British Columbia strip bonds with an annual yield to maturity (YTM) of 5%. MIC has also agreed to pay a cash settlement of $40,000. Currently, the annual GIC rate is 4%.

(b) Alternatively, MIC is willing to provide Myron with 12,000 shares of ITT, a Canadian public corporation, currently trading at $8, and a cash settlement of $40,000. The shares pay an annual 5% dividend; the company expects growth of about 4% per year. This assumes that the new vice president will improve the financial returns and reap greater rewards in the derivative market-place.

Myron feels like escaping for a few years. He's thinking of selling his home and purchasing a yacht outfitted with communications technology. According to the book, *Take Your Money and Run*, he could sever all ties (for about two years), transfer his assets and severance to a tax haven, and incorporate offshore. The company could rent a home in Canada for the children while they complete their education. The technology on board would permit his wife to communicate with her publisher (although she insists that she would have to spend at least four months of the year in Canada, visiting the children). Further, Myron can continue his adventurous trading in the options and derivative markets. One last problem: the CRA has disallowed his business loss of $90,000 in last year's income tax return. His trading in the options market generated losses of $90,000, including commission expenses. The CRA has assessed the loss as a capital loss because, in the prior year, Myron had reported his $22,000 in profits from trading in the options market as a capital gain and not as business income.

Draft a report to Myron, detailing and quantifying where possible, the income tax position he faces. Include the financial quantification of the two retirement packages he has been offered. Assume the tax rate on dividends equals approximately 25%.

 [For more problems and solutions thereto, see the DVD accompanying the textbook.]

CHAPTER 9 —
DISCUSSION NOTES FOR REVIEW QUESTIONS

(1) The payment was made to Ms. Tang "upon or after retirement of a taxpayer from an office or employment in recognition of her long service" and as such should qualify as a retiring allowance and be included in income. An Interpretation Bulletin states that "the cessation of employment for any reason is considered as being retirement or loss of employment". Therefore, even though she quit, this amount should still qualify as a retiring allowance.

ITA: 56(1)(a)(ii), 248(1) "retiring allowance"

IT-337R4, par. 2

(2) The accumulated sick days will qualify as a "retiring allowance" and be taxed as such. However, the unused vacation days will not qualify under this definition, according to the Interpretation Bulletin, and will be taxed as employment income.

ITA: 6(3), 56(1)(a)(ii), 248(1) "retiring allowance"; IT-337R4 par. 5

(3) Since the $3,000 per month is contained in the written agreement and the $1,200 mortgage payment is part of the "allowance," the full amount should be deductible. However, the deductibility for the mortgage payment is limited to ⅕ of the original principal. In this case, ⅕ × $120,000 = $24,000. After 20 months ($24,000/$1,200), Charles will no longer be able to deduct the payments related to the mortgage and Dee will no longer have to take them into income.

ITA: 60.1(2)

(4) Under this agreement, the $500 in monthly fees paid to the financial institution will qualify as an allowance since Mark does have the discretion as to where the $500 is paid. In addition, this amount is part of the monthly spousal maintenance payment specified in the agreement.

(5) The loan would have to be included in employment income when received. Such amounts are not awards and are not subject to the rules for scholarships and research grants. As a result, neither the full exemption for scholarships nor research expenses are available as deductions. Any repayment of this repayable award is deductible provided the conditions of that paragraph are met.

ITA: 5(1), 6(3), 8(1)(n); Income Tax Folio S1-F2-C3 — Scholarships, Research Grants and Other Education Assistance

ITA: 56(1)(n), 56(1)(o)

(6) The OAS Supplement would fall into the category of "social assistance payments" since it is based on an income test. As a result, the payments are included in net income, but there is a corresponding deduction to exclude it from taxable income. The effect of these two provisions is to raise Mrs. Smith's income to a point that no one can claim her as a dependant, but at the same time not to make Mrs. Smith taxable on this amount.

ITA: 56(1)(u), 110(1)(f)

(7) The $15,000 will be taxed in Mr. Singh's hands on an indirect payment and not in Mrs. Singh's hands.

ITA: 56(2)

(8) Defined benefit pension plans are approved by and registered with the CRA. Once the CRA has agreed to the terms of the plan, the amount that the company can deduct is determined by an actuary who certifies the amount that is necessary to fund the accruing benefits of the plan.

(9) The explanation is based on the fact that the two pension systems are integrated and the integration is based on how rich your pension plan is. The richness of your pension plan is determined by the Pension Adjustment calculation. For this system to work, the pension calculation has to come first. So, your maximum pension contribution is based on your current income. Then, early in the following year your pension adjustment (PA) is calculated. Finally, your RRSP limit is determined, based on your earned income and PA, both of which relate to the prior year.

(10) The Regulations set the withholding rates based on the amount of the withdrawal — 10% of the amount if it is $5,000 or less; 20% if the amount is between $5,000 and $15,000; and 30% if the amount exceeds $15,000. The rates are one-half of these amounts in Quebec. Based on this formula, the withholdings would be 30% of $20,000 or $6,000. Instead, if she were to withdraw four payments of $5,000, then the tax withheld would amount to only 10% of $20,000 or $2,000. In both cases the $20,000 withdrawn will have to be included in her income for the year and the same amount of ultimate tax will have to be paid. The tax will

ITR: 103(4), 103(6)

have to be funded from other sources to allow for the $20,000 to be spent for the car. Alternatively, the withdrawal will have to be increased for the amount of the tax to be paid. The necessary withdrawal would be $20,000/(1 − t), where t is her marginal tax rate.

(11) Since he left his RRSP to an adult child, the estate will have to pay tax on the basis that the full amount of the RRSP was included in income in the year of death. At a 50% tax rate, this will amount to $75,000 of tax which will come out of the residue or Jim's share of the estate. As a result, Kim will receive $150,000 of cash and Jim will receive the residue of the estate minus the $75,000 of tax and any other tax that may be payable. Mr. McDonald should have calculated the division of property based on the after-tax values to the estate.

(12) The following items would show up on her personal tax return:

(a) the $40,000 would be included in income as a retiring allowance; and

(b) the $8,000 of legal fees could be deducted.   ITA: 60(o.1)

The $32,000 (net of legal fees) retiring allowance is not eligible for a deduction on contribution to the RRSP. As a result, she will have an overcontribution which will attract a penalty of 1% per month in the RRSP, unless she removes the overcontribution on a timely basis.

CHAPTER 9

CHAPTER 9 — SOLUTIONS TO MULTIPLE CHOICE QUESTIONS

Question 1

(A) is the correct answer in this case, since no amount of the retiring allowance provides a   ITA: 60(*j*.1) deductible RRSP contribution.

(B), (C), and (D) incorrectly consider any amount of the retiring allowance to be deductible in this case when no amount is deductible.

Question 2

(C) is correct. The $6,000 is calculated as follows:

The lesser of:		
the 2016 RRSP dollar limit		$25,370
18% of earned income for 2015:		
Income from employment	$44,000	
RPP contributions	1,000	
Spousal support received	3,600	
Real estate rental income	1,400	
	$50,000 × 18%	$ 9,000
The lesser amount	$ 9,000	
minus 2015 PA	(4,000)	
add unused deduction room	1,000	
	$ 6,000	

(A) incorrectly uses $44,000 as earned income: 18% × $44,000 – $4,000 PA + $1,000 = $4,920.

(B) incorrectly excludes the unused deduction room: $9,000 – $4,000 = $5,000.

(D) incorrectly ignores the earned income calculation: $20,000 – $4,000 + $1,000 = $17,000.

Question 3

(A) is correct. The calculations are as follows:

	Meg	James	
Salary	$46,000		
Employment expenses	(2,800)		ITA: 8
Business income	—	$18,000	
Interest income	800	1,500	
Net income	$44,000	$19,500	
Earned income	$46,000	$18,000	ITA: 63

Since James has the lower net income ($19,500), he must claim the deduction, which is the least of:

(a) Eligible child care expenses: $15,000 + ($125 × 2 weeks) $15,250

(b) Eligible children:
$5,000 × 1 = $5,000
$8,000 × 2 = 16,000 . . . . $21,000

(c) ⅔ × James' earned income: ⅔ × $18,000 . . . . $12,000

Since Joanne is age 17, she is not an eligible child. The deduction for the overnight camp for Susie is restricted to $125 per week.   ITA: 63(3)

(B) is incorrect, because Meg cannot claim the deduction, since she has the higher net income.

(C) and (D) are incorrect because they are not the least amount calculated in (A) above.

Question 4

(B) is correct and is calculated as follows:

Moving van to transport household effects		$ 5,000
Travelling cost — self, spouse and two children		
Meals — flat rate ($51 × 4 persons × 5 days)	$ 1,020	
Car — flat rate (4,430 kms × $0.55)	2,547	
Hotel ($100 × 5 nights)	500	4,047
Legal fees — Vancouver house		900
Legal fees — Toronto house		1,100
Costs while waiting for Vancouver house —		
Hotel (15 days (max.) × $100)		1,500
Meals (15 days (max.) × 4 persons × $51)		3,060
		$15,607

The mileage rate is determined by the province in which travel began.

(A) incorrectly excludes the legal fees on the houses and uses $3,000 as travel costs: $15,607 − $2,000 − $4,047 + $3,000 = $12,560.

(C) incorrectly includes all the hotel costs and the house hunting trip and uses $3,000 as travel costs: $15,607 + $1,500 + $800 − $4,047 + $3,000 = $16,860.

(D) incorrectly includes all the hotel costs: $15,607 + 1,500 = $17,107.

Question 5

(D) is correct. The earned income that should be used to calculate her RRSP deduction for 2016 is her 2015 earned income, which is: ITA: 146(1)

	2015	
Salary	$100,000	
Taxable benefits	8,000	ITA: 6, 7
Travel expenses	(3,000)	ITA: 8
Business losses	(1,000)	
Rental income (net of expenses and CCA)	3,200	
Spousal support paid	(12,600)	
2015 Earned income	$ 94,600	ITA: 146(1)

CHAPTER 9

(A) and (C) are incorrect. The earned income that should be used to calculate her child care   ITA: 63(3)
expense deduction for 2016 is $118,000:

	2016
Salary	$110,000
Taxable benefits	8,000
Earned income	$118,000

ITA: 6, 7

ITA: 63(3)

(A) incorrectly includes 2016 salary only ($110,000).

(C) is the 2016 net income under Division B which includes amounts for travel expenses, RPP   ITA: 63(3)
contributions, business losses, rental income and spousal support which are not part of the earned
income calculation for the child care expense deduction.

(B) is Sahar's 2016 earned income for computing her 2017 RRSP deduction: ITA: 146(1)

	2016
Salary	$110,000
Taxable benefits	8,000
Travel expenses	(2,000)
Business losses	(1,200)
Rental income (net of expenses and CCA)	3,600
Spousal support paid	(12,000)
Net income under Division B	$106,400

ITA: 6, 7

ITA: 8

Question 6

(D) is correct. Deductible moving costs are: ITA: 62(3)

Moving van		$2,600
Travelling costs to move Natalie and family		
Meals — flat rate ($51 × 4 persons × 3 days)	$ 612	
Car — flat rate (1,000 kms × $0.47)	470	
Hotel ($100 × 2 nights)	200	1,282
Cost of maintaining vacant former residence (maximum amount)		5,000
Cost of changing address on legal documents		100
		$8,982

(A) $25,700 incorrectly includes all expenses listed, including only $900 for travelling costs.

(B) $16,007 incorrectly includes the actual cost of maintaining the former residence (an additional
$4,000) plus the $3,000 house hunting trip.

(C) $12,600 incorrectly includes all actual cost of maintaining the former residence (an additional
$4,000) and uses only $900 for travel.

CHAPTER 9 — SOLUTIONS TO EXERCISES

Exercise 1

The definition of "earned income" is found in two places in the Act, subsections 146(1) and 63(3). The definition found in subsection 63(3) relates to child care expenses. The definition of earned income contained in subsection 146(1) is used in the calculation of the RRSP contribution limit and is quite different from the definition contained in subsection 63(3). You will note that section 146, entitled "Registered Retirement Savings Plans", appears in Division G — Deferred and Other Special Income Arrangements. ITA: 63(3), 146(1)

The definition of "earned income" pertaining to the child care expense deduction can be seen to reflect the economic activity that the government is encouraging when taxpayers incur child care expenses. These are limited to: employment, carrying on business (in an unincorporated form), or studying where student income like a net research grant is obtained.

The definition of "earned income" pertaining to an RRSP can be seen to reflect, conceptually, a source of income that requires some amount of active involvement in the earning process, rather than a passive source, like a passive investment in stocks or bonds earning dividends or interest.

Exercise 2

The maximum amount that Don is able to deduct in respect of a spousal RRSP is his annual contribution limit, less any contributions made to his own RRSP in respect of the year.

Don's annual contribution limit for 2016 is calculated as the lesser of 18% of his 2015 earned income (i.e., $11,916 as calculated below) and the RRSP dollar limit for 2016, which is $24,930, less the PA reported by his employer in respect of 2015 of $6,084.

Don's earned income for 2015 is calculated as: ITA: 146(1)

Employment income — Subdivision a	$68,400	
Add: RPP contribution	2,800	$71,200
Rental loss		(5,000)
Earned income		$66,200
18% thereof		$11,916

Therefore, Don is able to deduct $5,832 (i.e., $11,916 – $6,084) of RRSP contributions in 2016. Since he has already contributed $5,000 to a spousal RRSP, he can either contribute $832 to his own RRSP, or an additional $832 to the spousal RRSP for 2016.

Exercise 3

To calculate the after-tax rate of return for the first investment alternative — the bond held outside of an RRSP — you must multiply the pre-tax rate of return by (1 – t). Therefore, the after-tax rate of return will be 2.216% (8% (1 – 0.46)), or $324. As the annual after-tax yield is reinvested at the same pre-tax 4%, the compounded yield is $3,574 (i.e., $15,000 (1.0216)^{10} – $15,000).

Inside the RRSP, the 4% interest compounds unhindered by tax, and in 10 years the RRSP amount grows to $7,204 (i.e., $15,000 (1.04)^{10} – $15,000); however, income taxes must be paid on withdrawal from the RRSP at 46% equalling $3,314 and yielding $3,890.

The RRSP approach produces the better after-tax yield, $3,890 versus $3,574 outside the RRSP.

Exercise 4

As this was a spousal RRSP, it is subject to the three-year rule. Douglas will be required to report $6,000 as his income. Under the three-year rule, Douglas's income is the lesser of (A) and (B). ITA: 146(1)

(A) Spousal RRSP contributions, current year $0; preceding two taxation years $6,000.

(B) RRSP withdrawn $10,000.

Donna will report the remaining $4,000 of income ($10,000 – $6,000).

While income is reported by Douglas, the income tax withholding of $2,000 remains as a credit in Donna's tax return.

Exercise 5

Mr. Reimer is able to contribute $20,900 to an RRSP for 2016 [(lesser of 18% of his earned income from 2015 (i.e., 18% of $120,000 = $20,900 and $25,370) less his 2015 PA of $700]. He may make this annual contribution to either his own or a spousal RRSP, as long as the total of the contributions does not exceed $20,200. These contributions may be made in the year or within 60 days of December 31, 2016.

He does not have to include the lump-sum transfer from his RPP in his income nor does he get an offsetting deduction, as long as it is eligible to be transferred.   ITA: 147.3(4), 147.3(9)

Mr. Reimer is not allowed to transfer any amount in this case to his RRSPs in respect of his retiring allowance.

Exercise 6

Allowable moving expense deduction

(A) 2016

Travelling cost — air fare	$ 1,300	ITA: 62(3)(*a*)
Household effects — transporting	1,000	ITA: 62(3)(*b*)
Selling costs of Vancouver residence		ITA: 62(3)(*e*)
— legal fees	500	
— real estate commission	10,000	
Allowable purchase cost of Montreal residence		ITA: 62(3)(*f*)
— legal fees	1,000	
— Quebec transfer tax	300	
Total potential deductions	$14,100	
Less		
Amount paid by the employer not included income	$ 5,000	ITA: 62(1)(*c*)
	$ 9,100	
Deduction restricted to income from new work location — 2016	$ 7,000	ITA: 62(1)(*f*)

(B) 2017

Balance deductible from income from the new location only in 2017	2,100	ITA: 62(1)
	$ 9,100	

Chapter 10

Computation of Taxable Income and Taxes Payable for Individuals

Learning Goals

Know, Understand and Explain

By the end of this chapter you will know, understand and be able to explain:

- The difference between net income for tax purposes and taxable income.
- Which deductions are used in the computation of net income for tax purposes and which deductions are used in the computation of taxable income.
- The difference between a tax credit and a tax deduction.
- The difference between a refundable and non-refundable tax credit.
- Non-refundable tax credits available to a taxpayer.
- Refundable tax credits available to a taxpayer.
- How computations of net income for tax purposes impact the calculation of refundable tax credits.
- The purpose of the minimum tax.
- Situations when minimum tax may apply.

Apply

By the end of this chapter you will be able to apply your knowledge and understanding to:

- Calculate the taxable income for an individual taxpayer.
- Calculate the tax owing for an individual taxpayer.
- Calculate tax credits for an individual taxpayer.

Analyze

By the end of this chapter you will be able to analyze:

- The choices in claiming the equivalent-to-married credit, caregiver credit and infirm dependant credit for a dependant.

Review Questions
¶10,800 in the Study Guide

Multiple Choice Questions
¶10,825 in the Study Guide

Exercise Questions
¶10,850 in the Study Guide

Assignment Problems
¶10,875 in the Study Guide

CHAPTER 10 — LEARNING CHART

Problem Descriptions

Textbook Example Problems

10-1	Employee stock option
10-2	Home relocation loan
10-3	Net capital losses
10-4	Deduction of loss carryovers
10-5	Deduction of loss carryovers
10-6	Personal tax credits for dependants
10-7	Medical tax credits
10-8	Medical tax credits for dependants
10-9	Transfer of education credits
10-10	Tax on Old Age Security
10-11	Transfer of credits to spouse
10-12	Taxable income and credits — ordering rules
10-13	Comprehensive
10-14	Comprehensive
10-15	Refundable GST/HST credit
10-16	Working income tax benefit
10-17	Minimum tax

Multiple Choice Questions

1	Employee stock option
2	Non-refundable credits
3	Transfer of education credits
4	Calculate taxable income and tax payable
5	Minimum tax

Exercises

1	Identify sources of income
2	Loss carryovers
3	Calculate income for tax purposes
4	Calculate income, taxable income, tax payable
5	Personal credits
6	Withdrawal from RPP
7	Transfer of credits to spouse
8	Transfer of dividends
9	Foreign and dividend tax credits
10	Minimum tax
11	Marginal tax rate
12	Minimum tax
13	Becoming resident in Canada
14	Calculate taxable income, personal credit base amount

Assignment Problems

1	Dependent credit
2	Tuition and education credits
3	Exempt income, non-capital loss
4	Income and taxable income, ordering rules

CHAPTER 10

Problem Descriptions

5	Credits
6	Dependent credit
7	Credits — single parent, infirm child
8	Medical expenses
9	Dividend election
10	Credits for U.S. university
11	Credits for U.S. and Canadian universities
12	Tax payable, refundable GST credit and CCTB
13	Pension vs. dividends, OAS claw back
14	Minimum tax
15	Stock option — Division C deduction
16	Loss carryover
17	Allowable business investment loss
18	Marginal tax rates
19	Maximum eligible dividend without tax
20	Pension splitting
21	Income, ordering rules
22	Income and taxable income, ordering rules
23	Income and taxable income, ordering rules
24	Income and taxable income, ordering rules

Study Notes

¶10,800 REVIEW QUESTIONS

(1) Ms. Gnu, a new client of yours, has brought in her tax information and is confused. In prior years, she has had some financial difficulties and has lost money in a number of her business ventures. As a result, she has some net capital and some non-capital losses. This year, she earned some income, but she does not know how to decide which losses to apply against this income. What advice do you have for her?

(2) Evan earns $150,000 of employment income and has come to you to talk about his investment income. He earns $10,000 of dividend income from a Canadian-resident public corporation in the year. He wants you to tell him what his marginal tax rate is on this dividend income.

(3) Phil earns $150,000 of employment income and has come to you to talk about his investment income. He earns $10,000 of interest income in the year. He wants you to tell him what his marginal tax rate is on this interest income.

(4) Karen earns $150,000 of employment income and has come to you to talk about her investment income. She realized a $10,000 capital gain in the year and wants you to tell her what her marginal tax rate is on this capital gain.

(5) Ms. Aarts is a painter who specializes in watercolours. In the artistic tradition, she does not make a great deal of money. In fact, she has never made over $20,000 of taxable income in any year. This year is no exception. She expects to have taxable income of $20,000 but she is also planning to donate one of her watercolours to a local charity to be used in one of their fundraising events. The value of the painting is $8,000 and her cost of the painting is $200. She has heard that there are special rules for artists making charitable donations of their work but she does not know if these rules will help her. She does not make any other donations. What is your advice?

(6) During the year Patricia had full-time employment income from employer A of $65,000 and from employer B of $60,000. Both employer A and employer B each deducted $2,544 from her salary for CPP. What impact will the CPP contributions for her employment income have on her personal tax return?

¶10,825 MULTIPLE CHOICE QUESTIONS

Question 1

Banbury Ltd. (BL) is a Canadian-controlled private corporation (CCPC). Brad King is one of BL's employees and deals at arm's length with BL. On April 30, 2013, Brad was granted an option to purchase 1,000 BL shares at $2 per share. Brad exercised the stock option on June 30, 2014, when the market price was $5 per share. In December 2016 Brad sold the shares for $7 each. The fair market value of the shares on April 30, 2013, was $2.50.

Which one of the following amounts represents the increase in Brad's taxable income resulting from the above transactions?

(A) $3,000 in 2014 and $1,000 in 2016

(B) $2,250 in 2014 and $1,000 in 2016

(C) $2,500 in 2016

(D) $4,000 in 2016

Question 2

Bob, a widower who is 65 years old, has correctly calculated his taxable income for 2016 as follows:

Employment income under Subdivision a	$10,000
Pension income (registered pension plan)	20,000
Old Age Security and Canada Pension Plans	10,000
Dividends from Canadian-resident public corporations (grossed up)	2,760
Interest income	5,000
	$47,760

What is the maximum amount (rounded to the nearest dollar) of federal income tax credits that Bob can claim on his 2016 tax return?

(A) $2,939

(B) $2,998

(C) $3,413

(D) $3,264

Question 3

In 2016, Shabir Hassam attended McGill University on a full-time basis for eight months, paying tuition fees of $3,900 for that period. In April 2016, Shabir moved back to Toronto to stay with his family and worked as a waiter. Shabir earned $10,500 in wages and $1,500 in tips during the summer. His moving costs were $200 to Toronto in April 2016 and $500 to Montreal in September 2016. Shabir also received a $1,500 scholarship from McGill in September 2016.

What is the maximum amount of federal personal income tax credits that Shabir can transfer to a parent in respect of his university education in 2016?

(A) $585

(B) $701

(C) $750

(D) $1,143

CHAPTER 10

Question 4

Kyle, who is employed by a CCPC, had the following sources of income for the year:

Salary	\$ 60,000
Dividends from Canadian-resident public corporation (amount received)	20,000
Employee stock option benefit	200,000
Capital gain	200,000

The stock option benefit relates to 50,000 shares that Kyle acquired under an employee stock option plan in January 2016 when the fair market value of the shares was \$10 per share. Kyle paid \$6 per share for the stock, which was the fair market value of each share at the time that the employee stock options were granted to him. He sold the stock when it was worth \$14 per share.

Kyle is married and his wife works full-time. Their three children attend university. Each child has transferred the \$5,000 maximum amount of education, tuition, and textbook credits to Kyle.

Based on this information, what is Kyle's federal Part I tax for the year under the regular rules, ignoring the minimum tax rules?

(A) \$66,410
(B) \$68,047
(C) \$70,555
(D) \$99,410

Question 5

Based on the information in Question 4, above, what is Kyle's minimum amount of federal tax for the year under minimum tax, after deducting minimum tax credits?   ITA: 127.53

(A) \$57,580
(B) \$55,330
(C) \$48,580
(D) \$39,580

¶10,850 EXERCISES

Exercise 1

ITA: 3

Paragraph 3(*a*) of the *Income Tax Act* requires that all non-capital sources of income be included. It is necessary to disclose each source of income in the computation of net income for tax purposes. Consider the following:

(a) Dividend income from a CCPC.

(b) Loss from a sole proprietorship.

(c) Cashier's income from a grocery store.

(d) Commissions earned from sales with a real estate company.

(e) Research consulting fees.

(f) Rental income earned on a single dwelling.

(g) Bonus income.

(h) Gain on the sale of land by a real estate development company.

(i) Profit from the sale of shoes earned in an incorporated company.

(j) Employment insurance income.

(k) Dividend income earned from a foreign investment.

(l) Tips earned as a hair stylist.

— *REQUIRED*

Identify the source of income for each of the above.

Exercise 2

ITA: 3, 111

The following information has been provided by your client, Ms. Campbell.

	2014	2015	2016
Capital gains (CG)	$37,500	$50,000	$11,250
Capital losses (CL) (excluding BIL)	15,000	—	22,500
Business investment loss (BIL)	—	30,000	—

Additional Information

(1) The above capital gains do not include capital gains from qualified farm property or qualified small business corporation shares.

(2) Ms. Campbell had a $7,500 net capital loss which was realized in 2012.

(3) Ms. Campbell has not had a taxable capital gain prior to 2014.

(4) Ms. Campbell had a property loss of $7,000 in 2015 and property income of $1,000 and $2,000 for 2014 and 2016, respectively.

— REQUIRED

(A) Determine Ms. Campbell's income from the sources indicated for 2014 to 2016 according to the ordering rules in section 3.

(B) Determine Ms. Campbell's taxable income from the sources indicated for 2014 to 2016 according to the ordering rules in Division C after amending the returns.

Exercise 3

ITA: 3, 111

Consider the following two taxpayer situations.

Taxpayer	A	B
Gross salary	$45,000	$15,000
Interest income	2,000	
Self-employed income (assume for tax purposes)	5,000	
Loss from business		(18,000)
Charitable donations	(280)	
Income tax paid	(15,000)	(3,200)
Net cash flow	$36,720	($6,200)

— REQUIRED

Compute each taxpayer's net income for the year, utilizing the aggregating formula of section 3 of the *Income Tax Act*. Where necessary, compute the net capital loss or the non-capital loss.

Exercise 4

ITA: Divisions B and C

Mr. Ethan Benjamin has provided you with a list of various sources of income, losses, deductions, and credits for the purpose of determining his basic federal tax.

Inclusions:

His share of tax profit from a partnership business	$10,000
Canadian bank interest	3,000
Retiring allowance from a former employer	20,000
Gross salary from new employer	60,000
Director's fee	5,000
Taxable capital gains	20,000
Taxable benefits from employment	3,000
Rental income from a triplex	25,000

Deductions, Losses, and Tax Credits:

Mortgage interest on triplex	23,000
Canada Pension Plan contributions tax credit	382
Property taxes and insurance on triplex	4,500
Non-capital losses from a previous year	4,000
Allowable capital loss for this year	2,000
Education and textbook tax credits transfer from son	80
Net capital losses from a previous year	5,000
Maintenance costs for triplex	1,500
Contribution to employer's registered pension plan	4,000
Basic personal and spousal tax credits	3,442
Fees to a professional engineering society	300
Employment Insurance premiums tax credit	143
Tuition tax credit for night course on computer applications	68
Charitable gifts tax credit	550
Canada employment tax credit	174

— REQUIRED

(A) Determine the income, taxable income and basic federal tax based on the above correct information using the ordering rules in sections 3, 111.1, and 118.92.

(B) Cross-reference each amount to the appropriate section of the Act.

Exercise 5

ITA: 118, 122.6, 122.61; IT-513R

Dan, age 50, supported the following persons during 2016:

	Net income for tax purposes
Wife, Dolly, age 45	$3,000
Son, Don, age 24...	3,800
Son, Dave, age 18, infirm and living with Dan and Dolly	3,200
Daughter, Doris, age 17.....................................	2,800
Son, Dan Jr., age 14	Nil
Mother, age 83, infirm and living with Dan and Dolly.............	7,000

Don is attending university; Dave has been unemployed most of the year; and Doris and Dan Jr. attend high school. Ages are given as of the end of 2016.

— REQUIRED

Determine Dan's total federal personal tax credits under section 118 for 2016.

Exercise 6

ITA: 8(1)(*m*), 56(1)(*a*), 118(3)

Sally was employed for a little under two years at the Banff Springs Hotel as a bellhop. When Sally resigned her position, she withdrew her total contributions of $800 from her employer's pension plan. Sally's contribution to this plan for her last year was $300.

— REQUIRED

Determine the tax consequences of the above situation.

Exercise 7

ITA: 118.8

Tina, age 72, has income for tax purposes from the following sources in 2016:

Pension income:		
Old Age Security pension	$6,850	
Canada Pension Plan	2,755	
Registered pension plan	350	$ 9,955
Investment income:		
Canadian bank interest..............................		100
Total Division B income		$10,055

— REQUIRED

Determine the amount Tina can transfer to her husband Tom in 2016.

Exercise 8

ITA: 82(3)

Henry, a resident of your province, cannot decide whether it would be advisable to elect to include in his income, his wife's cash dividends of $900 received from Canadian-resident public corporations. This is her only income for 2016.

— REQUIRED

Determine whether Henry should elect under subsection 82(3) for 2016 assuming his federal marginal tax rate is 29%.

Exercise 9

ITA: 126(1)

The following selected information has been taken from the 2016 tax return of Adam, who is a bachelor:

Income — Division B	$156,800
Taxable income	150,800
Basic federal tax	32,869

Included in the Division B income was foreign interest of $1,500. Withholding tax of $225 had been deducted by the foreign government. This income is not subject to an international tax agreement.

Also included in the computation of Division B income were $300 of dividends received from Canadian-resident public corporations. Included in the computation of taxable income were deductions for net capital losses carried forward of $6,000.

ITA: 111(1)(b)

— REQUIRED

Determine the amount of the federal foreign tax credit that can be claimed.

Exercise 10

ITA: Division E, E.1

Compute the federal tax at the top bracket, under minimum tax and regular Part I tax for 2016 on $100 of:

(A) interest;

(B) cash dividends from Canadian-resident public corporation;

(C) capital gains.

Exercise 11

ITA: 117(2), 120

Marginal tax rates, or the tax rate applicable to the next dollar of income earned, are relevant to many decisions. Jacob earns $95,000.

— REQUIRED

Calculate Jacob's marginal tax rate using the federal and notional provincial rates provided in this chapter.

Exercise 12

ITA: Division E, E.1

The following is a correct calculation of Betty's Division E tax payable for 2016:

Employment income		$160,000
Dividends from Canadian-resident public corporation		30,000
Gross-up @ 38%		11,400
Loss created by resource property shelter		(103,200)
Net income for tax purposes and taxable income		$ 98,200

Tax on first	$ 90,563		$ 16,075
on next	7,637 @ 26%		1,986
	$ 98,200		$ 18,061

Less tax credits:
Basic personal (15% × $11,474)	$1,721	
Employment Insurance premiums (max.) (15% × $955)	143	
CPP contributions (max.) (15% × $2,544)	382	
Dividend tax credit (6/11 × $11,400)	6,218	
Employment (15% of $1,161)	174	(8,638)
Division E tax		$ 9,423

— REQUIRED

Determine if Betty is subject to minimum tax in 2016.

Exercise 13

ITA: 63, 118

Mr. and Mrs. Ataila immigrated to Canada on May 1 (not a leap year). Mr. Ataila earned $12,400 in Argentina and $72,400 as a senior geologist in Canada. Mrs. Ataila is a homemaker, and mother of three children over the age of 6. Her child care expenses totalled $4,580 for the time she spent planning her entry into the workforce.

Mr. and Mrs. Ataila have approached you for assistance with their Canadian tax returns.

— *REQUIRED*

Discuss what you believe are the areas of their returns that they are most interested in.

Exercise 14

ITA: 63, 118

Pierino's wife died last year. Her income for the year was $28,000. Pierino has a 15-year-old dependent son, James. Pierino works for the Saskatoon Transit Commission and earns $65,000 yearly. He also has a part-time business operation on which he has a loss of $5,250. Pierino contributed $10,000 to his RRSP by transferring some shares in Public Co. Ltd. to his self-administered RRSP. The ACB of the shares was $6,000. He has $3,000 in net capital losses being carried forward.

— *REQUIRED*

Calculate Pierino's taxable income and the base amounts of his personal tax credits. Ignore any CPP and EI contributions.

CHAPTER 10

¶10,875 ASSIGNMENT PROBLEMS

Type 1 Problems

Problem 1

ITA: 118; IT-513R

Jack and Jill were married on December 1, 2016. Jill and her two children of a previous marriage moved into Jack's home. Jill's children are 14 and 16 and have no income.

Jack and Jill have the following income for tax purposes for 2016:

	Prior to the marriage	Subsequent to the marriage
Jack	$33,000	$3,000
Jill	9,800	800

You have been asked to:

(A) Determine the optimum personal tax credits under section 118 for both Jack and Jill for 2016.

(B) How would your answer change in 2017 if the income levels remain the same?

Problem 2

ITA: 118.6, 118.8, 118.9

Sammy, who was a resident of Canada and who attended the University of Alberta on a full-time basis for eight months during 2016, has employment income for tax purposes of $5,000. He paid tuition fees of $1,800 in 2016. Withheld from his income were $94 in Employment Insurance premiums and $74 in CPP contributions.

Determine the amount Sammy can transfer under section 118.8 or 118.9 to another qualified person.

List the potential persons to whom Sammy can transfer his tuition and education tax credits.

Problem 3

ITA: 2(2), 3, 111

Blake, a recent accounting program graduate, earned the following during the year:

Gross income from employment	$ 7,000
Provincial lottery winnings	2,500
Capital gain on ABC shares	1,200
Inheritance from grandmother	12,000
Interest income from inheritance	800

Blake has asked you to:

(a) Calculate his net income for tax purposes for the year.

(b) Calculate his taxable income for the year. Assume that Blake has a non-capital loss carryforward from last year of $3,000.

Problem 4

ITA: 3, 111

The following information has been provided by your client, Mr. Stanley Norman:

	2014	2015	2016
Employment income	$75,000	$80,000	$ 90,000
Property income (loss)	(4,000)	3,000	(6,000)
Capital gains (CG)	144,000	—	160,000
Capital losses (CL) (excluding BIL)	18,000	22,500	80,000
Business investment loss (BIL)	36,000	54,000	—

Additional Information

(1) The above capital gains do not include capital gains from qualified farm property or qualified small business corporation shares.

(2) Mr. Norman had a $21,000 net capital loss which was realized in 2011.

(3) Mr. Norman did not have a capital gain prior to 2014.

¶10,875

Dealing with each item line-by-line across the years, rather than one year at a time:

(A) determine Mr. Norman's income from the sources indicated for 2014 to 2016 according to the ordering rules in section 3, and

(B) determine Mr. Norman's taxable income from the sources indicated from 2014 to 2016 after amending the returns.

Problem 5

ITA: 56(1)(*u*), 56(1)(*v*), 74.1(1), 110(1)(*f*), 118, 118.3, 118.6, 118.9, 122.6, 122.61

Mrs. Plant, age 47, is married and has three children: Amanda, age 24, Joan, age 17, and Courtney, age 16. Her own income for tax purposes of $60,000 includes employment income of $58,000.

Amanda has been certified as impaired by a medical doctor. Her only income is $7,000 from social assistance payments relating to her disability. She took a university course on a part-time basis for four months. Mrs. Plant paid her tuition fees of $300.

Joan attended a university on a full-time basis in another city for eight months, had employment income for tax purposes of $4,200 from a summer job while living at home and received a $2,500 scholarship. Mrs. Plant paid Joan's tuition fees of $3,000 and Joan paid her own moving costs to and from the university which were $150 each way.

Courtney, who is attending high school, had employment income for tax purposes of $2,800 from summer employment and a part-time job.

Mr. Plant, age 50, has been certified as physically impaired and infirm as a result of a workplace accident. He has the following sources of income:

Worker's Compensation payment	$5,000
Cash dividends from shares of Canadian-resident public corporations purchased with Mrs. Plant's savings	4,000
Bank account interest earned from reinvestment of dividend income	100

Mrs. Plant has asked you to calculate the non-refundable tax credits available to her for 2016. Compute Joan's taxable income to determine if any of her tuition, education, and textbook tax credits will be available to Mrs. Plant. Prepare detailed calculations supporting your claim. All ages are given as of the end of 2016.

Problem 6

ITA: 118(4)

Angelina and Romeo are the divorced parents of Maria, who is 10 years old. Angelina and Romeo have joint custody and Maria lives every second month with the other. Both Angelina and Romeo have claimed Maria for the eligible dependent tax credit.

Is the claim by Angelina and Romeo allowed?

Problem 7

ITA: 118, 118.2–118.9; IT-513R

Mrs. Jackson, age 66, separated from her husband on October 17, 2016. She started receiving support payments from Mr. Jackson of $2,500 per month in November 2016. All of the support payments made commencing in November 2016 are considered to be pursuant to the divorce settlement. Of the $2,500 monthly payment, $1,000 is for the support of their daughter, Rachel. (In 2016, Mr. Jackson earned a salary of $100,000 per year and also earned other investment income.) Mrs. Jackson has income of $26,200.

Their eldest daughter Rachel is 40 and infirm and lives with Mrs. Jackson since she is severely mentally handicapped. She has been certified as impaired by a medical doctor. A part-time attendant helps care for Rachel at a cost of $12,000 per year. Rachel has no income.

Mrs. Jackson would like to know what tax credits related to her daughter Rachel are available to her.

Problem 8

ITA: 118.2

Mr. Jennings provides you with the following medical expenses and additional information for himself and members of his family who live with him, when he asks you to prepare his 2016 tax return.

Assume that you have correctly computed the incomes under Division B for 2016 as follows:

Mr. Jennings	$55,000
Mrs. Jennings	Nil
Son, age 19	8,000
Son, age 15	2,000
Daughter, age 14	1,800

Medical expenses for 2016:

February	Prescription drugs for daughter	$ 20
May	Doctor's bill paid for son, 15	15*
June	Chiropractor's bill for the past year	1150*
July	Glasses for Mr. and Mrs. Jennings	300
		$1,485

Medical expenses to March 31, 2017:

February	Orthodontist fee for daughter		$2,550
March	Expenses relating to older son's car accident:		
	Hospital	$1,500	
	Surgery	1,000	
	Drugs	200	2,700*

Additional expenses anticipated by May 31, 2017:

(a) Additional medical bills from son's accident	$ 750*
(b) Eyeglasses for his younger son and daughter ($225 each)	450
(c) Dental bills (⅔ for Mr. & Mrs. Jennings)	375
(d) Chiropractor's bill for the past year	1,050

---

* Excess over provincial plan payments.

Discuss the tax implications of Mr. Jennings claiming the above medical expenses for each of 2016 and 2017. Assume that all income amounts for 2017 will be the same as those for 2016.

Problem 9

ITA: 82, 118, 118.8

Mr. and Mrs. Reid, ages 55 and 50, received the following income during 2016:

Mr. Reid:

Employment income (commission)	$15,000
Employment expenses	(13,000)
Investment income:	
Canadian interest	2,000
Dividends received (in Cdn. $):	
Canadian-resident public corporations	1,000
U.S. corporations (net of 15% withholding tax)	680

Mrs. Reid:

Employment income	54,000
Investment income:	
Canadian interest	1,000
Dividends received from Canadian-resident public corporations	2,000

Calculate Mrs. Reid's federal tax (ignoring the foreign tax credit) under the following situations:

(A) No election to include spousal dividends.

ITA: 82(3)

(B) With an election to include spousal dividends.

ITA: 82(3)

Problem 10

Pamela is 38 years old and lives in Welland, Ontario. She commutes daily to Niagara University, in Niagara Falls, New York. She is completing a full-time Masters in Education that is 12 consecutive months in duration. Her tuition fees are the equivalent of C$20,000 per year.

Advise Pamela if she can claim the tuition fees on her personal income tax return.

Is Pamela eligible for the education and textbook credits?

Your answer should be supported with appropriate references to the Act.

ITA: 118.5(1), 118.6;
Income Tax Folio
S1-F2-C2 — Tuition Tax
Credit

Problem 11

Stuart presents to you the following information concerning tuition fees paid for 2014, 2015, and 2016

ITA: 118.5; Income Tax
Folio S1-F2-C2 — Tuition
Tax Credit

2014	Harvard University, Masters in Business Administration, fall term	$15,000
2015	Harvard University, Masters in Business Administration, winter and fall terms	30,000
2016	Harvard University, Masters in Business Administration, winter term	15,000
	Re-read fee for failed course	300
	Make-up course at Harvard for failed course, July–August	3,000
	Income tax course at University of Toronto, fall term; the tuition fee of $500 was paid through a scholarship that Stuart received from his father's employer, Universal Exports Inc.	500
	Fitness course taken at a local secondary school in Ontario	35

Discuss the tax implications of the above tuition fee payments.

Problem 12

Patty, a single parent of two children (ages nine and seven) works part-time as a clerk in a law office. She has provided you with the following information for 2016:

ITA: 117, 118, 121, 122.2,
122.5, 122.6–122.64, 180.1

Income:	
Workers' Compensation payments	$ 9,000
Employment income (Subdivision a)	35,000
Cash dividend from Canadian-resident public corporations	480
University scholarship received	600
Expenses:	
Canada Pension Plan contributions	1,559
Employment Insurance contributions	658
Cost of subsidized day care for the children (three days a week)	2,400
University tuition paid for a three-month evening course	600

Patty receives the Workers' Compensation payment because of the accidental death of her husband two years ago. Her two minor children have no income.

Patty had $700 of tax withheld from her employment income and has paid no income tax instalments.

Based on the information above, compute Patty's total federal tax for 2016 and her tax refund or balance due.

Determine if Patty is eligible for the refundable goods and service tax credit. Explain.

Problem 13

ITA: Division B, C, E

Clare and Alan, both age 70, widowers, and retired successful businesspeople, love to argue. The one fact that they agree upon is that they pay too much income tax. They both receive $6,850 of Old Age Security and $9,000 of Canada Pension Plan payments each year. Clare has $52,000 of income from a registered pension plan. Alan receives $52,000 in dividends from the active business income taxed at the low rate in his incorporated business, a CCPC, which is now managed by his son.

Determine which one of the two pays the most federal income tax for 2016.

ITA: 82(3)

Problem 14

ITA: Division E, E.1

Dawn, a client of yours, generally has employment income from her company and some investment income. In early 2016, you arranged Dawn's affairs such that she would crystallize her $500,000 capital gains exemption on qualified small business corporation shares. For 2016, her income is estimated as follows:

Employment income (CPP $1,931)	$ 42,500
Interest	12,800
Dividends from Canadian-resident public corporations	20,000
Gross-up @ 38%	7,600
Taxable capital gains	250,000
Interest expense	(10,000)
RRSP contribution	(14,500)
Capital gains deduction	(250,000)
Taxable income	$ 58,400

Calculate what effect, if any, minimum tax will have on Dawn's 2016 federal tax payable.

Type 2 Problems

Problem 15

Once again, you have been asked for advice on employee stock options by two different clients. This is a continuation of Assignment Problem 2 in Chapter 3 and Assignment Problem 2 in Chapter 7.

(1) Omer is part of the management team of a Canadian public company and is eligible for the employee stock option plan. A few years ago he received an option on 1,000 shares. The option requires him to pay the option price of $30 (the value at the time the option was granted) for the shares at the time he exercises his option.

Omer exercised the option three years ago when the shares were worth $35 and has sold the shares this year for $45. He has asked you to tell him the effect of this option on his taxable income for all the years.

(2) Hilda is part of the management team of a Canadian-controlled private company and is eligible for the employee stock option plan. A few years ago she received an option on 1,000 shares. The option requires her to pay the option price of $30 (the value at the time the option was granted) for the shares at the time she exercises her option.

Hilda exercised the option three years ago when the shares were worth $35 and has sold the shares this year for $45. She has asked you to tell her the effect of this option on her taxable income for all years.

¶10,875

Problem 16

Nate has come to you for tax advice for 2016. He has identified the following income for 2016 and would like you to calculate the effects of the above on his income, taxable income, and loss carry forward for the year.

Employment		$ 40,000
Lottery winnings		3,000
Stock option benefit		5,000
	Division C deduction for stock option	(2,500)
Business		(60,000)
Taxable capital gain		15,000
Allowable capital loss		(20,000)
Inheritance from his grandmother		12,000
Dividends	Cash	1,000
	Gross-up	170

Problem 17

Natalia has the following income for 2016:

Employment		$ 40,000
Stock option benefit		5,000
	Division C deduction for stock option	(2,500)
Business		(60,000)
Taxable capital gain		15,000
Allowable business investment loss		(20,000)
Dividends	Cash	1,000
	Gross-up	170

Calculate the effects of the above on Natalia's income, taxable income, and loss carry forward for the year.

Problem 18

The accounting firm you work for is preparing a booklet on personal tax, and the tax partner has asked you to prepare some of the material. She has asked you to calculate a generic marginal tax rate for individuals in the top tax bracket for each of the following types of income. Assume $10,000 of each type of income is earned.

Employment
Business
Interest
Eligible dividends
Other Canadian dividends
Capital gains

To be able to move this into the publication easily she has asked you to use the following format:

Tax Brackets	over $200,000
Tax Rates By Bracket	
Federal rate	33%
Provincial rate	17%
	50%

Federal + provincial dividend tax credit = gross up

Marginal Tax Rates	
Employment	%
Business	%
Interest	%
Eligible dividends	%
Other Canadian dividends	%
Capital gains	%

Problem 19

Peter and Shikha were at a party on the weekend where someone said that they earn a substantial amount a year in dividends and don't pay any tax. They want to know if this is true and, if it is, whether they can benefit from it.

You agreed to do some basic calculations to start the discussion.

You have decided that your assumptions will be:

— The individual's primary source of income is eligible dividends with a minor source of non-dividend income which could be used to absord excess tax credits from the dividends.

— They have federal personal tax credits of $1,721 and provincial personal tax credits of $1,147.

— For eligible dividends the provincial dividend tax credit is $5/11$.

— For non-eligible dividends the provincial dividend tax credit is $8/29$.

You will calculate the maximum they can earn without paying any net federal or provincial income tax. Also, do the same for non-eligible dividends as the primary source of income for the year.

Problem 20

Harry and Shia are married. Both are retired and over 65 years old. They have the following income in 2016:

	Harry	Shia
Company pension	$120,000	$ –
Canada Pension Plan	12,100	6,000
Old Age Security	6,850	6,850
Registered Retirement Income Fund		12,000

They have asked you to calculate the amount of federal tax they will pay on this income in 2016.

Part 1: Do not split pension income as allowed. Report it as shown above.

Part 2: Split pension income as allowed (refer to Ch. 9).

Hint: Only calculate the personal, married, age, and pension credits. Remember to calculate any tax on Old Age Security income.

Problem 21   ITA: 2(2), 3, 111

Jeffrey Lowe is an associate in a local law firm. He also has a number of sources of income from various investments and sideline businesses. Jeffrey has provided you with the following information for 2016:

Salary from law practice	$120,000
Business loss	(7,500)
Gross rents received from rental property	25,000
Operating expenses on rental property	(31,000)
Capital gain on sale of shares	10,000
Net interest income	9,000
Allowable capital loss (including allowable business investment loss of $6,000)	(11,000)
Contribution to RRSP	(1,000)
Share of net income from duplex rental property (owned by Jeffrey and his sister)	15,000
Net capital losses from 2010	(3,000)

Jeffrey has asked you to calculate his 2016 net income for tax purposes in accordance with the ordering rules in section 3 of the *Income Tax Act*.

Problem 22

ITA: Division B, C

The following tax information is extracted from Mrs. Hawkins' books and records:

Employment income (before effects of items below)	$72,000
Interest income	5,000
Capital gains (on securities)	9,900
Deductible carrying charges	1,000

The following balances are losses carried forward from December 31, 2015:

Non-capital loss arising — 2010	$24,000
— 2011	26,000
— 2014	28,000
Total non-capital losses	$78,000
Net capital loss arising in 2015	$12,000

During the latter part of 2016, Mrs. Hawkins moved from Montreal to Toronto to commence working for Leaves Co. Ltd. She received a $100,000 housing loan from Leaves Co. Ltd., which she used to help purchase a house in Toronto. Mrs. Hawkins received the interest-free loan on October 1, 2016.

Mrs. Hawkins previously worked for Les Habitants Co. Ltée (a public company). Prior to leaving Les Habitants Co. Ltée on April 15, Mrs. Hawkins exercised the stock option that she held in Les Habitants Co. Ltée. Mrs. Hawkins was able to purchase 2,000 listed common shares of Les Habitants Co. Ltée for $4 per share (the fair market value of the shares at the time the option was granted). The shares were trading at $10 per share at the time she exercised her option to purchase the shares.

Assume that the prescribed interest rate for the last quarter of 2016 is 1%.

Calculate Mrs. Hawkins' income and taxable income in 2016, in accordance with the ordering rules of Divisions B and C. Ignore any effects of any leap year.

Problem 23

ITA: 3, 111, 111.1

The following selected tax information has been taken from the books and records of your client, Mr. Weilman, who is 51 years old.

	2015	2016
Employment income	$ 47,000	$ 55,000
Other business income (loss)	(14,000)	(23,000)
Property income:		
Canadian interest	7,000	16,000
Rental income from real property (loss)	3,000	(4,000)
Capital gains (capital losses):*		
Listed personal property	6,000	20,250
Other personal-use property	2,000	(4,000)
Other capital property	6,000	(45,000)
Other deductions:		
RRSP	1,000	3,000
Support of former spouse	7,000	7,000

* The 2016 other capital property loss includes a business investment loss of $24,000.

The following balances are losses carried forward from December 31, 2014:

Non-capital loss arising in 2012	$33,000
Net capital loss arising in 2013	25,000
Listed personal property loss arising in 2012	5,000

Mr. Weilman was not a member of a registered pension plan and, hence, his pension adjustment for the relevant years was nil. His earned income for 2014 was $33,250.

Prepare a schedule for the calculation of income and taxable income for 2015 and 2016, in accordance with the ordering rules under Divisions B and C, after applying any loss carryforward and loss carryback provisions through an amended return. (Deal with each item line-by-line across the years, rather than computing income one year at a time.)

Problem 24

ITA: 245; Division B, C

Ms. Isabelle Cardin had a tumultuous year in 2016. She broke her engagement early in the year and quit her job. She moved to a resort area to take a waitress job and to start up a fitness instruction business. She has had the following items correctly calculated and classified as either inclusions, deductions or tax credits for the purposes of determining her taxable income and federal tax.

Inclusions:

Benefit received from Employment Insurance program	$ 600
Board and lodging provided by employer during busy season of resort	8,000
Bonus from resort employer	500
Business revenue from fitness instruction fees	2,000
Gratuities as a waitress	12,100
Interest on Canada Savings Bonds	775
Rental revenue	6,000
Salary received as a waitress	12,000
Taxable capital gain	3,750
Retiring allowance from previous employer	800

Deductions, Losses, and Tax Credits:

Allowable capital loss	4,500
Capital cost allowance on fitness business equipment	1,300
Capital cost allowance on rental building	1,200
Charitable gifts tax credit	26
Child care expenses	1,800
Canada Pension Plan contributions tax credits on employment earnings	215
Medical expenses tax credit	9
Business expenses of earning fitness instruction fees	900
Expenses of objection to a tax assessment	65
Interest on funds borrowed to pay expenses of earning fitness instruction fees	75
Maintenance on rental property	1,100
Mortgage interest on rental property	2,500
Moving expenses	1,700
Non-capital losses from previous year	600
Personal tax credit	1,721
Property tax on rental property	1,000
Employment Insurance premiums tax credit	92
Union dues	100
Canada employment credit	174

You have been asked to:

(A) Determine the income, taxable income and basic federal tax based on the above correct information using the ordering rules in sections 3, 111.1, and 118.92.

(B) Cross-reference each amount to the appropriate section of the Act.

 [For more problems and solutions thereto, see the DVD accompanying the textbook.]

¶10,875

CHAPTER 10 —
DISCUSSION NOTES FOR REVIEW QUESTIONS

(1) There is no ordering that is required to be followed when choosing among the different kinds of losses, except that the oldest losses are always applied first. Generally, the rule of thumb is that the most restricted losses are claimed first. The factors that would have to be taken into account in making this decision are as follows:

ITA: 111(3)(*b*)

(a) Does she have the kind of income needed to offset the losses? She would need net taxable capital gains to offset net capital losses.

(b) Which losses are going to expire first? Net capital losses can be carried back three taxation years and forward indefinitely and non-capital losses can be carried back three taxation years and forward twenty taxation years.

(c) What is the likelihood that she will realize the type of income needed in future years to offset those losses she decides not to claim this year? If she uses up her non-capital losses this year and not her net capital losses, what is the likelihood that she will have a taxable capital gain in the future?

(2) His marginal tax rate on dividend income would be:

Cash dividend	$10,000
Gross-up 38%	3,800
Taxable dividend	$13,800
Federal tax @ 29%	$ 4,002
Dividend tax credit @ $^6/_{11}$ × $3,800	(2,073)
Basic federal tax	$ 1,929
Provincial tax @ 17% of $13,800	2,346
Provincial dividend tax credit @ $^5/_{11}$ × $3,800	(1,727)
Total tax	$ 2,548

His marginal tax rate on these dividends is $2,548/$10,000 = 25.48%.

(3) His marginal tax rate on interest income would be:

Interest earned	$10,000
Federal tax @ 29%	$ 2,900
Provincial tax @ 17% of $10,000	1,700
Total tax	$ 4,600

His marginal tax rate on this interest is $4,600/$10,000 = 46%.

(4) Her marginal tax rate on capital gains would be:

Capital gain	$10,000
Taxable capital gain (½)	$ 5,000
Federal tax @ 29%	$ 1,450
Provincial tax @ 17% of $5,000	850
Total tax	$ 2,300

Her marginal tax rate on this capital gain is $2,300/$10,000 = 23%.

CHAPTER 10

(5) The Act allows an artist to designate the proceeds of the piece of art that is not   ITA: 118.1(7)
established to be cultural property at anywhere between the cost and the fair market value, in
this case between $200 and $8,000. Looking at the two alternatives:

(a) if she designates $200 she will report no net income since her proceeds equal her
    cost. However, she will receive a donation receipt for $200 which is worth a federal
    credit of $200 × 15% = $30;

(b) if she designated $8,000 as the proceeds, she would report an additional $7,800 in
    income and pay an additional federal tax of $7,800 × 15% = $1,170. However, she will
    also receive a donation receipt for $8,000 which will generate a federal credit of $200 ×
    15% + $7,800 × 29% = $2,292. On a net basis she would have a net federal credit from
    this alternative of $2,292 − $1,170 = $1,122.

On a net basis, she would be further ahead to designate the full $8,000 as the proceeds.
She would receive an incremental benefit of $1,092 (i.e., $1,122 − $30) plus the provincial tax
effect.

If the work of art is a cultural gift, the Act deems the artist to have received proceeds of   ITA: 118.1(7.1)
disposition equal to the cost. However, the legislation would entitle the artist to a credit based   ITA: 118.1(1)
on the certified fair market value of the work. As a result, no income needs to be reported on
the disposition and a credit based on the full value is available.

(6) Patricia will receive a personal credit of 15% times the maximum CPP contribution   ITA: 118.7
for the year of $2,544. The excess $2,544 will be refunded to her since it will be an overcon-
tribution.

CHAPTER 10 — SOLUTIONS TO MULTIPLE CHOICE QUESTIONS

Question 1

(C) is correct. Since BL is a CCPC and is at arm's length with Brad, the stock option benefit will be included in Brad's income in the year of sale (along with Brad's taxable capital gain). The stock option benefit is $3,000 (($5 – $2) × 1,000). Brad's taxable capital gain is $1,000 (½ × ($7 – $5) × 1,000). Since Brad held the shares for at least two years, he can claim a Division C deduction of $1,500 (½ × his $3,000 option benefit).

ITA: 7(1.1)

ITA: 110(1)(*d*.1)

(A) incorrectly includes the section 7 benefit in 2014 and ignores the deduction.

(B) incorrectly includes the employment benefit and the incorrectly calculated Division C deduction (at ¼ of the $3,000 benefit) in 2014.

ITA: 7, 110(1)(*d*.1)

(D) incorrectly ignores the Division C deduction.

ITA: 110(1)(*d*.1)

Question 2

(C) is correct and is calculated as follows:

Basic		$11,474	ITA: 118(1)(*c*)
Age: $7,125 – 15% × ($47,760 – $35,927)		5,350	ITA: 118(2)
Pension		2,000	ITA: 118(3)
Employment		1,161	ITA: 8(10)
	$19,985 × 15% =	$2,998	
Dividend tax credit: ⁶⁄₁₁ × $760		415	ITA: 121
		$3,413	

(A) incorrectly ignores the pension credit and the employment credit: ($11,474 + $5,350) × 15% + $415 = $2,939.

ITA: 118(3), 118(10)

(B) incorrectly ignores the dividend tax credit: ($11,474 + $5,350 + $2,000 + $1,161) × 15% = $2,998.

ITA: 121

(D) incorrectly ignores the income restriction on the age credit: ($11,474 + $7,125 + $2,000 + $1,161) × 15% + $415 = $3,264.

ITA: 118(2)

Question 3

(C) is correct. Shabir's net income and taxable income is calculated as follows:

Scholarship income (exempt)	$	Nil
Employment income		12,000
Moving expenses:		
to McGill University (limited to scholarship income)		Nil
to Toronto		(200)
		$11,800

Since Shabir's income is less than $11,474, his entire tuition fee, education, and textbook credits ITA: 118.9 can be transferred to his parent (up to a maximum of $5,000).

Tuition fee $3,900

Education credit: 8 × $400 3,200

Textbook credit: 8 × $65 520

[Note that the education and textbook tax credits are to be eliminated in 2017]

$7,620; max. $5,000 × 15% = $750

(A) incorrectly computes the credit base on tuition only ($3,900 × 15% = $585).

(B) incorrectly includes the scholarship in income and claims the full moving costs to McGill: $1,500 + $12,000 − $500 − $200 = $12,800. Since this income exceeds $11,474 ($12,800 − $11,474 = $326), then $4,674 ($5,000 − $326) can be transferred resulting in a credit of $701 to a parent.

(D) incorrectly ignores the $5,000 limit: $7,620 × .15 = $1,143.

Question 4

(A) is correct.

Salary	$ 60,000
Canadian dividends	20,000
Gross-up 38%	7,600
Stock option benefit	200,000
Taxable capital gain (½ × $200K)	100,000
Net income	$387,600
Stock option deduction (½ × $200K)	(100,000)
Taxable income	$287,600
Tax:	
first $200,000	$ 28,908
balance @ 33% of $149,014	46,317
Basic personal amount ($11,474 × 15%)	(1,721)
CPP (15% of $2,544)	(382)
EI (15% of $944)	(143)
Transfer of tuition, education, and textbook credits (15% of $5,000 × 3) [Note that the education and tuition tax credits will be eliminated in 2017.]	(2,250)
Employment (15% of $1,161)	(174)
Dividend tax credit (⁶/₁₁ × $7,600)	(4,145)
Federal tax	$ 66,410

(B) incorrectly omits the gross-up on the dividend and the dividend tax credit: $66,410 − (33% × $7,600) + $4,145 = $68,047

(C) incorrectly omits the dividend tax credit: $66,410 + $4,145 = $70,555

(D) incorrectly omits the stock option deduction: $66,410 + 33% × $100,000 = $99,410

Question 5

(A) is correct.

Taxable income	$287,600
Add:	
30% of capital gain	60,000
³⁄₅ of the stock option deduction	60,000
Deduct:	
Gross-up on dividends	(7,600)
Adjusted taxable income	$400,000
Minimum tax before minimum tax credit ($400,000 × 15%)	$ 60,000
Basic personal amount ($11,474 × 15%)	(1,721)
Employment ($1,161 × 15%)	(174)
CPP (15% of $2,544)	(382)
EI (15% of $955)	(143)
	$ 57,580

(B) incorrectly deducts the $2,250 transfer of tuition and education credits: $57,580 – $2,250 = $55,330.

(C) incorrectly omits the adjustment to add back the stock option deduction: $57,580 – 15% × $60,000 = $48,580.

(D) incorrectly omits the adjustment to add back the tax-free portion of the capital gain and the stock option deduction: $57,580 – 15% × $120,000 = $39,580.

CHAPTER 10 — SOLUTIONS TO EXERCISES

Exercise 1

(a) Property income

(b) Business income

(c) Employment income

(d) Employment income

(e) Business income

(f) Property income

(g) Employment income

(h) Business income

(i) Business income

(j) Other income

(k) Property income

(l) Employment income

ITA: 3

Exercise 2

(A)

	2014	2015	2016	
Income from non-capital sources (≥0):				ITA: 3(a)
Property income	$ 1,000	Nil	$ 2,000	
Net taxable capital gains (≥0).				ITA: 3(b)
Taxable capital gains				
(see Schedule 1, Part (A), below)	$18,750	$25,000	$ 5,625	
Allowable capital losses	(7,500)	Nil	(11,250)	
	$11,250	$25,000	Nil	
Total income	$12,250	$25,000	$ 2,000	ITA: 3(b)
Losses from non-capital source and ABIL:				ITA: 3(d)
Property loss	Nil	$(7,000)	Nil	
ABIL	Nil	(15,000)	Nil	
Division B income	$12,250	$ 3,000	$ 2,000	ITA: 3(e)
(B) Deduct: Net capital losses (see Schedule 1,				
Part (B) below for maximum)	(776)	Nil	Nil	
Non-capital losses	Nil	Nil	Nil	
Taxable income (max. equal to personal tax credit base)	$11,474	$ 3,000	$ 2,000	

SCHEDULE 1

	2014	2015	2016
(A) Net taxable capital gains			
Taxable capital gains (TCG)	$18,750	$ 25,000	$ 5,625
Allowable capital losses (ACL)	(7,500)	—	(11,250)
	$11,250	$ 25,000	$ (5,625)

(B) Net capital losses

ITA: 111(1)(b),
111(1.1)(a),
111(8)(a)

	2014	2015	2016
Lesser of:			
(i) Net TCGs for the year	$11,250	$25,000	Nil
(ii) Total of adjusted net CLs	$ 7,500	$ 6,288	$6,288
Lesser amount	$7,500	$6,288	Nil

(C) Loss continuity schedule

	2012	*2013*	*Total*
Net CL	$ 7,500	$5,625	$13,125
Utilized in 2014	(776)	N/A	(776)
Available in 2017	$ 7,724	$5,625	$12,349

Note: Only $766 of the Net CL was claimed in 2014 to bring taxable income down to equal the personal credit of $11,474 for that year. No Net CL was claimed in 2015 or 2016 as income was below the personal credit level.

Exercise 3

Taxpayer computation of net income for tax purposes	**A**	**B**	*ITA: 3, 111*
Paragraph 3(*a*)			
Section 5 Employment income	$45,000	$15,000	
Section 12 Interest income	2,000		
Section 9 Net income from a business	5,000		
Paragraph (*d*) Current-year business loss		(15,000)	
Net income for tax purposes	$52,000	0	
Non-capital loss carryforward			
Current business loss ($18,000) – loss utilized ($15,000) =		$(3,000)	

Charitable donations are a non-refundable tax credit and reduce taxes payable.

Exercise 4

DIVISION B

Par. 3(*a*)	*Subdivision a*				
	Sec. 5	Salary	$ 60,000		
	Par. 6(1)(*a*)	Taxable benefits	3,000		
	Par. 6(1)(*c*)	Director's fees	5,000	$ 68,000	
	Less:				
	Par. 8(1)(*i*)	Professional engineering fees	$ 300		
	Par. 8(1)(*m*)	Registered pension plan contributions	4,000	4,300	
				$ 63,700	
	Subdivision b				
	Sec. 9	Business income — share of partnership tax profits	$ 10,000		
	Par. 12(1)(*c*)	Canadian bank interest	3,000	13,000	
	Subdivision d				
	Par. 56(1)(*a*)	Retiring allowance		20,000	
		Total par. 3(*a*) income		$ 96,700	
Par. 3(*b*)	*Subdivision c*				
	Par. 38(*a*)	Taxable capital gain	$ 20,000		
	Par. 38(*b*)	Allowable capital loss	(2,000)	18,000	
				$114,700	
Par. 3(*d*)	*Subdivision b*				
	Ssec. 9(2):	Rental loss			
		Rental revenue	$ 25,000		
		Less: Expenses			
		Par. 20(1)(*c*) Mortgage interest	(23,000)		
		Par. 18(1)(*a*) Taxes and insurance	(4,500)		
		Par. 18(1)(*a*) Maintenance	(1,500)	(4,000)	

Division B income		$110,700
Par. 111(1)(*a*) Non-capital loss	$ 4,000	
Par. 111(1)(*b*) Net capital loss	5,000	(9,000)
Taxable income		$101,700

CHAPTER 10

Federal tax after credits	
Tax on $90,563	$ 16,075
Tax on next $11,137 @ 26%	2,896
Tax before credits	$ 18,971

Sec. 118(1)	Personal credits		(3,442)
Sec. 118(10)	Canada employment credit		(174)
Sec. 118.7	CPP contributions credit		(382)
Sec. 118.7	EI premium credit		(143)
Sec. 118.5	Tuition credit		(68)
	Education and textbook credit transfer [to be eliminated		
Sec. 118.6	in 2017]		(80)
Sec. 118.1	Charitable donation credit		(550)
Basic federal tax			$ 14,132

Exercise 5

(A) Personal tax credits		ITA: 118
Basic personal tax credit base	$11,474	ITA: 118(1)(a)
Dolly's tax credit base: $11,474 – $3,000	8,474	ITA: 118(1)(a)
Don:[1] over 18 years old and not infirm	Nil	ITA: 118(1)(d)
Dave: caregiver credit base:[2] $4,667 – ($3,200 – $15,940) + $2,121	6,788	ITA: 118(1)(d)
Mother: caregiver credit base (with family caregiver amount)[3]	6,788	ITA: 118(1)(c.1)
Total tax credit base[4]	$33,524	
Total personal tax credits @ 15%	$ 5,029	

— NOTES TO SOLUTION

[1] Don's father may claim the transferred tuition fee, education, and textbook tax credits, since Don's income tax will be completely offset by his basic personal tax credit.
ITA: 118.9(1)

[2] The infirm dependant tax credit would have virtually the same base of $6,788 (with the family caregiver amount), but a lower threshold of $6,807.

[3] The infirm dependant tax credit (with the family caregiver amount) would have a lower base of $6,595 (i.e., $6,788 – ($7,000 – $6,807)) The caregiver credit is better if conditions are met and only one of the two can be claimed in respect of the mother.
ITA: 118(4)(d)

[4] An impairment tax credit of $1,185 ($7,899 × 15%) is also available in respect of the mother and son Dave, if their impairment is certified by a medical doctor.
ITA: 118.3(1)

Exercise 6

$300 contribution is an employment deduction.	ITA: 8(1)(m)
$800 is pension income.	ITA: 56(1)(a)
A pension credit is not available since the amount is not from a life annuity, as	
required in the definition of "qualified pension income".	ITA: 118(3), 118(7)

Exercise 7

Tax payable by Tina:		
Division B income and taxable income		$10,055
Federal tax 15% of $10,055		$ 1,508
Less: basic personal tax credit	$1,721	
other tax credits (age ($1,069), pension (15% of $350))	1,122	(2,843)
Federal tax payable		Nil

Transferable tax credits available:

Age credit (15% of $7,125)	$1,069
Pension credit (15% of $350)	53
Total credits available to Tina's husband	$1,122
Less: federal tax payable net of basic personal tax credit ($1,508 – $1,721)	—
	$1,122

Exercise 8

Income increased by grossed-up dividend ($900 × 1.38)	$1,242
Increase in federal tax @ 29% of $1,242	$ 360

Less increase in tax credits:

Married credit with election [15% of ($11,474 – nil)]	$ 1,721	
Married credit without election [15% of ($11,474 – $1,242)]	(1,535)	$ 186
Dividend tax credit ($^6/_{11}$ × $342)	187	373
Net federal tax reduction		$ 13

ITA: 82(3)

Therefore, the election should be made in this case, although it is marginal.

ITA: 82(3)

Exercise 9

Federal foreign tax credit

lesser of:

(i) $225

(ii) $\dfrac{\$1,500}{\$156,800 - \$6,000} \times (\$32,869 + \$62^*) = \$328$ $\Big\}$ $225

* The dividend tax credit is equal to $^6/_{11}$ of the gross-up of $114 (i.e., 0.38 × $300).

Exercise 10

	Regular Part I Tax		Minimum Tax	
(A) $100 interest	($100 × .33)	$33	($100 × .15)	$15
(B) $100 cash dividend				
($138 grossed up)	$138 × .33 - $46		($100 × .15)	$15
	DTC (21)	$25		
(C) $100 capital gains ($50 taxable capital gains)	($50 × .33)	$17	($50 + $30) × .15	$12

Exercise 11

Jacob's marginal tax rate is 41% (26% + 15%) where the provincial marginal tax rate is assumed to be 15%.   ITA: 117(2), 120

Exercise 12

Taxable income		$ 98,200
Add: CCA loss on resource property shelter		103,200
		$201,400
Less: gross-up of dividends		(11,400)
Adjusted taxable income		$190,000
Minimum tax before minimum tax credit (15% of $190,000)		$ 28,500
Less basic minimum tax credits:		
Basic personal (15% × $11,474)	$1,721	
Employment Insurance premiums	143	
CPP contributions	382	
Employment	174	2,420
Minimum amount		$ 26,080

Betty's Part I tax will be her minimum amount of $26,080 with $16,657 ($26,080 – $9,423) carried forward and applied to reduce tax payable in a subsequent year.

Exercise 13

Since Mr. and Mrs. Ataila were resident in Canada for 245 days, their non-refundable tax credits will be prorated by 245/365. For Mr. Ataila this includes the basic personal tax amount of $11,474 and the spousal amount of $11,474, and the Canada Employment credit of $1,174. Mr. and Mrs. Ataila are considered residents of Canada only for the time since May 1, and will be taxed on their worldwide income. Any income earned during the four months prior to May 1 that they were non-resident will not be subject to tax in Canada.   ITA: 118, 63

The child care expenses are only deductible if Mrs. Ataila has earned income, is in attendance of full-time studies at an educational institution, or is mentally or physically unable to care for the children. If Mrs. Ataila attended full-time studies in order to obtain a job in the workforce, then her husband may claim the child care expenses.

Exercise 14

Pierino's taxable income is:

ITA: 118, 63

Salary from Saskatoon Transit	$ 65,000	
Business farm loss	(5,250)	
Taxable capital gain	2,000	(50% ($10,000 – $6,000))
Total income	$ 61,750	
RRSP contribution	(10,000)	
Net income	$ 51,750	
Net capital losses forward	(2,000)	(maximum of taxable capital gains)
Taxable income	$ 49,750	

Personal tax credit base amounts

Basic personal tax credit base	$ 11,474	
Canada employment credit	1,161	
Eligible dependant (ETM)	11,474	
	$ 24,109	

Chapter 11

Computation of Taxable Income and Tax After General Reductions for Corporations

Learning Goals

Know

By the end of this chapter you will know:

• The key components in the calculation of taxable income and tax payable for a corporation.

Understand and Explain

By the end of this chapter you will understand and be able to explain:

• Why the various items in Division C are deductible.

• How loss carry overs are restricted.

• How an acquisition of control impacts a corporation.

• Why the various taxes and tax reductions are part of the tax system.

Apply

By the end of this chapter you will be able to apply your knowledge and understanding to:

• Calculate taxable income including the carryover of losses.

• Calculate basic tax payable for a corporation.

• Calculate the tax consequences of an acquisition of control.

Review Questions
¶11,800 in the Study Guide

Multiple Choice Questions
¶11,825 in the Study Guide

Exercise Questions
¶11,850 in the Study Guide

Assignment Problems
¶11,875 in the Study Guide

CHAPTER 11

CHAPTER 11 — LEARNING CHART

Problem Descriptions

Textbook Example Problems

1	Calculate non-capital loss
2	Calculate taxable income and loss carryovers
3	Non and net capital losses
4	Acquisition of control
5	Acquisition of control
6	Acquisition of control
7	Calculate taxable income
8	Provincial abatement
9	Foreign tax credit
10	Investment tax credit
11	Investment tax credit

Multiple Choice Questions

1	Acquisition of control — year end
2	Acquisition of control — loss recognition
3	Acquisition of control — deemed CCA
4	Acquisition of control
5	Calculate taxable income
6	Calculate federal tax payable

Exercises

1	Calculate taxable income
2	Maximizing charitable donations
3	Calculate non-capital losses
4	Calculate net capital losses
5	Calculate net and non-capital losses
6	Calculate taxable income
7	Calculate taxable income
8	Acquisition of control
9	Business foreign tax credit
10	Calculate Part I tax — various sources of income
11	Investment tax credit

Assignment Problems

1	Taxable income
2	Permanent establishment
3	Tax payable, ITC
4	Acquisition of control
5	Acquisition of control
6	Acquisition of control
7	Schedule 1 reconciliation and taxable income
8	Tax payable — provincial allocation
9	Tax payable
10	Tax payable
11	Acquisition of loss company

Study Notes

¶11,800   REVIEW QUESTIONS

(1) Mr. Clements has been trying to prepare the corporate tax returns for his company and cannot seem to get the treatment of charitable donations sorted out. He cannot find the place to put the tax credit for the donations and he is not sure what the limits are. Can you help him?

(2) If a company finds that it has non-capital loss carryovers that are going to expire in the next few years, what tax planning steps can be taken to use up some of these losses without selling the company or buying another company?

(3) Mr. Jones has just bought all of the shares of a company that has some net capital losses being carried forward as well as accrued capital losses on some of its assets. What happens to them? Is there any relief?

(4) There are two basic types of restrictions on losses available for carryover. What are these restrictions and how do they affect the application of losses?

(5) Mr. Magee bought all the shares of Profitco Ltd. on July 1 of this year, and is expecting to combine the profitable operations of Profitco with the loss operations of his current corporation. However, for Profitco's deemed year-end of June 30, he hopes to offset the six months of profitable operations with a full year of CCA in order to minimize the tax liability. Profitco's normal year-end was December 31. Comment on his plan.

(6) What are the three main objectives of tax provisions affecting the taxation of corporations?

(7) MultiCo Inc. has permanent establishments in Ontario and Alberta. The Alberta operation normally accounted for 20% of the allocation of taxable income. However, in the current year, a salesman in Ontario sold a large order to a customer in Alberta and the goods were shipped directly from Ontario. How does this special sale impact the allocation to Alberta?

(8) Since residents of Canada are taxable on their world income, why does Canada give a foreign tax credit for taxes paid to another country?

(9) In the calculation of non-business foreign tax credit the "tax otherwise payable" calculation is reduced by the 10% federal abatement. Why?

(10) Lossco Inc. has a loss from operations for the year while at the same time earning interest of $5,000 from the United States on which $750 of tax was withheld. How can Lossco treat the $750 of foreign tax paid on its tax return?

¶11,825   MULTIPLE CHOICE QUESTIONS

Question 1

Helen acquired all of the voting shares of Lossco Inc. from a non-related individual on February 1, 2016 Lossco has always had a December 31 year end since its incorporation. Which one of the following statements is TRUE?

(A) Lossco had a deemed year end February 1, 2016.

(B) Lossco may select any date, within the 53-week period commencing February 1, 2016, as its new year end.

(C) Lossco must continue to have a December 31 year end unless the CRA grants permission for a change.

(D) Lossco had a deemed year end on January 31, 2016 and is required to keep January 31 as its year end for the future.

Question 2

Jim acquired control of Smart Ltd. from an unrelated person on May 15, 2016. The following information relates to the inventory and capital assets owned by Smart Ltd. at that time.

	Cost	FMV
Inventory	$120,000	$100,000
Land	200,000	140,000
Building	100,000	75,000
Marketable securities	20,000	30,000

For its taxation year ended on May 14, 2016, Smart Ltd. is required to recognize a capital loss of:

(A) $85,000

(B) $80,000

(C) $60,000

(D) $50,000

Question 3

On April 1, 2016, Calm Corp purchased 72% of the voting shares of X Ltd. from an unrelated person. The tax position of the fixed assets of X Ltd. at that time is summarized below.

	Cost	UCC	FMV
Automobiles (Class 10)	$100,000	$ 42,000	$45,000
Computer equipment (Class 45)	64,000	38,000	33,000
Computer software (Class 12)	30,000	Nil	5,000
Office furniture & equipment (Class 8)	80,000	58,000	48,000

The business loss of X Ltd. for the year ended March 31, 2016, will be increased by deemed CCA of:

(A) $7,000

(B) $10,800

(C) $15,000

(D) $23,000

Question 4

For its year ended December 31, 2015, its first year end since its incorporation, Lakehead Co. (Lakehead) reported the following income (losses) for tax purposes.

Business loss (retailer of widgets)	$ (20,000)
Capital loss	(6,000)

On January 1, 2016, Pacific Co. acquired control of Lakehead from an unrelated person and transferred its profitable gadget retailing business to Lakehead. For its year ending December 31, 2016, Lakehead is expected to have the following income/losses.

Business loss (widgets)	$ (3,000)
Business income (gadgets)	15,000
Taxable capital gain on sale of capital asset	6,000

Assuming widgets and gadgets are similar products, which one of the following statements is TRUE?

(A) For its year ending December 31, 2016, Lakehead will be able to deduct net capital losses of $3,000, provided the widget retailing business is carried on throughout the taxation year ended December 31, 2016 with a reasonable expectation of profit.

(B) For its year ending December 31, 2016, Lakehead will be able to deduct non-capital losses of $18,000 (maximum), provided the widget retailing business is carried on throughout the taxation year ended December 31, 2016, with a reasonable expectation of profit.

(C) For its year ending December 31, 2016, Lakehead will be able to deduct non-capital losses of $12,000 (maximum), provided the widget retailing business is carried on throughout the taxation year ended December 31, 2016, with a reasonable expectation of profit.

(D) For its year ending December 31, 2016, Lakehead will be able to deduct non-capital losses of $15,000 (maximum), provided the widget retailing business is carried on throughout the taxation year ended December 31, 2016, with a reasonable expectation of profit.

Question 5

During 2016, Curran Ltd, a public corporation, has net income for tax purposes of $600,000, including $100,000 of dividends from taxable Canadian corporations and $500,000 of retailing profits. It made $200,000 of charitable donations during the year. Income earned in a province was 90%.

What is Curran Ltd's taxable income for the year?

(A) $600,000

(B) $500,000

(C) $400,000

(D) $300,000

Question 6

Refer to the facts given in Question 5, above. What is Curran Ltd.'s federal tax payable for the year?

(A) $22,000

(B) $48,000

(C) $87,000

(D) $52,500

¶11,850   EXERCISES

Exercise 1

ITA: 110.1, 111

Generous Limited has income (loss) under Division B of $(7,350) in 2014 $22,050 in 2015, and $14,700 in 2016. During this period it made donations to registered charities of $2,625 in 2014, $4,700 in 2015, and $12,000 in 2016. It also made a donation of ecologically sensitive land valued at $19,700 to the Government of Canada in 2015. The company began operations in 2014.

— *REQUIRED*

Compute the corporation's taxable income for the years indicated.

Exercise 2

ITA: 110.1, 111

Determined Limited predicts, with reasonable accuracy, its income under Division B before capital cost allowances will be: $100,000 in 2014, $115,000 in 2015, and $132,250 in 2016. Capital cost allowances available are expected to be $200,000 in 2014, $170,000 in 2015, and $150,000 in 2016. It made charitable donations of $10,000 in 2010 and $11,500 in 2011, which it could not absorb before 2014.

— *REQUIRED*

How can the company maximize its charitable donation deduction while minimizing the taxes it pays in the period shown? (Hint: Take advantage of the loss carryover rules.)

Exercise 3

ITA: 111(8)

TPM Limited has computed the following income (loss) for the year ended December 31, 2016:

Loss from business	$(129,000)
Income from property including dividends of $10,750 received from taxable Canadian corporations	32,250
Capital gains	46,400
Capital losses	(12,000)
Business investment loss	(16,000)

The corporation has a net capital loss of $27,000 arising from 2010.

— *REQUIRED*

Compute the corporation's non-capital loss for the year.

Exercise 4

ITA: 111(8)

CLR Limited had a large allowable capital loss of $51,750 on one transaction during its taxation year ended December 31, 2016. In addition, the following information pertains to its situation for the year:

Income from business	$155,250
Income from property	17,000
Taxable capital gain	4,700
Allowable business investment loss (not included in above allowable capital loss)	(8,300)

— *REQUIRED*

Compute the corporation's net capital loss for the year.

Exercise 5

ITA: 111(1), 111(1.1)

Abigail Corporation has income from business of $55,500 and a taxable capital gain of $37,000 in 2016. It also has the following losses:

Non-capital losses (expiring beyond 2016)	$ 82,500
Net capital losses (2010)	$ 40,000

— REQUIRED

How much of the above losses will be available for carryforward after this year?

Exercise 6

ITA: 3, 110.1–112

Reconsider the example problem of FT Limited in this chapter in ¶11,160. If $3,378 less capital cost allowance had been taken in 2015, all $23,000 of the inter-company dividends could have been deducted, pursuant to section 112, in 2015.

— REQUIRED

Recalculate the taxable income of the corporation for the years indicated after taking $7,900 less in capital cost allowance for Class 8 in 2015. Comment on whether the corporation is in a better tax position at the end of 2015 with respect to capital cost allowance and taxable income under this alternative.

Exercise 7

ITA: 110.1, 111, 112

Plego Limited, a Canadian corporation, had its net income under Division B computed as follows for the year ending December 31:

Par. 3(*a*)	Income from non-capital sources:		
	Income from business operations		$ 66,625
	Income from foreign property		7,175
	Dividends from taxable Canadian		
	corporations		12,300
Par. 3(*b*)	Net taxable capital gains		30,750
Income under Division B			$116,850

During the year the corporation made charitable donations of $80,000. Its carryforward position from the previous year was as follows:

Charitable donations	$10,250
Non-capital losses	61,500
Net capital losses (realized in 2010)	27,000

— REQUIRED

Compute the corporation's taxable income for the current year.

Exercise 8

ITA: 111(4), 111(5),
111(5.1), 249(4)

In 2013, a chain of bakeries, called Buscat Ltd., commenced operation. The industry is fhighly competitive and because of Mr. Buscat's lack of marketing skills, the corporation incurred losses in the first three taxation years of operations as follows:

Taxation year end	Non-capital losses (business)	Capital losses
Dec. 31, 2013	$60,000	$12,000
Dec. 31, 2014	45,000	8,000
Dec. 31, 2015	25,000	4,000

On July 1, 2016, Mr. Buscat decided to sell 75% of his common shares to Mr. Bran, owner of Buns Plus Ltd. Mr. Bran has been in the business of supplying bread dough, pastry dough and bun bags for 10 years and has been very successful. Buns Plus Ltd. has two divisions: a bakery and a coffee shop, which it intends to transfer to Buscat Ltd.

The following income tax data relates to Buscat Limited's operations from January 1, 2016 to June 30, 2016:

(a) Business loss (before inventory valuation) $10,000
(b) Allowable capital loss 2,000
(c) Property loss (assets sold in April) 5,500
(d) Assets at June 30, 2016:

	Cost/ACB	UCC	FMV
Inventory	$ 85,000	—	$ 65,000
Land	155,000	—	195,000
Building (Class 1: 4%)	65,000	$45,000	75,000
Bakery equipment	100,000	86,000	70,000

During the later part of the 2016 calendar year, the bakery/coffee shop of Buns Plus Ltd. was transferred to Buscat Ltd. For the six-month period ending on December 31, 2016, Buscat Limited had net income of $90,000 from all its businesses.

The net income earned was as follows:

Buscat bakery	$(55,000)
Buns Plus bakery	130,000
Coffee shop	15,000
	$ 90,000

In the 2017 taxation year, Buscat Ltd. expects to earn $250,000, of which $65,000 will be from the original Buscat bakery business and $20,000 from the coffee shop business.

Prepare an analysis of the income tax implications of the acquisition of shares. In your analysis, consider the two election options from which an election choice is most likely to be made.

Exercise 9

ITA: 126

Exporter Limited is a Canadian public company carrying on a part of its business through an unincorporated branch in Japan. Its income from that business in Japan for the current taxation year ended December 31 was 75,593,884 yen. The corporation paid income tax instalments on that income during the year of 30,237,521 yen. During the year the exchange rate was 1 yen = C$0.008083.

During its current taxation year ended December 31, Exporter's income under Division B was $2.5 million excluding the income from Japan. During the year, the corporation received dividends of $100,000 from taxable Canadian corporations. This amount was included in the computation of Division B income. The corporation was also able to deduct $25,000 of its net capital losses carried forward. There was no foreign investment income during the year. Taxable income earned through a permanent establishment in Canada comprises 75% of total taxable income.

— REQUIRED

Compute the corporation's foreign business tax credit for the year.

Exercise 10

ITA: 110–112, 123, 124, 125.1, 126, 127

Maxprof Limited is a Canadian public company with the following income under Division B for its taxation year ended December 31, 2016:

Wholesaling income	$1,495,000
Foreign business profits (before $36,800 in taxes paid)	115,000
Dividends from taxable Canadian corporations	517,500
Dividends from foreign investments (before $25,875 in taxes withheld)	172,500
Canadian interest income (investment income)	345,000
Income under Division B	$2,645,000

During the year the company made donations of $69,000 to registered charities and $5,750 to federal political parties. It was carrying forward non-capital losses of $127,600. It is considered to earn 86% of its taxable income in Canada, as computed by the Regulation.

— REQUIRED

Compute the federal Part I tax payable for the year.

Exercise 11

ITA: 127

Consider the following data:

Qualified current expenditures eligible for investment tax credit	$90,000
Taxable income before qualified current expenditures	$300,000
Federal tax rate after abatement and reduction	15%

— REQUIRED

Compute the amount of the investment tax credit that will be deductible for the year and the net federal Part I tax payable after the investment tax credit.

¶11,875   ASSIGNMENT PROBLEMS

Type 1 Problems

Problem 1

ITA: 3, 110.1–112

The following data summarize the operations of Red Pocket Limited for the years of 2013 to 2016 ended September 30.

	2013	2014	2015	2016
Income (loss) from business	$54,000	$32,000	$(75,000)	$62,500
Dividend income — Taxable Canadian corporations	42,500	22,500	18,000	10,500
Taxable capital gains	11,000	2,500	5,000	9,000
Allowable capital losses	2,000	4,500	3,500	—
Allowable business investment loss	3,750	—	—	—
Charitable donations	23,000	9,000	3,000	13,000

The corporation has a net capital loss balance of $9,000 which arose in 2010.

Compute the taxable income for Red Pocket Limited for the years indicated and show the amounts that are available for carryforward to 2017.

Problem 2

ITA: 124; ITR: 400

The taxpayer, whose head office was in Manitoba, manufactured and sold various fans. Local sales agencies were maintained in Ontario and in Quebec. At the Ontario agency, two qualified representatives handled business under the company name. They were authorized to sign quotations. Contracts could be made, terms of payment arranged and credit given without reference to the head office in Winnipeg. The company name was displayed for public visibility, was used on calling cards, and was listed in the telephone directory. The Ontario agency, occupying one-half of a building with warehouse facilities, maintained an inventory worth about $6,000. Orders for standard-sized fans were filled from stock-in-trade. Orders for large fans were filled from the head office in Winnipeg. The Quebec agency was substantially similar to that in Ontario.

You have been asked to determine whether or not the company has a "permanent establishment" in the provinces of Ontario and Quebec. In reaching a conclusion, you should compare this situation with the case of *M.N.R. v. Sunbeam* discussed in this chapter.

61 DTC 1053 (Ex. Ct.)

Problem 3

ITA: 12(1)(*t*), 37, 127(5)–(11); ITR: 2900

Infotech is a public company in its first year of business in the information technology industry. It operates out of a plant in Ottawa, Ontario. In 2016, it incurred $2.2 million of SR&ED expenses which qualifies for deduction under subsection 37(1) of the Act.

Infotech's federal income tax rate after abatement is 15%. Its income before deducting the $2.2 million claim under section 37 is $3.2 million.

You have been asked to:

(A) Compute the maximum investment tax credit available to Infotech in 2016.

(B) Compute the company's net federal Part I tax payable after the investment tax credit, assuming a maximum section 37 deduction is claimed.

(C) Determine the amount, if any, of the investment tax credit carryover.

(D) Compute the company's deduction or income inclusion in the following year if no further SR&ED expenditures are made.

Problem 4

The president of Purchaser Inc. (Purchaser) is planning to have the company acquire all the shares of Target Inc. (Target) on September 1, 2016. He has asked you to calculate what losses will be available in Target after he acquires it and explain the future deductibility of those losses after the purchase. Target manufactures paper products, whereas Purchaser is a wholesaler of office supplies and equipment. Both companies are Canadian-controlled private corporations and have August 31 year-ends.

The loss carryovers of Target are expected to be as follows:

	Non-Capital Losses	Net Capital Losses
2012	$300,000	$ 50,000
2013	250,000	—
2014	200,000	—
2015	150,000	100,000
2016	50,000	—

On August 31, 2016, Target will have the following assets which are still on hand:

	Cost or Capital Cost	UCC — Aug. 31, 2016	FMV — Aug. 31, 2016
Manufacturing Equipment	1,000,000	NIL	300,000

Problem 5

ITA: 111(4), 111(5), 111(5.1), 111(5.2)

All of the voting shares of Lofty Limited, a manufacturer of widgets, have been acquired by Holdco Ltd., an investment holding company. At the time of the acquisition on March 10, 2016, Lofty Limited had non-capital business losses of $600,000 generated in 2015. Lofty Limited also had $20,000 of net capital losses carried forward from 2010. As well, at the time of the acquisition, it was discovered that the balance of undepreciated capital cost in its Class 8 was $70,000 while the fair market value of the assets in that class was only $40,000. The balance in its cumulative eligible capital account (being from the acquisition on August 31, 2015, of an exclusive customer list) was $50,000 while the fair market value of the customer list was $68,000. The corporation's inventory had a cost of $630,000, while its market value was $680,000. The book value of the corporation's receivables was $240,000, while its realizable value was estimated at $225,000. The corporation's only non-depreciable capital property, land, had accrued gains of $56,000 over its cost of $200,000. Lofty Limited has a December 31 year end.

The corporation had business losses of $3,000 from January 1 to March 9, 2016. This amount includes the normal calculation of cost of goods sold.

The holding company will inject added capital and augment the management of Lofty Limited in an attempt to turn Lofty's widget manufacturing business around.

What are the tax implications of the acquisition of the shares of Lofty Limited by Holdco Ltd., assuming the maximum election under paragraph 111(4)(e) is made?

Determine the minimum amount of elected proceeds under paragraph 111(4)(e) to offset expiring losses, if the accrued gains on the land were $100,000 instead of the $56,000 and Lofty Limited had an additional loss arising from property of $10,000.

Type 2 Problems

Problem 6

On November 1, 2016, Chris purchased all the issued shares of Transtek Inc. from an acquaintance, Tom. Transtek carries on a transmission repair business and has done so since its incorporation on January 1, 2015. In addition to the transmission repair business, Transtek rents out a small building it owns. Neither the transmission repair business nor the rental endeavour has been successful.

When Chris purchased Transtek, his financial projections indicated that Transtek would have significant income within two years. Chris credited Transtek's failure to Tom's brash personality and laziness. Chris, on the other hand, has a strong work ethic and has many contacts in the automotive industry to refer work to him.

The values of the capital assets owned by Transtek at the time of purchase by Chris are as follows:

	Repair shop		Rental property	
	Land	Building	Land	Building
FMV	$140,000	$230,000	$70,000	$120,000
Cost/ACB	80,000	150,000	90,000	120,000
UCC	—	147,000	—	120,000

Chris selected June 30, 2017, as the first fiscal year-end for Transtek after his purchase. The following is a schedule of Transtek's income (and losses) from its inception, January 1, 2015 through June 30, 2018.

Period	Transmission repair business	Rental income (loss)	Capital Loss
Jan. 1/2015–Dec. 31/2015....	$(40,000)	$(2,000)	$(10,000)
Jan. 1/2016–Oct. 31/2016.....	(60,000)	(5,000)	—
Nov. 1/2017–June 30/2017	(25,000)	6,000	—
July 1/2018–June 30/2018	54,000	11,000	—

You have been asked to discuss the tax implications of the acquisition of Transtek Inc. on November 1, 2016, ignoring all possible elections/options.

In addition, you have been asked to determine the tax consequences of the acquisition of Transtek Inc. under the assumption that:

(i) the maximum amount of all elections/options is utilized; and

(ii) the partial amount of all elections/options is utilized so that only enough income is generated to offset most or all of the losses which would otherwise expire on the acquisition of control.

Problem 7

ITA: 9–20, 38–55, 110.1–112, 111(4), 111(5), 111(5.1), 249(4)

The controller of Video Madness Inc. has prepared the accounting income statement for the year ended April 30, 2016:

VIDEO MADNESS INC.

INCOME STATEMENT

FOR THE YEAR ENDED APRIL 30, 2016

Sales.		$995,000
Cost of sales	$523,000	
Administrative expenses	185,000	(708,000)
Operating income		$287,000
Other income and expenses . . .		55,000
		$342,000
Provision for income taxes . . .		(102,000)
Net income		$240,000

Other Information

(1) Included in the calculation of "Administrative expenses":
    (a) Interest on late income tax payments . . . . $ 435
    (b) Amortization (maximum capital cost allowance of $149,500) 104,900
    (c) Club dues for the local Country Club 1,750
    (d) Federal political contributions 2,500
    (e) Donations to registered charities 22,500
    (f) Property tax with respect to vacant land not being used
        in the course of the business 3,000
    (g) Life insurance premium with respect to the president
        (the company is the beneficiary; not required for financing) 1,950

(2) Included in the calculation of "Other income and expenses":
    (a) Landscaping of ground around new premise 4,800
    (b) Fees paid with respect to the investigation of a suitable site for the
        company's manufacturing plant 5,500
    (c) Dividends received from taxable Canadian corporation 42,800
    (d) Gain from the sale of another piece of land, used in the business, sold
        for $200,000 in March (purchased for $73,800) 126,200
    (e) Loss on sale of investments held as capital property purchased for
        $85,000 and sold for $75,000 10,000

(3) Loss carryforwards from 2015 are:
    (a) Non-capital losses 73,800
    (b) Net capital losses (realized in 2010) 50,000

You have been asked to prepare a schedule reconciling the accounting net income to income for tax purposes and taxable income. Indicate the appropriate statutory reference for your inclusions or exclusions.

Problem 8

ITA: 123, 124, 126

Barltrop Limited is a Canadian public company involved in the software consulting business. Its controller provided you with the following information related to its 2016 taxation year ended December 31:

Income under Division B from consulting business including $100,000 earned in U.S. operations (before deducting $16,000 U.S. tax paid)	$264,000
Canadian investment royalty income	10,000
U.K. non-foreign affiliate dividend income (before $3,000 tax withheld)	20,000
Taxable dividend received from non-connected Canadian corporations	5,000
Taxable capital gains..	6,000
Charitable donations	100,000
Unused foreign tax credit in respect of U.S........................	3,000
Net capital losses carried forward arising in 2010	8,000

Barltrop Limited has permanent establishments in the United States, British Columbia, and Alberta. Its gross revenues and salaries and wages data have been allocated as follows:

	British Columbia	Alberta	United States.
Gross revenues...................	$3,000,000	$3,000,000	$4,000,000
Salaries and wages...............	500,000	300,000	200,000

Assume that the British Columbia and Alberta corporation tax rates are both 10%. Also, assume that taxable income for British Columbia and Alberta is computed on the same basis as federal taxable income.

Gross revenues exclude income from property not used in connection with the principal business operation of the corporation.

You have been asked to calculate the total tax payable by the company for the 2016 taxation year, including provincial tax. Show all calculations.

Problem 9

ITA: 123, 124, 125.1, 126, 127(5)

Up, Up and Away Limited is a public corporation that distributes hot air balloons in the Province of New Brunswick. For the year ended September 30, 2016, its accounting income statement was as follows:

Sales	$1,225,000
Cost of sales and other expenses including CCA	(725,000)
Operating profit	$ 500,000
Other income	198,500
Net income before taxes	$ 698,500
Provision for taxes	(200,725)
Net income	$ 497,775

Selected Additional Information

(1) Other income includes:

Dividends from taxable Canadian corporation	$ 85,000
Canadian interest income	52,500
Foreign interest income, net of withholding taxes of $10,000	61,000

(2) Up, Up and Away Limited has a non-capital loss carryforward of $255,545.
(3) Donations to registered charities were $9,755 (deducted from accounting income).

You have been asked to calculate the total taxes payable for 2016 using an 11% provincial rate of tax.

¶11,875

Problem 10

ITA: 123, 124, 125.1, 126, 127(5)

Tecniquip Limited is a public corporation whose head office is located in Toronto, Ontario. The activities of the corporation are carried on through permanent establishments in the provinces of Ontario and Alberta.

For the year ended December 31, 2016, Tecniquip Limited obtained the following results:

Income from distribution operations in Ontario	$1,000,000
Income from distribution operations in Alberta	1,040,000
	$2,040,000
Canadian-source interest income (investment)	32,000
Taxable capital gain	10,000
Taxable dividends from taxable Canadian corporations	15,000
Net income under Division B	$2,097,000

In computing income from distribution, the corporation claimed a deduction of $150,000 under subsection 37(1) of the Act for SR&ED. No SR&ED expenditures are expected to be made in 2017.

During the year, the corporation made charitable donations totalling $50,000 and claimed non-capital losses of $60,000 and the net capital losses carried forward from 2011 of $6,000.

You have been asked to calculate the federal Part I tax payable. Show all calculations, whether or not necessary to your final answer.

Type 3 Problems

Problem 11

Ian King has operated a successful office supply wholesaling business, King Enterprises Inc., for many years. Last week, he called to tell you that he is interested in putting an offer in on the shares of a company that is in some financial difficulty, Royal Forms Inc. ("Royal").

Royal is in the business of producing custom, as well as standard, forms for business use. In fact, Royal is a supplier of King Enterprises. This company has been in business for the past eight years, but has been losing money for the past six years. Last year they sold the land and building they used in their operations in a depressed real estate market, in order to get some cash. Their big problem seems to be that they are undercapitalized.

Ian sees this purchase as a real opportunity for him to pick up a company at a bargain price, turn it around to profitability and, at the same time, reduce King Enterprises' tax liability with the losses. He would like you to prepare a report for him on the tax issues before he decides whether to make an offer.

 [For more problems and solutions thereto, see the DVD accompanying the textbook.]

CHAPTER 11

CHAPTER 11 —
DISCUSSION NOTES FOR REVIEW QUESTIONS

(1) Charitable donations are tax credits only on personal tax returns. On corporate tax returns they are deductions under Division C. Donations up to 75% of net income plus 25% of the amount of a taxable capital gain and 25% of recapture in respect of gifts of capital property with appreciated value can be deducted in the year. If the charitable donations are in excess of this amount then the excess can be carried forward for five years.

ITA: 110.1

(2) Income can be increased in the current year by not claiming some of the optional deductions for tax purposes. For example, the deductions for the allowance for bad debts, CCA, CECA or scientific research and experimental development expenditures can be foregone in order to increase income. These deductions will be available in future years and will not be lost. Also, the CRA will allow the revision of some permissive deductions for prior years. In addition, the company could consider the sale of any redundant assets to generate income through recapture and/or capital gain.

IC 84-1

(3) Where there has been an acquisition of control, the corporation cannot carry over its net capital losses. To the extent that the corporation has *net* taxable capital gains in the year, it may take an optional deduction of net capital losses which may in turn increase the amount of non-capital losses. Accrued capital losses are deemed to be realized in the deemed year-end immediately preceding the acquisition of control. However, there may be some relief because the corporation is allowed to trigger, on an elective basis, enough unrealized accrued capital gains to use up the net losses that are going to expire.

ITA: 111(4), 111(8)

ITA: 111(4)
ITA: 111(8)

(4) The first restriction is on the type of income against which the loss carryover can be deducted, and the second restriction is on the number of years a loss can be carried over.

Net Capital Losses: Applied against taxable capital gains only; carried back 3 years and forward indefinitely.

Non-capital Losses: Applied against all sources of income; carried back 3 years and forward 20 taxation years.

(5) The deemed year-end applies whenever there is an acquisition of control even if the company acquired is not a loss company. Mr. Magee will not be able to claim a full year of CCA since CCA is prorated for a short fiscal year.

ITR: 1100(3)

(6) The three main objectives are:

(a) alleviate double taxation;

(b) prevent the avoidance of tax through the use of a corporation; and

(c) provide tax incentives to corporations.

See the text in ¶11,210 of Chapter 11 for details.

(7) The gross revenue from that sale will be attributed to Alberta since, even though the sale was handled from Ontario, the order was delivered to a province in which the company had a permanent establishment.

ITR: 402(4)(a)

(8) The theory is that the country where the income is earned has the first right to tax the income. Then, in order to prevent double taxation when Canada also taxes this income, a credit is given in Canada for the foreign taxes paid.

(9) Investment income may be taxed in the foreign country even though there is no permanent establishment in that country. Canada assumes that this investment income, other than from real property, is earned through its permanent establishment in Canada and, therefore, considers this income to be earned in a province for purposes of section 124. Foreign business income, on the other hand, is assumed to be earned in a permanent establishment in the foreign country and, therefore, is not eligible for the federal abatement.

(10) Since Lossco does not have any net income or Canadian income tax, it cannot claim a foreign tax credit. No carryover is allowed for non-business income tax. However, the corporation can deduct the foreign taxes which will increase its loss for the year. This deduction will at least provide the benefit of the foreign taxes being carried forward as part of the non-capital losses.

ITA: 126(1)
ITA: 20(12)

CHAPTER 11

CHAPTER 11 — SOLUTIONS TO MULTIPLE CHOICE QUESTIONS

Question 1

(B) is correct. Loss Co may select any date, within the 53-week period commencing February 1, 2016, as its new year end.

ITA: 249(4)(b), 249(4)(d)

(A) is incorrect, as the taxation year is deemed to have ended immediately before control was acquired. Since control was acquired on February 1, 2016, the year is usually deemed to have ended January 31, 2016. (Technically, it is possible to have an acquisition of control occur at a specific time, say, 10 a.m. on February 1, in which case, the taxation year can be deemed to have ended on February 1 at 9:59 a.m. Usually, a time is not specified, in which case, the taxation year is deemed to end the day before.)

ITA: 249(4)(a)

(C) is incorrect because the corporation is deemed not to have established a fiscal period yet. This being the case, the corporation is free to select any year end, within the 53-week limitation.

ITA: 249(4)(d)

(D) is incorrect for the same reason as (C).

Question 2

(C) is correct. The ACB of the land is reduced from $200,000 to $140,000, its FMV. The $60,000 reduction is deemed to be a capital loss for the taxation year ended May 14, 2016.

ITA: 111(4)(c), 111(4)(d)

(A) is incorrect as it includes the $25,000 accrued loss on the building which is depreciable property. Depreciable property is specifically excluded.

ITA: 111(4)(c)

(B) is incorrect as it includes the $20,000 accrued loss on the inventory which is not a capital property.

(D) is incorrect, because the $60,000 accrued loss on the land was reduced by the $10,000 accrued gain on the marketable securities. The recognition of the accrued gain on the marketable securities is not required. An election is available to recognize the accrued gain, if it is desirable.

ITA: 111(4)(e)

Question 3

(C) is correct. The UCC of the Class 45 computer equipment is reduced by $5,000, from $38,000 to $33,000. The UCC of the Class 8 office furniture and equipment is reduced by $10,000, from $58,000 to $48,000. The total of the two reductions, $15,000, is deemed to have been claimed as CCA in the year ended March 31, 2016.

ITA: 111(5.1)

(A) is incorrect as this amount adjusts the UCC of all the classes to the FMV of the classes. This amount includes an adjustment of $8,000 to increase the UCC of the Class 10 automobiles and the Class 12 assets to the FMV of the respective classes. The $8,000 is then subtracted from the $15,000 reduction calculated in (C). This is incorrect. The adjustment applies only to the classes where the UCC is higher than the FMV.

ITA: 111(5.1)

(B) is incorrect as it includes only 72% of the adjustment calculated in (C).

(D) is incorrect for the same reason as (A). The difference between (A) and (D) is that in (D) the positive and negative adjustments have been totalled, whereas in (A) they have been netted.

Question 4

(D) is correct. For its year ending December 31, 2016, Lakehead Co. will be able to deduct non-capital losses of $15,000 (maximum), provided the widget retailing business is carried on throughout the taxation year ended December 31, 2016 with a reasonable expectation of profit.

ITA: 111(5)(a)

(A) is incorrect as net capital losses incurred prior to the acquisition of control expire on the date control is acquired.

ITA: 111(4)(a)

(B) is incorrect. Non-capital losses realized prior to an acquisition of control cannot be deducted against taxable capital gains incurred after the acquisition of control. Non-capital losses are only deductible against income from the business in which the losses were incurred and income from a similar products or services.

ITA: 111(5)(a)

(C) is incorrect. The non-capital loss deduction has been limited to the income from a similar products or services net of the loss from the widget business. The netting of the widget business loss is not required.

ITA: 111(5)(a)

Question 5

(D) is correct.

Net income for tax purposes	$ 600,000
Canadian dividends	(100,000)
Charitable donations	(200,000) – not exceeding $450,000 (75% of net income)
	$ 300,000

ITA: 112

ITA: 110.1

(A) incorrectly makes no adjustments: $600,000.

(B) incorrectly omits the deduction for charitable donations: $600,000 – $100,000 = $500,000.

(C) incorrectly omits the section 112 deduction for Canadian dividends: $600,000 – $200,000 = $400,000.

Question 6

(B) is correct.

Taxable income as per the answer to Question 5	$300,000
Part I tax on taxable income	
Tax @ 38% on $300,000	$114,000
Deduct: Federal tax abatement (10% × 90% × $300,000)	(27,000)
	$ 87,000
Deduct: 13% rate reduction (13% of $300,000)	(39,000)
Total federal tax	$ 48,000

(A) incorrectly applies the rate reduction to $500,000 of business income: $87,000 – 13% of $500,000 = $22,000.

(C) incorrectly omits the 13% rate reduction.

(D) incorrectly calculates the rate reduction as 11.5% × $300,000 rather than 13% × 300,000: $87,000 – 11.5% of $300,000 = $52,500.

CHAPTER 11

CHAPTER 11 — SOLUTIONS TO EXERCISES

Exercise 1

	2014	2015	2016
Income under Division B	$(7,350)	$22,050	$14,700
Deduct: charitable donations limited by 75% of income above			
— carried forward	Nil	$ 2,625	Nil
— current	Nil Nil	4,700 (7,325)	$11,025[1](11,025)
unlimited charitable donation			
— carried forward	Nil	—	$ 3,675
— current	Nil Nil	$14,725[2](14,725)	— (3,675)[3]
non-capital loss from 2014[4]	Nil	Nil	Nil
Taxable income	Nil	Nil	Nil

— NOTES TO SOLUTION

[1] Limited to 75% of $14,700 = $11,025; $975 is available to carry forward five years to 2021.

[2] If the donation of the land gave rise to a capital gain, the taxable portion would be included in the amount of income under Division B.

[3] $1,300 ($19,700 – $14,725 – $3,675) is available to carry forward four more years to 2020.

[4] $7,350 is available to carry forward 20 taxation years to 2034.

Exercise 2

	2014	2015	2016
Option A: Claiming maximum charitable donations			
Income before CCA	$ 100,000	$115,000	$132,250
CCA	(200,000)	(101,667)[1]	(116,917)
Income (loss) under Division B	$(100,000)	$ 13,333	$ 15,333
Charitable donations:			
— Carried forward	Nil	(10,000)[1]	(11,500)[1]
— Current	Nil	Nil	Nil
Non-capital loss carried forward from 2014	N/A	(3,333)	(3,833)[2]
Taxable income	Nil	Nil	Nil
Option B: Non-capital loss utilization			
Income before CCA	$100,000	$115,000	$132,250
CCA	(107,167)[3]	(86,333)	(132,250)
Income (loss) under Division B	$ (7,167)	$ 28,667	Nil
Charitable donations:			
— carried forward	Nil	(21,500)	Nil
— current	Nil	Nil	Nil
Non-capital loss carried forward from 2014	N/A	(7,167)[3]	Nil
Taxable income	Nil	Nil	Nil
Option C: Maximum donation and non-capital loss utilization			
Income before CCA	$100,000	$115,000	$132,250
CCA	(107,166)	(101,667)	(116,917)
Income (loss) under Division B	$ (7,166)	$ 13,333	$ 15,333
Charitable donations:			
— Carried forward	Nil	(10,000)[4]	(11,500)[4]
— Current	Nil	Nil	Nil
Non-capital loss carried forward from 2014	N/A	(3,333)	(3,833)
Taxable income	Nil	Nil	Nil

● *Summary*

	Options		
	A	*B*	*C*
Total donations claimed	$ 21,500	$ 21,500	$ 21,500
Total CCA claimed	418,584	325,750	325,750
Unclaimed non-capital loss	92,834	Nil	Nil

— NOTES TO SOLUTION

[1] CCA amount selected to provide sufficient Division B income for a deduction of charitable donations (maximum of 75% of Division B income). The 2010 charitable donations would, otherwise, expire after 2015.

[2] $92,834 of non-capital loss from 2014 remains.

[3] Determined by looking forward to 2015 and creating the maximum non-capital loss in 2014 that can be fully utilized in 2015.

[4] Uses the five-year carryforward of charitable donations to the maximum — i.e., the $11,500 donations of 2011 may be carried forward to 2016, as in Option A.

Exercise 3

Sum of: loss from business		$129,000
allowable business investment loss		8,000
dividends deductible under sec. 112...........................		10,750
net capital loss deducted [$27,000 – $17,200 = $9,800 remaining]		17,200[1]
		$164,950
Less: income from property	$32,250	
net taxable capital gains [½ × ($46,400 – $12,000)]..........	17,200[1]	(49,450)
Non-capital loss for the year		$115,500

— NOTE TO SOLUTION

[1] The corporation may deduct the net capital loss from income even though it has no impact on the taxable income. However, the deduction is restricted to the net taxable capital gain for the year. Once deducted, the net capital loss can be included in the non-capital loss computation.

Exercise 4

Allowable capital loss (excluding ABIL)	$ 51,750
Less: taxable capital gain	(4,700)
Net	$ 47,050
Add: unutilized allowable business investment loss in respect of which the carryover period expires in the year (i.e., the 20th carryforward year)	Nil
Net capital loss for the year	$ 47,050

Exercise 5

	Option A[1]	Option B[1]
Income from business	$55,500	$55,500
Taxable capital gains	37,000	37,000
Income under Division B	$92,500	$92,500
Less: net capital losses....................	(37,000)[2]	(10,000)[2]
non-capital losses	(55,500)	(82,500)
Taxable income	Nil	Nil
Summary:		
Unutilized non-capital losses	$27,000	Nil
Unutilized net capital losses	3,000[2]	$30,000[2]

CHAPTER 11

— NOTES TO SOLUTION

(1) In Option A, maximum net capital losses are claimed before non-capital losses. In Option B, maximum non-capital losses are claimed before net capital losses.

(2)	Option A	Option B
2010 net capital loss	$40,000	$40,000
Utilized in 2016 (limited to TCG)	(37,000)	(10,000)
Available to carryforward	$ 3,000	$30,000

Exercise 6

	2015		2016
Net income (loss) per financial accounting statements	$ (53,000)		$126,000
Add total of items not deductible for tax purposes	127,700		240,700
	$ 74,700		$366,700
Less CCA ($3,378 less in 2015)	51,700		51,316
Income for tax purposes	$ 23,000		$315,384
Inter-company dividends	$23,000		$23,000
Charitable donations (max. 75% of income):			
Carried over	—		15,000
Current	Nil		15,000
Non-capital loss carryover	—	23,000	18,000 71,000
Taxable income		Nil	$244,384
Taxable income originally computed		Nil	$245,060

Conclusion:

This calculation produces better results. All of the inter-company dividends are fully deductible in 2015 with the reduction of the capital cost allowance by $3,378. Both options allowed, in total, an equal amount of non-capital losses and donations to be claimed over the two-year period. Although the original calculation enabled $2,702 (i.e., $55,078 + $50,640 – $51,700 – $51,316) more capital cost allowance to be claimed in total over the two years, the original calculation could not utilize $3,378 of the potential dividend deduction. This alternative increases the future CCA write-offs by $2,702 as shown below.

	Building Class 1: 6%	Equipment Class 8: 20%
Capital cost allowances were computed as follows:		
2016: UCC, January 1, 2016	$ 246,667	$ 182,578*
CCA (total deduction: $51,317)	(14,800)	(36,516)
2017: UCC, January 1, 2017	$ 231,867	$ 146,062
UCC originally computed	$ 231,867	$ 143,360

---

* $179,200 + $3,378.

Exercise 7

Division B income		$116,850
Less: charitable donations limited to 75% of $116,850 or $87,638		
— carried forward	$10,250	
— current	77,388[1]	(87,638)
dividends from taxable Canadian corporations		(12,300)
subtotal		$ 16,912
non-capital losses[2]		(16,912)
net capital losses[2] (not to exceed the taxable capital gains for the year)		(Nil)
Taxable income		Nil

—NOTES TO SOLUTION

[1] The balance of $2,612 in current charitable donations may be carried forward to the next five years.

[2] These carried-over losses may be claimed in a different sequence and in different amounts from that shown. For example, if there is little prospect of future capital gains, the corporation might make the following deductions:

subtotal	$16,912
net capital losses	(27,000)
non-capital losses	Nil
taxable income	Nil

The balance of the net capital losses may be carried forward indefinitely.

Net capital losses claimed are added to the non-capital loss balance carried forward.

Exercise 8

The data given in the problem statement can be summarized as follows:

carryforward losses	non-capital losses	net capital losses	expiration after deemed year-end
2013	$60,000	$6,000	
2014	45,000	4,000	
2015	25,000	2,000	
	$130,000	$12,000 ──────────→	$12,000

current deemed year-end losses	from non-capital sources	allowable capital losses	
ACL		$2,000 ──────→	2,000
business—operations	$10,000		
—inventory	20,000		
—equipment	16,000		
	$46,000		
property	$5,500 ─────────────────────────────→		5,500
			$19,500

potential elections	business income	taxable capital gain
recapture—building	$20,000	
TCG—land		$20,000
—building		5,000
		$25,000

The two election options to consider are the maximum election and the partial election.

(a) Maximum Election

If the maximum election is made, the $20,000 of recapture offsets the business loss, leaving $26,000 (i.e., $46,000 – $20,000) of net business loss. The $25,000 of taxable capital gain offsets the $19,500 of expiring losses, leaving $5,500 (i.e., $25,000 – $19,500) to offset the remaining $26,000 of business loss, leaving $20,500 of that business loss. As a result, the non-capital loss available for carry forward from June 30, 2016 is $150,500 (i.e., $20,500 + $130,000).

(b) Partial Election

If only a partial election is made to offset the $19,500 of expiring losses, the current business loss of $46,000 is not offset and, hence, is available to carry forward, along with the $130,000 of non-capital losses, from June 30, 2016 for a total of $176,000. If the election is made on the land, the ACB of the land can be increased without a tax cost.

(c) No Election

Note that if no election is made there is no income to offset the current business loss of $46,000 or the non-capital loss carryforward of $130,000. Therefore, the non-capital loss available to carry forward from June 30, 2016 is $176,000 (i.e., $46,000 + $130,000), which is the same as in the partial election, but there is no increase in any cost value.

Deemed Year-end

Buscat Ltd. is deemed to have a taxation year ending June 30, 2016, immediately before the acquisition of control by Buns Plus Ltd. on July 1, 2016 [ssec. 249(4)]. Tax returns will have to be filed for this short taxation year (i.e., six months) and amounts such as CCA will have to be prorated. In addition, the short taxation year will cause the counting of a carryforward year for the non-capital losses from 2013, 2014, and 2015.

Loss from Non-Capital Sources

Losses from non-capital sources for the deemed taxation year ended June 30, 2016, before any elections and options are computed as follows:

Loss from business	$ 10,000	
Add: Inventory loss [ssec. 10(1)] ($85,000 – $65,000)....................................	20,000	
Bakery equipment — Deemed CCA ($86,000 – $70,000).......................	16,000	
Total business losses..	$ 46,000	
Add: Property loss (will expire unless utilized by June 30, 2016)	5,500	
Total losses from non-capital sources...	$ 51,500	

Maximum Election

Division B income and taxable income

Par. 3(a)	Income from non-capital sources			Nil
Par. 3(b)	Net taxable capital gains:			
	Election on land [($195,000 – $155,000) × ½].................................		$ 20,000	
	Election on building [($75,000 – $65,000) × ½]		5,000	
			$ 25,000	
	Less: Allowable capital loss		(2,000)	
Par. 3(c)	Sum of par. 3(a) plus par. 3(b) less any Subdivision e deductions (nil)			$ 23,000
Par. 3(d)	Property loss...	$ 5,500		
	Business losses..	46,000		
		$ 51,500		
	Less: Building recapture...	(20,000)	31,500	
Sec. 3 income				Nil
Division C deductions:				
Net capital losses: 2013..		$ 6,000		
	2014..		4,000		
	2015..		2,000	$ 12,000	
Taxable income				Nil

Non-capital losses available for carryforward after acquisition of control:

Balance — July 1, 2016		
2013 non-CL	$ 60,000	
2014 non-CL	45,000	
2015 non-CL	25,000	$ 130,000

Non-CL from deemed taxation year before acquisition of control:		
Total par. 3(d) loss (see above calculation)...	$ 31,500	
Add: Net capital loss deducted	12,000	
	$ 43,500	
Less: Par. 3(c) income above	(23,000)	20,500
Total non-capital losses		$ 150,500

The $150,500 loss carryforward balance must "reasonably be regarded as its loss from carrying on a business."

2013, 2014, and 2015 loss carryforwards from a business as stated in the question...................	$ 130,000	
June 30, 2015 business loss net of recapture	$ 26,000	
Less portion of this loss used against par. 3(c) income*	(5,500)	20,500
		$ 150,500

* Par. 3(c) income..		$ 23,000	
Less:			
Property losses...	$ 5,500		
Net capital losses restored as business losses	12,000	(17,500)	
		$ 5,500	

The non-capital losses will expire in 20 taxation years, including the deemed taxation year, from the year of the loss as follows, assuming that Buscat Ltd.'s fiscal year-end after the acquisition of control returns to December 31.

2013 non-CL — on December 31, 2032

2014 non-CL — on December 31, 2033

2015 non-CL — on December 31, 2034

2016 deemed taxation year — on December 31, 2035

CHAPTER 11

The adjusted cost base/capital cost of the properties which were deemed to be sold at their fair market values would be:

	Capital Cost	UCC	Adjusted Cost Base
Bakery Equipment	$100,000	$ 70,000	$100,000
Land	n/a	n/a	195,000
Building* (Class 1)	70,000	70,000	75,000

*65,000 + ½ ($75,000 – $65,000).

In order for these non-capital losses to be deductible in subsequent fiscal periods, two conditions in subparagraph 111(5)(*a*)(i) must be met:

(a) the bakery business which generated the loss must be carried on throughout the taxation year in which the non-capital loss is deducted; and

(b) the bakery business must be carried on for profit or with a reasonable expectation of profit.

It would appear that both conditions will be met, since the Buscat business is being carried on and Buns Plus expects that the Buscat bakery business will earn a profit of $65,000 in 2017.

If the conditions of subparagraph 111(5)(*a*)(i) are met, then the non-capital losses may be deducted from income of the bakery business that generated the loss plus the income from the sale of similar products or services. If it can be assumed that the bakery business, transferred to Buscat Ltd., sells similar products and/or services as the Buscat bakery business, then the maximum $90,000 of non-capital losses can be deducted on December 31, 2016 as follows:

Lesser of:

(a) Net income for year		$ 90,000
(b) Income from: the loss business	Nil	
the sale of similar products	$130,000	$130,000

The remaining $60,500 ($150,500 – $90,000) of non-capital losses can be carried forward to 2017 subject to the deductibility tests discussed above.

Partial election

The minimum amount to be elected upon under paragraph 111(4)(*e*) (i.e., proceeds of disposition) should be an amount equal to two times the sum of:

(a) the allowable capital loss of $2,000 which is about to expire,

(b) the net capital losses of $12,000 which would otherwise expire, and

(c) the property loss of $5,500 which otherwise expires plus the adjusted cost base of the property to be elected upon.

If the land was chosen as the asset to trigger all of the taxable capital gain, then the deemed proceeds would be determined as:

[2 × ($2,000 + $5,500 + $12,000) + $155,000] or $194,000

The resulting taxable income computation would be:

Par. 3(a)	Non-capital sources of income			Nil
Par. 3(b)	Net taxable capital gain:			
	Land, $^1/_2$ ($194,000 – $155,000)	$ 19,500		
	Allowable capital loss	(2,000)	$ 17,500	
Par. 3(c)	Sum of par. 3(a) plus par. 3(b) less any Subdivision e deductions (nil)		$ 17,500	
Par. 3(d)	Property loss	$ 5,500		
	Business loss	46,000		
		$ 51,500		
	Less: Building recapture	Nil	51,500	
Sec. 3 income			Nil	
Division C				
Net capital loss			$ 12,000	
Taxable income			Nil	
Non-capital losses available for carryforward after the acquisition of control:				
Balance, July 1, 2016			$ 130,000	
Non-capital losses from the deemed taxation year ended June 30, 2015	$ 51,500			
Add: Net capital losses deducted above	12,000			
	$ 63,500			
Less: Par. 3(c) income above	(17,500)	46,000*		
Total non-capital losses		$ 176,000		

* Exactly equal to the business loss above.

Summary

The two alternatives presented above are summarized as follows for comparative purposes:

Taxable Income for the Deemed Taxation Year Ended June 30, 2016:

		Maximum election		*Partial election*	
Par. 3(a)	Income from non-capital sources (≥ 0)		Nil		Nil
Par. 3(b)	Net taxable capital gains (≥ 0):				
	Deemed taxable capital gains (elective):				
	land	$ 20,000		$ 19,500	
	building	5,000		Nil	
	Allowable capital loss	(2,000)	$ 23,000	(2,000)	$ 17,500
Par. 3(c)	Par. 3(a) + par. 3(b)		$ 23,000		$ 17,500
Par. 3(d)	Losses from non-capital sources and ABILs:				
	Loss from business	$ (46,000)		$ (46,000)	
	Recapture (elective): building	20,000		Nil	
	Loss from property	(5,500)	(31,500)	(5,500)	(51,500)
Division B income			Nil		Nil
Optional net capital loss deducted			(12,000)		(12,000)
Non-capital loss deducted			Nil		Nil
Taxable income			Nil		Nil

Non-Capital Losses Available for Carryforward at Deemed Taxation Year Ended June 30, 2016:

		Maximum election		*Partial election*	
Balance, Jan. 1, 2016		$ 130,000		$ 130,000	
Non-capital loss — June. 30, 2016:					
Par. 3(d) losses — see above	$ 31,500		$ 51,500		
Add: net capital losses deducted	12,000		12,000		
	$ 43,500		$ 63,500		
Less: par. 3(c) income — see above	(23,000)	20,500	(17,500)	46,000	
		$ 150,500		$ 176,000	
Less: losses utilized at June 30, 2016	Nil		Nil		
losses not utilized but expired	Nil	Nil	Nil	Nil	
Available for carryforward from June. 30, 2016		$ 150,500		$ 176,000	
Net Capital Losses Available for Carryforward		Nil		Nil	

The results of the above comparison of the two alternatives are further summarized as follows:

Options	(a)	(b)	Difference
Taxable income	0	0	0
Net capital loss deducted...	$ 12,000	$ 12,000	0
Total non-capital losses available for carryforward..................	150,500	176,000	$ 25,500
ACB of land	195,000	194,000	(1,000)
UCC of building (Class 1: 4%)...	70,000	45,000	(25,000)
ACB of building...	75,000	65,000	(10,000)

Option (b) is better if the additional $25,500 of non-capital loss can be offset by income generated in the next 20 years. The resultant lower ACB of the land under this option is only relevant on a disposition. The lower UCC on the building only represents a loss of CCA at a 4% declining balance rate. On the other hand, if an additional $25,500 of income cannot be generated in the next 20 years (i.e., business losses continue), alternative (a) is better. Note that 20 years is a long time to sustain continued business losses without generating at least $25,000 of business income. It is unlikely that alternative (a) is better, unless the land and building will be sold in the near future.

Exercise 9

Income from Japan in Canadian dollars (75,593,884 yen × .008083)		$ 611,025
Total income under Division B ($2,500,000 + $611,025)		$3,111,025
Less: Dividends deductible under sec. 112	$100,000	
Net capital losses carried forward (adjusted to current year inclusion rate)	25,000	125,000
Taxable income		$2,986,025
Tax @ 38%		$1,134,690
Less: Federal tax abatement (10% of 75% of $2,986,025)		(223,982)
General tax reduction @ 13% of 2,986,025		(388,183)
Net tax		$ 522,525

Foreign Business Tax Deduction

Least of: (a) amount paid (30,237,521 yen × .008083)	$ 244,410

$$\text{(b) } \frac{\text{income from Japan}}{\substack{\text{Div. B income minus s. 112 ded.} \\ \text{and net capital loss ded.}}} \times \substack{\text{tax otherwise} \\ \text{payable before} \\ \text{abatement}}$$

$$= \frac{\$611,025}{\$3,111,025 - (\$100,000 + 25,000)} \times \substack{(\$1,134,690 - \\ 388,183)} \qquad \$ 152,756$$

(c) Part I tax otherwise payable minus foreign non-business tax credit ($522,525 – nil) .... $ 522,525

Therefore, the foreign tax deduction is $152,756.

Exercise 10

Income under Division B..................................		$2,645,000
Less: Charitable donations............................	$ 69,000	
Taxable dividends deductible under sec. 112	517,500	
Non-capital losses.................................	127,600	714,100
Taxable income		$1,930,900
Tax @ 38%		$ 733,742
Less: Federal tax abatement (10% of 86% of $1,930,900)		166,057
		$ 567,685
Less: Non-business foreign tax credit (see Schedule 1)	$ 25,676	
Business foreign tax credit (see Schedule 2)..........	26,093	
Tax reduction (13% of $1,930,900)	251,017	
....		302,786
Part I tax payable.....................................		$ 264,899

Schedule 1: Non-business foreign tax credit

Lesser of: (a) amount paid .... $ 25,875

(b) $\dfrac{\text{foreign non-business income}}{\substack{\text{Div. B income minus s. 112 ded.}\\ \text{and net capital loss ded.}}} \times \substack{\text{tax otherwise payable}\\ \text{after abatement minus}\\ \text{general tax reduction}}$

$= \dfrac{\$172,500}{\$2,645,000 - (\$517,500 + 0)} \times \$316,668^{(1)}$ .... $ 25,676

Schedule 2: Business foreign tax credit

Least of: (a) amount paid .... $ 36,800

(b) $\dfrac{\text{foreign business income}}{\substack{\text{Div. B income minus s. 112 ded.}\\ \text{and net capital loss ded.}}} \times \substack{\text{tax otherwise payable}\\ \text{before deductions}\\ \text{minus general tax}\\ \text{reduction}}$

$= \dfrac{\$115,000}{\$2,645,000 - (\$517,500 + 0)} \times (\$733,742 - 251,017)$ $ 26,093

(c) $733,742 - $251,017 - $25,676 .... $457,049

— *NOTE TO SOLUTION*

(1) $733,742 - $166,057 - $251,017

Exercise 11

The total investment tax credit is 15% of $90,000 = $13,500.

Taxable income before qualified current expenditures	$300,000
Less: qualified current expenditures	90,000
Taxable income	$210,000
Net federal tax: @ 15% of $210,000	$ 31,500
Less: investment tax credit	$(13,000)
Part I tax payable	$ 18,500

Note that the $13,000 of investment tax credit will be brought into income in the following year.

CHAPTER 11

Chapter 12

Integration for Business and Investment Income of the Private Corporation

Learning Goals

Know

By the end of this chapter you will know:

- How the tax system works to integrate the tax on individual shareholders with the tax on private corporations for business and investment income.

Understand and Explain

By the end of this chapter you will understand and be able to explain:

- How the small business deduction helps to achieve the integration of business income.

- The rules for associated corporations.

- The investment tax credit for scientific research and experimental development.

- How investment income is taxed in a private corporation.

Apply

By the end of this chapter you will be able to apply your knowledge and understanding to:

- Determine if corporations are associated.
- Compute the small business deduction.
- Calculate the investment tax credit.
- Compute tax payable and refundable tax on investment income in a private corporation.
- Assess whether various types of income should be incorporated.

Review Questions
¶12,800 in the Study Guide

Multiple Choice Questions
¶12,825 in the Study Guide

Exercise Questions
¶12,850 in the Study Guide

Assignment Problems
¶12,875 in the Study Guide

CHAPTER 12 — LEARNING CHART

Problem Descriptions

Textbook Example Problems

1	Small business deduction
2	Specified investment business
3	Related groups of companies
4	Associated corporations
5	Associated corporations
6	Associated corporations
7	Associated corporations
8	M&P profits and small business deduction
9	Investment tax credits
10	Investment tax credits — indirect costs
11	Connected corporations
12	Refundable Part I tax
13	Refundable dividend tax on hand
14	Part I tax, RDTOH dividend refund

Multiple Choice Questions

1	Small business deduction
2	Identify type of income
3	General rate reduction
4	Part IV tax
5	Associated corporations
6	Associated corporations

Exercises

1	Identify type of income
2	Arm's length
3	Associated corporations
4	Sharing small business deduction
5	Associated corporations
6	Calculate Part I tax
7	Calculate Part I tax, RDTOH, dividend refund
8	Type of income, Part IV tax
9	Type of income
10	Investment income — personal vs. corporate
11	Interest income from U.S. subsidiary

Assignment Problems

1	Corporate tax rates
2	Explain small business deduction
3	Explain dividends
4	Explain investment income
5	Personal services business
6	Corporate tax — public vs. CCPC
7	Part IV tax
8	RDTOH, dividend refund
9	Active business vs. property income

Problem Descriptions

10	Associated corporations
11	Associated corporations
12	Associated corporations
13	Tax payable
14	SR&ED
15	Tax payable
16	Dividend refund
17	Comprehensive
18	Find the errors
19	Comprehensive
20	Identify types of income
21	Identify types of income
22	Incorporating investments
23	Incorporate or not
24	Share ownership

CHAPTER 12

Study Notes

¶12,800   REVIEW QUESTIONS

(1) Explain the purpose behind the concept of integration.

(2) It has been said that "ideal integration depends on the existence of two factors in the tax system". Briefly explain what they are.

(3) The dividend gross-up and tax credit has been described as the major tool of integration in the Act. Give a brief explanation of how it works in theory.

(4) What is the purpose of the small business deduction?

(5) On July 15th of this year, Mr. Smith bought all the shares of a company which was the Canadian subsidiary of a U.S. parent. There are no losses or ITCs being carried forward by the company. What advice would you have for Mr. Smith with regard to his choice of year-end for the acquired corporation?

(6) Give an example of when paragraph 125(1)(*b*) will give a lower limit for the small business deduction than paragraph 125(1)(*a*).

(7) List some tax and non-tax advantages of incorporation.

(8) List some tax and non-tax disadvantages of incorporation.

(9) Mr. Mould has just started up a manufacturing operation to supply parts to the auto industry. Given his need for start-up capital, he is happy that his tax rate is reduced by both the small business deduction of 17% and the general rate reduction of 13%. Comment.

(10) Are there any tax rules that prevent an individual from deferring tax on portfolio dividends by flowing them through a corporation?

(11) What are five tools that are used in the tax laws to integrate the taxation of investment income earned through a corporation?

(12) Theoretically, what does the 17% or 38% gross-up on dividends from taxable Canadian corporations represent?

(13) Theoretically, what does the dividend tax credit represent?

(14) Explain how integration theoretically works if a $1,000 capital gain is realized in a CCPC.

(15) Mr. Orville owns all the shares of Holdco which in turn owns all of the shares of Opco, a CCPC carrying on an active business in Canada. In recent years, Opco has done very well and its income is well in excess of the business limit. Last year Mr. Orville paid a dividend of $150,000 from Opco to Holdco. However, since he needed the cash in Opco to expand, he loaned the money back to Opco and charged 10% interest. The interest charged to Opco amounted to $15,000 in the year. How will this interest income be taxed in Holdco?

(16) A number of years ago a reorganization was undertaken so that now A Ltd. owns voting preferred shares in B Ltd. These preferred shares have only 7% of the votes and are now only worth 7% of the value. The other shares of B Ltd. are owned by the son of the only shareholder of A Ltd. Are A Ltd. and B Ltd. connected?

(17) Under paragraphs 186(1)(*c*) and (*d*), the recipient private corporation may choose to reduce the amount subject to the Part IV tax by applying otherwise available non-capital losses of the year or of a carryover year. Either the non-capital losses can be deducted from dividend income subject to Part IV tax or they can be deducted in the calculation of taxable income subject to Part I tax. What factors should be considered in deciding which option to choose?

¶12,825 MULTIPLE CHOICE QUESTIONS

Question 1

Concept Corp, a CCPC, correctly calculated its taxable income for its year ended December 31, 2016 as follows:

Income from retailing business carried on in Canada	$ 120,000
Loss from retailing business carried on in United States	(20,000)
Interest income from long-term bonds	30,000
Taxable capital gain from sale of a capital asset	5,000
Net income	$ 135,000
Non-capital losses	(3,000)
Taxable income	$ 132,000

Concept Corp and X Ltd. are associated corporations. X Ltd. claimed a 17% small business deduction on $385,000 for 2016. The taxable capital of Concept Corp and X Ltd. is significantly less than $10 million. Which one of the following amounts is the maximum 17% small business deduction for Concept Corp for 2016?

(A) $17,500

(B) $20,125

(C) $21,000

(D) $23,100

Question 2

M Ltd. provides management advisory services to ACC Ltd. and is not involved in any other business. Mr. Mud is the sole shareholder and only employee of M Ltd. Mr. Mud and his son each own 50% of the issued shares of ACC Ltd. Which one of the following statements is TRUE?

(A) If Mr. Mud would reasonably be regarded as an employee of ACC Ltd., but for the existence of M Ltd., then M Ltd. is carrying on a "personal services business".

(B) M Ltd. is carrying on a "personal services business", unless it employs in the business more than five full-time employees throughout the year, which it does not.

(C) M Ltd. is carrying on a "specified investment business".

(D) M Ltd. is carrying on an "active business".

Question 3

B Ltd. is a Canadian-controlled private corporation which distributes plastic bottles. The following information relates to its year ended December 31, 2016.

Active business income earned in Canada	$495,000
Net income, Division B	520,000
Taxable income	520,000

B Ltd. is not associated with any other corporation. B Ltd. did not earn any foreign business income nor any investment income. B Ltd.'s taxable capital is well below $10 million. Which of the following amounts is the maximum general rate reduction for the December 31, 2016 year:

(A) $2,600

(B) $3,250

(C) $53,089

(D) $67,600

Question 4

A Ltd., a private corporation, received dividends from B Ltd. and C Ltd. during its year ended December 31, 2016.

	B Ltd.	C Ltd.
Amount of dividend received by A Ltd.	$120,000	$120,000
Percentage of shares owned by A Ltd. (votes and value)	70%	8%
Dividend refund received by the payer of the dividend	$ 40,000	$400,000

A Ltd. and C Ltd. are not related. All three are taxable Canadian corporations. Which one of the following amounts is the Part IV tax payable by A Ltd.?

(A) $60,000

(B) $73,600

(C) $74,000

(D) $92,000

Question 5

Joanne owns 55% of the common shares of J Co. and Doug (her spouse) owns 55% of the common shares of D Co. Which of the following would *not* make J Co. and D Co. associated?

(A) If Joanne owned 25% of the common shares of D Co.

(B) If Doug owned 25% of the common shares of J Co.

(C) If a trust for their twin two-year-old daughters controls T Co. and no special elections were made.

(D) If J Co. and D Co. each owned 40% of the shares of R Co., a corporation carrying on a retailing business.

Question 6

In which of the following situations are X Ltd. and Y Ltd. NOT associated?

(A) Rod owns 10% of voting shares of X Ltd. and 50% of the voting shares Y Ltd. and Patrick owns 60% of the voting shares of X Ltd. and 10% of the voting shares of Y Ltd. Rod and Patrick are not related.

(B) The adult son of the controlling shareholder of X Ltd. controls Y Ltd. and owns 25% of the voting shares of X Ltd.

(C) A mother controls Company X. Her two adult daughters each own 30% of the voting shares of Y Ltd. Her adult son owns 25% of the voting shares of Y Ltd.

(D) A brother and sister each own 30% of the voting shares of Sibco Inc. A mother and father each own 20% of the shares. The mother and father each own 50% of the voting shares of Parentco Inc.

¶12,850   EXERCISES

Exercise 1

ITA: 125(7)

The taxpayer company carried on the business on a comparatively small scale of lending money on mortgages. The company was operated by two individuals who also owned and managed a number of other companies. All the companies operated out of the same office premises and used more or less the same office staff and equipment. The taxpayer company had no full-time employees. It was listed in the telephone directory but did no direct advertising. No attempt was made to keep track of the amount of time spent by the office staff on the work of each company and no specific charge was made for office space, use of telephones and equipment or staff.

The company made loans to potential borrowers referred to it by independent agents. Its clientele came mainly from those who found it difficult to obtain loans through the normal commercial channels. The agents had a general idea of the sort of loans which might be acceptable, but because those were relatively high-risk loans, the company had to examine them very carefully. Occasionally, an outside appraisal was made, but normally someone from the company would visit the property to examine it. Often considerable negotiations as to terms were involved. Post-dated cheques for five years would be obtained from borrowers and turned over to the bank as collateral for the company's line of credit.

For the year in question, the company held three mortgages involving $11,084. The sale of a small property, interest and other income resulted in total income of $4,609. Net income before taxes was shown as $3,479. The mortgages outstanding and net income of the company increased continuously from the year in question to the present time. During the year in question, the company's line of credit at the bank was estimated at $7,500 to $15,000, but it is now $25,000.

— *REQUIRED*

From the facts provided in the case, determine the type of business that is carried on by the company under the current legislation.

Exercise 2

ITA: 251

(A) By reference to provisions of the *Income Tax Act*, determine which of the following individuals or groups of individuals are not at arm's length with Alpha Corporation Limited:

(i) Mr. Beta, who owns 25% of the shares of Alpha and is not related to any other shareholders.

(ii) Mr. Beta and his brother, who together own 55% of the shares of Alpha and they are not related to any other shareholder.

(iii) Mr. Delta, who has an option to purchase all of the shares held by Mr. Beta and his brother anytime during the next three years.

(iv) Mr. Epsilon, who has an option to purchase all of the shares held by Mr. Beta and his brother from their estates within five years of their death.

(B) By reference to provisions of the *Income Tax Act*, determine under which of the following conditions Tau Corporation Limited and Lambda Corporation Limited do not deal with each other at arm's length:

(i) Tau is controlled by two brothers, A and B, and Lambda is controlled by A.

(ii) Three unrelated individuals together control Tau and one of these individuals controls Lambda.

(iii) Tau is related to Sigma Corporation Limited and Sigma is related to Lambda.

Exercise 3

ITA: 251, 256

Consider each of the following unrelated cases:

(A) Ava owns 55% of the shares of Jay-one Ltd. and 70% of the shares of Jay-two Ltd. Jay-one Ltd. owns 60% of the shares of Jay-three Ltd. The remaining shares in all three corporations are owned by persons unrelated to Ava.

(B) Abigail owns 30% of the common shares of Benco Ltd. and all of the shares of Rayco Ltd. The other 70% of the common shares of Benco Ltd. are owned by Abigail's cousin. However, Abigail's mother owns all of the voting preferred shares of Benco Ltd. and has sufficient votes to elect more than 50% of the Board of Directors of Benco Ltd.

(C) Adam owns 100% of the shares of Adamco Ltd. and 25% of the shares of Kidco Ltd. His daughter and son-in-law each own 20% of the shares of Kidco Ltd. and the remainder of the shares are owned by persons unrelated to all three.

(D) Sister One and Sister Two each own 50% of Sisco Ltd. and 25% of Cousco Ltd. Each sister has a daughter over the age of 18 who owns 25% of Cousco Ltd.

— *REQUIRED*

In each unrelated case, determine whether the corporations named are associated. Substantiate your answer by reference to specific provisions of subsection 256(1).

Exercise 4

ITA: 125(1), 256(1), 256(2.1)

Alpha and Beta are two sisters living in Halifax. While Alpha controls Taxit Ltd., Beta owns 25% of the shares of the corporation. Beta also owns 100% of the shares of Sibling Ltd. The active business income for Taxit during the current taxation year was $465,000 and for Sibling was $560,000. The taxation years for both corporations end December 31.

— *REQUIRED*

How much should each company claim as a small business deduction on their active business income for the taxation year?

Exercise 5

ITA: 251, 252, 256

The common shares of Chutzpah Enterprises Limited were owned by the three Chutzpah brothers as follows:

Aleph Chutzpah	40%
Bett Chutzpah	40%
Gimmel Chutzpah	20%

The common shares of Schlock Sales Limited were owned by the following:

Bett Chutzpah	45%
Dallied Chutzpah	45%
Unrelated person	10%

Aleph Chutzpah is married to Dallied Chutzpah.

— *REQUIRED*

Determine whether the two corporations are associated. Substantiate your answer by reference to specific provisions of subsection 256(1).

Exercise 6

ITA: 123–126

The following data pertains to Moosonee Company Limited, a Canadian-controlled private corporation for its fiscal year ended December 31, 2016:

Canadian-source business income	$110,000
Canadian investment income	7,000
Income under Division B	117,000
Taxable income all of which is earned in Canada	79,700

— REQUIRED

Compute the federal Part I tax payable plus provincial tax at a 5% rate for 2016 if all of the business income is considered to be active.

Exercise 7

ITA: 123–127, 129, 186

Ay Ltd. is a Canadian-controlled private corporation with a December 31, 2016 fiscal year end. The company operates in Alberta. Taxable income for the year is calculated as follows:

Canadian-source business income		$ 90,000
Dividends from CCPCs:		
Non-connected corporations		30,000
Wholly owned corporation which received a dividend refund of $4,000 as a		
result of paying the dividend		20,000
Canadian-source investment income		100,000
Canadian-source taxable capital gains		20,000
Income under Division B		$260,000
Less: donations	$ 40,000	
taxable dividends from CCPCs	50,000	
non-capital losses	20,000	
net capital losses	20,000	130,000
Taxable income		$130,000

The refundable dividend tax on hand account had a nil balance at the end of the previous year. No dividends were paid in the preceding year. Dividends of $70,000 had been paid during the year to the only shareholder, an associated corporation which has only income from investments.

— REQUIRED

(A) Compute the federal Part I tax and provincial tax at a 7% rate (using federal taxable income as the tax base) payable by the company for the 2016 taxation year.

(B) Compute the refundable dividend tax on hand balance at the end of the year and the dividend refund for the taxation year.

Exercise 8

ITA: 125, 129, 186, 256(1)

Sunlight Limited is owned 50% by H Ltd. and 50% by W Ltd. The two holding companies are 100% owned by Mr. Bennett and Mrs. Bennett, respectively. Sunlight Limited derives all of its income from active business carried on in Canada. It rents facilities from H Ltd. to which it pays $120,000 in annual rent, deducting this amount as a business expense. Sunlight also pays dividends to the two holding companies which is the only other income of those corporations.

— REQUIRED

(A) What is the nature of the rental income to H Ltd.?

(B) Is there a Part IV tax liability for the two holding companies on the dividends received from Sunlight Limited?

Exercise 9

ITA: 125, 129, 256

Janna Management Limited owns a building most of which it rents to Rayna Consulting Services Limited which carries on an active business. Janna and Rayna each own 50% of both corporations. Janna Management Limited also provides managerial, administrative and maintenance services to the unincorporated professional practice of Dr. Adam. The result of these transactions is that Janna Management Limited receives 60% of its income from rent and 40% from providing services and has available an excess business limit for the purposes of the small business deduction.

— REQUIRED

Determine the nature of its income and the deductions from tax available to Janna Management Limited.

Exercise 10

ITA: Part I, IV

Dana Toews lives in a province with a 15.5% corporate tax rate and owns an investment portfolio that generated the following Canadian-source income during the year:

Interest	$ 7,000
Portfolio dividends from CCPCs	15,000
Capital gains	6,000

Her cash needs require that $15,000 of the corporation's after-tax profits be distributed as a dividend. The corporation will retain and reinvest the remainder. She already has taxable income of $20,000 from other sources. She has federal personal tax credits of $1,800 and provincial tax credits of $1,200.

— REQUIRED

Compare the total tax on the income from the portfolio with the total tax if a corporation owned the securities.

Exercise 11

ITA: 123.3, 126, 129(1),
129(6), 256

Johnson & Co Ltd. holds all the issued shares in Johnson & Co (USA) Inc. Two years ago, the Canadian corporation advanced $100,000 in the form of a loan to the U.S. corporation. The U.S. corporation pays Johnson & Co interest at the rate of 5%. This 5% is comparable to the cost of borrowing at a U.S. bank, but is less than the prescribed interest rate under the Canadian Act. Assume that rate is 7%. (Ignore any subsection 17(1) considerations.)

— REQUIRED

Explain the tax obligations of the Canadian corporation relative to this 5% interest.

¶12,875 ASSIGNMENT PROBLEMS

Type 1 Problems

Problem 1

You are again working on the firm's tax publications and have been asked to compare the corporate tax rates for active business income earned by the following:

— a Canadian public company,

— a CCPC with income below $500,000 and

— a CCPC with income above $500,000.

Assume a generic provincial tax rate that you can support.

Problem 2

Still working on the publication you have been asked to calculate the small business deduction and then explain how it works.

(1) What is the purpose behind the small business deduction?

(2) Is this deduction a savings or a deferral? Explain

(3) The purpose behind the components of the calculation.

(4) The purpose behind the associated company rules.

(5) If income is over the annual business limit should the company declare a bonus to reduce the income back down to the annual business limit?

Your calculations should use the following assumptions:

— Active business income	$600,000
— Taxable income	300,000
— Business limit	200,000
— Personal marginal tax rate on employment income	50%
— Personal marginal tax rate on eligible dividends	31%
— Personal marginal tax rate on non-eligible dividends	42%

Compare the after-tax personal cash from the following:

1. Calculate the amount of bonus needed to reduce taxable income to the point where all of the taxable income is eligible for the small business deduction.

2. Assuming that the bonus is declared and paid, calculate the personal tax on the bonus received by the individual and their after-tax cash.

3. Assuming that the bonus is not declared, then calculate the amount of corporate tax the company will pay on the amount of the bonus identified in step 1. Then calculate the corporate after-tax cash on this bonus amount not paid. Pay this after-tax cash as a dividend and calculate the amount of personal tax on this dividend and their after-tax cash.

Problem 3

Staying with the tax publication, assuming Canadian portfolio dividends received are $100,000:

— Explain how Canadian dividend income is taxed in a public corporation.

— Explain how Canadian dividend income is taxed in a CCPC.

(1) Why are dividends deductible under Division C?

(2) What is the purpose of Part IV tax? Is it a permanent or temporary tax? To whom does it apply?

(3) Why might there be Part IV tax on dividends from connected corporations?

(4) What is the purpose behind the Refundable Dividend Tax On Hand (RDTOH)?

(5) Why doesn't Part IV tax apply to public companies?

(6) How does the Dividend Refund fit in?

Problem 4

Staying with the tax publication, assuming interest income of $10,000 and capital gains of $40,000:

— Explain how investment income, other than dividends, is taxed in a public corporation.

— Explain how investment income, other than dividends, is taxed in a CCPC.

(1) What type of income is included in Aggregate Investment Income (AII)?

(2) How is AII calculated?

(3) What is the purpose behind the Additional Refundable Tax (ART)?

(4) What is the purpose behind the Refundable Dividend Tax On Hand (RDTOH)?

(5) Why don't ART and RDTOH apply to public companies?

(6) How does the Dividend Refund fit in?

Problem 5

Compare the taxation of active business income and personal services business income assuming income of $100,000.

What is the purpose behind taxing "personal services business" income differently?

Compare the calculation of income and tax payable between an individual earning employment income and a corporation earning personal services business income.

Problem 6

First Gear Inc. is a corporation that distributes automotive parts in the Province of New Brunswick. For the year ended December 30, 2016, its accounting income statement was as follows:

Sales	$1,225,000
Cost of sales and other expenses including CCA	(725,000)
Operating profit	500,000
Other net income	208,500
Net income before taxes	708,500
Provision for taxes	(200,725)
Net income after tax	$ 507,775

CHAPTER 12

Selected Additional Information

(1) Other income includes:

Portfolio dividends from Canadian public corporation	$ 85,000
Canadian interest income on long-term bonds	123,500
	$208,500

You have been asked to:

(1) Assuming the company is a public company:

(a) Identify the different types of income and explain how each is taxed.

(b) Calculate the total federal taxes payable for 2016.

(2) Assuming the company is a CCPC:

(a) Identify the different types of income and explain how each is taxed.

(b) Calculate the total federal taxes payable for 2016.

Problem 7

ITA: 186

Ex Ltd., a Canadian-controlled private corporation, received a taxable dividend of $90,000 from its Canadian subsidiary Little Ex Ltd. The subsidiary had paid a total dividend of $120,000 and had received a dividend refund of $18,000.

Compute the Part IV tax payable by Ex Ltd.

Problem 8

ITA: 123–127, 129, 186

Why Limited is a Canadian-controlled private corporation operating solely in Newfoundland and Labrador. For its taxation year ended December 31, 2016, the company reported the following income under Division B:

Active business income	$ 85,000
Taxable capital gain	37,500
Canadian-source interest income	45,000
Taxable portfolio dividends from Canadian-resident public corporations	18,750
Income under Division B	$186,250

The corporation is carrying forward the following amounts:

Non-capital losses	$ 37,500
Net capital losses (arising in 2011)	52,000

The balance in the refundable dividend tax on hand account at December 31, 2015 was nil. On November 30, 2016, the company paid $112,500 in taxable dividends to its shareholders all of whom are individuals. The taxable portfolio dividends of $18,750 were received on November 1, 2016.

(A) Compute the federal Part I tax and provincial tax at an 8% rate payable by the company for 2016.

(B) Compute the refundable dividend tax on hand balance as at December 31, 2016 and compute the dividend refund for 2016.

Problem 9

ITA: 125(7)

The taxpayer company, a private corporation, owned and operated a small shopping centre from which it received rental income. There were seven separate tenants, only one of them being what is sometimes referred to as a "Triple A" tenant, namely, a Canadian bank. The corporation, through its principal officer, negotiated all the leases, took care of all the complaints from the tenants and arranged for the maintenance of the shopping centre. It required some activity by the company almost daily. The rental income of the company was mainly for use of the property, but also, to a much lesser extent, for services and other things supplied by the company such as heat, repairs, etc.

From the facts provided in the case, determine the type of income that the corporation derives from the business that it carries on under the current legislation.

Problem 10

ITA: 256

Consider each of the following unrelated cases, involving the ownership of the common shares of Canadian-controlled private corporations, for taxation years of all corporations ending on December 31:

(A) Leah Ltd. owns 55% of the shares of Elaine Ltd.

(B) Ms. Miriam owns 51% of the shares of Abigail Ltd. and 60% of the shares of Ethan Ltd.

(C) Ms. Irene and Mr. Mordechai each own 50% of the shares of Clare Ltd. In addition, they each own 50% of the shares of Philip Ltd. Ms. Irene and Mr. Mordechai are not related.

(D) Mrs. Lyn owns 60% of the shares of Jay Ltd. and Mrs. Sarah owns the other 40%. Mrs. Lyn and Mrs. Sarah each own 50% of the shares of Alex Ltd. Mrs. Lyn and Mrs. Sarah are not related.

(E) Janna Ltd., Rayna Ltd. and Adam Ltd. each own ⅓ of the shares of Stan Ltd. Janna Ltd. and Rayna Ltd. each own 50% of the shares of Jonathan Ltd.

(F) Ms. Ruth owns all of the shares of Rick Ltd. Ms. Ruth owns 25% of the shares of Daniel Ltd. and Ms. Ruth's daughter, Elana, who is over 18 years old owns the other 75%.

(G) Mr. Joshua owns 100% of the shares of Gord Ltd. and Ms. Dahlia owns 100% of the shares of Rosalyn Ltd. Mr. Joshua and Ms. Dahlia each own 30% of the shares of Rebecca Ltd. The other 40% of the shares of Rebecca Ltd. are owned by Eden, who is not related to any of the others. Mr. Joshua is the brother of Ms. Dahlia's husband.

(H) Mrs. Yael owns 60% of the shares of Benjamin Ltd. and 30% of the shares of Livi Ltd. Another 25% of the shares of Livi Ltd. are owned by Benjamin Ltd. and the remaining 45% of the shares of Livi Ltd. are owned by Joy, who is not related to any of the others.

(I) Ms. Daniella owns 60% of the shares of Elizabeth Ltd. and 25% of the shares of Ava Ltd. Ms. Samara, who is not related to Ms. Daniella, owns the other 75% of the shares of Ava Ltd. Ms. Daniella holds an option to buy all of the shares owned by Ms. Samara at any time in the next 10 years.

(J) Mr. and Mrs. Jonathan each own 50% of Isabelle Ltd. Mr. Jonathan and his two brothers and one sister each own 25% of Maya Ltd.

In each of the above *unrelated* cases determine whether the corporations are associated. Substantiate your answer by reference to the specific conditions in the provisions of section 256, and consider all possible alternatives.

Problem 11

ITA: 256

Consider each of the following unrelated cases, involving the ownership of shares of Canadian-controlled private corporations. Assume all of the issued shares are common shares unless specifically stated otherwise.

(A) Rachel and Monica, friends, each own 50% of the issued shares of A Ltd. In addition, Rachel owns 80% and Monica owns 20% of the issued shares of B Ltd.

(B) Charlie and Claudia are siblings. Charlie owns 80% of A Ltd. which in turn owns 40% of B Ltd. Claudia owns 60% of B Ltd.

(C) Bob, Bill, and Bert are three brothers who share equally the income of a professional partnership. The partnership owns 100% of the shares of A Ltd. Bert owns 100% of the shares of B Ltd.

(D) Anne and Barbara are sisters. They each own 100% of their respective corporations, A Ltd. and B Ltd. A Ltd. and B Ltd. each own 40% of the shares of C Ltd.

(E) Valerie, Brandon, and Claire are strangers. They each own ⅓ of the shares of A Ltd. Brandon owns 40% of the shares of B Ltd. The remaining 60% are owned by Claire. Claire also owns 100% of the shares of C Ltd.

(F) Valerie and her two nieces each own 25% of the shares of A Ltd. Valerie's husband, Dilon, and his nephew each own 50% of the shares of B Ltd. Dilon also owns the remaining 25% of the shares of A Ltd.

(G) Father owns 100% of the shares of F Ltd. His son, Sean, age 17, owns 100% of the common shares of S Ltd. F Ltd. owns 30% of the issued preferred shares of S Ltd. The preferred shares have the following characteristics:

- non-voting,
- dividend rate fixed at 6%,
- redeemable at $1,000 per share, and
- issue price $1,000 per share.

The prescribed rate of interest was 8% at the time the preferred shares were issued.

You have been asked to determine which of the corporations are associated and substantiate your answer by reference to specific provisions of the Act.

Problem 12

ITA: 256

Both corporations in this case were incorporated for the purpose of buying and selling anti-freeze products. Warren Packaging Limited sold its product ("Dual Duty") to wholesalers who serviced and supplied garages and service stations ultimately for the consumers. Its sole shareholder and president was Mr. Warren. Bradford-Penn Oil Inc. sold its product ("Viceroy") to retailers who sold it on a cash and carry basis to its clients. Mr. Warren's wife was the sole shareholder and president of the latter company.

In essence, both companies were directed by the same person in the same premises. They both had the same year-end. The product came in bulk from the same supplier and was packed in smaller quantities with the different brand names.

Management of the companies felt that it was too risky to have the same company distribute the anti-freeze product to both the wholesalers and the retailers. There was only one supplier of bulk anti-freeze available to the two corporations and that supplier marketed its own brand and, as a result, was also in competition with Warren Packaging and Bradford-Penn Oil. Maintaining the source of supply at a competitive price made the business risky.

Management also felt that it was necessary to have two companies with two different brand names to cover the wholesale market and the retail market. Experience had shown that if the same brand were supplied to both the wholesalers and the retailers, one or the other of the markets would be lost. Even if the same company name appeared on the package of the two different brands, it would be difficult to maintain both markets because of price differentials from the different outlets to the ultimate consumers.

In his testimony, Mr. Warren testified that he did not remember his counsellor discussing taxation with him when he decided to separately incorporate the two companies. He also testified that he had given a personal guarantee to the bank to obtain a loan for Warren Packaging Limited and he felt it was necessary to have a limited liability in that corporation. He believed that limited liability was accomplished by his wife's sole ownership of the shares of Bradford-Penn Oil Inc.

You have been asked the following:

(A) Would subsection 256(5.1) apply in this case and, if so, what would be the effect of that application?

(B) Assuming that subsection 256(5.1) does not apply, determine whether Warren Packaging Limited and Bradford-Penn Oil Inc. are associated. Provide reasons for your determination by reference to the legislation and to the facts of the case.

Problem 13

ITA: 123–126

The accountant, Ryan Mailling, of Double-D Retailing Ltd. (DRL), a Canadian-controlled private corporation, has requested your assistance with respect to the calculation of the company's Part I tax payable.

Ryan has provided you with the following information.

(1) DRL is not associated with any other corporation.

(2) For DRL's December 31 taxation year-end, the corporation correctly reported:

Active business income	$320,000
Investment income	
Canadian	17,000
Charitable donations	9,000
Net capital loss deducted	2,000
Non-capital loss deducted	10,000
Taxable income	316,000

(3) Taxable capital employed in Canada in 2015 was $11.9 million.

Ryan has asked you to calculate the federal Part I tax payable for the taxation year ended December 31, 2016. Show all calculations whether or not relevant to the final answer.

Problem 14

ITA: 37, 127(5)–(11), 127.1

Natalia, a resident of Canada, owns 100% of the shares of New Age Limited (NAL). NAL carries on scientific research and experimental development (SR&ED) activities with respect to finding the ingredients for a cream which will reduce fat and tone muscles when massaged into the skin.

During its fiscal year ended December 31, 2016, NAL incurred the following costs related to its SR&ED activities:

Salaries for research technicians and assistants	$600,000
Materials consumed	200,000
Supplies consumed	40,000
Small equipment purchased for the laboratory	80,000
A special machine purchased to mix the ingredients in a temperature controlled environment	100,000

The machine and the lab equipment will have no value when the research project is completed.

Additional overhead costs were incurred in 2016 because of the SR&ED project. The accounting system was not sophisticated enough to properly allocate these expenses. Overhead expenses for the year totalled $500,000.

NAL paid Natalia a bonus of $40,000 in 2016 in addition to her salary of $80,000. Natalia spent 25% of her time on the SR&ED project in 2016.

NAL does not expect to have any taxable income for 2016. It had taxable income of $100,000 in 2014. Its taxable capital does not exceed $10 million. It is not associated with any other corporation.

You have been asked the following:

(A) Which of the above costs incurred by NAL in 2016 qualify for deduction under subsection 37(1) as qualifying SR&ED expenditures?

(B) Determine the amount of ITCs and refundable ITCs for 2016.

Problem 15

ITA: 110.1–112, 123–126, 127(3)

Neville Ltd. is a Canadian-controlled private corporation which was incorporated in 2000 with a December 31 year end. In 2016, Neville Ltd. earned net income of $250,000 before taxes for accounting purposes. Included in the calculation of that amount were the following items:

Canadian active business income	$159,000
Dividends from taxable Canadian subsidiary corporations	8,000
Other Canadian investment income:	
— rental income	$115,000
— interest income	15,000
— royalty income	1,000
— taxable capital gain	9,000
Income under Division B	$307,000
Donations to registered charities	$ 60,000
The company also has the following balances at January 1, 2016:	
2010 Net capital loss	$ 10,000
Charitable donations carried forward from 2016	10,000

Neville Ltd.'s 100% owned subsidiary has used $350,000 of the business limit for the small business deduction in 2016. Together, Neville Ltd. and its subsidiary have $8 million of taxable capital in Canada.

You have been asked to calculate the federal Part I tax and provincial tax payable by Neville Ltd. for 2016. Show *all* calculations.

Problem 16

ITA: 123–127, 129, 186

The following selected information has been taken from the records of Sharp Ltd., a Canadian-controlled private corporation, for its fiscal year ended December 31, 2016.

(1) Income for tax purposes:

Active business income (retailing)	$160,000
Canadian bond interest	20,000
Taxable dividends received from taxable Canadian corporations	40,000
Taxable capital gains	30,000
Net income under Division B	$260,000

(2) Division C deductions claimed:

Donations	(2,000)
Net capital losses	(5,000)
Non-capital losses	(13,000)
Taxable dividends received from taxable Canadian corporations	(40,000)

(3) Taxable income $200,000

(4) Part I tax payable is $32,267 including additional refundable tax of $4,267. In computing Part I tax, the following deductions were made:

Small business deduction	$28,000

(5) Summary of taxable dividends received from taxable Canadian corporations:

Date received	Payer	% of voting shares owned	Amount of dividend received	Dividend refund received by payer corp.
Aug. 1, 2016	A Ltd.	6%	$20,000	$30,000
Oct. 1, 2016	B Ltd.	80%	20,000	5,000
			$40,000	

(6) Summary of dividends paid by Sharp Ltd.:

Type of dividend	Amount	Date declared	Date paid
Taxable dividend	$60,000	July 15, 2016	Aug. 15, 2016
Tax-free ssec. 83(2) dividend	20,000	Oct. 15, 2016	Nov. 15, 2016
Taxable dividend	24,000	Dec. 15, 2016	Jan. 15, 2017

(7) The refundable dividend tax on hand balance at December 31, 2015 was $12,000. The dividend refund for 2015 was $4,000.

You have been asked to:

(A) Compute the dividend refund for 2016.

(B) Explain what would change if Sharp Ltd. was a private corporation, and not a CCPC?

¶12,875

Problem 17

Multi Enterprises Ltd. is a Canadian-controlled private corporation whose fiscal period coincides with the calendar year. For the year 2016, the company's taxable income was calculated as follows:

Income from distributing net of CCA		$220,000
Dividends from taxable corporations:		
(a) connected corporation, dividend payment triggering a dividend refund of $2,750 to the wholly owned subsidiary		11,000
(b) non-connected corporation (portfolio dividends)		20,000
Taxable capital gain	$29,000	
Allowable capital losses	12,000	17,000
Royalties		9,000
Recapture of CCA on disposal of sales equipment		4,000
Income from rental of an apartment building (no full-time employees and tenants provide virtually all of their own services)		14,000
Interest charged on accounts receivable		5,000
Net income for tax purposes		$300,000
Less: net capital losses carried over	$ 7,000	
non-capital losses carried over	10,000	
donations	26,000	
dividends from taxable Canadian corporations	31,000	74,000
Taxable income		$226,000

At December 31, 2015, there was a nil balance in the refundable dividend tax on hand account. The company paid $72,000 in dividends during 2016 to individual shareholders.

It has been agreed that $200,000 of the business limit for small business deduction will be claimed by the parent, Multi Enterprises Ltd., leaving the remainder for the subsidiary.

The company has a permanent establishment in New Brunswick.

You have been asked to:

(A) Compute the federal Part I tax and assumed provincial tax at a 5% rate on federal taxable income payable by the company for 2016. Show in detail the calculation of all deductions in the computation, using a separate schedule for each special deduction. In calculating the small business deduction list all ineligible items of income, if any, and indicate the amount of the business limit available for the subsidiary.

(B) Compute the refundable dividend tax on hand balance as at December 31, 2016, showing, in detail, your calculations and compute the dividend refund for 2016.

Type 2 Problems

Problem 18

The controller of Tek Enterprises Ltd. provided you with the following information:

Tek Enterprises Ltd.
Income
For the fiscal year ended December 31, 2016

Canadian wholesaling income		$251,500
Canadian retail business income		90,000
Taxable capital gains		4,500
Interest income:		
Canadian long-term bonds	$20,000	
Interest on accounts receivable outstanding for more than 30 days in the Canadian retail business	5,000	25,000
Dividend income:		
From taxable Canadian corporations	$ 9,000	
From foreign corporations (before foreign tax of $1,800) (Tek Enterprises Ltd. owns less than 5% of the shares)	12,000	21,000
Net income		$392,000

Notes:

(1) Tek Enterprises Limited is a CCPC. It is not associated with any corporations.

(2) The following items were deducted in the computation of Canadian wholesaling income above:

SR&ED expenditures (current in nature) $50,000

(3) The taxable capital gain was calculated as follows:

	Marketable securities	Equipment	Total
Proceeds	$15,000	$ 200	$15,200
Cost	3,000	3,200	6,200
Gain (Loss)	$12,000	$ (3,000)	$ 9,000
			× ½
			$ 4,500

(4) The corporation has net capital losses (incurred in 2006) of $13,000.

You assigned a junior staff member to calculate the federal Part I tax payable for Tek Enterprises Ltd. The following is his calculation.

Net income	$392,000
Dividends	(21,000)
Donations	(75,000)
Net capital losses	(13,000)
Taxable income	$283,000

Basic federal tax (40% × $283,000)		$113,200
Abatement: Taxable income . . . . $283,000 × 10%		$ 28,300
		$141,500

Foreign tax credit:
Lesser of: (a) Foreign tax paid = $1,800

(b) $\frac{\text{Foreign income } \$12,000}{\$283,000 + \$21,000 + \$13,000} \times \$141,500 = \$5,356$ (1,800)

Small business deduction:
    17.5% × the least of: (a) Active business income:

Wholesaling business	$251,500	
Cdn. retail business	90,000	
	$341,500	
(b) $283,000 – 4 × $1,800 =	$275,800	
(c) Business limit:	$500,000	(49,525)

General rate reduction (13% × $283,000)	(28,300)
Federal Part I tax payable	$ 66,314

Write a memo in point-form explaining to the junior staff member the errors in his calculation. HINT: Do the calculations correctly and compare your results to the results of the junior staff member. Then explain the errors.

Problem 19

ITA: 123–127, 129, 186

Rob's Shameless Self-Promotion Sales (RSS-PS) Inc. is a Canadian-controlled private corporation located in London, Ontario. For its fiscal year ended December 31, 2016, the corporation had correctly calculated its income for tax purposes under Division B as follows:

CHAPTER 12

Canadian source:

Consulting income	$160,000
Advertising agency loss	(30,000)
Rental income from warehouse fully rented on a five-year lease	20,000
Retailing income	75,000
Interest on outstanding accounts receivable in retailing business	25,000
Recapture of CCA from sale of fixtures used in retailing business	25,000
Interest income from five-year bonds	75,000
Taxable capital gain	70,000
Dividends from non-connected taxable Canadian corporations	12,000
Division B net income for tax purposes	$432,000

Additional information:

RSS-PS Inc. made the following selected payments during the year:

Scientific research and experimental development (current expenses)	$100,000
Charitable donations	14,000
Taxable dividends	120,000

The balances in the tax accounts on December 31, 2015 were:

Charitable donations from 2013	$ 1,000
Non-capital losses from 2012	56,000
Net capital losses from 2012	12,000
Refundable dividend tax on hand	20,000
Dividend refund for 2015	9,000

RSS-PS Inc. allocated $370,000 of its $500,000 business limit to other associated corporations. The only scientific research and experimental development expenditures of the associated group were made by RSS-PS Inc.

Rob has asked you to:

(A) Compute the federal Part I tax and provincial tax at a 11.5% rate on federal taxable income for the 2016 taxation year, and

(B) Compute the dividend refund for 2016 and the amount of any RDTOH to be carried forward.

Problem 20

ITA: 125, 129, 186, 256

Carl owns 100% of the issued shares of Compunet. He incorporated Compunet earlier this year to provide computer consulting services to Vitamins Inc., a retailer of energy-producing vitamins. Prior to the incorporation of Compunet, Carl headed the computer service division of Vitamins Inc. One hundred per cent of the issued shares of Vitamins Inc. are owned by Carl's cousin, Vince.

Carl's daughter, Sulee, received a degree in computer science from the University of Toronto in April and has been employed by Compunet as a computer consultant since then. Sulee and Carl work well together. They are the only employees of Compunet.

¶12,875

Compunet owns a warehouse. One-half of the warehouse is rented to Vitamins Inc. and the remainder is rented to Mindblasters, a wholly owned subsidiary of Compunet. Mindblasters is a successful retailer of computer games.

During the current year, Compunet received taxable dividends from Mindblasters and paid taxable dividends to Carl.

Carl has asked you to determine the type(s) of income being earned by Compunet, the rate of tax for each type and any refunds available.

Problem 21

ITA: 125, 129, 256

Lemon Ltd. provides management services for Toys-4-U Limited (Toys), a retailer of educational toys, and for certain other corporations described below. Les Lemon is the sole shareholder and only employee of Lemon Ltd. Prior to this year, Les had been employed by Toys as vice-president of financial and administrative services.

Les owns all of the common shares of Rental Ltd. (Rental), which is in the business of renting commercial properties. Rental has no employees, except for Les, and subcontracts all maintenance and administrative services. Rental's income for tax purposes can be broken down as follows:

Lemon Ltd.	10%
Cheap Leasing Ltd. (see below)	25%
Arm's length parties.	65%
	100%

Les is also involved with Cheap Leasing Limited (Cheap), which is in the business of leasing educational equipment. The ownership of the common shares of Cheap is as follow:

Les Lemon	25 shares
Lucy Lemon, Les' wife	20 shares
Lemon Ltd.	30 shares
Larry Lemon, Les' uncle	10 shares
Arm's length parties.	15 shares

Cheap derives approximately 80% of its income from the educational equipment leasing business. The balance of its income is interest from a loan to Toys. Cheap has four employees in addition to Les.

All of the above corporations are Canadian-controlled private corporations and have December 31 year-ends.

You have been asked to identify the various sources of income for the above corporations indicating the reasoning behind your conclusions. Also indicate the *federal* tax rate and any refundable taxes applicable to each income source.

Problem 22

ITA: Part I, IV

Mr. Humphries, a resident of a province with a 40% effective combined federal and provincial corporate tax rate (before the additional refundable tax), has just won a lottery prize of $750,000. He is considering the following investment of these funds: $200,000 of bonds yielding 8% and $550,000 of common shares of Growth Unlimited Limited (a CCPC earning active business income less than the business limit), which pay a dividend to yield 5%. Having taken a course in security analysis, Mr. Humphries can predict with great confidence that he will realize a 10.5% capital gain on the shares within the year. Mr. Humphries currently has taxable income of $30,000. He has federal personal tax credits of $2,100, and provincial personal tax credits of $1,400.

Advise Mr. Humphries on whether he should use an investment corporation with a permanent establishment in the province of which he is a resident to hold the securities he proposes to purchase. Include in your analysis the realization of the predicted capital gain. Use 2016 rates. Also, consider any non-quantitative factors that may be relevant to the decision.

Type 3 Problems

Problem 23

You recently met Susan Taylor at a cocktail party. As a result of your conversation with her, Susan has come to you for tax advice. She wants to know how her income will be taxed. She also wants to know whether she should incorporate and earn the same types of income through a corporation called High Income Limited. She would be the sole shareholder and only employee of that corporation. Susan has received various types of income in 2016. These incomes are as follows:

- Interest income from GIC — $5,000

- Dividend income from a publicly traded corporation — $10,000

- Capital gains from selling public company shares — $20,000

- Susan owns 40% of all the issued and outstanding common shares of Stage Lighting Limited (Stage). Her best friend, Mary, who lives in Ontario, owns the rest of the common shares. The company is in the business of manufacturing customized lighting products. She received $20,000 in dividends (for which Stage *did not* receive any dividend refund) from Stage this year. All income earned by Stage is eligible for the small business deduction.

Susan would like to understand whether she should incorporate a holding company to earn the four different types of income mentioned above.

Susan runs a small fashion store selling high-end handmade scarves. The business is operated as a sole proprietorship. Active operations started four years ago and the business started to make sizable profit last year. The estimated taxable retail income in 2016 is $200,000. Susan would like to know whether she should incorporate this business.

Additional Information and Assumptions

Assume that the effective combined federal and provincial corporate tax rates for 2016 on the following types of income are:

- Active business income (ABI) (eligible for the small business deduction)

  38% – 10% – 17.5% + 5% (net provincial) 15.5%

- Specified investment business income

  38% – 10% + 10⅔% + 14% (provincial) – initially 52⅔%
  48⅔% – 30⅔% – ultimately when dividends paid 18%

- Capital gains

  Taxed portion is taxed as income from a SIB above
  Non-taxed portion 0%

The non-taxed portion of the capital gain is added to the capital dividend account. Dividends can be paid out of the balance of this account with no tax cost to the recipient shareholder.

Assume that, if the ABI increases to the point where it exceeds $500,000 (small business deduction), then the effective federal rate on the ABI in excess of the small business limit will be

- Combined federal and provincial rate:

  38% – 10% – 13% (general rate reduction) + 14 (provincial) 29%

Assume that the effective combined federal and provincial personal tax rates for 2015 are:

- The effective combined federal and provincial personal tax rate:

  Top marginal rates 33% (federal) + 17% (provincial) 50%

- Effective combined federal and provincial tax rate for dividends from:

  Low Rate Income Pool [for dividends paid after 2015] 41.5%
  General Rate Income Pool 31.0%

You have agreed with Susan that you will draft a memo analyzing the tax implications of the above situation. Your memo will address and conclude on the following issues:

(A) Based on the theory and a conceptual understanding of incorporation, determine whether Susan can save and/or defer income tax by incorporating a holding company to earn interest income, dividend income from a public company, capital gains from selling public company shares, and dividend income from Stage Lighting Limited.

(B) Based on the theory and a conceptual understanding of incorporation, determine whether Susan can save and/or defer income tax through incorporation of her fashion business.

(C) Discuss some of the general (i.e., not specific to Susan) quantitative and qualitative pros and cons of incorporation.

Problem 24

Mickey and Nicki Waterloo are husband and wife entrepreneurs. Most of the time, when they start a business, they will do so with another person, in order to let that person handle the day-to-day business matters and, also, to provide a potential buyer at some point in the future. Usually this other person will have a shareholding in the operating company, but Mickey and/or Nicki will maintain control. It is, also, usual for each company to have a shareholder agreement with a buy/sell provision that calls for a corporate repurchase on death, disability, bankruptcy, or retirement. Maximizing the use of the small business deduction is also a goal.

At this time, Mickey and Nicki have the following interests, which are all held through a holding company (Holdco) owned 100% by Mickey.

(1) Holdco owns 20% of a company called Sales Co. Inc. The other 80% is owned by Joe Shea, who runs the company. In order to finance the operations, Holdco has invested $100,000 in non-voting preference shares with a redemption value of $100,000 and a dividend rate of 8%.

(2) Holdco and Fred Smith have shared ownership of two companies. Holdco owns 90% of Retail One Inc. and 10% of Retail Two Inc., while Fred owns the other 10% of Retail One Inc. and 90% of Retail Two Inc.

Mickey and Nicki share ownership in two companies. Mickey owns 40% of Ours Inc., Nicki owns 100% of Mine Inc., and Mine Inc. own 60% of Ours Inc. Both Mickey and Nicki are actively involved in these businesses.

On the advice of their lawyer, they set up a discretionary trust for their two children, Dick, who is 12 years old, and Jane, who is 10 years old. This trust borrowed money from the bank (with personal guarantees from Mickey and Nicki) and bought treasury shares from a newly incorporated company, Kids Are Fun Inc. This company sells games through a retail store. It was capitalized with a loan from Nicki.

Advise Mickey and Nicki of the tax implications of the share ownerships outlined above on the small business deduction.

 [For more problems and solutions thereto, see the DVD accompanying the textbook.]

CHAPTER 12

CHAPTER 12 —
DISCUSSION NOTES FOR REVIEW QUESTIONS

(1) The purpose of integration is to avoid the double taxation of income earned through a corporation. Integration should cause the total tax paid by a corporation and its shareholders to be equal to the total tax paid by an individual who carries on the same economic activity directly and not through a corporation. The system should be neutral as to the form of organization used.

(2) Ideal integration depends on:

(a) When the corporation itself pays tax, the shareholder must include in income and pay tax on the full pre-tax income earned by the corporation and then get a full credit for all the income tax paid by the corporation.

(b) All after-tax income would have to be either paid out as dividends in the year earned or taxed in some manner at the shareholder level in that year to avoid the indefinite deferral of tax that might otherwise be available if the corporate rates were lower than individual tax rates. This would equate the position of the shareholder with the position of the proprietor, partner or owner of investments who must pay tax on income from his or her economic activity whether or not it is distributed.

(3) The gross-up is intended to add to the dividend received by the individual shareholder an amount equal to the total income tax paid by the corporation on the income that gave rise to the dividend. Thus, the grossed-up dividend is intended to represent the corporation's pre-tax income. The shareholder will pay tax on the grossed-up dividend at his or her personal rate. The tax credit is intended to give the shareholder credit for the total tax paid by the corporation on the shareholder's behalf. This procedure is intended to equalize the tax paid on the income that is flowed through the corporation to its shareholders with the tax paid on the same income that is earned directly. When the gross-up is 17% and the total (i.e., federal and provincial) corporate tax rate is 14.5%, integration is theoretically perfect. When the gross-up is 38% and the total (i.e., federal and provincial) corporate tax rate is 27.5%, integration is, also, theoretically perfect.

(4) Its purpose is to help small CCPCs retain capital in order to expand their businesses. This is accomplished by using a relatively low corporate tax rate after the small business deduction to defer tax until the income is paid out as a dividend.

(5) There is a deemed year end on July 14 as a result of the acquisition of control and he is deemed to acquire control at the commencement of that day. Mr. Smith can now choose any year end he wants and the company should qualify as a CCPC throughout the year.

ITA: 249(4), 256(9)

(6) Paragraph 125(1)(*a*) deals with Division B income (net of expenses) while paragraph 125(1)(*b*) starts off with taxable income. Therefore, if there are Division C deductions such as donations or loss carryforwards then paragraph 125(1)(*b*) could be lower.

(7) Some advantages of incorporation are:

- limited liability except for personal guarantees;

- tax savings if the combined corporate tax and the personal tax on the dividend is less than the personal tax would be on the same income;

- tax deferral if the corporate tax rate is less than the personal tax rate on that income;

- income splitting with family members as employees or shareholders (beware of the attribution rules and the tax on split income);

- estate freezing;

- availability of registered pension plans to the owner;

- separation of business and personal activities;

- greater flexibility as to the timing and type of income received personally;

- continuity of separate legal entity;

- deferral of accrued capital gains on transfer of shares to a spouse;

- access to financing;

- availability of capital gains exemption on QSBCS; and

- availability of deferral of capital gains on shares of an SBC.

(8) Some disadvantages of incorporation are:

- tax cost if combined corporate tax rate is over 14.5% for income eligible for the small business deduction and 27.5% for other business income;

- a prepayment of tax at lower levels of personal income on business income not eligible for the small business deduction;

- additional legal and accounting costs;

- inability to deduct losses against personal income — this disadvantage may be offset somewhat by the availability of the ABIL; and

- greater difficulty in accessing cash generated by the business for personal use.

(9) He will not be able to get the general rate reduction on income eligible for the small business deduction. In addition, the question does not indicate whether this venture is incorporated. If it is not, then these deductions are not available since they are only available to incorporated businesses. ITA: 125.1(1)(*a*)

(10) Part IV tax of 38⅓% on portfolio dividends prevents a significant deferral of tax.

(11) (a) Refundable Part I tax;

(b) Part IV tax;

(c) Dividend gross-up and tax credit;

(d) Refundable dividend tax on hand; and

(e) Dividend refund.

(12) The gross-up is intended to place the shareholder in an income position equivalent to that of the corporation before it paid corporate taxes. At an assumed corporate tax rate of 14.5% or 27.5%, the 17% or 38% gross-up, respectively, represents the underlying corporate tax. This is added to the after-tax dividend to tax, theoretically, the pre-tax corporate profits in the hands of the individual shareholder.

(13) The dividend tax credit is intended to give the shareholder credit against his or her taxes for the taxes paid by the corporation on the income from which the dividend was paid. Since the gross-up theoretically takes the dividend up to the pre-tax corporate income level, the dividend tax credit is needed to reduce the individual tax by the theoretical amount of corporate tax already paid on that income. At a corporate tax rate of 14.5%, for example, tax of $14.50 would be paid on corporate income of $100. The gross-up of 17% would take the individual's income on that dividend of $85.50 back up to the $100 of corporate pre-tax income level. Assuming a provincial dividend tax credit of ⁸/₂₉ of the gross-up, the total dividend tax credit would be 14.5% of the grossed-up dividend or $14.50. Thus the dividend tax credit represents the underlying corporate tax paid on the dividend.

(14) Of the $1,000 capital gain, $500 is not taxable and is allocated to the capital dividend account to be passed out to the shareholders tax-free as a capital dividend. This provides for the tax-free receipt of this $500 whether the capital gain is realized in the corporation or by the individual directly. ITA: 82(3)

The remaining $500 is theoretically taxed at an approximate initial rate of Part I tax of 40%. An additional refundable tax of 10⅔% is also levied and added to this account. Then,

30⅔% of the income is classified as refundable Part I tax and added to the refundable dividend tax on hand account. Dividend payments result in a return to the corporation of 38⅓% of dividends that are paid. This would leave an effective tax rate in the corporation on taxable capital gains of 20% which is higher than the 14.5% level at which integration works.

(15) Ordinarily the interest would be taxed at the full rate of 40% (38% – 10% + 12% provincial) plus the 10⅔% additional refundable tax under Part I with part of this being classified as refundable Part I tax and added to the refundable dividend tax on hand account. However, since the two companies are associated and the interest is being deducted against the active business income of Opco, the deeming rules will deem the interest income to be active business income and not eligible for the refundable tax treatment.

ITA: 129(6)

(16) While A Ltd. does not have more than 10% of the votes and value of B Ltd., A Ltd. does have control, since A Ltd. and the son of the only shareholder are related and do not deal at arm's length. Thus, over 50% of the voting shares belong to a person with whom A Ltd. does not deal at arm's length.

ITA: 186(2)

(17) The factors to be considered are:

- the same non-capital losses cannot be deducted under both provisions;

- the normal corporate tax rates under Part I are usually higher than the 38⅓% Part IV tax;

- the Part IV tax is a refundable tax and not a permanent tax like Part I tax;

- the non-capital losses would otherwise expire without any value; and

- the corporation is not expected to pay a dividend to claim the refund until years in the future.

CHAPTER 12 — SOLUTIONS TO MULTIPLE CHOICE QUESTIONS

Question 1

(B) $20,125 is correct. It is calculated as follows:

Least of:	(a)	income from an active business carried on in Canada	$120,000
		net of loss from an active business carried on in Canada	(0)
			$120,000
	(b)	taxable income	$132,000
	(c)	business limit: $500,000 – $385,000	$115,000

The least is (c): $115,000 × 17.5% = $20,125

(A) $17,500 is incorrect. The foreign business loss of $20,000 has been netted against the $120,000 of Canadian business income.

(C) $21,000 is incorrect. This amount is 17.5% of the Canadian active business income.

(D) $23,100 is incorrect. This amount is 17.5% of the taxable income.

Question 2

(D) is correct. M Ltd. is carrying on an active business. The business is not a personal services business as the services are provided to an associated corporation. M Ltd. and ACC Ltd. are associated. M Ltd. is not a specified investment business as the principal purpose is not to derive income from property. Thus, by default, it is carrying on an active business.

ITA: 125(7)
ITA: 256(1)(*d*)

(A) is incorrect. M Ltd. is not carrying on a personal services business for the reasons outlined above.

(B) is incorrect. M Ltd. is not carrying on a personal services business for the reasons outlined above.

(C) is incorrect. M Ltd. is not carrying on a specified investment business as the principal purpose is not to derive income from property.

Question 3

(B) $3,250 is correct. This amount is 13% of taxable income of $520,000 in excess of ABI eligible for the SBD, which is $495,000 (i.e., 13% of $520,000 – $495,000).

(A) $2,600 is incorrect. This amount is 13% of taxable income in excess of $500,000.

(C) $53,089 is incorrect. This amount is 13% × (Canadian ABI minus the SBD of $86,625 (i.e., 17.5% of $495,000)).

(D) $67,600 is incorrect. This amount is 13% × taxable income.

Question 4

(C) $74,000 is correct.

ITA: 186(1), 186(4)

Dividend received from non-connected corporation, C Ltd.:	
$120,000 × 38 1/3%	$46,000
70% of $40,000 dividend refund received by connected	
corporation, B Ltd.	28,000
	$74,000

B Ltd. is connected to A Ltd., because of *de jure* control and because A Ltd. holds more than 10% of B Ltd.

ITA: 186(2), 186(4)

CHAPTER 12

(A) $60,000 is incorrect. This amount is 70% and 8% of the dividend refunds received by B Ltd. and C Ltd., respectively.

(B) $73,600 is incorrect. This amount applies the Refundable Part I tax rate on investment income, 30⅔%, to the total dividends received.

(D) $92,000 is incorrect. This amount is 38⅓% × the dividends received and ignores the special rules for connected corporations.

Question 5

(D) is correct. Neither J Co. nor D Co. is associated with R Co., since neither Joanne nor David own at least 25% of the shares of R Co. through J Co. and D Co. Their ownership is only 22% (i.e., 55% of 40%). Hence, J Co. and D Co. cannot be associated through R Co.

ITA: 256(2)

(A) and (B) are incorrect because Joanne controls J Co. and her spouse controls D Co. Two corporations are associated under paragraph 256(1)(c), if related persons control each corporation and either person owns at least 25% of the shares of the related persons' corporation. Spouses are related by marriage.

ITA: 251(6)(b)

(C) is incorrect because if a trust for their twin daughters controls a third company, T Co., those shares are deemed to be owned by the beneficiaries. In addition, because those beneficiaries are minors, their shares are deemed to be owned by each of Joanne and Doug. Therefore, J Co. and T Co. are associated because they are deemed to be controlled by the same person (Joanne). The same is true for D Co. and T Co. (each deemed to be controlled by Doug). The two corporations are associated with each other unless an election is made to deem the third corporation (T Co.) to have a business limit of nil.

ITA: 256(1.2)(f)(ii), 256(1.3)
ITA: 256(1)(a)

ITA: 256(2)

Question 6

(C) is correct. X Ltd. and Y Ltd. are not associated because although X Ltd. is controlled by a person who is related to each member of the various groups of persons (i.e., a pair of the two daughters and one son or all three) who controls Y Ltd., there is no cross-ownership of at least 25%. Thus, X Ltd. and Y Ltd. are not associated.

ITA: 256(1)(d)

(A) is not correct. X and Y are associated. The same group (Rod and Patrick) controls both corporations. This group controls X Ltd., despite the fact that Patrick himself controls X Ltd. It does not matter that the individuals are not related.

ITA: 256(1)(b)
ITA: 256(1.2)(b)(i)

(B) is not correct because X Ltd. and Y Ltd. are associated because they are controlled by related persons (a parent and son are related by blood) and one of the persons owns not less than 25% of the shares of both companies.

ITA: 256(1)(c)
ITA: 251(6)(a)

(D) is not correct. Sibco and Parentco are associated. Sibco is controlled by a related group of two, three, or four of its shareholders. Parentco is controlled by the related group of the mother and father. Each member of any related group that controls Sibco is related to each member of the related group that controls Parentco. The mother and father, together, own at least 25% of the shares of both corporations.

ITA: 256(1)(e)

CHAPTER 12 — SOLUTIONS TO EXERCISES

Exercise 1

[Note: The facts of this case are those of *The Queen v. Rochmore Investments Ltd.* However, the legislation under which the case was decided did not contain a definition of "active business" or "specified investment business".]

76 DTC 6156 (F.C.A.)

Under the current legislation, "active business" is defined to exclude "a specified investment business" in such a way that if a business is not a specified investment business (and is not a personal service business), it is an active business. Note that the definition includes an adventure in the nature of trade and is only applicable in respect of the small business deduction.

ITA: 125(7), 248(1)

In this particular case, the facts indicate that it is carrying on a specified investment business. It would appear that the principal purpose of the corporation's business is to derive income from interest on mortgage loans. It does not appear to be carrying on the business of a credit union and it is not in the business of leasing movable property. If it did, the corporation would be considered to be carrying on an active business. Since the corporation had no full-time employees, it cannot escape the definition of a specified investment business, to be treated as an active business, through paragraph (*a*) of the definition, which requires more than five full-time employees.

ITA: 125(7)

The only possibility for escape is in paragraph (*b*) of the definition of "specified investment business". If the taxpayer company did not have more than five full-time employees because another corporation associated with it provided the services to the taxpayer corporation that would otherwise be performed by its own full-time employees, then the taxpayer corporation could be considered as carrying on an active business. In this case, the two principal operators of the taxpayer corporation own and manage a number of other companies. Further facts are required to determine if any of these other corporations are associated with the taxpayer corporation and if such an associated corporation provides services that would otherwise be provided by more than five full-time employees of the taxpayer corporation. This seems unlikely given the facts outlined in the case.

ITA: 125(7)

The taxpayer corporation, therefore, is likely carrying on a specified investment business. It is not carrying on a personal services business because it is not likely that the principals of the taxpayer corporation would reasonably be regarded as employees of the persons to whom the mortgage loans were made.

Exercise 2

(A) (i) Mr. Beta is at arm's length with the corporation because his 25% ownership does not give him control. However, paragraph 251(1)(*b*) could always apply if the facts indicate that the non-related persons are not dealing at arm's length at a particular moment in time.

ITA: 251(2)(*b*)

(ii) Mr. Beta and his brother are not at arm's length with the corporation. Mr. Beta and his brother form a related group; since they are siblings, each is related by blood.

ITA: 251(2)(*b*)(ii), 251(6)(*a*)

(iii) Mr. Delta is not at arm's length with the corporation because of the share purchase option. This provision deems Mr. Delta to control Alpha Corp. unless the exceptions in this subparagraph are met.

ITA: 251(5)(*b*)(i)

(iv) Mr. Epsilon is at arm's length with the corporation because of the exception, which is contingent on the death of Mr. Beta, unless paragraph 251(1)(*b*) applies, as described in (i), above.

ITA: 251(5)(*b*)(i)

(B) (i) The corporations are not at arm's length. This subparagraph applies where Lambda Corp. is controlled by a person (i.e., A) and Tau Corp. is controlled by a related group (i.e., A and B). A is related to himself for purposes of share ownership and to his brother.

ITA: 251(2)(*c*)(iii), 251(5)(*c*), 251(6)(*a*)

(ii) The corporations are at arm's length because subparagraph 251(2)(*c*)(iv) does not apply where there is an unrelated group of persons controlling one corporation, unless the person controlling the other corporation is related to each member of the unrelated group. For example, if two first cousins control one corporation and their grandfather controls the other, the two corporations would be related. Of course, factual non-arm's length can always apply as described in (A)(i), above.

(iii) The corporations are related and, hence, they are not at arm's length. This provision deems two corporations to be related where each corporation is related to another common corporation.

ITA: 251(3)

Exercise 3

(A) Jay-one Ltd. and Jay-two Ltd. are associated, both being controlled by the same person. Jay-one Ltd. and Jay-three Ltd., are associated. Since Ava has voting control of Jay-one Ltd. and Jay-one Ltd. in turn has voting control of Jay-three Ltd., then Ava controls Jay-three Ltd. Therefore, all three corporations are controlled by the same person. As a result of this application of the association rule in paragraph 256(1)(*b*), the election under subsection 256(2) is not available to Jay-one Ltd., because Jay-three Ltd. and Jay-two Ltd. are associated without subsection 256(2).

ITA: 251(1)(b), 256(1)(a), 256(1)(b)

(B) Benco Ltd. and Rayco Ltd. are associated. Benco Ltd. is controlled by Abigail's mother and Rayco Ltd. is controlled by Abigail. Abigail and her mother are related. Abigail owns at least 25% of the shares, which are not of a specified class, of both corporations.

ITA: 256(1)(a), 256(1)(c)

(C) Adamco Ltd. and Kidco Ltd. are associated. Adamco Ltd. is controlled by Adam. Kidco Ltd. is controlled by the group consisting of Adam, his daughter and his son-in-law. Adam is related to himself, to his daughter and to his son-in-law. Adam owns at least 25% of the shares which are not of a specified class of Kidco Ltd.

ITA: 252(1)(e), 256(1)(d), 256(1.5), 251(6)(a), 251(6)(b)

(D) Since both corporations are controlled by a group, paragraph 256(1)(*e*) is the only possibility for association. However, while Sisco Ltd. is controlled by a related group of sisters, Cousco Ltd. is not controlled by a related group. The two sisters as a group do not control Cousco Ltd. One sister and her daughter do not control the company. Finally, cousins and aunts and nieces are not related by the rules. Therefore, the condition in paragraph 256(1)(*e*) fails and the two corporations are not associated unless subsection 256(5.1) can be used with the argument that control in fact is exercised by Sister One and Sister Two through direct or indirect influence on their daughters or unless subsection 256(2.1) is invoked on the basis that one of the main reasons for the separate existence of the two corporations is to reduce taxes.

ITA: 251(6)(a)

ITA: 251, 252

Exercise 4

Taxit and Sibling are associated:

ITA: 256(1)(c)

— each corporation is controlled by one person;

— the person who controlled one was related to the person who controlled the other;

— one of these persons owned not less than 25% of the shares which are not of a specified class of each corporation.

Since the two corporations are associated, they must share the small business deduction on a maximum of $500,000 of active business income. The Act requires that the corporations file an agreement, in prescribed form, allocating the $500,000 business limit. If an agreement is not filed within the time period indicated in subsection 125(4), that subsection empowers the Minister to make an allocation.

ITA: 125(3)

They could each gain their eligibility for the small business deduction on a full $500,000 by having Beta reduce her holdings in Taxit to below 25% or by having Beta convert her holdings in Taxit to shares of a specified class (i.e., in essence, non-voting preferred shares). However, this strategy would work only as long as there are no factors present of the kind that would enable the deeming provisions to apply.

ITA: 256(2.1)

Exercise 5

Since neither corporation is controlled by one person, and both corporations are not controlled by the same group of persons, the only provision in subsection 256(1) that can potentially apply is paragraph 256(1)(*e*). That paragraph sets out three conditions, each of which must be met by the facts of the case for association.

(1) Each corporation must be controlled by a related group. — The group of brothers controlling Chutzpah Enterprises Limited is related. The group consisting of Bett and Dalled Chutzpah controlling Schlock Sales Limited are related as brother-in-law and sister-in-law or by paragraph 251(6)(*a*) and paragraphs 252(2)(*b*) and (*c*). Therefore, the condition is met.

ITA: 251(2)(a), 251(6)(a)
ITA: 251(6)(b)

(2) Each of the members of one of the related groups was related to all of the members of the other related group. — Consider the group consisting of Aleph and Bett Chutzpah which is a related group controlling Chutzpah Enterprises Limited and the group Bett and Dalled Chutzpah which is a related group controlling Schlock Sales Limited. Aleph is related to his brother Bett, as discussed above, and to Dalled. Bett is related to himself and his sister-in-law, Dalled, as discussed above. Therefore, the condition is met.

ITA: 251(2)(a), 251(6)(a), 256(1.5)

(3) One or more members of both related groups must own, either alone or together, not less than 25% of the issued shares of any class, other than a specified class, of shares of the capital stock of the other corporation. — Bett, who is a member of both related groups, owns alone the minimum 25% of the shares necessary to meet this condition. Common shares are not shares of a specified class.

ITA: 256(1.1)

Exercise 6

Part I tax payable

Part I Tax on Taxable Income

Taxable income	$ 79,700
Tax @ 38% on $79,700	$ 30,286
Deduct: Federal tax abatement (10% of $79,700)	7,970
Net	$ 22,316

Additional refundable tax (ART) — 10⅔% × lesser of:

(a) AII	$ 7,000	
(b) TI – SBD income amount (Schedule 1)	-	
Total		$ 22,316
Deduct small business deduction (see Schedule 1) ...	13,948	
General reduction (see Schedule 2)	Nil	13,948
Part I federal tax payable		$ 8,368
Provincial tax @ 5% of $79,700		3,985
Total tax payable		$ 12,353

Schedule 1: *Small Business Deduction*

17.5% of the least of:

Income from an active business	$110,000(I)
Taxable income	$ 79,700(II)
Business limit	$500,000(III)

Small business deduction — 17.5% of $79,700 = $13,948

Schedule 2: *General Reduction*

Taxable income		$ 79,700
Less: income eligible for the small business deduction	$79,700	
AII	7,000	(86,700)
Net		Nil
13% of Nil		Nil
Total		$ Nil

Exercise 7

(A) *Part I Tax on Taxable Income*

Tax @ 38% of $130,000	$ 49,400
Deduct: federal tax abatement (10% of $130,000)	13,000
Net	$ 36,400

Additional refundable tax (ART) — 10⅔% of lesser of:

(a) AII ($100K + $20K + $50K – $20K – $50K) = $100,000	
(b) TI – SBD income amount ($130K – $90K) = $40,000	4,267
Total	$ 40,667

Deduct: small business deduction (see Schedule 1)	15,750	
general reduction	Nil	15,750
Part I tax payable (federal)		$ 24,917
Provincial tax @ 7% of $130,000		9,100
Total tax		$ 34,017

Schedule 1: *Small Business Deduction*

17.5% of least of:

Income from active business	$ 90,000(I)
Taxable income	$130,000(II)
Business limit	$500,000(III)
Small business deduction — 17.5% of $90,000	$ 15,750

(B) *Refundable Portion of Part I Tax*

Least of:

(a) 30⅔% × aggregate investment income (30⅔% × $100,000)		$ 30,667
(b) Taxable income	$130,000	
Less: amount eligible for SBD	(90,000)	
30⅔% × $40,000 =		$ 12,267
(c) Part I tax		$ 24,917
Refundable portion of Part I tax — The least		$ 12,267

Part IV Tax on Taxable Dividends Received

Taxable dividends subject to Part IV tax:

Non-connected corporations × 38⅓ ($30,000 × 38⅓%)	$ 11,500
Connected corporations to the extent of share of dividend refund to payer	4,000
Total Part IV tax payable	$ 15,500

Refundable Dividend Tax on Hand

RDTOH at end of last year		Nil
Deduct: Dividend refund for last year	Nil	Nil
Add: Refundable portion of Part I tax		$ 12,267
Part IV tax		15,500
RDTOH at end of year		$ 27,767

Dividend Refund

Taxable dividends paid in year ($70,000 × 38⅓%)	$ 26,833(VI)
RDTOH at end of year	$ 27,767(VII)
Dividend refund — lesser of (VI) and (VII)	$ 26,833

Exercise 8

(A) Sunlight Limited and H Ltd. are associated. H Ltd. is controlled by one person, Mr. Bennett. He is related to each member of the group, H Ltd. and W Ltd. that controls Sunlight Limited, because he is related to H Ltd. which he controls and he is related to W Ltd., which is controlled by his wife. Also, he owns not less than 25% of the shares of Sunlight Limited through his ownership of shares in H Ltd. These shares are not specified shares. By a similar analysis, Sunlight Limited and W Ltd. are associated. *ITA: 256(1)(d)* *ITA: 251(2)(b)(i), 251(2)(b)(iii)* *ITA: 256(1.2)(d)*

Since the rental income would be deductible as an expense from the income of an active business of an associated payer, it will not be income from property of the recipient. It will be deemed to be income from an active business of the recipient, H Ltd. Since H Ltd. has only dividend income it will be eligible for the small business deduction in respect of the rental income as long as it is allocated a part of the business limit of the associated corporations. *ITA: 129(6)(a)(i)* *ITA: 129(6)(b)(i)* *ITA: 125(1)*

(B) Since Sunlight is connected with both holding companies there will be no Part IV tax liability unless Sunlight gets a dividend refund as a result of the dividends it pays. However, Sunlight earns only active business income which is not subject to refundable taxes and dividend refunds.

Exercise 9

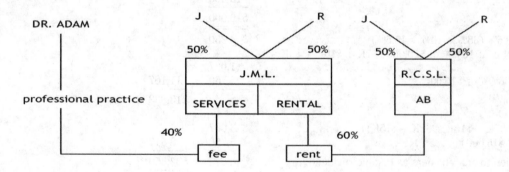

(A) Rent from RCSL:

(i) RCSL is associated with JML; *ITA: 256(1)(b)*

(ii) RCSL deducts the rent from its active business.

Therefore, the rent is deemed to be income of JML from an active business, eligible for the small business deduction. *ITA: 125(1), 129(6)(b)(i)*

(B) Services fee from Dr. Adam:

(i) JML's income from providing services would be considered income from an active business unless further facts indicate that it is carrying on a personal services business;

(ii) the business of providing services would be a personal services business if one or both of the shareholders of JML, who are specified shareholders (because they own at least 10% of the shares of JML), performed the services and would be regarded as an employee of the professional practice of Dr. Adam.

Therefore, if the services fee is considered income from an active business, it would qualify for the small business deduction.

Exercise 10

Interest income		$ 7,000
Dividends grossed up (1.17 × $15,000)		17,550
Taxable capital gains (½ × $6,000)		3,000
Incremental taxable income		$27,550
Federal tax on total taxable income of $47,550 (i.e., $27,550 incremental + $20,000 other income):		
Tax on first $45,282	$ 6,792	
Tax on next $2,268 @ 20.5%	465	$ 7,257
Less: dividend tax credit (²¹/₂₉ × 17% of $15,000)	$ 1,847	
other personal tax credits	1,800	(3,647)
Basic federal tax		$ 3,610
Provincial tax		
Tax on first $45,282	$ 4,395	
Tax on next $2,268 @ 12%	272	4,667
Less: dividend tax credit (⁸/₂₉ × 17% of $15,000)	$ 703	
other personal tax credits	1,200	(1,903)
Total tax on taxable income of $47,550		$ 6,374

Taxation of Income from Investment Portfolio through a Corporation

Corporation		*Available cash*
Interest income	$ 7,000	
Dividends	15,000	
Taxable capital gains	3,000	
Income	$25,000	$25,000[1]
Less: dividends [sec. 112]	15,000	
Taxable income	$10,000	
Tax under Part I @ 43.5% (38% − 10% + 15.5%)	$ 4,350	
Additional refundable tax at 10⅔% of $10,000 ($7K + $15K + $3K − $15K)	1,067	
Tax under Part IV @ 38⅓% of $15,000	5,750	11,167
Retained in corporation[1]		$13,833
Refundable tax:		
Part I (30⅔% of ($7K + $15K + $3K − $15K))	$ 3,067	
Part IV (38⅓% × $15,000)	5,750	8,817
Available for distribution to shareholders as taxable dividend		$22,650[2]

Shareholder		
Taxable dividend (per requirements)		$15,000
Gross-up (17% of $15,000)		2,550
Incremental taxable income		$17,550
Federal tax on total taxable income of $37,550 (i.e., $17,550 incremental + $20,000 other income):		
Tax @ 15%		$ 5,633
Less: dividend tax credit (²¹/₂₉ × 17% of $15,000)	$1,847	
other personal tax credits	1,800	(3,647)
Basic federal tax		$ 1,986
Provincial tax		
Tax @ 10%		$ 3,755
Less: dividend tax credit (⁸/₂₉ × 17% of $15,000)	$ 703	
other personal tax credits	1,200	(1,903)
Total tax on taxable income of $38,750		$ 3,838

Total Taxes Paid

Through corporation:

    Corporation after refund on $15,000 of dividends paid

        ($11,167 – 38⅓% × $15,000) .... $ 5,417

      Shareholder 3,838

Total .... $ 9,255

Received directly .... $ 6,374

—NOTES TO SOLUTION

[1] Ignores the non-taxable portion of capital gain which can be distributed tax free.

[2] Note that a dividend of $22,650 will result in a dividend refund of only $8,682 (i.e., $22,650 × 38⅓%), not the $8,817 that was added to the RDTOH for the year. This deficiency results from imperfections in the tax rates. A larger dividend of $23,000 (i.e., $8,817/38.33%) would have to be paid, using other sources of funds, to clear the RDTOH.

Exercise 11

The two corporations are considered associated for Canadian tax purposes. Generally, interest income received from an associated corporation that is deductible in computing that corporation's active business income would be considered active business income. However, as the interest is U.S.-sourced, and not from a "source in Canada", and is not deductible in computing active business income in Canada, it will be considered investment income to the Canadian corporation and not income from an active business. Hence, the small business deduction will not apply.

ITA: 256
ITA: 129(6)

The interest will be subject to the full corporate tax rate, including the 10⅔% additional refundable tax on investment income. The addition to RDTOH (30⅔%) will also apply.

ITA: 123.3, 129(1)

CHAPTER 12

Chapter 13

Planning the Use of a Corporation and Shareholder-Manager Remuneration

Learning Goals

Know

By the end of this chapter you will know:

- The common elements of compensation for a corporation's shareholder-manager.
- The basic elements of the capital gains exemption.
- The issues related to the general anti-avoidance rule.

Understand and Explain

By the end of this chapter you will understand and be able to explain:

- The issues related to the choice of different types of compensation for a shareholder-manager.
- The benefits of the capital gains exemption.
- The rewards and risks of income splitting using a corporation.
- Why the general anti-avoidance rule is designed the way it is.

Apply

By the end of this chapter you will be able to apply your knowledge and understanding to:

- Choose the compensation plan for a shareholder-manager.
- Determine whether the capital gains exemption applies.
- Calculate the capital gains exemption.
- Calculate the benefits and penalties from income splitting using a corporation.

Review Questions
¶13,800 in the Study Guide

Multiple Choice Questions
¶13,825 in the Study Guide

Exercise Questions
¶13,850 in the Study Guide

Assignment Problems
¶13,875 in the Study Guide

CHAPTER 13 — LEARNING CHART

Problem Descriptions

Textbook Example Problems

1	Shareholder benefit
2	Shareholder benefit
3	Shareholder loan
4	Shareholder loan
5	Shareholder loan — deemed interest benefit
6	Salary vs. dividends
7	Salary vs. dividends
8	Small business corporation
9	QSBC
10	QSBC — modified asset test
11	Capital gains deduction
12	Corporate attribution

Multiple Choice Questions

1	Shareholder loan
2	Shareholder loan
3	Deductibility of bonus
4	GAAR
5	GAAR
6	Corporate attribution
7	Small business corporation

Exercises

1	Bonus payable
2	Shareholder loan
3	Shareholder loan — series of transactions
4	Shareholder loan — car
5	Shareholder loan — car
6	Salary vs. dividend
7	Salary vs. dividend
8	Small business corporation
9	Capital gains deduction
10	Corporate attribution
11	GAAR
12	GAAR

Assignment Problems

1	QSBC shares
2	QSBC shares
3	Capital gains deduction
4	Corporate attribution
5	GAAR
6	GAAR
7	Shareholder benefit
8	Shareholder loans
9	Shareholder loans

Problem Descriptions

10	Shareholder loans
11	Incorporation, compensation
12	Incorporation, compensation
13	Salary/dividend planning
14	Owner/manager advice
15	Tax planning, GAAR

Study Notes

¶13,800   REVIEW QUESTIONS

(1) Mr. Smith owns a small manufacturing company that has suddenly become very profitable. This year his accountant has told him to declare a bonus to himself of approximately $150,000 in order to reduce his corporate income to the business limit. His dilemma is that he also needs the money in his business in order to finance expansion. What should he do?

(2) Mr. Jones owns a distributing company that is earning well over $500,000 each year. He has been declaring a bonus to himself each year but is now rethinking this strategy. What items should he consider when deciding whether to pay the bonus or leave the money in the company? Assume that the provincial corporate income tax rate is 13% on their income in excess of the small business deduction limit.

(3) What is the range of fiscal year-ends that might be chosen to allow the owner of a company to declare a bonus and be taxed on it personally in either of two calendar years?

(4) What are the five criteria for the deductibility of bonus accruals as decided in the *Totem Disposal* case?

(5) Mr. Chow is the sole shareholder of Chocobar Inc. His wife's brother has just come to him and asked to borrow some money in order to start up his professional accounting practice. Mr. Chow has decided to have Chocobar Inc. lend his wife's brother $20,000 on October 31, 2016, with interest only for the first two years and then principal payments of $10,000 per year starting in the third year. The fiscal year-end of the company is December 31. Discuss the tax implications of the loan.

(6) Ms. Jones is the President and sole shareholder of a construction company. She has two vice-presidents who are not related to her. As part of their compensation package she has agreed that all employees of the company are entitled to an interest-free loan from the company of up to $25,000. Ms. Jones herself has taken her $25,000 loan and bought a boat. Comment.

(7) If your province of residence were to declare a tax holiday for all CCPCs, what impact would this have on compensation for your owner-manager clients?

(8) How much personal tax will a single individual pay on $30,000 of non-eligible dividend income if that is his or her only source of income and his or her only non-refundable tax credit is his or her personal credit.

(9) Ms. Simpson owned 10% of the shares of a small business corporation that went out of business. Six months after it ceased business she sold her shares to an arm's length person, Mr. X, for $1. When she went to claim a loss on her investment she did not know how much she could write off. In order to have the loss treated as an ABIL, the company needed to be a small business corporation at the time of sale and at that time it did not have any assets used in an active business. She has not used any of her capital gains exemption before. Can you clarify this situation for her?

(10) What does the phrase "all or substantially all" mean?

(11) A corporation that has had 40% of its assets invested in term deposits for the last two years, and the balance in active business assets, qualifies as a "small business corporation" but not a "qualified small business corporation". Do you agree or disagree? Explain.

(12) Mr. Smith incorporated his company 20 years ago for $100 of share capital. It has prospered since then and it now has some excess capital. He has decided to have his wife set up an investment holding company and his company will lend her company $100,000 of cash for her to invest and thereby split income. Will the attribution rules apply?

¶13,825   MULTIPLE CHOICE QUESTIONS

Question 1

Stan owns 100% of the shares of S Ltd. which has a December 31 year end. He is also an employee of S Ltd. On January 1, 2016, S Ltd. loaned Stan $200,000 interest-free to assist him in purchasing a new home. Stan signed a promissory note for the loan. Under the terms of the note, the loan is to be repaid in five equal annual instalments commencing January 1, 2017. Such a loan is not available to other employees. Which *one* of the following statements is *true* under current tax administrative practice?

(A) Stan will have $200,000 included in his income in 2016.

(B) Stan will have $160,000 included in his income in 2016.

(C) An imputed interest benefit will be calculated for 2016 using a rate not in excess of the rate in effect at January 1, 2016, as the loan was used to purchase a home.

(D) The portion of the loan not repaid by December 31, 2017, will be included in Stan's income in 2018.

Question 2

In 2016, S Ltd., which has a December 31 year end, made the following loans to shareholders. All of the shareholders are resident in Canada and are not related to S Ltd. This was the first time that these shareholders had received a loan or had become indebted to S. Ltd. Since S Ltd. was not in the business of lending money, it was very careful, in each case, to ensure that *bona fide* arrangements were made at the time the loan was made for repayment of the loan within a reasonable time. Taking all this into consideration, which one of the following loan principal amounts will be included in the borrower's income in 2016?

(A) A loan to Mrs. A, a vice-president and 20% shareholder. The loan was made to assist Mrs. A in the purchase of newly issued shares of S Ltd. The loan was made on April 1, 2016, and repaid on April 1, 2017. No other employees have received similar loans.

(B) A loan made to B Ltd., a corporation which is a 20% shareholder of S Ltd. The loan was used to help B Ltd. repurchase some of its shares for cancellation and pay off a bank loan.

(C) A loan to Mrs. C, a vice-president and 20% shareholder. The loan was made to assist Mrs. C in the purchase of a home. The loan was made on April 1, 2016, and will be repaid on April 1, 2018. No other employees have received similar loans.

(D) A loan to Mr. D, an S Ltd. vice-president and 5% shareholder. Mr. D deals at arm's length with S Ltd. The loan was made to assist Mr. D in the purchase of a home computer for employment use. Five other employees of the company currently work at home and have received similar loans. None of the other employees are shareholders. Mr. D's loan was made on April 1, 2016, and will be repaid on April 1, 2018.

Question 3

In computing the net income on the financial statement of Fortelli Inc. for its year ended December 31, 2016, bonuses of $300,000 were accrued. On August 15, 2017, $100,000 of the bonus was paid to the owner-manager, and the remaining $200,000 of bonuses were paid to the sales staff on August 31, 2017. Which one of the following statements is *true*?

(A) If the $100,000 bonus, due to a related party, was not paid by December 31, 2018, it would be included in Fortelli Inc.'s income in the year 2019.

(B) The $100,000 bonus is not deductible in 2016, but the $200,000 bonus is deductible.

(C) An election is available to deem the bonus paid and loaned back to the corporation. This election can be used if the bonuses are not going to be paid by the appropriate deadline.

(D) The $300,000 bonus is not deductible in 2016.

Question 4

The Act contains a general anti-avoidance provision often referred to as the GAAR. Which one of the following statements concerning the GAAR is *false*?

(A) The tax benefit that results from an avoidance transaction will be denied.

(B) When the GAAR is applied, a penalty will be assessed, in addition to the tax owing plus interest.

(C) An avoidance transaction is any transaction that results in a tax benefit, unless the transaction can reasonably be considered to have a *bona fide* purpose other than obtaining the tax benefit.

(D) The GAAR applies to transactions that result in a misuse or abuse of the Act read as a whole.

Question 5

The general anti-avoidance provision, GAAR, is most likely to apply to which *one* of the following transactions?

(A) As part of an estate freeze, Bill had a trust for his adult children acquire 80% of the common shares of B Ltd. Until then, Bill had owned all the shares of B Ltd., a successful grocery retail outlet. Each year B Ltd. pays dividends to the trust which are paid to the children. The dividends are received by the children tax-free due to the dividend tax credit, since, as university students, they have no other income.

(B) Sam transferred his unincorporated pizza business, on tax-deferred basis, to a corporation, for the sole purpose of reducing tax by claiming the small business deduction.

(C) Paul gave his son a gift of $10,000 and the son invested it in dividend-paying shares. His son does not pay tax on the dividend income as he is a 19-year-old student with little other income. Paul will celebrate his 65th birthday two years after his son graduates. It is anticipated that Paul will receive a birthday gift of $10,000 from his son at that time.

(D) Mary owns all the shares of M Ltd., a CCPC which carries on an active business. For M Ltd.'s taxation year ended June 30, 2016, Mary accrued herself a bonus of $700,000 which reduced M Ltd.'s taxable income to $300,000.

Question 6

Mrs. Boehmer owns all the Class A common shares of a corporation which has an investment portfolio worth $500,000. The corporation has no other assets and has a December 31 year-end. On January 1 of the current year, Mr. Boehmer (Mrs. Boehmer's husband) subscribed for $1 million of Class B shares of the corporation and paid for them in cash. The purpose of this transaction was to income-split with his wife. The corporation earned $10,000 during the year and paid a $10,000 cash dividend to Mrs. Boehmer. Assuming the prescribed rate is 3% throughout the year, what is the minimum amount of income that Mr. Boehmer must report in the year in respect of his investment in the corporation?

(A) $10,000

(B) $11,800

(C) $15,000

(D) $30,000

Question 7

Ms. Prentice owns P Ltd., a Canadian-controlled private corporation with assets worth $4 million and liabilities amounting to $1 million. Sixty per cent of its assets are used in an active business carried on in Canada by the corporation and 20% are used in an active business carried on in Canada by a corporation controlled by Ms. Prentice's brother. The remaining assets (non-active business assets) earn investment income. Which of the following is the minimum amount of non-active business assets that P Co must sell in order for its shares to qualify as shares of a small business corporation? Assume that the after-tax proceeds on the sale will be used to pay off some of the corporation's liabilities.

(A) None

(B) $400,000

(C) $444,445

(D) $1,333,333

¶13,850   EXERCISES

Exercise 1

ITA: 78

Slipit Ltd. declared a bonus payable of $10,000 to Mr. Schneider, its president and majority shareholder, on September 30, 2016, its fiscal year end. If the bonus is paid it will be subject to withholding tax in the amount of $3,500.

— *REQUIRED*

(A) If the corporation is to get a deduction with no future consequences for the bonus payable, by what date must the bonus be paid?

(B) What are the consequences of not paying the bonus by this date?

(C) Assume that, instead of a bonus, the amount owing to Mr. Schneider is rent, properly included on the cash basis, on the only rental property he owns and rents to the corporation:

(i) If the corporation is to get a deduction with no future consequences for the rent payable, by what date must the rent be paid?

(ii) What are the consequences of not paying the rent by this date?

(iii) How can these consequences be avoided without paying the rent?

Exercise 2

ITA: 15(2), 80.4

Mr. Nesbitt relocated his private business, Leverage-Lovers Limited, to Alberta from Ontario at the end of May 2015. As a result of the move, the corporation made the following loans on June 1, 2016 to Mr. Nesbitt, the president and majority shareholder:

(a) a $75,000 loan at 2% interest per year with a five-year term but amortized over a 25-year period to purchase a house in the new location;

(b) a $5,000 loan at 5% interest per year with no definite term to buy furniture for the new house; and

(c) a $10,000 loan with no interest but with a five-year term to buy previously unissued, fully paid shares from the corporation.

The corporation uses the calendar year as its fiscal year and by the end of 2017 the loans described were still outstanding. Any interest required to be paid on the loans at the indicated rates was paid in 2016. Assume that the prescribed rates applicable to shareholder loans during 2016 were: 1st quarter, 4%; 2nd quarter, 3%; 3rd quarter, 4%; and 4th quarter, 4%. Ignore the effects of the leap year, if applicable.

— *REQUIRED*

Discuss the tax consequences in 2016 of the loan described, if Mr. Nesbitt received the loans:

(A) by virtue of his employment;

(B) by virtue of his shareholdings.

Exercise 3

ITA: 15(2), 20(1)(*j*)

Mr. Sims is a shareholder of Wonder Ltd. which has a December 31 year-end. Consider the following transactions in his shareholder loan account:

Date	Loan (repayment)	Balance
Dec. 31/Year 1	—	Nil
Jan. 31/Year 2	$ 20,000	$ 20,000
Apr. 30/Year 2	25,000	45,000
June 30/Year 3	(15,000)	30,000
Sept. 30/Year 3	(17,000)	13,000
Mar. 31/Year 4	(12,000)	1,000
Nov. 30/Year 4	10,000	11,000
May 31/Year 5	(11,000)	Nil
Nov. 30/Year 5	23,000	23,000
July 31/Year 6	(14,000)	9.000
Dec. 31/Year 6	—	9,000

— REQUIRED

(A) If it is assumed that these transactions result in the conclusion that there is a series of loans and repayments, compute the principal amounts that must be included or the repayments that may be deducted for each of the years indicated according to the guidelines in IT-119R4.

(B) If there has not been a series of loans and repayments, how would the amounts differ from the above? How would you argue there was no series of loans and repayments?

Exercise 4

ITA: 15(2), 80.4; ITR: 4300

Colton Marlach is a major shareholder and senior executive of Burlon Ltd. He was required to use a car about 60% for the duties of his employment. On April 1, under a plan available to the five other senior executives of the corporation, he was granted a loan of $35,000 at a rate of interest of 1% *per annum* and agreed to annual payments on the anniversary day of $7,000 for principal and monthly payments of interest at the end of each month. During the year, he faithfully made the monthly interest payments for seven months but neglected to make the interest payments for the last two months of the year.

— REQUIRED

What are the income tax consequences to the taxpayer? Assume that the prescribed rates were as follows:

first quarter 2%	third quarter 2%
second quarter 1%	fourth quarter 3%

Ignore the effects of the leap year, if applicable.

Exercise 5

ITA: 6(1)

Consider the data provided in Exhibit 13-4 in ¶13,100.

— REQUIRED

Analyze the situation if the business use of the car is 20,000 out of 30,000 km.

Exercise 6

ITA: 82(1), 117, 121, 123–125

Payton Hewitt is the sole shareholder and employee of Conduit Corporation Ltd. which operates a processing business in a province with a 4% corporate rate (i.e., a total corporate rate of 14.5%) on its income. The corporation has income of $20,000 before salaries and corporate taxes which is eligible for the small business deduction. Mr. Hewitt has no other income and has federal tax credits of $2,000 and provincial tax credits of $1,290. He requires all of the income generated by the business.

— REQUIRED

Consider the following three remuneration alternatives:

(A) all salary,

(B) all dividends, and

(C) $10,000 in salary and the remainder in dividends.

Compare the net cash to Mr. Hewitt for these alternatives ignoring employment income deductions available to an employee. Can the best of these alternatives be improved upon?

Exercise 7

ITA: 82(1), 117, 121, 123–125

Aaron Storey is a sole proprietor generating $80,000 in income before taxes from a processing business operating in a province with a 4% corporate rate (i.e., a total corporate rate of 14.5%). He requires $25,000 before taxes for living expenses and has federal personal tax credits of $2,100 and provincial tax credits of $1,400. He has no other source of income or deductions (except as assumed for (B)(iii), below). The business has a December 31 taxation year-end.

¶13,850

— REQUIRED

(A) Compute the tax that would be paid if he continues to operate the business as an unincorporated proprietorship.

(B) Compare your answer in (A) with the total tax that would be paid if he incorporates the business and remunerates himself by the following alternative methods:

(i) $25,000 in salary;

(ii) $25,000 in dividends; and

(iii) $3,435 in salary and $21,565 in dividends.

Ignore deductions available to employees. (Assume that the excess federal or provincial tax credits resulting from this case can be used against tax on other income.)

Exercise 8

ITA: 248(1)

Consider each of the following independent proportions of assets at fair market value. Assume the assets are owned by a Canadian-controlled private corporation. Active business assets refer to assets used principally in an active business carried on primarily in Canada.

	A	B	C	D
Active business assets	85%	50%	—	40%
Marketable securities	15	—	20%	20
Shares of a connected small business corporation	—	50	80	40
	100%	100%	100%	100%

— REQUIRED

Determine whether each of the above proportions meets the test of a small business corporation as defined in the Act.

Exercise 9

ITA: 110.6

Bobby Mills has provided you with the following information:

	2014	2015	2016
Taxable capital gains on sale of qualified small business corporation shares	$75,000	—	$300,000
Business investment loss (before ssec. 39(9) adjustment)	—	—	160,000
Interest income	—	$ 600	1,200
Grossed-up taxable dividends	—	140	—
Net rental income (loss).	—	(1,100)	(220)
Carrying charges	—	1,075	—

The 2014 taxable capital gain was fully offset by a capital gains deduction in that year.

— REQUIRED

Determine Bobby's capital gains deduction for 2016 supported by all the necessary calculations. Assume that there were no other capital transactions before 2014.

Exercise 10

ITA: 74.4

Mrs. Albert owns all of the outstanding common shares of a corporation, Prince Albert Inc., which operates a small retail store in Saskatoon. Her husband owns the building with a fair market value of $200,000, in which the store is located. He is planning to transfer it to Prince Albert Inc. in exchange for $60,000 of cash, a 5% demand note for $20,000 and preference shares for $120,000. The fair market value of the business assets (which are all of the assets excluding cash used to pay for the building) in the company immediately before the transfer is $600,000. Of the total space in the building, 20% is used in the retail business. The net rental income that Mr. Albert earned in the previous year was $20,000.

— REQUIRED

Determine the tax consequences, if any, to Mr. Albert for 2016, assuming the prescribed interest rate is a constant 4% and that the sale took place on January 1, 2016. The corporation's year-end is September 30. Dividends of $2,000 were paid on the preference shares in 2016.

ITR: 4301(c)

¶13,850

Exercise 11

ITA: 245

Gangster Production Ltd., a Canadian-controlled private corporation, paid its shareholder-manager, Herb, a salary of $250,000 which reduced the corporation's income to $499,500 for the taxation year. The amount of the salary is considered to be reasonable.

— *REQUIRED*

Determine whether the general anti-avoidance rule (GAAR) would apply in this situation.

Exercise 12

Over the past two years, your client, a lawyer in sole practice, has developed several software packages for the preparation of legal contracts. At a recent small-business seminar, your client learned that she could pay her spouse and children a salary. By doing so, your client's total tax paid as a family unit would drop substantially.

— *REQUIRED*

If tax is avoided, how would the general anti-avoidance rule affect the transactions?

¶13,875 ASSIGNMENT PROBLEMS

Type 1 Problems

Problem 1

ITA: 110.6

Karen owns all the common shares of K Ltd. which was incorporated in 2000 to hold her 85% interest in Cyber Corp. Cyber Corp. distributes computer equipment and games to retail stores in southern Ontario. Both corporations are CCPCs. The following is a balance sheet prepared as at December 31, 2016.

Cyber Corp.
Balance Sheet
as at December 31, 2016

Assets

Cash	$ 4,500
Marketable securities (FMV $700,000)	300,000
Accounts receivable (FMV $780,000)	800,000
Inventory (FMV $920,000)	920,000
Prepaid expenses (FMV $1,000)	1,000
Fixed assets (FMV $150,000)	140,000
	$2,165,500

Liabilities & Shareholders' Equity

Accounts payable and accrued liabilities	$ 600,000
Loans payable	400,000
Future income taxes	100,000
Share capital	1,000
Retained earnings	1,064,500
	$2,165,500

The relative values of Cyber Corp.'s assets have remained stable over the past three years. The marketable securities comprise Cyber Corp.'s investment portfolio which is not held as part of the corporation's business activities. The estimated value of the goodwill of the business is $200,000.

K Ltd. was recently offered $1,450,000 for the 85% interest in Cyber Corp. However, Karen has talked the prospective purchaser into buying the shares of K Ltd. instead of the shares of Cyber Corp., as she understands that by selling the shares of K Ltd. she is able to receive a tax-free capital gain.

K Ltd. has term deposits of $100,000 in addition to the shares of Cyber Corp.

Karen would like your advice on the following:

(A) Are the shares of K Ltd. qualified small business corporation (QSBC) shares?

(B) If the shares of K Ltd. are not QSBC shares, then suggest a method for purifying K Ltd. and indicate the tax consequences of your recommendations.

Problem 2

ITA: 110.6

Rogo Dan owns all of the common shares of Julie Inc. which in turn owns all of the shares of two other companies, Opco Inc. and RE Inc. Opco Inc. carries on an active business in Sudbury. RE Inc. owns real estate, of which 100% is used by Opco Inc. in its business. All three corporations are CCPCs. The following are further details:

Julie Inc. assets:	
Shares of Opco Inc. at FMV	$850,000
Shares of RE Inc. at FMV	800,000
Portfolio investments at FMV	75,000
Opco Inc. assets and liabilities:	
Active business assets at FMV	$900,000
Term deposits	50,000
Liabilities	100,000
RE Inc. assets and liabilities:	
Land and building at FMV	$800,000
Portfolio investments at FMV	200,000
Mortgage	200,000

The proportion of assets in each of the companies has been constant over the past three years. Rogo has owned the shares of Julie Inc. for the past five years.

Rogo would like your advice on the following:

(A) Does Julie Inc. meet each of the three tests necessary for its shares to be qualifying small business corporation shares.

(B) If the shares of Julie Inc. are not QSBC shares, then suggest ways of purifying Julie Inc. and indicate the tax consequences of your recommendations.

Problem 3

ITA: 110.6

Phil Zamboni realized taxable capital gains of $12,000 in 1999. This gain was offset by a capital gains deduction of $12,000 in that year.

In 2014, Zamboni received interest income of $825 and grossed-up taxable dividends of $200. He also incurred a net rental loss of $15,000 and carrying charges totalling $1,475 in 2014.

In 2015, Zamboni earned investment income of $200. He had a rental loss that year in the amount of $13,000 and carrying charges of $2,000. He also realized a business investment loss of $20,000 in December 2015.

In 2016, Zamboni sold the shares of Maps Unlimited Ltd., a qualified small business corporation, for a capital gain of $185,000 and he realized a capital loss of $21,000 on the sale of public company shares. He also received $1,650 in interest and incurred a net rental loss of $1,000 in 2016.

Zamboni had no other previous capital transactions, investment income, or investment expenses.

Phil has asked you to calculate his capital gains deduction for 2016 supported by all the necessary calculations.

Problem 4

ITA: 74.4

Bob Smith incorporated Smith Inc. 20 years ago and owns all of the shares himself. Smith Inc. is a "small business corporation" which carries on an active business in Victoria, B.C. Thirteen years ago, Bob felt that he would like to involve his wife Betty in the share ownership and, on the advice of his accountant, Holdco Inc. was incorporated with Bob and Betty each owning 50 common shares which they bought for $1 each with their own funds. Bob then transferred his common shares of Smith Inc., which were worth $600,000, to Holdco Inc. on a tax-free basis. As consideration for the transfer, Bob received 6% non-cumulative preference shares with a fair market value of $600,000.

On July 1, 2016, Smith Inc. sold some property that was used in the active business for net proceeds of $150,000. This amount was then paid as a dividend from Smith Inc. to Holdco Inc. on the same day. Bob and Betty plan to have the corporation invest this amount and use it as capital for their retirement. After the sale of the property and the payment of the dividend to Holdco Inc., Smith Inc. has a fair market value of $800,000 and is still a "small business corporation". Bob received $6,000 in dividends on his preferred shares of Holdco Inc.

Bob and Betty have asked you to explain the tax consequences of the 2016 transactions as they relate to the corporate attribution rules. Assume that the prescribed rate for 2016 was 4%.

ITR: 4301(c)

Problem 5

ITA: 245

Consider each of the following independent fact situations.

(1) Adam Aref has contributed the maximum amount to an RRSP on the first business day of each year in respect of the previous year and shortly thereafter has withdrawn the funds.

(2) Bill Sheridan loaned his wife $1,000,000 five years ago through a non-interest bearing promissory note. His wife invested the funds in GICs and earned $80,000 of interest income which was properly attributed to him, except for any compound interest. Bill gave his wife another cash amount to cover the income tax on the compound interest.

¶13,875

(3) Wells Ltd. is owned 100% by Mrs. Hogart. Stieb Ltd. is owned by Mrs. Hogart's husband and minor children. Wells Ltd. made an interest-free loan out of its taxable surplus to Stieb Ltd. such that the corporate attribution rule does not apply. Stieb Ltd. used the proceeds of the loan to earn property income.

(4) Traub has $200,000 of investments and a mortgage on his personal home for a similar amount. Traub sold the investments, paid off the mortgage, and reborrowed to acquire the investments.

(5) Andy made a loan to his adult child's corporation, Vancouver Hockey Puck Ltd., in order to avoid attribution, since the corporation used the funds to earn property income.

Discuss whether the general anti-avoidance rule (GAAR) applies to the above situations.

Problem 6   ITA: 245; IC 88-2

Consider each of the following independent fact situations:

(1) An individual transfers his or her unincorporated business to a corporation primarily to obtain the benefit of the small business deduction.

(2) An individual provides services to a corporation with which he or she does not deal at arm's length. The company does not pay a salary to the individual because payment of a salary would increase the amount of a loss that the company will incur in the year.

(3) A taxable Canadian corporation, which is profitable, has a wholly owned taxable Canadian corporation that is sustaining losses and needs additional capital to carry on its business. The subsidiary could borrow the monies from its bank but the subsidiary could not obtain any tax saving in the current year by deducting the interest expense. Therefore, the parent corporation borrows the money from its bank and subscribes for additional common shares of the subsidiary and reduces its net income by deducting the interest from its business.

(4) Profitco and Lossco are taxable Canadian corporations. Lossco is a wholly owned subsidiary of Profitco. Lossco has non-capital losses that would be deductible if Lossco had income. In order to generate income in Lossco from which its non-capital losses may be deducted, Profitco borrows from its bank and uses the monies to subscribe for common shares of Lossco. Lossco lends these monies to Profitco at a commercial rate of interest. Profitco repays the bank. The amount of share subscription is not in excess of the amount of monies that Lossco could reasonably be expected to be able to borrow for use in its business on the basis solely of its credit from an arm's length lender.

(5) Each of two private corporations owns less than 10% of the common shares of a payer corporation that is to pay a substantial taxable dividend. The payer corporation will not be entitled to a dividend refund on the payment of the dividend. None of the corporations is related to any of the others. The private corporations form a corporation, Newco, transfer their shares of the payer corporation to Newco in exchange for common shares of Newco, and elect under subsection 85(1) (assume that this is done correctly to avoid tax on the transfer) in respect of the transfer. Following the transfer of the payer corporation's shares to Newco, Newco will be connected with the payer corporation. The payer corporation pays the dividend to Newco, free of Part IV tax. Newco pays the same amount to the private corporations as a dividend, free of Part IV tax. The primary purpose of the transfer of the shares is to avoid the Part IV tax which would be payable if the dividend were received directly by the private corporations.

(6) The owner of land inventory has agreed to sell the property to an arm's length purchaser. The purchaser wants to buy the property for cash, but the owner does not want to have the profits recognized in the year of sale. The owner sells the land inventory to an intermediary company deferring receipt of the proceeds of disposition of the land for several years after the date of sale. In this way, a reserve can be claimed under paragraph 20(1)(n). The intermediary sells the land to the third party for cash. The owner receives interest from the intermediary in respect of the monies received by the intermediary from the third party.

For each of these fact situations, advise whether the part of the general anti-avoidance rule (GAAR) that asks the question "can it reasonably be considered that the transaction would not result, directly or indirectly, in a misuse of the provisions of the Act or an abuse having regard to the provisions of the Act read as a whole" applies.

Type 2 Problems

Problem 7

ITA: 15(1), 18(1)

Mia Gibbons is a vice-president of Pump You Up Ltd., a private corporation she started and currently owns with three of her university colleagues. Mia has recently signed a lease for an upscale downtown condominium which she intends to move into next month. It has been agreed that Pump You Up Ltd. will pay the $2,000 monthly rental for the condominium.

Mia has asked you to explain the income tax consequences of this arrangement to Mia and to Pump You Up Ltd.

Problem 8

Kristie owns 35% of Big City Developments Inc. (BCD), which has a December 31 year end. She is also an employee of the company. On March 31, Year 1, she purchased her shares of BCD from treasury for $150,000. BCD lent her all the funds for the share purchase at an interest rate of 2%. She is required to repay the loan at the rate of $25,000 each January 1.

On May 15, Year 1, BCD loaned Kristie $75,000 to purchase a new motor home and boat. Since she is a significant shareholder, she was not required to repay any of the loan in Year 1 or Year 2. At the end of Year 3, Kristie repaid $25,000 of the loan.

You have agreed to calculate the income tax implications to Kristie as a result of receiving these loans for Years 1, 2, and 3, assuming the prescribed rate of interest for shareholder loans was 3% throughout all the years. (Ignore the effects of a leap year, if applicable.)

Problem 9

ITA: 15(2), 20(1)(j),
20(1)(q), 67, 78, 80.4,
80.5, 147, 147.2

As the auditor for Skies Limited, a Canadian-controlled private corporation, you have discovered in your 2016 year-end audit several items that require further consideration. Mr. Scott is an 80% shareholder and president of the company which has a December 31 fiscal year-end.

The following items were expensed during the year:

Salary for Mr. Scott (assume equal to employment compensation)	$90,000
Royalty payable to Mr. Scott on material prepared for the corporation	54,000
Contribution to registered pension plan (money purchase plan) for Mr. Scott whose employee contributions are being matched by the corporation	3,000

The royalty was the only item not paid during the fiscal year. In fact, it was still unpaid at the time of the audit and Mr. Scott indicated to you that it could not be paid until sometime in 2016 when he anticipated that the company would have sufficient cash.

The records showed that the corporation had made several loans to Mr. Scott or to his son, age 30, who owns the other 20% of the shares of the corporation and is, also, an employee of the corporation. Each of the following was evidenced by a separate promissory note, duly signed and approved by the Board of Directors:

(a) a $180,000 non-interest bearing loan, dated August 1, 2016, repayable in $18,000 annual instalments, to permit Mr. Scott's son to purchase previously unissued, fully paid shares from the corporation at their fair market value;

(b) a $270,000 1% loan, dated June 1, 2016, repayable over 15 years in equal instalments of principal payable on the anniversary date, but with interest payable monthly, to enable Mr. Scott to purchase a new home, a few blocks from his old home; and

(c) a $24,000 2% loan, dated October 1, 2016, with no principal repayment arrangements, but with interest paid quarterly, to permit Mr. Scott to purchase a car to be used in his employment with the corporation.

Mr. Scott had repaid $4,800 of the car loan on May 31, 2017 and expressed the intention to repay $4,800 annually for four more years.

Any interest required to be paid on the loans at the indicated rates was paid in 2016. Assume the prescribed rates for 2016 were 2% for the first and second quarters, and 3% for the third and fourth quarters.

You have agreed to document your research and conclusions on the following:

(A) The deductibility of expenses contained in the foregoing information (excluding the shareholder loans).

(B) The tax implications of the shareholder loans if Mr. Scott and his son received the loans by virtue of being:

(i) shareholders,

(ii) employees.

You plan to support your answer with specific calculations where appropriate and provide reasons for your conclusions.

Problem 10

ITA: 15(2), 15(2.3), 15(2.4), 15(2.6), 20(1)(*j*), 80.4; ITR: 4300(7)

In 2016, Sunshine Publishing Ltd., a book publishing company with a fiscal year end on December 31, made a loan of $100,000 to Stuart Sunshine, the president and majority shareholder. Both Stuart and Sunshine Publishing Limited are Canadian residents.

This is the first loan that Stuart ever received from the company, and it helped him finance the purchase of a new home which was built just outside Toronto, 10 kilometres farther from the corporate headquarters than Stuart's previous home. The loan was made on May 1, 2016, and a mortgage agreement was signed on that date. This agreement requires that the $100,000 owing be repaid over five years in equal instalments of $20,000 on each anniversary date, starting on May 1, 2018, without interest. Early prepayments of principal are allowed.

Assume that the prescribed rates applicable to taxable benefits are: 1% for the first quarter of 2016, 2% for the second quarter, 3% for the third quarter, 2% for the fourth quarter, and 1% for all of 2017. (Ignore the effects of a leap year, if applicable.)

Stuart has asked you for the following advice:

(A) It is now December 2016 and Stuart has asked you to advise him on the tax consequences of the loan. It is not a company policy to make housing loans to employees and no other loans have been made to employees on similar conditions. What are the income tax consequences of this loan to Stuart in 2016 and 2017?

(B) If it was a company policy to make such loans to employees and other loans had been made to employees on similar terms and conditions, how would this change your answer to Part (A)?

(C) Assume the following facts: it was a company policy to make such loans to employees; other loans had been made to employees on similar terms and conditions; Stuart was a 9.5% shareholder rather than a majority shareholder; he was not related to any shareholders of the company; and the loan was to buy a rental property rather than a home. How would this change your answer to Part (B)?

Problem 11

ITA: 82(1), 117, 121, 123–125

Nancy Ball presently operates a retailing proprietorship with a December 31, year-end and makes $150,000 of net income for tax purposes annually. She is thinking of incorporating her business and has asked for your advice. She lives in a province where the provincial corporate tax rate is 5% of this type of federal taxable income. She has $2,100 of federal personal tax credits, $1,400 of provincial personal tax credits, and no other income.

You have agreed that you will do the following:

(A) Estimate the personal taxes that Nancy would pay currently on $150,000 of business income compared with the amount of corporate and personal taxes that would be paid if she incorporated her business and only took out a salary of $50,000? Ignore all payroll taxes (e.g., Canada Pension Plan premiums) when making your estimates.

(B) Based on your calculations in (A), estimate the amount of personal tax that Nancy defers by keeping the remaining after-tax retained earnings in her company this year? [Hint: compute the additional personal tax that she would pay on a dividend equal to the corporation's after-tax retained earnings.]

Problem 12

ITA: 82(1), 117, 121, 123–125

Mrs. Edwards presently operates a retailing proprietorship with a December 31 fiscal year end. She expects net income for tax purposes of $210,000 from the business. Since the business currently requires considerable amounts of working capital, she can only afford to withdraw $50,000 annually to meet her family's needs.

She lives in a province where the provincial corporate tax rate is 4% of federal taxable income. She is married and has two children (ages 18 and 19) who will start university soon. Her husband, who looks after their home, has no income and no interest in the business.

Mrs. Edwards has federal personal credits of $2,400, provincial personal tax credits of $1,600 and has no other income. She is contemplating the incorporation of her business. If she does so, she has been advised that if she makes all withdrawals from the business in the form of $50,000 salary, she will end up with enough after-tax to meet her family's needs. Although she is not considering it at present, she expects to pay dividends at a time when her other taxable income is at about the same level as it is currently.

You have agreed to do the following:

(A) Compare the total tax that Mrs. Edwards would pay in 2016 on the $210,000 earned personally with the total tax that would be paid if she incorporated her business and only took out a salary of $50,000. Ignore any Canada Pension Plan premiums payable on the income.

(B) Determine how much personal tax Mrs. Edwards will defer each year by keeping the remaining after-tax retained earnings in her company? [Hint: compute the additional personal tax that she would pay on a dividend equal to the corporation's after-tax retained earnings.]

(C) Compare the total income tax incurred by using a corporation to earn income with the personal tax incurred when the income is earned directly by Mrs. Edwards. Consider the corporate tax plus the personal tax on the salary and the dividend paid out of after-tax retained earnings. What is the absolute income tax cost or savings for Mrs. Edwards if she incorporates? Use the 18% gross-up for dividends.

(D) Assuming Mrs. Edwards chooses the incorporated form of business, calculate the additional tax savings that could be achieved by income splitting with her family members?

Problem 13

ITA: 82(1), 117, 121, 123-125.1

Iris Kroneman approaches you with the following information:

(a) She resides in a province with a 3% corporate tax rate (i.e., a total tax rate of 13.5%) where she owns and operates an incorporated business which generates income in the amount of $125,000 before taxes.

(b) She has federal personal tax credits of $2,100 and provincial personal tax credits of $1,400 including, among others, the marital status tax credit.

(c) She requires $65,000 before taxes for living expenses each year.

(d) She wants to maximize her Canada Pension Plan contributions each year. The CPP calculations are as follows:

Pensionable earnings (salary)	$54,900
Basic exemption	(3,500)
Maximum contributory earnings	$51,400
Employee rate	4.95%
Maximum contribution	$ 2,544

(e) She wants to make the maximum RRSP contribution based on the earned income you determine she should have. Assume that her earned income for 2015 is the same as for 2016.

You have agreed to determine the tax consequences of the salary/dividend combination for Ms. Kroneman that will achieve her goals.

Type 3 Problems

Problem 14

Herb Smith, the tax partner, has just talked to you about one of his clients, John Barwell. John has owned his retail store, Aurora Collectibles, for the past four years. Despite a recession, he has been able to do very well with the store by offering customers decorating advice along with the antiques and other unusual items that he sells. Last year, his store earned net income of $125,000.

When he first started the business, he set it up as a proprietorship and financed it with a loan of $100,000 from his wife, Alison, and a $75,000 bank operating loan. Currently, both of the loans remain unpaid, since both John and Alison enjoy a lifestyle that uses up all of their cash flow. Both John and

Alison agree that they are going to improve their spending habits. They want John to pay off the bank operating loan from the business earnings. Once this is done, any excess cash will be used by John to invest in some property that they will eventually move the store into.

Herb wants you to identify the tax issues and tell him what analysis you propose to do to help John and Alison. He doesn't want you to get into the numbers yet.

Problem 15

Charles Wong, the vice-president of Arctic Oil Corporation, loves to minimize his income taxes. He spends much of his time hiring tax professionals to seek loopholes in the *Income Tax Act*. One loophole that he discovered was as follows.

Since Arctic Oil Corporation is in a loss position this year, he has found a way to defer much of his employment income to the next year. It won't cost the firm any money at all and his corporation is even willing to loan him funds (interest free) to live on.

Arrangements like this lead to legislation of rules for "salary deferral arrangements" and provisions for the taxation of benefits received as low-interest loans. However, the business-purpose and the substance-over-form concepts were enacted in the general anti-avoidance rule to place a broad restriction on taxpayer behaviour. Charles is having less and less success in his pursuit of loopholes in the tax system.

You have realized that Charles needs to have a better understanding of the difference between tax minimization and effective tax planning. Charles may have to change his objective of tax minimization. In your opinion, a better understanding of the concept of substance over form may help him to avoid being caught under the general anti-avoidance rule. As his tax adviser, help Charles to understand this by explaining:

- the difference between tax minimization and effective tax planning;
- why he should change his tax minimization objective; and
- how he can avoid the application of the GAAR.

     [For more problems and solutions thereto, see the DVD accompanying the textbook.]

CHAPTER 13 —
DISCUSSION NOTES FOR REVIEW QUESTIONS

(1) Mr. Smith can pay the bonus within the 179-day limit and loan the net after-tax amount back to the company. If he actually does this, he should consider charging interest to the company in order to reduce payroll taxes by converting his salary into interest income. This will also protect his ability to claim a capital loss or an ABIL in the event the company was unable to repay the loan. He should also consider securing the loan. Another option is to leave the money in the corporation and pay tax at 28%. ITA: 78(4)

(2) (a) If he leaves the money in the company, the income over $500,000 will not be eligible for the small business deduction, but it will be eligible for the general rate reduction. The corporate marginal tax rate will be 28% (i.e., 38% – 10% – 13% + 13%), which is less than all but the lowest personal tax rate.

(b) If he declares and pays the bonus the personal marginal tax rate will be 50% (i.e., 33% + 17%).

(c) He can defer approximately 22.3% (see calculation below) of tax by leaving the income in the company to be taxed.

(d) If he leaves the income in the company to be taxed, he will have to pay tax on the dividend when he eventually pays it out. The combined tax rate at that point, assuming the 38% dividend tax credit, will be approximately 50.3% which is slightly above the 50% personal tax cost of paying out the bonus now. That small tax cost is offset by the deferral of tax until the dividend is paid.

(e) Calculation:

Corporate income	$1,000
Corporate tax @ 28%	(280)
After-tax income	$ 720
Dividend paid	$ 720
Gross-up (38%)	274
Taxable dividend	$ 994
Tax @ 50%	$ 497
Dividend tax credit	(274)
Net personal tax	$ 223
Net cash after tax	$ 497
Total tax ($280 + $223)	$ 503

(3) If he or she chooses a fiscal year-end on or after July 6, but no later than December 31, then the bonus can be paid within the 179 days in either this calendar year or on January 1 of the next calendar year. ITA: 78(4)

(4) The following are the five criteria for the deductibility of bonus accruals as decided in the *Totem Disposal* case:

- reasonableness of the bonus in relation to profit and services rendered;

- payment for real and identifiable service;

- some justification for expecting a bonus over regular salary (e.g., a company policy);

- reasonableness of the time between determining profit and establishing the bonus; and

- a legal obligation to pay the accrued bonus.

(5) Mr. Chow is related to his brother-in-law. Therefore, they are deemed not to deal with each other at arm's length and the brother-in-law is connected with Mr. Chow. As a result, the conditions in the shareholder loan rule are met and none of the exceptions are met. Therefore, the brother-in-law will be required to take the full amount of the loan into income in 2016 since none of it was repaid by December 31, 2017. In 2018 and 2019, the brother-in-law will be able to deduct the principal repayments. The imputed interest benefit included in his 2016 tax return can be removed through an amended return to eliminate the benefit.

ITA: 15(2.1), 251(2)
ITA: 15(2), 15(2.4)
ITA: 20(1)(j)

ITA: 80.4(3)(b)

(6) Since Ms. Jones is a shareholder and received a loan, the shareholder loan rules apply. Although Ms. Jones is an employee, the boat does not fit into one of the exceptions. Therefore, Ms. Jones will have to take the $25,000 into income unless she repays it within one year from the end of the taxation year in which she received the loan. If she has to include the principal in income then the imputed interest rules will not apply.

ITA: 15(2)
ITA: 15(2.4)(b)–(d), 15(2.6)
ITA: 80.4, 80.4(3)(b)

(7) This provincial tax holiday would bring the combined corporate tax rate on income eligible for the small business deduction down to 10.5%, which is below 14.5% and would provide a tax incentive to flowing active business income through a corporation, paying corporate tax and then paying dividends. Thus, there would then be an advantage to paying dividends instead of salary to the owner due to the fact that the dividend tax credit is greater than the underlying corporate tax.

(8) With the 17% dividend gross-up his taxable income would be $35,100. The federal tax would be $5,265 less the dividend tax credit of $3,693 and the personal credit of $1,721 (in 2016) leaving basic federal tax of nil. Provincial tax on $35,100 would be $3,510, less the provincial dividend tax credit of $1,407 (i.e., $^8/_{29}$ × $5,100) and the provincial personal tax credit of $1,147 (i.e., $11,474 × .10), leaving provincial tax of $956.

(9) It is true that in order to claim an ABIL the shares need to be shares in a small business corporation. However, the definition of small business corporation allows the status as a small business corporation to continue for 12 months for purposes of the ABIL provisions. Since she sold the shares within six months she should be able to claim the loss as an ABIL.

ITA: 248(1)
ITA: 39(1)(c)

(10) In several Interpretation Bulletins, the CRA states that the phrase means at least 90%. It should be noted that this phrase has not been specifically determined by the courts and it is unclear whether the courts would allow 85% or require 95% as the percentage necessary to meet this test. Practitioners generally use 90%.

IT-151R5, par. 31 (for example)

(11) This corporation is neither, since in order to meet the definition of "small business corporation" it has to meet the 90% test at the determination time. Since the corporation does not meet this test it is neither an SBC nor a QSBC.

(12) The preamble to the corporate attribution rule refers only to situations where "individuals have transferred or loaned property." In this case his corporation has loaned the funds to her corporation. It could not even be said that he did it indirectly since he has not loaned or transferred any money to his own corporation. Therefore, even though her corporation is not an SBC, the corporate attribution rules should not apply. However, GAAR should be considered.

ITA: 74.4(2)

CHAPTER 13 — SOLUTIONS TO MULTIPLE CHOICE QUESTIONS

Question 1

(B) is correct under administrative practice outlined in the text. If $40,000 of the loan is repaid within one year of the end of the year of S Ltd. in which the loan was made, then $160,000 must be included in the year of the loan. Subsequent repayments are deductible in the year of the repayment.

ITA: 15(2)
ITA: 15(2.6)
ITA: 15(2.4)

(A) is incorrect under administrative practice. Only the part of the loan ($160,000) that was not paid before the one-year limit will be included in Stan's income in 2016, the year he received the loan. The limit is one year after the end of the taxation year of the lender in which the loan was made. He does not meet the other criteria for exclusion. Since such a loan is not available to other employees, it is not reasonable to conclude that he received the loan because of his employment.

(C) is incorrect. There is no imputed interest benefit when the loan is included in income. If there was an imputed interest benefit the prescribed rate protection rule would not apply as the loan was not received because of his employment.

ITA: 80.4(1), 80.4(3)(*b*), 80.4(4)

(D) is incorrect. One year after the end of the calendar year in which the loan is received has no significance. The shareholder loan rule includes the loan in income in the year it is *received* unless it is repaid by one year after the end of the taxation year of the *lender* in which the loan was made, or the loan meets one of the specific exclusions.

ITA: 15(2)

Question 2

(C) is the correct answer. The shareholder loan rule would include the principal amount of the loan in Mrs. C's income in 2016 because none of the exception tests are met.

ITA: 15(2.2), 15(2.3), 15(2.4), 15(2.6)

(1) The exception test in subsection 15(2.2) does not apply because Mrs. C is resident in Canada.

(2) The exception in subsection 15(2.3) does not apply since the money is not lent in the ordinary course of money lending business.

(3) None of the exceptions for employees in subsection 15(2.4) are met, because it is not reasonable to conclude that the loan is received because of employment since no other employees have received similar loans.

(4) The exception in subsection 15(2.6) does not apply since the debt was repaid on April 1, 2018, which is more than one year from the end of S Ltd.'s December 31, 2016 fiscal year.

The loan in (A) would not be included in Mrs. A's income because the one-year repayment exception test applies: the debt is repaid on April 1, 2017, which is within one year from the end of S Ltd.'s December 31, 2016 fiscal year. Note, however, that the imputed interest benefit rule would apply to compute a deemed interest benefit on the loan.

ITA: 15(2.6)

ITA: 80.4(2)

The loan in (B) would not be included in B Ltd's income because the shareholder loan rule does not apply to corporate shareholders resident in Canada.

ITA: 15(2)

The loan in (D) would not be included in Mr. D's income because one of the exceptions for employees is met: Mr. D is not a specified employee and it is reasonable to conclude that the loan is received because of employment, since the computer is for employment use and other employees currently working at home have received similar loans. Since Mr. D is not a specified employee, the loan does not have to be for any specified purpose. A specified employee is an employee who is either a specified shareholder (i.e., generally, a person who owns at least 10% of the shares of any class of the corporation) or a person who does not deal at arm's length with the corporation. Since Mr. D owns only 5% of the shares of S Ltd. and deals at arm's length with the corporation, he is not a specified employee.

ITA: 15(2.4), 248(1)

Question 3

(D) is correct. Since the $300,000 bonus is unpaid on the 180th day after the end of the taxation year of Fortelli Inc. in which the expense was incurred, it is not deductible until 2017, the taxation year in which it is actually paid.

ITA: 78(4)

(A) is incorrect. This amount refers to the rules in subsection 78(1) for unpaid amounts due to related persons, other than pension benefits, retiring allowances, salary, wages, or other remuneration.

(B) is incorrect. Subsection 78(4) does not distinguish between amounts owed to related and unrelated persons.

(C) is incorrect for the same reason as (A).

Question 4

The correct answer is (B). There is no penalty. The tax benefit that would otherwise have been enjoyed is denied.

ITA: 245(2)

(A) is incorrect as it is true in accordance with subsection 245(2).

(C) is incorrect as it is true in accordance with subsection 245(3).

(D) is incorrect as it is true in accordance with subsection 245(4).

Question 5

(C) is correct. The purpose of the transaction seems to be the reduction or avoidance of tax on the income earned on the $10,000 gift. This transaction goes against the spirit of the Act, read as a whole, and falls within the definition of an avoidance transaction. Note that an attribution rule would apply if it was a loan instead of a gift.

ITA: 245(3)
ITA: 56(4.1)

(A) is incorrect. The transaction is an estate freeze which can reasonably be considered to have been undertaken for *bona fide* purposes other than to obtain the tax benefit. This transaction does not result in a misuse or abuse of the Act, read as a whole.

IC 88-2, par. 10

(B) is incorrect. The incorporation of a business and the claiming of a small business deduction by a CCPC is specifically provided for in the Act. This transaction does not result in a misuse or abuse of the Act, read as a whole.

IC 88-2, par. 11

(D) is incorrect. The Act will deny the deduction of the bonus to the extent it is in excess of a reasonable amount. To the extent the transaction is reasonable, it does not result in a benefit. Corporate tax will be reduced by the accrual, but Mary will pay tax on the income personally.

ITA: 67; IC 88-2, par. 18

Question 6

(D) is correct. All the conditions for corporate attribution are met. As a result, Mr. Boehmer is deemed to have income of 3% × $1,000,000 = $30,000.

ITA: 74.4

(A) incorrectly attributes the cash dividend received by Mrs. Boehmer to Mr. Boehmer: $10,000.

(B) incorrectly attributes the grossed up dividend received by Mrs. Boehmer to Mr. Boehmer: $11,700 [using the 17% gross-up].

(C) incorrectly computes the attributed amount to Mr. Boehmer based on $500,000: 3% × $500,000 = $15,000.

ITA: 74.4

Question 7

(C) is correct. In order to be a small business corporation, the percentage of assets used in an active business by the corporation and the corporation controlled by Ms. Prentice's brother must be at least 90%. It is now 80% (60% + 20%) or $3,200,000.

ITA: 248(1) "small business corporation"

Therefore total assets must be $3,200,000/90% or $3,555,555.

Therefore $444,445 ($4,000,000 – $3,555,555) of the non-active business assets must be sold.

(A) is incorrect because the corporation does not currently meet the 90% test.

(B) incorrectly assumes that 10% of the assets must be sold: 10% × 4,000,000 = $400,000.

(D) incorrectly ignores the assets used by the related corporation and calculates that since active business assets are $2,400,000 (60% × $4,000,000), total assets must be $2,400,000/90% or $2,666,666 to meet the 90% test. As a result, $1,333,333 ($4,000,000 – $2,666,666) of the non-active business assets must be sold.

CHAPTER 13 — SOLUTIONS TO EXERCISES

Exercise 1

(A) The bonus must be paid on or before 179 days from the end of the year in which it was deducted. In this case, it must be paid on or before March 28, 2017. (Administrative practice would allow payment on the 180th day.)

IT-109R2, par. 10

(B) If the bonus is not paid on or before March 28, 2017, the corporation may not deduct the bonus in its 2016 taxation year. The bonus may only be deducted when it is paid.

(C) (i) The rent must be paid within two years from the end of the year in which it was deducted. In this case, it must be paid by September 30, 2018.

(ii) If the rent is not paid by September 30, 2018, the corporation must add the $10,000 to its income for its 2019 taxation year beginning October 1, 2018. This does not cancel the payable, such that if the rent is ever paid, the shareholder will declare the rental income, but there will be no deduction for the corporation.

(iii) An election can be filed before the date on which the corporation must file its tax return for 2019. In this case, that date is March 31, 2020. If such an election is filed, Mr. Schneider will be deemed to have income of $10,000 and to have loaned that amount back to the corporation on October 1, 2018. When the loan is repaid to Mr. Schneider, there are no tax consequences since the amount of the loan has already been taxed. The election can be filed late. However, $2,500 (effectively, a late-filing penalty) will be added back to the income of the corporation for its 2019 fiscal year. Mr. Schneider's tax position is not affected by this late-filed election.

ITA: 78(1)(*b*)

ITA: 78(3)

Exercise 2

(A) *Employee*

Principal Amount

— Note that the shareholder loan rule applies in this case because he is a shareholder.

ITA: 15(2)

(a) House Loan

The Act would exempt the principal amount of this loan from income since Mr. Nesbitt received the loan in his capacity as an employee (i.e., by virtue of his employment), the purpose of the loan was to purchase a house and *bona fide* arrangements were made for repayment of the loan within a reasonable time;

ITA: 15(2.4)(*b*)

— however, an interest benefit on a "home purchase loan" would be included in income as shown in the calculation below.

ITA: 80.4

(b) Furniture Loan

There is no exemption from income for this loan because it was not repaid within one year of the 2016 taxation year of the corporation;

ITA: 15(2.3), 15(2.4), 15(2.6)

— since the loan is included in income in 2016, it is an exception for the purposes of the imputed interest benefit and, hence, there is no interest benefit.

ITA: 15(2), 80.4(3)(*b*)

(c) Share Purchase Loan

This loan is exempt from income because Mr. Nesbitt received the loan in his capacity as an employee and *bona fide* arrangements were made to repay the loan within a reasonable time;

ITA: 15(2.4)(*c*)

— since this type of loan is not an exception to the imputed interest rules, there is an interest benefit as shown in the calculation below.

ITA: 80.4

Interest Benefit

(a) interest on "home purchase loan" made to an officer or employee computed, at lesser of: (i) the prescribed rate in effect during the period in the year that the loan was outstanding, and (ii) the prescribed rate in effect at the time the loan was made. This "lesser of" choice can be made on a quarter-by-quarter comparison of tax rates. In this case, the 3% prescribed rate in June 2016, when the loan was received, is less than the rate for the other two quarters of 2016 in which the loan was outstanding. Therefore, the benefit would be based on the following calculation: *ITA: 80.4(1)(a), 80.4(4)*

June–Dec. 2016: 3% of $75,000 × $^{214}/_{365}$	$1,319

(b) interest on share purchase loan computed at prescribed rates in effect during the period in the year that the loan was outstanding   *ITA: 80.4(1)(a)*

June 2016: 3% of $10,000 × 30/365 = $ 25	
July–Sept. 2016: 4% of $10,000 × 92/365 = 101	
Oct.–Dec. 2016: 4% of $10,000 × 92/365 = 101	227
Subtotal	$1,546

(c) Less: interest paid on above loans (2% of $75,000 × 214/365) 879

Benefit calculated under ssec. 80.4(1) and included in employment income	$ 667	*ITA: 61(1)(a), 6(9)*
Less: deduction for imputed interest on loan to buy shares	227	*ITA: 20(1)(c), 80.5*
Net benefit under Division B	$ 440	

Since the loan to purchase the house is a "home relocation loan", the Act provides for a deduction from taxable income in Division C, calculated as the least of: *ITA: 248(1). 110(1)(j)*

(a) the net imputed interest on the home purchase loan computed under paragraph 80.4(1)(a) as the lesser amount above $1,319
    less: interest paid in respect of the year, ... 879 $ 440

(b) interest on $25,000 computed under paragraph 80.4(1)(a) as the lesser amount above ($25,000/$75,000 × $1,319) . . . . $ 440

(c) benefit deemed received under section 80.4 for the year . . . . . $ 667

Therefore, the deduction would be $440.   *ITA: 110(1)(j)*

(B) Shareholder

If Mr. Nesbitt received the loans by virtue of being a shareholder, then all the loans would be included in income in the year that the loans were received, unless the loans were repaid by the end of the fiscal year in which the loans were made. Where a loan is outstanding in the year in which the loan was made, there would be an imputed interest inclusion. However, the inclusion would be reversed on the filing of the amended return for the loan inclusion.   *ITA: 80.4(2)*
    ITA: 15(2)

For imputed interest, the main difference is that the benefit on the loan to purchase the house would be based only on the prescribed rate in effect during the period in the year that the loan was outstanding and reduced by the amount of interest paid on the loan by the shareholder in the period not later than 30 days after the corporation's year-end. This is because the calculation of the imputed interest benefit by virtue of shareholdings does not take into account the special rules for a "home purchase loan" or a "home relocation loan". Therefore, there would also not be a deduction available.   *ITA: 80.4(2), 80.4(7), 248(1)*
    ITA: 110(1)(j)

Exercise 3

(A) The CRA indicates that it examines the balance in the account at the end of each year of the lender considering a net increase as a loan to be included in the income of the borrower and a net decrease as a repayment to be deducted from the income of the borrower. This approach would result in the following: *IT-119R4, par. 34-35*

Lender's year end	Change from previous year	Income [ssec. 15(2.6)] or repayment [par. 20(1)(j)]
Year 2	$45,000	income
Year 3	(32,000)	repayment
Year 4	(2,000)	repayment
Year 5	12,000	income
Year 6	(14,000)	repayment

(B) If there is no series of loans and repayments, then repayments are considered to apply first to   IT-119R4, par. 27
the oldest loan outstanding unless the facts clearly indicate otherwise. Applying this approach would
result in the following:

Lender's year end	Net inclusion (or deduction)	Explanation
Year 2	$25,000	— only the $20,000 borrowed in year 2 is repaid within one year of year 2; the $25,000 loan was not fully repaid within one year, so it must be taken into income in year 2
Year 3	(12,000)	— repayment of $12,000 of the $25,000 year 2 loan previously included
Year 4	(12,000)	— repayment of part of balance of year 2 loan
	Nil	— Nov. 30/year 4 loan repaid within one year of year 4
Year 5	(1,000)	— repayment of remainder of April 30/ year 2 loan
	23,000	— full amount of Nov. 30/year 5 loan, since not fully repaid within one year of year 5
Year 6	(14,000)	— repayment of $14,000 of year 5 loan

Note that these methods of calculation are based on administrative practice and are not stipulated
by the Act. Note that based on these methods, while total inclusions net of deductions over the period
amount to $9,000 under each alternative, the time pattern of net inclusion is more favourable in this
case if there is no series of loans and repayments considered.

If the loans are all part of a single running loan account, they are likely a series of loans and
repayments. However, if the loans are for separate purposes, with differing repayment or other terms,
and the repayments relate to specific loans, the facts might suggest there was no series of loans and
repayments.

Exercise 4

Since he is a shareholder of the corporation, the shareholder loan rule applies and the loan that was   ITA: 15(2)
received by the taxpayer should be included in income. However, the Act provides an exclusion for the   ITA: 15(2.4)(*d*)
$35,000 principal amount of the loan because:

— the taxpayer is an employee of the lender;

— the loan is to enable him to acquire a motor vehicle to be used by him in the performance of his
employment duties;

— the taxpayer received the loan because of his employment, not because of his shareholdings,
since other employees were eligible for a loan; and

— *bona fide* arrangements were made, at the time the loan was made, for repayment within a
reasonable time.

Since the loan is a low-interest loan, the imputed interest benefit rule applies to impute an interest   ITA: 80.4(1)
benefit calculated as follows:

April 1 to June 30: $91/365 \times 1\%$ of $35,000 = ...	$	87
July 1 to Sept. 30: $92/365 \times 2\%$ of $35,000 = ...		176
Oct. 1 to Dec. 31: $92/365 \times 3\%$ of $35,000 = ...		265
Total	$	528
Less: interest *paid* (not payable) ($214/365 \times 1\%$ of $35,000)		205
Net interest benefit	$	323

The Act deems the imputed interest benefit of $323 to have been paid in the year. As a result, a part of the interest will qualify as a deduction of interest *paid* limited as follows:

ITA: 80.5
ITA: 8(1)(*j*), 67.2

Lesser of:

(a) interest deemed paid $323
    interest *paid* ($^{214}/_{365}$ × 1% of $35,000) .... 205 $ 528

(b) $\dfrac{$300}{30}$ × 214 days of interest paid $2,140

Lesser amount × 60% business usage (60% of $528) .... $ 317

Exercise 5

Shareholder-Manager Pays Tax on Benefit
Benefit from use of car:
  standby charge[1] (10,000 km/20,004 km × $^2/_3$ × $6,000) 2,000
  value of operating costs of personal use[2] 1,000   ITA: 6(1)(*e*)

Incremental taxable income .... $ 3,000

Tax @ 50% on $3,000 of incremental taxable income .... $ 1,500

Shareholder-Manager Leases Car Personally
Incremental taxable income ($2,880 + $6,000) .... $ 8,880
Less: deduction for business use of car [66⅔% of ($6,000 + $2,880)] .... (5,920)
Add: HST rebate (13/113 × $5,920)[3] 681

Incremental taxable income .... $ 3,641

Tax @ 50% on $3,641 of incremental taxable income .... $ 1,821

Tax net of HST rebate ($1,821 − $681) .... $ 1,140

Notice that the second alternative is the better by $360.

— *NOTES TO SOLUTION*

[1] This calculation assumes that business usage of 66⅔% meets the test that the primary distance travelled was for business. Generally, the term "primarily" has been interpreted by the CRA to mean more than 50%.

ITA: 6(2)

[2] The election includes a benefit of 50% of the standby charge of $2,000 (i.e., $1,000) which is less than 26¢ × 10,000 km or $2,600.

ITA: 6(1)(*k*)

[3] In reality, the HST rebate would have to be taken into income in the following year. Note that the present value considerations on the rebate have been ignored. Also, ignored is the effect of the input tax credit (ITC) received by the corporation if it incurs the annual lease and operating costs. If the corporation pays additional salary equal to its net costs for these items after ITC and, hence, if the shareholder manager must pay the HST from other sources, it can be shown that the shareholder-manager's after-tax retention is reduced by the after-tax equivalent of the HST costs. This would reduce the advantage of the second alternative.

Exercise 6

	Remuneration alternatives		
Corporation	*Salary*	*Dividends*	*Combination*
Income before salary and taxes	$ 20,000	$20,000	$ 20,000
Salary	(20,000)	—	(10,000)
Taxable income	Nil	$20,000	$ 10,000
Tax @ 14.5% (i.e., 38% − 10% − 17.5% + 4%)	—	(2,900)	(1,450)
Available for dividends	Nil	$17,100	$ 8,550
Shareholder			
Employment income (ssec. 8(1) deductions not considered) ...	$ 20,000	—	$ 10,000
Grossed-up dividends (1.17 × dividend)	—	$20,007	10,004
Taxable income	$ 20,000	$20,007	$ 20,004

	Remuneration alternatives		
	Salary	*Dividends*	*Combination*
Federal tax before dividend tax credit	$ 3,000	$ 3,001	$ 3,001
Dividend tax credit ($^{21}/_{29}$ of gross-up)	—	(2,105)	(1,053)
Personal tax credits	(2,000)	(2,000)	(2,000)
Basic federal tax*	$ 1,000	$ Nil	$ Nil
Provincial tax.....................	2,000	2,001	2,000
Provincial dividend tax credit ($^{8}/_{29}$ of gross-up)	—	(802)	(401)
Provincial personal tax credits	(1,290)	(1,290)	(1,290)
Total tax*	$ 1,710	Nil	$ 309
Summary			
Income before salary and taxes	$ 20,000	$20,000	$ 20,000
Less: tax paid by corporation	Nil	(2,900)	(1,450)
tax paid by shareholder	(1,710)	Nil	(309)
Net cash to shareholder	$ 18,290	$17,100	$ 18,241
Excess federal dividend and personal tax credits ($3,001 – $2,105 – $2,000)		$ 1,104	

* Cannot be negative.

Exercise 7

(A)

Taxation of Income from Sole Proprietorship

Income from business and taxable income		$80,000
Federal tax		
Tax on first $45,282	$ 6,792	
Tax on next $34,718 @ 20.5%	7,117	$14,430
Personal tax credits		(2,100)
Basic federal tax		$11,809
Provincial tax (12% of ($80,000 – $45,282) + $4,528)		8,694
Provincial personal tax credits		(1,400)
Total tax paid		$19,103

(B)

Taxation of Income through a Corporation

	Remuneration alternatives		
	All salary	*All dividends*	*Combination*
Corporation			
Income before salary and taxes	$ 80,000	$ 80,000	$ 80,000
Salary	(25,000)	—	(3,435)[3]
Taxable income	$ 55,000	$ 80,000	$ 76,565
Tax @ 14.5% (i.e., 38% – 10% – 17.5% + 4%)	(7,975)	(11,600)	(11,102)
Available for dividend	$ 47,025	$ 68,400	$ 65,463
Shareholder			
Salary[1] .... (A)	$ 25,000	—	$ 3,435
Dividend .... (B)	—	$ 25,000	21,565
Gross-up @ 17% of dividend	—	4,250	3,666
Income	$ 25,000	$ 29,250	$ 28,666
Federal tax	$ 3,750	$ 4,388	$ 4,300
Dividend tax credit ($^{21}/_{29}$ × gross-up) ...	—	(3,078)	(2,655)
Personal tax credits...............	(2,100)	(2,100)	(2,100)
Basic federal tax	$ 1,650	(790)	(455)[4]
Provincial tax	2,500	2,925	2,866
Provincial dividend tax credit ($^{8}/_{29}$ × gross-up)	Nil	(1,172)	(1,011)
Provincial personal tax credits	(1,400)	(1,400)	(1,400)

		Remuneration alternatives		
		All salary	All dividends	Combination
Total tax .... (C)		$ 2,750	$ (437)	Nil
Disposable income (A + B – C)		$ 22,250	$ 25,437	$ 25,000
Total Taxes paid Through corporation:				
Corporation		$ 7,975	$ 11,600	$ 11,102
Shareholder		2,750	(437)	Nil
Total		$ 10,725	$ 11,163	$ 11,102
Paid directly by proprietor		$ 19,103	$ 19,103	$ 19,103
Tax Saving (maximum[2])		$ 8,378	$ 7,940	$ 8,001

At these rates, all salary results in the biggest tax savings, assuming that dividends will be distributed when the owner-manager's income will be such that there will be no tax on the dividends.

—NOTES TO SOLUTION

[1] Assumes no deductions available to employee.

[2] Assumes amount retained in the corporation can be distributed as taxable dividends in amounts that will not attract tax after personal tax credits.

[3] Negative allowed only due to assumption in the required.

Exercise 8

In each of the cases, the test to be applied to the facts is whether all or substantially all (i.e., at least 90%) of the fair market value of the assets are:

(a) used principally in an active business carried on primarily in Canada by the corporation (or a related corporation);

(b) shares or debt of a connected SBC; or

(c) a combination of (a) and (b).

(A) This situation depends on whether the marketable securities are used in the active business or are passive investments not necessary to the active business. If the marketable securities are used in the active business, then the 90% test is met. This would be the case, for example, if the marketable securities represented a short-term investment of cash surpluses, awaiting the purchase of inventory for the next season.

(B) In this situation, the 90% test is met with a combination of active business assets and shares in a connected SBC.

(C) In this case, the marketable securities cannot be considered to be used in an active business, because the corporation has no other active business assets to carry on such a business. Since the shares of a connected SBC represent only 80% of the total fair market value of the corporation's assets, the 90% test is not met.

(D) Again, this case fits the definition of an SBC if the marketable securities are considered to be used in an active business. If the facts of this case so indicate, then the 90% test is met by a combination of active business assets (including the marketable securities) and the shares of a connected SBC.

Exercise 9

(A) Unused lifetime deduction in 2016:

Lifetime cumulative deduction limit	$ 406,800
Less: prior years' deductions:	
Capital gains deduction claimed in 2014	75,000
Capital gains deduction available for 2016	$ 331,800

(B) Annual gains limit for 2016:

Net taxable capital gains for 2016[1]		$ 225,000
Minus:		
Net capital losses deducted in 2016	Nil	
ABILs realized in 2016[1]	5,000	5,000
Annual gains limit for 2016		$ 220,000

(C) Cumulative gains limit for 2016:

Cumulative net taxable capital gains ($75,000 + $225,000)			$ 300,000
Minus:			
Cumulative net capital losses deducted		Nil	
Cumulative ABILs realized		$ 5,000	
Cumulative capital gains deductions		75,000	
Cumulative net investment loss:			
Investment expenses —			
Cumulative carrying charges	$ 1,075		
Cumulative net rental losses			
($1,100 + $220)	1,320		
	$ 2,395		
Investment income —			
Cumulative interest income			
($600 + $1,200)	(1,800)		
Cumulative grossed-up dividends	(140)	455	80,455
Cumulative gains limit for 2015			$ 219,545

(D) Least of (A), (B), (C) ... $ 219,545

—*NOTE TO SOLUTION*

[1]   Allowable business investment loss (ABIL):

BIL before ssec. 39(9) reduction			$ 160,000
Disallowed portion — Lesser of:			
(a) BIL		$ 160,000	
(b) Adjustment factor × cumulative CG deductions of previous years (2 × $75,000)	$150,000		
Minus: Cumulative disallowed BIL of prior years	Nil	$ 150,000	
Lesser of (a) and (b)			(150,000)
BIL after adjustment			$ 10,000
ABIL (½ × $10,000)			$ 5,000
Allowable capital loss (ACL):			
Disallowed portion of BIL			$ 150,000
ACL (½ × $150,000)			$ 75,000
Net TCG for 2015:			
TCG			$ 300,000
Less: ACL			75,000
Net TCG			$ 225,000

Exercise 10

The disposition of the real estate is a transfer for tax purposes in 2016. The facts do not provide enough details on the cost base to determine the tax effect of the disposition.

In this case it can likely be established that one of the main purposes of the transfer of the building may reasonably be considered to be to reduce the income of Mr. Albert and to benefit Mrs. Albert who is a designated person and a specified shareholder. Had Mr. Albert kept the building himself he would have earned $20,000 of rental income on which he would have been taxable. Instead, he will receive $1,000 of interest and $2,000 of dividends. Mrs. Albert benefited from the rental income since this will accrue to the common shares of the corporation. Therefore, it may be argued that the purpose test will have been met.

Furthermore, the corporation will no longer be a "small business corporation", since the fair market value of the assets of the corporation will be as follows: ITA: 248(1)

Retail assets, 75%	$600,000
Building, 25%	200,000
Total	$800,000

Even if 20% of the building (FMV $40,000) is classified as an active business asset, the corporation will still not be a small business corporation since all or substantially all of the fair market value of the assets are not used principally in an active business carried on primarily in Canada.

Mr. Albert's attributed amount	
FMV of the building transferred	$200,000
Less: cash received	(60,000)
Outstanding amount	$140,000
Interest imputed at 4%	$5,600
Less: interest received (5% of $20,000)	(1,000)
1.17 × dividends received	(2,340)
Attributed amount	$2,260
Mr. Albert would also have	
Interest income	1,000
Taxable dividends ($2,000 × 1.17)	2,340
Total income	$5,600

Exercise 11

The following comments are based on the application of the logic presented in Exhibit 13-11 to the facts of this situation.

(1) Does any other provision of the Act or other rule of law apply to stop the taxpayer from achieving the intended advantage? No, the amount paid is considered to be reasonable and, hence, is not prohibited. Remuneration is considered to be an expense incurred to produce income from business and, thus, is not prohibited.   ITA: 67 ITA: 18(1)(*a*)

(2) Does the transaction result, directly or indirectly, in a tax benefit, i.e., a reduction, avoidance or deferral of tax or an increase in a refund? On the one hand, corporate tax is reduced, but on the other hand the individual receives income subject to tax at a higher rate. However, the reduction of income to the corporation reduces the potential for double taxation on income taxed at more than a 27.5% rate in the corporation which may be considered to be a tax benefit. If it is concluded that there is no tax benefit, GAAR should not apply.   ITA: 245(1)

(3) Is the transaction part of a series of transactions, which would result, directly or indirectly, in a tax benefit? If the answer to question 2 is yes, then proceed directly to question 4.

(4) Can the transaction reasonably be considered to have been undertaken or arranged primarily for *bona fide* purposes other than to obtain the tax benefit? No, a tax reduction for the corporation was probably the primary purpose. On the other hand, it might be argued that, since the amount paid was reasonable, it is necessary remuneration.

(5) Can it reasonably be considered that the transaction would result directly or indirectly in a misuse of the provisions of the Act or an abuse having regard to the provisions of the Act read as a whole? No, "the Act recognizes the deductibility of reasonable business expenses".   IC 88-2, par. 18

Exercise 12

The general anti-avoidance rule allows for transactions or a series of transactions to be disregarded if they are without a *bona fide* purpose. If your client's spouse and children are not providing any services to her business, it is obvious that the transactions were arranged primarily to obtain a tax benefit with no *bona fide* purpose, and they will be disregarded by the CRA. Any tax benefit derived from the transactions will be eliminated. If there is some service being provided to justify a salary, the amount of salary must be reasonable in the circumstance or the deduction by your client can be disallowed without the need to apply the GAAR. In fact, if the unreasonable salaries are still taxed in the hands of the spouse and children, after the expense is disallowed, the result is worse than the application of the GAAR that disregards the payment.

Chapter 14

Rights and Obligations Under the Income Tax Act

Learning Goals

Know

By the end of this chapter you will know:

- The basic rules related to tax compliance.
    - Filing deadlines
    - Payment deadlines
    - Instalment payments
    - Appeal deadlines
- The tax issues related to death of a taxpayer.

Understand and Explain

By the end of this chapter you will understand and be able to explain:

- The basic rules related to tax compliance.
- How a deceased taxpayer is taxed.

Apply

By the end of this chapter you will be able to apply your knowledge and understanding to:

- Calculate instalments payable.
- Calculate penalties.
- Calculate the taxable income and tax payable for a deceased taxpayer.

Review Questions
¶14,800 in the Study Guide

Multiple Choice Questions
¶14,825 in the Study Guide

Exercise Questions
¶14,850 in the Study Guide

Assignment Problems
¶14,875 in the Study Guide

CHAPTER 14 — LEARNING CHART

Problem Descriptions

Textbook Example Problems

1	Reporting tax information
2	Installments — corporation
3	Penalties and interest
4	Net worth assessment
5	Obligation to withhold
6	Obligation to withhold

Multiple Choice Questions

1	Late filing penalty
2	Normal reassessment period — corporation
3	Notice of objection — individual
4	Final return due date
5	Installments — CCPC
6	Installments — individual

Exercises

1	Withholding tax requirements
2	Windfalls
3	Installments — individual
4	Installments — CCPC
5	Penalties — late filing
6	Notice of reassessment
7	Compare interest paid to and by CRA
8	Preparer penalties
9	Appeal procedure
10	Rents earned by non-resident
11	Interest on tax refunds
12	Death of a taxpayer
13	Death of a taxpayer

Assignment Problems

1	Filing deadlines
2	Deadlines for Notice of Reassessment
3	Notice of Objection
4	Back dating
5	Personal instalments
6	Corporate instalments
7	Notice of Reassessment
8	Preparer penalties
9	Withholding tax on rent
10	Withholding tax on compensation
11	GST/HST
12	Comprehensive
13	Death of a taxpayer

Study Notes

¶14,800   REVIEW QUESTIONS

(1) In each of the following situations indicate whether the answer is true or false and give a reference to the Act.

(a) The taxable income of Unco Inc., a corporation resident in Canada, was nil for the year. As a result, it did not have to file a corporate tax return.

(b) Mr. Austen sold his shares in a qualified small business corporation and realized a $200,000 capital gain. The full amount of the gain was eligible for the capital gains exemption leaving his taxable income at nil. He does have to file a tax return for the year.

(c) Instalments for individuals are due on the 30th of March, June, September, and December.

(2) Mr. Smith paid his first instalment on time but was unable to pay his second one on time. He paid both the second and the third instalments on September 15. Is there any way he can avoid the interest that was charged to him for the late payment on the second instalment?

(3) Bearings Inc. has been quite profitable, but this year the corporation realized a business loss that it is going to carry back to the third preceding year. They are also hoping to collect interest from the date they filed the return for that third preceding year. What do you think?

(4) Ms. Taylor received a Notice of Reassessment from the CRA to disallow certain expenses that she had claimed. She contacted her accountant who sent a letter to the CRA outlining the basis for the deduction. Both Ms. Taylor and her accountant feel that the deduction will be allowed. Should she also file a Notice of Objection?

(5) Murray Corp. has had a bad year. The corporation lost money for the first time in its history and some of its key employees have left. Because of all this confusion Murray Corp. was late in getting its financial records in shape and it did not file its corporate tax returns until seven months after the end of the year. Murray Corp. still needs the cash so it is waiting anxiously for the tax refund from the loss being carried back to the third preceding year. Do you think Murray Corp. will be disappointed?

(6) Describe the different tax returns that can be filed for a deceased individual.

¶14,825 MULTIPLE CHOICE QUESTIONS

Question 1

Jane filed her tax return for the 2015 taxation year on September 15, 2016. She enclosed with the return a cheque for $10,000, the balance of tax owing. Neither Jane nor her husband carried on business in 2015. Jane will be assessed a late filing penalty of:

(A) $500

(B) $900

(C) $950

(D) $1,000

Question 2

A Canadian-controlled private corporation received a notice of assessment for its taxation year ended December 31, 2015. The date of mailing on the notice of assessment was August 15, 2016. The normal reassessment period for the corporation's 2015 taxation year ends:

(A) December 31, 2018

(B) August 15, 2019

(C) December 31, 2019

(D) August 15, 2020

Question 3

Darol disagrees with the notice of assessment he received for his 2015 tax return. The date of mailing on the notice of assessment was October 16, 2016. The tax return was filed on June 15, 2016 as Darol carried on a business in 2015. The notice of objection must be filed by:

(A) December 31, 2016

(B) January 14, 2017

(C) April 30, 2017

(D) June 15, 2017

Question 4

Bill was a lawyer with a very successful law practice. He died March 31, 2016. Which *one* of the following is the due date for his 2015 tax return?

(A) April 30, 2016

(B) June 15, 2016

(C) June 30, 2016

(D) September 30, 2016

Question 5

The controller of X Ltd., a Canadian-controlled private corporation, estimates that the company's taxes payable for its year ended December 31, 2016, will be $200,000. Taxes payable for each of the previous three years was as follows:

2013 — $212,000

2014 — $180,000

2015 — $140,000 (taxable income was $600,000)

What is the minimum monthly instalment that X Ltd., which is not an eligible small CCPC, must pay in the 2016 taxation year and the due date for the final balance of tax?

(A) The minimum monthly instalment is $11,667 and the due date for the final balance of tax is February 28, 2017.

(B) The minimum monthly instalment is $16,667 and the due date for the final balance of tax is February 28, 2017.

(C) The minimum monthly instalment is $16,667 and the due date for the final balance of tax is March 31, 2017.

(D) The minimum monthly instalment is $15,000 and the due date for the final balance of tax is February 28, 2017.

Question 6

Ms. Jones is a retired partner in a law firm and has taxable income of $70,000 each year from the partnership, her RRIF and her investments. She expects to pay $25,000 in tax in respect of 2016. She paid $16,400 in tax in respect of 2015 and $15,300 in respect of 2014. No tax is withheld on any of this income.

Which of the following is the minimum amount that Ms. Jones should pay for her 2016 quarterly income tax instalments, in order to avoid any unnecessary interest costs?

(A) 4 payments of $6,250

(B) 2 payments of $4,100 and 2 payments of $6,250

(C) 2 payments of $3,825 and 2 payments of $4,100

(D) 2 payments of $3,825 and 2 payments of $4,375

¶14,850   EXERCISES

Exercise 1

ITA: 153(1)

List five payments from which the payer must withhold tax.

Exercise 2

Give two examples of a windfall that would reduce an estimate of income in a net worth assessment.

Exercise 3

ITA: 156(1)

In 2016, Mr. Owens projects his income to be $40,000 consisting of employment income of $25,000 and income from a small business, operated as a sideline, of $15,000. He expects that his tax liability will be $6,000 on the business income. During 2014 and 2015 he paid $3,000 and $4,000, respectively, in tax on the business income. Is he required to make instalments for 2016? If so, how much must he pay in instalments during 2016 so that he does not incur interest and when must each instalment be paid?

Exercise 4

ITA: 157(1)

A corporation that is not an eligible small CCPC uses the calendar year for its taxation year. In 2014, it paid tax of $158,400. By the end of March 2016, it had computed its tax for 2015 at $237,600. It estimates that it will have to pay $356,400 in tax for 2016. Is the corporation required to make instalments for 2016. If so, how much must it pay in instalments during 2016 and when must each be paid?

Exercise 5

ITA: 150(1), 162(1),
238(1)

X, Y, and Z filed their personal tax returns on May 5, 2016, for the 2015 year. X and Y are employees and Z is a proprietorship business owner. X determined that he owed $4,700 in tax on that date and enclosed a cheque for the $4,700; Y computed a refund of $2,000; and Z included a cheque for $3,500 relating to his balance of tax. What penalties and offences might each be liable for?

Exercise 6

ITA: 152(4), 163, 220(3.1);
IC 00-1R

Mr. DeHaan has approached you, on July 12, 2016, for some advice considering a reassessment notice for the 2013 year which he has received. Mr. DeHaan has misplaced the reassessment notice but assures you that it was dated June 15, 2016. In your conversation with Mr. DeHaan, he reveals that he has had considerable difficulty with the CRA in the past, and has had to pay penalties under the Act. Mr. DeHaan is positive that he has complied with the law in this situation and wishes to dispute the assessment.

ITA: 162, 163

— REQUIRED

(A) Determine what additional information you require from Mr. DeHaan before discussing the relative merits of the particular disputed items.

(B) Assuming you accept the engagement, what steps would you immediately take?

(C) Explain to Mr. DeHaan the penalty under section 163.

Exercise 7

ITA: 161, 164

Compare the calculation and tax treatment of interest paid on amounts owing to the CRA and interest paid on refunds by the CRA.

Exercise 8

ITA: 163.2; IC 01-1

You have been engaged by Sid Fisher, a self-employed new client, to prepare an income statement and his tax return. Sid has instructed you to prepare these based on a figure for his total revenue and a list of his business expenditures, which he has provided to you. Based on your quick review of these data, you concluded that the expenditures were consistent with Sid's type of business and the amounts appeared to be reasonable. You prepared the income tax return, showing $100,000 of total revenue and $70,000 of expenses.

Subsequently, Sid's return was selected for audit. The CRA determined that many of the expenses deducted in the return could not be substantiated by adequate records. The CRA concluded that some of these expenditures may not have been made. The CRA, also, discovered that only 65% of the actual revenues of the business had been reported.

— *REQUIRED*

Determine whether you are at risk of being assessed under the civil penalties provisions of the Act.   ITA: 163.2

Exercise 9

ITA: 165(1), 169, 172, 180

Outline briefly the full appeal procedure indicating the time allowed between steps in the procedure.

Exercise 10

ITA: 216, 220(3)

A non-resident individual owns a rental property in Canada and has paid non-resident withholding tax on the gross rental revenue since 2011. He has heard that he may be able to recover some of this withholding tax if he files Canadian income tax returns for those years. What would you advise him?

Exercise 11

ITA: 161

Mr. Steve Parrott's only source of income is from his dry cleaning business. In March and June of 2015, he paid instalments of $2,000 each in respect of his 2015 taxes. By September, he realized things were not going well and he would likely have a loss for the year. He, therefore, paid no further instalments.

On June 15, 2016, Steve filed his 2015 tax return claiming a loss and a refund of his $4,000 instalments. He also filed a T1A carrying the loss back to 2014. He expects a tax refund of $5,000 from the carryback.

— *REQUIRED*

What interest can Steve expect to receive on his tax refunds?

Exercise 12

ITA: 70, 104, 111

Sam Elder died on September 10, 2016. Discuss how the following are to be reported:

(A) $200, accrued but unpaid, interest on his bank account.

(B) $100 dividend declared on September 15, 2016 and paid on September 30 (the previous dividend was paid on March 30).

(C) CPP of $600 for August 2016, received on September 3 and $200 for the period September 1 to 10, received on October 4.

(D) Charitable donations for the period January 1 to September 10, 2016.

(E) Capital losses incurred in 2015 of $4,000, of which no amount was deducted in 2015.

(F) Income of $900 from a trust established on his wife's death, of which Sam was a beneficiary, for the year ended May 31, 2016.

(G) $50,000 in life insurance payable on Sam's death.

¶14,850

ITA: 70, 150

Exercise 13

After the 2015 personal tax season, the brother (Mr. Kaye) of one of your clients (Ms. Kaye) contacted you with respect to his sister. He indicated that his sister had passed away on May 2, 2016, at the age of 50.

Mr. Kaye indicated that his sister had the following income from January 1 to May 2, 2016:

(a) Salary — $22,000, of which $2,000 was vacation pay that had not been paid at the time of her death.

(b) Bond interest payable of $950 which had not been received at the time of death.

(c) Interest in her savings/chequing account of $150.

(d) Interest of $140 on a 60-day GIC which matured on May 15, 2016.

(e) Grossed-up dividend income of $1,380 on 100 Flying High shares, payable on April 30, 2016, but had not been paid at the time of her death.

(f) The fair market value of Flying High shares on May 2, 2016, was $25/share. These shares had been purchased for $10/share in 2009.

(g) Her RRSP had a value of $34,000 at the date of her death. In February 2016, Ms. Kaye made an RRSP contribution, in respect of 2016, of $9,000. Her earned income for 2015 was $80,000.

— *REQUIRED*

Discuss the tax implications and filing requirements as a consequence of Ms. Kaye's death.

CHAPTER 14

¶14,875 ASSIGNMENT PROBLEMS

Type 1 Problems

Problem 1

ITA: 150(1)

When must the tax returns for the following be filed: (a) a corporation, (b) a deceased person (terminal return only), (c) a trust, and (d) an individual?

Problem 2

ITA: 152(4)

An individual filed her 2015 tax return on April 30, 2016. The CRA responded with a notice of assessment mailed on May 27, 2016. If the CRA wishes to make an additional assessment of tax for 2015, by what date must it issue a notice of reassessment?

Problem 3

ITA: 165, 169

Rachel, a new client, requested some assistance with her personal income tax assessment. The CRA is claiming that her car expenses are not deductible because they were incurred to earn employment income. Rachel argues that the expenses were incurred to earn commission income in accordance with her employment contract and the *Income Tax Act*.

Outline the legal rights that Rachel has with respect to her assessment and the steps she should undertake with the CRA.

Problem 4

ITA: 163(2), 163.2

Mr. Turner visited his accountant Ms. Blackford, on March 31, 2016, to discuss the tax consequences of a recent transaction. On January 10, 2016, Mr. Turner received a dividend of $100,000 from Dot.com Ltd., a company he owns 100%.

Ms. Blackford explained that if he had transferred his shares of Dot.com Ltd. to a holding corporation on December 31, 2015, he could have deferred personal tax of $36,000 on the dividend until it was paid out of the holding corporation to him personally.

Ms. Blackford indicated that the documentation with respect to the transfer of the shares to the holding corporation and the payment of the dividend to the holding corporation can be back-dated to achieve the result desired.

What are the tax consequences of back-dating the documentation with respect to the transfer of the securities?

Problem 5

ITA: 156, 156.1, 161, 163.1

Bert Logan's daughter Amanda is an accounting student. After a brief review of Bert's previous tax returns she advised him that he would likely have to begin making income tax instalments for 2016; however, she was uncertain about how these instalments were to be calculated and the consequences of making inadequate instalments. Amanda called one of the tax specialists at her employer firm, First and Partners, for assistance.

Amanda provided the following information:

(a) 2014 actual tax liability was $8,750;

(b) 2015 actual tax liability was $7,640; and

(c) 2016 estimated tax liability is $5,520.

You have been asked to write a memo, in point form, for partner review explaining the options available to calculate instalment payments for Bert Logan and the consequences if incorrect instalments are made.

Problem 6

ITA: 157, 162, 163, 163.1

Ruffle Limited, a public company, specializes in the games business. For their fiscal year ended October 31, 2014, the company's tax liability was $54,024. Due to the success of the board game, Run About, the company's bottom line has increased significantly, resulting in a tax liability of $69,036 for the fiscal period ended October 31, 2015.

Ruffle Limited's climb to success came to a halt in the next fiscal year. Due to increased competition, profits are expected to decline significantly and the controller of Ruffle Limited estimates the tax payable for the fiscal period ending October 31, 2016 to be $45,000.

In addition, the controller informed you that, due to cash flow problems, the actual instalments for June, July, and August 2016 were $1,050 less than the amount required. The controller also indicated that in order to compensate for this shortfall an instalment payment of $4,500 was made in October 2016 and that the remaining outstanding balance would be included in the December remittance.

The controller has asked you, his tax accountant, to provide him with required instalments for the 2016 taxation year.

Problem 7

ITA: 161, 162, 163.1; IC 00-1R

On September 1, 2016, you started in your new position as manager of taxation for Malic Corporation, a large public company with a December 31 year-end. On the second day into the job, Maureen Smythe, the VP Finance, comes into your office with a folder entitled "Outstanding Items". She tells you that the folder was found in the bottom drawer of your desk when the office was cleaned up after the previous manager of taxation left. She is concerned about the following items found in the file:

(a) Paper-clipped to the corporation's notice of assessment for the 2010 taxation year (dated September 30, 2011), is a reassessment, dated April 30, 2016, that states that the corporation has been assessed additional tax for the 2010 taxation year in the amount of $722,500.

(b) A memo to the tax files from the previous manager stating that for the 2015 taxation year minimum instalments were made for January to October, no instalment was made in November, and an instalment of $1.45 million was made in December.

(c) A partially completed tax return for the 2015 taxation year indicating taxes payable of $10.76 million. The return had not been filed.

(d) A schedule of information from previous tax returns showing the tax liabilities for the 2012 to 2014 taxation years were $7.5 million, $5.4 million, and $9.2 million, respectively.

After reviewing the files Ms. Smythe leaves with you, you determine that you need to do the following:

(A) Comment on the validity of the CRA reassessment.

(B) Determine whether there is tax owing for the 2015 taxation year, calculate any late filing penalties, if any, and comment on any late installment penalties, if any.

The prescribed interest rate required by Regulation 4301, to be used for the purpose of computing imputed interest on employee and shareholder loans, is 1% for all of 2015 and assume 1% for all of 2016.

Problem 8

ITA: 163.2; IC 01-1

Bill, an accountant, lives in an exclusive neighbourhood where house prices are in excess of $1,000,000. He has recently become friendly with a new neighbour and in March the neighbour hired Bill to prepare his personal tax return. The neighbour gave Bill a T4 reporting $60,000 of income. Thinking that the income was on the low side, Bill asked if this was all the income he had and the neighbour replied that it was. Bill did not ask any further questions but prepared the tax return. When the neighbour's tax return was audited by the CRA, it was discovered that he had in excess of $300,000 in income for the year.

Advise Bill as to whether he is at risk of being assessed under the civil penalty provisions in the Act.

ITA: 163.2

Problem 9

ITA: 212(1), 215(3), 215(6), 216(1); IC 77-16R4

After several years of visiting Florida, Mr. Singh moved from Toronto to Florida on December 31, 2015, and became a non-resident of Canada. Mr. Singh decided to rent his house in Canada for the next few years. Mr. Singh has arranged with a relocation agency, Gone-Today-Here-Tomorrow, to collect the rent, pay all expenses and remit the balance to him quarterly. During 2016, the house was rented for $1,950 for January to June, and $2,150 for July to December. Expenses amounted to $1,550 per month.

You have been asked to discuss withholding tax and other tax implications concerning Mr. Singh's rental property.

Problem 10

ITA: 153

A Canadian university hires a well-known American lecturer to lecture on American history. The work will take approximately six weeks and she is to be paid $20,000.

You have been asked to determine whether there is a requirement to withhold Canadian tax on the $20,000.

Problem 11

ETA: 169(4), 169(5), 223; 225(1)–(4), 228(1)–(3), 237(1), 238(1), 238.1, 239(1), 243, 244(1), 245(2), 246(1), 248, 286(1)

Mr. E. Evans has decided to open a small car detailing company. The individual at the name registration office suggested that Mr. Evans walk down to the CRA office and pick up the information package with respect to tax filing, etc.

Mr. Evans had anticipated that the package of information obtained at the CRA office would include information on the harmonized sales tax ("HST"). Unfortunately, this information was not included in the package obtained. Mr. Evans approached you to explain the obligations of a registrant under the *Excise Tax Act*.

Provide the appropriate explanations.

Type 2 Problems

Problem 12

ITA: 153, 162(1), 162(2), 212(1)(*d*), 233.3; ITR: 108(1.11); IC 77-16R4

On January 10, 2015, you started your new job as controller for Bordessa Corporation, a Canadian-controlled private corporation with a December 31 year-end. On your first day, the president and owner-manager of the company has asked you to follow up on some personal and corporate tax concerns that he has.

(1) The company is the exclusive Canadian manufacturer and distributor of menswear designed by a famous U.S. designer and pays the designer a royalty equal to 10% of sales each quarter. Royalty payments are due one month after each quarter end (i.e., on April 30, July 31, October 31, and January 31). The company's financial statements show a 2015 royalty expense of $60,000. The financial statements also show the amount of royalties payable at the company's December 31, 2015 year-end to be $20,000 (the comparable number for December 31, 2014 is $10,000). According to the company's 2015 cheque register, however, only $45,000 has been paid to the menswear designer and only $5,000 has been paid to the CRA. The president wants to know how much the company should remit when it makes its January 31, 2016 payment to make up for unpaid royalties and withholding taxes it owes in respect of 2015.

(2) The company accrued a $100,000 bonus payable to the President on its financial statements. This bonus was declared by way of a director's resolution at the company's Board of Directors' last 2015 meeting. The president understands that his bonus must be paid within 180 days after the year-end in order for it to be deductible in 2015 and you have verified that this is correct. This is the first time the company has accrued such a bonus and the president wants to know the deadline for the remittance of payroll deductions on the bonus. You do a quick review of payroll remittances for 2014 and 2015 and find that they amounted to about $120,000 in each year.

ITA: 78(3)

(3) The president tells you that he filed his 2014, 2013, and 2012 tax returns yesterday (January 9, 2016) after receiving a demand to file these returns in December 2015. He is expecting a net refund of $5,490 (see the schedule below). He wants to know whether he will be assessed any penalties for late filing and what the amount of the penalties will be. He tells you that his wife is a self-employed medical doctor.

	Balance due (Refund $)
2012	(20,500)
2013	10,000
2014	5,010
Net refund expected	(5,490)

(4) During 2015, the president of the company inherited U.S. stock from a distant relative who lived in the U.S. The value of the stock at the date of the relative's death was C$120,000. The president has asked you if he has to report this on his 2015 tax return. The stock is held in safekeeping at a stockbroker's office in Toronto.

Report your findings to the president.

Problem 13

ITA: 60, 70, 118.93; IT-210R2, IT-212R3, IT-326R3

In early March, you were preparing your client list with respect to the personal tax return preparation season. When you came across Mr. Ricky's name you realized that Mrs. Ricky had called you regarding her husband's death. Mr. Ricky had passed away March 1, 2016, at age 62.

Mr. Ricky owned and operated a Canadian-controlled private corporation, Shining Ltd., involved in reconditioning cars. Mr. Ricky's 100 shares had an adjusted cost base and paid-up capital of $55,000. The fair market value of the shares at the date of death was $750,000. Seventy-five per cent of the shares were left to his wife and the rest of the shares were left to his 25-year-old son.

Mr. Ricky earned $15,000 per month in salary, which is paid by direct deposit on the last day of the month. A non-periodic bonus of $35,000 had been declared on February 15, 2016, but had not yet been paid at the time of his death. His accumulated vacation pay of $10,000 was due on the last day of the month, but was paid on March 10, 2016.

In addition to his shares, Mr. Ricky owned bonds which earned $5,500 of interest income in 2015 and accrued $917 of interest in 2016 to the date of his death. He owned another bond on which there was $500 in uncashed bond interest due on January 4, 2016, the anniversary date of that bond. Further, Mr. Ricky had owned two rental properties. Net rental income after capital cost allowance from January 1, 2015 to December 31, 2015 was $45,000 and net rental income before capital allowance was $4,000 for each of the months of January and February 2016.

Other Information:

(1) All assets of Shining Ltd. have been used in the active business of the corporation.

(2) The shares of Shining Ltd. have been owned by Mr. Ricky since 1999.

(3) Mr. Ricky had earned income in 2014 and 2015 of $95,000. He contributed to his RRSP the maximum amount allowed as a deduction in 2015. His RRSP was worth $295,000 at the time of his death. Mrs. Ricky is the designated beneficiary of his RRSP.

(4) Mr. Ricky had a savings/chequing account which earned $2,500 interest in 2015 and $150 during January and February 2016.

(5) Mr. Ricky had utilized $350,000 of his capital gains exemption.

(6) All of Mr. Ricky's other assets have been left to his wife, except for the two rental properties which are bequeathed to his 20-year-old daughter.

(7) The rental properties had a fair market value of $100,000 each. Both properties had the following details:

	Unit #1	Unit #2
Capital cost	$72,000	$83,000
UCC	50,000	52,000

The partner has asked you to prepare a letter, in draft form, to Mrs. Ricky explaining the tax implications and the filing requirements in respect of Mr. Ricky's death. Calculate taxable income for 2016.

 [For more problems and solutions thereto, see the DVD accompanying the textbook.]

CHAPTER 14 —
DISCUSSION NOTES FOR REVIEW QUESTIONS

(1) (a) False. All corporations resident in Canada have to file tax returns within six months of the end of the year.   ITA: 150(1)(a)

(b) True. An individual is required to file a tax return if he or she "has disposed of a capital property". Even if there is no taxable income or tax liability a return must be filed. In addition, Mr. Austen may lose his capital gains deduction in respect of this transaction, if he does not file the return.   ITA: 110.6(6), 150(1)

(c) False. Instalments must be paid on the 15th of each of those months.   ITA: 156(1)

(2) An instalment interest offset is available on prepaid or overpaid instalments. How-ever, this credit offset can only be applied against instalment interest owing; it is not refundable and may not be applied against any other debt. To benefit, he would have to pay the December 15 instalment on September 15 which would offset the fact that the June 15 instalment was three months late. In addition, the prescribed interest rate for the last quarter would have to be equal to or greater than the prescribed interest rate for the second quarter.   ITA: 161(2.2)

(3) They will not be able to collect interest for the last three years. Interest will not be paid for the period prior to the filing of the tax return for the year in which the request is made to carry the loss back.   ITA: 164(5)

(4) Since the accountant sent a letter to the CRA, it may take some time before a reply is received. If the reply is received late and there is disagreement, it may be too late to file a Notice of Objection. Therefore, it may be prudent to file the Notice of Objection in the first place unless the matter is a minor one.   ITA: 165(1)

(5) In order to amend the tax returns for the third preceding year the company would have had to file form T2A by the time the corporate tax returns are due for the loss year which is six months after the fiscal year end. However, Murray Corp. did not meet this deadline since it did not file until seven months after the year-end. Therefore, the CRA will not have to let the corporation carry the loss back at all. However, the loss will still be available to be carried forward.   ITA: 152(6)

(6) The following are the returns that can be filed:

(a) Terminal return — This return reports the income for the period in the year before the date of death and includes any gain or loss on the deemed disposition on death. Full personal credits may be claimed.   ITA: 70(1)

(b) Rights or things — "Rights or things" can be reported on a separate return to take advantage of the lower marginal tax brackets. Also, the full personal tax credits allowed can be claimed again.   ITA: 70(2), 118(1), 118(2)

CHAPTER 14 — SOLUTIONS TO MULTIPLE CHOICE QUESTIONS

Question 1

(B) is correct. The penalty is $900. The initial penalty rate of 5% is increased by 1% for each *complete* month after April 30, 2016, that the return was not filed to a maximum penalty of 5% + 4% = 9%.   ITA: 162(1)

(A) is incorrect as it includes only the initial penalty of 5% of the unpaid tax.

(C) is incorrect as it includes ½% for the half month of September. Only complete months should be counted for purposes of the penalty.

(D) is incorrect as it includes 1% for the month of September. Only complete months should be counted for purposes of the penalty.

Question 2

(B) August 15, 2019, is correct. The normal reassessment period for a CCPC ends three years after the day of mailing of a notice of assessment for the year.   ITA: 152(3.1)

(A) December 31, 2018, three years after the end of the taxation year, is incorrect. The three-year period commences with the date of mailing of the notice of assessment, not the last day of the fiscal year.

(C) December 31, 2019, four years after the end of the taxation year, is incorrect.

(D) August 15, 2020, four years after the day of mailing of a notice of assessment for the year, is incorrect. It would be correct if the taxpayer were a corporation other than a CCPC.   ITA: 152(3.1)

Question 3

(D) June 15, 2017, is correct. The notice of objection filing due date is one year after Darol's filing-due date for 2015.   ITA: 165(1)

(A) December 31, 2016, being one year after the end of the taxation year, is incorrect.

(B) January 14, 2015, being 90 days after the date of mailing of the notice of assessment, is incorrect in this case. For an individual and a testamentary trust, the due date is the later of this date and one year after the filing-due date for the tax return.

(C) April 30, 2017, being one year after the filing-due date for 2015 for an individual *not* carrying on a business, is incorrect. Darol's filing-due date for 2015 was June 15, 2016, as he carried on business in 2015.

Question 4

The correct answer is (D) September 30, 2016, being six months after the date of death.   ITA: 150(1)(*b*)

(A) is incorrect. It is the most common due date for 2015 personal tax returns. This date is not correct for two reasons: first, he has income from carrying on business, and second, he has at least six months from the date of death.   ITA: 150(1)(*a*)(i)

(B) is incorrect. It is the date the return would have been due if he had not died.   ITA: 150(1)(*a*)(ii)

(C) is incorrect as it is six months after the end of the year for which the return is being filed.

Question 5

(A) is correct. The minimum monthly instalment is the least of:

– $\frac{1}{12}$ of the estimated taxes payable: $\frac{1}{12} \times \$200{,}000 = \$16{,}667$

– $\frac{1}{12}$ of the prior year's taxes payable: $\frac{1}{12}$ of $140,000 = $11,667

– $\frac{1}{12}$ of the second prior year's taxable payable ($\frac{1}{12}$ of $180,000 = $15,000) for two months and 10 payments of $11,000 ($\frac{1}{10} \times$ [$140,000 – 2 × $15,000]).

The least of these is either the prior year method or the second prior year method. Only the prior year method ($11,667 per month) is listed as a choice in this question. Because X Ltd. had taxable income in the prior year of more than the small business deduction limit, it must pay its final balance due within two months of year end (February 28, 2017).

(B) and (C) incorrectly base the instalments on estimated taxes payable. (B) has the correct final due date. (C) incorrectly uses the balance-due day that is three months after the end of the year which is applicable only for Canadian-controlled private corporations that have taxable income that is less than the small business deduction limit in the prior year.

(D) incorrectly uses the amount for the first two payments of the second prior year method for all 12 payments but has the correct final due date for the balance due. (D) would have been a correct answer had it indicated that the payments for the last 10 months would be $11,000 per month.

Question 6

(D) is correct (two payments of $3,825 and two payments of $4,375). The minimum monthly instalment is the least of:

– ¼ of the estimated taxes payable: ¼ × $25,000 = $6,250

– ¼ of the prior year's taxes payable: ¼ of $16,400 = $4,100

– ¼ of the second prior year's taxable payable (¼ of $15,300 = $3,825) for two months and two payments of $4,375 (½ × [$16,400 – 2 × $3,825]).

(A) is incorrect because four payments of $6,250 is not the minimum payment.

(B) is incorrect because two payments of $4,100 and two payments of $6,250 is not the minimum amount. Four payments of $4,100 would result in the minimum amount.

(C) is incorrect because two payments of $3,825 and two payments of $4,100 is not the minimum amount. If the first two payments are $3,825, the last two payments must be $4,375. Alternatively, four payments of $4,100 can be made.

CHAPTER 14 — SOLUTIONS TO EXERCISES

Exercise 1

Subsection 153(1):

(a) salary or wages or other remuneration, including stock option benefits, from employment;

(b) a superannuation or pension benefit;

(c) a retiring allowance;

(d) a death benefit for long service from an employer;

(e) an Employment Insurance benefit;

(f) a benefit under a supplementary unemployment benefit plan;

(g) an annuity payment;

(h) a benefit from a deferred profit sharing plan;

(i) fees, commissions and other amounts for services;

(j) a payment under a registered retirement savings plan;

(k) certain amounts resulting from an income averaging annuity;

(l) a payment from a registered retirement income fund.

Exercise 2

Inheritance, gambling winnings, lottery prize, etc.

Exercise 3

As his net tax owing in the current year and one of the two preceding years is in excess of $3,000, he is required to make instalments.

Instalments of $750 (¼ × $3,000) must be paid by March 15 and June 15 and instalments of $1,250 (i.e., ($4,000 – 2 × $750) × ½) must be paid by September 15 and December 15. The balance of the tax liability must be remitted by the balance-due date of April 30, 2017.

Exercise 4

As the corporation's estimated taxes payable for the current year and the taxes paid for the preceding year exceed $3,000, instalments are required.

The Act would allow the following: ITA: 157(1)(a)(iii)

January 31 and February 28, 2016 — ¹⁄₁₂ of $158,400 or $13,200;

Last day of March to December 2016 — ¹⁄₁₀ of ($237,600 – 2 × $13,200) or $21,120;

Balance on the last day of the third month after the taxation year-end, where a small business deduction was taken by virtue of section 125 in the current or preceding year and the corporation and associated corporations' aggregate taxable incomes for the preceding year did not exceed the small business deduction limit, or, in this particular case, the last day of February 2017, as applicable to any other case.

Exercise 5

Subsection 150(1):

Y and Z will incur no penalties; furthermore, Y is not required to file since no tax is payable, unless he disposed of capital property.

Subsection 162(1):

Failure to file when required — 5% of unpaid tax plus 1% of unpaid tax per complete month past due for a first offence:

X — 5% of $4,700 or $235 plus 1% of $4,700 × nil = $235.

Y — 5% of nil or nil.

Z — no penalty as the return is not due until June 15. Interest charges on the unpaid tax from April 30 will, however, apply.

Subsection 238(1):

Failure to file as or when required — liable on summary conviction to a fine of $1,000 to $25,000 or a fine and imprisonment for up to 12 months;

— Y could be fined if there has been a demand to file under subsection 150(2).

Exercise 6

(A) Facts to be determined:

    (i) Date of mailing of 2013 original assessment in order to determine the three-year limit (i.e., the normal reassessment period for an individual).   ITA: 152(4)

    (ii) Obtain date of mailing of notice of reassessment.

(B) Steps to be taken:

    (i) Procure an engagement letter or a signed consent form which gives permission to discuss Mr. DeHaan's case with officials of the CRA.   Form T1013

    (ii) Start discussions with the CRA.

    (iii) File a Notice of Objection prior to the expiry of the 90-day period based upon the date of mailing determined above (i.e., September 12, 2016, if mailed on June 15, 2016).

    (iv) Warn Mr. DeHaan that certain second-time offences may carry heavier penalties than the first-time offence.

(C) A penalty of 10% of unreported income could be imposed on Mr. DeHaan, if the current reassessment is his second offence within three years of the first offence. Under the CRA's voluntary disclosure program, a valid voluntary disclosure may result in a waiver of penalties.   ITA: 163(1), IC 00-1R

Exercise 7

The Act computes interest at a basic prescribed rate plus 4% on amounts owing to the CRA from the earliest date the amount was due until the date it was paid: ITA: 161

    — the interest is not tax deductible.

Interest is computed at the same basic prescribed rate plus 2% on refunds by the CRA to non-corporate taxpayers and at the basic prescribed rate to corporate taxpayers: ITA: 164(3)

    — the interest is taxable;

    — if the interest relates to instalments, an interest offset is computed using the 4% addition, against interest owing on late instalments for interest earned on early instalments.   ITA: 161(2.2)

Both interest calculations are based on daily compounding.

Interest on the overpayment of taxes for individuals will start to accrue 30 days after the later of the balance due day for the return (i.e., April 30, 2017 for 2016 returns) or the date the return is filed.

An individual's refund interest accruing over a period can be offset by any arrears interest that accrues over the same period, to which the refund interest relates. Hence, only the excess refund interest is taxed to the individual.

Exercise 8

The CRA has commented on this type of situation. The conclusion is that the good faith defence is available, since the income statement reveals nothing that would lead you to question the validity of the information provided to you. As a result, the preparer penalty would not apply in your situation.   IC 01-1

Use of the flowchart presented in the chapter may be helpful in analyzing this situation and reaching this conclusion.

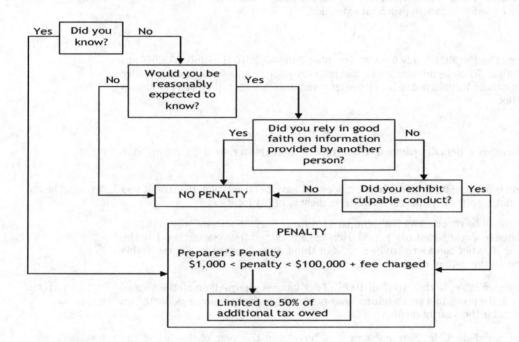

Exercise 9

(a) Notice of objection: ITA: 165(1)

— to be filed by *individual* taxpayers and graduated rate estates by the later of:

(i) one year after the filing-due date, which is normally April 30 or June 15 except for trusts and deceased persons, and   ITA: 248(1)

(ii) the 90th day after the mailing date of the notice of assessment;

— to be filed within 90 days of mailing of notice of assessment for all other taxpayers;

— a prescribed form is not required.

(b) Appeal to the Tax Court of Canada: ITA: 169

— after 90 days of date of decision on notice of objection or 90 days after the mailing of the notice of objection if there has been no response to it;

— may be able to elect informal procedure under subsection 18(1) of the *Tax Court of Canada Act*.

(c) Appeal to the Federal Court of Appeal (section 17.6 of the *Tax Court of Canada Act*):

— within 30 days from date of mailing of decision of the Tax Court of Canada only if that taxpayer chose the general procedure in the Tax Court of Canada.

(d) Appeal to Supreme Court of Canada:

— on recommendation of Federal Court of Appeal;

— with permission of Supreme Court of Canada.

Exercise 10

A tax return may be filed by a non-resident within two years after the end of the year that rents were paid. In that return, rental income for the year, net of expenses, would be reported and any withholding tax paid in the year in respect of rental revenue would be considered taxes paid for the year.

ITA: 216

This individual is eligible to file this return for 2014, 2015, and 2016. The 2011, 2012, and 2013 rents do not fall into the eligible filing period. However, the Minister may extend the time for filing a return. The individual may consider requesting such an extension.

ITA: 216
ITA: 220(3.2)

Exercise 11

Steve will receive interest on the $9,000 only from 30 days after June 15, 2016 (i.e., July 15, 2016) to the date the cheque was mailed. When he determined he had paid excess instalments, he could consider requesting that the instalments be transferred to his employer remittance account, if he has employees from whom he withholds tax.

Exercise 12

(A) The accrued interest is a periodic payment to be reported on the terminal T1 return, due April 30, 2017.

ITA: 70(1)

(B) Since the dividend is not payable until declared, it does not have to be accrued. Because it was declared after death, it is not a right or thing. Therefore, it is income of his estate.

ITA: 70(1), 70(2)

(C) The $800 of CPP would be reported on the terminal T1 return, since no amount was unpaid at the date of death that related to a *completed* pay period. Hence, CPP earned from September 1 to the date of death on September 10 is not considered to be a right or thing, since it is not legally receivable for a completed pay period on the date of death.

(D) The donations are creditable, to the extent of 100% of net income reported, on all the year of death returns combined or in the preceding year's return. Only personal tax credits may be deducted on each of the separate returns for the year of death.

ITA: 118(1), 118(2)
ITA: 118.93

(E) Net capital losses are deductible from any source of income in the year of death and the preceding year.

ITA: 111(2)

(F) Trust income of $900 for the year ended May 31, 2016 must be reported on the terminal return. An election is permitted to report the trust income payable to Sam for the stub period, June 1, 2016 to September 10, 2016 on a separate return, also due April 30, 2017. The personal tax credits can be deducted on this return.

ITA: 104(23)(*d*)

ITA: 118(1), 118(2)

(G) Life insurance proceeds received on death are not taxable.

Exercise 13

Ms. Kaye's 2016 terminal personal tax return is required to be filed by April 30, 2017. In Ms. Kaye's 2016 return all accrued income earned on a periodic basis during the period January 1 to May 1, 2016 should be included. In addition, all capital property (such as her Flying High shares) is deemed to have been disposed of at the fair market value. A claim for the full personal tax credits can be made on the terminal return even though Ms. Kaye died on May 2, 2016. The RRSP contribution of $9,000 is deductible on her 2016 terminal return, since it is less than the maximum amount (i.e., lesser of $22,000 and 18% of $80,000).

ITA: 150(1)(*d*)
ITA: 70(1)
ITA: 70(5)

Ms. Kaye's 2016 terminal return will include the following:

Salary	$22,000
Bond interest	950
Savings account interest	150
GIC interest	140
Dividend income	1,380
Taxable capital gain [½ ($25 − $10) × 100]	750
RRSP accumulation	34,000
RRSP contribution	(9,000)
Taxable income	$50,370

Ms. Kaye's legal representative can report amounts which were receivable but not received at the date of death, on a separate tax return, called a "rights or things" return, instead of on the terminal return.

ITA: 70(2)

The unpaid vacation pay of $2,000, interest payable of $950 and $1,380 of grossed-up dividend income would qualify as income from "rights or things." Personal tax credits equal to the amounts claimed in the terminal return may be claimed again on the "rights or things" return. This return is due on the date that is the later of one year after death and 90 days after assessment of any return for the year of death.

Alternatively, the legal representative can assign the income from "rights or things" to a particular beneficiary.

ITA: 70(3)

Chapter 15

Corporate Distributions, Windings-Up, and Sales

Learning Goals

Know

By the end of this chapter you will know:

• The basic provisions of corporate surplus and the implication of its distribution.

Understand and Explain

By the end of this chapter you will understand and be able to explain:

• The tax paid or tax-free components of corporate surplus.

• The process for analyzing the tax consequences of selling the assets or shares of a corporation.

Apply

By the end of this chapter you will be able to apply your knowledge and understanding to:

• Calculate the corporate surplus components and the tax consequences of its distribution.

• Calculate whether the shareholders should sell shares or assets of a corporation.

Review Questions
¶15,800 in the Study Guide

Multiple Choice Questions
¶15,825 in the Study Guide

Exercise Questions
¶15,850 in the Study Guide

Assignment Problems
¶15,875 in the Study Guide

CHAPTER 15

CHAPTER 15 — LEARNING CHART

Problem Descriptions

Textbook Example Problems

1	Capital dividend account
2	Share attributes — tax consequences
3	Capital dividend
4	Wind-up calculations
5	Assets vs. shares

Multiple Choice Questions

1	Capital dividend
2	Redemption of shares
3	Winding-up consequences
4	Winding-up — available for distribution
5	Paid-up capital
6	Sale of goodwill — tax consequences

Exercises

1	Capital dividend account
2	Capital dividend account
3	Withdrawing cash from a corporation
4	Stock dividend
5	Independent situations — tax consequences
6	Winding-up
7	Winding-up
8	Winding-up

Assignment Problems

1	Capital dividend account
2	Capital dividend account
3	Deemed dividends
4	Redeem vs. sell shares
5	Wind up of a corporation
6	Sale of assets with wind-up
7	Sale of assets with wind-up
8	Corporate distribution
9	Assets vs. shares
10	Purchase of asses vs. shares
11	Corporate distribution

Study Notes

¶15,800   REVIEW QUESTIONS

(1) Assuming that you are working in a province in which only par value shares can be issued, what journal entry would you use to record the issuance of 100 common shares, which had a par value of $100 each, for $30,000?

(2) In jurisdictions without par value shares, how is the paid-up capital determined?

(3) What are "high-low" shares?

(4) What are the five basic components of the capital dividend account?

(5) Calculate the effect on the capital dividend account as a result of the sale of unrecorded goodwill this year for $100,000. The only other transaction in eligible capital property took place three years ago when a customer list was purchased for $10,000. The balance in the CEC account is now approximately $6,000.

(6) Smith Co. has total PUC of $10,000. It decided to make a distribution of capital in the amount of $9,000, but when it actually paid out the $9,000, the PUC was only reduced by $8,000. What are the tax consequences?

(7) What are the three components of a distribution on the winding-up of a corporation where the only shareholder is an individual?

(8) Glee Co. is a CCPC that is in the process of being wound up under the general winding-up rule. One of its assets is a building that has an accrued terminal loss. The lawyer has suggested that subsection 13(21.2) will apply to deny the terminal loss to the corporation on winding-up. What do you think?   ITA: 88(2)

(9) Technically, on the winding-up of a corporation under the general winding-up rule, how are the proceeds of disposition of the shares calculated?   ITA: 88(2)

¶15,825   MULTIPLE CHOICE QUESTIONS

Question 1

Which one of the following statements is FALSE?

(A) A capital dividend is usually received tax-free.

(B) A corporation must elect to pay a capital dividend, not later than the day the dividend is paid.

(C) If a private corporation has had more capital gains than capital losses, it will probably have a balance in its capital dividend account.

(D) The payment of a capital dividend by a private corporation will trigger a dividend refund: one dollar refund for each three dollars of capital dividends paid.

Question 2

Mr. Andrews owned Class A special shares of Atlantis Ltd. with the following characteristics:

Fair market value	$60,000
Cost	20,000
Paid-up capital	10,000

These shares were redeemed. Which one of the following best describes the tax consequences of the redemption to Mr. Andrews?

(A) A capital gain of $40,000

(B) A dividend of $40,000

(C) A dividend of $50,000 and a capital gain of $40,000

(D) A dividend of $50,000 and a capital loss of $10,000

Question 3

X Ltd. had $40,000 available for distribution to its sole shareholder, Xavier, on winding-up. The balances in the tax accounts of X Ltd. were as follows:

Share capital (paid-up capital)	$ 2,000
RDTOH	Nil
Capital dividend account	8,000
Other surplus (LRIP taxed at low CCPC rate)	30,000
	$40,000

Xavier paid $1,000 for the shares of X Ltd. when he purchased them two years ago. Which one of the following statements is TRUE?

(A) The winding-up can occur on a tax-deferred basis. Xavier will be able to defer the recognition of any income for tax purposes.

(B) Xavier will have dividend income of $30,000 which will be grossed-up to $35,400 for tax purposes. In addition, he will have a capital gain of $1,000.

(C) Xavier will have dividend income of $30,000 which will be grossed-up to $35,400 for tax purposes. In addition, he will have a capital gain of $9,000.

(D) Xavier will have a capital gain of $39,000 on the winding-up of X Ltd.

Question 4

Art, the sole shareholder of Art's Variety Inc. with a November 30 year end, has decided to wind up the corporation, effective December 1. The balance sheet as at that date is anticipated to be as set out below.

CHAPTER 15

Assets

Cash..	$ 45,000
Refundable dividend tax on hand	30,000
Land, at cost (FMV, $850,000)	250,000
Building, at UCC (FMV, $780,000; cost, $380,000)	180,000
	$505,000

Liabilities & Equity

Liabilities	$ 20,000
Paid-up capital	5,000
Capital dividend account.....................................	10,000
Other surplus	470,000
	$505,000

Art's Variety Inc. is a Canadian-controlled private corporation. It pays tax at a combined federal and provincial rate of 14.5% on business income in the winding-up period and 50⅔% including the additional refundable tax on investment income.

The amount available for distribution to Art on the windup will be:

(A) $1,655,000

(B) $1,372,667

(C) $1,556,000

(D) $1,858,333

Question 5

At the beginning of its first taxation year, Newco Ltd., a newly incorporated company, issued 100 common shares to Mr. A for $10,000. On June 1 of the same year, Newco issued an additional 100 common shares to Mr. B for $15,000 (which is the fair value of the shares on that date). On December 30 of the same year, Mr. C acquired all of Mr. A's common shares for $20,000. At the end of this year (December 31), which of the following statements is true?

(A) The total paid-up capital of the common shares is $25,000, ½ of which is attributable to each of Mr. C and Mr. B.

(B) The total paid-up capital of the common shares is $35,000, ½ of which is attributable to each of Mr. C and Mr. B.

(C) The total paid-up capital of the common shares is $25,000, $10,000 of which is attributable to Mr. C and $15,000 of which is attributable to Mr. B.

(D) The total paid-up capital of the common shares is $35,000, $20,000 of which is attributable to Mr. C and $15,000 of which is attributable to Mr. B.

Question 6

C Co. is a Canadian controlled private corporation with a December 31 year-end. During the year it sold all its assets including goodwill. The goodwill was sold for fair market value: $1 million. The cost of the goodwill and the company's cumulative eligible capital account was Nil. Which of the following is a correct statement?

(A) C Co. will report a taxable capital gain of $500,000 and its capital dividend account will increase by $500,000.

(B) C Co. will report active business income of $500,000 and its capital dividend account will increase by $500,000.

(C) C Co. will report active business income of $750,000 and its capital dividend account will increase by $250,000.

(D) C Co. will report a taxable capital gain of $500,000 and its refundable dividend tax on hand account will increase by $153,333.

¶15,850   EXERCISES

Exercise 1

ITA: 89(1)

The following capital properties have been sold by a Canadian-controlled private corporation during the year ended December 31:

	A	B	C
Proceeds of disposition	$4,000	$1,000	$2,000
Cost	2,000	2,000	2,000
Selling expenses	400	100	200

— *REQUIRED*

Compute the effects of the dispositions on the capital dividend account.

Exercise 2

ITA: 89(1)

Action Ltd., a Canadian-controlled private corporation, sold the following two capital properties during the fiscal year ending December 31:

	Cost	Proceeds	Selling costs
Property 1	$75,000	$110,000	$11,000
Property 2	40,000	11,000	5,500

— *REQUIRED*

Compute the effects of these sales on:

(A) the net income for tax purposes, and

(B) the balance in the capital dividend account.

Exercise 3

ITA: 83, 84

Mr. Duong, the sole shareholder of Investment Limited, a Canadian-controlled private corporation, requires some cash for other personal investment transactions. Investment Limited's share capital is composed of 100 common shares with an ACB and PUC of $1 per share and 1,000 6% preferred shares with an ACB and PUC per share of $15 and a retractable value of $75 per share. Mr. Duong is considering the following alternatives:

(a) Mr. Duong would cause Investment Limited to redeem 800 preferred shares at $75 per share.

(b) Mr. Duong would cause Investment Limited to pay a cash dividend of $60,000 on the common shares. Investment Limited has a capital dividend account of $75,000.

(c) Mr. Duong would cause Investment Limited to make a non-dividend cash distribution of $60,000 on the preferred shares.

— *REQUIRED*

Discuss the tax implication of the above transactions.

Exercise 4

ITA: 54, 84(3), 248(1)

A Canadian-controlled private corporation with no GRIP balance has paid a dividend this year in the form of 10 first preference shares each having a redemption value of $1,000 and a paid-up capital value of $1.00.

— REQUIRED

(A) What are the tax consequences of the receipt of the dividend by an individual shareholder?

(B) What are the tax consequences to the corporation?

(C) What are the tax consequences to the individual shareholder of a sale at their fair market value of the shares received?

(D) What are the tax consequences to the individual shareholder of a redemption of the shares received?

Exercise 5

ITA: 53(1)(*b*), 53(2)(*a*), 84(1), 84(3), 84(4)

The following situations deal with Canadian-controlled private corporations and their non-arm's length shareholders. However, each transaction, described below, is separate and distinct from the other transactions unless the contrary is stated.

(a) X Ltd. issued to the daughter of its only shareholder retractable special shares (preferred shares) with a PUC of $150 and a redemption value of $1,000 for $100 cash.

(b) A, the sole shareholder of A Ltd., gave the corporation land with an FMV of $150,000.

(c) Y, the controlling shareholder of Y Ltd., converted debt of $20,000 for preferred shares with a PUC and redemption value of $2,000 plus cash of $20,000.

(d) Z, the sole common shareholder of Z Ltd., is considering causing the corporation to make a payment as a return of capital (PUC). The shares have an FMV of $50,000, PUC of $10,000 and ACB of $20,000:

(i) payment is for $5,000;

(ii) payment is for $18,000.

— REQUIRED

Discuss the tax consequences of the above transactions.

Exercise 6

ITA: 54, 83(2), 84(2), 88(2), 89(1)

Flare Limited is a Canadian-controlled private corporation, founded 20 years ago by Mr. Siewert who holds all of the outstanding shares. The following balance sheet reflects the position of the corporation after selling all assets and paying all liabilities:

Flare Limited

BALANCE SHEET

as at December 31, 2016

Cash	$ 950,000	Capital stock (PUC)	$ 625,000
RDTOH	50,000	Capital dividend account	150,000
		Other surplus	225,000
			$1,000,000
Total assets	$1,000,000		

— REQUIRED

(A) Determine the components of the distribution to Mr. Siewert.

(B) Compute the taxable capital gain or allowable capital loss on the disposition of Mr. Siewert's shares on January 1, 2017, assuming that their adjusted cost base was $350,000.

¶15,850

Exercise 7

ITA: 54, 83(2), 84(2), 88(2), 89(1)

Twilight Ltd., a CCPC with no GRIP balance, has been wound up this year and its only shareholder has surrendered her shares. She received $30,000 in total from the corporation for her shares which had a cost to her equal to their paid-up capital of $2,000. The company had elected a capital dividend on a dividend of $2,000. All business income of the CCPC has been taxed only at the low rate.

— *REQUIRED*

What are the tax consequences to the shareholder if she will be taxed on any income from the winding-up at a combined 33% federal and 17% provincial marginal rate of 50%?

Exercise 8

ITA: 54, 83(2), 84(2), 88(2), 89(1)

Dwight Limited is a Canadian-controlled private corporation which will be wound up by its only shareholder, Mr. Warren, who bought the shares at their paid-up capital value of $2,000. As at December 31, 2016, its balance sheet appears as follows:

Dwight Limited

BALANCE SHEET

as at December 31, 2016

Assets		Liabilities	
Cash	$ 20,000	Bank loan	$ 47,000
RDTOH	10,000	Wages payable	3,000
Inventories at cost		Total	$ 50,000
(FMV: $220,000)	200,000		
Land at cost		*Shareholder's Equity*	
(FMV: $70,000)	40,000	Paid-up capital	$ 2,000
Buildings at UCC		Surplus	318,000
(cost: $200,000;		Total	$370,000
FMV: $300,000)	60,000		
Equipment at UCC			
(Cost: $100,000;			
FMV: $80,000) ...	40,000		
Total	$370,000		

The balance in the corporation's capital dividend account was nil as at the above balance sheet date. The assets are to be liquidated, the liabilities paid and the net proceeds distributed to Mr. Warren effective January 1, 2017.

— *REQUIRED*

(A) Compute the amount available for distribution to the shareholder assuming the corporation pays corporate tax at the rate of 15% on the first $500,000 of active business income, 28% on active business income not eligible for the small business deduction, and 40% initially on any other income, plus the additional refundable tax on investment income, from the winding-up. The balance in the corporation's GRIP is nil.

(B) Determine the components of the distribution to the shareholder.

(C) Compute the taxable capital gain or allowable capital loss on the disposition of Mr. Warren's shares assuming that their adjusted cost base was $1,000.

(D) Discuss the HST implications on the wind-up of Dwight Limited.

CHAPTER 15

¶15,875 ASSIGNMENT PROBLEMS

Type 1 Problems

Problem 1

ITA: 89(1)

Sabres Limited, a Canadian-controlled private corporation whose fiscal year-end is December 31, provides you with the following data concerning its tax accounts and capital transactions for 2015. The balance in its capital dividend account was nil on January 1, 2016. Ms. Tsakiris, a Canadian resident, is the sole shareholder.

Sabres Limited is considering winding up the corporation and wishes to determine the impact of the sale of all its capital assets on its tax surplus accounts. The following capital assets are recorded in the books of account:

Assets	Cost	UCC/ CEC	Estimated proceeds	Estimated selling costs
Investments	$60,000		$ 22,000	$ 500
Land	40,000		200,000	10,000
Building	70,000	$ 45,000	125,000	6,000
Equipment	35,000	Nil	8,000	400
Customer lists (Note 1)	40,000	16,000	60,000	—

Additional Information

(1) The balance in the cumulative eligible capital account reflects the purchase of the customer lists in 2006 for $40,000 less the tax write-offs for 2006 to 2015, inclusive.

(2) In addition to the above assets, there is $35,000 of goodwill which will also be sold.

You have been asked to determine the effect on income and the capital dividend account balance immediately after the above transactions.

Problem 2

ITA: 89(1)

You have been asked to compute the capital dividend account of Granatstein Ltd., a Canadian-controlled private corporation incorporated in 2001. You have reviewed the tax returns of the corporation for the period January 1, 2001 to December 31, 2016, and made the following notes:

2002 Disposed of bonds resulting in a capital gain of $5,000.

2003 Received taxable dividend of $2,000 and capital dividend of $5,000.

2004 Disposed of shares resulting in a capital loss of $4,000.

2007 Disposed of equipment resulting in a capital gain of $6,000 and recapture of $3,000.

2008 Eligible capital property was purchased for $40,000.

2009 Sold vacant land and reported capital gain of $100,000.

2010 2009 capital gain on sale of vacant land was reassessed by the CRA as income. Granatstein Limited did not fight the reassessment.

2011 Sold shares resulting in a capital gain of $20,000.

2012 Received life insurance proceeds of $100,000 on a life insurance policy on the life of the company president purchased in 2006. As at January 1, 2012, the policy had an adjusted cost basis of $20,000.

2013 Paid capital dividends of $50,000.

2014 Sold a customer list for $100,000. The company's cumulative eligible capital balance at the time of the sale was $25,000.

2016 Sold shares resulting in a capital gain of $37,500.

Calculate the balance in Granatstein Ltd.'s capital dividend account showing *all* calculations, and explain why you omitted any of the above amounts in your answer.

Type 2 Problems

Problem 3

ITA: 53(1)(*b*), 84

The following situations deal with a Canadian-controlled private corporation and its shareholders. Each transaction described below is separate and distinct from the other transactions.

(a) Capital Inc. issued 135 preferred shares with PUC equal to $110 each for $11,050 cash and assets with a FMV of $2,800.

(b) Plastics Ltd. has shares with a FMV of $35,000 and a PUC of $5,500. Plastics Ltd. is considering making the following paid-up capital reductions on these shares. Their shareholders have an ACB of $16,000 for their shares:

    (i) payment of $3,750; and

    (ii) payment of $8,750.

(c) Festivals Ltd. has 4,500 common shares with a PUC of $22,500. In March of this year the corporation declared and distributed a 15% stock dividend in common shares with a PUC of $3,375.

(d)(i) The sole shareholder of Baker Corp. Ltd. contributed assets worth $38,400 to the corporation in return for cash of $15,400 and preferred shares with a PUC of $23,000 (redemption value of $23,000).

    (ii) A year later, the sole shareholder redeemed the preferred shares.

Discuss the tax consequences for deemed dividends for each of the above transactions.

ITA: 84

Problem 4

ITA: 54, 84(3), 84(6)

Ms. Chiu owns all of the 100 Class B shares issued by Chiu Ltd., a small business corporation, which was formed by Ms. Chiu about 15 years ago. Her son owns all the Class A shares. The current fair market value of the Class B shares is $100 per share. The paid-up capital value of the shares and their adjusted cost base to Ms. Chiu is presently $5 each. Ms. Chiu would like to know the tax consequences if (a) her shares are redeemed by Chiu Ltd. for their fair market value or, alternatively, (b) she sells her shares to her son for their fair market value.

Ms. Chiu has also sold 100 common shares of Bellco Limited, a company whose shares are listed on a designated stock exchange. She has found out Bellco Limited, itself, had purchased her shares through the exchange for $4.10 each. The paid-up capital value of the shares was $1 each and their cost to Ms. Chiu three years ago was $1.25 each.

Ms. Chiu has asked you to explain the tax implication of the above transactions.

Problem 5

ITA: 54, 83(2), 84(2), 88(2)

J. Tilkenhurst Limited (JTL) is a Canadian-controlled private corporation which was started in 2004 by Mr. Santosh Prasad with an initial investment in common shares of $18,000. Mr. Prasad has decided that it's time to retire and move to his retirement home in Saskatoon, Saskatchewan. Therefore, Mr. Prasad wishes to have JTL sell the assets at their fair market value and then wind up JTL.

The following is a projected tax balance sheet prior to the sale of the assets and the distribution of the resulting net cash as at the intended date of the winding-up:

J. Tilkenhurst Limited
BALANCE SHEET
as at December 31, 2016

Cash		$ 15,000
RDTOH		6,000
Accounts receivable	$60,000	
Less: reserve for doubtful accounts	5,000	55,000
Inventory		110,000
Marketable securities		26,000
Land		85,000
Building — UCC		23,000
Equipment — UCC		10,000
Customer list — CEC account balance		20,600
		$350,600

CHAPTER 15

Liabilities	$ 45,000
Future income taxes	41,000
Common shares (PUC)	18,000
Capital dividend account (no unabsorbed negative amounts)	12,000
Other surplus	234,600
	$350,600

Additional Information

(1) The corporation is taxable at a total 15% corporate tax rate for the first $500,000 of active business income, a 28% rate on active business income not eligible for the small business deduction, and an initial 40% rate for all other income, plus the 10⅔% additional refundable tax on investment income. The corporation has a GRIP balance of nil.

(2)

Assets	Cost	FMV
Accounts receivable	$ 60,000	$52,000
Inventory	110,000	127,000
Marketable securities	26,000	26,000
Land	85,000	150,000
Building	66,000	97,000
Equipment	30,000	6,000
Customer lists*	42,453	70,000

> * The customer lists were acquired in 2007 from a similar business which was acquired that year. The balance in the CEC account includes the maximum cumulative eligible capital amounts in each year.

(3) The books of account do not reflect unrecorded goodwill with an estimated fair market value of $60,000. This is in addition to the customer lists.

(4) The accounts receivable are to be sold to a factoring company.

You have agreed to prepare an analysis of the income tax implications of the sale of the assets and the winding-up of JTL for Mr. Prasad.

Problem 6

ITA: 54, 83(2), 84(2), 84(2.1), 89(1)

Ms. Bast owns all the common shares of Batterup Ltd., a Canadian-controlled private corporation, which started operations in 2003. Batterup Ltd. has been quite profitable in recent years. As a result, Three-Strikes Ltd., a Canadian public corporation, has offered Ms. Bast $252,500 for the assets, excluding cash, as at December 31, 2016. The offer price reflects unrecorded goodwill of $47,500. Ms. Bast wants to wind up the company after the sale of the assets.

The *pro forma* balance sheet of Batterup Ltd. as at December 31, 2016, is as follows:

Assets	Cost	UCC	FMV
Cash......................	$ 2,500		
Accounts receivable (net)	8,750		$ 7,500
Inventory	22,250		15,500
Land	11,000	—	45,000
Building	35,000	$ 7,500	95,000
Equipment	45,000	22,000	10,000
Marketable securities	14,250	—	32,000
	$138,750		$205,000

Liabilities	
Current liabilities	$ 54,000
Future income taxes	5,000

Shareholder's Equity	
Paid-up capital	10,000
Capital dividend account........	4,000
Retained earnings	65,750
Total liabilities and equity........	$138,750

Additional Information:

(1) Batterup Ltd. pays corporate tax at the overall rate of 15% on active business income eligible for the small business deduction, 28% on active business income not eligible for the small business deduction, and an initial 40% rate for investment income, plus the 10⅔% additional refundable tax on investment income. The corporation has a GRIP balance of nil.

(2) The reserve for doubtful accounts at December 31, 2016 was $1,500.

(3) Batterup Ltd. and Three-Strikes Ltd. elected under section 22.

You have agreed to do the following for Ms. Bast:

(A) Compute the amount available for distribution to the shareholder.

(B) Determine the components of the distribution to the shareholder.

(C) Compute the taxable capital gain or allowable capital loss on the disposition of Ms. Bast's shares on the winding-up. (Assume the adjusted cost base of Ms. Bast's common shares is $10,000.)

(D) Explain the conditions for and advantages of using a section 22 election.

Problem 7

ITA: 54, 83(2), 84(2), 88(2), 89(1)

You have been approached by one of your clients, Mr. Sidney Chow, for help in determining what will be the tax consequences if he sells all his assets in his corporation (at their fair market value) in 2016 to someone who will continue the business. However, Mr. Chow is not sure if he should wind up his corporation at this time. The following tax balance sheet for Chow Enterprises Ltd. has been prepared as at December 31, 2016.

Chow Enterprises Ltd.

BALANCE SHEET

as at December 31, 2016

Cash		$ 10,000
RDTOH		5,000
Accounts receivable	$30,000	
Less: reserve for doubtful debts	5,000	25,000
Land		55,000
Building (Class 1) — UCC		95,000
Equipment (Class 8) — UCC		12,000
Shares in Bell Canada — cost		15,000
Goodwill — cumulative eligible capital balance		18,000
		$235,000
Liabilities		$ 35,000
Future income taxes		12,000
Common shares — PUC		20,000
Capital dividend account		8,000
Other surplus		160,000
		$235,000

~ditional Information

(1) Mr. Chow owns all the common shares of the corporation, which he acquired in 2001 for $20,000 when the business was incorporated.

(2)

Assets	Cost	FMV
Accounts receivable	$30,000	$ 18,000
Land	55,000	150,000
Building — Class 1	170,000	320,000
Equipment — Class 8	30,000	3,000
Shares in Bell Canada	15,000	26,000
Goodwill	50,000	120,000

CHAPTER 15

Goodwill was acquired in 2006 in connection with a similar business which was purchased that year. The fair market value reflects the goodwill for the combined businesses. The maximum amortization has been deducted for tax purposes.

(3) The corporation is taxable at a total 15% corporate tax rate for the first $500,000 of active business income, a 28% rate on active business income not eligible for the small business deduction, and an initial 40% rate for any other income, plus the 10⅔% additional refundable tax on investment income. The corporation has a GRIP balance of nil.

(4) The accounts receivable are to be sold to a factoring company.

You have agreed with Sidney that you will:

(A) Compute the effect of the sale of the above assets on the various tax accounts in 2016, ignoring any potential normal business transactions.

(B) If he should decide to wind up beginning in 2017, ignoring any subsequent business transactions,

(i) determine the components of the distribution to him; and

(ii) compute the taxable capital gain or allowable capital loss on the disposition of his shares.

(C) Indicate briefly the tax consequences of leaving the proceeds in the corporation and investing the money in high-yielding securities.

(D) Discuss the HST implications on the sale of assets and the subsequent winding-up.

Problem 8

ITA: 14, 38, 82, 83(2), 117, 121, 123, 124, 129

Mr. Liu incorporated a company in 2016 in a province with a 15% corporate tax rate on active business income eligible for the small business deduction, a 28% total corporate tax rate on other active business income, an initial 40% corporate tax rate on investment income before the 10⅔% additional refundable tax, and a 50% combined personal tax rate (including a 17% personal provincial tax on income rate), taking one share with a paid-up capital value of $1 and a note representing a loan to the company of $499,999. The company, Luck Unlimited Limited, a private corporation, purchased the assets of a business in the same year for $500,000. The purchase price was allocated to the land and building of the business in the amount of $400,000 and to goodwill in the amount of $100,000. However, before the business had commenced, the company sold the assets of the business for $700,000, including $170,000 for goodwill.

Mr. Liu has asked you to determine how much of the $700,000 received in the corporation he would retain if he removed all of this amount from the corporation. Assume that the sale of land and building was considered to result in a *capital gain*.

Problem 9

ITA: 54, 83(2), 84(2), 84(2.1), 89(1)

Ms. Debbie, the sole shareholder and president of Shining Limited, a CCPC, has been considering selling her common shares to Let's-Make-a-Deal Ltd., a CCPC. However, Ms. Debbie recalls reading somewhere that one should compare a share sale with an asset sale to determine which would result in higher after-tax cash flow.

Ms. Debbie provides you with the following information:

(1) The cost of Ms. Debbie's common shares in Shining Limited was $120,000.

(2) Shining Limited pays tax at the overall rate of 15% on the first $300,000 (assuming that the other $200,000 is allocated to an associated corporation) of active business income, 28% on additional active business income, and 40% on all other income, plus the 10⅔% additional refundable tax on investment income. The corporation has a GRIP balance of nil.

(3) Ms. Debbie's combined federal and provincial personal tax rate is 50%, including a personal provincial tax on income rate of 17%. The provincial dividend tax credit is ⁸⁄₂₉ of the 17% gross-up on dividends from the LRIP and ⁵⁄₁₁ of the gross-up on dividends from the GRIP.

(4) Financial information concerning Shining Limited on December 31, 2016 is as follows:

Assets	Book cost	UCC	FMV
Cash (required as working capital)	$ 23,000		
Marketable securities (required as working capital)	58,000		$ 54,000
Inventory	41,000		50,000
Land.	154,000		210,000
Building (Note)	213,700	$195,000	440,000
Goodwill	Nil		85,000
	$489,700		$839,000

Liabilities			
Current liabilities	$ 43,000		
Future income taxes	4,800		
Paid-up capital	120,000		
Capital dividend account	48,000		
Retained earnings	273,900		
	$489,700		

(5) Shining Limited earned active business income of $50,000 during the year.

NOTE: The original cost of the building in Class 1 was $410,000. Book cost of $213,700 is net book value after accumulated amortization.

You have agreed to do the following analysis:

(A) If Ms. Debbie sells all of the assets, except cash, to Let's-Make-a-Deal Ltd., pays the outstanding liabilities, and then winds up Shining Limited, determine the net amount available for distribution to her, showing all computations.

(B) Determine the components of the distribution to Ms. Debbie.

(C) Determine the amount, including principal, Ms. Debbie would retain from this distribution.

(D) Determine a selling price for the Shining Limited shares that results in the same after-tax net cash retained as the net cash from sale of assets followed by a wind-up, as determined in Part (C). You will consider the payment of a capital dividend before the sale of shares. Also, assuming that the shares of Shining Limited are QSBCS at the time of their sale, you will consider the use of Ms. Debbie's capital gains deduction, none of which she has used before.

(E) Based on the indicated fair market value of the net assets, you will determine the maximum price a Canadian-controlled private corporation should be willing to pay for the shares of Shining Limited. You will assume that the CCPC pays tax at the low rate of 15% on all of its business income, that it uses an after-tax discount rate of 10%, and that it does not expect to sell the fixed assets of Shining Limited for a very long time. Also, you will assume that if the purchaser bought the assets, it would have to invest $23,000 in cash to meet working capital requirements.

Type 3 Problems

Problem 10

Glenda is considering the purchase of a family-run catering business, called Palace Catering Ltd. The corporation specializes in the planning, preparation, and hosting of professional dinners, parties, and activities. Although Glenda is qualified for operating and managing the business, there is a high probability that profits from operating this business will not begin for a couple of years. She is wondering if she should purchase the net assets from the corporation or 100% of the shares presently held by the vendor family. The corporation had a proven record of profits until two years ago, when the death of the chef, along with the retirement of two employees resulted in a loss of business. The accumulated non-capital loss carryforward is $84,000.

Glenda's plan for the new business is to carry on catering. She is also toying with the idea of producing dessert cakes for sale to hotels and restaurants. Over the next two years she expects she could make profits on the sale of cakes of $4,000 and then $18,000. Thereafter, she estimates profit from the cakes of about $25,000 annually.

Glenda plans to use an 8% small business loan to purchase the business. If there are any further operating losses she will use the proceeds from her bond investment to finance the business over the next few years. From January 1 to August 31 of the current year, Glenda earned $38,000 as senior hostess at the Professional Club in Saskatoon, and $12,000 in interest income.

Glenda would like your advice on what should be considered in deciding on a share purchase or an asset purchase.

Problem 11

Ottawa Associates Inc. is a business that was set up 25 years ago by Grant Carter to provide consulting services to the federal government. When the economy was good, the company was able to generate substantial profits and, even now, with a slow economy, the profits are approximately $550,000 before tax. Grant now feels that the company is worth $1,200,000 based on the income it is generating.

Grant is 50 years old this year. When he started the business, another shareholder, John Price, owned the other 50% of the shares. Each had put $10,000 of cash into the corporation as share capital. Initially, their working relationship had been excellent, but John had wanted to branch out into other areas of consulting, while Grant wanted to concentrate on government consulting. Fifteen years ago, they had agreed to go their own separate ways and Grant had bought John's shares from him for $30,000.

Grant's wife, Betty, does not work in the business directly. However, she does receive a salary for her work as secretary-treasurer of the corporation and for the time she spends on charitable activities, which is sometimes of benefit to Grant in his business. Grant would like to involve Betty in the ownership of the business, unless there are any problems with this.

Grant and Betty's two children, Scott and Kelly, are 21 and 16 years old, respectively. Scott is in university at Queen's and Kelly is in high school in Ottawa. At this point, it is not certain whether Scott and Kelly will join Grant in the business, but both are open to the possibility. Both work in the business during the summer holidays and are paid enough to cover their schooling costs.

Grant and Betty are now planning to build the cottage they have always wanted. They feel they need a place to unwind on the weekends and, also, they want a place for the children to come back to once they have left home. They see the cottage as a family gathering place. The land and construction costs are going to be approximately $200,000. Although they have that much extra cash in the corporation, they do not want to pay tax on the dividends to get the cash out. As a result, they plan to take out a mortgage to finance the cottage and pay it off over 10 years from Grant's bonus cheques.

Please provide your recommendations. Assume a total corporate tax rate on income not eligible for the small business deduction of 28% (i.e., 15% federal and 13% provincial). Assume that Grant is in the 50% marginal tax bracket.

 [For more problems and solutions thereto, see the DVD accompanying the textbook.]

CHAPTER 15 —
DISCUSSION NOTES FOR REVIEW QUESTIONS

(1) Dr.: Cash $30,000
    Cr.: Share capital $10,000
    Cr.: Contributed surplus $20,000

(2) In these jurisdictions, the paid-up capital is the "stated capital" as determined by the directors of the corporation under corporations law. Generally, this stated capital will be the fair market value of the consideration for which the shares were issued. However, these statutes provide that, in connection with certain non-arm's length transactions, the corporation may establish an amount which is less than the consideration for which the shares were issued as the stated capital and such amount as so determined will then be the amount of PUC for tax purposes.

(3) In no par value jurisdictions, in certain non-arm's length situations, the stated capital (PUC) can be set at less than the fair market value of the consideration received by the corporation. In these situations, the PUC may be kept low to avoid certain penalty provisions of the Act. This will result in the redemption value of the shares being high to represent the value of the assets transferred and the PUC being low to avoid tax penalties or to benefit from a deemed dividend on redemption rather than a capital gain, since the tax on dividends is lower than the tax on an equal amount of capital gain. This ignores the capital gains exemption.

(4) The five basic components of the capital dividend account are:

(a) the non-taxable portion of net capital gains;

(b) capital dividends received from other corporations;

(c) the untaxed portion of the proceeds of eligible capital property;

(d) proceeds from life insurance policies net of their adjusted cost base; and

(e) capital dividends paid, which reduce the account.

(5)

CEC balance	$6,000
Proceeds ($^3/_4 \times$ $100,000)	(75,000)
	$(69,000)
Previous CECA claims (($^3/_4 \times$ $10,000) – $6,000)	1,500
	$(67,500)
Income (($^2/_3 \times$ $67,500) + $1,500)	$46,500
Capital dividend account ($^2/_3 \times$ $67,500)	$45,000

Conceptually, the $45,000 added to the CDA is one-half of the economic gain of $90,000 (i.e., $^1/_2$($100,000 – $10,000)).

Even though the goodwill may not relate to the customer list, the two are both included in the same calculation as long as they both relate to the same business.

(6) The $8,000 reduction in capital will not cause a deemed dividend. However, the extra $1,000 of payment will be a deemed dividend since it is considered to be a distribution out of taxable surplus.

ITA: 84(4)

CHAPTER 15

(7) The three components of a distribution are: ITA: 88(2)

   (a) paid-up capital which is returned tax-free;

   (b) a capital dividend to the extent of the capital dividend account and the election of   ITA: 83(2)
      a capital dividend; and

   (c) a taxable dividend to the extent of the balance.

(8) On the winding-up of the corporation, subsection 13(21.2) does not apply. There-   ITA: 69(5)(*d*)
fore, the terminal loss will be allowed as a deduction to the corporation.

(9) The Act provides the definition of "proceeds of disposition" for purposes of the   ITA: 54
calculation of capital gain or loss. The proceeds do not include the deemed dividend on the   ITA: 84(2)
winding-up distribution. Therefore, the proceeds are calculated as the amount distributed
less the deemed dividend.

CHAPTER 15 — SOLUTIONS TO MULTIPLE CHOICE QUESTIONS

Question 1

(D) is false. Only taxable dividends paid are included in the computation of dividend refunds.   ITA: 129(1)

(A) is true.   ITA: 83(2)(*b*)

(B) is true.   ITA: 83(2)

(C) is true.   ITA: 89(1) "capital dividend account" (*a*)

Question 2

(D) is correct.

Redemption amount	$ 60,000
PUC	(10,000)
Dividend	$ 50,000

ITA: 84(3)

Redemption amount	$ 60,000
Dividend	(50,000)
Proceeds of disposition	$ 10,000
ACB	(20,000)
Capital loss	$(10,000)

ITA: 54

(A) is incorrect. This amount ignores the redemption deemed dividend.   ITA: 84(3)

(B) is incorrect. This amount calculates the dividend using the cost as opposed to the PUC.

(C) is incorrect. The dividend has not been subtracted from the redemption amount to arrive at the proceeds of disposition.

Question 3

(B) is correct.

Funds available for distribution	$ 40,000
PUC	(2,000)
Deemed dividend	$ 38,000
Elected amount of capital dividend	(8,000)
Taxable dividend	$ 30,000

ITA: 84(3)

Funds available for distribution	$ 40,000
Deemed dividend	(38,000)
Proceeds of disposition	$ 2,000
ACB	(1,000)
Capital gain	$ 1,000

ITA: 54

(A) is incorrect. Only subsidiaries in which the parent company owns at least 90% of the shares can wind up on a tax-deferred basis.

(C) is incorrect. The capital dividend has not been subtracted in the calculation of the proceeds.

(D) is incorrect. The ACB has been subtracted from the funds available to arrive at a $39,000 capital gain. The general winding-up rule and the deemed dividend on winding-up have been ignored.   ITA: 84(2), 88(2)

Question 4

(C) $1,556,000 is correct.

	Deemed proceeds	Business income	Investment income	CDA	RDTOH
Opening balance		Nil	Nil	$ 10,000	$ 30,000
Cash	$ 45,000				
Land	850,000		$300,000	300,000	
Building	780,000	$200,000	200,000	200,000	
	$1,675,000		$500,000	$510,000	
Liabilities	$ (20,000)	× 14.5%	× 50⅔%		
Tax	(282,333)	$ 29,000	$253,333		$153,333
RDTOH	183,333				$183,333
	$1,556,000				

(A) $1,655,000 is incorrect. The tax and RDTOH have not been accounted for. Only the liabilities were deducted.

(B) $1,372,667 is incorrect. The RDTOH has been omitted.

(D) $1,858,333 is incorrect. The liabilities and the income tax have not been deducted in the computation of the amount available for distribution.

Question 5

(A) is correct. The total paid-up capital of the common shares is $25,000, ½ of which is attributable to Mr. C and ½ is attributable to Mr. B. The total paid-up capital of the common shares is

100 common shares issued to Mr. A	$10,000
100 common shares issued to Mr. B	15,000
	$25,000

(B) and (D) are incorrect. The total paid-up capital of the common shares is not $35,000. The sale by Mr. A to Mr. C for $20,000 does not affect the paid-up capital of the shares.

(C) is incorrect because the $25,000 total paid-up capital of the common shares is split equally among the shares and is not based on the issue price of the shares.

Question 6

(B) is correct. The ¾ × the proceeds would be deducted from the CEC pool which would cause it to have a negative balance of $750,000. The Act states that this negative balance should be multiplied by ⅔, which makes it $500,000. The definition of the capital dividend account requires the tax-free portion of the gain ($500,000) to be included in the capital dividend account.

ITA: 14(1)(b)
ITA: 89(1) "capital dividend account" (c.2)

(A) and (D) are incorrect because there is no taxable capital gain on the sale of goodwill. As well, the reference in (D) to the refundable dividend tax on hand account is incorrect. The account is not affected.

(C) is incorrect as it does not take into consideration the business income inclusion or paragraph (c.2) of the definition of "capital dividend account".

ITA: 14(1)(b), 89(1)

CHAPTER 15 — SOLUTIONS TO EXERCISES

Exercise 1

	A	B	C
Proceeds of disposition	$ 4,000	$ 1,000	$ 2,000
Less: adjusted cost base	(2,000)	(2,000)	(2,000)
selling expenses	(400)	(100)	(200)
Capital gain (loss)	$ 1,600	$(1,100)	$ (200)
Adjustment to CDA (½ × capital gain (loss))	$ 800	$ (550)	$ (100)

Exercise 2

(A) Net income for tax purposes	Property 1		Property 2	
Proceeds of disposition		$110,000		$ 11,000
Less: ACB	$75,000		$40,000	
selling costs	11,000	86,000	5,500	45,500
Capital gain (loss)		$ 24,000		$(34,500)
Taxable capital gain (allowable capital loss)		$ 12,000		$(17,250)
(B) Adjustment to CDA (½ × capital gain (loss))		$ 12,000		$(17,250)

Exercise 3

(A) Where Investment Limited redeems the preferred shares, Mr. Duong will have a deemed dividend equal to: ITA: 84(3)

Redemption amount	$60,000
Less: PUC (800 × $15)	12,000
Deemed dividend	$48,000

ITA: 84(3)

Mr. Duong will not have a capital gain on the transactions because the adjusted proceeds of disposition equals the ACB of shares as demonstrated below:

Proceeds of disposition	$60,000	
Deemed dividend	48,000	ITA: 84(3)
		ITA: 54 "proceeds of disposition" (j)
Adjusted proceeds of disposition	$12,000	
Less: ACB (800 shares × $15)	12,000	
Capital gain	Nil	

(B) The dividend payment of $60,000 will be a taxable dividend unless Investment Limited makes an election to treat the cash dividend as a distribution from the capital dividend account. Where this election is made, the dividend will be tax-free to Mr. Duong. ITA: 83(2)

(C) A non-dividend distribution to Mr. Duong in excess of the PUC of the preferred shares will result in a deemed dividend of $45,000 (i.e., $60,000 – $15,000). The ACB of the shares will be reduced by the non-taxed portion of the payment of $15,000. The PUC of the shares must be reduced by the $15,000 in this case to reflect the tax-free distribution of PUC If PUC is not reduced by $15,000 in this transaction, an additional $15,000 will be treated as a deemed dividend. ITA: 84(4)
ITA: 53(2)(a)(ii)
ITA: 84(4)(a)

Exercise 4

(A) The amount of the stock dividend is $1.00 per share and must be grossed up and included in income of the shareholder. Thus, income would total $11.70 (1.17 × $1.00 × 10 shares). The dividend tax credit would be available on the $1.00 amount of the stock dividend or about $0.17 total (including provincial tax effect) per share. The adjusted cost base of the shares on the acquisition date would be $10.00 in total (i.e., $1.00 per share).

(B) The corporation will be deemed to have paid a dividend of $10.00 for determining its dividend refund and other amounts dependent on dividends paid.

(C)	P of D (10 shares @ $1,000 FMV)	$10,000	
	ACB (see (A), above)	(10)	
	Capital gain	$ 9,990	
	Taxable capital gain (eligible for capital gains deduction)	$ 4,995	
(D) (i)	Redemption amount (10 shares @ $1,000)	$10,000	
	PUC (10 shares @ $1.00)	(10)	
	Deemed dividend on redemption	$ 9,990	ITA: 84(3)
(ii)	Proceeds of disposition (above)	$10,000	
	Less: deemed dividend	(9,990)	ITA: 54 "proceeds of disposition" (j)
	Adjusted proceeds of disposition	$ 10	
	ACB	(10)	
	Capital gain	Nil	

Exercise 5

(a) This transaction would cause an immediate deemed dividend of $50 since the daughter could immediately retract the shares and receive $150 tax free whereas the price paid for the shares was only $100.   ITA: 84(1)

Deemed dividend		ITA: 84(1)
PUC increase	$150	
PUC decrease	(Nil)	
	$150	
Increase in net assets	(100)	
Deemed dividend	$ 50	ITA: 84(1)

This $50 deemed dividend would be added to the ACB of the preferred shares acquired by the daughter.

In addition, there would be a subsection 84(3) deemed dividend on the ultimate redemption of the preferred shares as calculated below:

Redemption of shares			
Redemption amount		$1,000	
PUC — Special share		(150)	
Deemed dividend on redemption		$ 850	ITA: 84(3)
Proceeds of disposition		$1,000	
Less: deemed dividend		850	ITA: 54 "proceeds of disposition" (j)
Adjusted P of D		$ 150	
ACB			
— original cost	$100		
— ssec. 84(1) deemed dividend	50	(150)	ITA: 53(1)(b)
Capital gain		Nil	
Economic consequences			
Redemption amount		$1,000	
Actual price paid		(100)	
Economic gain on redemption		$ 900	

Tax results:

Deemed dividend	$ 50	ITA: 84(1)
Deemed dividend	850	ITA: 84(3)
Total gain taxed ($1,000 – $100)	$ 900	

(b) As long as there is no capital gain or loss triggered on the transfer, the gift of land to the corporation should have no other immediate tax consequences. The accounting and tax records would show an increased balance in the contributed surplus account. However, the withdrawal of this contributed surplus can only be in the form of taxable dividend subject to the gross-up and tax credit mechanism. However, the Act permits the capitalization of the contributed surplus into PUC as long as the amount did not arise under one of the corporate tax-free rollover provisions, discussed in the next few chapters.

ITA: 84(1)(*c*.3)

(c) Y has received $2,000 more in consideration than the cancelled debt (i.e., $2,000 + $20,000 versus $20,000); therefore, Y will have an income inclusion of:

PUC increase	$2,000	
Net asset increase ($20,000 – $20,000)	Nil	
Deemed dividend	$2,000	ITA: 84(1)

The cost of the shares is nil since the $20,000 cash cancelled the debt; however, there will be an increase in ACB equal to the deemed dividend of $2,000.

ITA: 53(1)(*b*)

(d) (i) Since the payment of $5,000 is less than the PUC of the outstanding share(s) (i.e., $10,000), there are no immediate tax consequences because this payment is a return of the original investment in the corporation with tax-paid funds. However, the adjusted cost base of the shares is reduced to $15,000 (i.e., $20,000 – $5,000) by the amount of the return of capital which would result in a potential higher capital gain on the ultimate disposition of the shares.

ITA: 53(2)(*a*)(ii)

Deemed dividend		ITA: 84(1)
PUC before distribution	$10,000	
PUC after distribution	(5,000)	
PUC decrease (not an increase)	$ 5,000	
Adjusted cost base		
ACB prior to distribution	$20,000	
Distribution amount	(5,000)	
New ACB	$15,000	

(ii) Since the payment of $18,000 exceeds the PUC of the outstanding share(s), there will be a deemed dividend of $8,000. However, the ACB of the share(s) will only be reduced by the non-taxed portion of the payment to $10,000.

ITA: 84(4)

Exercise 6

(A)
Funds available for distribution to shareholder	$1,000,000	
Less: paid-up capital	(625,000)	
Deemed dividend on winding-up	$ 375,000	ITA: 84(2)
Less: capital dividend elected	(150,000)	ITA: 83(2), 88(2)(*b*)(i)
Taxable dividend (sufficient to clear RDTOH)	$ 225,000	

(B) Taxable capital gain (allowable capital loss) to Mr. Siewert:
Proceeds on winding-up	$1,000,000	
Less: deemed dividend	(375,000)	ITA: 54 "proceeds of disposition" (*j*)
Proceeds of disposition	$ 625,000	
ACB	350,000	
Capital gain	$ 275,000	
Taxable capital gain (½)	$ 137,500	

CHAPTER 15

Exercise 7

Funds available for distribution	$30,000	
Less: paid-up capital	(2,000)	
Deemed dividend or winding-up	$28,000	ITA: 84(2)
Less: capital dividend elected	(2,000)	ITA: 83(2), 88(2)(b)(i)
Deemed taxable dividend	$26,000	

Capital gain or loss on disposition of shares:

Actual proceeds from distribution	$30,000	
Less: deemed dividend	(28,000)	ITA: 54 "proceeds of disposition" (j)
Proceeds of disposition	$ 2,000	
Cost	(2,000)	
Capital gain (loss)	Nil	
Taxable capital gain	Nil	

Net cash retained:

Funds distributed		$30,000
Tax on incremental income from distribution:		
Deemed taxable dividend	$26,000	
Gross-up (17% × $26,000)	4,420	
Taxable capital gain	Nil	
Incremental taxable income	$30,420	
Combined federal and provincial tax @ 50%	$15,210	
Less: combined dividend tax credit in province @ ($21/29$ + $8/29$) × .17 × $26,000	(4,420)	10,790
Net cash retained		$19,210

Exercise 8

(A)

	Proceeds	Income Bus.	Income Invest.	C.D. a/c	RDTOH
Opening balances		Nil	Nil	Nil	$ 10,000
Cash	$ 20,000	Nil	Nil		
Inventories	220,000	$ 20,000	Nil		
Land[1]	70,000	Nil	$ 15,000	$15,000	
Buildings[2]	300,000	140,000	50,000	50,000	
Equipment[3]	80,000	40,000	Nil		
Liabilities	(50,000)				
Income taxes[5]	(62,933)	$200,000[4]	$ 65,000		19,933
RDTOH[6]	29,933				$ 29,933
	$607,000		$65,000		

(B) Funds available for distribution to shareholder	$607,000	
Less: paid-up capital	2,000	
Deemed dividend on winding-up	$605,000	ITA: 84(2)
Less: capital dividend elected	65,000	ITA: 83(2)
Deemed taxable dividend (clears RDTOH)	$540,000	

(C) Taxable capital gain to Mr. Warren		
Actual proceeds on winding-up	$607,000	
Less: deemed dividend	605,000	
Proceeds of disposition	$ 2,000	
Cost	(1,000)	
Capital gain	$ 1,000	
Taxable capital gain (½ × $1,000)	$ 500	

(D)

Where a corporation is wound up and the general winding-up rules of the Act apply, the supply of property on the wind-up is subject to HST. HST is payable on any taxable supplies of property. However, an election may be available, in which case the payment of HST is not required. In order to qualify, a registrant must have sold or transferred all or substantially all of the assets used in a commercial activity that is part of a business carried on. Since Dwight Ltd. is being wound up by Mr. Warren it would qualify for this election.

ITA: 88(2)

ETA: 167(1)

— NOTES TO SOLUTION

(1) Proceeds on sale of land	$ 70,000
Cost	(40,000)
Capital gain	$ 30,000
Taxable capital gain (½ × $30K) (investment income)	$ 15,000
Capital dividend account (½ × $30K)	$ 15,000

(2) Actual proceeds on sale of building	$300,000
UCC	(60,000)
Gain	$240,000
Recapture ($200K – $60K) (business income)	$140,000
Taxable capital gain (½ × ($300K – $200K)) (investment income)	$ 50,000
Capital dividend account (½ × ($300K – $200K))	$ 50,000

(3) Actual proceeds on sale of equipment	$ 80,000
UCC	(40,000)
Gain	$ 40,000
Recapture ($80K – $40K) — fully accounts for gain (business income)	$ 40,000

(4) The $500,000 business limit for the small business deduction must be prorated for the number of days in the taxation year. Since the winding-up may take some time to complete, this solution assumes that the corporation maintains its eligibility for the small business deduction in the year in which the sale of assets occurs. In this case, there would be no need to bonus down to the business limit for the small business deduction, given active business income of $200,000.

IT-73R6, par. 9

(5) Income taxes		
15% × ABI ($200,000)	$30,000	
50⅔% × investment income ($65,000)	32,933	$ 62,933
RDTOH (26⅔% of $65,000)		$ 19,933

(6) Assumes a minimum $77,413 (i.e., 29,933/38⅔%) is to be distributed as a taxable dividend to produce a refund of the full RDTOH.

CHAPTER 15

Chapter 16

Income Deferral: Rollover on Transfers to a Corporation and Pitfalls

Learning Goals

Know

By the end of this chapter you will know:

- The basic provisions of the Income Tax Act that relate to the transfer of property to a corporation on a tax-deferred basis.

- The basic provisions of the Income Tax Act that relate to the transfer of shares of a corporation in both non-arm's length and arm's length transactions.

Understand and Explain

By the end of this chapter you will understand and be able to explain:

- The basic tax consequences of the transfer of property to a corporation by a shareholder on a rollover basis.

- The means that a corporation can use to pay for the property transferred.

- Potential traps or pitfalls on the transfer of shares to a corporation.

Apply

By the end of this chapter you will be able to apply your knowledge and understanding to:

- Calculate the tax consequences of the transfer of property to a corporation on a rollover basis.

- Use the rollover tools to accomplish a taxpayer's objectives.

Review Questions
¶16,800 in the Study Guide

Multiple Choice Questions
¶16,825 in the Study Guide

Exercise Questions
¶16,850 in the Study Guide

Assignment Problems
¶16,875 in the Study Guide

CHAPTER 16 — LEARNING CHART

Problem Descriptions

Textbook Example Problems

1	Elected amounts — 85(1)
2	Consideration received — 85(1)
3	PUC of shares received — 85(1)
4	Comprehensive — 85(1)
5	Non-arm's length sale of shares

Multiple Choice Questions

1	Sale of depreciable asset to a corporation
2	Non-share consideration
3	Capital cost of asset to corporation
4	ACB of share consideration
5	Section 22
6	Non-share consideration

Exercises

1	Elected amount, income, non-share consideration
2	Cost and PUC of consideration
3	Comprehensive 85(1)
4	Gifting
5	Transfer of depreciable property
6	Comprehensive 85(1)
7	Transfer of depreciable property
8	Non-arm's length sale of shares
9	Non-arm's length sale of shares
10	Sale of shares by a corporation

Assignment Problems

1	Section 85 elected amounts
2	Transfer of assets to a corporation
3	Transfer of assets to a corporation
4	Transfer of assets to a corporation, sale or redeem shares
5	Transfer of assets to a corporation
6	Transfer of assets to a corporation, gifting
7	Transfer of assets to a corporation
8	Estate freeze
9	Sale of shares by corporation

Study Notes

¶16,800 REVIEW QUESTIONS

(1) In tax terms, what does the word "rollover" mean and how does it impact on both the transferor and the transferee?

(2) Della Inc. is a corporation that was incorporated in Delaware, U.S.A., in 1965 and has been resident in Canada since 1973 when its sole shareholder, Mr. Della, moved to Canada. During this year, Mr. Della wanted to transfer some land and a building, that was capital property to him, to Della Inc. for use in the business. He did transfer the property to the corporation and used section 85 to defer the accrued gain. Comment on whether there is any technicality that would not allow him to use section 85.

(3) When using section 85, the elected price is very important since it is used in the determination of four things that arise on the transfer. What are they?

(4) Since the tax value and the fair market value are usually fixed, what is the one decision variable that you can use that will have an effect on the limits of the elected transfer price range?

(5) When using section 85, what is the maximum amount of boot that should be taken in order to maximize the deferral?

(6) Ms. Smith heard at a party last night that she can avoid the "half-year rule" for CCA by first purchasing the equipment personally and then selling it shortly thereafter to her corporation and electing under section 85. She thinks that the corporation will then be able to claim the full CCA in the first year instead of only one half. What do you think and why?

ITR: 1100(2)

(7) How is the cost of the consideration taken back by the transferor in a section 85 transfer determined?

(8) Bar Ltd., a CCPC, owns shares in Lite Ltd., a small business corporation, that have gone down in value. Bar Ltd.'s problem is that it cannot sell the shares because there is no market. Bar Ltd. then decides that it will sell the shares to a company owned by the wife of the sole shareholder of Bar Ltd., called Spouse Ltd., claim an ABIL and at least be able to withdraw from Spouse Ltd. the fair market value of the shares of Lite Ltd. Bar Ltd. does not own any shares in Spouse Ltd. Since there is no gain to defer, they will not elect under section 85. Comment on this strategy.

(9) Using section 85, what is the amount that determines how much the transferor can withdraw from the company on a tax-free basis?

(10) Ms. Smith has decided to transfer some portfolio shares to her wholly owned company in exchange for more shares of the company. The shares have a cost of $5,000 and a fair market value of $8,000. She plans to elect at $8,000 and take back shares with a PUC and redemption amount of $10,000. What are the tax consequences to Ms. Smith and her company?

(11) If the optimal value of the boot is equal to the tax value of the property transferred under section 85, what will the ACB and PUC of the shares taken back be?

(12) Given that FMV is often not easily arrived at when transferring assets under section 85, what protection can you use to avoid a one-sided adjustment by the CRA if their value is different than yours?

(13) What is the purpose behind section 84.1?

(14) Mr. Blythe got a good deal a few years ago on the shares of a company that he just bought. He paid $10,000 for the shares even though the PUC of the shares is $100,000. Today the company is worth $100,000 again thanks to his hard work. Mr. Blythe has never used his QSBC share capital gains exemption. How can he get money out of the company without paying any personal tax?

¶16,825   MULTIPLE CHOICE QUESTIONS

Question 1

Pauline plans to sell a depreciable asset to a corporation owned by her husband. The characteristics of the assets are as follows:

FMV	$3,000
Capital cost	2,200
UCC	800

Which *one* of the following statements is *true*?

(A) The gain will be deferred due to the spousal rollover since the corporation is owned by Pauline's husband.

(B) Pauline should file a section 85 election and elect at $2,200 to defer the tax on the sale.

(C) Pauline should file a section 85 election and elect at $800 to defer the tax on the sale.

(D) If a section 85 election is not made, the capital cost and UCC of the asset to the corporation will be $3,000.

Question 2

Steve plans to sell a non-depreciable asset which has a mortgage of $15,000 to S Ltd. S Ltd. is a taxable Canadian corporation. Steve owns all the shares. Steve and S Ltd. will file an election under section 85. S Ltd. will assume the mortgage. For proceeds, Steve would like to receive a non-interest bearing note for the maximum amount possible without incurring adverse tax consequences. The balance of the consideration will be in shares of S Ltd. Steve considers any tax incurred an adverse consequence. The asset has the following characteristics:

FMV	$100,000
ACB	40,000

What is the maximum amount of the note that Steve should take?

(A) $100,000

(B) $85,000

(C) $40,000

(D) $25,000

Question 3

Susan sold a Class 1 depreciable asset to a corporation that she controls in exchange for a non-interest bearing demand loan of $100,000 and preferred shares redeemable for $80,000 in total. Susan and the corporation filed a section 85 election electing for the transfer to take place at $120,000. The characteristics of the asset were as follows:

FMV	$180,000
Capital cost	100,000
ACB	100,000
UCC	75,000

The capital cost of the asset to the corporation is:

(A) $120,000

(B) $110,000

(C) $90,000

(D) $75,000

CHAPTER 16

Question 4

Sylvia is the sole shareholder of Strained Ltd., a taxable Canadian corporation. Sylvia transferred a non-depreciable capital property having an adjusted cost base of $40,000 and a fair market value of $50,000 to Strained Ltd. in exchange for the following package of consideration.

Cash	$ 3,000
Debt	2,000
Preferred shares (FMV and legal stated capital)	15,000
Common shares (FMV and legal stated capital)	30,000
	$50,000

Sylvia and Strained Ltd. made a joint election under section 85, electing a transfer price of $40,000.

The cost to Sylvia of the common shares received as consideration is:

(A) $35,000

(B) $23,000

(C) $23,333

(D) $20,000

Question 5

Which one of the following is an advantage for a vendor and purchaser using a section 22 election to transfer accounts receivable rather than electing under section 85?

(A) The vendor will realize a loss that may be a superficial loss.

(B) The vendor will realize a loss that is a capital loss.

(C) The vendor will not be required to add the prior year's doubtful debts reserve to income.

(D) The purchaser will be able to take a doubtful debts reserve on the accounts receivable.

Question 6

Rebecca transfers land to R Co and makes a joint election with R Co under section 85 of the *Income Tax Act* in the amount of $50,000. The land has a cost of $50,000 and a fair market of $210,000. Rebecca takes back a demand promissory note of $60,000 and redeemable, retractable preference shares worth $150,000 in value. The tax consequences of this transaction are that:

(A) Rebecca is deemed to dispose of the land for proceeds of $50,000.

(B) R Co.'s cost of the land is $50,000.

(C) Rebecca's cost of the preference shares is $150,000.

(D) R Co.'s cost of the land is $60,000.

¶16,850   EXERCISES

Exercise 1

ITA: 85(1), 85(5.1)

Consider the following cases involving the transfer of capital assets to a corporation for consideration including both common shares and boot.

	A	B	C	D	E	F	G
Fair market value	$120	$100	$ 80	$100	$110	$100	$ 80
Adjusted cost base	N/A	75	N/A	75	N/A	75	N/A
Capital cost	100	N/A	100	N/A	100	N/A	100
UCC of class	200	N/A	50	N/A	150	N/A	50
FMV of class	170	N/A	110	N/A	140	N/A	110
Boot	150	200	80	50	80	90	20

— REQUIRED

(A) Compute the minimum elected amount possible given these data.

(B) Compute the effects on income given these data.

(C) Indicate the maximum boot that should be taken in each case to maximize the deferral of taxation.

Exercise 2

ITA: 85(1), 85(2.1)

Dee transferred capital property to Dee Ltd. The capital property had an adjusted cost base of $5,000 and a fair market value of $10,000. Dee could receive any of the following packages of consideration:

	A	B	C
Notes at fair market value	$5,000	$2,500	$4,000
Preferred shares at fair market value and LSC	4,500	7,500	—
Common shares (LSC)	500	—	6,000

— REQUIRED

(A) Given an elected amount of $5,000, what would be the cost of each item of consideration under each possible package of consideration?

(B) What will be the PUC for tax purposes under each possible package of consideration?

Exercise 3

ITA: 13(7)(e), 84(3), 85(1), 85(2.1), 110.6

Last year Mr. Good purchased a business location including land for $150,000 and a brick building for $436,224. He operated the business as a sole proprietorship for a year taking maximum capital cost allowance on the building. On your advice, this year he incorporated the business using section 85 to transfer the land and building to the corporation without triggering any of the gain that had accrued on these assets during the year. The following is a summary of the transfer under section 85.

				Consideration		
	Tax value	Appraised FMV	Elected amount	Assumed mortgage	New debt	Common shares
Land	$150,000	$375,000	$150,000	$150,000	—	$225,000
Building (UCC)	427,500	525,000	427,500	97,500	$330,000	97,500
	$577,500	$900,000	$577,500	$247,500	$330,000	$322,500

— *REQUIRED*

(A) What are the tax consequences of electing a transfer price of $577,500 as indicated?

(B) (i) Compute the cost of the consideration received from the corporation.

(ii) Compute the PUC for tax purposes of the common shares.

(C) (i) What are the tax consequences to Mr. Good if the corporation redeems the debt issued by the corporation for $330,000 and he sells his shares in the corporation for $425,000?

(ii) What are the tax consequences to Mr. Good if the corporation redeems the common shares for $425,000?

Exercise 4

ITA: 85(1)(*e*.2), 85(2.1)

Mother owned some debt securities which she transferred to a corporation in which Daughter (age 29) owns all of the common shares. These securities cost Mother $100,000 and had a fair market value at the time of transfer of $125,000. Section 85 was used to transfer the securities at an elected amount of $100,000. As consideration for the securities transferred, Mother received a note having a value of $100,000 and a preferred share having a fair market value and an LSC of $1,000.

— *REQUIRED*

What are the tax consequences of this transaction and how could they have been avoided?

Exercise 5

ITA: 85(1)(*e*.1), 85(2.1)

Ron Roberts, who owns 100% of Rollover Ltd., has come to you concerning transferring some additional assets to the corporation. The following facts relate to the transfer:

Asset #1
Capital cost	$10,000
Undepreciated capital cost	5,000
Fair market value	20,000

Asset #2
Adjusted cost base	$ 8,000
Fair market value	14,000

Ron wishes to take back one no par value common share and $18,000 cash.

— *REQUIRED*

Discuss the tax implications of the proposed transaction.

Exercise 6

ITA: 22, 85

Mrs. Designer has provided you with the following balance sheet and additional information relative to her unincorporated ladies' fashion business.

Mrs. Designer

(A Proprietorship)

BALANCE SHEET

May 31, 2016

Cash		$ 4,000	Accounts payable		$ 14,000
Short-term investments		10,000	Mortgage payable		
Accounts receivable	$ 12,000		(current maturity) . . .		6,000
Allowance for doubtful					$ 20,000
accounts	(2,000)	10,000			
Inventory		5,000			
Prepaid insurance		500			
		$ 29,500			
Building cost	$ 80,000		Mortgage payable	$ 60,000	
Accumulated			Current portion	(6,000)	$ 54,000
depreciation	(18,000)	$ 62,000	Proprietor's equity		47,500
Land, cost		30,000			$101,500
		$ 92,000			$121,500
		$121,500			

Additional Information

(1) Incomes for tax and financial accounting purposes have always been the same.

(2) The proprietorship began to carry on business about seven years ago.

(3) The May 31, 2016 fair market value of various assets owned by the proprietorship are:

Short-term investments	$ 5,000
Accounts receivable	9,000
Inventory	25,000
Prepaid insurance	400
Building	60,000
Land	26,500
Goodwill	44,000

Effective June 1, 2016, Mrs. Designer wants to transfer her business assets to a corporation (Hi-Fashion Co. Ltd.) in which her husband owns 100% of the common shares.

She has indicated that, provided the company assumes the business debts, she would receive the balance in debt and preferred shares (stated value $100) as full consideration.

— *REQUIRED*

(A) Determine which assets should not be transferred to the corporation under section 85 and those that should not be transferred at all and give reasons.

(B) Determine the amounts to be elected on the various assets to avoid any taxes.

(C) Determine the consideration to be received without any tax consequences.

(D) Determine the adjusted cost base of the consideration in part (C), above.

(E) Determine the tax PUC of the preferred shares received.

(F) Determine the cost/capital cost of the transferred assets for the corporation, Hi-Fashion Co. Ltd.

Exercise 7

ITA: 13(7)(*e*), 85(1), 85(2.1), 110.6

In 2016, Ms. Kvetch transferred a depreciable capital property (the only one in its class) to a corporation which she controls. The property had an undepreciated capital cost of $27,000, a capital cost of $30,000 and a fair market value of $100,000. She elected to transfer the property under section 85 at $80,000 in order to offset the resultant taxable capital gain with a net capital loss of $25,000. As consideration for the property, she received a note for $80,000 and common shares with a stated value of $20,000.

— *REQUIRED*

What are the income tax implications of this transaction?

¶16,850

Exercise 8

ITA: 84(3), 84.1, 85

Mr. Newberry, a Canadian resident, owned all of the common shares with a paid-up capital value and cost of $75,000 in an operating company, Opco Ltd. He transferred these shares under section 85 to a company, Broco Ltd., owned by his brother at a time when the value of the Opco Ltd. shares was $800,000. As consideration for the shares transferred he received a note with a principal amount of $500,000 and preferred shares with a paid-up capital and fair market value of $300,000 such that an elected amount of $500,000 was possible under section 85. Mr. Newberry offset all of the resultant $425,000 of capital gain with his available QSBC share capital gains exemption. Both Opco Ltd. and Broco Ltd. are Canadian-controlled private corporations.

— *REQUIRED*

(A) What are the tax consequences of the transfer to Mr. Newberry?

(B) What are the tax consequences if the preferred shares received from his brother's corporation are redeemed by that corporation for their fair market value?

(C) What are the tax consequences if the preferred shares are sold in an arm's length transaction for their fair market value?

Exercise 9

ITA: 54, 84(3), 84.1

Ms. Erin owns all of the common shares of Davpet Ltd. The shares have a PUC and cost of $1,000. Their current fair market value is $300,000. The shares are qualified small business corporation shares and she is anxious to crystallize her capital gains exemption on the accrued gain in these shares. Her father owns all of the common shares of Lenmeag Ltd., a Canadian-controlled private corporation, and is willing to use that corporation to assist her in her plans.

— *REQUIRED*

(A) Determine the immediate tax consequences, if Ms. Erin sells her common shares in Davpet Ltd. to Lenmeag Ltd. for their fair market value, receiving a $300,000 note from Lenmeag Ltd. which will ultimately be repaid in cash. Her father will allow her to continue to manage Davpet Ltd. and she will ultimately inherit the shares of Lenmeag Ltd. to reacquire control of Davpet Ltd.

(B) Determine the tax consequences, alternatively, if she sells her shares of Davpet Ltd. to Lenmeag Ltd. for their fair market value of $300,000, receiving $300,000 of the common shares of Lenmeag Ltd. No section 85 election is made.

Exercise 10

ITA: 55(1)–(6)

Vendco Ltd. owns all of the shares of Preyco Ltd. The shares of Preyco have a total adjusted cost base of $100,000 and a fair market value of $1,000,000. Since its incorporation in 1993, Preyco has realized and retained $700,000 of income and has no refundable taxes.

Vendco wishes to sell its shares in Preyco to Purchco. It causes Preyco to borrow $900,000 from the bank and to pay a dividend on its shares of $900,000. This reduces the fair market value of Preyco's shares to $100,000 and Purchco buys the shares for this amount.

— *REQUIRED*

What are the tax consequences of these transactions?

¶16,875 ASSIGNMENT PROBLEMS

Type 2 Problems

Problem 1

ITA: 85(1)

The following assets are to be transferred under section 85 for consideration including common shares plus boot as indicated below:

	Fair market value	ACB/ Capital cost/ ECE	UCC/ CEC
Land	$ 75,000	$60,000	—
Marketable securities	65,000	55,000	—
Building*	95,000	85,000	$70,000
Equipment	50,000	65,000	40,000
Furniture and fixtures	10,000	15,000	7,000
Licence**	100,000	82,500	60,000

* Only asset in class.
** Indefinite life.

For each of the assets transferred:

(A) Assess whether they qualify for transfer under section 85.

(B) Determine the minimum possible elected amounts.

(C) Indicate the maximum non-share consideration (boot) that can be taken and not create any income.

(D) Compute the effects on income.

(E) Determine what would happen if the non-share consideration on the land was $70,000 and the equipment was $45,000.

Use the following format:

				Consideration		
Asset	Tax Value	FMV	Elected Amt	New Debt	Pref Shares	Income

Problem 2

ITA: 85(1)

Elijah Pitts operates a simple but profitable business as a proprietorship. Given the level of profits he is attaining, he would like to incorporate. The latest balance sheet of his proprietorship follows.

Elijah Pitts Enterprises
Balance Sheet (condensed version)
(Tax value basis)
December 31, 2016

Assets	
Cash	$ 5,000
Accounts receivable (trade)	15,000
Office equipment (UCC)	10,000
	$30,000

Liabilities

Bank loan (operating)	$ 4,000
Accounts payable	5,000
	9,000
Proprietorship Equity	$21,000
	$30,000

He advises you that the current value of the office equipment is $12,000, that he fully expects to collect all of the receivables, and that the value of the goodwill is $20,000. If he does incorporate, he prefers to minimize any tax liability that incorporation might bring.

Design in detail what you believe to be the optimum plan for transferring the assets to the corporation, including any section 85 rollover. Indicate the tax values of the assets owned by the corporation.

Problem 3

ITA: 85(1)

Pete Hallman is the sole proprietor of a hardware store, The Handyman Shop. Pete has decided to incorporate the business but wishes to minimize any income inclusions on the transfer of his business to the new corporation.

The Handyman Shop has the following assets:

	Tax value	FMV
Cash	$22,000	$22,000
Inventory (cost: $44,000)	39,500	39,500
Furniture and fixtures (cost: $12,000)	6,000	8,000
Building ($75,000 cost)	45,000	55,000
Land	8,000	30,000

As consideration for the transfer of the above assets, Pete would like to take back the maximum amount of debt and the balance in the form of common shares. There is no goodwill value in the business.

Determine the appropriate transfer price under section 85 for the assets which can and should be transferred. Determine the amount of debt and share consideration that Pete can accept without any adverse tax consequences. Compute the adjusted cost base and the PUC for tax purposes of the common shares received as consideration.

Problem 4

ITA: 84(3), 85

Ms. Hart has just met with you to talk about incorporating her business and having her husband participate in its future growth in value. She is a Canadian resident and has provided you with the balance sheet and additional information concerning her unincorporated active retail clothing business.

She has chosen November 10, 2016 as the date when she wishes to transfer all of her business assets and liabilities to a corporation (Hart Ltd.) in which her husband, also a Canadian resident, owns 100% of the common shares. She wants your advice on how to do this with the minimum amount of personal tax.

She insists on receiving the following package of consideration:

(1) The maximum amount of debt (to the nearest $100); and

(2) Voting, redeemable, retractable preferred shares for the balance of the consideration with a legal stated capital equal to their fair market value.

¶16,875

The following financial information concerning the business as of November 10, 2016, was provided:

	Tax value	Fair market value
Shares in public companies (note 1)	$ 11,000	$ 6,000
Accounts receivable (net allowance) (note 2) . . .	13,000	10,000
Inventory	8,000	9,000
Land (held as inventory)	100,000	220,000
Prepaid property insurance	600	600
Building (Class 1, cost $90,000).	70,000	150,000
Land (capital property)	140,000	160,000
Goodwill	nil	80,000

Additional Information:

1. The shares are capital property to Ms. Hart. Ms. Hart owns less than 1% of each public company.

2. The tax reserve for doubtful debts taken in the previous year was $1,000. The original cost of the accounts receivable before deducting the reserve was $14,000.

3. The unincorporated business has liabilities of $60,000 which are to be assumed by Hart Ltd.

You have to provide Ms. Hart with the following:

(A) An analysis, with explanations as necessary, of the income tax consequences of selling the assets to Hart Ltd. without electing under section 85 or section 22, showing all calculations whether or not relevant to the final answer.

(B) A more tax-effective manner in which to achieve her objectives. You will explain your recommendation in detail, including the income tax implication for Hart Ltd., as well as for Ms. Hart.

(C) The tax consequences if Ms. Hart sells her preferred shares to a third party for their fair market value.

(D) The tax consequences if Hart Ltd. redeems Ms. Hart's preferred shares for their fair market value.

Problem 5

ITA: 85

Joe Schmaltz has carried on a retail business for about 20 years. He intends to transfer the business assets and liabilities to a corporation, Schmaltz Enterprises Ltd. (SEL), in which he will own all of the voting preferred shares. His three children, all in their 20s, have already subscribed for all of the common shares in equal numbers. The balance sheet of the proprietorship and certain additional information are provided as follows:

Assets	Balance sheet, April 30, 2016	Fair market value April 30, 2016
Cash	$ 12,000	$ 12,000
Accounts receivable (Net of $10,000 allowance)	110,000	102,000
Inventories.	90,000	100,000
Shares of Supplyco Ltd.[1]	36,000	40,000
Land	96,000	103,000
Buildings[2]	48,000	144,000
Equipment[2]	72,000	60,000
Goodwill	—	90,000
	$464,000	$651,000

Liabilities[3]	
Bank loan	$ 30,000
Accounts payable	31,000
Accrued liabilities	6,000
Mortgage on land and building	84,000
	$151,000
Proprietor's equity	313,090
	$464,000

Notes to Balance Sheet

$^{(1)}$ These shares represent a 2% ownership in the common shares of Supplyco Ltd. which is a small business corporation.

$^{(2)}$ Fixed assets are recorded at original cost less accumulated financial accounting depreciation. Tax data follow:

	Original cost	UCC
Buildings	$ 95,000	$42,000
Equipment	110,000	57,000

No single piece of equipment is worth more than its cost.

$^{(3)}$ Liabilities are to be assumed by the corporation. In addition, Joe Schmaltz will receive as consideration for the transfer of assets under section 85 the maximum in notes payable by the corporation to permit the maximum deferral of taxation on the transfer and voting retractable preferred shares.

You have been asked to:

(A) Indicate which assets should not be transferred to the corporation at all.

(B) Indicate which assets should be transferred to the corporation, but cannot or should not be transferred under section 85 and explain why.

(C) Assuming that the appropriate procedure has been adopted to take advantage of the provisions of section 85 of the Act, indicate the elected amounts which should be used in order to defer any taxation upon the transfer of the business to the company and the effect of the consideration package as expressly requested by your client. He has $3,000 of net capital losses that he would like to use on the transfer.

(D) Determine Joe's cost on the consideration and the PUC for tax purposes of the shares he receives for the transfer of assets.

(E) Without re-doing all of the calculations, indicate the tax consequences of having the corporation issue the maximum debt, as indicated above, but only $150,000 of voting, retractable preferred shares.

(F) Advise on the tax consequences, if on a subsequent assessment the CRA determines that the value of the goodwill was $120,000? What protection from this eventuality can be implemented?

Problem 6

ITA: 85

Mr. Schminkie, the sole proprietor of a small manufacturing business wishes to have his wife involved in the business on an equal basis. Mr. Schminkie's barber advised him that this is possible by incorporating a company and having Mr. and Mrs. Schminkie subscribe for all the common shares equally. Then, Mr. Schminkie could transfer all the assets of the business to the newly formed company, taking back Class A and Class B non-voting preference shares as consideration. Mr. Schminkie thought this was a wonderful idea and proceeded with incorporating the company.

The assets and liabilities of the proprietorship and certain additional information are provided as follows:

Assets	Balance sheet Dec. 31/16	Fair market value Dec. 31/16
Cash	$ 20,000	$ 20,000
Accounts receivable$^{(1)}$	90,000	85,000
Inventories	86,000	86,000
Shares in Public Co.	50,000	20,000
Land — Parcel I$^{(3)}$	200,000	339,000
Building$^{(2)}$	15,000	75,000
Land — Parcel II$^{(4)}$	20,000	45,000
Equipment$^{(2)}$	35,000	5,000
Auto$^{(2)}$	10,000	12,000
Goodwill	—	60,000
	$526,000	

Liabilities[5]

Bank loan	$169,000
Accounts payable	43,000
Mortgage on building	30,000
	$242,000
Proprietor's equity	284,000
	$526,000

Notes to Balance Sheet

[1] The accounts receivable are net of a $6,000 reserve for doubtful accounts which represents the closing reserve for the previous fiscal period.

[2] Fixed assets are recorded at original cost less accumulated financial accounting depreciation. Tax data is as follows:

	Original cost	*UCC*
Building	$60,000	$15,000
Equipment	80,000	35,000
Auto	16,000	11,000

[3] Parcel I of land is the property upon which the building used in the business is sited.

[4] Parcel II of land was acquired in 2015. Mr. Schminkie purchased it with the intention to sell as soon as the fair market value exceeded $50,000. Mr. Schminkie speculates this will occur by April 19, 2016, at which point he will sell for the quick profit.

[5] Liabilities are to be assumed by the corporation.

You have been asked to do the following:

(A) Indicate which assets should not be transferred to the corporation at all.

(B) Indicate which assets should be transferred to the corporation, but cannot or should not be transferred under section 85 and briefly explain why.

(C) For the assets which can be transferred under section 85 to the corporation, indicate the maximum amount of debt in addition to the shares that can be taken as consideration to defer all possible capital gains, losses, other income and other available adverse tax consequences given the consideration to be taken. The corporation will issue a maximum of $200,000 Class A retractable non-voting preference shares with a dividend rate of 5% and the remainder of the share consideration will be Class B retractable, non-voting preference shares with no dividend entitlement.

(D) Determine Mr. Schminkie's cost of the consideration and the PUC for tax purposes of the preferred shares that he receives for the transfer of assets.

(E) Compute the tax consequences of a redemption of the preferred shares of the corporation at their fair market value after the transfer of assets to the corporation.

(F) Advise on what could be done to avoid a benefit problem, if the Class B consideration is limited to an authorized share capital amount of only $50,000 and the Class A consideration remains the same.

Problem 7

ITA: 84.1, 85(1)

Mrs. Andrews, a Canadian resident, has just told you about a proposed transaction she is planning to undertake shortly. She would like your advice on her plan.

She recently set up Von Trapp Holdings Limited (Holdings) with 100 common shares, which she owns and are worth $1 each. The plan is for her to sell her shares in Plummer Enterprises Inc. (Plummer) to Holdings in order to crystallize her capital gains exemption and for her to have a holding company to accumulate capital away from the risks of the business. She has never claimed the capital gains exemption in the past.

Mrs. Andrews currently owns 100% of the outstanding common shares of Plummer. Plummer is a small business corporation and meets all the tests for the shares to be qualified small business corporation shares. Plummer and Holdings are both Canadian-resident corporations. She purchased the Plummer shares in 1996 from an unrelated third party for their then fair market value of $200,000.

The fair market value of the Plummer shares today is $4 million. The paid-up capital of these shares is $1,000.

CHAPTER 16

Mrs. Andrews plans to transfer her shares of Plummer to Holdings on December 3rd and has been advised by someone else to jointly elect under section 85 with Holdings and take back the following consideration:

Mrs. Andrews will jointly elect under section 85 with VHL and will take back the following consideration:

(a) non-interest bearing note for $200,000, and

(b) voting preference shares which are retractable for $3.84 million and have a dividend rate of 6%.

Advise Mrs. Andrews on the tax implications of the proposed transaction, supported by your computations.

Problem 8

ITA: 84(3), 84.1, 85

Mrs. Domm owns all 100 common shares of Low-Cal Caterers Inc. (Low-Cal), a Canadian-controlled private corporation with a December 31 year-end. Low-Cal was incorporated in 1997 when Mrs. Domm invested $250,000 in common shares with a paid-up capital of the same amount. The Low-Cal shares are now valued at $2,000,000. She has already used up $324,176 of her capital gains exemption on other shares.

Mrs. Domm would like to freeze the present value of Low-Cal so that any future increase in value would accrue to her 20-year-old son, Sam. She proposes that Sam incorporate a new corporation, Sam Pickings Holdings Ltd. (Sam Pickings), with $100 of his own money by acquiring all the common shares of the new corporation.

Mrs. Domm would then transfer her common shares in Low-Cal to Sam Pickings using a section 85 election in order to defer the inherent gain on these shares. Mrs. Domm would like to receive as consideration a non-interest-bearing note for $774,176 and the balance of the fair market value for 1,000 6% non-cumulative, voting preference shares with a retraction value, fair market value, and paid-up capital of $1,225,824. Since she would also like to use all of her remaining capital gains exemption (of $524,176 for QSBC shares), she proposes that the elected amount under section 85 be $774,176. You have determined that both Low-Cal and Sam Pickings are small business corporations at the present time and that Low-Cal meets all the conditions for QSBC shares.

You have agreed to do the following:

(A) Describe the tax consequences to Mrs. Domm of the proposed section 85 transfer of the Low-Cal common shares to Sam Pickings.

(B) Advise on how you would change the above proposed consideration package so that Mrs. Domm achieves her objectives as stated above.

(C) Describe the tax consequences if Mrs. Domm sold to Sam Pickings for cash or debt just enough of the 100 common shares of Low-Cal common shares to realize a capital gain of $524,176 in order to utilize her capital gains exemption as described above.

(D) Indicate the tax consequences for parts (A) and (B) if Mrs. Domm:

(i) redeems all the preference shares in Sam Pickings for their fair market value; or

(ii) sells all the preference shares in Sam Pickings to an arm's length party for their fair market value.

Problem 9

ITA: 55(1)–(6)

Holden Limited has received an offer from an unrelated corporation, Corporate Raider Inc., to purchase all of Holden's common shares in a wholly owned subsidiary, Profits Galore Ltd. All three corporations are Canadian-controlled private corporations and have December 31 year-ends.

The common shares of Profits Galore Ltd. have an adjusted cost base and paid-up capital of $500,000 and a fair market value of $2.4 million. Profits Galore Ltd. has realized and retained income for tax purposes of $900,000 since its incorporation in 1999. All of this realized income was derived from active business assets.

Holden Limited has come to you for your comments on two acquisition alternatives proposed by Corporate Raider Inc.

Plan A would first have Profits Galore Ltd. borrow from the bank $1.9 million and, then, immediately pay a dividend to its parent corporation, Holden Limited, for the same amount. Corporate Raider Inc. would then purchase the common shares of Profits Galore Ltd. from Holden Limited for the residual fair market value of $500,000. Then, Corporate Raider would inject $1.9 million into Profits Galore Ltd. through a common share subscription so that the bank loan could be repaid.

Plan B would have Holden Limited transfer its common shares in Profits Galore Inc. to Corporate Raider Inc. on a tax-free basis by jointly electing under section 85 at a transfer price of $500,000. Holden Limited would accept as consideration only special shares of Corporate Raider Inc. with a paid-up capital of $500,000 and a redemption/retraction value of $2.4 million. These shares would represent 15% of all the voting rights and fair market value of Corporate Raider Inc. Holden Limited would, then, retract the special shares which it holds in Corporate Raider.

Holden Limited has asked you to describe the tax implications of the above acquisition alternatives supported by any relevant calculations.

 [For more problems and solutions thereto, see the DVD accompanying the textbook.]

CHAPTER 16 —
DISCUSSION NOTES FOR REVIEW QUESTIONS

(1) In general, a rollover allows for a partial or complete deferral of the recognition of income on the transfer of property from one person to another. The transferor, in return for the property transferred, should receive a package of consideration, the total fair market value of which should be equal to the fair market value of the property transferred. The transferor is the one who is deferring the recognition of income. The transferee usually steps into the position of the transferor in terms of the tax value of the asset received. Therefore, on the ultimate disposition of the asset by the transferee, the income will be recognized. Examples of rollovers include subsections 73(1), 85(1), 88(1) and sections 51 and 86.

(2) In order to use section 85, the corporation must be a "taxable Canadian corporation", which is defined to be a "Canadian corporation" that is not exempt from tax. A "Canadian corporation" is defined to include a company that is resident in Canada and was either incorporated in Canada or resident in Canada since before June 18, 1971. In this case, Della Inc. has been resident in Canada only since 1973 and, therefore, is not a Canadian corporation and not a taxable Canadian corporation. Although the real estate is capital property to Mr. Della and, thus, it is "eligible property", this property cannot be transferred using section 85 since the transferee is not a taxable Canadian corporation.

ITA: 85(1.1)
ITA: 89(1)

(3) The following are the four uses of the elected price:

    (a) it is the proceeds of disposition to the transferor;

    (b) it is the cost of the property to the corporation;

    (c) it is used to determine the ACB of the package of consideration taken by the transferor from the corporation in return for the assets transferred to the corporation; and

    (d) it is used to calculate the paid-up capital of the shares taken as consideration by the transferor from the corporation.

(4) On the transfer, the only decision variable you have is the non-share consideration or boot. If the boot is higher than the tax cost (lower limit) for the particular asset transferred, then the elected amount is increased. The boot cannot, however, raise the elected amount above fair market value.

ITA: 85(1)(b), 85(1)(c)

(5) The maximum "boot" that should be taken in order to maximize the deferral is the tax value of the asset transferred. If, however, the asset being transferred is shares and section 84.1 applies, the maximum boot should be the greater of the PUC and the modified ACB (removing any CGE element) of the shares transferred.

(6) She may have heard about a regulation which allows the transferee to avoid the half-year rule as long as the transferor was not dealing at arm's length with the corporation at the time of the transfer (which is true in this situation) and the property was owned continuously by the transferor (Ms. Smith) for the period from a day that was at least 364 days before the end of the taxation year of the corporation in which the asset was acquired to the date the property was transferred to the corporation. For example, if the transfer happened April 1st and the taxation year end of the corporation was December 31st, Ms. Smith would have to have owned the property continuously from January 1st of that year through to April 1st.

ITR: 1100(2), 1100(2.2)

(7) The elected transfer price is equal to the total cost of the consideration taken back. This elected amount is allocated among the different types of consideration in the following manner:

First: to non-share consideration (boot) up to the FMV of that property as long as that FMV does not exceed the FMV of the assets transferred to the corporation;

ITA: 85(1)(f)

Second: to preferred shares up to the FMV of those shares after the transfer but only to the extent that there is a balance left after the boot has been deducted from the elected amount; and

ITA: 85(1)(g)

Third: to common shares to the extent that the elected amount exceeds the FMV of the boot and the cost allocated to the preferred shares.

ITA: 85(1)(*h*)

(8) Normally, the sale of shares in an SBC would allow Bar Ltd. to claim the loss as a business investment loss. However, the ABIL is denied, since it must sell to an arm's length person. Bar Ltd. and Spouse Ltd. do not deal at arm's length since they are related. Therefore, the loss would be an ordinary capital loss.

ITA: 39(1)(*c*)
ITA: 251

However, in this case, Bar Ltd. is transferring the shares to a corporation controlled by the sole shareholder's wife, an affiliated person; therefore, the superficial loss will be denied to Bar Ltd. However, Spouse Ltd. can take advantage of the ability to add the loss to the cost base of the Lite Ltd. shares now owned by Spouse Ltd. The rule applies whenever a taxpayer disposes of capital property to an affiliated person, including a corporation that was controlled, directly or indirectly in any manner whatever, by the taxpayer, by the spouse of the taxpayer or by other affiliated persons. Section 84.1 will not apply as a corporation; Bar Ltd is transferring the shares to a non-arm's length corporation.

ITA: 53(1)(*f*), 54, 251.1
ITA: 40(2)(*g*)

ITA: 40(2)(*g*)

(9) The "elected amount" determines how much can be withdrawn tax-free since this is the starting point for determining the ACB and the PUC of the shares. In addition, it is the amount that is used to determine how much boot to take back on the transaction to fully defer the accrued income (except when 84.1 applies).

(10) The elected amount is correct since the upper limit is the FMV of $8,000. Ms. Smith will realize a capital gain of $3,000. The company will have a cost in the portfolio shares of $8,000 which is the elected amount. There will be a paid-up capital reduction to reduce the PUC to $8,000. Thus, on redemption, she will have a deemed dividend for $2,000 (i.e., $10,000 of redemption value – $8,000 of PUC).

ITA: 85(1)(*b*)

ITA: 85(2.1)

(11) If boot is equal to the elected amount and equal to the tax value of the property being transferred, then the ACB and PUC of the shares will be nil.

ITA: 40(2)(*g*), 54 "superficial loss"
ITA: 53(1)(*f*)
ITA: 85(1)(*e*.2)

(12) Price adjustment clauses are often used to provide for an adjustment to the consideration taken back in the event that the assessed value is different than what was originally used. The courts have determined that the price adjustment clause will only be recognized if the parties have reasonably and in good faith attempted to determine fair market value. The CRA's position on them is outlined in an Interpretation Bulletin.

IT-405

(13) The provision is designed to prevent an individual from stripping the fair market value in excess of the greater of his or her modified ACB or the PUC out of the company by selling the shares to a non-arm's length corporation.

(14) He can reduce the PUC of the shares by $100,000. This will cause his ACB in the shares to become negative $90,000 which will give rise to an immediate capital gain. Alternatively, he can transfer his shares to a holding company under section 85 and take back a note for $100,000 and one share with a nominal value of, say, one cent. Section 84.1 will not give rise to a deemed dividend, since the boot does not exceed the greater of the modified ACB and the PUC. In either case, he can use his capital gains exemption to shelter the gain.

ITA: 40(3), 53(2)(*a*)(ii), 84(4)

CHAPTER 16 — SOLUTIONS TO MULTIPLE CHOICE QUESTIONS

Question 1

(C) is correct. Electing at $800, the UCC of the transferred asset, will defer recapture as well as the capital gain.   ITA: 85(1)(e)

(A) is incorrect. The spousal rollover applies to transfers to a spouse or a spousal trust, but never to a corporation.   ITA: 73(1)

(B) is incorrect. Electing at $2,200 will defer the capital gain, but recapture of $1,400 will be incurred.

(D) is incorrect. Since the corporation will have acquired the depreciable asset from a non-arm's length individual, $2,600 (i.e., $2,200 + ½ ($3,000 – $2,200) is the maximum amount that the capital cost could be.   ITA: 13(7)(e)

Question 2

(D) $25,000 is correct. In order to defer the gain, Steve will elect at $40,000, the ACB of the asset. The elected amount cannot be less than the non-share consideration. Since S Ltd. assumed the mortgage of $15,000, an additional $25,000 of non-share consideration is the maximum that can be taken.   ITA: 85(1)

(A) $100,000 is incorrect. This amount would result in a capital gain of $60,000 as well as a shareholder benefit of $15,000.   ITA: 15(1)

(B) $85,000 is incorrect. This amount would result in a capital gain of $60,000.

(C) $40,000 is incorrect. This amount would result in a capital gain of $15,000.

Question 3

(B) $110,000 is correct. Since the corporation has acquired the depreciable property from a non-arm's length individual, the capital cost is limited to the transferor's capital cost, $100,000 plus the taxable capital gain on the transfer, $10,000. This totals $110,000.   ITA: 13(7)(e)

(A) $120,000, the elected transfer price, is incorrect for the same reason that (B) is correct.

(C) $90,000, the transferor's UCC plus the taxable capital gain on the transfer, is incorrect. The starting point is the transferor's capital cost, not UCC.   ITA: 13(7)(e)

(D) $75,000, the transferor's UCC, is incorrect for the same reason that (B) is correct.

Question 4

(D) $20,000 is correct.

Elected transfer price		$40,000
Allocated to non-share consideration:		
Cash	$3,000	
Debt	2,000	$ 5,000
Allocated to the preferred shares, up to their FMV		15,000
Allocated to the common shares, remainder		20,000
		$40,000

ITA: 85(1)(g)
ITA: 85(1)(h)

(A) $35,000 is incorrect. The elected amount, in excess of the non-share consideration, has all been allocated to the common shares.

(B) $23,000 is incorrect. None of the elected amount has been allocated to the cash.

(C) $23,333 is incorrect. The allocation between the preferred and common shares has been done based on proportionate values.

Question 5

(D) is correct because a section 22 election ensures that the purchaser will be able to take a doubtful debts reserve on the accounts receivable.

(A) and (B) are incorrect because a section 22 election ensures that the loss to the vendor is a business loss rather than a capital loss or superficial loss. If no section 22 election is made, the vendor will realize a loss that is a capital loss. Further, if the vendor and purchaser are affiliated persons, the loss will be denied and will be a superficial loss.

ITA: 54

(C) is incorrect because the vendor is always required to add the prior year's doubtful debts reserve. It does not matter whether or not a section 22 election is made.

ITA: 12(1)(*d*)

Question 6

(D) is correct. Because the promissory note is $60,000, the elected amount is deemed to be $60,000. The elected amount determines the proceeds of disposition to Rebecca, R Co.'s cost of the land, the cost of the consideration to Rebecca, and the paid-up capital of the shares issued as consideration after the paid-up capital reduction.

ITA: 85(2.1)

(A) is incorrect because the proceeds to Rebecca are deemed to be $60,000 not $50,000 as discussed above.

(B) is incorrect because R Co.'s cost of the land is deemed to be $60,000, not $50,000 as discussed above.

(C) is incorrect because Rebecca's cost of the preference shares is zero. It is calculated as the elected amount minus the boot ($60,000 – $60,000 demand note).

ITA: 85(1)(*g*)

CHAPTER 16 — SOLUTIONS TO EXERCISES

Exercise 1

	A	B	C	D	E	F	G
(A) Minimum elected amount or deemed proceeds	$120	$100	$80	$75	$100	$90	$50
(B) Proceeds	$120	$100	$80	$75	$100	$90	$50
Cost	100	75	100	75	100	75	100
Capital gain	$20	$25	Nil*	Nil	Nil	$15	Nil
Taxable capital gain (½)	$10	$13	Nil	Nil	Nil	$8	Nil
Lesser of cost or proceeds	$100		$80		$100		$50
UCC of class	200		50		150		50
Recapture	Nil		$30		Nil		Nil
Income from shareholder benefit	$30	$100	Nil	Nil	Nil	Nil	Nil
(C) Maximum "boot"	$100	$75	$50	$75	$100	$75	$50

ITA: 15(1)

---

* No capital loss on depreciable property.

Exercise 2

(A) Cost of consideration received:

	A	B	C
Elected transfer price	$5,000	$5,000	$5,000
Allocated to note up to FMV	5,000	2,500	4,000
Allocated to preferred up to FMV	Nil	$2,500	Nil
Allocated to common shares	Nil	Nil	$1,000

(B)

		A		B		C
LSC before reduction		$5,000		$7,500		$6,000
Reduction in PUC						
(a) Increase in LSC of all shares		$5,000 (A)		$7,500 (A)		$6,000 (A)
(b) Elected amount	$5,000		$5,000		$5,000	
Less: boot	5,000		2,500		4,000	
Excess, if any		Nil (B)		$2,500 (B)		$1,000 (B)
Total reduction in PUC (A – B)		$5,000		$5,000		$5,000

ITA: 85(2.1)

(c) Allocation of reduction to different classes:

Preferred shares

$$\$5,000 \times \frac{\$4,500}{\$5,000} = \quad \$4,500$$

Common shares

$$\$5,000 \times \frac{\$500}{\$5,000} = \quad \$\,500$$

Tax PUC			
Preferred shares	Nil	$2,500	
Common shares	Nil		$1,000

Note how the PUC after reduction is equal to the amount of the $5,000 ACB of the original capital property that has not been recovered through the notes received as consideration.

Exercise 3

(A) The elected amount becomes the proceeds of disposition of the assets transferred by Mr. Good. Since his adjusted cost base on the land and his undepreciated capital cost on the building are equal to these proceeds, there will be no capital gain on that land and no recapture on the building. The corporation is deemed to acquire these assets at a cost equal to the elected amount. On the building, the corporation is deemed to have a capital cost of $436,224 and to have taken capital cost allowance of $8,724 making it liable for future recapture and for a potential future capital gain if ultimate proceeds exceed $436,224. This places the corporation in the same position as Mr. Good was in with respect to the building prior to the transfer.

(B) (i) The cost of the debt and shares taken as consideration would be computed as follows:

Elected transfer price		$577,500
Allocated to debt:		
— mortgage assumed	$247,500	
— new debt issued	330,000	577,500
Allocated to shares		Nil

(ii) LSC before reduction ..... $322,500   *ITA: 85(2.1)*

Reduction in PUC			
(1) Increase in LSC of all shares		$322,500 (A)	
(2) Elected amount	$577,500		
less: boot ($247,500 + $330,000)	577,500		
Excess, if any		Nil (B)	
Total PUC reduction (A – B)			(322,500)
Tax PUC after reduction			Nil

(C) (i) If the new debt is redeemed for $330,000, given its adjusted cost base in Mr. Good's hands of $330,000, there would be no gain or loss. However, on the disposition of the shares, the following would result:

Proceeds of disposition	$425,000
Adjusted cost base	Nil
Capital gain	$425,000
Taxable capital gain	$212,500

(ii)	Redemption amount	$425,000
	Less: PUC	Nil
	Deemed dividend	$425,000

ITA: 84(3)

Redemption amount	$425,000
Less: deemed dividend	425,000
Proceeds of disposition	Nil
Less: adjusted cost base	Nil
Capital gain	Nil

ITA: 54 "proceeds of disposition" (j)

Exercise 4

The benefit rule would apply. The amount of the benefit would be equal to: *ITA: 85(1)(e.2)*

Fair market value of property transferred		$125,000
Less greater of:		
(a) fair market value of all consideration received	$101,000	101,000
(b) elected amount	$100,000	
Benefit		$ 24,000

The proceeds of disposition of the securities to Mother would be increased by the amount of the benefit, $24,000, to $124,000 resulting in a capital gain of $24,000 on the transfer. The cost of the property to the corporation would also be increased by $24,000 to $124,000. However, the cost of the consideration received would be as follows:

Elected amount	$100,000
Allocated to note (up to FMV)	100,000
Allocated to preferred share	Nil

Thus, the cost of the consideration received or of the shares owned by Daughter, which would increase in value by $24,000, is not increased by the amount of the benefit resulting in potential double taxation.

The $1,000 LSC of the preferred share would not be reduced and would equal tax PUC.

Reduction in PUC   ITA: 85(2.1)

(a)	Increase in LSC..		$ 1,000 (A)
(b)	Elected amount (as increased by benefit)	$124,000	
	Less: boot	100,000	
	Excess, if any		24,000 (B)
	Total PUC reduction (A – B)		Nil

ITA: 257

To avoid the problem of the $24,000 benefit being potentially taxed twice, Mother should have taken more share consideration in the amount of $24,000 such that the fair market value of all consideration received was equal to the fair market value of the property transferred. The PUC of these shares will be reduced to nil by the above formula, but this will not have any immediate tax consequences.   ITA: 85(2.1)

Exercise 5

Elected amount	*Range*
Asset #1	$5,000–$20,000
Asset #2	$8,000–$14,000

However, the Act forces the minimum elected amount to be $18,000 because of the non-share consideration taken in that amount.   ITA: 85(1)(b)

Assign the elected amount as follows:

Asset #1	$ 5,000
Asset #2	13,000
	$18,000

Note that the minimum amount is assigned to the depreciable asset to avoid recapture being fully taxed.

Income

Asset #1	P of D	$ 5,000
	ACB	10,000
	CL	Nil
Asset #2	P of D	$13,000
	ACB	8,000
	CG	$ 5,000
	TCG	$ 2,500

Under corporate law[1], the paid-up capital of the one common share would be equal to the net fair market value of the assets transferred to the corporation. In this case, the PUC would be $16,000 (i.e., $20,000 + $14,000 – $18,000). However, the Act will reduce the PUC as follows: ITA: 85(2.1)

(a)	Increase in legal PUC of all shares on the transfer to the corporation..		$16,000 (I)
(b)	Elected amount	$18,000	
	Less: non-share consideration ("boot")...............	18,000	
	Excess, if any		Nil (II)
	Total PUC reduction (I – II)		$16,000

Since there is only one class of shares issued, there is no prorating of this reduction. As a result, the PUC of the share will be reduced to nil (i.e., $16,000 – $16,000) for tax purposes. The PUC is reduced to nil, because all of the tax-paid cost in UCC of $5,000 and ACB of $8,000 has been recovered through cash.

— NOTE TO SOLUTION

[1] Where the transferor and the corporation do not deal at arm's length, the legal stated capital (the initial PUC) can be less than the fair market value of the transferred assets at the discretion of the corporate directors.

Exercise 6

(A) Items not transferred under subsection 85(1):

Cash	$ 4,000	(not capital property)
Short-term investments	5,000	(capital loss denied)
Accounts receivable	9,000	(use section 22[1])
Prepaid insurance	400	(business loss of $100)
Building	60,000	(terminal loss of $2,000 denied)
Land	26,500	(capital loss denied)
Total	$104,900	(assume proprietorship debt of $74,000 and take back new debt for the balance of $30,900)

The building may not be transferred using the rules in section 85 because of the unrealized terminal loss. A stop-loss rule applies to deny the loss. The corporation will acquire the building with a UCC of $60,000 which is equal to its fair market value and the amount paid by the corporation. **ITA: 13(21.2)**

If the short-term investments can be considered assets used in the active business of the corporation, they can be transferred to the corporation. However, the capital loss will be considered to be a superficial loss because the corporation is affiliated with the transferor, Mrs. Designer. Therefore, a stop-loss rule will deny the loss to Mrs. Designer. The amount of the loss will be added to the cost of the investments to the corporation, such that the corporation's ACB of the investments will be $10,000. **ITA: 54** **ITA: 40(2)(*g*), 53(1)(*f*)**

Section 85 need not be used when there is no accrued income to defer. If the short-term investments cannot be considered as assets used in an active business, then they should not be transferred to the corporation, because it will seriously jeopardize the qualification of the shares of the corporation as QSBCSs.

The land need not be transferred under section 85 for the same reasons as the short-term investments, because of the accrued capital loss. While the loss will be denied to Mrs. Designer, the corporation will acquire the land for $26,500 of consideration, but hold it with an ACB of $30,000 which was Mrs. Designer's tax position in the land before the transfer.

(B) and (C) Items transferred under subsection 85(1) and consideration:

				Consideration				
	Tax value	FMV	Elected amount	Assumed debt[2]	New debt	Pref. shs.	Income
Inventory	$ 5,000	$25,000	$ 5,000	Nil	$ 5,000	$20,000	Nil
Goodwill	Nil	44,000	1	Nil	Nil	44,000	$0.50
	$ 5,000	$69,000	$ 5,001	Nil	$ 5,000	$64,000	

Since the corporation will qualify as a small business corporation, the Act will not apply to attribute income or capital gains back to Mrs. Designer. **ITA: 74.4, 248(1)**

(D) Elected transfer price.		$ 5,001
Allocated to debt consideration:		
debt assumed	Nil	
new debt	5,000	5,000
Allocated to ACB of preferred shares		$ 1

(E) LSC before reduction $64,000

Reduction in PUC   ITA: 85(2.1)

    (i) Increase in LSC of all shares . . . . $64,000 (A)

    (ii) Elected amount . . . . $ 5,001

        Less: boot 5,000

        Excess, if any . . . . 1 (B)

        Total PUC reduction (A – B) . . . . (63,999)

    Tax PUC after reduction . . . . $ 1

The $1 of PUC after the reduction represents the amount of tax-paid cost that has not been recovered through boot received from the corporation. The $1 of income resulting from the transfer of the goodwill is a tax-paid cost. A total of $5,000 of total tax-paid cost was recovered through boot.

(F) For those assets *not* transferred under subsection 85(1) and not subject to the specific provisions discussed below, the cost for tax purposes to the corporation would be equal to the fair market value of the consideration:

Cash . . . . $ 4,000

Prepaid insurance 400

Building 60,000

             $64,400 = debt consideration

Under section 22, the purchaser, Hi-Fashion, would record the accounts receivable at their face value of $12,000 which would be their adjusted cost base for tax purposes. Under the conditions of section 22, the corporation must include in its income the business loss of $3,000 recognized by the transferor (i.e., difference between the face value ($12,000) and the fair market value ($9,000)). Hi-Fashion is now entitled to set up a reserve to offset any potential doubtful debts (i.e., $3,000), plus an amount equal to any further decline in value. In addition, the corporation is now eligible to write off any realized bad debts since it has included an amount in income in respect of these receivables.

The ACB of the short-term investments and the land to the corporation will be their fair market value plus the denied superficial loss. Therefore, the ACB of the short-term investments will be $10,000 ($5,000 FMV + $5,000 denied loss) and that of the land will be $30,000 ($26,500 FMV + $3,500 denied loss). This puts the corporation in the same tax position on these assets as Mrs. Designer was in before the transfer.

The capital cost and, therefore, the ACB of the building in the corporation is $80,000.

For the inventory that has been transferred under subsection 85(1), the cost base would be the elected amount (i.e., inventory — $5,000). The goodwill, which is eligible capital property, would have a cost base of 75 cents (i.e., ¾ × $1.00).

—NOTES TO SOLUTION

[1] Reserve of $2,000 from last year must be brought into income this year. There will be a full business loss of $3,000 (i.e., face value of $12,000 less fair market value of $9,000) using section 22.

[2] The $104,900 of debt consideration for the assets not transferred under subsection 85(1) could include all assumed liabilities of $74,000, leaving none to be assumed in the subsection 85(1) transfer.

Exercise 7

An elected transfer price of $80,000 will result in the following: ITA: 85(1)

Recapture ($27,000 – $30,000)	$ 3,000
Taxable capital gain [$\frac{1}{2}$ ($80,000 – $30,000)]	25,000
Income	$28,000
Less: net capital loss	25,000
Incremental taxable income	$ 3,000

ACB of consideration received:

Note	$80,000
Common shares	Nil

PUC of common shares: ITA: 85(2.1)

LSC of shares issued	$20,000
Less: PUC reduction	

ITA: 85(2.1)

(a) increase in LSC		$20,000 (A)
(b) elected amount	$80,000	
boot	80,000	
excess, if any	Nil (B)	
(A – B)		$20,000
PUC for tax purposes		Nil

Capital cost of transferred property to corporation for CCA and recapture purposes is equal to the aggregate of:

(a) capital cost to transferor		$30,000
(b) proceeds of disposition to transferor	$80,000	
less: capital cost of property transferred	30,000	
excess, if any	$50,000	
$\frac{1}{2}$ of excess		25,000
Deemed capital cost to corporation		$55,000

ITA: 13(7)(e)(i)

The capital cost used for future CCA write-offs, which shield business income from full tax, will be increased by the taxable capital gain triggered, but not, in effect, the untaxed portion of the capital gain.

Capital cost of the depreciable property for future *capital gains* purposes (equal to elected amount) is $80,000.

Exercise 8

Part (A)

Section 84.1 applies because Mr. Newberry is a Canadian resident and is not at arm's length with his brother who controls the corporation to which the Opco shares were transferred. Therefore, Mr. Newberry is not at arm's length with the corporation. In addition, Opco Ltd. is connected with Broco Ltd., since Broco owns all of its outstanding common shares.   ITA: 251(2)(b)(iii)
ITA: 186(2)

CHAPTER 16

PUC reduction: ITA: 84.1(1)(*a*)

(a) Increase in LSC of brother's corporation	$ 300,000 (A)	
Less:		
(b) Greater of:		
(i) PUC of operating company shares .... $75,000 ⎤		
(ii) Modified ACB* of operating company shares .... $75,000 ⎦	$ 75,000	
Less: FMV of boot	500,000	
Excess, if any	Nil (B)	
PUC reduction (A – B)	$ 300,000	
PUC after reduction	Nil	

The PUC after reduction is nil because all of the $75,000 hard cost in the operating company shares has been recovered in boot from the brother's corporation.

Deemed dividend: ITA: 84.1(1)(*b*)

Sum of:		
(a) Increase in LSC of brother's corporation	$ 300,000 (A)	
(b) FMV of boot	500,000 (D)	
(A + D)	$ 800,000	
Less sum of:		
(c) Greater of:		
(i) PUC of operating company shares .... $ 75,000 ⎤		
(ii) Modified ACB* of operating company shares .... $ 75,000 ⎦	$ 75,000 (E)	
(d) PUC reduction	300,000 (F)	ITA: 84.1(1)(*a*)
(E + F)	375,000	
Deemed dividend (A + D) – (E + F)	$ 425,000	

* Adjusted actual cost.

This deemed dividend is equal to the excess of the $500,000 in boot received from the brother's corporation over the $75,000 of hard cost in the operating company shares transferred.

Capital gain or loss on disposition of Opco Ltd. shares:		
Elected amount and proceeds of disposition for operating company shares	$ 500,000	ITA: 85(1)
Less: deemed dividend	425,000	ITA: 54 "proceeds of disposition" (*k*)
Adjusted proceeds of disposition for operating company shares ...	$ 75,000	
Less: ACB of operating company shares	75,000	
Capital gain (loss) if any, (not denied*)	Nil	ITA: 40(2)(*g*)
ACB of Broco Ltd. shares received:		
Cost of shares of Broco Ltd. after allocation of $500,000 elected amount to "boot"	Nil	ITA: 85(1)(*g*)

* He is not affiliated with Broco Ltd. by the definition of "affiliated person" in section 251.1, since he does not control, directly or indirectly, Broco Ltd.

Part (B)

Ultimate redemption of shares of brother's corporation		
Redemption amount	$ 300,000	
Less: PUC	Nil	
Deemed dividend on redemption	$ 300,000	ITA: 84(3)
Proceeds of disposition	$ 300,000	
Less: deemed dividend on redemption	300,000	ITA: 84(3)

Adjusted proceeds of disposition	Nil	ITA: 54 "proceeds of disposition" (*j*)
Less: adjusted cost base	Nil	
Capital gain (loss)	Nil	

Summary of income effects:

Sec. 84.1 deemed dividend	$ 425,000	
Redemption deemed dividend	300,000	ITA: 84(3)
Capital gain (loss) on transfer	Nil	ITA: 85(1)
Capital gain (loss) on redemption	Nil	
Net economic effect	$ 725,000	

Note that $725,000 represents the accrued gain on the Opco Ltd. shares at the time of the transfer.

Part (C)

Ultimate arm's length sale of shares of brother's corporation

Proceeds of disposition	$ 300,000	
Less: adjusted cost base	Nil	
Capital gain	$ 300,000	

Summary of income effects:

Sec. 84.1 deemed dividend	$ 425,000	
Capital loss on transfer	Nil	ITA: 85(1)
Capital gain on arm's length sale	300,000	
Net economic effect	725,000	

Again, the $725,000 represents the accrued gain in the Opco Ltd. shares at the time of the transfer.

Exercise 9

For either alternative involving the sale of the Davpet Ltd. shares, the conditions of section 84.1 are met. Davpet Ltd. is a corporation resident in Canada and its shares are held as capital property by Ms. Erin, a Canadian resident. These shares are sold to a non-arm's length corporation, Lenmeag Ltd., since Ms. Erin is related to her father who controls Lenmeag Ltd. The two corporations are connected, since all of the shares of Davpet Ltd. are owned by Lenmeag Ltd. after the sale.

(A) Since no new shares of Lenmeag Ltd. were issued in this alternative, there is no PUC reduc-. tion. However, there will be an immediate deemed dividend computed as follows:

Deemed dividend:

ITA: 84.1(1)(*b*)

Sum of:

(a) Increase in LSC of Lenmeag Ltd. shares		Nil	(A)
(b) FMV of "boot"		$300,000	(D)
(A + D)		$300,000	

Less sum of:

(c) Greater of:			
(i) PUC of Davpet Ltd. shares	$1,000		
		$1,000	(E)
(ii) Modified ACB of Davpet Ltd. shares	$1,000		
(d) PUC reduction		Nil	(F)
(E + F)		1,000	
Deemed dividend (A + D) – (E + F)		$299,000	

ITA: 84.1(1)(*a*)

This deemed dividend represents the excess of the $300,000 in boot received from Lenmeag Ltd. over the $1,000 in PUC of the Davpet Ltd. shares.

Proceeds of disposition for the Davpet Ltd. shares will be reduced so that there will be no capital gain against which to offset the QSBC share capital gains deduction, as follows:

ITA: 54 "proceeds of disposition" (*k*)

Consideration in debt received on sale	$300,000
Less: sec. 84.1 deemed dividend	299,000
Adjusted proceeds of disposition	$ 1,000
ACB of Davpet Ltd. shares	(1,000)
Capital gain	Nil

ITA: 54 "proceeds of disposition"(*k*)

When the $300,000 debt is repaid by Lenmeag Ltd., there will be no further tax consequences. However, the plan is ineffective, because Ms. Erin will have to pay tax on a deemed dividend of $299,000 at the time of the sale of her shares instead of the intended capital gains.

(B) In this alternative, there will be a PUC reduction, computed as follows:

PUC reduction:

ITA: 84.1(1)(*a*)

(a) Increase in LSC of Lenmeag Ltd.	$300,000 (A)
Less:	
(b) Greater of:	
(i) PUC of Davpet Ltd. shares $1,000	
	$ 1,000
(ii) Modified ACB of Davpet Ltd. shares . . . $1,000	
Less: FMV of "boot"	Nil
Excess, if any	1,000 (B)
PUC reduction (A – B)	$299,000
PUC of new Lenmeag Ltd. shares after reduction ($300,000 – $299,000)	$ 1,000

The PUC of $1,000 after reduction represents the $1,000 of hard cost in the Davpet Ltd. shares transferred. None of that $1,000 of cost was recovered through boot on this transfer.

Since no "boot" was received, there will be no deemed dividend. As a result, proceeds of disposition for the Davpet Ltd. shares are equal to the $300,000 common share consideration received from Lenmeag Ltd. The result is the following:

Proceeds of disposition for Davpet Ltd. shares	$300,000
ACB	1,000
Capital gain	$299,000
Taxable capital gain (½ × $299,000)	$149,500
Less: Capital gains deduction for QSBCS	149,500
Effect on taxable income of Ms. Erin	Nil

The ACB of the Lenmeag Ltd. shares acquired by Ms. Erin will be equal to the $300,000 fair market value of the shares in Davpet Ltd. given up. As a result, when the shares of Lenmeag Ltd. are either sold or redeemed the $300,000 ACB of the shares will shield an equal amount from being taxed as a capital gain and the objective of crystallizing the QSBC share capital gains exemption will be accomplished without an immediate capital gain or deemed dividend on the sale of the Davpet Ltd. shares.

Exercise 10

Of the $900,000 dividend received by Vendco, $700,000 can be attributed to post-1971 earnings of Preyco and, therefore, can be received by Vendco without tax consequences under Part I and Part IV of the Act. The other $200,000 of the total dividend received will be deemed to be a gain of the dividend recipient.

These results are equivalent to Vendco's receiving a dividend from Preyco, of $700,000 without tax consequences and then selling the shares of Preyco to Purchco for their fair market value of $300,000 (i.e., $1,000,000 – $700,000). With an adjusted cost base of $100,000 for the shares, a capital gain of $200,000 would result.

Chapter 17

Income Deferral: Other Rollovers and Use of Rollovers in Estate Planning

Learning Goals

Know

By the end of this chapter you will know:

- The basic provisions of the Income Tax Act pertaining to corporate rollovers that are useful in many planning situations.

Understand and Explain

By the end of this chapter you will understand and be able to explain:

- The tax consequences of the various rollovers discussed and their uses in various planning situations.

- The use of rollovers to execute an estate freeze.

Apply

By the end of this chapter you will be able to apply your knowledge and understanding to:

- Determine the tax consequences of a wind-up or an amalgamation.

- Determine the tax consequences of a basic estate freeze.

- Determine whether an estate freeze achieves a client's goals.

Review Questions
¶17,800 in the Study Guide

Multiple Choice Questions
¶17,825 in the Study Guide

Exercise Questions
¶17,850 in the Study Guide

Assignment Problems
¶17,875 in the Study Guide

CHAPTER 17 — LEARNING CHART

Problem Descriptions

Textbook Example Problems

1	Share-for-share exchange
2	Reorganization of capital
3	Reorganization of capital
4	Reorganization of capital

Multiple Choice Questions

1	Amalgamation, wind-up
2	Wind-up
3	Reorganization of capital
4	Share-for-share exchange
5	Estate freeze
6	Estate freeze

Exercises

1	Share-for-share exchange
2	Reorganization of capital
3	Reorganization of capital
4	Amalgamation, wind-up
5	Convertible property

Assignment Problems

1	Sections 85 and 85.1
2	Capital reorganization
3	Capital reorganization, gifting
4	Amalgamation vs. wind-up
5	Sections 85, 86, 84.1
6	Estate planning
7	Estate freeze
8	Estate planning

Study Notes

¶17,800   REVIEW QUESTIONS

(1) What legal documents need to be filed in order to accomplish a reorganization of capital rollover?   ITA: 86

(2) What are some of the occasions on which a reorganization of capital rollover might be used?   ITA: 86

(3) What adjustments are there as a result of a deemed dividend that arises on a reorganization of capital rollover?   ITA: 86

(4) Legally, what happens to two corporations that are amalgamated?

(5) At the time of amalgamation there is a deemed year-end for tax purposes. What are some of the other tax rules that are impacted by this deemed year-end?   ITA: 87(2)(*a*)

(6) Acme Co. is a CCPC with a January 31 year-end. The owners want to change the year-end of the company to July 31 to allow bonuses to be paid either in this year or the next. It is now July and they do not have time to receive clearance from the CRA so they incorporate another company and amalgamate it with Acme on July 31 to create a new year-end. Do you have any problems with this tactic?

(7) In order for the subsidiary wind-up rollover to apply, what ownership criteria need to be met?   ITA: 88(1)

(8) Ms. Sweeney purchased 1,000 convertible preferred shares at a total cost of $10,000. These shares gave her the right to convert each preferred share into two common shares. She exercised her conversion right at a time when the common shares were trading at $10 each. What is the ACB of her new common shares?

(9) What is the primary purpose of estate freezing?

(10) What might be some of the secondary objectives of an estate freeze?

(11) What are the three principal methods of freezing the value of growth assets?

(12) What are the basic steps involved in doing a Holdco freeze?

(13) When doing an estate freeze on the shares of a small business corporation in favour of a spouse, what is one of the biggest dangers? Assume that the freeze was done correctly.

(14) Describe when a "reverse or asset freeze" would be used and the steps you would take to accomplish it.

¶17,825 MULTIPLE CHOICE QUESTIONS

Question 1

P Ltd. is a profitable taxable Canadian corporation with a December 31 fiscal year end. It has a wholly owned subsidiary, L Ltd., with a June 30 fiscal year end. L Ltd. has a significant 2011 non-capital loss balance. Therefore, consideration is being given to either amalgamating P Ltd. and L Ltd. or winding up L Ltd. into P Ltd. in order to utilize the loss. The amalgamation or the winding-up will take place on November 1, 2016. Which *one* of the following statements is *true*?

(A) The newly amalgamated corporation can utilize the non-capital loss in its deemed year ended October 31, 2016.

(B) The newly amalgamated corporation cannot utilize the non-capital loss until its taxation year commencing one year after the amalgamation.

(C) If a winding-up takes place, P Ltd. can utilize the non-capital loss in its taxation year commencing January 1, 2017.

(D) If a winding-up takes place, P Ltd. can utilize the non-capital loss in its taxation year ended December 31, 2016.

Question 2

On September 1, 2013, X Ltd. acquired all the shares of Y Ltd. for $500,000. At that time, Y Ltd. had land with a fair market value of $130,000 and a cost of $100,000. On September 1, 2016, a winding-up of Y Ltd. into X Ltd. took place. At the time of the winding-up, the tax values of Y Ltd.'s assets totalled $420,000. The fair market value of the land at this time was $300,000. X Ltd. received $15,000 of dividends from Y Ltd. between September 1, 2013 and September 1, 2016. The adjusted cost base of the land after the winding-up cannot exceed:

(A) $100,000

(B) $130,000

(C) $165,000

(D) $180,000

Question 3

In the course of the reorganization of the capital of A Ltd., Chris exchanged all his common shares of A Ltd. (which are capital property to him) for the package of consideration outlined below.

Cash.	$ 135
Preferred shares (50 shares redeemable at $100 each)	5,000
	$5,135

At the time of the exchange, Chris' common shares had an ACB of $2,000 and a FMV of $5,135. Which one of the following best describes the tax consequences to Chris as a result of the exchange?

(A) Chris will have no capital gain on the disposition of his common shares and the ACB of his preferred shares is $2,000.

(B) Chris will have no capital gain on the disposition of his common shares and the ACB of his preferred shares is $1,865.

(C) Chris will have a capital gain of $3,135 on the disposition of his common shares and the ACB of his preferred shares is $5,135.

(D) Chris will have a capital gain of $135 on the disposition of his common shares and the ACB of his preferred shares is $2,135.

Question 4

Shelly exchanged her shares of Abigail Inc., a public corporation, for shares of Clare Ltd., another public corporation, when Abigail Inc. was taken over by Clare Ltd. Her shares of Abigail Inc. had the following characteristics:

FMV	$12,000
ACB	7,000
PUC	5,000

Section 85.1 is often used in take-over situations. Which one of the following statements with respect to the rollover in this case is FALSE?

(A) When there are many diverse shareholders, a share-for-share exchange rollover is easier to accomplish than a subsection 85(1) rollover because there is no need for each shareholder to file an election.   ITA: 85.1

(B) The ACB of Shelly's shares of Clare Ltd. is $7,000.

(C) The ACB of the Abigail Inc. shares acquired by Clare Ltd. from Shelly is $5,000.

(D) Non-share consideration, up to the PUC of the exchanged shares, $5,000, could have been received by Shelly without any adverse tax consequences to her.

Question 5

Mr. Winters owns 100% of the shares of ABC Co., a small business corporation. He would like to freeze the value of this company for tax purposes at today's value and transfer future growth to his children without giving up control over the company. He does not want to pay tax any sooner than he has to. His will currently leaves everything to his wife. Which of the following plans will achieve his objectives?

(A) His children should subscribe to common shares of a holding company and he should transfer his shares of ABC to this holding company, electing under section 85 at tax cost and taking back voting redeemable retractable preferred shares as consideration.

(B) He should change his will to leave his shares of ABC to his children rather than his wife.

(C) He should gift the ABC shares to his children during his lifetime.

(D) He should sell the ABC shares to his children at fair market value, taking back debt as consideration.

Question 6

Which of the following techniques will allow Mr. Singh to use up his $824,176 capital gains exemption on the accrued gain on shares of a qualified small business corporation? The shares were issued to him 20 years ago for $1 and are worth $1 million now.

(A) A reverse asset freeze.

(B) An internal freeze, using section 86.

(C) A holdco freeze, taking back boot of $1.

(D) A holdco freeze, taking back boot of $824,177.

¶17,850   EXERCISES

Exercise 1

ITA: 85.1

Magnamous Publico Ltd., a widely-held public corporation, has offered to exchange its common shares, currently trading on a designated stock exchange at $14.70 per share, for the common shares of Targetco Ltd., another widely-held public corporation. The shares of Targetco Ltd. trade currently on the same stock exchange in the range of $12 to $12.25 each. Magnamous Publico Ltd. has offered to exchange one of its common shares for every two common shares tendered by shareholders of Targetco Ltd.

Mr. Stewart owns 1,000 shares of Targetco Ltd. which he bought several years ago for $11.25 each. Their paid-up capital value is $11 per share. On the announcement of the exchange offer their value on the market rose to $12.35. Mr. Stewart is interested in the exchange offer, but does not wish to realize any of the accrued gain on his shares of Targetco Ltd. Upon taking up the exchange offer, Mr. Stewart indicates that he will never own more than 10% of the shares of Magnamous Publico Ltd.

— REQUIRED

What are the tax consequences to Mr. Stewart and to Magnamous Publico Ltd. of taking up the exchange offer?

Exercise 2

ITA: 86

Aaron Chui owned some Class A preferred shares of a corporation that reorganized its capital structure. He exchanged all these shares which had an adjusted cost base and paid-up capital of $20,000 and a fair market value of $30,000 for the following consideration:

Cash	$6,750
Fair market value of Class B preferred shares (LSC: $10,000)	17,550
Fair market value of common shares (LSC: $3,250)	5,700

— REQUIRED

What are the tax consequences to Mr. Chui as a result of this exchange?

Exercise 3

ITA: 86(2)

Mrs. Janna and her daughter Rayna, respectively, own 75% and 25% of the 100 common shares of Adam Ltd. The total fair market value of all the shares of the corporation is $600,000. The shares were acquired by both individuals at a total cost of $1,000 on incorporation about 18 years ago.

Mrs. Janna is now prepared to freeze the future growth of her ownership in the corporation, so that the future growth will be passed on to her daughter. Mrs. Janna will give up all of her common shares for preferred shares of Adam Ltd. having a legal stated capital of $750 and a fair market value of $350,000. As a result, Rayna will own all of the common shares.

— REQUIRED

What are the tax consequences under section 86 to Mrs. Janna on the proposed transaction?

Exercise 4

ITA: 87, 88(1)

M&M Limited owns all of the shares of Acme Limited. The cost of the shares to M&M was $750,000 and they now have a fair market value of $1,000,000. Acme's only asset is land which cost it $500,000. The land had a fair market value of $900,000 when the shares of Acme were purchased by M&M (at a bargain price!) and the land now has a fair market value of $1,000,000.

— REQUIRED

Determine the income tax consequences to M&M Limited and Acme Limited of using either an amalgamation or a winding-up of a subsidiary to combine.

ITA: 87, 88

Exercise 5

ITA: 51

Charlie owns $10,000 of debentures of Charlie's Cars Ltd. They were purchased several years ago at their face value and are convertible into 16 common shares of the corporation for each $100 of debentures owned at the option of the holder. When the common shares traded on the market at $100 each, Charlie exercised the conversion privilege.

— REQUIRED

What are the tax consequences of this conversion?

¶17,875   ASSIGNMENT PROBLEMS

Type 1 Problems

Problem 1

ITA: 85, 85.1

Jason purchased all of the common shares of Quality Appliances Ltd., a Canadian-controlled private corporation, about 20 years ago, for $500,000. The paid-up capital of the shares was $25,000. These shares have recently been valued at $1,250,000.

Big Distributors Ltd., a Canadian, arm's length corporation, has offered to buy all of Jason's shares. The following alternatives have been presented to Jason:

(a) $250,000 in cash and $1,000,000 of FMV in common shares of Big Distributors Ltd.

(b) $1,250,000 of FMV in Big Distributors Ltd.'s common shares.

Jason is at arm's length with Big Distributors Ltd. and, after acquiring its shares, will neither control Big Distributors Ltd. nor own more than 50% of the FMV of its shares.

Jason has asked you to advise him on:

(A) The tax consequences to him if these transactions are conducted using the provisions of section 85.1.

(B) The tax consequences to him if these transactions are conducted using the provisions of section 85.

Problem 2

ITA: 84(1), 84(3), 86

Matt owns common shares of Maeb Inc. The adjusted cost base and paid-up capital of these shares is $300,000 and the FMV is $900,000. In the course of a capital reorganization, the following two packages of consideration were offered in exchange for the shares:

(a) Cash	$ 10,000
Bond	80,000
FMV and LSC of Class A preferred shares	810,000
Redeemable and retractable at FMV	
(b) Cash	$500,000
FMV and LSC of Class A preferred shares	400,000
Redeemable and retractable at FMV	

Advise Matt on the tax consequences to him as a result of the above proposed reorganizations.

Problem 3

ITA: 86(2)

Mr. Fresser, age 67, owns 80% of the common shares of Fresser Ltd., a CCPC. The other 20% is owned by his daughter, Elana, who has worked in the business with Mr. Fresser for the past 22 years.

When the business was incorporated and capitalized, the 1,000 common shares were issued to Mr. Fresser and his daughter for $62,500 in total. They now have a fair market value of $625,000. Mr. Fresser proposes a capital reorganization in which he would give up his common shares in return for $90,000 in cash and $300,000 in retractable voting preferred shares with a legal stated capital of $300,000 which he could redeem at his convenience. As a result, Elana could own all of the outstanding common shares.

Advise Mr. Fresser on:

(A) The tax consequences to him of section 86 on the proposed transaction.

(B) The tax consequences to him of subsequently redeeming the preferred shares for their fair market value.

Type 2 Problems

Problem 4

ITA: 87, 88(1)

Norm Bass has just met with you to ask your advice on the possible merger of his two companies. Norm, a Canadian resident, owns 100% of Normpar Inc., which in turn owns 100% of Jonsub Inc. Both are Canadian companies located in Saskatchewan and both have December 31st year ends.

The shares of Jonsub were purchased five years ago at a cost of $4,000,000. The first few years were profitable and in the second year of ownership Jonsub paid a dividend of $500,000 to Normpar, but the last two years have not been good as Jonsub has realized non and net capital losses. It is unlikely that Jonsub will generate sufficient income to absorb the losses in the foreseeable future. However, Normpar expects to generate sufficient business income and taxable capital gains to absorb all of Jonsub's losses.

Norm has heard that he could amalgamate the two companies or wind up Jonsub into Normpar, so Normpar could offset its income with the losses.

Norm would like your advice on when Normpar can gain access to the losses of Jonsub if the two companies merge on June 30, 2016, either by amalgamating or by winding up Jonsub into Normpar. After the transaction they want to retain the December 31st year end. Norm is also concerned about what will happen to the $4.0 million ACB that Normpar has in the shares of Jonsub after an amalgamation or wind up.

The balance sheet of Jonsub Ltd. immediately before the merger is as follows:

Assets:

Cash	$ 80,000
Accounts receivable (net of $30,000 reserve)	800,000
Inventory at cost (FMV $920,000)	920,000
Land at cost (FMV $2,000,000)	1,200,000
Building at UCC (FMV $500,000)	300,000
Equipment at UCC (FMV $150,000)	200,000
Goodwill (FMV $500,000)	0
Total current assets	$3,500,000

Liabilities and shareholder's equity:

Accounts payable and accrued liabilities	709,000
Loans payable	700,000
Share capital	1,000
Retained earnings	2,090,000
	$3,500,000

Other Information

(1) The fair market value of the land and building at the time Normpar Ltd. acquired control were $1.9 million and $400,000 respectively.

(2) The fair market value of goodwill developed by Jonsub Ltd. (i.e., not purchased) was $300,000 at the time Normpar Ltd. acquired control.

(3) Jonsub has the following losses:

Taxation year of loss	Non-capital loss	Net capital loss
2014	$43,000	$14,000
2013	7,000	10,000

Advise both Jonsub and Normpar on the tax consequences of either an amalgamation or a winding-up.

ITA: 87, 88(1)

Problem 5

ITA: 84.1, 85, 86

Ms. Knight owns all of the common shares of Knight Manufacturing Limited (KML) that she acquired 20 years ago from an arm's length person. These shares have a paid-up capital of $100,000 and their adjusted cost base is $400,000. Their current fair market value is $1.7 million and it is anticipated that this value will continue to grow rapidly. Ms. Knight is considering freezing the value of KML at $1.7 million by holding non-growth debt and preferred shares and having her adult children own the common shares. Ms. Knight would like to use up her remaining (QSBC share) capital gains exemption of $500,000.

You have agreed to advise Ms. Knight on the following matters:

(A) One method of freezing the future growth of her KML common shares is to transfer her present common shares to a newly formed holding company, Knight Holdings Ltd. (KHL). She would take from the holding company as consideration for the shares, debt in the amount of $900,000 and voting preferred shares with a legal stated capital and fair market value of $800,000. What are the tax consequences of this plan and how can the adverse tax consequences be avoided? Show all calculations.

(B) What are the tax consequences if the preferred shares in KHL received in (A) are:

(i) sold in an arm's length transaction for their fair market value?

(ii) redeemed by the corporation for their fair market value?

(C) As an alternative, Ms. Knight is considering a capital reorganization of KML in which she would receive $900,000 in debt and $800,000 in voting preferred shares in return for her common shares. The $800,000 amount of preferred shares represents their legal stated capital, fair market value and retractable value. What are the tax consequences to Ms. Knight on the reorganization? How can the adverse tax consequences be avoided?

(D) What are the consequences if the shares received by Ms. Knight on the reorganization in (C) are:

(i) sold in an arm's length transaction for their fair market value?

(ii) redeemed by the corporation for their fair market value?

(E) Compare the alternatives in (B) and (D) in terms of their total "net economic effects":

(i) with the adverse tax consequences of the plan as outlined, and

(ii) with the tax consequences of the plan that avoids these adverse tax consequences.

Type 3 Problems

Problem 6

Georgette is the president and sole shareholder of Vitality Plus Canada Ltd., a wholesale make-up and vitamin distributor. Twenty years ago, after the birth of her third child, Georgette invested $20,000 into the corporation and worked out of her home. Her corporation presently has the Canadian distribution rights for Vitality Plus, a European make-up line that continues to grow in popularity each year.

The company's net income (pre-tax) is approximately $320,000 per year, and Georgette's $100,000 salary is more than sufficient for her needs. The company shares have a current fair market value of approximately $680,000.

Candice, Georgette's eldest daughter, is 26 years of age and currently works full-time for the business. Since Candice lives at home, Georgette pays her a small salary of $22,000 per year. Candice would eventually like to take over the business but Georgette is not quite ready to retire and still wonders if her other two daughters, aged 20 and 22, would be interested in joining the company. At the same time, Georgette would like to slow down and spend more time with her fiancé, whom she will soon marry.

Georgette, a single mother for several years, has a portfolio of Canadian public utility shares worth about $250,000. The unrealized capital gain on those shares is $120,000. She also has a self-directed RRSP valued at approximately $490,000.

Georgette would like you to prepare a report outlining how she could plan for her new marriage and retirement over the next few years. Consider the options for estate planning arrangements that will assist Georgette in transferring her business to other family members.

Problem 7

Gil and Ruth George have been friends of yours for many years. They have come to you for advice on their estate plan since they want a second opinion to make sure it is going to do what they hope.

Orillia Resorts Inc. (Resorts) is a company purchased by Gil about 20 years ago to operate a tourist resort. Gil originally paid $200,000 for all 1,000 common shares of the company, which is now worth $2.4 million as a result of the increase in the value of lakefront property. The common shares have a paid-up capital of $1,000.

They have found that they are no longer able to look after the resort, now that they are both 68 years old. Also, they feel that they would like to spend their summers travelling instead of working 14 hours a day. They have had discussions with their lawyer and, on her recommendation, are now in the process of transferring the business to their only child, their daughter Gale, who has been working in the business and is ready to take over.

Gil has never used his capital gains exemption. The only assets in Resorts are the property and equipment used in the business. They have not accumulated any investments personally so they will still be relying on the business for their retirement income. As a result, they would like to keep voting control as long as they have an investment in the company.

The plan proposed by their lawyer has the following steps:

1) Gil will exchange his common shares of Orillia Resorts Inc. for 2,400 voting Class A preference shares. Then Gale will purchase 1,000 common shares from the company for $1 per share. The preference shares are redeemable and retractable at $1,000 each with a non-cumulative dividend rate of up to 7%.

2) Gil will then transfer the preference shares of Orillia Resorts Inc. to a holding company (Holdco) in exchange for 13,864 Class B preference shares of Holdco plus a note for $1,024,176. On this transfer, he will elect under section 85 at a value of $1,024,176 to use up his capital gain exemption. The preference shares are redeemable and retractable at $100 each with a non-cumulative dividend rate of up to 7%.

3) Ruth will pay $1,000 for 1,000 common shares of Holdco so she can receive dividends in their retirement years.

The plan is that Orillia Resorts Inc. will pay a 7% dividend each year to Holdco and then Gil and Ruth will decide how much they will take out of Holdco to live on. This will give them some investment assets outside of the business to provide some security for them in retirement.

Gil and Ruth would like your advice on the following issues:

1) Does the freeze work technically?

2) Is there a better plan?

Problem 8

Whyte Co. Inc. is a manufacturing company started by Bill and Betty Whyte about 25 years ago when they each paid $50 for 50 shares in the company. Since that time, it has grown significantly and now competes on a global basis.

Bill is 60 years old and Betty is 59 years old. They are both actively involved in the business and each owns 50% of the shares. However, they now want to start winding down their involvement in the business, so they can spend some time travelling together while they are still young. Betty and Bill have three children, Sandra (age 32), Paul (age 29), and Joan (age 26).

Sandra is actively involved in the business and is vice president, Operations. She is married to Jason and they have no children. Neither Paul nor Joan is involved in the business, nor do they plan to be. They each have their own career.

Betty and Bill are financially well off. Their personal net worth is as follows:

Cash	$ 10,000
Marketable securities	180,000
Loans to Whyte Co.	100,000
Residence	300,000
Cottage	120,000
RRSP	450,000
Real estate used in Whyte Co.	2,800,000
Whyte Co shares	4,500,000
Total	8,460,000
Mortgage on real estate	150,000
Net worth	$ 8,310,000

Bill and Betty have thought about estate planning and feel that their children will be well taken care of. They want to be fair to each of them, so they are going to leave everything to them equally in their wills, but they want Sandra to own the business and benefit from the future growth in value. They have group life insurance through the company for $200,000 each. Otherwise, they do not like to spend money on life insurance. When they think about retirement, they think they will need after-tax income of about $200,000 per year to do the things they want to do.

Bill and Betty would like you to present them with a plan that will accomplish their goals. As part of that, they specifically want you to address the following issues:

1) How should they structure the ownership to let Sandra benefit from the future growth in value?

2) How will they continue to receive income from the business in their retirement?

3) How can they be fair to all three children after they both die?

 [For more problems and solutions thereto, see the DVD accompanying the text-book.]

CHAPTER 17 —
DISCUSSION NOTES FOR REVIEW QUESTIONS

(1) Either articles of amendment or supplementary letters patent need to be filed with the incorporating jurisdiction in order to reorganize the capital of the corporation. Nothing needs to be filed with the CRA.

(2) Some of the uses of a reorganization of capital rollover include:

ITA: 86

(a) an estate freeze to allow the children to benefit from future capital appreciation;

(b) a reduction in the value of the common shares to allow a purchaser to buy common shares for a nominal amount; and

(c) a reduction in the value of the common shares to allow employees to buy shares at a reduced value.

(3) A deemed dividend may arise under the reorganization of capital rollover where the redemption proceeds (the reduced PUC of the new shares plus the non-share consideration) exceeds the paid-up capital of the old shares. The deemed dividend results in an adjustment to the proceeds of disposition. As a result, the proceeds will be reduced by any deemed dividend.

ITA: 54 "proceeds of disposition" (j), 84(3), 86
ITA: 84(3)
ITA: 84(3), 86(1)(c)

(4) For corporate law purposes, the two predecessor corporations are deemed to continue to exist as an amalgamated corporation. The amalgamated corporation is deemed to have existed previously as the predecessor corporations. Property owned by the predecessor corporations continues to be the property of the new amalgamated corporation. Liabilities enforceable against the predecessor corporations are now enforceable against the new amalgamated corporation.

(5) The deemed year-end as a result of an amalgamation has an impact on:

(a) unpaid amounts — the deemed year-end will count for purposes of section 78;

(b) CCA will have to be prorated;

ITR: 1100(3)

(c) the small business deduction business limit ($500,000) will have to be prorated for a short taxation year; and

ITA: 125(5)

(d) the short taxation year will count as one of the carryforward years available.

ITA: 111

(6) The CRA has indicated that, if an amalgamation is undertaken with a shell corporation solely to effect a year-end change, the GAAR would be applied. Therefore, this is considered to be an offensive transaction as far as the CRA is concerned.

IC 88-2
ITA: 245

(7) In order for the rollover on winding up a subsidiary to apply, not less than 90% of the issued shares of each class of the capital stock of the subsidiary need to be owned by the parent, which is a taxable Canadian corporation, and all of the shares of the subsidiary that were not owned by the parent immediately before the winding-up were owned at that time by persons with whom the parent was dealing at arm's length.

ITA: 88(1)

(8) Her new ACB is the total ACB she had on her preferred shares divided by the total number of new common shares. In this case her new ACB on the common shares would be $10,000 divided by 2,000 or $5 per share.

ITA: 51

(9) The primary purpose of estate freezing is to freeze all or part of the value of growing assets at their current fair market value in preferred shares held by a taxpayer. Future growth in these assets accrues to someone else, usually the next generation of family members through ownership of common shares. The result will be that this future growth will not be taxed in the hands of the taxpayer on a disposition or at his or her death.

(10) Some secondary objectives of an estate freeze would be to:

(a) defer any immediate tax cost on the freeze transaction and establish the amount of the tax liability on death;

(b) maintain control over the asset that has been frozen;

(c) maintain a source of income from the asset being frozen;

(d) split income with low tax-rate family members; and

(e) use up the QSBC share capital gains exemption on the asset being frozen, if possible.

(11) The three principal methods of freezing the value of growth assets are:

(a) holdco freeze;   ITA: 85

(b) internal freeze; and   ITA: 86

(c) reverse or asset freeze between corporations.   ITA: 85

Refer to the text for details of these methods.

(12) The basic steps involved in a Holdco freeze are:

(a) incorporate the holding company;

(b) transfer the shares of an operating corporation to the holding corporation using section 85 to avoid incurring an immediate tax cost; and

(c) have the transferor take back, as consideration for the growth asset, debt and preferred shares of the holding company. The preferred shares will have certain characteristics to achieve the freezor's objectives including a fixed retraction value which will freeze the value. Other features would revolve around desired voting control, income and security.

(13) One of the biggest dangers of doing an estate freeze on the shares of an SBC in   ITA: 74.4(2)
favour of a spouse or minor children is that the corporation will subsequently lose its SBC status and the corporate attribution rules will apply to deem an interest benefit on the transferor. Remember that the corporation only has to accumulate over approximately 10% of the FMV of its assets in non-active business assets in order to fall offside. This may be done easily if the company is generating excess cash and invests it. Keep in mind that the   ITA: 74.4(2)
corporate attribution rules only apply if "one of the main purposes of the transfer or loan may reasonably be considered to be to reduce the income of the individual and to benefit, either directly or indirectly, by means of a trust or by any other means whatever, a person who is a designated person in respect of the individual". Thus, before the corporate attribution rule applies, this purpose test must be met.

(14) A "reverse or asset freeze" would be used to transfer some or all of the growth assets of a corporation in which the taxpayer owns common shares to a new corporation owned by family members who will benefit from the future growth through their ownership of the new corporation's common shares. The consideration taken back on the transfer will usually consist of non-growth assets such as debt and preferred shares with a fixed retraction value. For example, an operating company owns land and building that are used in the business and the present shareholders want the increase in value of the land and building to go to their adult children.

The steps that would be taken are as follows:

(a) a new company would be incorporated with the adult children subscribing for the common shares usually for a nominal amount;

(b) the existing corporation would then transfer the growth assets to the new corporation using section 85 to defer any tax; and

(c) the transferor corporation will take back, as consideration for the growth assets, debt and preferred shares of the new corporation. The preferred shares will have certain characteristics to achieve the freezor's objectives including a fixed retraction value which will freeze the value. Other features would revolve around desired voting control, income and security.

CHAPTER 17 — SOLUTIONS TO MULTIPLE CHOICE QUESTIONS

Question 1

(C) is correct. On winding-up, the losses of the subsidiary are not available to the parent, until the parent's taxation year commencing after the commencement of the winding-up. Thus, the losses of L Ltd. would first be available to P Ltd. in its taxation year commencing January 1, 2017.   ITA: 88(1.1)

(A) is incorrect. The predecessor corporations are deemed to have a year end immediately before the amalgamation, October 31, 2016. The amalgamated corporation first exists on November 1, 2016.

(B) is incorrect. The amalgamated corporation can utilize the losses in its first taxation year commencing November 1, 2016.   ITA: 87(2.1)

(D) is incorrect for the reasons (C) is correct.

Question 2

(B) is correct.

X Ltd's adjusted cost base of the shares of Y Ltd.	$500,000
Less: Cost amount of Y Ltd.'s assets	(420,000)
Dividends paid to X Ltd.	(15,000)
Potential bump	$ 65,000

ITA: 88(1)(*d*)

The ACB of the land can be bumped by $30,000, up to its FMV at the time X Ltd. acquired control of Y Ltd., $130,000.   ITA: 88(1)(*d*)

(A) is incorrect. The bump available on a winding-up has not been applied.   ITA: 88(1)(*d*)

(C) is incorrect. The full amount of the bump available has been allocated to the land. The ACB of the land cannot be bumped above the FMV of the land when X Ltd. acquired control of Y Ltd.   ITA: 88(1)(*d*)

(D) is incorrect for the same reason as (C). In addition, the potential bump has not been reduced by the dividends received from X Ltd.

Question 3

(B) is correct. Since Chris exchanged all his common shares as part of a reorganization of capital, the rollover applies automatically. The cost of the preferred shares is equal to the cost of his common shares, less the non-share consideration: $2,000 – $135 = $1,865. For purposes of calculating the capital gain on the disposal of the common shares, proceeds are defined as the cost of the new shares, plus non-share consideration received: $1,865 + $135 = $2,000. As the proceeds equal his ACB, there is no capital gain.   ITA: 86(1)(*b*) ITA: 86(1)(*c*)

(A) is incorrect. The ACB of the preferred shares has not been reduced by the non-share consideration received.

(C) is incorrect. The tax-deferral provisions have been ignored.

(D) is incorrect. A capital gain equal to the non-share consideration has been recognized.

Question 4

(D) is correct as it is false. The provision specifically states that subsection 85.1(1) does not apply where consideration other than shares of the particular class of the purchaser was received by the vendor. Therefore, in the absence of any other election being made, Shelly would have a capital gain of $5,000 on the exchange if she received any non-share consideration.   ITA: 85.1(2)

(A) is incorrect as it is true. Section 85.1 is automatic; no election is required.

(B) is incorrect as it is true.   ITA: 85.1(1)(*a*)

(C) is incorrect as it is true.   ITA: 85.1(1)(*b*)

Question 5

(A) is the correct answer because this plan will freeze the value of his interest in ABC for tax purposes (since preferred shares don't grow in value) and transfer future growth to his children (because common shares do grow in value) without giving up control (because the preferred shares are voting). There will be no tax on the transfer since he will be electing at tax cost.

(B) is incorrect because changing his will to leave his shares of ABC to his children does not achieve his objective of freezing the value of his interest and having no tax on the transfer.

(C) is incorrect because gifting the ABC shares to his children results in the loss of control and immediate tax on the accrued capital gain because the gift results in a deemed disposition at fair market value.

ITA: 69

(D) is incorrect because, although a sale at fair market value taking back debt as consideration will defer tax somewhat because of the capital gains reserve, there will be tax on the accrued gain payable over the 5-year period and there is a loss of control.

ITA: 40

Question 6

(C) is correct, assuming an election is made at $824,177. The boot must be limited to $1 because the Act will cause any boot in excess of this amount to be a deemed dividend not a capital gain. That is why (D) is incorrect.

ITA: 84.1(1)

(A) is incorrect because a reverse asset freeze involves a transfer by a company rather than an individual. Hence, the $824,176 capital gains exemption cannot be used.

(B) is incorrect because an internal freeze using section 86 involves an automatic rollover. Hence, the $824,176 capital gains exemption cannot be used. However, while it is possible to accomplish an internal freeze with the crystallization of his capital gains exemption using section 85 as discussed in the textbook, that was not a choice offered in this question.

ITA: 86

CHAPTER 17 — SOLUTIONS TO EXERCISES

Exercise 1

Section 85.1 applies because shares of a Canadian corporation (Magnanimous, the purchaser) are being issued to a taxpayer (Mr. Stewart, the vendor) in exchange for capital property (shares of Targetco) of Mr. Stewart. Since Mr. Stewart wishes to fully defer the accrued gains in his shares he should not include any amount in his income on the disposition of his Targetco shares as a result of the exchange. Mr. Stewart and Magnanimous are at arm's length before the exchange. Furthermore, Mr. Stewart will neither control nor own more than 50% of the fair market value of all of the outstanding shares of Magnanimous after the exchange.

The tax consequences to Mr. Stewart will be as follows:

Proceeds of disposition for Targetco shares ($11.25 × 1,000)	$11,250
ACB of Targetco shares	(11,250)
Capital gain	Nil
ACB of Magnanimous shares received by Mr. Stewart in exchange	$11,250

As a result, the ACB of the 1,000 shares of Targetco given up by Mr. Stewart becomes the ACB of the 500 shares acquired in the exchange and the accrued capital gain on the Targetco shares is deferred. The ACB per share of the Magnanimous shares held by Mr. Stewart will be $22.50 (i.e., $11,250/500).

Magnanimous will have acquired the 1,000 Targetco shares from Mr. Stewart at an ACB equal to the lesser of:

FMV of Targetco shares before exchange (1,000 × $12.35)	$12,350
PUC of Targetco shares before exchange (1,000 × $11.00)	$11,000

The provision will apply to limit the addition to the PUC of Magnanimous shares on their issue in exchange to the amount of the PUC of the Targetco shares received (i.e., $11.00 per share). **ITA: 85.1(2.1)**

Exercise 2

There is no deemed dividend, because the redemption amount paid, consisting of cash for $6,750 and total reduced PUC of the new shares for $13,250, does not exceed the PUC of the old shares of $20,000. (See calculations (4) and (5) below.) **ITA: 84(3)**

Issuance of New Shares
(1) Reduced PUC: **ITA: 86(2.1)(a)**

LSC increase for all new shares		$13,250
Less: PUC of old class A preferred shares	$20,000	
Less: boot	6,750	13,250
PUC reduction		Nil
Total reduced PUC (class B preferreds, $10,000; commons, $3,250)		$13,250

(2) Cost of class B preferred and common shares received:

Adjusted cost base of old shares	$20,000
Less: fair market value of non-share consideration	6,750
Cost of Class B preferred and common shares received	$13,250
Cost of non-share consideration (boot) received (equal to FMV)	$ 6,750	**ITA: 86(1)(c)**

Allocation of cost of new shares:
Class B preferred shares:

$$\frac{\text{FMV of class B preferred shares}}{\text{FMV of all shares}} \times \text{cost of new shares}$$

$$= \frac{\$17,550}{\$17,550 + \$5,700} \times \$13,250 = \underline{\underline{\$10,000}}$$

Common shares:

$$\frac{\text{FMV of common shares}}{\text{FMV of all shares}} \times \text{cost of new shares}$$

$$= \frac{\$5,700}{\$17,550 + \$5,700} \times \$13,250 = \underline{\underline{\$3,250}}$$

Redemption of Old Shares

(1) Proceeds on redemption of old shares: ITA: 84(5)(*d*)

    Boot or non-share consideration . . . . $ 6,750

    Reduced PUC of the new shares — see above   13,250   ITA: 84(5)(*d*)

    Redemption proceeds $20,000

    Deemed dividend on redemption: ITA: 84(3)

    Redemption proceeds $20,000

    Less: PUC of old shares   20,000

    Deemed dividend on redemption . . . .   Nil   ITA: 84(3)

(2) Proceeds of disposition of old shares: ITA: 86(1)(*c*)

    Cost of all new shares (above) $13,250

    Plus: cost of all non-share consideration (equal to FMV) 6,750 $20,000

    Less: deemed dividend . . . .   Nil   ITA: 84(3)

    Proceeds of disposition of old shares $20,000

    Capital gain or loss on disposition of old shares:

    Proceeds of disposition of old shares $20,000

    Adjusted cost base of old shares   20,000

    Capital gain (loss)[1] . . . .   Nil

Net economic effect:

    Deemed dividends on redemption . . . .   Nil   ITA: 84(3)

    Capital gain (loss) on disposition of old shares . . . .   Nil

    Accrued capital gain on new shares:

    FMV ($17,550 + $5,700) $23,250

    ACB . . . .   (13,250) $10,000

    Net economic effect $10,000

This $10,000 reflects the accrued gain (i.e., $30,000 – $20,000) on the old shares before the reorganization.

— NOTE TO SOLUTION

[1] Capital losses on a redemption are denied where the corporation is still affiliated with the shareholder (e.g., where the shareholder or the shareholder's spouse still controls the corporation after the exchange).   ITA: 40(3.6)

Exercise 3

The benefit rule will apply in this case because the FMV of Mrs. Janna's common shares ($450,000, i.e., 75% of $600,000) is greater than the FMV of the preferred shares received on the reorganization ($350,000) and it is reasonable to regard the $100,000 excess as a benefit that Mrs. Janna desired to have conferred on a related person, her daughter.   ITA: 86(2)

There is no deemed dividend, as shown by the following: ITA: 84(3)

Issuance of New Shares

(1) Reduced PUC: ITA: 86(2.1)(a)

LSC increase for new preferred shares		$750
Less: PUC of old common shares	$750	
Less: boot	Nil	750
PUC reduction		Nil
Reduced PUC ($750 – Nil)		$750

(2) The cost of the preferred shares received will be equal to: ITA: 86(2)(e)

ACB of common shares		$ 750
Less: cost of non-share consideration	Nil	
benefit	$100,000	100,000
Cost of preferred shares		Nil

Since no boot was taken back on the exchange the final PUC of the preferred shares will be $750.

Redemption of Old Shares

(1) Redemption amount:

Non-share consideration	Nil	
PUC of preferred shares received	$ 750	$ 750
Less: PUC of common shares given up		(750)
Deemed dividend on redemption		Nil

ITA: 84(3)

(2) The deemed proceeds of disposition of Mrs. Janna's common shares will be equal to the lesser of: ITA: 86(2)(c)

(a) Cost (equal to FMV) of non-share consideration	Nil
Plus: benefit	$100,000
	$100,000
(b) FMV of common shares given up	$450,000

There will be a capital gain on the disposition by Mrs. Janna of her common shares equal to:

Deemed proceeds of disposition (lesser of (a) and (b), above)	$100,000
ACB of common shares (75% of $1,000)	(750)
Capital gain	$ 99,250

The following net economic effect can be aggregated from the foregoing:

Deemed dividend on redemption		Nil
Capital gain on disposition of common shares		$ 99,250
Accrued capital gain on preferred shares:		
FMV	$350,000	
ACB	Nil	350,000
Net economic effect		$449,250

ITA: 84(3)

This $449,250 reflects the accrued gain (i.e., 75% of ($600,000 – $1,000)) on the common shares held by Mrs. Janna, before the reorganization. Note how $99,250 is realized immediately on the reorganization and the remainder will be realized on the disposition of the preferred shares.

Furthermore, Mrs. Janna has lost the ability to recover $100,000 in tax-paid cost, because the cost of the preferred shares is nil, having been reduced by the benefit. The $100,000 is tax-paid cost because it reflects the $750 of cost in the common shares, plus $99,250 of capital gain realized on the disposition of those shares and included in income. At the same time, Rayna has had the benefit of a $100,000 increase in the value of her shares without any increase in their adjusted cost base. Therefore, the $100,000 of gain will be taxable in her hands on the disposition of her common shares.

Exercise 4

If either section 87 or subsection 88(1) is used:

(A) Acme Limited will be deemed to have proceeds of disposition on the land of $50,000, so the capital gain will be deferred.

(B) M&M will be able to "bump" the cost base of the land on its books

ITA: 88(1)(*d*)

— the "bump" would be computed as follows:

M&M's ACB of Acme's shares		$750,000
Less the sum of:		
(I) cost amount of Acme's assets	$500,000	
(II) dividends paid by Acme to M&M	Nil	500,000
Increase in ACB of land		$250,000

— this "bump" cannot exceed:

fair market value of the land at the time control was acquired	$900,000
less: ACB of the land	500,000
maximum "bump"	$400,000

— therefore, the ACB of the land to M&M will be $750,000 after a "bump" of $250,000.

Exercise 5

Adjusted cost base of common shares equal to adjusted cost base of the debentures at the time of conversion	$10,000

Adjusted cost base of each common share:

Number of shares received on conversion ($\frac{\$10,000}{\$100} \times 16$)	1,600
ACB of each share ($10,000/1,600)	$ 6.25

Chapter 18

Partnerships and Trusts

Learning Goals

Know

By the end of this chapter you will know:

- The basic provisions of the Income Tax Act that relate to partnerships and trusts.

Understand and Explain

By the end of this chapter you will understand and be able to explain:

- How a partnership and a trust are established.
- How income earned within a partnership is computed.
- How income of a partnership is taxed.

Apply

By the end of this chapter you will be able to apply your knowledge and understanding to:

- Calculate the income of a partner from a partnership.
- Calculate income of a partnership.
- Calculate taxable income and tax payable of a trust.

Review Questions
¶18,800 in the Study Guide

Multiple Choice Questions
¶18,825 in the Study Guide

Exercise Questions
¶18,850 in the Study Guide

Assignment Problems
¶18,875 in the Study Guide

CHAPTER 18 — LEARNING CHART

Problem Descriptions

Textbook Example Problems

1   Partnership income allocation
2   Partnership income flow through
3   Transfer of partnership property to a corporation
4   Transfer of property to a partnership
5   Taxable income of trust and beneficiary
6   Attribution

Multiple Choice Questions

1   Partnership income flow through
2   ACB of a partnership interest
3   Trust
4   Testamentary trust
5   Types of trusts
6   Testamentary trust

Exercises

1   Partnership income flow through
2   Disposal of partnership interest
3   Taxable income of trust and beneficiary

Assignment Problems

1   Partnership income, ACB
2   Partnership income, ACB, disposition
3   Partnership income, incorporation
4   Transfer of assets to a partnership
5   Trusts
6   Establish a trust, income allocation, personal tax
7   Estate freeze
8   Merging two businesses
9   Advice on estate plan

Study Notes

¶18,800 REVIEW QUESTIONS

(1) What does the term "partnership" mean and where would you find the definition?

(2) A limited partner can deduct in full losses allocated to that partner by the partnership. True or false? Explain.

(3) An older man, Dadd, and his son, Ladd, wish to carry on a business as a partnership. Dadd is going to contribute land, building and equipment and cash while Ladd is going to contribute energy. They have agreed that they will split the profit from the business on a 50/50 basis; however, they would allocate any capital gain on the land and building fully to Dadd. In addition, any losses in the first five years are to be allocated fully to Dadd. What are your comments on the allocation of the gains and losses?

(4) Assume that you are a partner in a partnership and you are entitled to 25% of the income. How would your income allocation and adjusted cost base be affected by a $1,200 capital gain realized by the partnership?

(5) Assume that you are a partner in a partnership and you are entitled to 25% of the income. How would your income allocation and adjusted cost base be affected by a $100,000 receipt from a life insurance policy on the death of one of your partners?

(6) Ms. Jones is about to become a partner in a partnership and she wants to contribute some property on a rollover basis. There are 13 other partners involved although one of them has just moved to the United States for a four-year assignment. Should Ms. Jones have any concerns about the availability of the rollover?

ITA: 97(2)

(7) What is a trust?

(8) Comment on this statement: "Trusts are taxed in much the same way as partnerships; they are both conduits of income and neither is liable to pay tax".

(9) How is a testamentary and an *inter vivos* trust created?

(10) What is a discretionary trust and how does it work?

(11) One method of transferring the tax liability from the trust to the beneficiary is to either pay out the income or make it payable to the beneficiaries. What types of income retain their source for purposes of calculating the taxable income and tax payable of the beneficiary?

ITA: 104(6)

(12) Ms. Betty is the sole beneficiary of a trust that arose on the death of her father. He died on March 15, 2015. When does the trust file its first tax return? When does Ms. Betty report the income that is allocated to her by the trust in its first tax year end?

¶18,825   MULTIPLE CHOICE QUESTIONS

Question 1

Bert & Ernie
Partnership Income Statement
For the year ended December 31, 2016

Income:

Consulting fees		$300,000
Dividends received from low-rate income of a CCPC		40,000
Gain of sale of shares of taxable Canadian corporations		120,000
		$460,000

Expenses:

Salaries to staff	$50,000	
Capital cost allowance on equipment	15,000	
Office rent	10,000	
Charitable donations	20,000	$ 95,000
Net income		$365,000

The dividends were received from a CCPC whose income was eligible for the small business deduction.

Bert and Ernie each took drawings of $30,000 in the year.

Bert and Ernie share income from the partnership equally. Bert has no other source of income in 2016. Bert will have taxable income in 2016 of:

(A) $186,100

(B) $182,500

(C) $167,500

(D) $165,900

Question 2

On January 1, 2016, Ann and Bob formed a partnership to provide window cleaning services. The partners each contributed $5,000 and agreed that all income and losses would be shared equally. For the fiscal period January 1 to December 31, 2016, the following information is available.

(1) The partnership earned income for tax purposes of $200,000. Included in this amount is a taxable capital gain of $40,000.

(2) The partnership made charitable donations of $12,000.

(3) Ann took draws totalling $70,000.

(4) Ann contributed additional capital of $14,000 to the partnership.

The adjusted cost base of Ann's partnership interest at January 1, 2017, is:

(A) $23,000

(B) $43,000

(C) $63,000

(D) $69,000

Question 3

Al Smith settled a trust in favour of his two children on May 1, 2016. He settled the trust with marketable securities worth $50,000. His adjusted cost base for the marketable securities was $20,000. Al, his wife, and a family friend were named as trustees. His two children are ages five and six. Which one of the following statements is FALSE?

(A) The tax return for the first year of the trust is due March 31, 2017.

(B) The trust is entitled to a deduction in computing its income for amounts paid to the children during the year.

(C) Income in the trust will be subject to a 33% federal rate of tax.

(D) Al can defer the recognition of the capital gain on the transfer of the securities to the trust.

Question 4

The James Stewart family trust was created on and as a consequence of the death of James Stewart on May 1, 2016. Which one of the following statements with respect to the trust is TRUE?

(A) The trust must have a December 31 year-end.

(B) The income in the trust will be subject to the same graduated rates of tax applicable to individuals.

(C) The trust return is due six months after the year-end of the trust.

(D) The trust is not entitled to claim a dividend tax credit for dividends received and retained in the trust.

Question 5

Which of the following types of trusts has a deemed disposition of all its assets at fair market value on the settlor's death?

(A) An *inter vivos* trust

(B) A joint partner trust

(C) An alter ego trust

(D) A discretionary trust

Question 6

Which of the following is **not** an advantage of providing for testamentary trusts in your will for each of your children with a giftover to your grandchildren on each child's death?

(A) Income-splitting using the available designations.   ITA: 104(13.1), 104(13.2)

(B) Avoiding a deemed disposition of assets at fair market value on the child's death that would result if the assets were left directly to the child.

(C) Avoiding the deemed disposition of assets at fair market value on the transfer of assets to the trust on death.

(D) Providing your children with beneficial ownership over their inheritances, but giving control over their inheritances to the trustees of each trust.

¶18,850 EXERCISES

Exercise 1

ITA: 96, 110.1, 118.1, 121

The following income statement was prepared for Bob and Stan Tax Services, a partnership of two individuals who share income equally:

Bob and Stan Tax Services
INCOME STATEMENT
for the year ended December 31, 2016

Gross revenue from operations		$400,000
Less: Amortization on office furniture	$ 3,750	
Donations to charities	5,500	
Dues to Canadian Tax Foundation	550	
Employees' salaries	67,220	
Fringe benefits for employees	11,500	
Heat, light and water	2,400	
Interest expense	725	
Membership in fitness club	1,250	
Office rent	9,000	
Office supplies	2,250	
Repairs and maintenance	575	104,720
		$295,280
Dividends received from a CCPC that has no GRIP balance		4,000
Capital gain		5,000
Net income		$304,280

Additional Information

(1) Maximum capital cost allowance on the furniture for the year is $4,300.

(2) The partners each took drawings of $54,000 in the year.

(3) The dividends were received from a CCPC, all of whose income was eligible for the small business deduction.

— REQUIRED

Bob is your client. He has received personal investment income consisting of $3,500 in dividends from Canadian public companies and $1,200 in interest income. Determine his taxable income for 2016 and analyze the nature of his income.

Exercise 2

ITA: 53(1)(*e*), 53(2)(*c*)

Five years ago, a partnership was formed between David and Katie to carry on a professional accounting practice. Both partners made an initial contribution of $50,000 at that time agreeing to make equal drawings and to share equally in the profits and losses of the practice. The following data pertain to the partnership business during the period from its inception to the present:

Income of the partnership during the period	$450,000
Losses of the partnership during the period	15,000
Net taxable capital gains included in the above income	20,000
Drawings by the partners in the period	176,000
Capital dividends received by the partnership	4,000
Charitable donations made by the partnership	27,000
In 2016, Katie will retire from the partnership and will receive in full settlement of her partnership interest	250,000

— REQUIRED

What are the tax consequences to Katie of the disposition of her partnership interest in 2016?

Exercise 3

On January 1, 2016, Mr. Ruester settled a trust for the benefit of his two children, Rebecca and Robert, both over the age of 18, neither of whom has other income. Robert attends, for eight months a year, a university in Canada where tuition is $3,500 per year. All tuition for 2016 was paid in respect of that year. Under the terms of the trust, the trustees have complete discretion to allocate the accumulated income to the beneficiaries in any manner they wish. The trust earned income from cash transferred to the trust by Mr. Ruester. For the 2016 taxation year, the trust received the following income:

Interest	$11,500
Dividends from public corporations	9,000
Capital gain	9,000

The trustees paid the income, and made the appropriate designations as follows:

	Interest	Dividend	Capital gain
Rebecca	$5,500	$3,000	$3,000
Robert	1,500	3,000	3,000
Total paid	$7,000	$6,000	$6,000
Total income accumulated in trust	$4,500	$3,000	$3,000

— REQUIRED

Compute the taxable income and the federal taxes payable of the trust and each beneficiary.

¶18,875 ASSIGNMENT PROBLEMS

Type 2 Problems

Problem 1

ITA: 53(1)(e), 53(2)(c)

Mr. Clancy has come to you with a question about his interest in the partnership Ludlum, Clancy, Follet & Associates. He has provided you with the following information:

Ludlum, Clancy, Follet & Associates
INCOME STATEMENT
for the year ended December 31, 2016

Gross revenue		$880,250
Less:		
Professional staff employee salaries	$229,000	
Office salaries	74,000	
Rent	42,000	
Office supplies	17,000	
Client entertainment	5,075	
Capital cost allowance	16,222	
Donations to charities	25,000	408,297
		$471,953
Dividend income:		
Dividends from Canadian public companies	25,000	
Net income for accounting purposes		$496,953

Mr. Clancy has come prepared with some additional information. The adjusted cost base of his partnership interest was $45,792 at the beginning of the year. His drawings for the year were $77,500. Mr. Clancy is one of four equal partners in the partnership.

Mr. Clancy is not married and does not have children. He is 31 years old. His only income is from the partnership.

Mr. Clancy wants to know what his tax position is based on the current structure.

You have agreed to do the following :

(A) Compute the partnership income for the year, the income to be allocated to him, and the nature of the income.

(B) Compute his taxable income and tax payable for 2016. Ignore CPP.

(C) Compute the adjusted cost base of his partnership interest.

(D) Compute his after-tax personal cash.

(E) Discuss the CPP and EI implications.

Problem 2

ITA: 53(1)(e), 53(2)(c)

About five years ago, Isabelle, Eden, Samara, and Joy formed a partnership to carry on a snow removal and landscape business. All the partners, except Isabelle, made an initial contribution of $40,000. Isabelle made an initial contribution of $80,000. Each agreed to share in the profits and losses of the business based on their initial capital contribution. At the end of the 2016 fiscal year of the partnership, Isabelle and Samara decided to go their separate ways. Samara received $125,000 for her partnership interest, while Isabelle received $250,000. The tax records for the five years ended December 31, 2015 reflected the following cumulative amounts:

Income (before capital gains) from operations for tax purposes	$750,000
Losses	80,000
Capital gains (to 2015)	10,000
Drawings by the partners	730,000*
Charitable donations (added back to Division B income for tax purposes)	15,000

* Isabelle, $170,000; Eden, $150,000; Samara, $250,000; and Joy, $160,000.

Financial results for the year ended December 31, 2016, are as follows:

Net income per financial statements	$60,000
Charitable donations (deducted from accounting income)	2,000
Drawings:	
Isabelle	10,000
Samara	5,000
Eden	5,000
Joy	4,000

Other Information

(1) Isabelle is single, and has interest income of $2,500 for the year 2016.

(2) Samara has interest income of $6,600, and is allowed a deduction of $16,000 for child care in 2016. She has made an RRSP contribution in 2016 of $2,700 (her 2015 earned income was $15,000).

You have agreed to do the following:

(1) Compute the partnership income for the year ended December 31, 2016, and the income to be allocated to the partners.

(2) Advise on the tax consequences to Samara and Isabelle as a result of the disposition of their partnership interests in 2016.

(3) Compute Samara's and Isabelle's taxable income and tax payable for 2016 using the hypothetical provincial tax rate table presented in Chapter 10, ¶10,250.

Problem 3

Brenda and Sasha are equal partners in an interior decorating business in Kenora, Ontario. Their income statement for the year ended December 31 shows:

S&B Interior Decorators
INCOME STATEMENT
December 31, 2016

Revenue	$300,000
Expenses	200,000
Income before gain on asset sale	$100,000
Gain on asset sale	35,000
Net income	$135,000

They have each asked you to prepare their personal income tax return, and to that end have provided you with the following additional information.

- Brenda was paid a salary of $6,000 and it is included in the expenses.

- A $1,000 donation to a registered charity is included in the expenses.

- The asset sold was a piece of land they had purchased in hopes of having their own building from which to operate their business; those plans fell through when the bank wouldn't advance the necessary loans. The $35,000 represents the net gain after real estate broker and legal fees of $5,000.

- Each partner uses (and personally pays for) his/her own car in the business. Brenda's auto expenses for business use are $1,500 and Sasha's is $3,500.

- The business was originally started by Brenda. Sasha bought in several years later. He borrowed $35,000 from the bank to purchase his partnership interest and has paid $1,800 in interest on the bank loan.

- Included in revenue is $1,000 in interest earned on a GIC.

- Sasha's son is employed in the business and his wages of $2,000 are included in the expenses. He cleans up the store on weekends and does odd jobs. The $2,000 is considered reasonable, no T4 slip has been issued to him by the business.

- S&B's December 31 balance sheet shows that Brenda had drawings of $42,000 and Sasha had drawings of $35,000.

You have agreed to do the following:

(a) Identify the amount of any income, including the types of income, that each of Brenda and Sasha will include in their income tax returns. Identify any other items that will be included in their income tax returns.

(b) Brenda and Sasha are considering incorporating their partnership. What is the most significant property that needs to be considered on a section 85 rollover of their business?

Problem 4

ITA: 22, 97(2)

Adam and Amit formed a partnership this year to operate a retail store specializing in gag gifts. Adam, who has been in the business for about 13 years as a sole proprietor, owns the following assets:

	Cost amount	Fair market value
Accounts receivable	$17,500	$ 17,000
Inventory	22,000	22,000
Store fixtures (cost: $17,500)	16,000	19,500
Leasehold improvements (cost: $37,500)	33,500	35,000
Goodwill	—	40,000
	$89,000	$133,500

Adam will transfer these assets to the partnership on November 1, 2016, in exchange for a 60% partnership interest. Amit will contribute $59,000 in cash and marketable securities with a fair market value of $30,000 in return for a 40% interest. The marketable securities were purchased about 12 years ago at a cost of $25,000.

You have agreed to advise Adam and Amit on the following:

(A) How can Adam's and Amit's assets be transferred to the partnership with the minimum amount of tax? What is the cost to the partnership of the assets?

(B) What is the maximum non-partnership consideration that Adam and Amit can receive without adverse tax consequences?

(C) What is the adjusted cost base of the partnership interest to each of Adam and Amit, assuming that the only consideration received for the transferred assets is a partnership interest?

Problem 5

Part A

ITA: 117(2), 122, 248(1)

For each of the following trusts settled by Mrs. A:

— explain the tax consequences of the transfer of property by Mrs. A to the trust;

— identify the rate of tax payable by the trust; and

— explain the tax consequences of the transfer of property from the trust to the beneficiary.

(a) On June 1, 2016, Mrs. A settled a painting on her daughters, B and C, in trust for her grandchildren. The painting has a cost to Mrs. A of $500 and a fair market value of $7,000.

(b) Mrs. A provides in her will that her shares of ABC Co. are to be held in trust for her grandchildren. These shares have a cost to Mrs. A of $10,000 and a fair market value of $35,000.

(c) Mrs. A's will provides that her remaining properties will be inherited by her daughters, B and C. On her death the properties are held in her estate until distributed to the daughters.

Part B

ITA: 70(6)

Mr. B died on March 15, 2016. Mr. B's will provides that the residue of his estate is to be transferred to a trust for the benefit of his wife, Mrs. B, a resident of Canada. The will provides that the income of the trust is to be paid to Mrs. B. The will also allows the executors to pay out capital for the benefit of Mrs. B. On Mrs. B's death, the trust's assets are to be distributed to the Bs' children. Mr. B's assets include shares of XYZ Inc., a public company, which were purchased about 25 years ago for $1,000 and have a fair market value at his death of $100,000.

You have agreed to advise the executor as follows:

(A) Explain the tax consequences to Mr. B arising out of the transfer of the ABC Inc. shares to the trust for Mrs. B.

(B) Explain the tax consequences to the trust of holding the shares and earning dividend income.

(C) Explain the tax consequences if the shares are transferred to Mrs. B.

(D) Explain the tax consequences if the shares are held by the trust at the time Mrs. B dies.

(E) How would your answer to (A) be different if Mr. B's will provided the trustees with the power to encroach on capital for the benefit of the Bs' children?

Part C

ITA: 104(13.1), 104(13.2), 108(1)

Mrs. Jones died about six years ago. Under the terms of her will, an investment portfolio was settled on Mr. Shiah and Mrs. Clive, as trustees, for the benefit of her daughter, Hilary Jones. In 2015, the trust will have substantial income comprised almost exclusively of capital gains. The trust has a non-capital loss carryforward which arose three years ago.

Hilary's income from other sources is substantial with the result that any allocation of income from the trust to her will increase her overall tax liability.

Is there any strategy that can be adopted by the trustees in order to reduce the taxes payable in respect of a distribution to Hilary?

Problem 6

ITA: 104

On January 1, 2015, Mr. Bilodeau settled a trust for his daughter Jane, who became age 17 in 2015. The trust was documented by a written agreement. There are three trustees, Mr. Bilodeau, Mrs. Bilodeau, and a long-time family friend. The trust provided that the trustees had complete discretion to distribute any portion of the capital or annual income of the trust to the beneficiary.

Mr. Bilodeau transferred the following assets into the trust on January 1, 2015:

(a) $250,000 cash; and

(b) 1,500 shares of Successful Retailers Ltd., a corporation that is incorporated in Canada and is a CCPC with no GRIP balance. The original cost of the shares about 23 years ago when they were purchased by Mr. Bilodeau was $17 per share. At the date of transfer the fair market value was $500 per share.

The trust immediately purchased a 6% bond with the $250,000 cash. Interest of $15,000 is payable on December 31st.

The amount of dividends paid on the Successful Retailers Ltd. shares for each of 2015 and 2016 is $30,000. The dividends were received only from income eligible for the small business deduction.

In each year, the trust is to "accumulate" 60% of the income earned and pay out the remainder before capital cost allowance to the beneficiary to meet her financial needs. Mr. Bilodeau is in the top tax bracket. Jane does not have any income other than from the trust.

The trustees have asked you to do the following:

(A) Outline the income tax consequences to Mr. Bilodeau of the transfer of property to the trust in 2015.

(B) Calculate the amount of net income allocable to each and the taxes payable by each of Mr. Bilodeau, Jane and the trust in 2015 and 2016. Use the hypothetical individual tax rate table presented in Chapter 10, ¶10,250.

(C) Advise on the steps that could have been taken when the trust was established to minimize the income allocable to Mr. Bilodeau.

Problem 7

ITA: 84(1), 85, 86, 104, 129(6)

Gordon Willows is 60 years old. He is the president and sole shareholder of Amazing Results Inc. ("Amazing"). Amazing was incorporated about 25 years ago. At the time of incorporation, Gordon subscribed for 100 common shares without par value for subscription proceeds of $100. These are still the only shares that are issued and outstanding.

Amazing has been involved in the lobbying business and achieves results for its clients which are considered to be simply amazing. Amazing has just been involved in a very successful high-profile lobbying effort. Business is booming. Amazing has been a very profitable company. It is estimated that the fair market value of the shares is $8 million today. Gordon believes that the value of the shares of Amazing will increase dramatically over the next two years to about $13 million.

Included in Amazing's assets is land and building (the "real estate") which is located steps away from the provincial legislature. The real estate was purchased about 20 years ago for $200,000 and is estimated to be worth about $7,000,000 today. The cost and value of the real estate is allocated 50/50 between land and building. The undepreciated capital cost of the building as at today's date is $35,000. It is estimated that the property will be worth about $12 million within five years.

Gordon is divorced with three children. Wendy is 35 years old and very active in the business. Her intention is to make a career out of Amazing. Wayne, who is 32 years old, is an artist with no interest in Amazing. Winona, who is 28 years old, is in a PhD program in accounting. She has stated her intention is to become a researcher at a top university.

Gordon would like to retire from active involvement in Amazing within the next 10 years. He estimates that he will continue to require an income of $200,000 per year thereafter. He wants to take action now so that, in the event of his death, he will not be taxed on the expected growth of Amazing in the next five years.

Gordon has decided that a plan should be implemented to ensure that Wendy will benefit from the future growth of Amazing. At the same time, he wants to be fair to Wayne and Winona by providing them with some benefits from the growth of his estate in the future. He wants to maintain sufficient control over Amazing during his life in the event that Wendy does not fulfil his expectations of her involvement in the business. Gordon tells you that his neighbour has "frozen" everything in favour of his children as a means of saving taxes. Gordon would like to freeze everything too. Gordon has never claimed a capital gains exemption.

Advise Gordon of the tax consequences and merits of the following proposals to achieve his objectives:

(i) Gordon would transfer the shares of Amazing, using section 85, to a corporation (Holdco) of which Wendy holds the common shares. He would receive as consideration preferred shares with a PUC of $100 and a redemption value of $824,276.

(ii) The same as in (i); however, the consideration for the transfer would be a promissory note of Holdco for $824,276 and fixed-value preferred shares of Holdco with a redemption value and legal stated capital of $7,175,724.

(iii) Gordon would exchange the shares of Amazing for a newly created class of fixed-value preferred shares of Amazing. He has been advised that under corporate law the stated capital of the fixed-value preferred shares can be $8 million. He would like the paid-up capital to be $8 million since he understands that paid-up capital can be returned to him tax-free.

(iv) Gordon would cause Amazing to transfer its land and building to a new corporation in exchange for preferred shares of the new corporation having a fair market value of $7,000,000 and then lease the real estate back from the new corporation. The common shares of the new corporation would be owned by Wayne and Winona.

Suggest to Gordon an alternative to his plans, taking into consideration his age and objectives.

Type 3 Problems

Problem 8

Kay Sega is a pharmacist and owner of a well-established and unincorporated pharmacy in a Saskatoon mall. Lamia Savitz is a nutritionist and owner of an unincorporated health food store that is located in the same neighbourhood shopping mall. Kay and Lamia both realize that they share many of the same products and customers. They are currently considering combining the two stores to not only save on costs but also to provide opportunities for growth and tax deferral. Kay heard, at a local investment seminar, that tax rates for corporations are much lower than for partnerships. Last year, each earned the following:

- Pharmacy net income from a business $160,000

- Health food store net income from a business $110,000

Advise Kay and Lamia on the alternative methods that would permit the merger to take place. Which alternative will attract the least tax, over time?

Problem 9

Cora Dusk owns 100% of the common shares of a corporation, Cee Ltd. These shares have an original cost of $1,000, a paid-up capital of $1,000 and a fair market value of $1.8 million. At the current time, the common shares are the only shares of Cee Ltd. that are issued and outstanding.

Cora is a Canadian resident, 70 years old and a recent widow. She wants to freeze the value of her common shares of Cee Ltd. in favour of a trust for her children and grandchildren. Cora has a 40-year-old daughter, Jordan, and a 35-year-old daughter, Susanne. All of Cora's grandchildren are under the age of 10. Her current will leaves these shares equally to Jordan and Susanne.

Cee Ltd. carries on a real estate rental business and has nine full-time employees throughout the year, including Cora, Jordan and Susanne. The company qualifies as a small business corporation and the shares which Cora owns meet all the tests to be qualified small business corporation (QSBC) shares.

Cora's plan is to settle one trust for her daughters and grandchildren with $100. The trust would use the $100 to subscribe and pay for 100 common shares of a holding company (Holdco Inc.) at a cost of $1 each. The trustees of the trust will be Jordan, Susanne and the family's lawyer and decisions would be made by a majority of trustees. The trust agreement would allow the trustees discretion as to the allocation of income to beneficiaries on an annual basis. The trust agreement would provide that, at the end of 21 years, the trust capital would be distributed equally to the children of Jordan and Susanne.

Cora would then sell her common shares of Cee Ltd. to Holdco Inc. Since she wants to crystallize the $400,000 remainder in 2016 (after indexation) of her lifetime QSBC capital gains exemption when she freezes the value of her shares, she plans to make an election under section 85 of the Act in the amount of $401,000. She will receive $401,000 of debt, with the balance of the consideration being Holdco Inc. shares with a fair market value and legal stated capital of $1,399,000 from Holdco Inc. in return for her common shares of Cee Ltd.

Cora currently pays tax at the top marginal rate, but Jordan and Susanne do not because of child care expenses, RRSP contributions and other deductions and tax credits.

Cora has asked you for your comments on her stated plans and whether you have any ideas for improvement or alternatives for her to consider.

 [For more problems and solutions thereto, see the DVD accompanying the text-book.]

¶18,875

CHAPTER 18 —
DISCUSSION NOTES FOR REVIEW QUESTIONS

(1) The term "partnership" is not defined in the *Income Tax Act*. The term "partnership" is defined in the provincial Partnership Acts. The Ontario *Partnership Act*, for example, provides that a "partnership is a relation that subsists between persons carrying on a business in common with a view to profit."

(2) False. The amount of losses a limited partner can deduct in computing income in respect of losses allocated by the limited partnership is limited. The losses can only be deducted to the extent of the limited partner's "at-risk amount" as defined. Generally, the losses may be deducted by a limited partner only to the extent that the total of his or her investment in the partnership plus his or her share of the partnership profit exceeds any amount owing to the partnership by him or her and so on. To the extent that limited partnership losses are restricted, they can be carried forward indefinitely and deducted, but only against income from the limited partnership that gave rise to the loss. `ITA: 96(2.1)` `ITA: 96(2.2)` `ITA: 111(1)(e)`

(3) Because Dadd and Ladd do not deal at arm's length, the anti-avoidance rule must be considered. The issue is whether the allocation is reasonable in the circumstances having regard to the capital invested in or work performed for the partnership by the members thereof, or such other factors as may be relevant. For example, the allocation of the capital gain to Dadd may be reasonable given that it was his property in the first place. Since Dadd is the only one with capital and cash invested in the partnership, any losses may be his losses, as the losses impair his capital in the partnership. Arguments can be made that the allocation is reasonable in the circumstances. `ITA: 103(1.1)`

Because the decision has been made to allocate income on a 50/50 basis but to allocate all of the losses to Dadd, reference should also be made to another anti-avoidance rule. There should be no problem with this allocation on the basis that the principal reason for the allocation cannot reasonably be considered to be the reduction or postponement of the tax otherwise payable under the Act. `ITA: 103(1)`

(4) Income is calculated at the partnership level and then allocated to the partners. A $600 taxable capital gain would be included in the income of the partnership, of which your share is $150 (25% × $600). Your adjusted cost base will be increased by $300, being your share of the taxable capital gain of $150 and your share of the non-taxable portion of $150. `ITA: 53(1)(e)`

(5) Income is calculated at the partnership level and then allocated to the partners. A $100,000 receipt would not be included in the partnership's income, since life insurance proceeds are not taxable. The adjusted cost base of your partnership interest will be increased by your share or $25,000. `ITA: 53(1)(e)`

(6) A rollover is available only on a transfer to a Canadian partnership. This is defined to include only those partnerships where all the members are resident in Canada at the particular time. In this case, Ms. Jones will need to determine whether the partner in the United States is still considered a resident of Canada for purposes of the Act. If not, the rollover will not be available. `ITA: 97(2)` `ITA: 102`

(7) A trust is a relationship whereby a person (who is called a trustee) is bound to deal with property (which is called the trust property) over which he or she has control for the benefit of persons (who are called the beneficiaries) any of whom may enforce the obligation according to the terms of the trust document. A trust is created when a person (called the settlor) transfers property to a trustee.

(8) While it is true that trusts are conduits by allowing certain types of income to flow through to the beneficiaries and retain their character for tax purposes (for example, dividends, capital gains, foreign income), the income of a trust may be subject to tax. Trusts are taxed as an individual on any income that is not paid or payable to the beneficiaries. The rate of tax paid depends on whether the trust is an *inter vivos* trust or a testamentary trust. `ITA: 104(2), 104(6)`

CHAPTER 18

(9) A testamentary trust is created as a consequence of the death of an individual. An *inter vivos* trust is one that is created during the lifetime of an individual. An *inter vivos* trust may also be created for tax purposes where a person other than the deceased has contributed property to a testamentary trust.

(10) A discretionary trust is a trust where the trustee is given the power of choice. The trustee may be given the power to determine the date of distribution of trust property, whether income or capital is to be paid to a beneficiary, how much is to be paid to a beneficiary and in what proportions among a group of beneficiaries it is to be paid. This feature gives the trust a great deal of flexibility and is a very useful planning tool for income splitting and estate equalization purposes.

(11) The special treatment applies to the following types of income:

(a) taxable dividends from a Canadian corporation which allows the beneficiary to use the dividend gross-up and tax credit;   ITA: 104(19)

(b) net taxable capital gains which are eligible for the capital gains deduction available in respect of qualified shares of a small business corporation and qualified farm property (note that net capital losses do not flow through to the beneficiary);   ITA: 104(21)–(21.3)

(c) non-taxable dividends which are excluded from the computation of taxable income;   ITA: 104(20)

(d) foreign income and related foreign tax paid to allow the beneficiary to claim the foreign tax credit; and   ITA: 104(22)

(e) superannuation and pension benefits.   ITA: 104(27), 104(28)

(12) The trust would file a tax return for the fiscal period ending on December 31, 2015 on or before March 31, 2016 (that is, 90 days after the end of the trust's year). She would report the income allocated to her for the December 31, 2015 taxation year on her 2015 personal tax return, i.e., the calendar year in which the fiscal year end of the trust fell. A testamentary trust that is created by will is not an "estate" and so cannot be a graduated rate estate with an off calendar year end.   ITA: 104(13), 104(14)

CHAPTER 18 — SOLUTIONS TO MULTIPLE CHOICE QUESTIONS

Question 1

(D) $165,900 is correct.

Net income per financial statement		$ 365,000
Add: Donations		20,000
Sale of shares — Taxable capital gain	$ 60,000	
— Accounting gain	(120,000)	(60,000)
		$ 325,000
Bert's share		× ½
		$ 162,500
Dividend gross-up: $20,000 × 17%		3,400
Taxable income		$ 165,900

(A) $186,100 is incorrect. The only adjustment that was made was for the dividend gross-up.

(B) $182,500 is incorrect. All of the adjustments have been ignored: donations, net accounting/tax gain, and the dividend gross-up.

(C) $167,500 is incorrect. All adjustments were made except for the dividend gross-up, which, at 25%, was incorrect on dividends from a CCPC out of its LRIP.

Question 2

(C) $63,000 is correct.

Contributions — initial	$ 5,000
— additional	14,000
Share of profit	100,000
Share of non-taxable portion of capital gain	20,000
Share of charitable donations	(6,000)
Drawings	(70,000)
ACB	$ 63,000

(A) $23,000 is incorrect. The capital gain has been excluded completely.

(B) $43,000 is incorrect. The non-taxable portion of the capital gain has not been included.

(D) $69,000 is incorrect. The ACB has not been reduced by Ann's share of the charitable donations.

Question 3

(A) is true. The tax return is due 90 days after the year-end of the trust. *Inter vivos* trusts are taxed on a calendar year basis. ITA: 150(1)(*c*), 249(1)(*b*)

(B) is true. The trust is entitled to the deduction. ITA: 104(6)

(C) is true. The tax rate is 33%. ITA: 122(1)

(D) is false. Al is deemed to have received proceeds equal to the fair market value of the marketable securities transferred to the trust. Therefore, Al is required to recognize the $30,000 capital gain. ITA: 69(1)(*b*)

Question 4

(A) is true. The taxation year of a testamentary trust that is not a graduated rate estate must have a   ITA: 104(2), 122(1)
calendar year end.

(B) is false. Only a graduated rate estate is taxed as an individual and only for the first 36 months   ITA: 104(23)
from the date of death. A testamentary trust that is created by will is not an "estate" and cannot be a
graduated rate estate.

(C) is false. The trust return is due 90 days after the end of the fiscal period of the trust.   ITA: 150(1)(*c*)

(D) is false. The trust is entitled to claim a dividend tax credit for dividends received from taxable   ITA: 104(2), 121
Canadian corporations.

Question 5

(C) is correct. An *alter ego* trust has a deemed disposition on the settlor's death.   ITA: 248(1)

(A) is incorrect. An *inter vivos* trust generally has a deemed disposition at fair market value at the
end of 21 years, unless it is a joint partner trust (described in (B)), in which case the deemed
disposition takes place on the partner (i.e., spouse or common-law partner) beneficiary's death.

(B) is incorrect. A joint partner trust has a deemed disposition on the death of the partner (i.e.,
spouse or common-law partner).

(D) is incorrect. A discretionary trust would always have a deemed disposition at fair market value
at the end of 21 years, since it cannot be a joint partner trust (which, by definition, must pay the income
out to the beneficiary and, therefore, cannot be discretionary).

Question 6

(C) is correct. Avoiding the deemed disposition is not an advantage. You cannot avoid the deemed   ITA: 104(4)
disposition at FMV if the beneficiaries of the testamentary trust are your children.

(A) is incorrect because income-splitting through distributions to beneficiaries is an advantage.   ITA: 104(13.1), 104(13.2)

(B) is incorrect, because avoiding the deemed disposition on the child's death is an advantage.

(D) is incorrect, because providing your children with beneficial ownership but not control over
their inheritance is an advantage.

CHAPTER 18 — SOLUTIONS TO EXERCISES

Exercise 1

Partnership's net income for financial accounting purposes		$304,280
Deduct: Capital gain		5,000
		$299,280
Add: Amortization on office furniture	$ 3,750	
Donations	5,500	
Membership in fitness club	1,250	
Taxable capital gain (½ × $5,000)	2,500	13,000
		$312,280
Deduct: Capital cost allowance		4,300
Income to be allocated (Division B)		$307,980
Bob's share of income from partnership		$153,990
Add: Gross-up of Bob's share of partnership dividends		
(17% × $4,000 × ½)	$ 340	
Grossed-up personal dividends ($3,500 × 1.38) . . .	4,830	
Personal interest income	1,200	6,370
Bob's net income (Division B) and taxable income		$160,360

Analysis of Bob's income:

	Personal	Partnership	Total
Grossed-up dividends	$4,830	$ 2,340	$ 7,170
Interest	1,200	—	1,200
Taxable capital gains	—	1,250	1,250
Business income		150,740	150,740
Total	$5,575	$154,330*	$160,360

* $153,990 + $340 gross-up

Notes:

(1) Drawings taken by the members of a partnership do not constitute a business expense but are a method of distributing partnership income to members of the partnership.

(2) Charitable donations are not deductions in computing the income of a partnership but are used as the basis for computing the charitable donations tax credit for an individual partner.

(3) Fees paid to a fitness club are non-deductible expenses.   ITA: 18(1)(*l*)

(4) Bob will be eligible for the following federal dividend tax credit:

— on share of partnership dividends (²¹/₂₉ × $340)	$	246
— on personal dividends (⁶/₁₁ × $1,330)		725
Total	$	971

Exercise 2

Adjusted cost base of Katie's partnership interest:

Contributions			$ 50,000
Add:	Share of profits excluding taxable capital gain (½ ×		
	($450,000 – $20,000))	$215,000	
	Share of full capital gain (½ × $20,000 × ²/₁)	20,000	
	Share of capital dividends (½ × $4,000)	2,000	237,000
			$287,000
Deduct:	Share of losses (½ × $15,000)	$ 7,500	
	Drawings (½ × $176,000)	88,000	
	Share of donations (½ × $27,000)	13,500	109,000
ACB of partnership interest			$178,000

Capital gain on disposition of partnership interest:

Proceeds of disposition	$250,000
ACB	178,000
Capital gain	$ 72,000
Taxable capital gain (½ of $72,000)	$ 36,000

Exercise 3

	Trust	Rebecca	Robert
Income			
Interest	$ 4,500	$ 5,500	$ 1,500
Taxable capital gain	1,500	1,500	1,500
Taxable dividends	4,140	4,140	4,140
Net income/taxable income	$10,140	$11,140	$ 7,140
Federal tax (@ 33% for trust and 15% for individuals)	$ 3,346	$ 1,671	$ 1,071
Personal tax credit @ 15% of $11,474	—	(1,721)	(1,721)
Tuition credit and education credit	—	—	Nil
Dividend tax credit @ 6⁄11 of $3,000 × .38	(622)	(622)	(622)
Total tax	$ 2,724	$ Nil	Nil

Note: None of the tuition and education tax credits were claimed by Robert. Federal tuition and education tax credits of $750[1] are transferable to a parent, or the unused amount of $1,083 less any amount transferred to a supporting person may be carried forward. The definition of tax payable and the ordering rules require that the personal, tuition and education tax credits be deducted before the dividend tax credit which is lost in this case.

ITA: 118.9(1)

ITA: 118.61

ITA: 118.81, 118.92

—NOTE TO SOLUTION

[1] Lesser of:
   (a) $750 (federal) = $750

   (b) (15% × $3,500) + (15% of (($400 + 65) × 8)) = $1,083

	$ 750
Minus ($1,071 – $1,721)	Nil
Net amount transferred to parent	$ 750

Chapter 19

International Taxation in Canada

Learning Goals

Know

By the end of this chapter you will know:

- The basics of Canadian taxation of non-residents.
- The Canadian tax law applicable to cross-border transactions.
- Canadian taxation of residents with foreign investments.

Understand and Explain

By the end of this chapter you will understand and be able to explain:

- The taxation of non-residents with Canadian investments or business dealings.
- The tax treatment of cross-border transactions between Canadian residents and foreign persons.
- The taxation of Canadian residents earning income from foreign investments.
- The basic application of tax treaties.

Apply

By the end of this chapter, you will be able to apply:

- Your knowledge and understanding of the key provisions applicable to non-residents, cross-border transactions, and foreign income earned by Canadian residents.
- Your knowledge and understanding of the impact of a tax treaty on the taxation of various sources of income earned by non-residents in Canada.
- The provisions of the *Income Tax Act* applicable to cross-border loans and transactions.
- Your knowledge and understanding of foreign investment by Canadian residents.

Review Questions
¶19,800 in the Study Guide

Multiple Choice Questions
¶19,825 in the Study Guide

Exercise Questions
¶19,850 in the Study Guide

Assignment Problems
¶19,875 in the Study Guide

CHAPTER 19 — LEARNING CHART

Problem Descriptions

Textbook Example Problems

1	Taxation in Canada of U.S. corporation
2	Branch tax
3	Sale of shares of CCPC
4	Going non-resident — RRSP
5	Canadian rent paid to non-resident
6	Part-year resident
7	Deemed acquisition on becoming resident
8	Deemed disposition of becoming non-resident
9	Transfer pricing
10	Thin capitalization
11	Cross-border shareholder loans
12	Low-interest cross-border loans
13	Low-interest cross-border loans
14	Dividends from non-foreign affiliates
15	Dividends from foreign affiliates
16	Investment income in foreign corporation

Multiple Choice Questions

1	Disposal of Canadian real estate
2	Income in year of immigration
3	Foreign partnership income
4	RRSP on emigration
5	Dividend from foreign subsidiary
6	Individual owns U.S. condo
7	Investment income in foreign corporation

Exercises

1	Deemed disposition on becoming non-resident
2	Foreign tax credit
3	Income earned in Canada by non-resident
4	Low-interest cross-border loans
5	Immigration — moving expenses
6	Dividends from foreign corporation
7	Rental property owned by non-residents

Assignment Problems

1	Canadian income of non-resident individual
2	Sale of property by non-resident individual
3	Canadian income of non-resident corporation
4	Canadian income of non-resident individual
5	Individual becoming a non-resident
6	Transfer pricing

CHAPTER 19

Problem Descriptions

Study Notes

¶19,800   REVIEW QUESTIONS

(1) Describe two objectives that international tax treaties strive to achieve.

(2) Distinguish between a part-year resident and a non-resident.

(3) Briefly explain the intention behind the "transfer pricing" legislation.

(4) Briefly explain the "thin capitalization rules" and what they are designed to prevent.

(5) Is a non-resident who owns shares in a Canadian corporation taxable on the disposition of those shares? Does the purchaser have a withholding requirement?

(6) Can a part-year resident claim the full amount of personal tax credits in the year of arrival/departure?

(7) How would you calculate the gain on the disposition of a rental property that an immigrant to Canada owned in the country he/she emigrated from for five years prior to coming to Canada and is disposing after his or her move? If the rental property was located in Canada how would your answer change?

(8) When is a non-resident employer required to withhold and remit Canadian tax from an employee's employment income?

(9) What withholding tax rate applies to dividends from a Canadian corporation to a shareholder resident in the United States?

(10) When is it best for a non-resident to make a section 217 election for Canadian RRSP benefits received?

(11) Would a non-interest-bearing loan by a Canadian corporation to its non-resident parent company result in a Canadian tax liability?

(12) What is the purpose of deeming that an immigrant has disposed of and reacquired all of his or her capital property on entering Canada?

(13) Under what circumstances might a non-resident be entitled to the same or similar total personal tax credits that are allowed to a resident?

(14) When and how much of a foreign tax credit can be claimed by a Canadian resident for withholding taxes paid to a foreign jurisdiction on dividend income?

(15) What is the purpose of the FAPI rules related to foreign passive income?

(16) How would you describe exempt surplus and its treatment for Canadian tax purposes?

(17) What is the purpose of filing an election under subsection 93(1) when a Canadian corporation disposes of shares of a foreign affiliate?

¶19,825   MULTIPLE CHOICE QUESTIONS

Question 1

Jari Kitsopolous is a resident of Greece. Last year, he disposed of real estate located in Saskatchewan for a gain. Jari will pay Canadian income taxes at which of the following rates?

(A) Federal tax based on the tax rate schedule plus Saskatchewan taxes.

(B) Federal tax based on the tax rate schedule plus an additional federal tax.

(C) Withholding tax only at 25%.

(D) Withholding tax only at $33^{1}/_{3}$%.

Question 2

Prior to immigrating to Canada, Mai Kim had money on deposit in a Canadian bank and earned $1,000 interest. After taking up Canadian residence, she immediately used that deposit towards a down payment on a home. Which of the following is the correct tax treatment of the $1,000 interest earned in the year of immigration?

(A) She pays a 25% non-resident tax and the interest is excluded from the Canadian tax return for the period of residency.

(B) She does not pay any Canadian tax in relation to the interest.

(C) The income is included in her Canadian tax return for the period of residency, but she receives a foreign tax credit for any taxes paid in her previous country of residence.

(D) The income is included in her Canadian tax return for the period of residency based on a proration calculated as the number of days resident divided by 365 days.

Question 3

Antonio Sperilli immigrated to Canada from Brazil last year, but continues to be a partner in a Brazilian business. What is the correct tax treatment of any income earned from the partnership?

(A) It is subject to tax only in Brazil.

(B) It is included in Antonio's Canadian income tax return, but any Brazilian taxes are deductible from the partnership income.

(C) It is included in Antonio's Canadian income tax return, but a foreign tax credit may be claimed in Antonio's Brazilian tax return for any Canadian income taxes paid.

(D) It is included in Antonio's Canadian income tax return, and a foreign tax credit may be claimed for any Brazilian taxes paid.

Question 4

Betty Albright emigrated from Canada to the United States last year. At the time that she gave up her Canadian residence, she held an RRSP with a fair market value of $100,000. Which of the following statements is true?

(A) The RRSP is taxable Canadian property and Betty will have to file a Canadian non-resident tax return when she disposes of the RRSP.

(B) There is a deemed disposition of the RRSP at fair market value on emigration.

(C) There will be a withholding tax at the time Betty terminates the RRSP and has it paid to her.

(D) Non-resident withholding tax should be paid, at 25%, from the income earned in the RRSP after emigration.

Question 5

Maxwell Rock Ltd. is a Canadian incorporated entity with a December 31 year-end. The corporation has a gravel pit operation owned and operated in Collingwood, Ontario. The company expanded operations into the United States this year through a 100% acquisition of a U.S. incorporated company with gravel pits operating in Michigan. The U.S. corporation also has a mining operation in Paraguay. In the U.S. corporation's first taxation year-end since acquisition, it earned C$100,000 of business income from its Michigan operation and C$200,000 of business income in Paraguay. At the end of its tax year, the U.S. company paid a dividend to Maxwell Rock Ltd. of C$150,000. Which of the following statements is true?

(A) Maxwell will include the C$150,000 dividend in taxable income for the year in which the dividend was received. A foreign tax credit can be claimed for the withholding tax paid to the U.S. government on the dividend.

(B) Maxwell will include the C$150,000 dividend in Division B income for the year in which the dividend was received. An offsetting deduction of C$100,000 will be available for the portion of the dividend paid from exempt surplus.

(C) Maxwell will include the C$150,000 dividend in Division B income for the year in which the dividend was received. An offsetting deduction will be available in computing taxable income for C$150,000 because the dividend was from exempt surplus.

(D) Maxwell will include the C$150,000 dividend in Division B income for the year in which the dividend was received. A deduction will be available in computing taxable income for the underlying tax paid by the U.S. company on the business income earned in the United States and Paraguay.

Question 6

Bob Smith is a Canadian resident and owns a condominium in Arizona that he and his family use during their winter holidays. The property is left vacant the rest of the year. What is Bob's filing obligations regarding this property?

(A) Bob is required to file Form T1135 reporting foreign property ownership.

(B) Bob is exempt from filing a Form T1135 as the property is personal-use property.

(C) Bob is required to file a Form T1135 only if the property has a cost of over $100,000.

(D) Bob needs to file a U.S. Form 1040NR (non-resident income tax return) and declare the ownership of the property to the U.S. Internal Revenue Service.

Question 7

Jane Alison, a resident of Canada, sold $100,000 of her Canadian mutual funds and invested the funds in common shares of a newly incorporated U.S. corporation. Jane's friend, Tori, also a Canadian resident, invested $500,000, and a third friend, a U.S. resident, invested $400,000 in common shares of the corporation. The $1 million was invested in fixed income securities with future plans to invest in U.S. stock markets. Which statement is correct regarding the interest income on the investments?

(A) It will not be taxed in Canada until dividends are paid to the shareholders. A foreign tax credit will be available for the U.S. withholding tax.

(B) It will not be taxed in Canada until dividends are paid to the shareholders. An offsetting deduction will be available under Division C because the dividend will be paid from taxable surplus.

(C) It will not be taxed in Canada until dividends are paid to the shareholders. An offsetting deduction will be available under Division C because the dividend will be paid from exempt surplus.

(D) It will be included in income of the Canadian shareholders annually because the company is a controlled foreign affiliate.

¶19,850   EXERCISES

Exercise 1

Alan Croupier is moving to Venezuela on August 1. In anticipation of this move, he has sold all of his assets except for 1,000 common shares in Tell Canada (a TSX listed company). The shares have a value of $40,000 and his adjusted cost base is $28,000. What is Alan's tax position on these shares should they remain unsold at the time of his departure?

— *REQUIRED*

Are there any alternatives available to Alan in respect to the Tell Canada shares in the year of departure?

Exercise 2

A non-resident is liable for Canadian taxes where they are employed in Canada, carry on business in Canada, or dispose of taxable Canadian property. In most countries, the non-resident will also be subject to tax in his or her country of residence on this same income. Tax treaties will alleviate the double taxation burden by allowing for foreign tax credits.

— *REQUIRED*

As the income will be taxed in two countries, does the taxpayer claim a foreign tax credit in both countries? If not, in which country is a foreign tax credit claimed?

Exercise 3

Sam-son Industries Inc. is a small American company located in Minneapolis, Minnesota. Sam-son sells various items by mail-order, mostly advertising trinkets such as pens, telephone diaries, post-it notes, and similar items, to Canadian businesses. Last year was the first year the company did this and profits on its Canadian sales amounted to $76,000. The company did not have sales representatives enter Canada during the year. The principals of Sam-son are worried about their liability for Canadian income tax and have come to you for advice.

— *REQUIRED*

Advise Sam-son on their Canadian tax liability. Include an explanation of your rationale.

Exercise 4

Johnson & Co Ltd., a Canadian-controlled private corporation, holds all the issued shares in Johnson & Co (USA) Inc. Two years ago, the Canadian corporation advanced $100,000 in the form of a loan to the U.S. corporation. The U.S. corporation pays Johnson & Co interest at the rate of 1%. This 1% is comparable to the cost of borrowing at a U.S. bank, but is less than the prescribed interest rate under the Canadian Act. Assume the prescribed rate is 2%.

— *REQUIRED*

Describe the tax obligations of the Canadian corporation relative to this 1% interest.

Exercise 5

Mary Jane is a Canadian citizen and has been living and working in Singapore for the past 11 years. Mary Jane moved back to Canada on October 13, 2016 and incurred $8,000 in moving expenses. Mary Jane paid her own moving expenses and did not receive a reimbursement from her new employer. She earned $35,000 in employment income from October 13 to December 31, 2016.

— *REQUIRED*

Advise Mary Jane if she is entitled to claim her moving expenses.

Exercise 6

Canco is a Canadian incorporated manufacturer and wholly owned subsidiary of a U.S. incorporated company. In 2014, Canco invested C$500,000 of excess cash in a newly incorporated Dutch company (Dutchco) and received an 80% common share interest in the entity. The U.S. parent invested C$125,000 for the remaining 20% interest. All except C$200,000 was used to acquire a distribution business. The distribution business will distribute products manufactured in Canada and the United States to European customers. For its December 31, 2015 year end, Dutchco earned C$30,000 from the distribution business and C$12,000 in interest on a money market account holding the C$200,000 of excess cash. For its December 31, 2016 year end, Dutchco earned C$50,000 from the distribution business and C$12,000 in interest. The company paid a C$50,000 dividend to its shareholders in February 2016. Dutchco paid corporate tax of 20% on its income each year. Withholding tax of 5% applied to the dividend paid to Canco.

— *REQUIRED*

Determine the Canadian tax consequences of the investment in Dutchco and the dividend received in 2016.

Exercise 7

Mr. and Ms. Doe are citizens and residents of China. They purchased a condominium in their names in Waterloo, Ontario, for their son, Joe. Joe moved to Waterloo in August 2016 to attend university and rented two rooms to his friends, Sam and Harry, who are both Canadian residents. Joe will live in Canada for at least four years while attending school. Sam and Harry each pay rent of $400 per month to Joe, who deposits the funds into his parents' Canadian bank account. Joe pays the mortgage, utilities, and property taxes for the property from this account. His parents will occasionally withdraw excess funds from the account.

— *REQUIRED*

(A) Discuss the Canadian tax implications associated with the rental of the property and any options available to the non-residents.

(B) What will happen if the condominium is sold in the future?

(C) Would it have been better for Joe's parents to give or lend Joe funds to purchase the condominium in his name?

¶19,875 ASSIGNMENT PROBLEMS

Type 2 Problems

Problem 1

Andrew English has agreed to play professional soccer with the Toronto Metros of the Canadian Soccer League starting March 1, 2017. Andrew lives in England and will live in Canada temporarily for the five months of the soccer season. His three-year contract calls for an annual salary of $95,000. At the time of signing this contract in England in the fall of 2016, the Metros gave Andrew a signing bonus of $25,000. Andrew's agent was paid $5,000 to represent him in negotiating the contract. Andrew will earn C$100,000 playing soccer in England during the other seven months.

Determine Andrew's Canadian income tax obligations. What deductions/credits may he claim against Canadian income?

Problem 2

Kresna Dubchuk lives in Kenya and is in the process of selling her Canadian real property, situated in New Brunswick, which has been rented to various tenants over the last 10 years. The selling price of the property is $100,000 and her ACB is $35,000. She will incur $6,500 in real estate commissions and $500 in legal fees in connection with the sale.

A few days after complying with the requirements concerning the proposed disposition of the property, Kresna receives a copy of a proposed assessment from the CRA from the agent collecting the rent on her behalf in Canada. The assessment is for income taxes, plus penalties and interest for the past three taxation years.

(A) Describe and detail Kresna's Canadian tax obligations arising on the sale of this property.

(B) What is the probable cause of the proposed assessment? Can you offer Kresna and her agent any professional assistance with regard to the proposed assessment? If so, detail what you might advise her.

Problem 3

A corporation resident in the United States (USCO) recently expanded its sales activities in Canada. Up until two years ago, the company had been selling small amounts of product directly to Canadian customers. The Canadian sales resulted from U.S. tradeshows, industry magazines, and the company's website. USCO did not have a sales force in Canada or a direct advertising program. Starting last year, USCO hired three sales employees to work from an office rented by USCO in Toronto. The company uses an independent wholesaler and bonded warehouse in Mississauga to keep a supply of its products on hand. Shipping instructions are faxed to the warehouse. Invoicing is done in Dallas and payments are remitted to the U.S. head office. All purchase orders are subject to approval and acceptance by USCO's home office.

The Canadian balance sheet and income statement for USCO's second year of operations ending December 31 was as follows:

Balance Sheet (000s)

Assets		Liabilities/Equity	
Cash (Cdn currency)	$ 50	Accounts payable	$ 400
Accounts receivable	150	Bank loan (used to purchase fixed assets)	150
Inventory	400	Tax liability	104
Fixed assets (UCC)	200	Home office account	146
Total assets	**$800**	**Total liabilities/equity**	**$800**

Income Statement (000s)		
Sales		$ 500
Expenses		
Sales expenses	$ 120	
Office expenses	30	
Advertising	90	
Total expenses		240
Pre-tax profit		260
Tax provision		104
After tax profit		**$ 156**

For its first year of operations ending December 31, the Canadian operations incurred a taxable   ITR: 808
loss of $4,000 and had an investment allowance, as defined in the Regulations, of $2,000.

The aggregate FMV of the assets is $820,000 (Cash — $50,000, A/R — $150,000, Inventory — $410,000, Fixed Assets — $210,000). The $50,000 cash balance was the lowest balance outstanding for the year.

Assume an Ontario income tax rate of 13%.

(A) How will USCO be taxed under Canadian domestic tax law?

(B) Without considering the Canada–U.S. Tax Convention, calculate USCO's total federal and provincial Canadian tax liability under Parts I and XIV of the Act. Assume that pre-tax profit represents taxable income.

(C) Would USCO be considered to have a permanent establishment under paragraphs 1, 2, or 5 of Article V of the Canada–U.S. Tax Convention? How does paragraph 6, Article X of the Canada–U.S. Tax Convention impact the Canadian tax return for the company? Perform calculations to reflect the impact.

Problem 4

Sally Juarez is retired and lives in Mexico, but virtually all of her investment assets, and her income, are Canadian. In 2016, Sally realized the following income (all Canadian except as identified):

Dividends on shares in Canadian Public Co Ltd.	$ 5,000
Interest on deposit in bank	8,000
Gain on sale of raw land (assume business income)	60,000
Gain on sale of Public Co Ltd. shares	15,000
Gain on sale of real estate	30,000
Share of income from business partnership	7,000
Mexican pension income	20,000

Sally has paid $7,500 in Canadian withholding tax on the property gains.

Without considering the implications of the Canada–Mexico Tax Convention, calculate Sally's taxable income earned in Canada and tax owing (refund). Identify any other Canadian tax requirements. Assume any business income was earned in a province where the personal tax rates are the hypothetical rates shown in ¶10,250 of Chapter 10. Ignore any CPP/QPP implications.

Problem 5

Cal Murphy is emigrating from Canada to take up residence in Jakarta, Indonesia. At the time of his departure, Cal will have the following Canadian assets:

	FMV	Cost
Principal residence	$250,000	$135,000
RRSP	75,000	N/A
20% interest in CCPC (active)	45,000	1,000
GIC at TrustCo	15,000	15,000

Cal has been impressed by the capital appreciation he has made on his residence, so he intends to keep it and rent it out for $1,500 monthly. He intends to sell it at some future opportune time but believes this will be many years from now. The expected expenses for the mortgage, taxes, repairs, insurance, and sundry for the house are expected to be about $1,200 a month. Cal's brother, Joseph, will be collecting the rents for him and depositing them to Cal's Canadian bank. This money will be kept at the bank in a savings account in case of any unanticipated expenses.

His 20% shareholding in the CCPC is not easily liquidated, and so he is retaining it, for now, to earn about $5,000 in annual dividend income. He is anxious to dispose of the shares, but has not yet found a prospective purchaser, despite a fairly exhaustive attempt to do so. The $45,000 fair market value was determined by a chartered business valuator.

Cal is not at all sure what to do with the RRSP. He can liquidate it either before or after his planned departure date. Cal intends to renew the GIC when it matures as he is uncertain as to the Indonesian banking system, and won't transfer the money to an Indonesian bank until he's done some research.

Cal and his wife separated last year, and Cal has custody of their only child, who will be moving to Indonesia with Cal. Cal receives $500 in monthly child support and Mrs. Murphy will continue to pay the support to Cal in Indonesia.

Cal has engaged you to advise him of his current (year of departure) and any future Canadian tax obligations.

Identify and advise Cal of his current and future Canadian tax position. Ignore the Canada–Indonesia Tax Convention in your analysis. Include any options or alternatives he may have available and any planning advice you think appropriate.

Problem 6

Samsystems Inc. (SI) is a Canadian-controlled private corporation and a leading edge developer and manufacturer of furniture components with subsidiaries worldwide. You are the tax manager for SI. The controller of the corporation is very concerned that the corporation's intercompany transactions do not meet the transfer pricing requirements of the Act. In a recent meeting, the controller provided you with the following information concerning the company's transactions with foreign corporations.

ITA: 247

Transactions with Samsystems Netherlands Inc. (SNI)

SI sells metal drawer slides to its newly acquired, wholly owned subsidiary and Netherlands resident, SNI. SNI was acquired by SI in July and has two divisions: a manufacturing division that manufactures ergonomically designed furniture components, and a distribution division that distributes curtain rod products purchased from Thailand and now drawer slides purchased from SI, as well. All products purchased by the distribution division are sold to arm's length European distributors.

Until the purchase of SNI, SI was selling drawer slides directly to European distributors for all European sales. Now all European sales are through SNI. Over the next two years, SNI plans to replace the use of distributors in the European market and sell SI's slides directly to original equipment manufacturers. SNI does not own any trademarks related to the sale of SI products. SNI is responsible for collection of receivables from European distributors. However, SI is responsible for all warranty costs associated with the sale of its products by SNI. All patents for Canadian-manufactured products are owned by SI.

For Canadian sales, SI sells drawer slides to arm's length distributors in Canada. All international sales of the slides are sold by subsidiaries of SI (including SNI) in various countries.

A subsidiary of SI, U.S. resident Samsystems United States Inc. (SUSI) (see below), manufactures a similar drawer slide to SI's. These slides are sold by the U.S. company to arm's length distributors in the U.S. market.

For its taxation year ending December 31, SNI's distributor division earned a gross margin of 30% and an operating profit of 5% of sales for its sales of SI product. For sales of curtain rods, the division earned a gross margin percentage of 35% and an operating profit of 8% of sales.

Transactions with SUSI

SUSI was acquired by SI through a share purchase in July. For several years prior to the acquisition, SUSI had purchased ergonomic furniture components from SI for distribution to original equipment manufacturers in the U.S. After the acquisition of SUSI, SI continued to sell these products to the company. SUSI does not own any trademarks for the sale of SI's product and does not distribute products for any other entity. SI sells its ergonomic products in Canada through arm's length Canadian distribution companies.

Advise the controller on the possible transfer pricing methodologies that could be applied to the above transactions under section 247. Indicate why discarded methodologies would not be appropriate. Describe how you would apply these methodologies and indicate what additional information you will need from the client to help you determine the appropriate methodology.

Problem 7

Ergold Ltd. is a Canadian subsidiary of a Swedish company. The company is a distributor of automated milking machines to dairy farmers in Canada. Its sole supplier is the Swedish parent company. The current transfer pricing policy between Ergold Ltd. and its parent company has resulted in losses in Canada for its years of operation since incorporation as follows:

Year Ended December 31	Taxable Loss	Gross Revenue
2014	$ 200,000	$ 3,000,000
2015	$ 400,000	$ 6,500,000
2016	$ 850,000	$ 9,500,000

The company does not appear to have any internal or external uncontrolled comparable transactions that would allow you to apply a traditional transaction method. In discussions with some of your colleagues in your Toronto office transfer pricing group, you have discovered that recent transfer pricing studies have concluded, using the transactional net margin method, that similar distributors operating in Canada earn an operating margin percentage of 5% of sales. You mention this to the controller. He indicates that he does not believe that there is much of a concern as he has heard that because of the company's small size there would not be any penalties applicable if the CRA were to audit. Ergold's effective tax rate is approximately 28%.

How would you respond to the controller? How can you convince the controller that he should consider having your firm prepare a transfer pricing report to provide it with documentation to support its transfer pricing?

Problem 8

Witmold Ltd., a subsidiary of a U.S. corporation, received a loan from the U.S. parent company of $6 million on December 2, 2015 to purchase manufacturing equipment. The company started making loan payments of $72,500 per month on January 2, 2016. On July 15, due to a problem collecting from its major customer, the company borrowed an additional $600,000 from the U.S. parent. This loan was a 2% loan and was repaid 14 days after receipt when the customer paid the accounts receivable.

Because of the above problem, the company did not make its August to October payments on the loan but began making payments again in November. Witmold Ltd. plans to catch up and make its August to October payments sometime in 2017. The total interest expense booked to the financial statements for 2016 was $458,808 for both loans.

In November 2016, Witmold's controller realized that, due to thin capitalization restrictions, the interest deduction on the loan for tax purposes would be limited. As a result, on November 30, 2016, $500,000 of the loan balance was converted to paid-up capital of the common shares held by the U.S. parent company. There were no other share capital transactions during the year. Witmold's comparative balance sheet for its December 31, 2016 taxation year was as follows:

	2016	2015
Assets		
Cash	$ 250,000	$ 6,200,000
A/R	300,000	500,000
Inventory	1,200,000	800,000
Fixed assets	6,600,000	400,000
Total assets	**$ 8,350,000**	**$ 7,900,000**
Liabilities		

Accounts payable	$ 450,000	$ 300,000
Loan to parent	5,345,300	6,039,452
Equity		
Retained earnings	1,754,700	1,260,548
Common stock	800,000	300,000
Total liabilities & equity	**$ 8,350,000**	**$ 7,900,000**

The details of the loan balance after each payment for 2016 was as follows:

Date	Loan Balance
02-Dec-15	$6,000,000
02-Jan-16	5,966,952
02-Feb-16	5,933,687
02-Mar-16	5,900,203
02-Apr-16	5,866,499
02-May-16	5,832,573
02-Jun-16	5,798,424
02-Jul-16	5,764,051
02-Aug-16	5,801,951
02-Sep-16	5,840,101
02-Oct-16	5,878,502
02-Nov-16	5,844,655
30-Nov-16	5,380,524
02-Dec-16	5,310,382
02-Jan-17	5,272,800

Compute the amount of interest that the company will be able to deduct for tax purposes for its December 31, 2016 taxation year end.

Problem 9

Ronal Canada Ltd. is a Canadian subsidiary of Ronal Inc., a U.S. multinational public corporation. You are the tax manager responsible for reviewing the corporate tax return and tax provision for the Canadian company for its December 31, 2016 taxation year end. During your review, you ask for a detailed summary of the intercompany receivable balance of $6.5 million on the company's financial statements. The controller has provided you with the following information:

Receivable from Ronal Argentina Ltd.	$4,100,000
Receivable from Ronal Germany Ltd.	540,000
Receivable from Ronal Switzerland Ltd.	1,860,000
Total intercompany receivable	$6,500,000

The receivable from Ronal Argentina Ltd. relates to a 1% loan made by Ronal Canada Ltd. to Ronal Argentina Ltd. October 1, 2013. The loan was repaid in January 2017. Ronal Argentina Ltd. is a wholly owned subsidiary of Ronal Inc.

The receivable from Ronal Germany Ltd. is a trade receivable related to the sale of goods by Ronal Canada Ltd. to Ronal Germany Ltd. in November 2016. Ronal Germany Ltd. usually pays its trade payable within 90 days of receiving an invoice. Ronal Canada Ltd. sells goods to related companies under the same terms as sales to its regular customers. Ronal Germany Ltd. is a wholly owned subsidiary of Ronal Inc.

The receivable from Ronal Switzerland Ltd. relates to a sale of a piece of equipment to Ronal Switzerland Ltd. December 1, 2015 to be used in its ongoing manufacturing operations in Zurich. Ronal Switzerland is not required to pay interest on the payable to Ronal Canada Ltd. Ronal Switzerland Ltd. is a wholly owned subsidiary of Ronal Canada Ltd.

The controller indicated that, on January 15, 2015, Ronal Canada Ltd. had used excess cash of $5 million to invest in common shares of a subsidiary of Ronal Inc., Ronal Luxembourg Ltd. Ronal Luxembourg used the funds to make a non-interest-bearing loan to Ronal Germany Ltd. on that same day.

(a) Does subsection 15(2) and/or subsection 80.4(2) apply to the receivable from Ronal Argentina? If so, how will this impact Ronal Canada Ltd.'s tax provision? Consider the application of subsection 227(6.1) in your response.

(b) Does subsection 17(1) or 17.1(1) apply to the receivable from Ronal Argentina? If so, how will this impact Ronal Ltd.'s tax provision?

(c) Does subsection 15(2) and/or subsection 80.4(2) apply to the receivable from Ronal Germany Ltd.? Does subsection 17(1) or 17.1(1) apply to this loan? If so, how will this impact Ronal Ltd.'s tax provision?

(d) Does subsection 15(2) and/or subsection 80.4(2) apply to the receivable from Ronal Switzerland Ltd.? Does subsection 17(1) or 17.1(1) apply to this loan? Does 212.3(2) apply to this loan? If so, how will this impact Ronal Ltd.'s tax provision?

(e) Does subsection 17(1) or 17.1(1) apply to the investment in Ronal Luxembourg? Does 90(6) apply to the loan to Ronal Germany? Does 212.3(2) apply to the investment in Ronal Luxembourg? If so, what advice could you provide to the client?

Problem 10

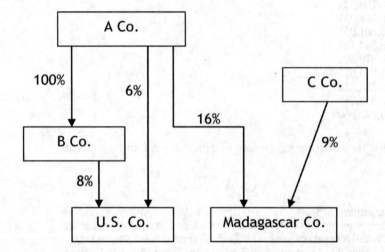

A Co., B Co., and C Co. are Canadian resident corporations. C Co. is not related to either A Co. or B Co. B Co.'s share capital consists of 1,000 common shares. The companies have a December 31 year end.

A Co. and B Co. received dividends of C$36,000 and C$48,000, respectively, out of a total dividend of C$600,000 paid by U.S. Co. on December 31, 2016. U.S. Co.'s taxation year end is October 31.

U.S. Co. was incorporated in the United States in 2014, issuing 100 common shares to its shareholders. The share structure of the corporation has not changed since incorporation. The company is operated and managed from the U.S. The company's only business is the manufacturing of auto parts supplied to various customers, including A Co. U.S. Co. earned net income from its operations of C$900,000 from the time of incorporation up to its October 31, 2016 taxation year end. U.S. Co. paid U.S. federal and state tax of C$180,000 on those earnings. U.S. Co. has not paid any dividends and has not incurred capital gains or losses in previous years. The company does not own shares in any other company.

Madagascar Co. is a cut-and-sew sweatshop. For its first taxation year ending December 31, 2016, the company earned C$500,000 net income from its operations. On this net income, the company paid a 20% tax to the government of Madagascar. The company does not own shares in any other company and did not incur any capital gains or losses in the year.

Madagascar Co. paid a dividend to shareholders of C$222,000 on January 31, 2017; this is the first dividend payment made by the company. A Co. and C Co. received dividends of C$35,520 and C$19,980, respectively. A dividend withholding tax of 3% applied to the dividends.

Part A

Determine whether the corporation paying the dividend is a foreign affiliate of the Canadian company receiving the dividend.

ITA: 95(1)

Part B

Depending on your response in Part A, determine whether a Division C deduction is available to the Canadian corporation in respect of the dividend. If not, how will the dividend be treated for tax purposes?

ITA: 113(1)
ITA: 126(1)

Part C

If a Division C deduction is available, follow these steps to calculate the deduction:

(1) Compute the relevant surplus balances for the company showing all components.

ITR: 5907

(2) Compute the portion of the full amount of the dividend (whole dividend) paid out of each surplus balance.

ITR: 5901

(3) Compute the portion of the dividend received by the Canadian shareholder out of each surplus balance.

ITR: 5900

(4) If needed, compute the foreign tax applicable to the portion of the dividend received by the Canadian shareholder out of taxable surplus. (Refer to the definition of "underlying foreign tax").

ITR: 5900(1)(*d*)
ITR: 5907

(5) Calculate the Division C deductions.

ITA: 113(1)

Part D

What is the rationale for the double taxation elimination mechanism applied under Parts B and C?

Part E

How would the dividends be treated if they were paid to Canadian resident individuals instead of corporations?

Ignore foreign exchange differences in your solution.

Problem 11

Mallot Co. is a Canadian-resident corporation owning 60% of the common shares of Trotter Inc., a U.S.-incorporated company operating and managed out of Chicago. Mallot Co. owns 60 common shares of the company that were issued to it for a capital contribution of US$60,000 at the time of incorporation.

The other 40% of Trotter Inc. is owned by Mr. Tellus, a Canadian resident. Trotter Inc. has been operating a medical supplies business since its incorporation on January 1, 2010 and has an October 31 year end. Mr. Tellus owns 40 common shares of the company that were issued to him for a capital contribution of US$40,000.

You are filing the December 31, 2015 tax return for Mallot Co. and have been provided with the following information:

(1) Trotter Inc. had earnings (losses) from its active business operations in the United States and related tax liabilities (refunds) since incorporation as follows:

Taxation Year End	Earnings (Loss) (US$)	Tax Paid (Refunded) (US$)
October 31, 2012	$200,000	$50,000
October 31, 2013	$100,000	$25,000
October 31, 2014	$100,000	$25,000
October 31, 2015	($200,000)	($50,000)
October 31, 2016	$50,000	$12,500

(2) In the October 31, 2013 taxation year end, Trotter Inc. sold some equipment used in its operations incurring a capital gain of US$100,000 on which it paid a tax of US$20,000. It also paid a dividend of US$100,000 to shareholders that year.

(3) On October 31, 2014, Trotter Inc. received a dividend for US$200,000 from a wholly owned subsidiary, N, located in the Nepal. N has a December 31 year end and was acquired in an arm's length transaction in 2014 for US$50,000. You have been told that the dividend represented all of

¶19,875

N's active business income for 2014 and that no underlying income tax on the income and no withholding tax on the dividend was paid to the Nepal's government. U.S. domestic tax of US$50,000 was paid by Trotter Inc. on the dividend.

(4) On September 1, 2016, Trotter Inc. disposed of 100% of its shares in N to the controlling Canadian shareholder of Mallot Inc. and incurred a capital gain on the sale of US$150,000 on which it paid tax of US$15,000. You have been told that all of the assets of N were used in its active business operations. N earned active business income of US$50,000 in 2015 and US$50,000 to the date of disposition in 2016.

Assume that the Canadian dollar is on par with the US dollar.

Compute the surplus balances for Trotter Inc. as of December 31, 2016.

Problem 12

Ragyun Co. (Ragyun) is incorporated and operates in Hungary. The structure of the corporation is as follows:

All unrelated Canadian residents:

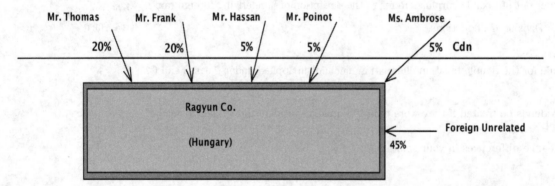

Ragyun was formed on January 1, 2016 and has an October 31 year end. The company was formed to hold a patented technology that the Canadian shareholders developed in Canada and transferred to the corporation at the time of incorporation. The technology was valued at $55,000 at the time of transfer. The foreign unrelated shareholders contributed cash of $45,000 at the time of incorporation for common shares. The company holds the patented technology, a small amount of cash, and investment properties.

Ragyun's income for 2016 included a $20,000 gain on the sale of shares in another foreign entity, Maya Inc. Ragyun owned 1% of the shares of Maya Inc. as a speculative investment. Also included in income was a $10,000 gain on the sale of shares of Tech Inc., a corporation that Ragyun owned in Hungary. Tech Inc. is an engineering firm (whose activities and assets relate only to the engineering business) that provided services to Ragyun in the final development phase of the technology. Because of a dispute with the firm, Ragyun sold the 60% share interest to another shareholder of Tech Inc. Ragyun's income also included $5,000 of dividend and interest income from investments in mutual funds, and $25,000 in royalties from licensing the technology to unrelated foreign corporations.

Ragyun has two employees. One is responsible for administration and accounting for the company, and the other is responsible for marketing and arranging licence agreements.

Ragyun paid tax of $7,200 on its income to the Hungarian taxing authorities for the 2016 taxation year-end. On January 31, 2017, Ragyun paid a dividend of $52,800 to its shareholders. A 15% withholding tax applied to dividends paid to the Canadian shareholders.

Part A

Is Ragyun a foreign affiliate or controlled foreign affiliate (CFA) of Ms. Ambrose?

Part B

Is Ragyun a foreign affiliate or controlled foreign affiliate (CFA) of Mr. Frank?

Part C

Calculate foreign accrual property income (FAPI) for Ragyun for 2016. Calculate the impact of the FAPI on Mr. Frank's taxable income for 2016 and the adjusted cost base of his shares.

Part D

How will the January 31, 2017 dividend affect Mr. Frank's taxable income for 2017 and the adjusted cost base of his shares?

Part E

How will the January 31, 2017 dividend affect Ms. Ambrose's taxable income for 2017?

Part F

How would your response to C and D above change if Mr. Frank were Frank Corporation, a Canadian resident corporation with a December 31 year end?

 [For more problems and solutions thereto, see the DVD accompanying the textbook.]

CHAPTER 19 —
DISCUSSION NOTES FOR REVIEW QUESTIONS

(1) One objective of international tax treaties is to eliminate double taxation. This is accomplished by ensuring that income is not taxed in more than one country or by providing a foreign tax credit for the taxes paid in the other country. The second objective of the treaties is to prevent tax evasion. This is accomplished through "sharing of information" provisions in the treaties. Treaties facilitate information exchange and promote resolution of disputes related to domestic tax laws of the two countries.

(2) A part-year resident is a taxpayer who either becomes a permanent resident of Canada or relinquishes permanent resident status at some point in the year. This taxpayer is taxable in Canada on worldwide income only during the period of residency. Non-Canadian source is not taxable in Canada for the period during the year that the taxpayer is not a resident of Canada. A non-resident is a person who is resident somewhere other than Canada and is taxable in Canada only on Canadian employment or business income, or taxable capital gains on taxable Canadian property. Part XIII withholding tax may apply to certain other types (passive sources) of Canadian-source income earned by a non-resident.

ITA: 2(3)
ITA: 114

(3) The transfer pricing rules are intended to ensure that transactions between Canadian taxpayers or partnerships and non-arm's length non-resident persons occur at an arm's length price, i.e., the price that would be used between unrelated persons. In that way, profits cannot be exported beyond the Canadian tax authorities.

ITA: 247(1)

(4) The thin capitalization rules are designed to prevent the erosion of Canada's tax base through deductible interest payments on loans to Canadian corporations by non-residents. By under-capitalizing a Canadian subsidiary, a foreign parent could receive interest that would otherwise be profits of the subsidiary that are taxable in Canada instead of the subsidiary repatriating profits through dividends.

ITA: 18(4)

(5) A non-resident is taxable on the disposition of taxable Canadian property (TCP). TCP is defined in the Act and includes shares of an unlisted corporation resident in Canada, if more than 50% of the fair market value of the share was derived from real or immovable property situated in Canada, or Canadian or timber resource properties at any time in the prior five years. Listed shares of a Canadian resident corporation are TCP only if, at any time in the prior five years, the non-resident and non-arm's length persons owned not less than 25% of the shares of the corporation and more than 50% of the fair market value of the shares were derived from real or immovable property situated in Canada, or Canadian or timber resource properties. The relevant tax treaty would need to be considered to determine whether a treaty article overrides the domestic law. Unless the shares are treaty-protected property, the purchaser of the shares is required to withhold and remit 25% of the purchase price unless the non-resident obtains a certificate of compliance and remits a tax payment of 25% of the gain on the property to the CRA no later than 10 days after the disposition.

ITA: 248(1)

(6) Some personal tax credits are prorated for the portion of the year the individual is resident in Canada, for example, the basic personal tax credit, age credit, etc. Other credits can be claimed in full, for example, the donation credit, medical expense credit, etc.

(7) If the rental property were located in the country from which the individual was emigrating, the individual would be taxable only on the taxable capital gain resulting from the appreciation in value from the time he or she moved to Canada. The cost base used to calculate the gain would be the fair market value of the property at the date of the move to Canada. If the property were a rental property located in Canada, the property would be taxable Canadian property and would be exempt from the deemed disposition rules when the individual immigrated to Canada. As a result, on disposition of the property, the individual would be taxable on the taxable capital gain calculated using the original purchase price of the property as the adjusted cost base.

ITA: 128.1(1)(c)

(8) A non-resident employer is required to withhold and remit tax from **remuneration** paid to an employee related to duties performed in Canada. The employee will file a Canadian tax return to include the Canadian employment income less any income exempt from tax under the relevant Canadian tax treaty. The tax withholdings will be applied against any taxes payable on the return. Employers resident in countries that have a tax treaty with Canada which exempts the employment income from Canadian tax can apply for a withholding tax waiver. The exemption to the income tax withholding requirement for non-resident employers applies to a qualifying non-resident employer for qualifying non-resident employees. A qualifying non-resident employer must be resident in a treaty country and needs to obtain certification to be eligible for the waiver. A qualifying non-resident employee is an employee who is resident in a treaty country, is exempt from Canadian tax under the treaty on the employment income and works in Canada for less than 45 days in the calendar year or is present in Canada for less than 90 days in any 12-month period during which the salary is paid.

ITA: 153(1), (6), (7); ITR: 102

(9) The withholding tax rate is 25%. However, under the Canada–U.S. Income Tax Convention this rate is reduced to 5% if the shareholder owns at least 10% of the voting stock of the corporation and 15% in all other cases.

ITA: 212(1)
Article X Canada–U.S. Tax Convention

(10) There would only be a benefit to a section 217 election where the individual's tax calculated under Part I on those benefits would be less than the 25% withholding tax rate (or the reduced rate under the relevant tax treaty).

ITA: 212(1)(l), 217

(11) If the loan is not repaid within one year of the end of the taxation year in which the loan was made, Part XIII tax will apply to a deemed dividend to the shareholder equal to the loan balance. Subsection 17(1) will not apply where Part XIII tax is paid (and not refunded on a repayment of the balance). A refund of the Part XIII tax may be requested within two years of the calendar year in which a repayment of the balance occurs (in which case, subsection 17(1) could apply).

ITA: 15(2), 214(3)(a)

It would be possible for the non-resident and the Canadian-resident corporation to file an election to treat the loan as a "pertinent loan or indebtedness". In such case, subsection 15(2) and section 17 would not apply to the loan. Instead, the amount included in computing income of the Canadian corporation each year is the greater of the interest computed on the balance at a high prescribed rate and all amounts of interest payable by the Canadian corporation for a debt obligation owing by the Canadian corporation that was used to fund the loan.

ITA 17.1(1); ITR 4301(b.1)

(12) The purpose of the deemed disposition/acquisition rule is to provide a tax cost base from which future income/gains are determined for Canadian income tax purposes. Properties that are taxable in Canada irrespective of the residency status of the owner are exempt from the deemed disposition/acquisition rule, e.g., real property situated in Canada.

ITA: 128.1(1)

(13) Non-residents who are filing a Canadian income tax return for employment income, business income, or because they have disposed of taxable Canadian property, are entitled to claim the same personal tax credits available to a resident where their Canadian-source income represents 90% or more of their world income.

ITA: 118.94

(14) A Canadian resident individual may reduce Part I taxes payable by a foreign tax credit for tax withholdings up to a rate of 15%. Withholding taxes in excess of 15% are deductible in computing Division B income. A Canadian resident corporation may claim a foreign tax credit for withholdings unless the dividends are received from a foreign affiliate, in which case Division C deductions apply.

ITA: 113(1), 126(1)
ITA: 20(11)

(15) The FAPI rules prevent a Canadian resident from deferring tax on investment income by holding investments offshore in controlled foreign affiliates. The rules require the Canadian investor to pay tax on the foreign investment income as it is earned each year instead of when it is received as a dividend.

ITA: 91(1)

(16) Exempt surplus of a foreign affiliate represents income or gains for which Canada relinquishes its right to tax. Active business income earned in countries with which Canada has a treaty or tax information exchange agreement as well as the non-taxable portion of capital gains become exempt surplus of a foreign affiliate [other than the non-taxable portion of gains included in hybrid surplus for dispositions of shares in foreign affiliates that are excluded property]. The taxable portion of gains on the disposition of properties used principally to gain or produce active business income in a designated treaty country is also included in exempt surplus.

ITR: 5907, "exempt earnings"

(17) A subsection 93(1) election allows a Canadian corporation to access the surplus accounts of the foreign affiliate being sold without having to pay dividends on the shares of the foreign affiliate in advance of the sale. If the foreign affiliate has exempt surplus, the exempt surplus can be deemed to have been paid as a dividend to the Canadian corporation and received tax free. The dividend will also reduce the proceeds of disposition and thus the capital gain on the disposition of the shares of the affiliate.

CHAPTER 19 — SOLUTIONS TO MULTIPLE CHOICE QUESTIONS

Question 1

(B) is correct. Jari is taxed as a non-resident on the disposition of taxable Canadian property. The tax is federal tax on the rate schedule plus 48% of tax otherwise payable. The Canada–Greece tax treaty does not override Canada's right to tax the taxable capital gain.

ITA: 2(3), 115, 120(1)

(A) is not correct. Income earned in a particular province for a non-resident includes only employment income and income from carrying on business.

ITR: 2602(1)

(C) and (D) are not correct. Non-residents are taxable on gains from the disposition of taxable Canadian property under Part I of the ITA. Withholding tax is exigible under Part XIII.

ITA: 2(3), 115(1)

Question 2

(B) is correct. The interest was earned while Mai was a non-resident, before she became a resident of Canada. Withholding tax does not apply to interest paid by a Canadian resident bank to unrelated non-residents.

ITA: 2(3), 212(1)(*b*)

(A) is incorrect. Only interest that is not fully exempt interest paid to a non-arm's length person and participating debt interest is subject to 25% withholding tax.

ITA: 212(1)(*b*)

(C) and (D) are incorrect. The interest was not earned during her period of residency.

Question 3

(D) is correct. As a resident of Canada, Antonio is taxed in Canada on his worldwide income. Canada provides a foreign tax credit to alleviate potential double taxation of the income.

ITA: 126(2)

(A) is incorrect. As a resident of Canada, Antonio is subject to tax on his worldwide income.

(B) is incorrect. Deductions for business foreign tax credits are not available in Division B of the ITA.

(C) is incorrect. Business income is sourced to the country in which the business activities are carried on (or where a permanent establishment is located under treaty). Brazil has jurisdiction to tax the income, and Canada provides a foreign tax credit for the Brazilian tax.

Question 4

(C) is correct. There are no tax consequences until Betty receives payments from her RRSP/RRIF, at which time, the payer will withhold tax on each payment. The withholding tax rate is 25%, but is reduced to 15% under treaty for annuity payments if the RRSP is matured and converted to an annuity.

212(1)(*l*)
Article XVIII

(A) is not correct. Taxable Canadian property, as defined, does not include RRSPs.

ITA: 248(1)

(B) is not correct. Excluded rights or interests are exempt from deemed disposition at the time of emigration.

ITA: 128.1(10)

(D) is not correct. Only payments out of an RRSP are subject to withholding tax.

ITA: 212(1)(*l*)

Question 5

(B) is correct. The exempt surplus balance of Maxwell Rock Ltd. will be $100,000 at the end of the year. The business income earned in Michigan is the net earnings for the year from an active business carried on by it in a designated treaty country and would be exempt surplus of the U.S. company. The business income earned in Paraguay is included in taxable surplus because the income is being earned in a country that is not a designated treaty country. Of the $150,000 dividend paid to Maxwell, $100,000 will be considered to have been paid from exempt surplus and $50,000 will be considered to have been paid from taxable surplus. The exempt surplus portion of the dividend is fully deductible in computing taxable income.

ITR: 5901
ITA: 113(1)(*a*)

(A) is incorrect. Dividends received by a corporation from a foreign affiliate are not eligible for a foreign tax credit.

ITA: 126(1)

(C) is incorrect. Only $100,000 of the dividend is paid from exempt surplus.

(D) is incorrect. A deduction will be available in computing taxable income for the underlying tax paid associated with the dividend paid by the U.S. company from business income earned in Paraguay but not from business income earned in the United States. The business income earned in the United States is exempt surplus and is fully exempt from tax in Canada when paid as a dividend.

ITA: 113(1)(b)

Question 6

(B) is correct, for the reason stated in the question.

(A) and (C) are incorrect for the reason stated in (B).

(D) is incorrect. Bob would only need to file a U.S. form 1040NR in relation to an income producing property.

Question 7

(D) is correct. The company will be a controlled foreign affiliate of each of the Canadian shareholders because (i) it is a foreign affiliate (each Canadian shareholder owns not less than 1% of the shares and not less than 10% of the shares with related persons) of the company, and (ii) it is a controlled foreign affiliate because it is controlled by less than five unrelated Canadian residents (Jane and Tori). The income of the corporation will be FAPI because it will be considered income from property. The shareholder's participating percentage of the income as of the end of the affiliate's taxation year will be included in Division B income. A deduction for the related U.S. tax paid on the income calculated using the relevant tax factor will also be available.

ITA: 95(1)

ITA: 91(1)
ITA: 91(4)

(A) is incorrect. The income will be taxed annually. Dividends paid to the Canadian shareholders will be included in Division B income. Foreign tax credits will be available against Part I tax for U.S. tax withholdings. An offsetting deduction will be available for the lesser of the amount of the dividend and the cumulative total of prior year's net income inclusions for FAPI.

ITA: 12(1)

ITA: 126(1)
ITA: 91(5)

(B) is incorrect. The income will be taxed annually. An offsetting deduction for a dividend is not available under Division C because the dividend is not received by a corporation. Division C deductions are only available to Canadian resident corporations.

ITA: 113(1)

(C) is incorrect. The income will be taxed annually. An offsetting deduction for a dividend is not available under Division C because the dividend is not received by a corporation.

ITA: 113(1)

CHAPTER 19 — SOLUTIONS TO EXERCISES

Exercise 1

Alan is deemed to have disposed of the shares on emigration at their fair market value of $40,000. Given his ACB of $28,000, he will have a capital gain of $12,000, and a taxable capital gain of $6,000.

Alan can elect to defer paying the tax that results from the deemed disposition rule. The election must be made on or before the balance due date for the year in which emigration takes place. If the election is made, the payment of the tax can be deferred without interest until the properties are actually sold. Since security is not required for up to $100,000 of capital gains resulting from the deemed disposition rule, Alan will not be required to post security with the CRA.

ITA: 220(4.5), (4.51)

Exercise 2

No, a foreign tax credit is not claimed in both countries. To do so would eliminate the taxes on the income altogether. The country (the source country) where the income is sourced has the first right of taxation and consequently, a foreign tax credit is allowed only in the other country (the residence country).

A non-resident will pay the Canadian income taxes on income from duties of office and employment performed in Canada, income from business carried on in Canada, and on taxable capital gains on taxable Canadian property. These taxes will then be used as a foreign tax credit in the country of residence. Note that some countries will recognize CPP/QPP contributions as taxes, in addition to any income taxes paid to Canada. Note that treaties can limit or eliminate a country's jurisdiction to tax source income. The country of residence will provide a tax credit only if taxes are paid.

ITA: 2(3)

Exercise 3

Canada levies tax on non-residents who carry on business in Canada. Carrying on business in Canada is distinguishable from carrying on business with Canada. While Sam-son solicits sales from Canadians, it does not solicit sales in Canada through an agent or servant. Given these facts, Sam-son is not carrying on business in Canada and is not liable for Canadian income taxes on the $76,000 profit originating from within Canada.

ITA: 2(3)

Exercise 4

The interest is U.S. sourced and will be considered investment income to the Canadian corporation.

The interest will be subject to the full corporate tax rate, including the $10\frac{2}{3}\%$ additional refundable tax on investment income. The addition to RDTOH ($30\frac{2}{3}\%$) will also apply.

Subsection 17(1) requires an interest income inclusion equal to interest computed using the prescribed rate less the actual interest included in income on the loan. If the interest paid is considered to be computed at a reasonable rate, an income inclusion is not required. Imputed income will not arise if the 1% rate being paid is comparable to the U.S. borrowing rate.

The foreign affiliate dumping provision does not apply because Johnson & Co. Ltd. is not controlled by a non-resident corporation.

ITA: 212.3(1)

Exercise 5

The Act defines "moving expenses" as including any expenses incurred as, or on account of, travel costs in the course of moving the taxpayer from the old residence to the new residence, cost of transporting or storing household effects, cost of meals and lodging, etc. It appears Mary Jane's expenses would qualify under this definition; however, the move must be an eligible relocation as defined by the Act. The definition of "eligible relocation" only includes relocations that are both from and to a residence in Canada unless the person is a student or person absent from but a resident of Canada.

ITA: 62(3)

ITA: 62(1); 248(1)
ITA: 62(2)

Exercise 6

Dutchco is a foreign affiliate of Canco as Canco owns not less than 10% of the shares of the company. Dutchco is a controlled foreign affiliate of Canco as it is controlled by a Canadian resident.

Dutchco is earning income from an active business in a country with which Canada has a tax convention. This income would be treated as exempt surplus. The company is also earning income from property. This income would be treated as FAPI and would become part of Dutchco's taxable surplus.

For 2015 and 2016, Canco must include, in respect of each share it owns in Dutchco, the share's participating percentage of FAPI less a deduction for the foreign accrual tax applicable to the FAPI income inclusion.

Income Inclusion	$ 9,600	80% of $12,000	ITA: 91(1)
Deduction	$(7,680)	20% of $9,600 multiplied by the relevant tax factor of 1/(38% – 13%)	ITA: 91(4)
2015 Income Inclusion	$ 1,920		

The net income inclusion is added to the adjusted cost base of the shares of Dutchco held by Canco, i.e., $500,000 + $1,920 = $501,920.

Income Inclusion	$ 9,600	80% of $12,000	ITA: 91(1)
Deduction	$(7,680)	20% of $9,600 multiplied by the relevant tax factor of 1/(38% – 13%)	ITA: 91(4)
2016 Income Inclusion	$ 1,920		

The net income inclusion is added to the adjusted cost base of the shares of Dutchco held by Canco, i.e., $501,920 + $1,920 = $503,840.

When the dividend is paid in 2016, it will be included in Canco's Division B income. A deduction is available for the portion of the dividend prescribed to have been paid from exempt surplus. Exempt surplus includes exempt earnings for any taxation year ending in the period that starts with the first day of the taxation year in which Dutchco became a foreign affiliate and ends at the time the dividend is paid. FAPI is included in taxable surplus in a similar manner. The exempt surplus and taxable surplus balances of Dutchco at the time of the dividend would be as follows: — ITA: 12(1), 90(1)

	Exempt Surplus	Taxable Surplus	
Income for December 31, 2015 taxation year end of the affiliate	$30,000	$12,000	ITR: 5907(1)
Income/profits tax paid to Netherlands tax authorities	($ 6,000)	($ 2,400)	
Balance February 2015	$24,000	$ 9,600	

Surplus balances are not impacted by 2016 income amounts because the dividend was paid within the first 90 days of 2016. — ITR: 5901(2)(a)

The portion of the whole dividend of $50,000 deemed to have been paid out of exempt surplus would be $24,000. The portion of the whole dividend deemed to have been paid out of taxable surplus would be $9,600. The remainder, of $16,400, would be considered to have been paid from pre-acquisition surplus.

The 2016 income inclusions less deductions for Canco related to the dividend would be as follows:

Dividend Income	$ 40,000	$50,000 × 80%	ITA: 12(1), 90(1)
Deduction	$(19,200)	$24,000 × 80%	ITA: 113(1)(a)
Deduction	$ (5,760)	Lesser of: (1) $5,760 [$2,400 × 80% × (1/(38% – 13%) – 1], and (2) $7,680 [$9,600 × 80%]	ITA: 113(1)(b)
Deduction	$ (1,536)	Lesser of: (1) $1,536 [$9,600 × 80% × 5% × 1/(38% – 13%)], and (2) $1,920 [$9,600 × 80% less: paragraph 113(1)(b) deduction of $5,760]	ITA: 113(1)(c)
Deduction	$ (1,920)	Lesser of: (1) $1,920 [$9,600 × 80% – paragraph 113(1)(b) deduction of $5,760], and (2) 2015 net FAPI inclusion of $1,920 added to the ACB of the shares	ITA: 91(5)
Deduction	$(13,120)	$16,400 × 80%	ITA: 113(1)(d)
Net Inclusion (Deduction)	$ (1,536)		

The subsection 91(5) deduction reduces the adjusted cost base of the shares of Dutchco held by Canco. The adjusted cost base of shares after the February 2016 dividend and FAPI inclusions/adjustments for 2016 is $501,920.

The portion of the dividend paid from exempt surplus, i.e., $19,200, and pre-acquisition surplus, i.e., $13,120, is not taxed in Canada. The portion of the dividend paid from FAPI, i.e., $7,680 ($40,000 − $19,200 − $13,120), is taxed in Canada less a deduction for the underlying foreign tax, i.e., $5,760, and for the withholding tax, i.e., $1,536. There is a further deduction of $1,920 to reverse the prior year's FAPI inclusion (preventing double taxation of the passive income earned in the CFA), limited to the total amount of the taxable surplus dividend, net of the deduction for underlying tax.

Exercise 7

(A) The rents paid by Sam and Harry to Joe's parents are subject to a 25% withholding tax. Joe appears to be acting as an agent for his parents in collecting the rents and would be required to deduct and withhold the tax from the rents received and submit it to the Receiver General. Failure to withhold can result in interest charges and a penalty of 10% to 20% of unremitted withholdings.

ITA: 212(1)(d), 215(3), 227(8), 227(8.3)

Joe's parents can file a Canadian tax return within two years of the end of the year to obtain a refund of any Part XIII tax paid in excess of the Part I tax payable (using graduated tax rates) on the net rental income (rents less mortgage interest, CCA, utilities, and property taxes).

ITA: 216(1)

Alternatively, an undertaking (NR6) to file an income tax return can be filed prior to the first rental payment for the year indicating Joe's parents' intent to file a Canadian tax return within six months of the end of the year. In that case, withholding tax can be reduced to 25% of the net rents received (i.e., rents less mortgage interest, utilities, and property taxes). The return must be filed within six months of the end of the year or Joe will become liable for the excess of 25% of the rents received less the withholdings remitted to CRA.

ITA: 216(4)

(B) If the condominium is sold in the future, Joe's parents will have disposed of taxable Canadian property. They will be required to file a personal tax return to report the taxable capital gain on the disposition of the property. They will also be required to file a separate personal tax return to report any recapture on the disposition of the property. The Canada–China Tax Convention would need to be reviewed to determine if the taxable capital gain on the disposition of the property is treaty exempt. Assuming not, the purchaser would be required to withhold 25% of the proceeds paid for the land and 50% of the proceeds paid for the building within 30 days of the end of the month of the purchase, unless Mr. and Mrs. Doe have obtained a clearance certificate and paid 25% of the estimated (or actual) capital gain on the disposition of the property plus an estimate of the tax on the recapture related to the disposition of the property.

ITA: 248(1)

ITA: 116(1), (5)

(C) It appears that Joe will become a resident of Canada under common law and will be taxed on his worldwide income. If Joe were to own the condominium, it may be possible for him to treat the property as his principal residence. He would need to be able to argue that the income-producing use is ancillary to the main use of the property as a principal residence, and he would not be able to claim CCA on the property. The rents paid to him by the roommates would not be subject to withholding tax. If Joe's parents were to loan him the funds to purchase the property, the attribution rules would not apply, as the rules only apply to individuals who are residents of Canada. Any interest Joe were to pay on loans from his parents would be subject to withholding tax, as the interest would be paid to a non-arm's length person. The Canada–China Tax Convention may reduce the rate to 10%.

ITA: 212(1)(b)

CHAPTER 19